D1592659

A Thousand Years of Christianity in Ukraine

An Encyclopedic Chronology

ERRATA

Page	Column	Line from top	Printed	Should be
9		22	Gobulinsky	Golubinsky
31	1	26	Julian calendar	Gregorian calendar
34	1	12-13	proclaimed at the Ecumenical Council	proclaimed the Ecumenical Council
35	13	13	Merseberg	Merseburg
40		6	Thessalonkika	Thessalonika
53	1	25	is canonized. Along with	along with
54	1	26-28	A sword is carved on his tombstone with the inscription Honorem meum nemini dabo ("I will not yield my honor to anyone).	(delete)
57	2	48	<u>15 June 1173 -</u>	<u>10 May 1173 -</u>
64	2	20	12th century.	12th century in Polotsk.
83	2	44	Iona...1448-1461	(delete)
97	1	42	<u>23 January 1588 -</u>	<u>23 January 1589 -</u>
102	2	26	<u>1 June 1595 -</u>	<u>12 June 1595 -</u>
109	2	1	METROPOLITAN	METROPOLITANS
110	2	7	(1576-1594)	(1576-1607)
113	1	11	Wlasdyslaw IV	Wladyslaw IV
120	2	39-40	Hetman of Ukraine	Hetman of Ukrainian Kozaks
129	2	4	(Caption) (1637-45)	(1637-40)
135	1	1	<u>10 June-20 July 1954 -</u>	<u>10 June-20 July 1654 -</u>
135	1	7	<u>28 July 1954 -</u>	<u>28 July 1654 -</u>
163	2	12	Rafayil	Raphael
200	1	42	1807-1814	1808-1814
200	2	36	1818-1858	1816-1858
236	2		(Caption) Vasyl Romanyuk	Rev. Vasyl Romanyuk
239	2	25	Resurection	Resurrection
250	2	21	<u>October 1963 -</u>	<u>23 December 1963 -</u>
255	1	16	<u>3 October 1974 -</u>	<u>5 October 1971 -</u>
262	1	12-13	are under the jurisdiction of the Moscow Patriarchate	(delete)
263	1	5-6	HIERACHY OF THE UKRAINIAN AUTOCEPHAOUS CHURCH IN THE DIASPORA	HIERARCHY OF THE UKRAINIAN AUTOCEPHALOUS CHURCH IN THE DIASPORA METROPOLITANS
266	1	21	Yosyf Shmondyuk...1976-79	Yosyf Shmondyuk...1976-78
270	1	51	Thesslonika	Thessalonika
271	2	41	Laskiv (1980)	Laskiv (1880)
275	1	2	Mykhayil...988-922	Mykhayil...988-992
276	1	13	Isidore (Izydor)...1439-42	Isidore (Izydor)...1436-42
281	1	45	Andriy Sapelak...1961-78	Andriy Sapelak...1961-
281	1	49	Yosyf Martynets...1958-71	Yosyf Martynets...1958-78
283	2	41	Rozymovsky	Rozumovsky
286	2	46	Sichnysky,	Sichynsky,
290	2	17	Chruch"	Church"
291	2	29	Ressurection"	Resurrection"
303	2	24	Prince of Kiev	Voevoda of Kiev
304	2	22	Policarp	Polikarp

A Thousand Years of Christianity in Ukraine

An Encyclopedic Chronology

Compiled and Edited
by
Osyp Zinkewych and Andrew Sorokowski

Smoloskyp Publishers
and
The National Committee to Commemorate the Millenium of Christianity in Ukraine
New York • Baltimore • Toronto
1988

A Thousand Years of Christianity in Ukraine

An Encyclopedic Chronology

Library of Congress Catalog Card Number: 88-61255
ISBN: 0-914834-58-4

Published by V. Symonenko Publishers,
Smoloskyp, Inc.
A non-profit organization

Smoloskyp, P.O. Box 561, Ellicott City, Md. 21043, U.S.A.

Smoloskyp Trust, P.O. Box 430, Sta. "E," Toronto, Ont., M6H 4E3, Canada

National Committee to Commemorate the Millennium
of Christianity in Ukraine
63 Fourth Avenue, New York, N.Y. 10003

Printed in the United States of America
by
UKRAPRINT, Inc., P.O. Box 304, Woodstock, Md. 21163, U.S.A.

Contributors

Yaro Bihun, Rostyslav Chomiak
Karen and Orest Deychakivsky
Andrew Fedynsky, Olenka Hanushevska-Galadza
Eugene Iwanciw, Jaroslawa Zelinsky Johnson
Marta Kolomayets, Mykola Koropetsky
Christine Kowalsky, Daria Kuzyk
Valentyna Limonchenko, Rev. Taras R. Lonchyna
Marta D. Olynyk, George Sajevych
Marta Sawczuk, Peter Skorupsky
Oleksander Voronyn, Wiacheslaw Wyshnewsky
Yuriy Zelinsky

Preface

This is the first book to present the history of Christianity in Ukraine in simple chronological form. Heretofore, this history has been dismembered, its component facts scattered among various accounts of Russian or Polish, Catholic or Orthodox history, often in a light unfavorable to Ukraine or ignoring her altogether. The purpose of this book is to reassemble these facts in simple, objective form, so that the general reader as well as the scholar may consider Ukrainian church history as a coherent whole.

It would be quixotic to attempt to separate Christian history from political history. Christian history is primarily the history of Christian Churches, and Churches are by their nature both divine and human institutions. As a human institution, every Church interacts with other institutions in society, and thus participates in political life. Indeed, throughout much of the history of Europe, Churches themselves have played major roles on the political stage. Furthermore, as an institution every Church also has its internal political life.

For much of her history Ukraine has played a role in the politics of other, more powerful states, achieving statehood herself for only limited periods after her glorious princely era. Similarly, the fortunes of her Churches, as well as their internal politics, have often been determined by external factors. Ukrainian church history must therefore be considered in the context of East European political history.

But notions of history have themselves served as political tools. The powers that have ruled Ukraine and sought to control her church life have manipulated the writing of her history to suit their political purposes. Ukraine's church history has been taken out of her hands and grafted onto the histories of her more powerful neighbors. This is a compelling reason finally to present the history of Ukrainian Christianity as a distinct subject deserving of separate attention.

The need for a history of Ukrainian Christianity is particularly urgent today, when Ukraine is under the control of a government hostile in principle to all religions and Churches. The Soviet Union opposes religion as a delusion concocted to distract the oppressed from the class struggle; it opposes churches as tools of oppression. Yet seventy years after the Revolution, both religion and Church remain alive in the U.S.S.R., while the ideological rationale for their suppression has lost its meaning. As a result, Soviet policy has wavered among different approaches to this bewildering problem. Separation of Church from State and School, proclaimed in 1918, did not significantly weaken the power of religion and, in any case, was soon violated by the State. The all-out attack on religion in the 1920s and 1930s failed. But control and manipulation of some Churches, combined with repression of others, has proved a viable if not altogether a successful policy, especially since World War II. Aside from its external propaganda and foreign-policy role, the state-controlled Russian Orthodox Church has played an important internal role. It has served as an integrating factor in Soviet society, promoting the assimilation of the predominantly Orthodox Ukrainians and Byelorussians with the Russians. This step is to be followed by the fusion of all three into a single, Russian-speaking — and atheist — Soviet nation.

In this process, the Russian Church is given the role first of executioner, then of victim. For by helping to create the new Soviet Man it is ultimately undermining the religious and national values that it has traditionally represented. Indeed, in the long run neither the Russian Church nor the Russian nation stands to gain from this enterprise. For just as a nationalism that has swollen to imperialism negates its own basis by denying other nations' right to exist, so a Church that participates in the denial of other Churches' religious liberty sows the seeds of its own destruction.

The exploitation of Churches for political purposes is accompanied by the exploitation of their history. By drawing a straight line from the Church of Kievan Rus' through the Muscovite Church to the modern Moscow Patriarchate of the Russian Orthodox Church, the Soviet regime enhances its own prestige as well as that of the Church that serves it. Thirsting for legitimacy, the Communist leaders lay claim to the political charisma of the Kievan princes. Simultaneously, this distortion in effect removes the Ukrainian Churches from the stage of history. The Russian Orthodox hierarchy, naturally interested in raising its own prestige, cooperates in this effort. Moscow, which arose only in the twelfth century, and only on the periphery of Kievan Rus', presents itself as its only true successor. The Muscovite Church, which arose in the fourteenth century, is presented as the logical and inevitable continuation of the Kievan Church. Indeed, as early as the 1500s Muscovite publicists were promoting their state as the heir to Rome and Byzantium. The Galician and Kievan Metropolitanates of the Ukrainian Church, the direct successors of the medieval Kievan Church, are simply left out of the picture.

Later attempts by Ukrainian historians to reconstruct their Church history from medieval to modern Kiev are branded as separatist and nationalistic. Yet it was the Muscovite state that separated from the Kievan realm, and it was the Muscovite Church that, declaring autocephaly in 1448 and a Patriarchate in 1589, separated from the Kievan Church. These acts laid the foundations of the modern Russian Empire and of the Church which has contributed so heavily to the development of an imperial ideology. Quasi-historical myth is a prime element of that ideology.

Today's Soviet regime understands the power of historical consciousness. Having annihilated the Ukrainian Autocephalous Orthodox Church in the 1930s and the Ukrainian Greek-Catholic Church in the 1940s, having destroyed or converted 14,332 church buildings and killed or imprisoned thousands of clergy and believers, it knows that brute force alone cannot subjugate a nation or its faith. Thus the mythology of the "Russian Millennium" is created not only to glorify the Russian Church and State, but to deprive the Ukrainians and Byelorussians of a sense of their own religious and national identity. For to erase a people's historical consciousness is to eradicate their spirit.

While in 1888 the Tsarist regime had enough sense of historical propriety to celebrate the 900th anniversary of the Baptism of Rus' in Kiev — where, after all, it had happened — this year's Millennium is being observed principally in Moscow, capital of the Soviet state and seat of the Russian Orthodox Patriarchate. Meanwhile, the elimination of a thousand years of Ukrainian history is proceeding apace. A steady flow of publications denigrates the Ukrainian Churches, while the Millennium is billed as an exclusively Russian Orthodox occasion. The international dissemination and acceptance of this unhistorical concept deprives the Ukrainian Churches of their birthright, of the historical basis for their survival.

Thus it is only an irony, and not a contradiction, that an atheist regime should celebrate a Christian anniversary. For the very concept of an exclusively Russian Orthodox Millennium is a negation of religious liberty, and the fulfillment of a Soviet political goal. It represents the abuse of a Christian anniversary to deprive the Ukrainian Churches of the vital sources of historical tradition.

It is only in the West that the Ukrainian Orthodox, Catholic and Protestant Churches can today function freely. With limited resources, they must try to reconstruct their history and offer it to a world already under the spell of Russian nationalist historiography and no small dose of Soviet political propaganda. It is therefore ironic that the Ukrainian Churches should be accused of nationalism and politicization. In the face of a centuries-long onslaught by an imperial Church and State, they seek only to vindicate their rights and regain their patrimony. Ukrainians wish to have their own Churches on their own land — a right long enjoyed, however imperfectly, by the Russian nation and by two other peoples in the U.S.S.R., the Armenians and the Georgians. This principle of autocephaly, fundamental among the Eastern Churches, responds to a deep spiritual and psychological need in all peoples to worship God in their own language and in harmony with their own cultural traditions.

Given current political realities and the state of religious liberty in the Soviet Union, no serious effort to present the history of Christianity in Ukraine in an objective manner can be expected there in the near future. Yet the cause of religious liberty could greatly benefit from such an effort. Thus it is left to Ukrainians in the West to take the first steps. It is most fitting that the task is undertaken during the celebration of the Millennium of Christianity in Kievan Rus'-Ukraine. This book, dedicated to the Millennium, is such a beginning.

The Editors

Explanatory Note

This book is divided into ten chapters. Each chapter consists of a chronology preceded by brief summaries of the political situation in Eastern Europe, the religious situation in Europe generally, and the political situation in Ukraine during the period in question. This places the chronology in context. Each section also contains a list of metropolitans and bishops who reigned during that period, and a list of churches and monasteries built.

The enumeration of churches and monasteries is intended as a register of religious monuments, many of which are no longer standing. The frequent wars and invasions that have ravaged Ukraine over her thousand-year history have taken their toll in ecclesiastical architecture. Furthermore, Soviet anti-religious policy has resulted in the destruction or desecration of thousands of churches and monasteries during the past seventy years, while no new Ukrainian churches have been built. The editors therefore consider it important to register those church buildings that still remain. In the tenth section, a list is also provided of those churches known to have been destroyed, so as to give the reader some notion of Ukraine's lost religious and architectural heritage. Insofar as possible, photographs of both destroyed and surviving churches and monasteries have been provided. These photographs suggest the importance of the church building in the life of the Ukrainian people, and illustrate the role of Christianity in the development of a highly sophisticated national architecture.

The entries in the chronologies have been prepared on the basis of available documents and published materials. The principal sources, preceded by the abbreviations used in citations in the text, are as follows:

Acta Patriarchatus	Miklosich and Muller, eds. *Acta Patriarchatus Constantinopolitani.* Vienna, 1860
Bugoslavsky	S.A. Bugoslavsky. "K literaturnoy istoriyi 'Pamyati i Pokhvaly' knyazyu Vladimiru." *Izvestiya otdeleniya russkogo yazyka i slovesnosti Imperatorskoy Akademii Nauk,* Vol. XXIX, 1924.
Chubaty	Mykola Chubaty. *Istoriya Khrystiyanstva na Rusy-Ukraini.* Vol. I, Rome-New York, 1965.
Galician-Volynian Chronicle	Teofil Kostruba, translator and editor. *Halytsko-Volynsky Litopys.* Vol. I-II, Lviv, 1936.
Gobulinsky	E. Golubinsky. *Istoriya Russkoy Tserkvi.* Vols. I-II, Moscow, 1900-11.
Hrushevsky	Mykhaylo Hrushevsky. *Istoriya Ukrayiny-Rusy.* Vols. I-XI, Kiev, 1905-13.
Hypatian Chronicle	*Letopis po Ipatskomu spisku.* St. Petersburg, 1871.
Ilarion	Mytropolyt Ilarion. *Ukrayinska Tserkva za chas ruyiny.* Winnipeg, 1956.
Likhachev	D.S. Likhachev, ed. *Povest vremennykh let (Po Lavrentyevskoy letopisi 1377 g.).* Vol. I, Moscow-Leningrad, 1950.
Makariy	Makariy, Mitropolit Moskovskiy. *Istoriya Russkoy Tserkvi.* Vols. I-XII, St. Petersburg, 1881-91.
Martyrology	*Martyrology of the Ukrainian Churches.* Vol. I: *Ukrainian Orthodox Church;* Vol. II: *Ukrainian Catholic Church.* Baltimore-Toronto, 1985-87.
Nestorian Chronicle	*Letopis Nestora po spisku monakha Lavrentiya.* St. Petersburg, 1903.
Petukhov	E. Petukhov. *Serapion Vladimirsky.* St. Petersburg, 1888.
Ponomarev	Ponomarev. *Pamyatniki drevnye-russkoy tserkovno-uchitelskoy literatury.* St. Petersburg, 1894.
Velyky	A.H. Velyky. *Z Litopysu Khrystiyanskoyi Ukrayiny.* Vols. I-IX, Rome, 1968-77.
Vlasovsky	I. Vlasovsky. *Narys Istoriyi Ukrayinskoyi Pravoslavnoyi Tserkvy.* Vols. I-IV, New York-Bound Brook, 1956-66.

The terms "Ukraine," "Rus'-Ukraine," and "Kievan Rus'" are commonly used in a political sense. "Ukraine" is also a geographical term, which has denoted somewhat different territories at different times in history. In general, "Ukraine" is used in this work in the broadest sense, to denote both the state and its territory as they existed at various periods. For the medieval period, "Rus'" or "Kievan Rus'" is used for the state and territory, as well as the people. The term "Ruthenian" is also sometimes used for the early modern Ukrainian people and their culture, as well as for the Byelorussian people and culture of that period (16th-17th centuries). This term, which is simply a variant of "Rus'," is frequently used with regard to the Ukrainians of Galicia up to the twentieth century, and to the Ukrainians of Transcarpathia up to the present.

The term "Rus'" should not be confused with the term "Russia." The land and people now properly referred to as "Russian" were known as "Muscovite" until the eighteenth century. Their state and Church arose in the 12th-14th centuries on the northeast periphery of Rus'. In the eighteenth century, Muscovy appropriated the name "Rus'" in a new form, "Rossiya," to symbolize its conquest of the old Rus' lands. Thus, in the nineteenth and early twentieth centuries "Russia" referred to the Muscovites' empire, which included Ukraine and Byelorussia. Today, however, "Russia" and "Russians" refer only to the state and people descended from Muscovy and the Muscovites: the Russian Soviet Federated Socialist Republic and the Russian people (excluding Ukrainians, Byelorussians, and the other peoples of the Soviet Union). We use these terms in the historical context.

The term *oblast,* used throughout the book, denotes a Soviet administrative region. The Ukrainian S.S.R. is divided into twenty-five oblasts.

The term "synod" usually denotes a meeting of bishops. The term *sobor,* which is translated in some works as "council," usually denotes a major meeting of hierarchy, clergy and laity. The principal *sobors* mentioned in this book are the two that took place in Berestya (Brest) in 1596, and the *sobors* of the Ukrainian Autocephalous Orthodox Church held in October 1921 and 1927 in Kiev.

Ukrainian geographic names are transliterated, with the exception of four with established English equivalents: Dnieper, Galicia, Kiev, and Ukraine. The name "Ukraine," however, is used without the preceding article "the." Non-Ukrainian place names are generally given in the language of the country in which the place is found today (e.g., Pinsk, Vilnius), unless there is a common English form (e.g., Moscow, Rome, Warsaw). However, some names of places on historically Ukrainian ethnic territory are transliterated from the Ukrainian forms, even though they are not within the present Ukrainian S.S.R. (e.g., Peremyshl, not Polish Przemysl; Pryashiv, not Slovak Presov). The names of some cities have changed; the principal ones follow:

Former name(s)	*Present name*	*Former name(s)*	*Present name*
Katerynoslav Novorossiysk		Oleksandrivsk	Zaporizhzhya
Sicheslav	Dnipropetrovsk	Proskuriv	Khmelnytsky
Kremyanets	Kremenets	Rivne	Rovno
Krystynopil	Chervonohrad	Stanyslaviv	Ivano-Frankivsk
Luhansk	Voroshylovhrad	Yelysavethrad	Kirovohrad
Mukachiv	Mukacheve	Zhovkva	Nesterov

The towns of Yuriyiv and Bilhorod, near Kiev, no longer exist.

The given names of individuals are only anglicized if there is an accepted English form (e.g., Peter the Great), or in the case of saints (e.g., St. Peter). Accordingly, names of churches or monasteries bearing saints' names will usually be in the English form (e.g., St. George's Church). Some other names of churches or monasteries have commonly accepted English equivalents. Following is a list of the most important ones transliterated from Ukrainian with their English equivalents.

Ukrainian	*English*	*Ukrainian*	*English*
Blahovishchenska	Annunciation	Stritennya	Presentation of Christ at the Temple
Bohoyavlenska	Theophany	Troitska	Trinity
Desyatynna	Tithes	Uspenska	Dormition (Assumption of the Mother of God)
Pecherska Lavra	Caves Monastery (Kiev)	Voskresenska	Resurrection
Pokrovska	Protection (Mary the Protectress)	Vozdvyzhennya	Elevation of the Cross
Prechystoyi Bohorodytsi	Immaculate Mother of God	Voznesenska	Ascension
Preobrazhenska	Transfiguration	Vvedenska	Presentation of the Blessed Virgin Mary
Pyatnytska	Holy Friday		
Rizdva Bohorodytsi	Nativity of the Mother of God		
Spaska	Savior		

Of the many sources of the illustrations in this book, the following deserve special mention:

Museum-Archives of the Ukrainian Autocephalous Orthodox Church in the U.S.A., South Bound Brook, New Jersey.
Z.I. Khyzhnyak. *Kyyevo-Mohylyanska Akademiya.* Kiev, 1981.
H.N. Lohvyn. *Po Ukrayini; Starodavni Mystetski Pamyatky.* Kiev, 1968.
Hryhor Luzhnytsky. *Ukrayinska Tserkva mizh Skhodom i Zakhodom.* Philadelphia, 1954.
Paul Robert Magosci. *Ukraine: A Historical Atlas.* Toronto-Buffalo-London, 1985 (reproductions of maps).
Martyrology of the Ukrainian Churches. Vol. I: *Ukrainian Orthodox Church.* Vol. II: *Ukrainian Catholic Church.* Baltimore-Toronto, 1985-87.
National Geographic. Vol. 171, No. 5, May 1987 (lower map on p. 208).
Pamyatniki Gradostroitelstva Ukrainskoy SSR. Vols. I-IV, Kiev, 1983-1986.
Smoloskyp Archives. Baltimore, Maryland.

Contents

I. The Beginnings of Christianity in Ukraine 1st-10th Centuries (to 988)

General Characteristics of the Period

1. THE POLITICAL SITUATION IN EASTERN EUROPE

The political situation in Eastern Europe during the first ten centuries of the Christian era was characterized by a series of migrations and conquests and the development of intersecting and shifting trade routes over land and along rivers. A portion of Eastern Europe was under the Roman Empire, which became Christian in 313. After the founding of Constantinople, which became the capital in 330, portions of Eastern Europe became part of, or were influenced by, what came to be known from the seventh century as the Byzantine Empire.

In the second and third centuries the predominantly Slavic population of Eastern Europe came under the rule of the migrating Goths, who reached the Black Sea and then separated into the Ostrogoth and Visigoth confederations. In the fourth century, these were pushed south and west by the Huns from the East, who reached Dacia (present-day Romania) and settled in what is today Hungary. After the death of Attila, the Hun Empire split and weakened. The Germans defeated the Huns at the Battle of the Nedao in 454.

At this time, the Slavs spread west and south to the Elbe and the Danube. In the mid-sixth century, a Mongolian group called the Jouan Jouan joined with the White Huns and, having been defeated by the Turks, entered Eastern Europe. Known as the Avars, this group was paid by the Roman emperor Justinian to subdue the Slavs and the remaining Huns. The Avars ruled from the Volga to the Danube, and moved west as far as the Elbe.

As Avar power declined in the seventh century, the Slavs freed themselves of their rule, as did the Huns. The latter formed the Kingdom of Great Bulgaria on the Sea of Azov. At the same time the Khazar state arose on the Volga. The Bulgars split into two states — one on the Volga, north of the Khazars, the other on the Danube. The Magyars appeared next on the scene. In the ninth century the Franks expanded east into Slav territory.

The ninth and tenth centuries saw the rise of Rus' and Poland, and the incursion of the Pechenegs (Patzinaks) from the East. Great Moravia flourished until its destruction by the Magyars, who then settled in what is today Hungary. The Danube Bulgarian kingdom thrived under King Simeon. Byzantium's defeat of the Arabs at Mayyafariqin in 863 assured its place as a center of trade.

During this time trade passed along a route between the Black Sea and the Mediterranean, and from the Near East along the silk route to the Far East. North-south routes along the Volga, and later the Dnieper, connected the Baltic commercial sphere with the Black Sea and the Mediterranean. Eastern Europe was a source of slaves, furs, amber, honey and wax.

2. THE RELIGIOUS SITUATION IN EUROPE

The first ten centuries in Europe saw the rise and spread of Christianity. Also important was the rise of Islam, which influenced events in Europe and prevailed in parts of the continent. States adhering to various forms of Christianity and Islam rose upon the ruins of the Roman Empire and beyond.

In the Roman Empire, Christians suffered several waves of persecution, from those under Nero in 64 to those under Diocletian in 303. Emperor Galerius issued an edict of toleration of Christians in 310. Constantine converted to the Christian faith in 312 and, with Licinius, confirmed Galerius' edict in 313.

In the first centuries of Christianity various sects and heresies arose: Gnosticism and Montanism in the second century, Sabellianism in the third, Arianism and Apollinarianism in the fourth, Nestorianism and Pelagianism in the fifth, and Monothelitism in the seventh. These heresies generally involved interpretations of the nature of the Trinity, of Christ, and of divine grace. From 727 iconoclasm, introduced by the Byzantine emperor Leo III, resulted in the destruction of countless icons, until it was condemned at Nicaea in 787 and finally defeated in 843.

The supreme authority of the Papacy was not declared until the fifth century, by St. Leo. It reached its height of prestige under Pope Gregory the Great (590-604). For centuries the popes vied for power with secular rulers. Although the Pope crowned Charlemagne Holy Roman Emperor in 800, later the purported testament of Constantine was used to justify the Papacy's secular authority.

After the split of the Roman Empire into East and West in 395, the Church began to develop somewhat differently in Rome and Byzantium. The Eastern Church, tied closely to the Byzantine emperor, gained some security at the expense of independence; the Western Church, steering a more independent course, was exposed to the vagaries of politics.

Christianity spread to the German tribes — Burgundians, Lombards, Vandals, Visigoths, and others — in the fourth century, but in its heretical Arian variant. The Frankish king Clovis, on the other hand, converted to Catholicism in 496. The Burgundians turned from Arianism to the Catholic faith in 516, as did the Visigoths of Spain in 589; the Lombards did likewise in 653. The faith spread to England (St. Augustine, 596), the Netherlands (650), present-day Germany (St. Boniface, 724), and Denmark and Sweden (Anskar, 826-829).

In 796 the defeated Avars converted to Christianity, and in 828 the advancing Franks brought the faith to what is today Czechoslovakia. In the 860s SS. Cyril and Methodius brought Eastern Christianity to the Slavs of Great Moravia, but the Moravian princes turned to Latin Christianity instead. While in the ninth century the Bulgarians and the Serbs became Eastern Christians, the Croats adopted Western Christianity, as did the Magyars after their defeat by the Germans at Lechfeld in 955, and the Poles in 966. Despite Bishop Adalbert's mission on behalf of the Holy Roman Emperor, Kievan Rus' chose the Eastern, Byzantine form of the faith in 988.

The rise of Islam in the seventh century had political consequences too: the Muslims invaded Visigoth Spain in 711 but stopped near Tours in 732. The Umayyads remained in Spain for over three centuries. The Aghlabids and Fatimids held Sicily in the ninth and tenth centuries, respectively. The Volga Bulgars adopted Islam in 922. The Khazars adopted the Jewish faith of their Mediterranean trading partners.

3. THE POLITICAL SITUATION IN UKRAINE

Various peoples settled in the Black Sea region before the formation of Rus' and its official acceptance of Christianity in 988. While the Scythians and Sarmatians settled the interior, the Black Sea coast was dotted with Greek colonies, later protected by Byzantium.

Around the year 200 the Goths arrived from the north. They were Christianized by the fourth century, when they were exposed to the raids of the Huns. In the following century the Alans appeared. Of the sedentary Slavs, whose homeland included a part of present-day Ukraine, the Antes formed a confederation in southern and southwestern Ukraine which lasted from the fourth to the seventh centuries. Next came the Bulgars, who established themselves on the Volga.

In the sixth century the Avars conquered the Slavs, using them as soldiers and commanders. Around this time Kiev was founded by Prince Kyi at a crossing of north-south and east-west trade routes. In the seventh century the Khazars established a state on the Volga, which lasted to the tenth century.

In the eighth century the Arabs reached a height of power and influence in the Mediterranean world. Both Muslims and European Christians sought trade routes to the Slav lands, which were a rich source of slaves and other goods. While the Arab and Jewish trading companies, which controlled the eastern Mediterranean, approached Ukraine through the Black Sea, the European Christian traders were forced to sail through the Baltic and along the north-south river routes. With their Scandinavian allies, known as Varangians, the Christians came to control the trade routes in Ukraine by about 830.

At this time Ukraine was inhabited by various Slavic tribes, such as the Polyanians, Derevlyanians, Ulychians, Tivertsians, Siverians, Kryvychians, Dulebians and White Croats.

The first mention of Rus' in the records dates from 555 (in Syrian and Armenian writings) and from 839 (in the *Annales Bertiniani*). Who they were and how they arose, however, remains a matter of dispute. Some scholars maintain that they were Normans (Varangians), pointing to the invitation of the Frisian-Danish Ryuryk (Hraerekr) by the three northen towns of Ladoga, Byeloozero and Izborsk to be their ruler. Later, Ryuryk's descendants moved south to Kiev and ruled over the Slavs there. Others, however, hold that the Rus' were Slavic. A recent theory views the origin of Rus' in the symbiosis of the Varangian sea nomads and the Turkic steppe nomads. The former served the dominant international trading organization called "Rus'," based near Rodez (Rutenicis) in southern France. The pivotal event was the marriage of the Turkic Khazar ruler, who had unsuccessfully tried to overthrow the Jewish religion of his state, to a daughter of the prestigious Scandinavian Ynglingar clan in a Rus' trading settlement. This elevated the clan into a nascent state taking the name of Rus'.

In 860 the Rus' leaders Askold and Dyr attacked Byzantium. In 907 Oleh (Helgi) likewise campaigned against Byzantium, concluding a peace treaty in 911. Ihor (Ingvar), a descendant of Ryuryk, defeated the Khazars, took Kiev around 930 and attacked Byzantium in 941 and 944, concluding a peace treaty after the latter campaign. With the aid of the Polyanians, who lived in central Ukraine, he subdued the Derevlyanians. About this time trade switched from the Volga route to the Dnieper. As a result, Kiev grew in importance.

Ihor's widow Olha became a Christian around 955. Her pagan son Svyatoslav campaigned in the 960s against the Khazars, Danube Bulgars, and others. The Rus' were defeated by the Byzantines at Silistria in 971, and Svyatoslav died in a Pecheneg ambush in 972. Svyatoslav's son Volodymyr enlisted Varangian aid and had his brother Yaropolk murdered in 980. He thus took control of Rus'. Yet it was the pagan Volodymyr who later converted and made Christianity the official Rus' religion around 988.

How and why this came about is uncertain. Eventually, by providing a high culture, with a uniform written religious language, Christianization helped the multi-ethnic and multilingual Rus' fill the political vacuum left by the defeated Avars. But the immediate incident leading to Volodymyr's adoption of Christianity seems to have been his marriage to Anna, the Byzantine emperor's sister, in exchange for Rus' military aid. A condition of marriage was his personal conversion and, apparently, the "Baptism of Rus'," which took place in Kiev in 988.

9TH-10TH CENTURY RULERS OF KIEVAN RUS'

Kyi	ca. 560
Askold and Dyr	ca. 860-882
Oleh	882-912
Ihor	912-945
Olha (Regent)	945-957
Svyatoslav Ihorevych	957-972
Yaropolk Svyatoslavych	972-978
Volodymyr Svyatoslavych	978-1015

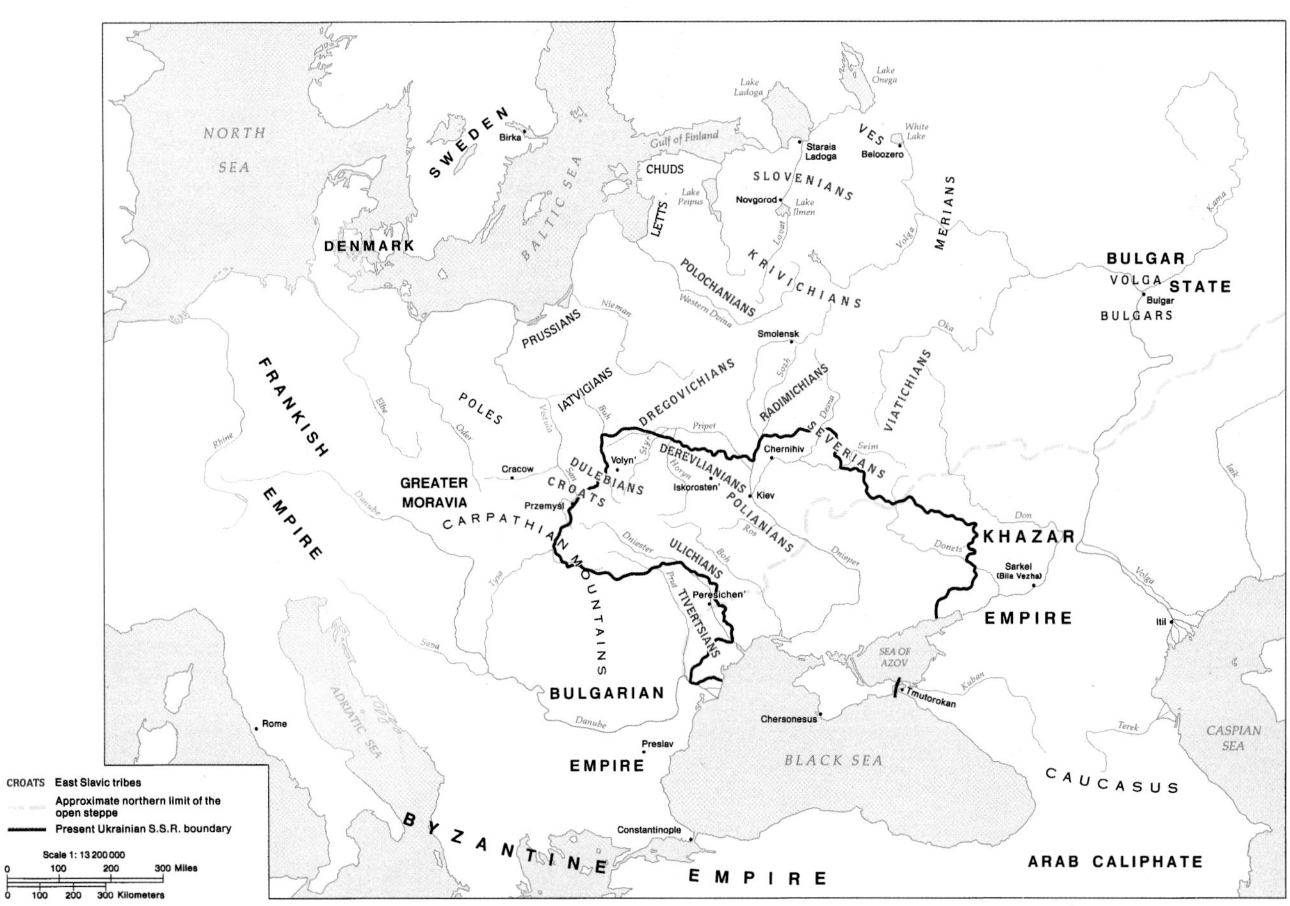

East Slavic and adjacent tribes and states in the 9th century.

Chronology

1st century — According to the Church history of Eusebius, Bishop of Caesarea (d. ca. 340), St. Andrew the Apostle, brother of St. Peter, preached the Gospel in Scythia, which included the Crimean Peninsula, the Dnieper River watershed and the area around Lake Ilmen. *The Tale of Bygone Years* describes St. Andrew's journey and prophecy thus:

> When Andrew was teaching in Sinope and came to Korsun [Chersonesus] in the Crimea, he learned that the mouth of the Dnieper River was nearby. Wishing to go to Rome, he sailed to the mouth of the Dnieper, and then traveled upstream. By chance he stopped beneath the hills along the banks and upon arising one morning, he observed to his disciples: "Do you see these hills? God's blessing will shine upon them, on this spot a great city shall rise and God shall build many churches here." He went into the hills, blessed them, raised a cross and, after praying, descended from the hill on which Kiev was later built, and continued his journey up the Dnieper. (*Nestorian Chronicle,* p. 3).

In the 4th to 5th centuries, Lucius, a collector of apocryphal legends about Christians living in the 1st century, gathered stories about the preachings of St. Andrew the Apostle and his disciples Rufus, Alexander and Filomen on the north-eastern shores of the Black Sea and the Sea of Azov.

The first apostles proselytized in the provinces of the Roman Empire, from the western shores of the Black Sea all the way to Chersonesus ("Korsun" in Slavic sources) on the Crimean Peninsula. The eastern parts of the Black Sea constituted the Bosporus kingdom and were under the protectorate of Rome. Scythia (Sarmatia) stretched to the north of the Black Sea. The city of Chersonesus and the Western part of the Crimea were places to which the Roman authorities exiled the first Christians, who often suffered martyrdom there.

94 A.D. — The fourth pope, Clement (ca. 92-101), the Roman patrician Domitilla as well as several hundred Christians are exiled to Chersonesus by Emperor Trajan (53-117). According to the Church history of Origen and Eusebius, St. Clement was exiled for having converted several prominent Romans. In Chersonesus, Pope Clement converted "all the people," founded 75 Christian communities and became the prelate of the Chersonesus Eparchy.

101 — Clement, Pope of Rome, suffers a martyr's death in Chersonesus, in the Crimea. Because of his missionary work, the Emperor ordered Clement to be executed and his body thrown into the sea. A 12th century work, *Song of Praise for the Roman Clement,* describes how St. Clement's body was weighed down with a heavy anchor and thrown into the sea. According to this work, his disciples' prayers caused a parting of the waters, opening a path to his body, which lay in a beautiful underwater church. Ever since then, the story goes, on the anniversary of St. Clement's death the sea would part for a few days so that the pilgrims might revere his relics.

Many faithful also died, while others went into the catacombs. Later, Pope Clement was canonized; in 988 Volodymyr the Great brought some of Clement's relics to Kiev, where he was proclaimed the patron saint of the Church of the Tithes of Our Blessed Mother.

St. Clement the Pope, who died a martyr's death in exile in Chersonesus (present-day Kherson, Crimean oblast) in 101. Mosaic from St. Sophia Cathedral in Kiev, 11th century.

2nd century — The Crimean Christian community is replenished by Christian, Greek and Jewish exiles, banished by Emperor Trajan.

2nd-3rd centuries — The Goths, who migrated from Scandinavia in the 1st century, settle on the southern shores of the Baltic Sea and the lower portion of the Vistula River, then move to the area between the Don and the Dniester rivers, settling southward, along both banks of the Dnieper river. They destroy the Greek colonies along the Black Sea as well as all signs of Christianity. However, Christians captured by the Goths spread their religion among their captors. Once the Roman Empire recognized Christianity early in the 4th century, a large portion of the Goths also converted.

3rd century — The first Scythian Eparchy is established in the city of Toma (later called Constance). It serves Christians along the Black Sea between the Dniester and Dnieper rivers. Evanhelic is the Scythian bishop during the time of Diocletian's persecution of the Christians (284-292).

3rd-5th centuries — The Church historians Tertullian (ca. 155-ca. 222), Athanasius of Alexandria (ca. 295-373), John Chrysostom (d. 405), Jerome (d. 420) and Origen (ca. 185-ca. 254) consider Scythia (Sarmatia) to be one of the countries where Christianity is established. Jerome writes: "Chilly Scythia is warmed by the fires of faith."

The authors of the apostolic catalogues, Hippolytus of Rome, Dorotheus of Tyre, Sophronius and Epiphanius of Cyprus, provide information in their catalogues about the work of St. Andrew in Scythia.

310-325 — Herman, Patriarch of Jerusalem, sends two bishops to the Crimea: Basil, who preaches and worked largely among the Greeks, and Ephraim, who preaches among the neighboring Scythians. Both evangelists are martyred.

313 — After the proclamation of the Edict of Milan, Christians in the Roman Empire are legally permitted to practice their religion.

325 — Theophilus, bishop of the Goths, and Kadym, bishop of Bosporus, participate in the first Ecumenical Council in Nicaea.

341 — Ulfilas (Wulfila), the first Goth to become a bishop, is consecrated by John Chrysostom and becomes the prelate of the Gothic eparchial cathedral in the city of Doros, in the Crimea. He develops the Gothic alphabet and translates the Gospels into that language. During his reign as bishop, Christianity spreads significantly among the Tivercians and the Ulychians, are then under Gothic rule.

375 — During the Huns' invasion of the lands north of the Black Sea, Christianity suffers many losses and enormous destruction; however, it spreads even among the Huns.

381 — The Bishop of Chersonesus, Eutherius, participates in the second Ecumenical Council in Constantinople.

That same year the Gothic princess Haafa, Prince Ermininingold and Bishop Ioann, as well as several presbyters and monks, are martyred in the Crimea.

431 — The bishop of Chersonesus participates in the third Ecumenical Council in Ephesus.

451 — The bishop of Chersonesus participates in the fourth Ecumenical Council in Chalcedon.

The Patriarch of Jerusalem sends Bishops Aphodar, Eugenius and Elpidius to the Crimea.

The Chersonesus and Bosporus Eparchies in the Crimea come under the jurisdiction of the Jerusalem Patriarchate.

5th century — Bishops Basil, Yephrem, Eugenius, Elpidius, Ahaphodor (Aphodar), Eutherius and Kapiton are martyred.

4th-8th centuries — Small stone and marble crosses are widespread among the Christians in the Crimea (especially Chersonesus), in the Kiev region and in Volynia. Crosses dating from between the 4th and 5th centuries are not symmetrical and have no images; those dating from the 6th century depict the suffering of Christ, while 7th-century crosses show Christ's crucifixion, together with other references to his death. These crosses were discovered during archeological digs in the above-mentioned areas in the 19th and 20th centuries.

555 — Syrian and Armenian writings first use the term "Rus'," to refer to the lands north of the Caucasus. In later years the term was applied to the lands of Tmutorokan (Tmutorokan Rus') and to the areas around present-day Chernihiv and Pereyaslav.

Inkerman Monastery of the Caves in Inkerman (Crimea oblast), established by the Byzantines in the 5th-6th centuries, with additions in the 8th-9th centuries. It had eight above-ground and cave churches, which were interconnected by stone steps and ladders, including the Church of St. Clement the Pope and the Church of St. Martin the Pope.

ca. 560 — According to *The Tale of Bygone Years,* the brothers Kyi, Shchek and Khoryv found Kiev. It is possible that Kyi was the first tribal prince of the Polyanians.

6th century — St. Eutherius is banished from Chersonesus and subsequently martyred on an island near the mouth of the Dnieper.

May 655 — Constans II, the Byzantine emperor, exiles Pope Martin (649-655) to Chersonesus in the Crimea, where he suffers martyrdom in September of that same year. Pope Martin had presided over the Lateran Council (649) that condemned the heresy of Monotheletism. He was later canonized by both the Catholic and Orthodox Churches.

787 — Bishop Stephen of Sugday (Surozh) takes part in the 7th Ecumenical Council in Nicaea.

8th century — The Greek writings *Life of St. Stephen of Surozh* and *Life of Gregory of Amastrydia* mention that Rus' soldiers, as well as their Prince Bravlin, converted to Christianity.

End of the 8th century — Chersonesus becomes a Metropolitan See composed of two eparchies: Sugday (Surozh) and Fulla. Bishop Stephen is canonized after his death and succeeded as Bishop of Surozh by Philaret. Christian communities are organized in the middle and upper Dnieper areas. In the 20th century archeologists discovered Christian burial grounds in those areas dating from the 8th century.

860 — The first bishop is assigned to Rus' to minister to Christian communities composed of Varangians and Slavs. SS. Cyril and Methodius visit Khazaria on the orders of Byzantine emperor Michael III and Patriarch Photius. According to the *The Tale of Bygone Years,* they stop at Chersonesus in the Crimea, where they meet a "Rusyn" and discover a Gospel and a Psalter written in the language of Rus'. With the help of Bishop Georgiy in Chersonesus, they discover the relics of St. Clement, Pope of Rome. They take some of the relics with them on their return trip. The Moravian-Pannonian work, *Lives of Constantine the Philosopher,* describes St. Cyril's stay in Chersonesus:

> There he found a Gospel and a Psalter written in the language of Rus'. He met a man and conversed with him in that language, learning many things from him and, using various vowels and consonants in his language, composed a prayer to the glory of God. (M. Chubaty, Vol. 1, p. 92).

After his return trip from Chersonesus, St. Cyril, with the assistance of his brother Methodius, develops a Slavic alphabet called Cyrillic (although some scholars maintain that St. Cyril developed the Glagolithic alphabet, while the script that came to be named after him existed before his time). The brothers translated many religious works into this new language, which became the basis for the Ukrainian alphabet, as well as for several other Slavic alphabets.

867 — The Kievan princes Askold and Dyr accept Christianity.

SS. Cyril and Methodius present Pope Adrian II

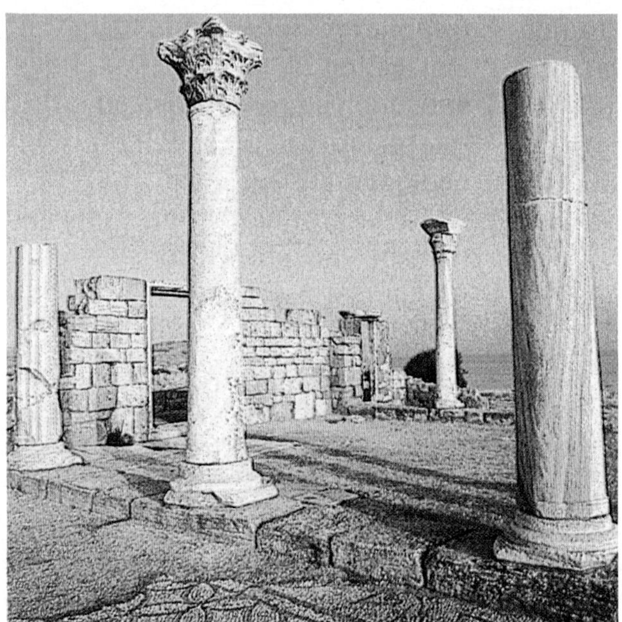

Ruins of the basilica in Chersonesus (Crimea oblast), built in the 6th century and existing till the 10th century. It was built on the site of a small church from the 5th century.

SS. Cyril (Constantine) and Methodius. Miniature from the Radziwill Chronicle.

with some of the relics of St. Clement, who was martyred in the Crimea in the 1st century. Patriarch Photius of Constantinople (858-867 and 878-886) described Christianity in Rus' in his *Circular Epistle* (no. 35):

> And not only did that nation [the Bulgars] redeem their previous dishonor by their faith in Christ... [but also] the so-called Rus', who, having vanquished their neighbors, became proud and raised their hands against the Roman state — even they have now converted from their Hellenic [pagan] and impure teaching, to which they had adhered until now, to the pure, true Christian faith and with love have become our vassals and friends... And the desire and fervor for faith so grew in them that they accepted a bishop as pastor and revere Christians with great sincerity and care. (Photius, *Epistolae.* Migne, Patrologia Graeca, Vol. CII, p. 736).

In Chapter 9 of his work, *On Ruling the Empire,* "On the Ruthenians Who Come from Rus' to Constantinople in Their Dugout Vessels," the Byzantine emperor Constantine VII Porphyrogenitus (913-959) wrote:

> And the warlike and pagan people of Rus', through means of generous gifts of gold and silver and silk garments from Emperor Basil I, were induced to negotiate and conclude a peace treaty, participate in Holy Baptism and accept an archbishop, who was consecrated by Patriarch Ignatius. The archbishop who came to the country for the above-mentioned purpose was welcomed with good will.

In their chronicles the Greek authors John Zonaras, Michael Glycas and Theophanes's Continuators Scylitzes-Cedrenus (Georgius Monachus) wrote that Rus' converted to Christianity (during the reign of Askold and Dyr) and that Byzantium sent an archbishop there. *The Tale of Bygone Years* makes no mention of this conversion. Some scholars conclude that the conversion referred to was that of Tmutorokan and not Kievan Rus'.

8th-9th centuries — Pope Leo III (795-816) and later, Pope Benedict III (855-858) prepare special epistles to the "Clerics of Rus'," who were Arians and kept apart from other Christians.

874 — Patriarch Ignatius of Constantinople sends his bishop to Rus' (probably Tmutorokan Rus').

879 — First mention of a Rus' Eparchy in the Crimea, which was juridically subordinate to the Patriarchate of Constantinople.

880 — Ibn Khurdadbeh, Arabian author, relates that the Ruthenians that came to Baghdad were Christians.

882 — Oleh, Prince of Novgorod, conquers Kiev, kills the Kievan princes Askold and Dyr (who were probably Christians), liquidates the first eparchy in Kiev and forces the Christians back to paganism. According to *The Tale of Bygone Years:*

> They killed Askold and Dyr and brought them to a hill and buried them at the top of the hill, now called Uhorska, where Olma's Court now stands. The Church of St. Nicholas was built on their gravesite [there are some historians who speculate that Prince Askold took the name Nicholas at his baptism], and Dyr was buried behind St. Irene's [Church]. (*Nestorian Chronicle,* p. 11).

9th century — Eparchies are established in the following cities in Tmutorokan Rus' along the Black Sea and the Sea of Azov: Doros in the Crimea (a Gothic metropolitanate), Khotdziron (Fullye), Astil (Itil, capital of the Khazar Empire), Khovalyes (on the Caspian Sea), Onoguron (east of the Sea of Azov), Retey (at the mouth of the Terek River), Unnon (where the Huns lived, north of the lower Terek River), Tamatarkha (Tmutorokan, the Greek name of the capital of the Tmutorokan Rus' Kaganate). (Carl de Boor, *Nachtrage zu den Notitiae Episcopatum.* Zeitschrift fur Kirchengeschichte XII, 1891, p. 520.)

The Kievan Eparchy, subordinate to the Byzantine emperor Leo VI the Philosopher (886-918), was the sixth largest of the eparchies under his jurisdiction.

Christianity was widespread in Peremyshl and Pannonia (then part of Moravia), at the time when St. Methodius was the archbishop of Moravia and Pannonia (869-870, 873-885).

Beginning of the 10th century — An eparchy of the Greater Moravian Church is established in Peremyshl, which in the previous century had belonged to White Croatia, then ruled by Hungary.

The Byzantine emperor Constantine Porphyrogenitus noted that during his journey along the Dniester River he could see the ruins of six cities and "among the ruins, church crosses carved in stone." During his reign, the Kievan Eparchy was listed as No. 60 on the list of eparchies under the jurisdiction of the Patriarchate of Constantinople.

911 — The treaty between Prince Oleh of Kiev and the Greeks, notes that merchants and soldiers from Rus' are constant visitors to Byzantium and that Christian Greeks often visit Rus'.

945 — In the treaty between Prince Ihor of Kiev and the Greeks, appropriate mention is made of the Christians in Rus', who occupied an equal, or even perhaps a dominant position, in the government and in the entourage of the prince. This treaty, the first document of Kievan Rus', officially recognizes Christianity in that nation. When the Byzantine emperor Roman agrees to pay a large tribute in exchange for peace, his envoys, along with the envoys from Rus' who drafted the treaty in Constantinople, come to Kiev. There Prince Ihor takes an oath in their presence. The *Chronicle* states:

St. Olha, Princess of Kievan Rus' (954-964). She was the first ruler of Rus' to personally accept Christianity.

> The next day Ihor called the envoys and went to the top of the mountain where stood [a statue of] Perun; and he laid down his weapons and shields and gold and went to take the oath, together with those Rus' subjects who were pagan; while the Christian Rus' went to take the oath in St. Elias Church, which stands above the creek, in the vicinity of the Pasynech square and the quarter of the Khazars. This was, in fact, a parish church, since there were many Christians among the Varangians. Ihor, having concluded the treaty with the Greeks, sent the envoys home... Ihor then began ruling in Kiev, having peace with all the countries. (*Nestorian Chronicle,* p. 25-26.)

Upon the death of Grand Prince Ihor, his wife Olha becomes the ruler of Kiev, because of their son Svyatoslav's minor age. During her reign Christianity spreads significantly in Kievan Rus'.

955 — Olha converts to Christianity. The *Chronicle* describes this event:

> Olha set out for Greece and came to Tsarhorod [Con-

stantinople]. At that time Constantine, son of Leo, was emperor; and Olha came to him. And the emperor saw that she was beautiful and intelligent and, while talking with her, told her: "You are worthy to rule together with us in our capital." She, realizing the meaning of these words, told the emperor: "I am a pagan and if you want me baptized you will have to do this yourself; if not, then I will not be baptized." And the emperor, together with the Patriarch, baptized her. Having been enlightened, her body and soul rejoiced. And the Patriarch taught her about the faith and said: "Blessed are you among the women of Rus', because you have chosen the light and left behind the darkness. The descendants of Rus' will bless you throughout many generations." And he gave her instructions about the Church, prayer, fasting, charity and purity of the body. She, with head bowed, stood and listened to the teachings, taking it all in like a sponge, and bowing to the Patriarch said: "May your prayers, Your Holiness, protect me against the nets of evil." And at baptism she was given the name Helen, the name of the ancient empress, mother of Constantine the Great. And the Patriarch blessed her and dismissed her... She got ready to go home and went to the Patriarch to ask for his blessing for the journey and said to him: "My people and my son are pagan — may God preserve me from all evil." And the Patriarch said: "My faithful child! You were baptized in Christ, you trust in Christ and Christ will protect you the way he protected Enoch in olden times..." And the Patriarch blessed her and she left in peace to go to her land, and came to Kiev. The blessed Olha from her childhood had sought wisdom in this world and found the priceless pearl — Christ. (*Nestorian Chronicle,* pp. 30-32.)

According to some historians, Princess Olha was baptized by her priest Hryhoriy, between 954 and 955. According to others, she was baptized in 957, while still others maintain she was not baptized until 959. The *Continuator Reginonis* under the year 959 writes thus about the baptism of Olha:

> Envoys of Helen, Queen of the Rugi [Helenae reginae Rugorum], who was baptized during the reign of Emperor Romanus [920-944], in Constantinople, had approached the king in a devious manner, it later developed. She requested that bishops be consecrated and priests be ordained for her people. (*Continuator Reginonis,* Monumenta Germaniae Historica, Vol. I, p. 624.)

The monk Yakov Mnikh (second half of the 11th century) wrote in his work, *In Memory and Praise of Volodymyr, Prince of Rus',* about the baptism of Olha:

> And so Olha, the blessed Princess of Rus', after the death of her husband Ihor, the Prince of Rus', was enlightened by God's grace in her heart... Although a woman, she had man's wisdom and having been enlightened by the Holy Spirit and understanding the true God, Creator of Heaven and Earth, she went to the land of the Greeks, to Tsarhorod [Constantinople], where the rulers were Christian and Christianity was firmly established, and having arrived asked to be baptized and having accepted Holy Baptism, she returned to the land of Rus', to her home, to her people, with great joy, sanctified in spirit and body and carrying the sign of the true cross. (Bugoslavsky, p. 149.)

The Kievan princess Olha by the Byzantine emperor in 955. Miniature from the Radziwill Chronicle.

956 — Pope John XII, and Emperor Otto I create two new dioceses in the Magdeburg Eparchy, one for Poland and another for Rus'.

957 — Princess Olha pays an official visit to the Byzantine Emperor Constantine Porphyrogenitus. The emperor himself describes Olha's visit in great detail. A dish used by Princess Olha was preserved in Constantinople. The dish had a precious stone from Olha and the word "Christ" engraved; hoping that it would bring them good luck, people made rubbings from the engraving. Once she accepted Christianity, Olha toured all the towns of Rus' preaching the Gospel.

959 — Princess Olha sends emissaries to the Holy Roman Emperor Otto I regarding the appointment of a bishop for Kievan Rus'.

Bishop Adaldag of Frankfurt consecrates the monk Libusius as bishop of Kievan Rus', but he dies shortly thereafter and never leaves for Kiev.

962 — On orders from Pope John XII, Wilhelm, the archbishop of Mainz, consecrates the monk Adalbert as the bishop of Kievan Rus'. The bishop leaves for Kiev the same year, but returns soon thereafter because of an unfriendly reception in Kiev.

24 July 969 — Princess Olha dies in Kiev. There are many legends about her life and death. The monk Yakov (Mnikh) describes her miracles:

> In the grave where the honorable and blessed body of the Blessed Princess Olha lay, there is a stone from the Church of our Blessed Mother of God. That church, made of stone, was built by Prince Volodymyr to honor the Blessed Mother of God and is the grave of the Blessed Princess Olha. At the top of the grave a window was cut out and through it one can see the body of the Blessed Olha, which lies uncorrupted; and for whomever comes there with faith this window is opened and the uncorrupted body, lying intact, can be seen and one wonders at this miracle of the body being unaffected after so many years... That is how God honors His servant, Olha, Princess of Rus', named Helen at the time of her baptism. After her sacred baptism this Blessed Princess Olha lived for another 15 years and having served God with her good deeds died on July 11 in the summer of 6477 [969] and delivered her honorable soul into the

hands of Our Lord and God, Christ. (Bugoslavsky, p. 151.)

977 — For the first time in the history of Kievan Rus' emissaries, sent by Pope Benedict VII (974-983), arrive in Ukraine. Their mission has not been ascertained, but some scholars speculate that during their stay in Kiev they baptized Yaropolk Svyatoslavovych, Grand Prince of Kiev, son of Svyatoslav.

Monument of St. Olha, first Christian Princess of Kievan Rus'-Ukraine in Kiev. Built in 1911 by Ivan Kavaleridze. Destroyed by the Soviet authorities in the 1920s.

Monument of St. Olha in Bound Brook, N.J. Built at the see of the Ukrainian Orthodox Metropolitanate in the USA in 1987, by Petro Kapshuchenko.

Church and Monastery Construction in the 1st-10th Centuries

CHURCH CONSTRUCTION

CRIMEA: 5th-7th century — In Chersonesus (Korsun), there were more than ten basilicas, chapels and churches. The most important were the basilica in Kruze, St. Peter's (Uvarovska) and the Western basilica. Basilicas were rectangular structures with an apse (a semi-circular area for the altar). This kind of structure was common in the West, in the Balkans (Bulgaria and Greece) and in the eastern provinces (Syria, Asia Minor). This style was not characteristic of Constantinople at that time. In Chersonesus there is also the Chapel with the Ark (so named by archeologists during excavations). An ark with the relics of a saint, along with reliefs depicting Christ and Sts. Peter and Paul, was found in the chapel.

6th-10th centuries — The Northern Basilica, found on the seashores in Chersonesus. A "basilica within a basilica" was built in the central nave of basilicas from the 6th century.

758-8th century — Church of St. John the Precursor, built from stone in Kerch; Cathedral of St. Sophia in Sugday (Surozh); Church of the Presentation in Feodosia; Church of the Assumption, built at the Monastery in Bakhchisaray; large and a small church carved from the lower section of the great cliffs at the cave monastery Shchuldan, in the village of Zalisne; church built in a cave at the monastery Chelter-Koba, near the village Male Sadove; St. Clement's Church, carved out of a cliff in the form of a three-naved basilica, at the cave monastery at Inkerman; church built at the cave monastery Kachi-Kalon in the village of Bashtanovtsi on the banks of the River Kachi; a cave church, Tepe-Kermen, carved out at the northeastern part of the cave town of Tepe-Kermen.

882 In *The Tale of Bygone Years* the Church of St. Irene in Kiev is mentioned for the first time.

9th century — The Church of St. Nicholas, built on the grave of Prince Askold in Kiev; St. Clement's Church in Chersonesus; two churches (one three-naved, the other in rotunda form) in the settlement of the Old Cathedral near Volodymyr-Volynsky.

945 — *The Tale of Bygone Years* mentions the wooden church of St. Elias in Kiev, where representatives of Prince Ihor took an oath on the occasion of the signing of the treaty with the Greeks.

981 — During the campaign of Volodymyr Svyatoslavych, Grand Prince of Kiev (still a pagan at that time), for the

Church of St. John the Baptist in Kerch (Crimea oblast), built in 758 and rebuilt during later centuries.

Cherven cities (now the Kholm region and Volynia), the church at the Old Cathedral settlement, near Volodymyr-Volynsky, is destroyed.

9th-10th centuries — In Chersonesus many churches in the cupola style, as well as miniature churches, are built; the Church of the Holy Trinity in the village of Zymne in Volynia.

MONASTERY CONSTRUCTION

CRIMEA: 8th century — Dormition (Panahiya) Monastery, built into a cliff in Bakhchisaray; cave monastery Shuldan, carved out from the lower cliffs in the village of Zalisne; cave monastery at Inkerman, carved from the side of a mountain, with churches above and underground, linked by stone steps; cave monastery Kachi-Kalon in the village of Bashtanovtsi on the bank of the Kachi River.

891 — Balaklavan St. George's Monastery, founded by the Greeks, near present-day Sevastopol. According to legend, the monastery was built on the spot where St. George appeared and saved a group of Greeks during a storm at sea.

Volodymyr-Volynsky: Svyatohirsky Monastery in the village of Zymne.

Ruins of the "Basilica in a basilica" in Chersonesus (Crimea oblast), built in the 6th century. Its 6th-century frescos remain. The new basilica, built in the 10th century on the location of the old, stood until the 14th century.

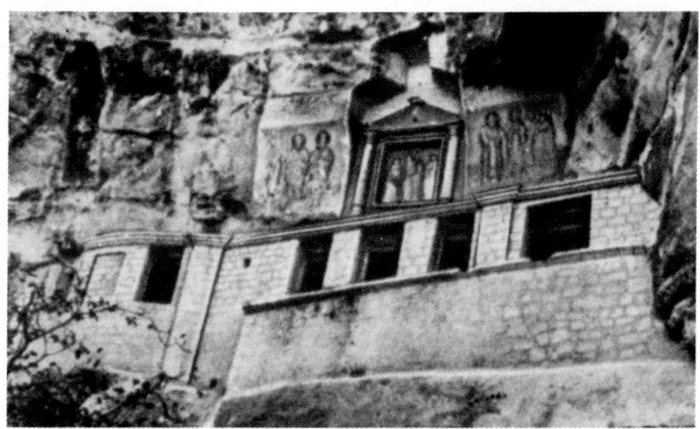

Dormition Cave Monastery (Uspensky) in Bakhchisaray (Crimea oblast), built in a rock in the 8th century.

II. The Age of Volodymyr the Great and Yaroslav the Wise: the Introduction and Development of Christianity in Kievan Rus'-Ukraine

General Characteristics of the Period

1. THE POLITICAL SITUATION IN EASTERN EUROPE

The end of the tenth century and the first half of the eleventh in Eastern Europe saw the rise of Poland, Hungary, and Bohemia, and the destruction of the Bulgar state. The Rus' state reached its zenith. On the east lay the Volga Bulgars and the Patzinaks (Pechenegs), who were decisively vanquished in 1036. The Alans and the Khazars, who had earlier been defeated by Svyatoslav, presented no major threat to Rus'.

Poland expanded under Boleslaw the Brave, taking territory from the Germans, the Magyars and Rus'. In 1019 Boleslaw took the Cherven cities of Galicia. After his death in 1025, this area was re-taken by Rus'. Under Casimir the Restorer, however, Poland enjoyed friendly terms with Rus' ruler Yaroslav the Wise.

Although in 1000 the Venetians took Istria, elsewhere in southeast Europe the Byzantine Empire made advances. The Byzantines took the Crimea in 1016. In 1018 they destroyed Bulgaria, which had developed a rich Eastern Christian culture. They reduced the Serbs to vassals, though the Croats lay outside their domain. In 1043 the Serbs revolted.

In the north, the Rus' cities of Polotsk and Novgorod developed a certain degree of autonomy. Novgorod was given its own charter after its prince, Yaroslav, moved his capital to Kiev in 1036. The city also gained a certain ecclesiastical autonomy. Novgorod obtained a foothold near the Gulf of Finland when Yuriyev (the present Tartu) was founded in 1030.

The spread of Christianity in Eastern Europe created a demand for tallow and wax for liturgical use. Bohemia became Western Europe's main source of gold. In the north, the Vikings and Varangians ceased plundering to participate in the lively North Sea trade in fish, wine, beer, salt and metals. To the south, the old Byzantine maritime trade routes between East and West were taken over by the Venetians.

2. THE RELIGIOUS SITUATION IN EUROPE

For some time the Papacy had been suffering a decline in its temporal power, becoming dependent on the central Italian barons. But around 1000 the Church recovered and began enjoying a new prosperity and prestige. In 1045 the German emperor came to the aid of the Papacy, enabling it to attain a position of strength. Gradually it became independent of secular rulers, at times even asserting its superiority over them.

At the same time, Western monasticism, exemplified by the Benedictines, reversed its decline with the Cluniac Reform. In Germany, the emperors introduced reforms of the secular clergy, encouraging piety, continence, and literacy.

In Spain, the Umayyad caliphate fell in 1031. Arabs and Berbers set up their own emirates, fragmenting Muslim resistance to the Christian onslaught from the north. Castile took over Leon in 1037, strengthening the political and military unity of the Christians.

Relations between the Eastern and Western Church, however, deteriorated during this time. In 1054 the Roman legate threw a bull of excommunication directed against the Patriarch upon the altar of St. Sophia in Byzantium. In turn the Patriarch excommunicated the Roman delegation. This decisively split the Church into what came to be known as the Great Schism (Catholicism and Orthodoxy).

Byzantine Christianity advanced in Eastern Europe. In 991 the population of Novgorod was baptized. In Suzdal, however, the pagans revolted in 1024 and were subdued by Yaroslav the Wise. In 997 the Magyars under King Stephen accepted the Christian faith.

3. THE POLITICAL SITUATION IN RUS'-UKRAINE

In 988 Rus' was still a loosely-knit confederation of principalities peopled by various tribes who spoke different languages. It had no firm territorial base. Gradually, the concept of Rus' spread to include the peoples ruled by the Christian descendants of Ryuryk. In the mid-eleventh century Rus' became a full-fledged medieval state firmly based on a specific territory — the areas of Kiev, Chernihiv and Pereyaslav — with its capital at Kiev, and possessing the "high" culture concomitant with its Christian state religion.

Volodymyr had strengthened his ties with Byzantium through his personal acceptance of the new faith and his marriage to Anna, the Emperor's sister, and a Greek Metropolitan had arrived in Kiev to administer the new Church.

The threat from the East, however, did not abate. In 992, 995 and 997 Volodymyr waged campaigns against the Pechenegs. Nor was there peace among the Rus' princes. When Volodymyr died in 1015, civil war broke out. Svyatopolk "the Damned" battled Yaroslav of Novgorod. In the confusion, the Poles took Kiev in 1018. In the following year Yaroslav succeeded in taking the capital. Defeated by Mstyslav near Chernihiv in 1024, Yaroslav retreated to his base at Novgorod. Seven years later he conquered the Cherven cities to the west. Polotsk went its own way.

For a dozen years, Rus' was divided between Yaroslav and Mstyslav, the latter holding Chernihiv. But when Mstyslav died in 1036, Yaroslav became master of the realm. He defeated the Pechenegs, re-united Rus' and settled in Kiev. The stage was set for a new era in the history of Rus'.

Yaroslav's state could now become fully Christian and Slavic. The canonization of Borys and Hlib around 1020 had prepared the ground for a native Christian culture. Kiev's St. Sophia, a marvel of architecture, as well as a showcase for mosaics and murals, was built around 1036. The city itself, admirably situated on the north-south river trade route, grew and prospered. Slavic translations of Greek texts were imported from Bulgaria, which Byzantium had destroyed as a state in 1018. The Church Slavonic language and alphabet developed by SS. Cyril and Methodius was adopted. The *Rus'ka Pravda,* a law-code influenced by Christian ethics, was compiled. The new Church even exhibited some independence when Ilarion (Hilarion) was appointed the first native metropolitan without consultation with Byzantium.

In 1043 Kievan Rus' launched an unsuccessful attack on Byzantium, and a reconciliation took place two years later. Yaroslav's son Vsevolod married the daughter of Emperor Constantine Monomachus. Other dynastic marriages established ties with ruling houses of Western Europe.

Yaroslav the Wise died in 1054, the year of the Great Schism. It was also the end of peace in the Rus' realm, and the beginning of its disintegration and decline.

RULERS OF KIEVAN RUS'-UKRAINE DURING THE 10TH-11TH CENTURIES

Volodymyr Svyatoslavych the Great 978-1015
Svyatopolk I Volodymyrovych "the Damned"....... 1015-1019
Yaroslav I Volodymyrovych the Wise 1019-1054

Chronology

978 — Prince Volodymyr emerges victorious from the fratricidal war among the sons of Svyatoslav the Conqueror, having defeated his brother Yaropolk with the help of the Varangians. Yaropolk had been tolerant of Christians, and scholars have speculated that he may have secretly converted to Christianity. During the early years of his reign in Kiev, Volodymyr had been devoted to paganism, perhaps merely because it was contrary to Prince Yaropolk's policy of tolerating Christianity. More likely, Volodymyr may have adhered to pagan worship in order to establish a strong political base among the predominately pagan population and to unite the various tribes. The earliest Ukrainian historical record, *The Tale of Bygone Years,* tells of Volodymyr's creation of an entire pantheon of pagan gods, including some non-Slavic ones:

> And he set up idols on the hills outside the castle with the hall: one of Perun, made of wood with a head of silver and a mustache of gold, and others of Khors, Dazhboh, Stryboh, Symarhl, and Mokosha. The people offered sacrifices to them, calling them gods (Nestorian Chronicle, p. 43).

983 — Volodymyr compels the nation to worship the pagan gods. After his victory over the Yatviagians, Volodymyr commands that a boy and a girl be sacrificed to the pagan gods. The son of a Christian Varangian is chosen, but when the father refuses to allow his son to be sacrificed, both are killed by an enraged mob. The father and son are the first known Rus' martyrs for their faith.

983-987 — Prince Volodymyr steadily comes under the influence of Christians and gravitates away from paganism. Of Volodymyr's five wives, four are Christians.

986 — Prince Volodymyr receives delegations from the Volga Bulgars, who are Moslems; from the German Catholics; from the Khazars, who practice Judaism; and the Byzantine Greeks. Each delegation extolls its faith, but the Greeks make the greatest impression on Volodymyr.

987 — Prince Volodymyr assembles his boyars and elders to discuss the need of conversion from paganism to a new faith. This event is described in *The Tale of Bygone Years:*

> In the year 6495 [987] Volodymyr summoned together his boyars and the city elders and said to them, "Behold, the Bulgars came to me, saying: Accept our faith. Then

came the Germans and praised their own faith. After them came the Jews. Finally the Greeks appeared, criticizing all other faiths but praising their own, and they spoke at length, telling the history of the whole world from its beginning. Their words were artful, and it was wondrous to listen and pleasant to hear them. They preach about another world. 'Whoever,' they said, 'adopts our religion and then dies shall arise again and live forever. But whosoever embraces another faith shall be consumed with fire in the next world.' What is your opinion on this subject, what do you counsel?" The boyars and the elders replied, "You know, O Prince, that no man condemns that which is his own, but praises it instead. If you desire to find out for certain, send your servants to look and inquire about who has what kind of religion and how he serves God." (Nestorian Chronicle, pp. 47, 48.)

After visiting the Bulgars on the Volga, and the Germans, Volodymyr's emissaries travel to Constantinople to meet with the Emperors Basil and Constantine. Upon their return they give the following report from their sojourn in Constantinople, as recorded in *The Tale of Bygone Years:*

"Then we went to the land of the Greeks and they led us to the place where they worship their God, and we knew not whether we were in heaven or on earth. For on earth there is no such splendor or such beauty, and we are at a loss how to describe it. We only know that God dwells there among men, and their service is fairer than the ceremonies of other nations. We cannot forget such beauty, for every man, after tasting something sweet, is afterward unwilling to accept that which is bitter; and so we also can no longer live here as pagans." Then the boyars said, "If the Greek faith were evil, it would not have been accepted by your grandmother Olha, and she was wiser than all others." Volodymyr then inquired: "Where should we be baptized?" And they replied, "Wherever you wish." (Nestorian Chronicle, p. 49.)

988 — Prince Volodymyr leads an assault on the Crimean city of Chersonesus (Korsun), a major Byzantine colony. After taking the city, he demands that the Byzantine emperors give him their only sister, Anna, in marriage. The emperors finally agree, but insist upon a precondition to the marriage: that Volodymyr convert to Christianity. At that time, Volodymyr has temporarily lost his eyesight as a result of illness. *The Tale of Bygone Years* provides the following account of the restoration of his vision and his conversion to Christianity:

Volodymyr and his retinue entered the city, and he sent envoys to the Emperors Basil and Constantine, with the message, "Behold, I have captured your famous city. I have heard that you have an unwedded sister. Unless you give her to me as wife, I shall do to your capital what I have done with this city." When the emperors heard this they were fearful, and sent to him the following reply: "It is not becoming for Christian women to be given in marriage to pagans. If you are baptized, you shall have her as wife, inherit the kingdom of God, and be our companion in the faith. If you do not do this, we will not be able to give you our sister in marriage." When Volodymyr heard this, he told the envoys of the emperors, "Tell your emperors this: I will be baptized, for I have already learned about your religion and I love your faith and your services, which have been described to me by the men we sent." When the emperors heard this they rejoiced and persuaded their sister, Anna, whom they sent to Volodymyr. They then requested Volodymyr to submit to baptism before they should send their sister to him, but Volodymyr desired that the princess should herself bring priests to baptize him. The emperors complied with this request, and sent forth their sister, accompanied by some dignitaries and priests. Anna did not want to go. "It is as if I were going into captivity," she lamented, "better were it for me to die at home." But her brothers protested, "Through your agency God may turn the land of Rus' to repentance, and you will relieve the Greek lands from the danger of grievous war. Do you not see how much harm the Rus' have already brought upon the Greeks? If you do not go, they may bring on us the same misfortunes as they did in Korsun." They overcame her hesitation only with great difficulty. The princess embarked upon a ship, and after tearfully embracing her kinfolk, set forth across the sea and arrived at Korsun. The natives came forth to greet her, and conducted her into the city, where they settled her in the palace.

Baptism of Grand Prince Volodymyr in Chersonesus (Korsun, Crimea oblast). Miniature from the Radziwill Chronicle.

By divine agency, Volodymyr was suffering at that moment from a disease of the eyes and could see nothing. He sorrowed greatly and did not know what to do. The princess declared to him: "If you desire to be relieved of this disease, you should be baptized with all speed, otherwise you will not be rid of this disease." When Volodymyr heard this, he said, "If this proves true, then truly the God of the Christians is great," and gave orders that he should be baptized. The bishop of Korsun, together with the princess's priests, after announcing the tidings, baptized Volodymyr, and as the bishop laid his hand upon him, he straightway received his sight. Upon experiencing this sudden cure, Volodymyr glorified God, saying, "I have now perceived the one true God." When his retinue beheld this miracle, many of them were also baptized.

Volodymyr was baptized in the Church of St. Basil, which stands in Korsun in a square in the center of the city, where the Korsunians trade. The palace of Volodymyr stands beside this church to this day, and the palace of the princess is behind the altar. After his baptism, Volodymyr took the princess in marriage. Those who do not know the truth say he was baptized in Kiev, while others assert this event took place in Vasylkiv, while still others mention other places.

Hereupon Volodymyr took the princess and Anastasius and the priests of Korsun, together with the relics of St. Clement and of Phoebus, his disciple, and also selected sacred vessels and icons for the service. In Korsun he founded a church on the mound which had been heaped up in the middle of the city with the earth removed from his embankment; this church is still standing to the present day. While returning Volodymyr took two bronze statues and four bronze horses, which now stand behind the Church of the Holy Virgin [in Kiev] and which the ignorant think are made of marble. As a dowry for the princess, he gave Korsun to the Greeks, and then departed for Kiev. (Nestorian Chronicles, pp. 50-52.)

Upon returning to Kiev, Prince Volodymyr directed that his twelve small sons be baptized. Many boyars accepted Christianity together with them. The first baptism in Kiev took place on the spot where the Pochayna and Dnieper rivers join and which was later called Khreshchatyk.

The Tale of Bygone Years relates the following about the official Christianization of Rus':

When the prince arrived [in Kiev], he directed that the idols should be toppled, and that some should be cut to pieces and others burned. He ordered Perun to be bound to a horse's tail and dragged down Borychev to the Ruchay River. He appointed twelve men to beat the idol with sticks, not because he thought the wood was sensitive, but to affront the demon who had deceived man in this guise, that he might receive chastisement at the hands of men. "Great art thou, O Lord, and marvelous are thy works! Yesterday he was honored of men, but today held in derision." While Perun was being dragged along the Ruchay to the Dnieper, the unbelievers wept over it, for they had not yet received Holy Baptism. After they had thus dragged the idol along, they cast it into the Dnieper.

Then Volodymyr sent heralds throughout the whole city to proclaim that if any inhabitant, rich or poor, did not betake himself to the river, he would become the prince's enemy. When the people heard these words, they wept with joy and exclaimed in their happiness: "If this were not good, the prince and his boyars would not have accepted it." On the morrow, the prince went forth to the Dnieper with the priests of the princess and those from Korsun, and a countless multitude assembled. They all went into the water: some stood up to their necks, others to their breasts, and the younger near the bank, some of them holding children in their arms, while the adults waded farther out. The priests stood by and offered prayers. There was joy in heaven and on earth to behold so many souls saved. And the devil spoke quietly: "Woe is me! I am driven out hence! I thought to have my dwelling-place here, since the apostolic teachings could not be heard in this land. Nor did this people know God, and I rejoiced in the service they rendered unto me. But now I am vanquished by the ignorant, not by apostles and martyrs, and my reign in these regions is at an end."

When the people were baptized, they returned each to his own abode. Volodymyr, rejoicing that he and his subjects now knew God himself, looked up to heaven and said, "O God, who has created heaven and earth, look down, I beseech thee, on this thy new people, and grant them, O Lord, to know thee as the true God, even as the Christian nations have known thee. Confirm in them the true and inalterable faith, and help me, O Lord, against the devil, so that, hoping in thee and in thy might, I may overcome his malice." Having spoken thus, he ordered that churches should be built and established where pagan idols had previously stood. He thus founded the Church of St. Basil on the hill where the idol of Perun and the other images had been set, and where the prince and the people had offered homage. They began to build churches

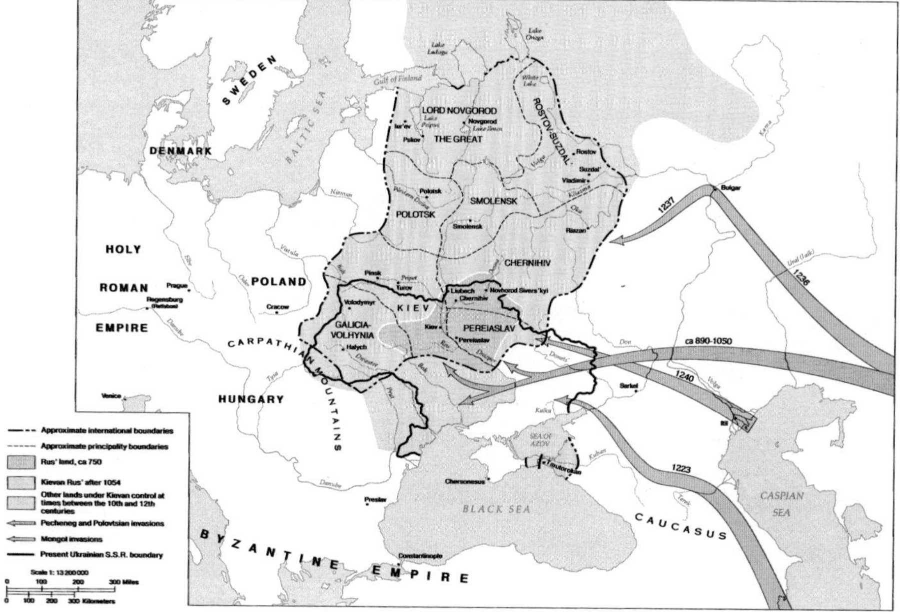

Kievan Rus' in the 11th century.

The "Baptism of Ukraine," by Petro Andrusiv. Painted on the occasion of the millennium of Christianity of Rus'-Ukraine.

in other cities and to assign priests to them and to lead the people of entire cities and villages to baptism. Blessed be the Lord Jesus Christ, who gave love to the land of Rus', and illumined it with Holy Baptism. (Nestorian Chronicle, pp. 52-53.)

In addition to the record in *The Tale of Bygone Years,* the conversion of Kievan Rus' to Christianity is chronicled in other historical works from the 10th-11th centuries.

The Church Code of St. Volodymyr (11th century) states:

In the name of the Father, the Son and the Holy Ghost. I, the Grand Prince Vasyliy, named Volodymyr, son of Svyatoslav, grandson of Ihor [and] the blessed Olha, received Holy Baptism from the Greek emperors Constantine and Basil and the Patriarch Photius, and brought the first metropolitan, Mykhayil, to Kiev, so that he would baptize all of Rus'. (Makariy, Vol. 1, p. 273.)

(The compilers and transcribers of the Code erroneously included in the text a reference to Patriarch Photius, who occupied the patriarchal seat in Constantinople during the periods 857-867 and 878-886.)

Nestor, the noted 11th-century chronicler of Kievan Rus', wrote thus in *A Narrative about Saints Borys and Hlib:*

In those times there was a prince named Volodymyr, who ruled Rus'. He was a fair man who showed compassion toward lesser men, orphans, and widows. He was a pagan by faith. God moved him and caused him to become a Christian, like the ancient Plakyda. For Plakyda was a just and merciful man, an Alan by faith, as has been written of him. When the cross of the Lord Jesus Christ appeared before him, he bowed and said: "Lord, who are you and what do you tell your servant?" And the Lord said to him: "I am Christ, whom you, not knowing, worship; now go and be baptized." And later, taking his wife and children with him, he was baptized in the name of the Father, the Son, and the Holy Ghost. And he was given the name Eustachius. And that Volodymyr also saw a vision of God, leading him to become a Christian. He was given the name Vasyliy. After his christening, Volodymyr atoned for his past: "I was like an animal, creating much evil, living a pagan life, like a naked beast." (Chubaty, Vol. I, p. 217).

Yakov Mnikh, a monk who lived during the eleventh century, wrote thus in his work, *In Memory and Praise of Volodymyr, Prince of Rus':*

And so I, a humble monk, had heard from many of the pious Volodymyr, [ruler] of all Rus', son of Svyatoslav, and, after compiling what I could from those who knew of his good deeds, I wrote of how God's love illuminated the heart of Volodymyr, Prince of Rus'... Volodymyr heard of his grandmother Olha and how she travelled to Constantinople and received Holy Baptism there... Volodymyr's heart was set on fire by the Holy Spirit and he longed for Holy Baptism. Seeing the desire in Volodymyr's heart, God showed his greatness and looked down from the heavens with His mercy and munificence and illuminated the heart of Volodymyr, the Prince of Rus', causing him to receive the Christian Faith... Volodymyr, grandson of Olha, baptized himself, his children, and all of the land of Rus' and its cities... (Makariy, Vol. I, p. 255.)

Contemporary writers, as well as later historians (Ademar, Dlugosh (1415-80), and El-Maknin (1223-1302), wrote that Greek bishops had travelled to Rus' (Some wrote that only the Greek bishop of Chersonesus came) and christened the people of Rus'. Certain sources from the 13th century state that the Patriarch of Constantinople, Nicholas II Chrysoberges, and the general Synod sent Metropolitan Mykhayil to Kiev, and that he baptized the people of Rus'.

According to church tradition, the date of the christening of Kiev is August 14 (August 1 by the Julian calendar). In fact, history suggests that the events and dates associated with the christening of Kievan Rus' may differ somewhat from the account in *The Tale of Bygone Years.* This new chronology, recently suggested by historians, is set forth below:

987 — An uprising against the Byzantine emperors is led by Bardas Phocas, a warlord, who proclaims himself emperor. At the request of Basil II and Constantine VIII, Volodymyr dispatches 6,000 soldiers to assist in quelling the revolt. As a precondition of this assistance, Volodymyr asks for the hand in marriage of the emperors' sister, Anna. By this time, Volodymyr had already converted to Christianity.

989 — Volodymyr's army defeats Bardas Phocas. However, the Byzantine emperors renege on their promise to give Anna in marriage to Volodymyr. Volodymyr reacts to this treachery by launching an assault on the city of Chersonesus (Korsun), which he captures after a siege of several months. He threatens to attack Byzantium unless he obtains Anna's hand in marriage. Ultimately, the emperors capitulate to Volodymyr's demand. The marriage of Volodymyr and the Greek princess takes place in Chersonesus.

Bas-relief "Baptism of Kievan Rus'" on the Stone pedestal of the monument of St. Volodymyr the Great in Kiev. Built in 1853.

During the siege of Chersonesus, Volodymyr is visited by emissaries of Pope John XV, who bring a gift — the relics [the head] of St. Clement. The delegation probably has a missionary purpose but, having accepted the faith, Volodymyr remains loyal to the Eastern Church.

989 or 990 — Volodymyr returns to Kiev and proclaims his intention to christen the entire nation. After a period of preparation, he proceeds to baptize the Kievans in the Dnieper River. Contrary to the account in *The Tale of Bygone Years,* the christenings are not in all cases voluntary. This is alluded to by Metropolitan Ilarion in his *Sermon on Law and Grace:*

> Some who went to be baptized went not out of love but out of fear for him who ordered the baptisms, because his [Prince Volodymyr's] faith was tied to his authority.

989 — Construction is begun in Kiev on the Cathedral of the Holy Mother of God (the Church of the Tithes), the first stone church built in Rus'.

(According to the alternate chronology, the construction of the Church of the Tithes began in 990 or 991.)

Volodymyr endeavors to create an educated stratum of society, from which he can recruit priests and literate advisors. According to *The Tale of Bygone Years:*

> He took the children of the best families and sent them for instruction in book-learning. The mothers of these children wept bitterly over them, for they were not yet strong in faith, but mourned as for the dead.

Volodymyr the Great oversees the spread of Christianity to all parts of his vast domain. Historians have noted that there was great resistance in the cities of Novgorod, Murom, and Rostov, as well as in the northern territories. In what is known today as Ukraine and Byelorussia, no resistance was noted.

Representatives of Pope John XV arrive in Kiev, bringing with them the relics of saints as gifts for Volodymyr the Great.

988-990 — Christianity in Ukraine expands around Kiev and the settlements along the Dnieper, Desna, Oster, Trubezh, Sula, and Stuhna rivers.

990 — Metropolitan Mykhayil and six bishops, in the company of Volodymyr the Great's uncle, Dobrynya, and Anastas Korsunyanyn, travel to Novgorod to do missionary work. Encountering great resistance to their efforts to Christianize the people, the large Christian delegation succeeds in baptizing only a part of the population of Novgorod. The following saying is a legacy of the efforts to christen Novgorod: "Putyata [a military commander] baptized them with the sword and Dobrynya [Volodymyr's viceregent] baptized them with fire."

991 — Metropolitan Mykhayil and four bishops, together with Dobrynya and Anastas Korsunyanyn, visit Rostov, in the northern territories. After an unsuccessful attempt to baptize the residents of Rostov, the metropolitan and three of the bishops return to Kiev. Bishop Theodore remains in Rostov, but soon he, too, is compelled to escape to Suzdal, having failed to overcome the resistance of the heathens. After this failure, Bishop Ilarion comes to Rostov from Constantinople but, after a short time, he, too, escapes and returns to his homeland.

Emissaries from Pope John XV visit Kiev again. Later, Volodymyr the Great sends his envoys to Rome.

992 — Mykhayil, the first Metropolitan of Rus', dies. He is interred in the Church of the Tithes, but in 1103 his remains are transferred to Antoniy's cave and, in 1730, moved again to the main Church of the Assumption of the Kievan Monastery of the Caves.

The new Kievan metropolitan, Leontiy, ordains the first bishops for cities in Kievan Rus' — Chernihiv, Volodymyr-Volynsky, Bilhorod, Novgorod and Rostov.

11-12 May 996 — In Kiev the Church of the Tithes is consecrated. *The Tale of Bygone Years* describes that event:

> Volodymyr, upon seeing his church completed, entered it and prayed to God, saying, "Lord God! Look down from heaven, behold and visit thy vineyard, and protect what thy hand hast planted. Make these new people, whose heart thou hast turned unto wisdom, to know Thee, the true God." After he had offered this prayer, he added, "I bestow upon this church of the Holy Virgin a tithe of my property and of my cities..." So he gave the tithe to Anastasius of Korsun. (Nestorian Chronicle, p. 55.)

(Anastasius of Korsun was, in all likelihood, the most important of the priests that Volodymyr brought with him from Korsun after marrying Princess Anna, and to him fell the honor of being the pastor of the newly-built Kievan church.)

With the tax of one-tenth of all wealth going to the Church of the Tithes and all the other churches of Kievan Rus', Volodymyr bestowed on them a privilege enjoyed by no church or patriarchal cathedral in Greece.

1000 — Representatives of Pope Sylvester II, together with emissaries of the Czech and Magyar kings, arrive in Kiev. The purpose of their mission is not known.

1001 — Volodymyr the Great sends envoys to Rome (to Pope Sylvester II), to Egypt (to the Patriarch of Alexandria), and to Babylon (to the Patriarch of Antioch), that they may, according to the Chronicle of Nikon, "observe the lands and their customs."

The exchange of representatives between Rome and Kievan Rus' demonstrates that Volodymyr maintained friendly relations with the Western Church, even though, the Kievan Metropolitan See, initially autonomous, was tied to Byzantium since 1037.

10th-11th centuries — The grand princes, Volodymyr and his son Yaroslav, found the Monastery of the Assumption on Mt. Athos in Greece. Subsequently,

Monument of St. Volodymyr the Great, Baptizer of Kievan Rus'-Ukraine, in Kiev. Built in 1853. Height 20.4 m. Sculptors V. Demut-Malynovsky and P. Klodt. Architect O. Ton.

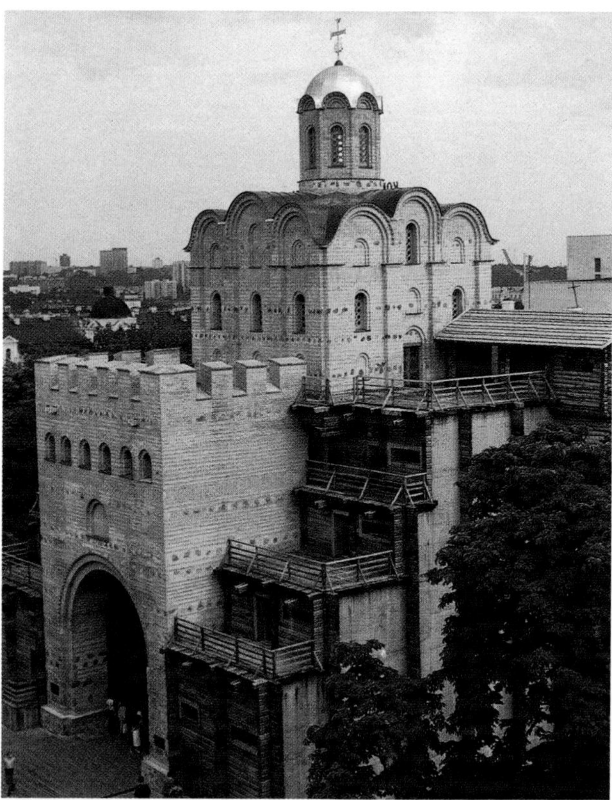

The Golden Gate with the Annunciation Church Above-the-Gate in Kiev. Construction of the triumphal and defensive gate and church began in 1037. The gate and the church were destroyed by the Mongols in 1240 and later restored. The population of Kiev and the hierarchy of the Ukrainian Church triumphantly greeted Hetman Bohdan Khmelnytsky at the gate in 1648 after his victories over Poland. After Ukraine's annexation to Russia, the gate and the church fell into disrepair and were covered by earth in 1750. The Golden Gate and the church were restored in 1982 and converted into a museum and concert hall.

the monastery of St. Panteleimon was added to it. Together, they became known as the Monasteries of Rus'.

1004 — The Monk Adrian, of the Paulician sect, which rejects numerous Christian dogmas and does not recognize the church hierarchy, visits Kiev. Soon thereafter Metropolitan Leontiy excommunicates the monk from the Church. Adrian is put in prison, where he renounces his errors.

1007 — En route to visit the Pechenegs, Archbishop Bruno of Querfurt, an emissary of Pope John XVIII, stops in Kiev and spends a month at the court of Volodymyr the Great. During his return trip home he stops again in Kiev and ordains a bishop for the Pechenegs.

ca. 1007 — Volodymyr the Great and Metropolitan Leontiy disinter the theretofore undisturbed relics of Princess Olha. With great ceremony, the relics are transferred to the Church of the Tithes.

1008 — Archbishop Ioann becomes Metropolitan of Kiev.

1011 — Princess Anna, wife of Volodymyr, dies in Kiev. She is buried in the Church of the Tithes.

16 July 1015 — Volodymyr the Great dies in Kiev. In the quarter century from the Christening of Kievan Rus' until his death, he oversaw the conversion to Christianity of approximately half of the Kievan state. The process of converting the people to Christianity did not always proceed smoothly. The farther north one went, the more difficult was the missionary work.

By introducing the Christian faith into Kievan Rus', Volodymyr led his country into the great family of nations and opened it to the cultures of the world. With the acceptance of Christianity in Kievan Rus', literature, church architecture, and art began to develop. Volodymyr built many churches, including the Kiev cathedral, the Church of the Tithes. The people fondly remembered him as a great and powerful, yet humane and accessible, leader. Reflecting the nation's sentiments, the ancient sagas refer to Volodymyr as the "Beautiful Sun." Volodymyr the Great was buried with great ceremony in the Church of the Tithes, alongside Princess Anna. Subsequently, he was proclaimed a saint of the Church.

A later metropolitan, Ilarion, dedicated his historical work, *The Sermon on Law and Grace... Praise for Our Kagan Volodymyr,* to the prince during a ceremony at Volodymyr's tomb in the Church of the Tithes in 1043. In his sermon, which is one of the oldest works of Ukrainian church literature, Ilarion wrote:

> How did you come to believe? How did you come to burn with Christ's love? How did you come to possess a wisdom surpassing that of all wise men, to love that which cannot be seen and to reach toward heaven? How did you find Christ? How did you give yourself to Him?.. Tell us, your servants, tell us, our teacher, from where

Head of a youth. Fragment of the oldest fresco from the 10th century still remaining. It was found in the ruins of the Tithes (Desyatynna) Church in Kiev, destroyed by the Soviets in the 1930s.

did the breath of the Holy Ghost come to you? You never saw Christ, nor did you walk with him: how, then, did you become his disciple? Others, who had seen him, did not become believers, but you did not see, and yet you believed. You did not see the apostle who, having come to your land, with his abject poverty and nakedness, his hunger and thirst, brought humility to your heart. You did not see how demons were cast out in the name of Christ, the ill returned to health, fire changed to ice, the dead resurrected. Not having seen all of that, how did you come to believe? What a strange miracle! Other kings and rulers, having learned of all this from holy men, not only did not believe, but subjected them to torture and martyrdom. But you, O blessed one, came to Christ without all that. Guided solely by your own good sense and sharp mind, you concluded that there is only one God, the Creator of all that is visible and invisible, heavenly and of the earth, and that He sent down his Beloved Son for our salvation. And with these thoughts you strode into the holy waters. (Ponomarev, p. 69.)

1015 — Prince Svyatopolk murders his younger brothers, Borys and Hlib, whom he regarded as potential opponents. The body of Borys is buried in the Church of St. Basil, in Vyshhorod. The Church added them to the register of saints, and honors their memory jointly on August 6 (July 24 by the Julian calendar), the day on which Borys was killed. The day of Hlib's death, September 18 (September 5), is observed separately.

1018 — Poland seizes the western part of Kievan Rus', including the Cherven cities and with them the seat of the Eparchy of Peremyshl. It was through the Peremyshl Eparchy that Rus' received much religious literature written in Slavic.

1019 — Yaroslav, later known as "The Wise," becomes Grand Prince of Kiev. Whereas his father, Volodymyr the Great, spread Christianity throughout his vast realm, Yaroslav dedicates himself to expanding churches and enlarging the ranks of the clergy, building monasteries and schools, and promoting education.

Reception on the occasion of the blessing of SS. Borys and Hlib Church in Vyshhorod. Miniature from the Sylvester anthology.

SS. Borys and Hlib. 16th-century icon from the Holy Spirit Church in the village Potelychi (Lviv oblast).

1020 — The body of Prince Hlib is discovered near Smolensk. The relics are transported with great ceremony to Vyshhorod, where they are interred in the Church of St. Basil, next to the grave of Hlib's brother Borys. After a fire destroys the Church of St. Basil, the relics of the saints are transferred to another location, and there Prince Yaroslav the Wise, the brother of the martyrs, later builds the Church of SS. Borys and Hlib.

1021 — Historical accounts mention the first Service ever celebrated in Rus' in honor of SS. Borys and Hlib. The Service, written by Metropolitan Ioann, is regarded as the first church composition of Kievan Rus'.

1026 — The martyred princes Borys and Hlib are canonized through the efforts of Metropolitan Ioann. A church is built in their honor in Vyshhorod and a holiday proclaimed in their memory.

1030 — Yaroslav orders 300 children from the families of deacons and priests in Novgorod to be taken for training for the priesthood.

1031 — Prince Yaroslav the Wise liberates the Cherven cities, including the Eparchy of Peremyshl, from Poland.

1.

2.

3.

4.

Coins of Grand Princes of Kiev of the 10th-11th centuries with the Ukrainian national symbol, the trident, and the cross. Coins of Prince Volodymyr the Great: 1. Gold of type I, 2. Silver of type II, 3. Silver of type III, 4. Silver of type IV, 5. Coins of Prince Svyatopolk, 6. Silver coins of Prince Yaroslav the Wise.

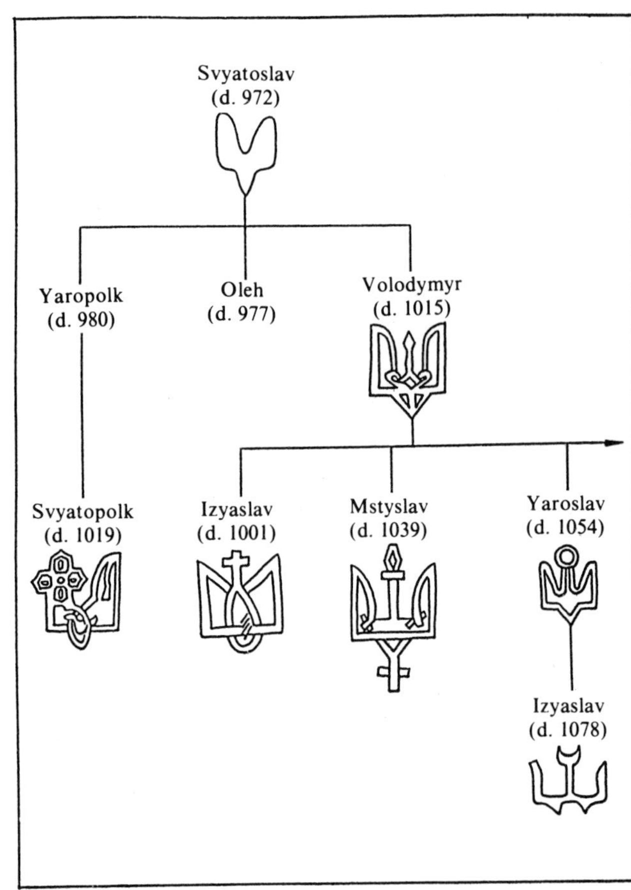

Genealogical scheme of old Ukrainian coins of the Princes of Kiev of the 10th-11th centuries with the Ukrainian symbol, the trident, and the cross. Classification by M. Sotnikov and I. Spasky.

5.

6.

The representation of the family of Grand Prince Yaroslav the Wise in the Cathedral of St. Sophia in Kiev. XIth-century fresco.

1035 — Patriarch Alexius the Studite ordains Theopemptos Metropolitan of Kiev.

1037 — The Feast of the Protection of the Most Holy Mother of God (Pokrov) is established in Kievan Rus', as Prince Yaroslav the Wise builds the Annunciation Church atop the Golden Gates in Kiev.

Prince Yaroslav the Wise establishes the first library in Kievan Rus' at the Church of St. Sophia. He recruits transcribers and translators skilled in Greek, Bulgarian, Hebrew, and other languages to work in the library. The original collection numbers approximately 950 volumes, primarily religious works.

1039 — According to *The Tale of Bygone Years,* Metropolitan Theopemptos consecrates the Church of the Holy Mother of God, built by Volodymyr the Great.

1044 — Prince Yaroslav transfers the remains of Princes Yaropolk and Oleh, killed during the struggle for power that followed the death of Svyatoslav the Conqueror, to the Church of the Tithes.

Grand Prince Yaroslav the Wise of Kiev.

Sarcophagus of Grand Prince Yaroslav the Wise of Kiev, 11th century. St. Sophia Cathedral in Kiev.

1051 — Ilarion, the priest of the Church of the Savior in the village of Berestiv, where the Kievan Monastery of the Caves stands, is elected Metropolitan by a Synod of bishops assembled in Kiev on Prince Yaroslav's orders.

1050-1059 — Construction of the Monastery of the Caves begins in Kiev. A historical account associates them with Metropolitan Ilarion who, while still a priest, would spend long periods of time in a cave he had dug, "praying secretly to God." The monastery was founded on the site by Antoniy, a monk from Lyubech, near Chernihiv. He and Teodosiy, who later became Hegumen of the Monastery of the Caves, are regarded as the founders of monasticism in Ukraine.

20 February 1054 — Yaroslav the Wise dies in Vyshhorod, near Kiev. This event is recounted in *The Tale of Bygone Years:*

> The end of Yaroslav's life drew near, and he gave up his spirit to God on the first Saturday after the feast of St. Theodore. Vsevolod had his father's body prepared and, laying it upon a sled, brought it to Kiev, accom-

panied by priests, who sang the customary hymns. The people mourned for him, and, having brought his body, laid it in a marble sarcophagus in the Church of St. Sophia. (Nestorian Chronicle, p. 75, 76.)

Iryna, the wife of Yaroslav the Wise, was the first princess of Rus' to enter the monastic life. She died on February 10, 1050.

16-25 July 1054 — The Christian Church splits into the Eastern and Western Churches, or the Orthodox and Catholic Church. Pope Leo IX excommunicates Patriarch Michael I Cerularius, accusing him of ten heresies. In reply, on July 20, the Patriarch declares the Pope anathema. The Eastern Patriarchs cease to mention the Pope in their services.

Principal Ecclesiastical Activities

1. THE KIEVAN METROPOLITANATE DURING THE 10TH-11TH CENTURIES

The First Ecumenical Council in Nicaea (325) and the Fourth in Chalcedon (451) decided that metropolitans would be elected by provincial synods of bishops, confirmed and ordained by the Patriarch. The Patriarch of Constantinople, proclaimed at the Ecumenical Council in 518, was responsible for overseeing the activities of the metropolitans and the metropolitan sees and was empowered to discipline the metropolitans. However, the Patriarchs were not authorized to demote metropolitans without the approval of the Church council.

Notwithstanding the decisions of the Nicaea and Chalcedon Councils, the Patriarchs of Constantinople selected and ordained Kievan metropolitans who had not been elected by a provincial synod of Ukrainian bishops of Kievan Rus'. The exceptions to this practice were Metropolitan Ilarion (1051-1054), Klym Smolyatych (1147-1154), and Hryhoriy Tsamblak (1415-1419), all of whom had been elected by a Synod of Rus' bishops without the consent of the Patriarch. For this reason, the Patriarch never confirmed them.

The first four metropolitans of this period — Mykhayil, Leontiy, Ioann, and Teopempt — were designated for Kiev and confirmed by the Patriarch without the participation of the bishops of Kievan Rus'. The first two metropolitans could not have been chosen from among the bishops of Rus', because there were no established eparchies in the young Christian state, while the bishops of the 10th and early 11th centuries were exclusively engaged in missionary work.

From the inception of the Kievan Metropolitan See, its seat was the city of Kiev. However, the metropolitan resided in the nearby town of Pereyaslav. It was not until 1037, after the construction of the Church of St. Sophia during the reign of Prince Yaroslav the Wise, that the metropolitan's residence was relocated to Kiev.

METROPOLITANS OF KIEV (988-1054)

The following list of the first metropolitans of Kievan Rus'-Ukraine (988-1054) is arranged in accordance with church tradition. Certain church historians have disputed the names of some metropolitans and the dates when they served. Nevertheless, sufficient source materials exist to confirm the accuracy of the names and dates listed below.

Mykhayil 988-992
Leontiy 992-1008
Ioann 1008-1035
Teopempt 1035-1049
Ilarion (Hilarion) 1051-1054

2. EPARCHIES IN THE KIEVAN METROPOLITANATE

The dates below represent the year in which the eparchy was established or, where this information is not available, the dates when the eparchy is mentioned in the chronicles for the first time:

WITHIN THE BORDERS OF PRESENT-DAY UKRAINE:

Kiev 988
Tmutorokan 868
Volodymyr-Volynsky 991
Bilhorod 992
Chernihiv 992
Yuriyiv 1032

WITHIN THE BORDERS OF PRESENT-DAY BYELORUSSIA:

Polotsk .... 10th century
Turov .... 10th century

WITHIN THE BORDERS OF PRESENT-DAY RUSSIA:

Novgorod 992

WITHIN THE BORDERS OF PRESENT-DAY POLAND:

Peremyshl 899

BISHOPS OF EPARCHIES WITHIN KIEVAN RUS'

History has recorded only a few of the names of the bishops of the Kievan Metropolitanate who served during the 10th and 11th centuries. Certain bishops came to Kievan Rus' from Constantinople, others from Bulgaria, while some were ordained by the metropolitans in Kiev. The following bishops have been identified:

Bilhorod: Mykyta (992)

Chernihiv: Neofit (992)

Novgorod: Ioakym Korsunyanyn (992-1030), Luka Zhydyata (1035-1059)

Rostov: Teodor (992), Ilarion (10th century)

Volodymyr-Volynsky: Stefan (992)

Church and Monastery Construction

CHURCH CONSTRUCTION

The first churches built in Ukraine were erected prior to the official acceptance of Christianity in 988. Many churches in Kiev and other cities of Rus' were built by Volodymyr the Great and Yaroslav the Wise. The German historian, Thietmar of Merseberg (975-1018), in his work, *Chronicon,* and the Polish historian, Mechow, both wrote that during the period following the acceptance of Christianity between 300 and 400 churches were built in Kiev alone. This figure probably included small churches and chapels that were established in private homes.

The chronicles report the construction of many churches in Ukraine during the 10th and 11th centuries. The following list is arranged according to the present-day administrative division of Ukraine:

KIEV OBLAST. Kiev: The first Church of St. George the Conqueror (988), built by Prince Volodymyr the Great; Church of St. Basil (988), built by Volodymyr the Great, destroyed by fire in 1020; Church of St. Turov the Martyr (10th century); Church of the Tithes (Desyatynna) of the Holy Mother of God (990-996), built by Volodymyr the Great on the site where the first Christians (the Varangians Teodor and Ioann) were martyred in Kiev; Church of the Apostles SS. Peter and Paul (1008), built by Metropolitan Ioann; Church of St. Sophia (1036), built by Yaroslav the Wise on the site of his victory over the Pechenegs; Church of the Annunciation of the Holy Mother of God (1037), built by Yaroslav the Wise above the Golden Gates of Kiev; the second Church of St. George the Conqueror, built by Yaroslav the Wise; Church of St. Irene (1037), built by Yaroslav the Wise. ***Berestiv:*** Church of the Holy Apostles (11th century). ***Bilhorod:*** Church of the Divine Transfiguration (10th century), built by Volodymyr the Great. ***Pereyaslav:*** Church of the Holy Cross (1008), built by Metropolitan Ioann. ***Vasyliv:*** Church of the Divine Transfiguration (996), built by Volodymyr the Great. ***Vyshhorod:*** Church of St. Basil (988), built by Volodymyr the Great; Church of SS. Borys and Hlib (1020), built by Yaroslav the Wise.

CHERNIHIV OBLAST. Chernihiv: Church of the Divine Transfiguration (1036-1050), built by Chernihiv Prince Mstyslav Volodymyrovych and Svyatoslav I Yaroslavych.

CRIMEA OBLAST: The Old Church (10th century).

KRASNODAR KRAY. Tmutorokan: Church of the Most Holy Mother of God (1022), built by Prince Mstyslav Volodymyrovych at the place of the victory over the Kasoh (Cherkess) Prince Rededya.

ROVNO OBLAST. Dorohobuzh: Church of the Dormition (11th century).

MONASTERY CONSTRUCTION

KIEV OBLAST. Kiev: Monastery of the Archangel Michael (988-992), the first monastery of Kievan Rus', built by Metropolitan Mykhayil; Monastery of the Most Holy Mother of God (996), adjoining the Church of the Tithes, built by Volodymyr the Great; Monastery of St. Sophia (1017), built during the reign of Volodymyr the Great, destroyed by fire; Monastery of the Caves (1051), founded by the monks Antoniy and Teodosiy; Convent of St. Irene (11th century), built by Yaroslav the Wise. ***Vyshhorod:*** Monastery of the Divine Transfiguration (10th century), built by monks who had come to Kiev with Metropolitan Mykhayil.

CHERNIHIV OBLAST. Chernihiv: Monastery of the Holy Trinity and the Prophet Elias (11th century).

KHMELNYTSKY OBLAST. Bakota: Monastery of the Cliffs (11th century).

VINNYTSYA OBLAST. Lyadova: Monastery of the Cliffs (11th century).

Christian Kiev of the 10th-13th centuries — churches and monasteries. Model by Yuriy Aseyev.

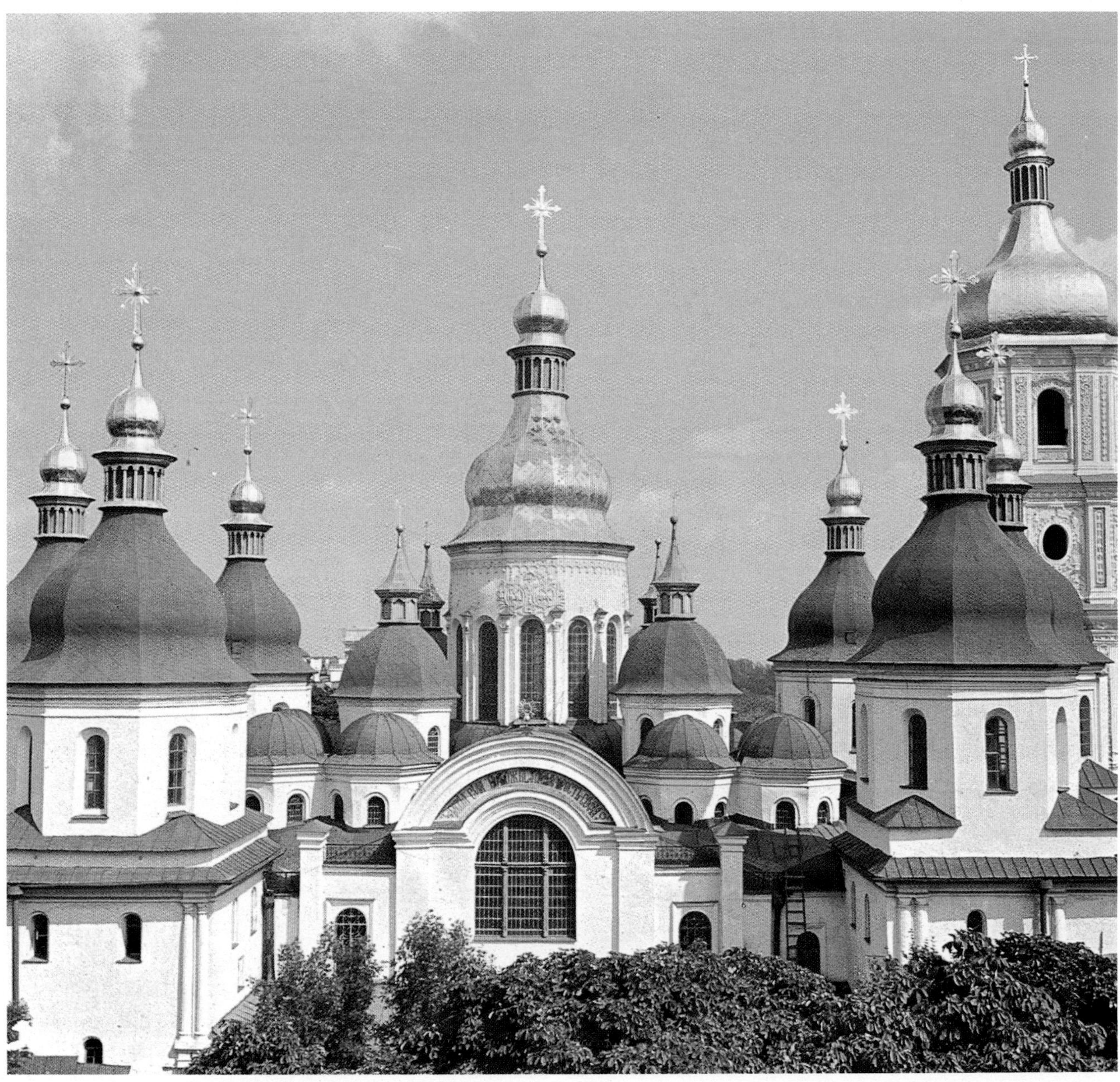

St. Sophia Cathedral in Kiev. Built by Grand Prince Yaroslav the Wise of Kiev in 1036, in commemoration of the victory over the Pechenegs, to serve as the Metropolitan Cathedral of Kievan Rus'. During the next seven centuries the Cathedral was the center of the religious, cultural-educational and national-political life of Ukraine. Princes received foreign envoys in the cathedral, chronicles were written there and the first library in Ukraine was established. The Romanesque style of the structure remained until the 17th century. The Cathedral came temporarily under the Uniate Metropolitan in the 16th century. In 1640 Metropolitan Petro Mohyla established a monastery by the cathedral. During 1685-1707 the cathedral was rebuilt in the Ukrainian Baroque style according to plans by the architect J. Mancini, and restored in the 18th and 19th centuries. In 1731 the new iconostasis in the Baroque style was installed. The first All-Ukrainian Orthodox Sobor, where the hierarchy of the Ukrainian Autocephalous Orthodox Church was renewed was held in the cathedral in 1921.
The Soviets transformed the cathedral into an architectural-historical monument in 1934. The Cathedral was open briefly during World War II and shortly thereafter closed again.

Christ Pantocrator. Mosaic from the 12th century in the main dome of St. Sophia Cathedral in Kiev.

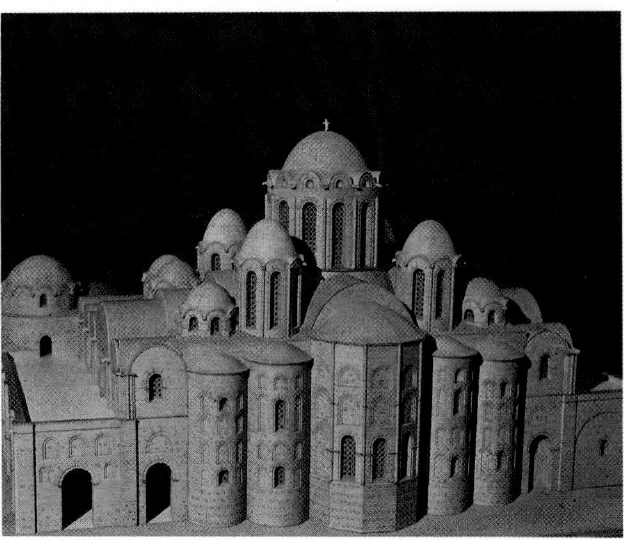

St. Sophia Cathedral in the 11th century. Model by Yuriy Aseyev and others.

The Eucharist. Mosaic fragment from the 11th century. St. Sophia Cathedral in Kiev.

The Mother of God. From the composition "Deisus." Mosaic fragment from the 11th century. St. Sophia Cathedral in Kiev.

Christ the Priest. Mosaic from the 11th century.
St. Sophia Cathedral in Kiev.

The Oranta. Mosaic from the 11th century. Ceiling over the main altar of St. Sophia Cathedral in Kiev.

The Oranta. Fragment.

St. Michael Golden-domed (Mykhaylivsky Zolotoverkhy) Catheral in Kiev, built by Svyatopolk Izyaslavych, grandson of Prince Yaroslav the Wise, in 1108-1113. It was sacked and partially destroyed by the Mongols and Tatars in 1240. Princes Svyatopolk Izyaslavych (1113) and his wife Varvara, Svyatopolk Yuriyevych (1190), Hlib Yuriyevych of Turov (1196), Metropolitans Yov Boretsky (1631) and Isaya Kopynsky (1640) and other famous persons from the history of Ukraine are buried here. The Cathedral and the St. Michael Monastery were destroyed by the Soviets in 1934-1935. Some frescos and mosaics were transferred to St. Sophia Cathedral, but most, the mosaic "St. Demetrius of Thessalonkika" were taken among them to Russian museums in Moscow and Leningrad.

The "Eucharist." 12th century. Mosaic from the St. Michael Golden-domed Cathedral, destroyed by the Soviets. Preserved in the St. Sophia Cathedral in Kiev.

St. Demetrius of Thessalonika. Mosaic from the 11th-century St. Michael Golden-domed Cathedral, destroyed by the Soviets. The mosaic was sent to the Tretiyakovsky Gallery in Moscow.

SS. Theodore and George, 11th century. Relief from the St. Michael Golden-domed Cathedral in Kiev, destroyed by the Soviets.

St. Cyril Church in Kiev, built in the mid-12th century by Princess Mariya Mstyslavivna, wife of Prince Vsevolod Olhovych of Chernihiv, in memory of her husband. Buried in the church is the hero of the *Tale of Ihor's Host* (*Slovo o polku Ihorevim*) — Prince Svyatoslav Vsevolodovych of Kiev. The Church was repaired in 1605, 1687-1697 and in the mid-18th century after the fire of 1734. Frescos and a painting from the 12th century as well as paintings by M. Vrubel, I. Yizhakevych, M. Murashko and others, may be found in the church. The Church was converted into a concert hall by the Soviets in 1965.

Interior of the St. Cyril Church in Kiev (12th century).

St. Thaddeus. 12th-century mosaic from St. Michael Golden-domed Church, destroyed by the Soviet authorities in 1934-35.

Holy Trinity Church Above-the-Gate of the Kiev Monastery of the Caves, built in 1106-1108. After the destruction of the Dormition Cathedral by the Mongols in 1240, it became the main church of the Monastery. The most complete edition of the *Patericon of the Kievan Monastery of the Caves* was compiled in 1462 in this church. In 1631 Metropolitan Petro Mohyla opened a school by this church, which a year later together with the Kiev Brotherhood school constituted the Kiev Mohyla Collegium. The church was rebuilt and restored many times. Paintings by Ukrainian artists of the 18th century may be found there.

Askold's Grave in Kiev, painting by Taras Shevchenko (1846). Built at the location of the death of Princes Askold and Dyr of Kiev in the 9th century. A masonry church was built in 1810 on the spot of the old wooden church. A Ukrainian historical cemetery surrounds the church; the cemetery was destroyed by the Soviets in the 1930s.

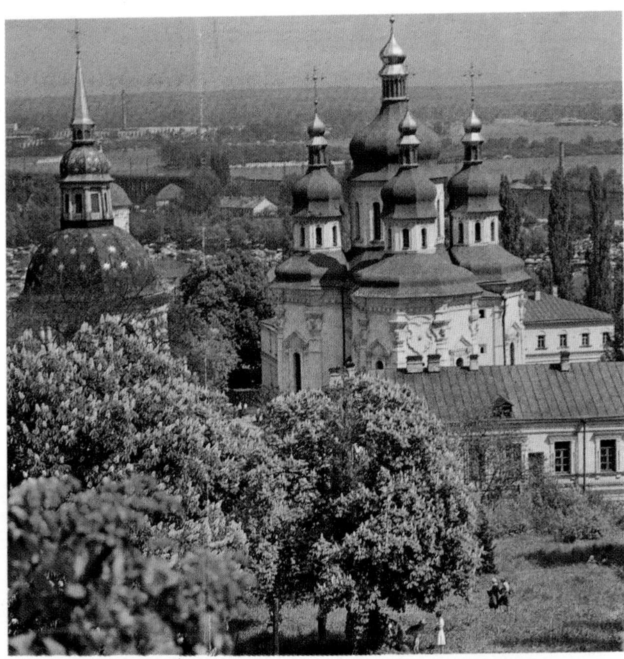

Vydubytsky Monastery in Kiev, founded in the late 11th century by Prince Vsevolod Yaroslavych. It was razed by the Polovtsians in 1096. St. Michael Cathedral was built there in 1070-1088. The monastery lost its original appearance when the St. George Cathedral and the Refectory were built in 1696-1701, and further when the Hetman of Ukraine, Danylo Apostol, built a belfry in Ukrainian Baroque style in 1727-1733. The Soviets destroyed iconostases in the churches and the cemetery in the 1930s, and the monastery was adapted to house the Archeological Institute in 1963.

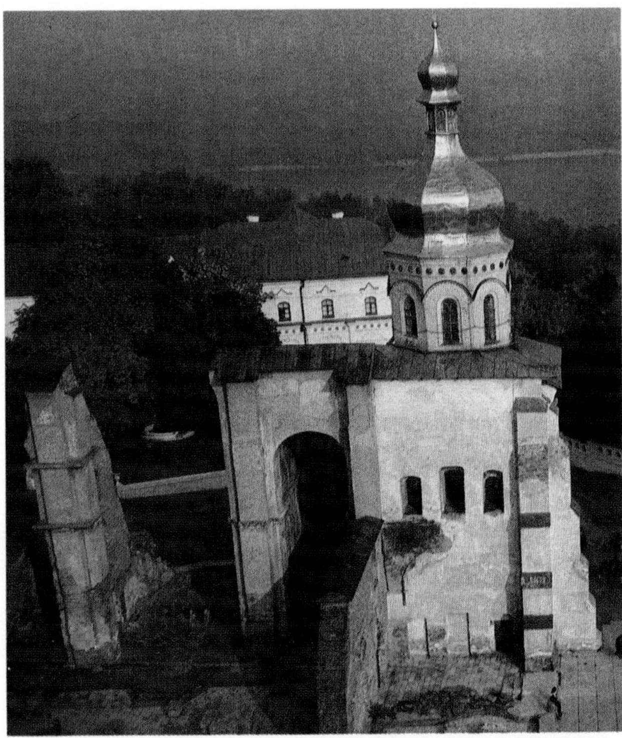

Dormition Cathedral of the Kievan Monastery of the Caves, built in 1073-1078. The painting of the interior was done by the eminent artists of Kievan Rus' Alimpiy and Hryhoriy. The Cathedral was destroyed by the Mongols in 1240. After the restoration in 1723-1729, the Cathedral acquired Ukrainian Baroque lines. The interior of the Cathedral was painted in the 1730s by artists under the direction of S. Lubensky and renewed in 1772-1776 by artists of Z. Holubovsky. In the cathedral are buried many famous Ukrainians: Yelisey Pletenetsky, Zakhariya Kopystensky, Pamvo Berynda, Metropolitan Petro Mohyla, Innokentiy Gizel, Prince Konstantyn Ostrozky and others. Before their retreat from Kiev in World War II, the Soviets dynamited the Cathedral. Only one part of the cathedral remains — side altar of St. John the Theologian.

Holy Savior Church in Berestiv of the Kiev Monastery of the Caves, built in the 1070s and restored in Ukrainian Baroque style in 1640-1642.

St. Elias (Illinska) Church in Chernihiv, built in the 12th century and rebuilt in the Baroque style in 1649.

Holy Friday Church in Chernihiv, built by Petro Mylonih in the 12th century. The church was partially destroyed by the Mongols in 1239 and by the Soviets in the 1930s. It was restored in 1670-90, again after a fire in 1750, and was rebuilt in the 19th century. In 1962 the Soviets declared it an architectural-historical monument.

St. Tekla. Fresco from the 11th century. Holy Savior Cathedral in Chernihiv.

Holy Savior-Transfiguration Cathedral in Chernihiv. Built in 1036, it was partially destroyed by the Mongols in 1239 and by the Soviets in the 1930s. Rebuilt in 1791-1799, it is one of the oldest churches still standing. It is renowned for its iconostasis, built in 1793-98 by the architect Yasnyshyn and the Nizhyn woodcarvers S. Voloshenko and S. Bilopolsky. Paintings by the Ukrainian artist O. Murashko may be found in the cathedral.

The Last Judgement. Fresco from the 11th century. Holy Savior Cathedral in Chernihiv.

St. George's Dormition Cathedral in Kaniv (Cherkasy oblast). Built by Prince Vsevolod in 1144, it was rebuilt in the classical style in 1805-10 and renamed Dormition in 1883. Graffiti from the 12th century may be found on its walls. Transformed by the Soviets in 1970 into a museum of folk decorative art.

Dormition Cathedral of the Yeletsky Monastery in Chernihiv, built in 1016 by Prince Svyatoslav Yaroslavych. Partially destroyed by the Mongols in 1239, it was rebuilt in 1449-1499. It was seriously damaged in 1611 and rebuilt in 1671-1679 in the Ukrainian Baroque style. Ornaments from the 12th century, the fresco "The Last Judgement" and paintings from the 18th century may be found there. The church and the whole monastery was converted by the Soviets into an architectural historical monument.

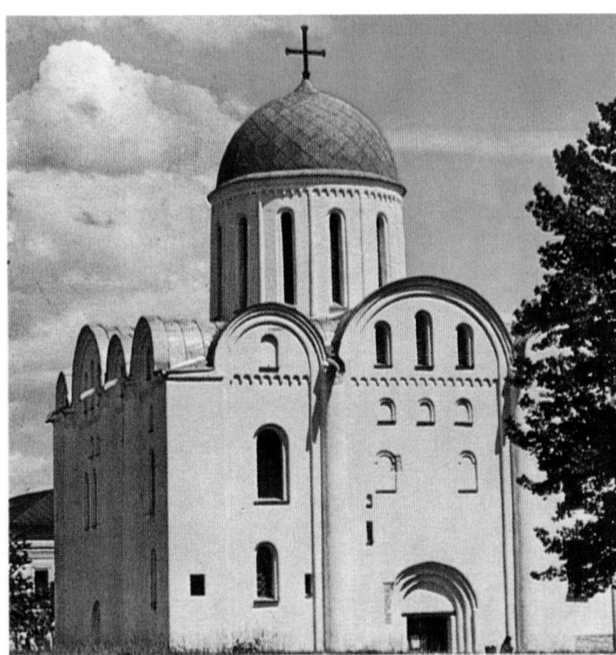

SS. Borys and Hlib Cathedral in Chernihiv, built in 1120-1123. It was forcibly converted into a Polish Catholic Dominican church in the 1620s and returned to the Ukrainian Orthodox Church in the 1640s. It was rebuilt in the Ukrainian Baroque style in the late 17th century and restored in 1857. Partially destroyed, especially the interior, by the Soviets in the 1930s and converted into a museum in 1972.

Remains of St. Michael's Church in the city of Oster (Chernihiv oblast), built in 1098.

A rock monastery in the village of Lyadova (Vinnytsya oblast), built in the 11th century. In the 18th century it belonged to the Uniate Order of St. Basil. It includes three cave churches — the Church of the Beheading of St. John the Baptist, the Church of St. Paraskeva Friday and the Church of St. Anthony of the Caves.

The Dormition Cathedral in Volodymyr-Volynsky (Volynia oblast), built by Grand Prince Mstyslav Izyaslavych in 1160. This is the only church in Volynia remaining from the Kievan Rus' period. In 1896-1900 the cathedral was rebuilt in its original 12th-century form.

A rotunda church in Horyany, a suburb of Uzhhorod (Transcarpathian oblast), built in the 12th-13th centuries. St. Nicholas Church was added to it in the 15th century.

Holy Mountain Monastery in the village of Zymne (Volynia oblast), built in the 11th century and rebuilt during the 1460s.

St. Hlib. Slate icon from the 11th century. Tmutorokan.

Vyshhorod Mother of God. Byzantine icon from the 11th-12th century. Moved to Vladimir-on-the-Klyazma, also known as "Our Lady of Vladimir."

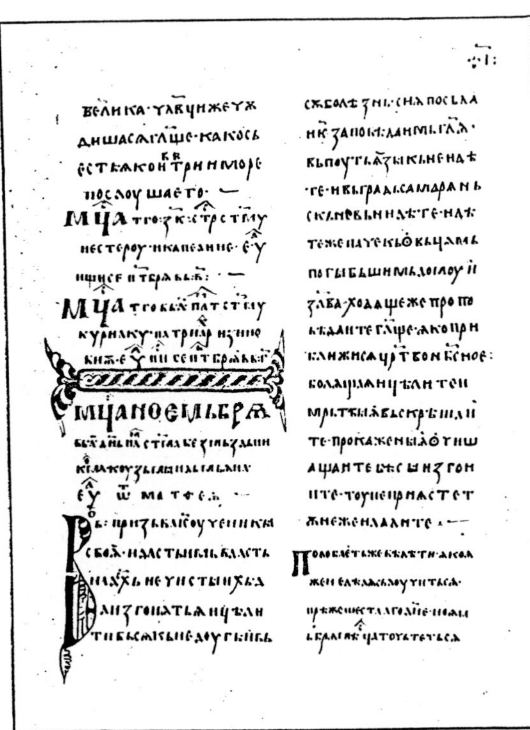

A page from the "Rheims Gospels," early 11th century. The oldest manuscript book of Kievan Rus'-Ukraine still remaining. It is in Rheims, France.

Panagia. Icon from 12th century.

Christ marrying Prince Yaropolk of Kiev and Princess Iryna. Miniature from the Trier psalter, 1078-1087.

A rock monastery in the village of Bakota (Khmelnytsky oblast), built in the 12th century. Carved into the rock are inscriptions in Old Slavonic from the 12th century.

III. Christianity in Kievan Rus'-Ukraine during the 11th — 13th Centuries (1054-1240)

General Characteristics of the Period

1. THE POLITICAL SITUATION IN EASTERN EUROPE

In 1060, the Polovtsians (Cumans) entered southern Rus' from the east. In 1068, they defeated Rus', took Tmutorokan and the Crimea and began raiding southeastern Europe. In the process they pushed the Pechenegs westward.

Meanwhile, the Seljuks, a Ghuzz offshoot which revolted in 1037 against the Moslem Ghazanids, pushed into Asia Minor. They routed the Byzantine army at Mandzikert (1071). On the Balkan front, however, Byzantium subdued the rebellious Serbs and destroyed the Pechenegs in 1122. In 1176, Byzantium again faced the Seljuk Turks, at Myriocephalum, and again was defeated.

At about this time, the Germans regained some of the lands taken earlier by Poland. Between 1102 and 1124, the Poles succeeded in subduing the Pomeranians. In 1138 Poland was split into separate principalities.

The Hungarians, who had taken Croatia in 1097, seized Dalmatia on the Adriatic from the Venetians in 1108; however, the Byzantines later took both Croatia and Dalmatia, only to lose them to the Hungarians in 1188. Serbia and Bulgaria regained their independence from the recently defeated Byzantines. During the twelfth century the Byzantine Empire entered into an alliance with the Holy Roman Empire and secured a peace with the Norman kingdom of Sicily.

At the start of the next century, the Fourth Crusade touched on Eastern Europe when the Crusaders took Dalmatian Zara for the Venetians and in 1204 sacked Constantinople itself.

In the north, the Knights of the Sword took Riga in 1201 and advanced up the Dvina. Meanwhile, the Teutonic Knights began their mission against the Prussians, whom they forcibly converted to Christianity. In 1220 Novgorod took Karelia.

The northern principalities of the Kievan realm, Novgorod and Rostov-Suzdal, which expanded to become Vladimir-Suzdal, became increasingly independent as they profited from their river routes to the Baltic as well as to the oriental commercial spheres. Galicia and Volynia, too, profited from their economically advantageous position. Kiev gradually lost control of the rest of Rus'.

The Flemish heirs of the Vikings and Varangians controlled the Baltic and North Sea trade. The major commodities were fish — an obligatory food for Christians — and English wool. The wool was brought to Flemish weavers; later, it was supplied to the textile industry of northern Italy. Meanwhile, the German Hanseatic League took over the Baltic and then the North Sea trade, driving out the Flemish merchants. The Dvina and Oder connected the Baltic with the Dniester, which flows to the Black Sea, where Genoa and Venice had established trading colonies. Thus, commerce passed between the Mediterranean and Baltic-North Sea regions. Direct access by central Rus' to Byzantium, however, was cut off by the Pechenegs, forcing Rus' traders to resort to other routes and markets and shifting their attention to the Baltic region.

In the early years of the thirteenth century, Leszek the White of Poland sided with the Pope and the Guelph alliance. He defeated Prince Roman of neighboring Galicia-Volynia, thus extending his influence over the politics in that area.

The Mongols and Tatars appeared on the eastern horizon in the 1220s, defeating the Rus' and the Polovtsians, conquering the Volga Bulgars, and vanquishing Vladimir-Suzdal in 1237-38. In 1239-40, they dealt a virtual death-blow to Kievan Rus'.

2. THE RELIGIOUS SITUATION IN EUROPE

After 1054, the Eastern (Orthodox) Church based in Byzantium developed independently of the Western (Catholic) Church under Rome. The Roman Church prevailed in northern, central, east-central and southern Europe, and in northern Spain. Its main difficulty was its recurring conflict with the German emperor. In 1077 the Pope prevailed and the Emperor was forced to do public penance. But thereafter the fortunes of the Church and Empire were reversed more than once. Eventually, the Emperor recognized an "anti-Pope," while the Pope recognized a kind of "anti-emperor." This situation was resolved when the Pope and the Emperor reached a compromise in 1122.

In the eleventh century, the Normans began to make their presence felt in various parts of Europe. In 1066, William began his conquest of England. From 1061 to 1091, the Normans took Sicily from the Muslims.

In Asia Minor, the Seljuk Turks, unlike their Fatimid predecessors, took an intolerant view of Christian pilgrimages to the Holy Land. Responding to this situation and to a Byzantine request for mercenaries, Pope Urban II launched the First Crusade in 1095. It set out in the following year with thirty thousand French and Italian troops.

The Orthodox Church held sway over those parts of Anatolia held by the Byzantine emperor, much of Trans-Caucasia, part of the Balkan peninsula, and those parts of Rus' not invaded by the Polovtsians. The Byzantine Empire shrank under the Seljuk onslaught and Venetian advances, and Orthodox influence consequently weakened. In Greece and parts of Asia Minor the Venetians created the Latin Empire. However, due to the efforts of the Kievan Metropolitanate, Orthodox Christianity spread to the north and east of Kievan Rus'.

In Spain, the tide had turned in favor of the Christians in the North. The crowns of Aragon and Navarre were united in 1076. In 1085, the Christians took Toledo. The "Reconquista" had begun. However, the Murabits united the scattered Muslim emirates in Spain, facilitating resistance to the Christian advance. In the twelfth century, the Chrisitians held most of Spain; the Muwahid Muslim caliphate held out in the South. In 1212, Castile and its northern allies finally defeated the Muwahids at Los Navos de Tolosa.

In 1166, the Waldensian movement for the reform of the Catholic Church arose in Lyons. The Third Lateran Council in 1179 condemned the Catharis, a heretical group in northern Italy influenced by Manichaeism. Similar groups existed in southern France (the Albigenses) and in the Balkans (the Bogomils). In 1209, the Papacy hired freebooters to suppress the Albigenses. The campaign, which went on for some twenty years, soon escaped the Pope's control and was marked by pillage and massacres. The Fourth Lateran Council of 1215 again condemned the Albigenses, as well as the Waldensians.

At about this time, monastic life in the Western Church was enriched by the founding of the Mendicant Friars by St. Francis of Assisi in 1209, and of the Dominicans in 1215. The latter sent a mission to Rus' in 1221 and established a province there in 1228.

The Third Crusade began in 1189, the Fourth in 1202. The Crusades sparked conflicts with the Orthodox Church, especially with the sack of Byzantium in 1204. At this time papal power reached its peak. However, the Pope's struggle with the German emperors continued. As pro-papal Guelphs and pro-imperial Ghibellines struggled over the northern Italian towns, the loose imperial confederation was weakened.

3. THE POLITICAL SITUATION IN RUS'-UKRAINE

After the death of Yaroslav the Wise in 1054, Kiev remained the center of Rus'-Ukraine. However, Yaroslav's realm began to disintegrate, although Volodymyr Monomakh succeeded in bringing it together one last time. Afterward, the descendants of Yaroslav partitioned the Kievan realm into fifteen principalities. Those representing today's Ukrainian territory were Kiev, Chernihiv, Pereyaslav, Volodymyr-Volynsky and Galicia (Halychyna). During the latter half of the eleventh and early twelfth centuries, Rus' expanded northward, but was cut off on the south by the nomadic Polovtsians and Pechenegs. In 1187, the name *Ukraina,* signifying "borderland," appears in the chronicles for the first time.

The Polovtsians (Cumans) moved into southern Rus' in 1060, defeating her forces in 1068 and later taking Tmutorokan and the Crimea. During the many internecine wars of the time, Rus' princes often obtained the help of the Polovtsians against each other. However, they did combine forces to defeat the Polovtsians during 1110-13. In 1185, Prince Ihor Svyatoslavych led a campaign against the Polovtsians. This was the basis of the epic poem *The Tale of Ihor's Host.*

Yaroslav the Wise left a statute defining the order of succession to the princely thrones of Rus'. The procedure proved unworkable and resulted in frequent warfare among the princes of Rus'. Sons of members of the ruling dynasty who had not lived to take their allotted thrones (princes without domains known as the *izhoyi*) posed a special problem. From 1054 on, the sons of Yaroslav the Wise — Svyatoslav, Vsevolod and Izyaslav — ruled their principalities of Rus' in harmony. But later, Svyatoslav and Vsevolod combined against Izyaslav. Svyatoslav ruled in Kiev from 1073 until his death in 1076. Izyaslav then returned to the capital, but died two years later. The continuing strife among the princes of Rus' prompted Volodymyr Monomakh of Pereyaslav to call them to a meeting at Lyubech in 1097, where a new succession system was agreed upon. It proved more practical; it also signaled the ultimate partition of the Kievan realm into separate principalities.

During his reign (1113-25), Volodymyr Monomakh united the land of Rus' and issued new laws. In his *Instructions to Children* (1117), he argued for the unity of the Kievan Rus' state. Volodymyr Monomakh threw the Polovtsians back to the Volga and strengthened his ties with Western Europe through his marriage to the daughter of the English King Harold II and through the marriage of his daughter to Koloman of Hungary. His sister was married to a Saxon margrave and afterwards to the German emperor Heinrich IV. Volodymyr's granddaughter was married to the Byzantine emperor John II Comnenus.

The Kievan era of the history of Rus' can be said to have begun to disintegrate at about 1132. Other cities arose in the northeast, northwest and west. In 1139 the Realm of Rus' was split. The descendants of Volodymyr Monomakh — the Monomakhovychi of Pereyaslav — and of Yaroslav the Wise — the Olhovychi of Chernihiv — battled for supremacy for the next hundred years.

In 1147 a growing principality in northeast Rus', the city of Moscow, was founded. This was the germ of the Muscovite state and later of the Russian Empire.

In 1169, Prince Andrei Bogolyubsky of Suzdal sacked Kiev, devastating the city and plundering its churches and monasteries. He seized church treasures and brought them to his capital of Vladimir-on-the-Klyazma.

In the 1140s the Galician principality, with its capital at Halych, arose in western Rus'. Conveniently located at the headwaters of rivers flowing to the Black Sea as well as of rivers flowing north to the Baltic, crossed by East-West trade routes, and well provided with the valuable commodity of salt, Galicia prospered. It reached its zenith during the reigns of Volodymyrko (1141-52) and Yaroslav Osmomysl

(1152-87). In 1199, Prince Roman Mstyslavych of Volodymyr-Volynsky united his realm with Galicia, thereby creating the Galician-Volynian State.

Roman died in battle with Leszek the White near the Vistula in 1205. The Galician and Volynian boyars began to struggle among themselves and in 1213 the Galicians put boyar Volodymyr Kormylchych on the throne. In the following year, the Poles and Hungarians intervened to depose Kormylchych and replace him with the Hungarian Koloman. Only in 1219 was order restored by Mstyslav Romanovych (the Daring) of Novgorod, who took the Galician throne at Halych. Roman's son Danylo united Volynia, and, after Mstyslav's death in 1228, battled with the Hungarians, the Galician boyars and Prince Mykhaylo of Chernihiv. In 1237, Danylo re-united Galicia and Volynia under his rule; his final triumph came eight years later.

In the meantime, a new danger appeared from the east. In 1221-22, the Alans and Polovtsians were defeated by a reconnaissance party of the Mongols sent by Genghis Khan. The Mongols dealt the people of Rus' a staggering blow on the Kalka River in 1223. As political confusion weakened Kiev, the Mongols assaulted Suzdal in the north in the 1230s, returning to Kievàn Rus' proper in 1239. In 1240, they devastated Kiev. The age of Kievan Rus' was over.

4. 11TH-13TH-CENTURY RULERS OF KIEVAN RUS'

(1054-1240)

Izyaslav Yaroslavych	1054-68, 1069-73, 1076-77
Vseslav of Polotsk	1068-69
Svyatoslav Yaroslavych	1073-76
Vsevolod Yaroslavych	1077-93
Svyatopolk Izyaslavych	1093-1113
Volodymyr Vsevolodovych Monomakh	1113-25
Mstyslav I Volodymyrovych	1125-32
Yaropolk Volodymyrovych	1132-39
Vsevolod II Olhovych	1139-46
Ihor Olhovych	1146-47
Izyaslav II Mstyslavych	1147-54
Yuriy Volodymyrovych Dolgoruky	1154-57
Izyaslav Davydovych of Chernihiv	1157-58, 1161
Rostyslav Mstyslavych of Smolensk	1159-67
Mstyslav Izyaslavych of Volodymyr-Volynsky	1167-69
Hlib Yuriyevych	1169-71
Roman Rostyslavych of Smolensk	1171, 1175-76
Svyatoslav Vsevolodovych	1177-97
Ryuryk Rostyslavych	1197-1202, 1205-10
Roman Mstyslavych of Volodymyr-Volynsky	1202-05
Vsevolod Svyatoslavych of Chernihiv	1210-12
Mstyslav Romanovych (the Daring) of Smolensk	1212-23
Volodymyr Ryurykovych of Smolensk	1223-35, 1238-39
Yaroslav Vsevolodovych	1236-38
Mykhaylo Vsevolodovych of Chernihiv	1238-39
Rostyslav Mstyslavych of Smolensk	1239
Danylo Romanovych of Halych	1240

This is a simplified chronology. For numerous reasons, such as battles, there were short gaps, usually months, in the reigns of many rulers of Kievan-Rus'. Temporary substitutions upon the throne and variations in historiographic data explain instances of overlapping dates.

Chronology

1067 — The Blessed Antoniy, co-founder of the Kievan Monastery of the Caves, arrives in Chernihiv and establishes the Monastery of the Blessed Virgin Mary (Holy Mother of God).

5 May 1072 — The relics of the holy martyrs Borys and Hlib are transferred to the newly built church in Vyshhorod near Kiev. Taking part in the solemnities are the sons of Yaroslav the Wise — Izyaslav, Svyatoslav and Vsevolod — Metropolitan Heorhiy of Kiev, Bishop Petro of Pereyaslav, Bishop Mykhayil of Yuriyiv, Bishop Neofit of Chernihiv, Bishop Nykyta of Bilhorod, Hegumen Teodosiy of the Kievan Monastery of the Caves, Hegumen Herman of the Monastery of the Holy Savior, Hegumen Sofroniy of the Monastery of St. Michael, and Hegumen Mykolay of the Pereyaslav monastery.

According to the account of this event in *The Tale of Bygone Years,* when the casket was opened, the church "was filled with fragrance, with unusual aroma; they who saw it glorified God. And the Metropolitan was overcome with fright because he was not yet steadfast in his belief in [Borys and Hlib] and he prostrated himself [before them] asking forgiveness." (Metropolitan Heorhiy asked forgiveness because the Patriarch of Constantinople had not canonized Borys and Hlib, and they were not acknowledged as saints in Byzantium. They had been declared saints by the Ukrainian hierarchy only.)

10 July 1073 — Antoniy (Pechersky), co-founder (with the Blessed Teodosiy) of the Kievan Monastery of the Caves, dies. Both are later canonized.

1073 — Bishop Leontiy, a native of Kiev, dies a martyr's death in Rostov. He is later canonized.

1073 — The builders of the Cathedral of the Dormition of the Kievàn Monastery of the Caves come to Kiev from Constantinople and bring with them the relics of seven holy martyrs: SS. Artemiy, Polievkt, Leontiy, Akakiy, Arefa, Yakiv and Teodor.

3 May 1074 — The Blessed Teodosiy, Hegumen of the Monastery of the Caves, dies in Kiev. He organized monastic life in Kievan Rus', introducing the Studite Order from the Studion Monastery in Constantinople. On his initiative, the construction of the Cathedral of the Dormition was begun. It stood for about nine centuries and was partially destroyed by the Soviets in 1941.

Spring 1075 — Banished by his brothers from Kiev,

Nestor the Chronicler, by L. Tarasevych.
From "Patericon of the Kievan Monastery of the Caves," Kiev, 1702.

Prince Izyaslav Yaroslavych sends a mission, headed by his son Yaropolk-Petro, to Pope Gregory VII, asking for papal help in his struggle for the throne of Kiev. The Pope declares full support for Izyaslav, crowns Yaropolk King of Rus' and gives Izyaslav assurances of his royal rights with respect to Kiev.

17 April 1075 — Pope Gregory VII sends a letter to Prince Izyaslav Yaroslavych, addressing him as "King of Rus'," and, on April 20, sends a letter on behalf of Izyaslav to the Polish king Boleslaw II, addressing Boleslaw as "Prince of Poland."

1080s — Anti-Pope Clement (1080-1100) sends a mission, headed by a bishop, to Ioann II, Metropolitan of Kiev, to explore chances of unity. Following discussions with the envoys, the Metropolitan writes a letter to the Pope, addressed "From Ioann, Metropolitan of Rus', to Clement, Pope of Rome," in which he expresses a positive attitude toward the Pope's efforts to unite the Western and Eastern Churches while expressing criticism of the Latin Church and personages.

1088 — Metropolitan Ioann II (1077-88) dies in Kiev. He was descended from the Greek family Prodrom. He was known for his polemical and canonical works, his letter to Anti-Pope Clement, opposition to Teodosiy of the Caves, outspokenness against Latin Catholics and his ban on marrying Latin Catholics. He was the author of *Tserkovni Pravyla* (Church Rules).

9 May 1089 — A new feast is added to the calendar of the Kievan Metropolitanate — the summer feast of St. Nicholas, proclaimed by Pope Urban II that year. The Patriarchate of Constantinople did not sanction this feast.

1089 — The Abbess of the Convent of St. Andrew (Yanchyn) in Kiev — a daughter of Grand Prince Vsevolod Yaroslavych — goes with a diplomatic mission to Byzantium to ask for a new Metropolitan of Kiev. The Patriarch of Constantinople consecrates Ioann III as the new Metropolitan, and he returns with the mission to Kiev.

1090 — After the death of Ioann III, Yefrem II becomes the Metropolitan of Kiev. He is known for building churches in Pereyaslav and a hospital, introducing free medical care in the cities under his jurisdiction, as well as for his work for the good of the Ukrainian Church. It is believed that he was a native of Kievan Rus'.

14 August 1091 — Metropolitan Yefrem II canonizes Teodosiy of the Caves and establishes a holiday to commemorate the transfer of Teodosiy's relics against the wishes of Byzantium.

1094 — The daughter of the Polovtsian Khan Tugorkan accepts Christianity and marries Grand Prince Svyatopolk Izyaslavych.

1095 — The Polovtsians sack the Kievan Monastery of the Caves and its vicinity and capture many monks, the Blessed Yevstratiy among them. All the captives are sold to merchants in Kherson who, starving them, demand that they renounce Christ. All die a martyr's death. After the sack of Yuriyiv by the Polovtsians, the eparchy is moved to the city of Svyatopolch, where it remains until 1103, returning at that time to a rebuilt city of Yuriyiv.

End of the 11th century — The *Hypatian, Nikon* and *Trinity* chronicles mention the existence of a Metropolitanate in Pereyaslav. No details are available; it is believed, however, that there were Greek metropolitans of Kiev who fell into disfavor with the Kievan grand princes during 1054-68 and 1073-85.

Early 12th century — Under Polovtsian occupation, the Tmutorokan Principality is lost to the Kievan State. Consequently the Tmutorokan Eparchy is lost to the Kievan Metropolitanate and comes under the direct jurisdiction of the Patriarch of Constantinople.

12th century — Christian thought and faith infuse all aspects of statecraft and personal life. Princes and nobles hold the belief that monastic life is the only form of Christian experience that leads to salvation. A number of princes and members of their families join monastic orders, rejecting secular power to completely devote themselves to the service of God.

1103 — The relics of Metropolitan St. Mykhayil (died 992) are transferred from the Church of the Tithes in Kiev to Antoniy's Cave in the Monastery of the Caves.

6 December 1104 — During the reign of Svyatopolk Izyaslavych, the new Metropolitan, Nykyfor, arrives in Kiev from Constantinople.

1105 — The Kievan iconographer and calligrapher Hryhoriy dies. He wrote and illustrated the *Ostromyr Gospel* (1056-57). He is later canonized.

Metropolitan Nykyfor nominates the monks Amfilokhiy, Lazar and Myn of the Kievan Monastery of the Caves as bishops of Volodymyr-Volynsky, Pereyaslav and Polotsk, respectively.

1106 — Prince Svyatoslav (Mykola Svyatosha) of Chernihiv, becomes the first Ukrainian prince to join the Kievan Monastery of the Caves.

1106-08 — Hegumen Danylo leads a large pilgrimage from Kievan Rus' to the Holy Land. He described the journey in his chronicle, *The Life and Travels of Danylo, Hegumen from the Lands of Rus'.* (Published in the anthology *Palestinian Circular,* St. Petersburg, 1885, Vol. 1, No. 3.)

1108 — Teodosiy (Pechersky) (ca. 1036 — May 3, 1074) is canonized. Along with Antoniy (Pechersky), he founded monastic life in Kievan Rus'-Ukraine. He was Hegumen of the Kievan Monastery of the Caves and author of many epistles, sermons and prayers.

Princess Varvara (Barbara), daughter of the Byzantine emperor Alexius Comnenus and wife of the Grand Prince Svyatopolk Izyaslavych of Kiev (1093-1113), brings the relics of St. Barbara from Constantinople. The relics are placed in the monastery of the Church of St. Michael (destroyed in 1934 by the Soviets).

1110 — The Venerable Kuksha suffers a martyr's death while spreading Christianity among the pagan Vyatychian tribe.

19 January 1113 — Hegumen Teoktyst of the Monastery of the Caves is consecrated Bishop of Chernihiv. The monk Prokhor takes his place as Hegumen.

1113 — Metropolitan Nykyfor I begins attacks against Roman Catholicism through his pastoral letters.

7 July 1114 — The Kievan iconographer and mosaicist Alipiy dies. He is the first ancient Ukrainian artist to be mentioned in the chronicles; later he is canonized.

10 November 1114 — Nestor (b. ca. 1047), renowned writer and chronicler of Kievan Rus', dies. He is the author of *A Discourse on the Princes Borys and Hlib, Life of the Venerable Teodosiy,* and *The Tale of Bygone Years.*

1115 — The relics of the first saints of Kievan Rus'-Ukraine, SS. Borys and Hlib, are transferred to the Church of St. Volodymyr the Great in Vyshhorod. This is the greatest national-religious observance of Kievan Rus' held during the reign of Volodymyr Monomakh.

Hegumen Sylvester, the chronicler, described the event:

> In 6623 (1115), the brothers gathered — the Rus' Grand Prince Volodymyr, known as Monomakh, his sons Vsevolod and Davyd Svyatoslavych, and his brother Oleh — and decided to move the relics of Borys and Hlib, for they had built a stone church to pay respect and homage to the relics and to give them eternal rest. First, the

Blessed Antoniy of the Caves (ca. 982-1073), founder of monastic life in Kievan Rus'-Ukraine and of the Kievan Monastery of the Caves (left).

Blessed Theodosius of the Caves (ca. 1036-1074), Hegumen of the Kievan Monastery of the Caves, organizer of monastic life in Kievan Rus', author of works about monastic life. By L. Tarasevych. From *Patericon of the Kievan Monastery of the Caves,* Kiev, 1702.

church was consecrated on Saturday, May 1, and on the next day the saints were brought there.

There was a huge gathering of people from all parts, as well as Metropolitan Nykyfor with all the bishops: Teoktyst of Chernihiv, Lazar of Pereyaslav, the priest Nykyta of Bilhorod and Danylo of Yuriyiv; and with the hegumens: Prokhor of the Monastery of the Caves, Sylvester of St. Michael, Sava of the Church of the Holy Savior, Hryhoriy of St. Andrew, Petro of Klov, and other hegumens.

...When morning came, the Metropolitan, bishops and hegumens, all dressed in sacred vestments, lit candles and came with blessed incense to the caskets of the saints, took the coffin of Borys and placed it on a wagon, and princes and noblemen pulled it with ropes and then, when the monks came to the front with candles and with the priests, hegumens and bishops right before the coffin, the princes pulled the coffin between the barriers which had been placed there. They were unable to get through the throng, which had broken down the barriers. Masses of people occupied the city and its expanses, so that it was frightening to see such a large number of people. (Likhachev, Vol. I., p. 199.)

19 August 1120 — St. Teoktyst, Bishop of Chernihiv and friend of the Chernihiv prince Davyd Svyatoslavych, dies. A sword is carved on his tombstone with the inscription *Honorem meum nemini dabo* (I will not yield my honor to anyone).

1121 — The Bishop of Bilhorod Nykyta becomes Metropolitan of Kiev. Nykyta was consecrated bishop by Metropolitan Nykyfor I in 1115.

1122 — Bishop Amfilokhiy of Volodymyr-Volynsky dies at the Monastery of the Caves. He is later canonized.

An earthquake severly damages the Church of St. Michael in Pereyaslav.

23-24 June 1124 — During the time of the Great Fire, approximately six hundred churches burn down in Kiev.

1126 — Metropolitan Nykyta I dies in Kiev. He is known for "byzantizing" the Ukrainian church and for his attacks against the Roman Catholics.

1127 — A congress of clergy of Rus' meets in Kiev, headed by Hryhoriy, Hegumen of the Monastery of St. Andrew. Not a single bishop takes part. The participants attempt to settle the differences between the princes of Kiev and Chernihiv.

1130 — During the rule of Mstyslav I Volodymyrovych, Grand Prince of Kiev, the new metropolitan, Mykhayil, arrives in Kiev from Constantinople, bringing along a large group of Greek clergy, who are to take the leading posts in the Church. He appoints Nifont, Teodor and Manuyil (Emmanuel) as bishops of Novgorod, Volodymyr-Volynsky and Smolensk, respectively. These new bishops are proponents of Byzantine politics in the Ukrainian Church. Mykhayil remains metropolitan for fifteen years and in 1145 leaves for Byzantium for unknown reasons.

14 April 1132 — Mstyslav Volodymyrovych (b. June 1, 1076), Grand Prince of Kiev, dies. Mstyslav built the St. Theodore (Fedorivsky) Monastery in Kiev. He is later canonized.

1139 — The Kievan grand prince Vsevolod II Olhovych issues a decree on taxes for the Church. One-tenth of all income raised by the principality is reserved for the Church, setting a standard for future tax rates.

With the assumption of power by Vsevolod II Olhovych as the Grand Prince of Kiev, a struggle emerges between two factions in the Church — the "Rus' faction," which favors making the Church independent, and the "Byzantine faction" of Metropolitan Mykhayil.

27 October 1143 — Prince Svyatoslav of Chernihiv

Anthology of Svyatoslav
Miniature, Kiev, 1073.

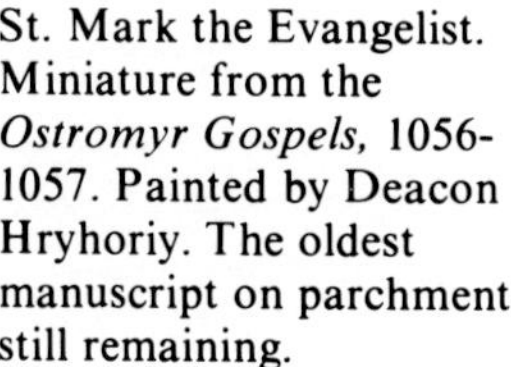

St. Mark the Evangelist. Miniature from the *Ostromyr Gospels,* 1056-1057. Painted by Deacon Hryhoriy. The oldest manuscript on parchment still remaining.

(b. 1080), dies. He was an ecclesiastical leader in Kievan Rus', becoming Brother Mykola Svyatosha at the Kievan Monastery of the Caves. He built the Church of the Holy Trinity Over-the-Gates (Nadbramna) and a hospital by the Church of St. Nicholas at the Monastery. He is later canonized.

1145 — Mykhayil, Metropolitan of Kiev, leaves his metropolitanate and moves to Constantinople, whence he came in 1130. Before his departure, he forbids the celebration of Liturgy at the Cathedral of St. Sophia without the presence of the Metropolitan. His departure from Kiev is considered a demonstration of protest following a dispute with the Grand Prince of Kiev.

1146 — Patriarch Michael II dies in Constantinople. For a short time, Kiev is left without a prince or metropolitan, until Prince Izyaslav Mstyslavych of Pereyaslav triumphantly enters Kiev. Bishops and clergy greet him at the Cathedral of St. Sophia in honor of his assumption of authority over Kievan Rus'. Recognizing the vital role played by the Church in the lives of the people and accepting that Metropolitan Mykhayil would not be returning to his metropolitanate, Izyaslav decides to have a Kievite become the metropolitan for only the second time in the history of the Kievan realm.

27 August 1147 — Grand Prince Izyaslav II Mstyslavych convenes a synod of bishops of Rus'-Ukraine to elect a new metropolitan. The leading candidate is Klym (Clement) Smolyatych, a monk at the Zarubsky Monastery near Kiev. The main proponent of convening a synod when the Patriarchate in Constantinople is vacant is Onufriy, Bishop of Chernihiv. He establishes the canonical and legal authority of the synod and presides over its sessions.

According to the *Hypatian Chronicle:*

> That year, Izyaslav installed Klym Smolyatych as Metropolitan, taking him from the Zarubsky Monastery. He was an ascetic monk and a scholar and philosopher such as Rus' has never seen. The Bishop of Chernihiv said, "I know that the gathered bishops have the authority to install a metropolitan." The following bishops gathered [for the synod]: Onufriy of Chernihiv, Teodor of Bilhorod, Yevfymiy of Pereyaslav, Damyan of Yuriyiv and Teodor of Volodymyr-Volynsky.
>
> Nifont of Novgorod and Manuyil of Smolensk said: "There is nothing in the law which allows bishops to install a metropolitan without the Patriarch; only the Patriarch can do that. We will not bow to your [Metropolitan Klym's] will, nor will we serve you, for you have not received the blessings of St. Sophia [in Constantinople], nor those of the Patriarch. When you correct these matters and receive the blessings of the Patriarch, then we will bow to you.
>
> We have a letter from Metropolitan Mykhayil that

Vestments of the Kievan metropolitan of Rus'-Ukraine from the 10th-12th centuries. Reconstructed by Petro Tolochko from church frescoes of the period and from the Radziwill Chronicle.

forbids us to celebrate the Divine Liturgy in St. Sophia [in Kiev] without the Metropolitan." This hurt him [Metro-politan Klym] severly. Onufriy of Chernihiv said, "I know we have the authority to install [a metropolitan], for we have the head of St. Clement [relic of Pope Clement], just as the Greeks install [metropolitans] by virtue of the arm of St. John." And so, having considered carefully, the bishops installed the Metropolitan [Klym] by authority of the head of St. Clement. (*Hypatian Chronicle*, pp. 340-341.)

All six bishops whose eparchies were within the borders of contemporary Ukraine voted for the installation of Klym Smolyatych. Voting against were Bishops Nifont of Novgorod and Manuyil of Smolensk, whose sees were beyond the Ukrainian lands. The Kievan *Hypatian Chronicle* describes the election of Klym Smolyatych in great detail, while the *Laurentian Chronicle* of Suzdal and the *Novgorod Chronicle* only mention the event.

1147 — Bishop Nifont of Novgorod does not mention the Metropolitan of Kiev, Klym Smolyatych, in Liturgies and recognizes only the Patriarch of Constantinople.

Brother Harasym of the Hnyletsky Monastery comes to Vologda. There, in a remote corner of the forest, he builds the Holy Trinity Church and founds a monastery.

The Dobryliv Gospels, 1164. Made in the Galician-Volynian state.

1148 — Grand Prince Izyaslav II Mstyslavych of Kiev imprisons Bishop Nifont of Novgorod, who comes to Kiev as an envoy of Prince Yuriy Dolgoruky.

1149 — Prince Yuriy Dolgoruky of Suzdal captures Pereyaslav and Kiev and demands the removal of Kiev Grand Prince Izyaslav II Mstyslavych and Kievan Metropolitan Klym Smolyatych. Finding themselves in mortal danger, both flee to Volodymyr-Volynsky.

1150s — As a result of constant conflict with the Polovtsians, the Pereyaslav principality, begins to lose its significance as a political-religious center in eastern Rus'-Ukraine. With the decline of Pereyaslav, a new focus of ecclesiastical-religious life emerges — the Rostov Eparchy — along with a new political focus — Suzdal, despite the fact that in the middle of the twelfth century, Christianity is not yet firmly established in these lands, where the vast majority of the people do not even know the language of Rus'.

1154 — On the Alta River, near Pereyaslav, the Polovtsians burn the Church of SS. Borys and Hlib.

The departure of Klym Smolyatych as Metropolitan of Kiev marks the end of the struggle of some elements of the hierarchy and the clergy to make the Ukrainian Church autocephalous.

ca. 1155 — St. Bernard, Abbot and co-founder of the Clairvaux Monastery of the Roman Church, is sent as a missionary to Kievan Rus' with the aim to convert Rus' to the Latin rite. In a letter to him, Bishop Maciej of Cracow (1143-66) writes that the people of Rus' are as plentiful as the stars and that they believe in Christ, but follow a "heretical" rite which is neither Greek nor Roman.

1156 — Metropolitan Konstantyn I of Kiev participates in the Patriarchal Synod in Constantinople.

Theodosius the Greek dies. He was the hegumen of the Kievan Monastery of the Caves (1142-56) and author of numerous epistles and sermons.

1157 — During the reign of Prince Yuriy Dolgoruky in Kiev, a new metropolitan, Konstantyn I, returns from Constantinople in 1155. He is designated by the Patriarch of Constantinople to head the Kievan Metropolitanate. Konstantyn removes the participants of the Synod of 1147, by which Klym Smolyatych was chosen to be Metropolitan of Kiev — Bishop Teodor of Volodymyr-Volynsky, Bishop Damyan of Yuriyiv, Bishop Teodor of Bilhorod and Bishop Yakym of Turov — from their eparchies and excommunicates Izyaslav, Grand Prince of Kiev.

1158 — Prince Andrey Bogolyubsky, son of Grand Prince Yuriy Dolgoruky, transfers the Icon of the Mother of God from Vyshhorod near Kiev to Vladimir-on-the-Klyazma. According to legend, the icon was painted by the Apostle Luke. In the fifth century, Emperor Theodosius the Younger transferred it from Jerusalem to Constantinople.

1159 — The Kievan Grand Prince Rostyslav Mstyslavych removes Konstantyn I from the Kievan Metropolitanate. The latter goes to Chernihiv, where he dies in disgrace a year later. Before his death, he repents for his sins against the Ukrainian Church. Rostyslav sends emissaries to the Patriarch of Constantinople to seek a new metropolitan.

1160s — Prince Andrey Bogolyubsky of Vladimir-Suzdal initiates efforts to sever the Suzdal Eparchy from the Kievan Metropolitanate. He builds a grand cathedral in Vladimir-on-the-Klyazma and sends emissaries to the Patriarch of Constantinople, with an appeal to establish a separate Vladimir-Suzdal Metropolitanate, which would report directly to the Patriarch of Constantinople. The Patriarch rejects his appeal. Andrey then appeals to have the bishop of Vladimir consecrated by the Patriarch and not by the Metropolitan of Kiev — a proposal which the Patriarch also rejects.

In the 1160s, there is a great polemic in Kievan Rus' over the issue of fasts. Rostyslav Mstyslavych, Grand Prince of Kiev, along with the princes of Chernihiv, Pereyaslav and Suzdal, sends emissaries to consult with Constantinople on the issue. A debate is held in the presence of the Emperor between the Bulgarian Archbishop Adrian and Leon, the Bishop of Rostov, who counselled the faithful to observe the fast on all holidays. The polemic on fasts is an indication of the kind of issues that were imposed on Christians in Kievan Rus' by the Greek metropolitans and bishops.

In addition to the polemic on fasts, the twelfth century also is known for polemics on Christian traditions and contacts with pagans. The Kievan metropolitans of the time, Greeks by origin, maintained that marriages with those of the Latin faith were contrary to the "true faith." According to some chronicles, the polemic resulted in a ban on eating from the same dishes as Latins, it being said that only in the Orthodox faith can one achieve salvation. These bans and teachings did not have any significant impact on the faithful. Numerous princes, for example, married women of the Latin faith.

31 July 1160 — Brother Ioan Zatvornyk dies at the Kievan Monastery of the Caves. He is later canonized.

1161 — The new Metropolitan, Teodor, arrives in Kiev from Constantinople. He dies 10 months later.

1163 — After Metropolitan Teodor's death, Grand Prince Rostyslav attempts to return Klym Smolyatych to the Metropolitanate of Kiev. To add legality to this act, he dispatches envoys to the Patriarch of Constantinople, Lucas Chrysoberg, asking for his blessing for Metropolitan Klym. Having learned about Metropolitan Teodor's death, the Patriarch consecrates Ioann IV as the new Metropolitan and sends him to Kiev. The Prince's envoys meet the new Metropolitan in Olesha and return with him to Kiev, abandoning the Grand Prince's mission. An indignant Rostyslav tells the Patriarch's envoys that if the Patriarch will continue to appoint new metropolitans without the knowledge and agreement of the Prince, they will not be received in Kiev; instead, metropolitans will be chosen from the realm of Rus' and according to the wishes of the Grand Prince.

1164 — The new Metropolitan, Ioann IV, arrives in Kiev from Constantinople.

The relics of Bishop Leontiy are discovered during construction of a new church in Rostov. He was martyred by pagans in 1073; and subsequently canonized.

1165 — The first mention is made in the chronicles of the first bishop of Halych, Bishop Cosma, although it is believed that Oleksiy was the first bishop.

1166 — With the blessing of Metropolitan Ioann IV, Illya, Bishop of Novgorod, receives the title of archbishop.

1167 — On the initiative of Grand Prince Mstyslav Izyaslavych, Konstantyn II is consecrated in Constantinople as the new Metropolitan and is received in Kiev with great honors. (According to some sources, Metropolitan Konstantyn II was a native of Kievan Rus'.)

Summer 1167 — Envoys of (Anti-) Pope Paschalis III arrive in Kiev.

8 March 1169 — Prince Andrey Bogolyubsky of Suzdal treacherously attacks Kiev in order to eliminate it as the political and religious center of Kievan Rus'. His intention, after destroying Kiev, is to elevate Vladimir-on-the-Klyazma to that position. The *Hypatian Chronicle* describes Prince Andrey's sack of Kiev:

> Kiev was captured on Wednesday, March 8, during the second week of Lent. The city was plundered throughout two days: the Hill, the Podil, the monasteries, the Cathedral of St. Sophia and the Tithe Church [Desyatynna] of the Mother of God. No one showed any mercy. Churches were burned, Christians were killed and others were bound, while the women were forcibly taken from their husbands and led away into captivity. Children saw their mothers and wailed. The invaders took a great deal of wealth; from the churches they took icons, books, and vestments and all the church bells... the evildoers set fire to the Monastery of the Caves and the Church of the Tithes, but God, through the intervention of the Blessed Virgin, saved them from great misfortune. All the people of Kiev were enveloped by great terror, longing, constant sorrow and unceasing tears. (*Hypatian Chronicle*, Vol. II, pp. 545-546.)

15 June 1173 — Princess Yevfrosiniya, granddaughter of Volodymyr Monomakh and Abbess of the Convent of the Holy Savior, which she founded, dies during a pilgrimage to Jerusalem.

1174 — The first mention is made in the chronicles of the title *archimandrite* for the Hegumens of the Kievan Monastery of the Caves.

29 June 1174 — In the castle Bogolyubov (from which came the name Bogolyubsky), Prince Andrey Bogolyubsky of Vladimir-Suzdal dies at the hands of

Armies of Prince Andrey Bogolyubsky of Vladimir-on-the-Klyazma, conquer Kiev. Miniature from the Radziwill Chronicle.

his boyars. He sacked Kiev in 1169, burned and plundered its churches and monasteries, and tried to establish a separate Metropolitanate in Vladimir-on-the-Klyazma. All the treasures that he obtained by robbing different lands were in turn taken by the boyars. Prince Andrey was later canonized by the Russian Orthodox Church.

17 March 1178 — Harasym Volohodsky, a monk at the Hnyletsky Cave Monastery, dies. He is later canonized.

1182 — Lavrentiy Zatvornyk Volohodsky is consecrated Bishop of Turov. He wrote twelve sermons and twenty-four prayers. He is later canonized.

Archimandrite Polikarp of the Kievan Monastery of the Caves dies. A renowned church figure in Rus'-Ukraine, he is later canonized.

1187 — The relics of the Abbess Yevfrosiniya are transferred from the Convent of the Holy Savior in Jerusalem to the Kievan Monastery of the Caves.

1190s — Antoniy Pechersky (983-1073), founder of the Kievan Monastery of the Caves (in 1020), is canonized.

1191 — Davyd Rostyslavych, Prince of Smolensk, transfers the remains of SS. Borys and Hlib to the monastery in Smyadin near Smolensk.

1199 — Grand Prince Ryuryk Rostyslavych builds a wall on the Dnieper side of the Vydubytsky Monastery. This wall was admired by all of that time. It was constructed by local builder Petro Mylonih.

1203 — The former Grand Prince, later Prince of Novgorod, Ryuryk Rostyslavych, together with the Polovtsians, sacks Kiev. According to the description in the chronicles, churches and monasteries are destroyed, icons smashed, and treasures and books plundered. The Polovtsians are commanded by their leaders Konchak and Danylo Kobyakovych.

1207 — Pope Innocent III sends a large mission headed by Cardinal Gregory to Ukraine. He calls upon the hierarchy and clergy of Rus'-Ukraine to join the Roman Church.

Beginning of the 13th century — The first Catholic missionaries — Franciscans, Dominicans and Cistercians — arrive on Ukrainian lands. They service foreigners primarily engaged in trade, preach the Gospel and attempt to convert the local population to the Roman rite. This marks the beginning of the establishment of the first Latin Bishoprics in Kievan Rus'. These bishops were independent of Ukrainian hierarchs.

1223 — The Patriarch of Constantinople, Germanus II, and the Synod of Metropolitans of Byzantium send an edict to Metropolitan Kyrylo I of Kiev, forbidding him to ordain slaves to the priesthood.

17 January 1227 — Pope Honorius III calls on all Princes of Kievan Rus' to join the Roman Church. In his epistle he asks them whether they are ready to receive a papal legate and the rules of the Catholic faith from him.

1231 — With the permission of Grand Prince Volodymyr Ryurykovych, the Dominican Monastery of the Virgin Mary is established in Kiev. Martin of Sandomierz is its first prior.

1232 — Pope Gregory IX sends a special message to the monks of the Dominican Order in Rus'-Ukraine. All Roman Catholics, not only the Dominicans, can openly exercise their religion in Rus'-Ukraine. They have their own church in Kiev. The majority of Roman Catholics come from Poland, Hungary and Bohemia.

1233 — Volodymyr Ryurykovych deports the Dominicans from Kiev and forbids them to return to his principality. This is due to the Dominicans' latinization policy among the local population with the aim of converting people to the Latin rite.

1234 — Pope Gregory IX establishes a diocese for the Latins in Rus'-Ukraine.

1239 — Bishop Symeon dies at the hands of the Tatars in Pereyaslav, which they destroyed. Also destroyed was Chernihiv.

6 December 1240 — The third sack of Kiev occurs, this time by the Tatars and Mongols. The Church of St. Basil or of the Three Holy Hierarchs, built by Grand Prince Svyatoslav Vsevolodovych in 1184, is destroyed. The monasteries devastated are: Klovsky (or St. Stefan's), built by Hegumen Stefan of the Kiev Monastery of the Caves during 1074-78; Mykolayivsky, built by Prince Mstyslav Volodymyrovych in 1113; and the Hnyletsky Monastery (the Monastery of the Blessed Virgin), built near the end of the eleventh century.

The monasteries that sustained greatest damage are: the Monastery of the Caves, of St. Theodore, Yanchyn (St. Andrew's), the Savior in Berestiv, St. Simeon, St. Cyril and the Vydubytsky. In Chernihiv, the

Yeletsky (Dormition) Monastery, built by Grand Prince Svyatoslav Yaroslavych in the eleventh century, and the Dormition Monastery of the Holy Mount (Svyatohirsky) on the northern Donets River, built in the thirteenth century, are destroyed.

Some of these churches and monasteries were rebuilt in later centuries or were replaced by new structures. Information about other destroyed churches and monasteries has not survived.

The *Trinity Chronicle* describes the sack of Kiev:

> That year 6748 [1240] the Tatars conquered Kiev and [destroyed the Cathedral of] St. Sophia and robbed all the monasteries, taking icons, crosses and all priceless vestments, and killed by the sword all people old and young. And this tragedy took place just before Christmas, on St. Nicholas' Day.

Kiev cross-enkolpion from the 12th-13th centuries. Found during excavations in 1974.

According to the description in the *Galician-Volynian Chronicle,* the last defenders fortified themselves in the Church of the Tithes (Desyatynna). Their defense was not strong and the faithful tried to hide from the Tatars in the choir loft of the church. The building could not hold their weight and collapsed, burying many of them alive.

The collapse of the Church of the Tithes is considered to be a symbol of the end of the Kievan Rus'-Ukraine epoch.

Principal Ecclesiastical Activities

1. THE KIEVAN METROPOLITANATE DURING THE 11TH-13TH CENTURIES

The head of the Kievan Metropolitanate (the Metropolitan Eparchy), was the Metropolitan of Kiev, who was appointed by the Patriarch of Constantinople. During this period only one metropolitan was elected against the wishes of the Patriarch — Metropolitan Klym (Clement) Smolyatych, installed by the synod of bishops in 1147.

Sometimes, different primary sources give differing dates for the years of office of the Kievan metropolitans.

METROPOLITANS OF KIEV (1054-1240)

Yefrem I	1054
Heorhiy	1062-72
Ioann II	1077-88
Ioann III	1089-90
Yefrem II	1090-96
Mykolay	1097-1102
Nykyfor I	1104-21
Nykyta I	1121-26
Mykhayil I	1130-45
Klym Smolyatych	1147-54
Konstantyn I	1155-58
Teodor	1161-62
Ioann IV	1164-66
Konstantyn II	1167-72
Mykhayil II	1171-82
Nykyfor II	1182-97
Matviy	1200-20
Kyrylo I	1223-33
Yosyf I	1237-40

2. NEW EPARCHIES IN THE KIEVAN METROPOLITANATE

As Christianity developed and took root on the territory of Kievan Rus'-Ukraine, new eparchies were established in the following towns:

WITHIN THE BORDERS OF PRESENT-DAY UKRAINE:

Halych	1157 (or 1167)
Pereyaslav	1072
Peremyshl *	1220
Uhrovsk (Kholm)*	1220
Yuriyiv	1072

WITHIN THE BORDERS OF PRESENT-DAY BYELORUSSIA:

Polotsk	1105
Smolensk**	1137

WITHIN THE BORDERS OF PRESENT-DAY RUSSIA:

Ryazan	1207
Rostov	End of the 11th century
Vladimir-on-the-Klyazma	1214-1215

The Tmutorokan Eparchy, established in the ninth

century, first belonged to the Goth Metropolitanate, and later to the Kievan. In the early 12th century, it fell under the direct jurisdiction of the Patriarch of Constantinople.

During the destruction of Kiev by the Mongols and Tatars in 1240, when nearly all the lands of Rus'-Ukraine fell under their rule, the Kievan Metropolitanate consisted of the following eparchies in cities within the borders of present-day Ukraine: Bilhorod, Halych, Chernihiv, Peremyshl*, Pereyaslav, Yuriyiv, Kholm* and Volodymyr-Volynsky. Eparchies corresponding to cities in present-day Byelorussia were Turov and Polotsk; those corresponding to cities in present-day Russia were Novgorod, Rostov, Ryazan, Smolensk,** and Vladimir-on-the-Klyazma.

* Uhrovsk (Kholm) and Peremyshl are part of present-day Poland.

** Smolensk was later incorporated into Russia.

BISHOPS OF EPARCHIES WITHIN KIEVAN RUS'

Dates given below indicate when the bishops were first mentioned in the chronicles or indicate period in office.

Bilhorod: Stefan (1072); Luke (1089); Nykyta (1115-21); Teodor (Fedir) (ca. 1147).

Chernihiv: Neofit (1072); Ioann (1080-1112); Teoktyst (1113-20); Heraklid (n.d.); Panteleymon (1140); Onufriy (1143-47); Teotekn (1147); Yevfymiy (1148); Antoniy (1158-68); Porfyriy (1187); Porfyriy (1230-38); Neofit (1238).

Halych: Cosma (ca. 1165); Oleksiy (ante 1165).

Novgorod: Nifont (1130); Illya (1160s).

Pereyaslav: Petro (1072); Yefrem (1090); Lazar (1105-18); Sylvester (1118-23); Ioann I (1123-25); Mark or Markel (1126-34); Yevfymiy (1141); Symeon (1239).

Polotsk: Myn (1105); Cosma (1147); Mykolay (1182).

Rostov: Leontiy (1073); Teodor (1169).

Smolensk: Manuyil (1130).

Turov: Yakym (1157); Lavrentiy Zatvornyk (1182).

Volodymyr-Volynsky: Amfilokhiy (1105-22); Teodor (1130-47).

Yuriyiv: Mykhayil (1072); Antoniy (1098); Maryn (1091); Danylo (1114-22); Damyan (ca. 1147).

3. SYNODS AND ASSEMBLIES OF BISHOPS OF THE KIEVAN METROPOLITANATE

Kiev was the seat of the Metropolitanate — the center of the Church of Kievan Rus'-Ukraine until the middle of the thirteenth century. All bishops within the land of Rus' were appointed in Kiev. The synods and bishops' conferences were held here. Kiev was the center of spiritual life in the great realm of Rus'-Ukraine for almost four centuries. The largest number of churches and monasteries were built in this city, and the largest number of ecclesiastical works were written there. It was called the "Jerusalem" of Rus'.

During the eleventh through thirteenth centuries, several synods of bishops and many assemblies of bishops from the entire territory of the Kievan realm were held in Kiev. The most significant among these were the following:

1072 — An assembly on the occasion of the transfer of the relics of SS. Borys and Hlib to the new church in Vyshhorod. Taking part in the meeting are Metropolitan Heorhiy, Bishop Petro of Pereyaslav, Bishop Mykhayil of Yuriyiv, and others.

1147 — A synod to elect a new Metropolitan of Kiev. Participating are Bishop Onufriy of Chernihiv, Bishop Teodor of Bilhorod, Bishop Yevfymiy of Pereyaslav, Bishop Damyan of Yuriyiv, Bishop Teodor of Volodymyr-Volynsky, Bishop Nifont of Novgorod, Bishop Manuyil of Smolensk, and, it is believed, Bishop Cosma of Polotsk. By a majority vote the synod elects Klym Smolyatych as the Metropolitan of Kiev.

1150 — An assembly for the triumphal arrival in Kiev of Grand Prince Izyaslav Mstyslavych after his victory over Prince Yuriy Dolgoruky. Izyaslav is greeted by Metropolitan Klym Smolyatych and the bishops.

1160 — A synod to deal with the expulsion of Bishop Nestor of Rostov by Prince Andrey Bogolyubsky of Vladimir-Suzdal. The synod investigates all charges brought by the Prince and finds Bishop Nestor not guilty.

1168 — A synod to review the issue of fasting on Wednesdays and Fridays. The differences on this question are so great that the synod does not pass a single resolution regarding fasting. Later, the Patriarch of Constantinople reviews the same issue.

1169 — A synod in the matter of Bishop Teodor of Rostov, who is accused of heresy and theft. In spite of the defense of the bishop by Prince Andrey Bogolyubsky, the synod finds the bishop guilty and sentences him to death.

1182 — An assembly for the tonsure of priest Vasyliy (Basil) as hegumen of the Kievan Monastery of the Caves. Taking part in the ceremony is Metropolitan Nykyfor II, Bishop Lavrentiy of Turov and Bishop Mykolay of Polotsk.

1183 — An assembly on the occasion of the consecration of the place for a new church of St. Basil (Vasyliy). Bishops of Bilhorod and Yuriyiv, and probably others, come to Kiev to participate with Metropolitan Nykyfor II in the ceremonies and later to attend the reception given by Grand Prince Svyatoslav Vsevolodovych.

4. THE CHURCH AND RULERS OF KIEVAN RUS'

The metropolitan, bishops and clergy played an important role in the life of the realm, in the development of education for its people, in ensuring health care, and in the relations among the princes.

The hierarchy and the clergy always received the new grand prince. They sanctified his enthronement in Kiev with special ceremonies and they blessed him during the divine services.

During hard times and attacks by pagans upon Ukrainian territory, the clergy called on the faithful to defend their homeland and faith. When the need arose, the clergy served as active intermediaries in disputes among the princes.

The following are examples found in the chronicles about the important role played by the hierarchy of the church in the life of the realm.

1096 — At a time of Kievan Rus' decline under the constant attacks of the Polovtsians and during a dispute among the princes, Grand Prince Svyatopolk Izyaslavych, and then Prince Volodymyr Monomakh of Pereyaslav, send a letter to Prince Oleh of Chernihiv, in which they write: "Come to Kiev to (help) establish order in the land of Rus', make an appeal to the bishops, the hegumens, our parents, and the citizens of the town, to defend the land of Rus' from the pagans."

1111 — Metropolitan Nykyfor I and the hegumens of Kievan monasteries obtain the release of Prince Yaroslav Svyatopolkovych of Volodymyr-Volynsky, who was imprisoned by Grand Prince Svyatopolk Izyaslavych.

1127 — Hegumen Hryhoriy of the Monastery of St. Andrew in Kiev averts the danger of war between Grand Prince Mstyslav Volodymyrovych and Prince Vsevolod Olhovych of Chernihiv.

1135 — Metropolitan Mykhayil I of Kiev reconciles Grand Prince Yaropolk Volodymyrovych with the citizens of Novgorod. In 1136 he reconciles Yaropolk with the princes of Chernihiv of the House of Olhovych, and in 1140 he reconciles Prince Vyacheslav Volodymyrovych of Chernihiv with Grand Prince Vsevolod Olhovych.

1146 — Bishop Onufriy of Chernihiv threatens to excommunicate princes who might oppose the Grand Prince of Kiev, Ihor Olhovych.

1154 — The boyars of Kiev send a delegation headed by the Bishop of Kaniv to Prince Izyaslav Davydovych of Chernihiv, inviting him to the Kievan throne.

1175 — Metropolitan Mykhayil II, bishops and clergy, come with church banners and crosses to meet the new Grand Prince of Kiev, Roman Rostyslavych.

1195 — Metropolitan Nykyfor II is a successful mediator in peace talks between Grand Prince Ryuryk Rostyslavych and Prince Vsevolod Yuriyevych of Suzdal.

1210 — Metropolitan Matviy becomes a successful mediator in the peace negotiations between Princes Olhovych of Chernihiv and Vsevolod Yuriyevych of Suzdal.

1226 — Metropolitan Kyrylo I settles a dispute between Princes Oleh of Kursk and Mykhayil of Chernihiv.

1230 — Metropolitan Kyrylo I, Bishop Porfyriy of Chernihiv and Hegumen Petro of the Monastery of the Holy Savior in Berestiv settle a dispute between Princes Mykhayil of Chernihiv and Yuriy Vsevolodovych of Suzdal.

St. Michael the Archangel, from the "Annunciation," a mosaic from the 11th century.
St. Sophia Cathedral, Kiev.

Church and Monastery Construction in the 11th-13th Centuries

CHURCH CONSTRUCTION

Builders in Kievan Rus'-Ukraine were renowned craftsmen, who proved capable of resolving the most complex architectural and engineering problems. They readily learned the architectural techniques of Byzantium and creatively adapted them to local traditions.

St. Panteleimon Church in Halych (Ivano-Frankivsk oblast), built in 1200.

Church of the Nativity of Jesus in Halych (Ivano-Frankivsk oblast), the oldest church still standing in Western Ukraine. Built in the 12th century. Destroyed many times, it was rebuilt in 1600 and restored in 1926.

The wooden structures they built have not survived, but other architectural monuments, such as churches and monasteries made of stone and other durable materials, have been preserved. The structures of Kievan Rus' had a common character, although individual schools and tendencies characteristic of different parts of Ukraine are discernible.

Typical construction of churches in the first half of the twelfth century involved a six or four-columned configuration with cross-bearing domes on a one-story structure. In some areas there were churches with a single apse and a single nave and, more rarely, those with cupolas. This trend in architecture is known as the royal-monastic style. In these structures more emphasis was placed on the interior of the church than on the facade.

By the end of the twelfth century a new style had evolved, in which the main emphasis was placed on the exterior. It was characterized by a pyramidal quality, a precipitous dynamism directed upward, which coincided with the development of the Gothic style in the West.

Many churches on the territory of Ukraine were built during the 11th-13th centuries. The only information on some of them is their mention in the chronicles; more details are available on others, such as the dates of construction and the names of their founders.

The following churches are listed according to the present-day administrative divisions of Ukraine.

KIEV OBLAST. Kiev: Cathedral of St. Demetrius (1060s); Church of St. Michael (1069), built by Grand Prince Vsevolod Yaroslavych; Church of St. Peter (1070s); Church of St. Simeon (1073-76), built by Grand Prince Svyatoslav Yaroslavych; Church of the Blessed Virgin Mary of Pyrohoshcha (1132-36), built by Grand Prince Mstyslav Volodymyrovych; Church of St. Andrew of the Yanchyn Monastery (1131); Church of St. Cyril (1140) built by Princess Maria Mstyslavna, wife of the Grand Prince Vsevolod Olhovych; Church of St. Gregory (1146); Church of St. Basil or of the Three Holy Hierarchs (1184), built by Grand Prince Svyatoslav Vsevolodovych on the site of a wooden church built by Volodymyr the Great; Church of St. Catherine (12th century); Church of the Elevation of the Cross (1215). ***Bilhorod:*** Church of the Holy Apostles (1114). ***Pereyaslav:*** Church of the Holy Cross (1008); Church of St. Michael (1089); Church of St. Andrew and St. Theodore, built by Metropolitan Yefrem of Kiev; Church of the Blessed Virgin Mary (1098) and SS. Borys and Hlib on the river Alta (1117), built by Prince Volodymyr Monomakh; Church of the Dormition; Church of the Zarubsky Monastery. ***Vyshhorod:*** Church of SS. Borys and Hlib (11th century), built by Prince Oleh Svyatoslavych of Chernihiv.

St. Nicholas Church in Lviv, built in the 13th century. It burned a few times and was destroyed, but was restored in the 17th and 19th centuries and in 1924-1925.

CHERKASY OBLAST. Cherkasy: Cathedral of the Dormition (1144). ***Kaniv:*** Church of the Dormition of St. George (1144), built by the Grand Prince of Kiev, Vsevolod Olhovych.

CHERNIHIV OBLAST. Chernihiv: Cathedral of the Holy Savior (1024), built by Prince Mstyslav Volodymyrovych of Chernihiv; Church of the Dormition of the Yeletsky Monastery (1060); Illinska (Elijah) (1078); Pyatnytska (12th century); Church of the Archangel Michael (1098); Church of SS. Borys and Hlib (1120- 23), built by Prince Davyd Svyatoslavych of Chernihiv; Church of St. Michael (1165-77); Church of the Annunciation (1186), built by the Grand Prince of Kiev, Svyatoslav Vsevolodovych (it has not survived). ***Novhorod-Siversky:*** Cathedral of the Holy Savior (1180-90), built by Prince Ihor Svyatoslavych of Novhorod-Siversky. ***Oster:*** Church of St. Michael (11th century).

CRIMEA OBLAST. Tape-Kermen: Church of the Caves of Donors (13th century).

IVANO-FRANKIVSK OBLAST. Halych: Church of the Dormition (12th century), built by Prince Yaroslav Volodymyrovych; Church of St. Panteleymon (1190-1200); Church of the Holy Savior; Church of the Nativity (13th to 14th century); Cathedral of the Dormition (1157-87), built by the Galician grand prince Yaroslav Osmomysl. ***Rohatyn:*** Church of the Nativity (12th century). ***Shevchenkove:*** Church of St. Panteleimon (13th century).

LVIV OBLAST. Lviv: Church of St. Nicholas (13th century).

VOLYNIA OBLAST. Lutsk: Church of St. Demetrius (12th century); Cathedral of St. John (13th century). ***Lyuboml:*** Church of St. Heorhiy (13th century). ***Volodymyr-Volynsky:*** Cathedral of the Dormition (1160), built by Prince Mstyslav Izyaslavych of Volodymyr-Volynsky; Church of St. Demetrius; Church of St. Basil (13th-14th centuries); a cathedral on the Luh River near Volodymyr-Volynsky (it has not survived).

ZAKARPATSKA OBLAST. Uzhhorod: Rotunda Church (12th-13th century).

ZHYTOMYR OBLAST. Ovruch: Church of St. Basil at the St. Basil Monastery (1190), built by Prince Ryuryk Rostyslavych.

PRESENT-DAY POLAND. Kholm: Cathedral of St. John Chrysostom; Church of the Blessed Virgin Mary and the Holy Trinity (13th century), built by King Danylo Romanovych of Galicia; Church of SS. Cosmas and Damian; Church of SS. Peter and Paul. ***Peremyshl:*** Cathedral of St. John (1124).

MONASTERY CONSTRUCTION

Many monasteries were built on the territory of Ukraine during the 11th-13th centuries. Detailed information is available about some of them. About others there is only a mention of their existence in the chronicles. The list of known monasteries is given according to the present-day administrative divisions of Ukraine.

MONASTERIES

KIEV OBLAST. Kiev: St. Demetrius (1057), built by Grand Prince Izyaslav Yaroslavych; St. Michael (1069), built by Vsevolod Yaroslavych; Monastery of the Holy Savior in Berestiv (1072); St. Simeon (1073-77), built by Grand Prince Svyatoslav Yaroslavych; Klovsky or St. Stephan (1074-78), built near the Klov River by Hegumen Stefan of the Monastery of the Caves; Vydubytsky (1076-77), built by Grand Prince Vsevolod Yaroslavych; Hnyletsky or the Monastery of the Blessed Virgin Mary (end of the 11th century); St. Theodore (beginning of the 12th century), built by Grand Prince Mstyslav Volodymyrovych; St. Cyril (beginning of the 12th century), built by Grand Prince Vsevolod Olhovych; Gold-domed Monastery of St. Michael (1108), built by Grand Prince Svyatopolk Izyaslavych; Hospice Monastery of the Holy Trinity (1113), built by Prince Davyd Svyatoslavych of Chernihiv; Mykolayivsky (1113), built by Grand Prince Mstyslav Volodymyrovych; St. Basil; Monastery of the Resurrection. ***Pereyaslav:*** St. Michael or Yefremiy (1089), built by Bishop Yefrem; SS. Borys and Hlib on the river Alta (11th century); St. John (12th century).

CRIMEA OBLAST. Ternovka: Chelter-Marmara Monastery of the Caves (13th century).

CHERNIHIV OBLAST. Chernihiv: Elijah or Trinity (1069), built by Prince Svyatoslav Yaroslavych of Chernihiv; Redeemer-Transfiguration (11th century); Yeletsky Assumption (11th century), built by Prince Svyatoslav Yaroslavych; Blessed Virgin Mary; SS. Borys and Hlib.

CHERNIVTSI OBLAST. Neporotove (Kuchelmyna): Monastery of the Cliff (12th-13th century).

IVANO-FRANKIVSK OBLAST. Halych: St. John; Lelesiv (near Halych).

KHARKIV OBLAST. Donets: Holy Mount Monastery of the Dormition (middle of the 13th century).

KRASNODAR KRAY. Tmutorokan: Blessed Virgin Mary (11th century), built by Hegumen Nikon of the Kievan Monastery of the Caves.

ROVNO OBLAST. Dorohobuzh: Monastery of the Holy Savior. ***Peresopnytsya:*** Nativity of the Mother of God (13th century).

VOLYNIA OBLAST. Lutsk: Zhydychynsky. ***Volodymyr-Volynsky:*** Holy Mount (Monastery of the Dormition) in the village of Zymne on the river Buh (11th century); St. Michael (13th century); Holy Apostles.

PRESENT-DAY POLAND. Uhrovsk (near Kholm): St. Daniel.

Monasteries were built also in the towns of Cherven and Synevidsk.

CONVENTS

Kiev: Convent of the Holy Martyr Irene (beginning of the 11th century); St. Andrew (Yanchyn) (1086), founded by Princess Anna (Yanka) and built by Grand Prince Vsevolod Yaroslavych; St. Lazar (11th century); St. Nicholas; Convent of the Holy Savior, founded by Princess Yevfrosiniya in the 12th century.

IV. The Church in the Galician-Volynian State during the 13th-15th Centuries (1199-1458)

General Characteristics of the Period

1. THE POLITICAL SITUATION IN UKRAINE*

After the sack of Kiev in 1240, the focus of southern Rus' economic, political and cultural life shifted west to the Galician-Volynian State. In the 13th and 14th centuries, while Vladimir-Suzdal and then Moscow, emerged and grew powerful in the north, Galicia-Volynia flourished in the southwest.

The supremacy of Prince Danylo (reigned 1237-1264) in Galicia-Volynia was assured when he defeated Rostyslav (son of Prince Mykhaylo of Chernihiv) and his Hungarian allies near Yaroslav in 1245. But Danylo ruled as a vassal of the Mongol Golden Horde, which ruled over all the Rus' lands except for Turov-Pinsk and Polotsk. The Mongols generally succeeded in preventing the formation of alliances among the Rus' princes.

Danylo defeated the Lithuanian Yatvyagians, siding with the Mazovians and the Teutonic Knights. He also allied himself with the Hungarians and the Pope of Rome, from whom he accepted a crown in 1253. Thus he became King of Rus', an equal among the sovereigns of the European feudal order.

Danylo's western contacts strained his relations with the Mongols, from whom he never secured full independence. He also had to contend with his own boyars. In this struggle he was helped by the burghers of newly-founded cities like Lviv.

Danylo's son, Lev, assumed the throne upon his father's death in 1264, and established his capital in Lviv, a new city named in his honor. While Danylo's brother Vasylko (died 1270) and Vasylko's son Volodymyr (ruled 1270-1289) held Volynia, Lev reigned in Galicia, trying to maintain good relations with the Mongols. In 1267-1268 a union between Galicia-Volynia and Lithuania was concluded. Lev's son Yuriy captured the Lublin area from the Poles in 1293. In 1299 Lev helped the Hungarian king Andrew III subdue his nobles. Lev died and was succeeded by Yuriy around 1301.

The Galician-Volynian Chronicle breaks off in 1289, leaving a gap in the history of this state. Exact dates are unavailable and the early years of the 14th century remain obscure. The establishment of a Metropolitanate of Galicia in 1303 may have signaled a new Byzantine orientation. It seems that Lev II and Andriy ruled jointly from 1316 to 1323. Boyar unrest increased, facilitating Hungarian, Polish, and Lithuanian intervention. The Mongols, provoked by the Galician-Volynian alliance with the Teutonic Knights, attacked the state in 1316 and again in 1323. Lev and Andrew were apparently both killed in the latter assault. Thus the male side of the Romanovych dynasty, the Galician branch of the Ryurykides, died out.

From 1323 to 1340 Boleslaw, a Romanovych on his mother's side, ruled the realm as Yuriy II. A convert from Roman Catholicism to Orthodoxy, he nevertheless failed to gain full support from the boyars. Yuriy II supported the Teutonic Knights against the Poles and Hungarians. He introduced the Magdeburg Law, a municipal legal system of self-government, and its privileges to a number of Rus' cities, primarily Syanok. With his death in 1340 the Romanovych dynasty came to an end, and civil war broke out in the land.

* For the political situation in Eastern Europe, see part III, section 1 and part V, section 1; for the religious situation in Europe, see part III, section 2 and part V, section 2.

2. 13th-15th CENTURY RULERS OF THE GALICIAN-VOLYNIAN PRINCIPALITY 1199-1458

UKRAINIAN RULERS

Roman Mstyslavych 1198-1205
Volodymyr Ihorevych, Roman Ihorevych,
Svyatoslav Ihorevych, Mstyslav Mstyslavych 1206-1211
Volodyslav Kormylchych 1212-1214
Mstyslav Udatny 1219-1228
Danylo Romanovych, king 1228-1233, 1237-1264
Rostyslav Mykhaylovych 1233-1237
Lev I Danylovych 1264-1301

Yuriy I Lvovych, king 1301-1315
Andriy Yuriyevych, Lev II Yuriyevych 1315-1323
Yuriy II Troydenovych 1323-1340
Dmytro Detko 1340-1349

KINGS OF HUNGARY

Koloman 1214-1218
Louis I 1378-1382

KINGS OF POLAND

Casimir III 1349-1370
Wladyslaw Opolski, prince 1370-1378
Jadwiga 1382-1386
Wladyslaw II 1386-1436
Jagiello Wladyslaw III 1436-1444
Casimir IV 1447-1492

Galicia was incorporated into the Polish kingdom in 1387; from then on, it no longer existed as a separate state.

Chronology

The Galician-Volynian state was created in 1199 as a result of the unification of the Galician and the Volodymyr-Volynian principalities by Prince Roman Mstyslavych. Until the year 1340 it was viewed as a distinctly separate Ukrainian principality, with its own state emblem, currency and laws. Its most outstanding ruler, King Danylo Romanovych (1237-1264) incorporated great parts of Kievan Rus', including Kiev, into his state. However, in 1340, after the death of Yuriy II, the last of the Romanovych line, the Galician-Volynian state ceased to exist. Ukrainian traditions and rites came into constant conflict with Muscovy on one side and Roman Catholic Poland on the other. Several times, at the initiative of the Muscovite princes and metropolitans based in Moscow, the Metropolitanate of Galicia was closed.

1204 — Constantinople is captured and plundered by the Crusaders. Patriarch John X Camaterus flees to Thrace. Pope Innocent III sends envoys to the Galician king, Roman Mstyslavych, to discuss his acceptance of a union with the Apostolic See.

1214 — The Hungarian king, Andrew, conquers Galicia and notifies the Pope falsely that the population of that state is ready to be converted to Roman Catholicism, if allowed to retain its traditional rites. In 1215 King Andrew's six-year-old son Koloman is crowned king of Galicia. After his accession to the Galician throne, the bishop and some priests are driven out of Halych. The church is forcibly taken over by Latin-rite priests.

1218 — The eparchy of Peremyshl is taken over by the bishop of Novgorod, Antoniy Dobrynya Yadrenkovych.

1230 — The Pope creates the first Roman Catholic diocese in Halych, against the will of the population.

1247 — Danylo Romanovych informs the Pope, through emissaries (headed by Plano de Carpini) returning from a mission to the Golden Horde, that he is ready to embrace a union with the Apostolic See on the condition that the bishops and priests of Galicia are allowed to retain the rites of the Greek faith and to receive Holy Communion in the current manner. In September, the Pope informs Danylo and his brother, Vasylko, that he will meet their demands, and sends the Prussian Archbishop Henry to Halych. The hierarch will appoint new bishops and priests from among the local population and will order that all the wealth confiscated by the Roman Catholic priests be returned to the Ukrainian Church. In November, the Pope sends two Roman Catholic bishops to Halych to crown Danylo. However, Danylo, who has not yet received papal help in his war against the Tatars, refuses to accept the crown.

1249 — Deprived of papal aid against the Tatars during two years of negotiations, Danylo dismisses the papal legate, Albert, and facing the danger from the Tatars, break off relations with the Apostolic See.

1252 — The Hungarian King, Bela, reconciles Prince Danylo and the Pope.

1253-54 — Pope Innocent IV dispatches emissaries to Prince Danylo; they bring a wreath, a scepter, and a crown. The coronation of the first Ukrainian prince of the Galician-Volynian principality takes place in Dorohychyn. The *Galician-Volynian Chronicle* describes the coronation in this manner:

> Thus he accepted the crown from God, from the Church of the Holy Apostles and from the altar of St. Peter, from his father Nykentiy [Innocent IV] and from all his bishops. For Nykentiy cursed all who besmirched the Greek Orthodox faith and wanted to call a council on Orthodoxy and the unification of the Church. Danylo received the crown in the town of Dorohychyn, as he was departing for war. (Galician-Volynian Chronicle, Vol. II, p. 46.)

After Danylo's coronation, the Pope issues a bull to all the Christians in Bohemia, Moravia, Serbia, and Pomerania urging them to join the King of Rus', Danylo, under the sign of the cross, in the war against the Tatars.

1255 — Danylo rebuilds the churches of St. John, the Holy Trinity and the Immaculate Conception, all of which had burned down in the town of Kholm, and redecorates them with precious icons.

1257 — Having accepted his crown from the Pope, Danylo continues to profess the Orthodox faith. In a letter to Danylo, the displeased Pope berates him for this, urges him to repent and threatens him with anathema.

1289 — Volodymyr Vasylkovych, Prince of Volynia, donates two icons of Christ the Savior, decorated with gold, silver and precious stones, to the Cathedral of the Immaculate Conception in the city of Volodymyr-Volynsky.

1299 — After the latest destruction of Kiev by the Tatars, Metropolitan Maksym moves the seat of the Kievan Metropolitanate to Vladimir-on-the-Klyazma. The eparchies of Kiev, Volynia and Galicia are left without the spiritual care of a metropolitan. A struggle for the creation of its own see begins in the Galician-Volynian principality.

1303 — After long and persistent efforts on the part of King Yuriy Lvovych of Galicia-Volynia, Patriarch Athanasius I creates a separate Galician Metropolitanate. In a catalog of archbishops' cathedrals, compiled during the reign of Emperor Andronicus Palaeologus II (1282-1328), the following passage about the founding of this metropolitanate can be found:

> Galicia, an eparchy of Rus', was incorporated into the metropolitanate by Emperor Andronicus Palaeologus II during the reign of the Holy Patriarch Athanasius, in 6811 (1303). (Holubinsky, Vol. III, p. 97.)

The metropolitanate included the sees of the following cities: Halych, Peremyshl, Volodymyr-Volynsky, Lutsk, Kholm (formerly Uhrovsk) and Turov. The Galician Metropolitanate, as it appeared on the metropolitanate list of the Constantinople Patriarchate is listed as the eighty-first. Nifont was the first Metropolitan of Galicia.

1317 — During the reign of the Lithuanian King Gediminas (1315-1341), Emperor Andronicus II and Patriarch John XIII Glykys, create a separate Lithuanian Metropolitanate based in Novogrudok. It includes the eparchies of Polotsk, Pinsk, and, later, Turov. Theophilus becomes the first Lithuanian Metropolitan.

ca. 1328 — At the demand of Moscow's Metropolitan Teognost, Patriarch Isaias closes the Lithuanian Metropolitanate, and then the Galician one.

March 1330 — With the permission of Patriarch Isaias, Metropolitan Teognost arrives in Galicia-Volynia from Moscow. He remains there over a two-year period (until May 1332). He consecrates Teodor Bishop of Halych, and by his presence he wishes to underscore the closing of the Galician Metropolitanate and its subordination to him.

April 1331 — Patriarch Isaias re-opens the Galician Metropolitanate and recognizes Bishop Teodor as Metropolitan of Galicia. The latter goes to Constantinople and takes part in a Synod of Greek metropolitans. In August Metropolitan Teognost arrives in Constantinople from Moscow with envoys bearing expensive gifts for the emperor and Patriarch from the Muscovite Grand Prince, Ivan Kalita I. At their demand, the Patriarch closes the Galician Metropolitanate once again, and deprives Teodor of the status of metropolitan, leaving him the title of bishop. Returning to Halych Bishop Teodor, against the wishes of the Patriarch, remains the Metropolitan of Galicia, until 1347.

1337-41 — The new Patriarch, John XIV Calecas, reinstates the Galician Metropolitanate, recognizes Teodor as the Metropolitan of Galicia, and confirms the illegality of its closing. The Galician Metropolitanate is composed of five eparchies at this time: Halych, Peremyshl, Lutsk, Volodymyr-Volynsky and Kholm.

1340 — The Galician boyars poison Prince Yuriy II Troydenovych, the last ruler of the Galician Romanovych dynasty; they suspect him of spreading the Roman Catholic faith. The Galician-Volynian State ceases to exist as a federation of Galicia and Volynia. Volynia is taken over by the Lithuanian King Gediminas (1316-41), and Galicia is conquered by the Polish King Casimir III (1333-70). In this manner the Ukrainian lands are divided among two different states. Part of Kievan Rus', including Kiev and Volynia, falls under the rule of Lithuania. Constant attempts on the part of the Muscovite principality and the new religious center in Moscow are made to incorporate them on political and religious grounds. Galicia falls under the rule of the Catholic Polish kings. Roman Catholic colonists, Dominicans, and Franciscans begin to settle *en masse* on the Ukrainian lands of Galicia. They engage in missionary work and build Roman Catholic churches and monasteries. The Ukrainian population, which professes Eastern Orthodox Christianity, retains and defends its traditions and rites against the spread of Catholicism. A religious struggle, which lasts for many centuries, begins in Galicia. The eastern Ukrainian lands, under Lithuanian rule, are deprived of the spiritual leadership of a metropolitan. The metropolitans, designated by the Patriarch, are generally Greek, although they bear the title "Metropolitan of Kiev and All Rus'." They abandon Kiev, the seat of the Metropolitanate, and as early as 1299 move it to Vladimir-on-the-Klyazma, and later to Moscow. Despite this division, which is of a political nature, the Ukrainian population in both the eastern and western lands retains its own Kievan form of Christianity, which differs from Eastern Greek and Western Roman Catholic Christianity.

1345 — A separate Roman Catholic vicariate, with representation in Lviv, Horodok, Halych, Kolomyya, and Snyatyn, is created for Galicia.

1347 — The Muscovite prince Simon Ivanovich and Metropolitan Teognost send emissaries to Emperor John VI Cantacuzene and Patriarch Isidore I Kakkinos. They bring large sums of money and demand the closing of the Galician Metropolitanate. Metropolitan Teognost also brings accusations against Teodor, Metropolitan of Galicia, which result in a court hearing presided over by the Patriarch in Constantinople. In August-September the Galician Metropolitanate is closed for the third time, "forever and ever," by the decision of the emperor and Patriarch. The eparchies of Volynia, under the rule of the Lithuanian king, come under the jurisdiction of Metropolitan Teognost of Moscow.

14 March 1351 — Pope Clement VI orders all the income of the Catholic Church in Poland to be handed over to King Casimir. These monies are to be used for proselytizing the Roman Catholic faith and the creation of seven Roman Catholic dioceses headed by a metropolitan.

1355 — Patriarch Callistus I ordains the monk Roman in Constantinople as the Galician and Lithuanian Metropolitan with his see in Kiev. However, the patriarch does not create a metropolitanate either for Galicia or Lithuania. Roman is in charge of the metropolitanate until his death in 1361.

5 May 1358 — King Casimir establishes the first two Roman Catholic dioceses in Peremyshl and Volodymyr-Volynsky.

20 May 1359 — King Casimir institutes a new Roman Catholic diocese in Kholm.

1361 — When King Casimir organizes a Roman Catholic archdiocese in Lviv, the Ukrainian cathedral is converted into a Polish Roman Catholic cathedral.

The Pope appoints Christian as the first Roman Catholic archbishop of Lviv.

The Patriarchal Synod in Constantinople, during the reign of Patriarch Callistus I, orders the metropolitanates of Galicia and Lithuania to remain closed and places them under the jurisdiction of Aleksey, the Metropolitan of Moscow.

1363 — The new Patriarch Philotheus cancels the order closing the Galician Metropolitanate and its subordination to Metropolitan Aleksey.

1370 — The Polish king's governor in Galicia, Prince Wladyslaw Opolski (1370-1378), with the approval of Pope Gregory XI, orders all the Ukrainian Orthodox eparchies in Galicia to be closed. Roman Catholic dioceses are established in cities where they did not exist. The only city that remains without a Roman Catholic diocese is Halych.

The bishops, boyars and faithful, disturbed at the attempts to replace Orthodoxy with Catholicism in Galicia, demand the establishment of a separate metropolitanate for Galicia. As a result, King Casimir writes a letter to Patriarch Philotheus:

> Since time immemorial Galicia has been famed for its metropolitanate and has been the seat of metropolitans since time immemorial. The first metropolitan was God-fearing Nifont, the second metropolitan — Petro, the third metropolitan — Havryil, and the fourth metropolitan was Teodor. They were all metropolitans of Galicia. For God's sake, for our sake, and that of the Holy churches, grant your blessing to this man [Antoniy]. Make him a metropolitan, so that the law of the Rus' shall not perish. And if God will not show this man His mercy, and you will not give him your blessing, then later on, when the need arises to baptize the Rus' into the Latin-Catholic Church, have no complaints against us, since there is no metropolitan in Rus', and the world cannot live without laws (*Acta Patriarchatus,* Vol. I, p. 577).

May, 1371 — The Patriarchal Synod in Constantinople reopens the Galician Metropolitanate and designates as metropolitan Bishop Antoniy, the candidate of King Casimir. At that time he was the only bishop on Ukrainian lands under Polish rule. Metropolitan Aleksey, whose title was Metropolitan of Kiev and All Rus' and whose seat was in Moscow, did not consecrate a single bishop for the Ukrainian lands. Metropolitan Antoniy was only Metropolitan of Galicia and had under his jurisdiction the eparchies of Peremyshl, Kholm, Volodymyr-Volynsky and Turov. At this time the Lithuanian king Algirdas also asked the Patriarch to designate a separate Lithuanian Metropolitanate, since Metropolitan Aleksey was not attending to his religious and church obligations in Lithuania.

1375 — During the reign of King Louis, the Roman Catholic Church begins a forcible attack on the Ukrainian Church in Galicia. Halych becomes the seat of the Roman Catholic Metropolitanate. Roman Catholic bishops are appointed to those sees that were created during the reign of Casimir, but which had remained long unoccupied. They now begin active missionary work. In Halych they seize the Ukrainian cathedral, and all the confiscated wealth of the Ukrainian eparchy is transferred to the Roman Catholic archbishop. The Orthodox cathedral in Peremyshl is razed and a Roman Catholic one is built in its place. At the same time the Ukrainian Church in Galicia is also under attack by Metropolitan Aleksey of Moscow, who sends false reports to the Patriarch about the Ukrainian bishops.

1378 — Instructed by Pope Urban VI, the Dominicans take over some Orthodox monasteries in Galicia and Wallachia during the reign of the Polish kings. The Orthodox Church in Galicia, which was a state Church in the Galician-Volynian principality, becomes a humiliated second-class church. The Roman Catholic faith, which was only practiced by the Poles and Germans, generally colonists, becomes the privileged religion, wholeheartedly supported by the Pope and the Polish kings.

1381 — Pope Urban VI appoints a Roman Catholic inquisitor for Galicia and Wallachia.

1389 — Patriarch Antony IV appoints Cyprian, of Bulgarian origin, Metropolitan of All Rus'. His metropolitanate includes all the Ukrainian, Byelorussian, Lithuanian, and Muscovite lands, except those of Galicia.

1390 — The Polish Queen Jadwiga establishes the monastery of the Holy Cross in Cracow for the Benedictines from Prague, who are to conduct mass in the Slavonic language and spread Latin-rite Catholicism among the Ukrainian population in the Polish kingdom.

The eparchy of Moldavia is incorporated into the Galician Metropolitanate.

1391 — The Metropolitan of Halych Antoniy dies. On the orders of the Patriarch, the affairs of the metropolitanate are run by Abbot Simeon.

1393 — Patriarch Antony IV consecrates Ioann, Bishop of Lutsk, metropolitan of Galicia. He is a candidate of King Wladyslaw V. After learning this, Metropolitan Cyprian of Moscow sends envoys to Constantinople with slanderous information about Ioann. The Patriarch orders an investigation and a trial, but Metropolitan Ioann leaves Constantinople and returns to Galicia, where he performs his spiritual functions for the next several years.

1397 — Patriarch Antony IV sends his exarch, Archbishop Michael of Bethlehem, who speaks Ukrainian, to Galicia. At the same time he demands that the king remove Metropolitan Ioann from his post.

1401 — The decline of the Metropolitanate of Galicia begins: for many years it has been at the center of the struggle between the Polish Roman Catholic and the Muscovite Orthodox Churches and has been closed and reopened several times. On the orders of Patriarch Matthew I, the Polish king Wladyslaw V Jagiello places Ioann, the last Galician Metropolitan, in the hands of Cyprian, Metropolitan of Moscow. He is taken to Moscow, where he is imprisoned for the rest of his life. Metropolitan Cyprian arbitrarily begins to call himself "Metropolitan of Lviv, Galicia and All Rus'."

1412 — The new Metropolitan of Rus' leaves Moscow for Halych and takes charge of the Galician metropolitanate on the instructions of Patriarch Euthymius II. Some historians consider that the Galician Metropolitanate was incorporated into the Metropolitanate of All Rus' in 1407, under Metropolitan Fotiy I.

1413 — With the approval of the king, Metropolitan Fotiy of Moscow puts his assistant Ihnatiy Krekhovych in charge of the Galician Metropolitanate. Not wishing to have an Orthodox assistant to the Metropolitan in Galicia, the king instructs that his seat be transferred to the Basilian monastery in Krekhiv.

On the orders of the king, the Polish Roman Catholic bishop forcibly seizes the Ukrainian cathedral of St. John in Peremyshl. The bodies of princes and boyars are removed from the crypts of the cathedral, where they were buried.

14 November 1415 — Vitautas, Grand Prince of Lithuania, convenes a synod of bishops in Novogrudok in order to elect a new Metropolitan of Kiev without the blessing of the Patriarch. The following bishops take part in the synod: Bishop Teodosiy of Polotsk, Bishop Isaakiy of Chernihiv and Bryansk, Bishop Dionysiy of Lutsk, Bishop Herasym of Volodymyr-Volynsky, Bishop Pavlo of Peremyshl, and Bishop Kharyton of Kholm. Hryhoriy Tsamblak is unanimously elected the new Metropolitan. He is the third Ukrainian metropolitan to be elected without the consent and the blessing of the Patriarch by Ukrainian and Byelorussian bishops. The first was Metropolitan Ilarion (elected 1051), and the second was Klym Smolyatych (elected 1147).

1415 — The eparchies of Galicia are administered by Metropolitan Hryhoriy Tsamblak (1415-1419), "Metropolitan of Kiev, Galicia and All Rus'" with his seat in Kiev.

1420 — After the death of Metropolitan Hryhoriy Tsamblak and following negotiations between Metropolitan Fotiy of Moscow and the Lithuanian Prince Vitautas (Witowt), the Kievan and Galician Metropolitanates fall under the jurisdiction of Metropolitan Fotiy.

1432 — After a lengthy struggle for their rights, the Orthodox parishes of Lviv obtain a charter from the king permitting them to practice their religion, not to convert to Roman Catholicism, and guaranteeing that their churches and property will be protected by the laws.

22 March 1433 — Wladyslaw III, King of Poland and Hungary, issues a proclamation in Buda stating that the Ukrainian clergy has the same rights and privileges as the Roman Catholic clergy.

1433 — In Cracow, a statute granting the Ukrainian Orthodox nobility the same rights and privileges as the Roman Catholic Polish nobility is promulgated.

1436-1458 — Galician church affairs are managed by appointees of the Metropolitan of All Rus'.

1439 — The first Brotherhood is founded in Lviv, at the Church of the Holy Dormition. The Brotherhood, a religious-civic organization, protects the Church against the inroads of Roman Catholicism, supports priests, maintains the churches, and takes care of the sick and poor.

16 Janaury 1458 — After fifty years without its own bishops, Galicia obtains its first Metropolitan, who is appointed and consecrated by Pope Calixtus III. The new Metropolitan, Makariy, a Serb from the monastery of St. Cyprian in Constantinople, comes to Halych. Unable to conduct the affairs of the Metropolitanate and encountering resistance from the Roman Catholic archbishop of Lviv, he leaves his metropolitanate after one year. Some contemporary sources state that Makariy was consecrated not as a metropolitan, but as a bishop and that he never came to Halych.

3 September 1458 — The successor to Pope Calixtus III, Pope Pius II, who temporarily renewed the Galician Metropolitanate, appoints Hryhoriy Metropolitan of Kiev, Halych and All Rus'. He is from the monastery of St. Demetrius in Constantinople. The church in Galicia is ruled by metropolitan vicars whose seat is in Krylos.

Principal Ecclesiastical Activities

1. THE GALICIAN METROPOLITANATE DURING THE 13TH-15TH CENTURIES

Many facts and documents, that would help bring to light additional facts and events, in particular the investitures and the activities of metropolitans and bishops, are missing from the history of the Galician Metropolitanate.

The following lists of the metropolitans of Galicia and the bishops of the Galician Metropolitanate were compiled on the basis of various source materials. Some historians might differ as to the names and dates of some of the metropolitans and their terms of office.

The Galician Metropolitanate was opened and closed several times. It existed in 1302-03—1328; 1337-41—1347; 1371—1401. All the metropolitans were appointed and consecrated by the Patriarch of Constantinople. Some of the metropolitans were nominated by the Ukrainian princes of Galicia, but when Galicia came under Polish rule the hierarchs were nominated by Polish kings.

METROPOLITANS OF GALICIA

Nifont	1302-03—1305
Petro, also Metropolitan of Kiev and All Rus'	1308-1326
Havryil	1317-26—1328
Teodor	1331-1347
Roman, also the Lithuanian Metropolitan	1355-1361
Antoniy	1371-1391
Ioann	1393-97-98
Symeon, Administrator	1391-1393
Ihnatiy Krekhovych, Administrator	1413
Makariy	1458

2. BISHOPS OF THE GALICIAN METROPOLITANATE

There is very little original source material dealing with the bishops of the Galician Metropolitanate. The following list provides only the names of those bishops who were mentioned in manuscripts or other documents of that period:

Halych: Teodor (1330); Makariy (1458).

Kholm: Hryhoriy (1328); Kharyton (1414).

Lutsk: Teodosiy (1328); Tryfon (1331); Ioann (1393); Teodor (1397); Sava (1401); Dionysiy (1414).

Peremyshl: Antoniy Dobrynya Yadrenkovych (1218-1225); Ilarion (1254); Avraam (1271); Yeremiya (1282); Serhiy (1283-1287); Memnon (1288); Ilarion (1292-1302); Heorhiy (1315); Marko (1330-1341); Kyrylo Voloshyn (1353); Ilarion (1366-1385); Vasyliy (1385); Atanasiy (1391-1407); Pavlo (1415); Atanasiy Drohoyovsky (1422); Iliya (1422-1442); Oleksander (1442-1467); Ioann Boretsky (1442-1476).

Volodymyr-Volynsky: Atanasiy (1328); Yona (1389); Hohol (1405); Danylo (1446-49).

Holy Trinity Church in the village of Nyzhankovychi (Lviv oblast), built of wood in the 15th century.

Holy Friday Church in the village of Stara Sil (Lviv oblast), built in 1440. A typical example of wooden church architecture of the Boyko school.

Volynia Mother of God. 13th-14th centuries. Icon from the Protection of the Blessed Virgin Mary Church in Lutsk (Volynia oblast).

St. George the Dragonslayer. 14th-century icon from the church in the village of Stanylya (Lviv oblast).

Mother of God. 15th-century icon from the village of Krasiv (Lviv oblast).

Church and Monastery Construction in the 13th-15th Centuries

When the Ukrainian princes ruled the Galician-Volynian principality, the Chronicles provided information about the building of new churches and monasteries. After the destruction of Kievan Rus' by the Mongols in 1239-41, and later, the fall of Galicia to Polish rule, the construction of churches and monasteries ceased completely. In some cases churches were even destroyed. Between the years 1240 and 1500 there were 44 monasteries in Galicia. The following churches are listed by city.

Church of the Nativity of the Mother of God in the city of Rohatyn (Ivano-Frankivsk oblast), built in the 14th-15th centuries. Its inside walls were painted by Ya. Pankevych in 1869.

CHURCH CONSTRUCTION

IVANO-FRANKIVSK OBLAST. Halych: Church of the Holy Savior (13th-14th century).

LVIV OBLAST. Lviv: Church of St. Nicholas (13th century).

TERNOPIL OBLAST. Kremenets: Church of the Annunciation of the Blessed Mother of God (13th century), built by Volodymyr Vasylkovych, Prince of Volodymyr-Volynsky.

VOLYNIA OBLAST. Lutsk: Church of St. John (13th century). ***Lyuboml:*** Church of St. Gregory (13th-14th centuries). ***Volodymyr-Volynsky:*** Church of St. Demetrius (13th-14th centuries); Church of St. Basil (13th-14th centuries).

PRESENT-DAY POLAND. Kholm: Church of St. John Chrysostom; Church of the Blessed Virgin Mary; Church of the Holy Trinity (1237-1264), built by King Danylo Romanovych; Church of SS. Cosmas and Damian (13th century); Church of SS. Peter and Paul (13th century).

MONASTERY CONSTRUCTION

LVIV OBLAST. Lavriv: Holy Savior (13th century), built by Prince Lev I Danylovych; St. Onufriy (12th-13th centuries). ***Lviv:*** St. Gregory (13th century), founded by Prince Lev I Danylovych; St. Onufriy (14th century). ***Sambir:*** Holy Savior (13th century), founded by Prince Lev I Danylovych; on the banks of the river Rat, Ratsky (13th century), founded by Metropolitan Petro. ***Synevidsk:*** St. Mary Monastery (13th century).

VOLYNIA OBLAST. Lutsk: Polonynsky (1262), built near the town of Polonne by King Danylo Romanovych. ***Volodymyr-Volynsky:*** St. Michael (13th century), founded by King Danylo Romanovych; Monastery of the Holy Apostles (13th century), built by Volodymyr Vasylkovych, Prince of Volodymyr-Volynsky.

TRANSKARPATHIAN OBLAST. Mukachiv: St. Nicholas (14th century).

PRESENT-DAY POLAND. Peremyshl: St. Nicholas (13th-14th centuries); Holy Savior (13th-14th centuries); Dormition of the Blessed Virgin Mary (13th century). ***Uhrovsk:*** St. Daniel (1264), built by King Danylo Romanovych.

Univ Monastery in the village of Mizhhirya (Lviv oblast), established by Prince Fedir Lyubartovych in 1400. A rare example of the defensive style in Ukrainian church architecture.

V. The Church during the Decline of Kievan Rus' in the 13th-15th Centuries (1240-1458)

General Characteristics of the Period

1. THE POLITICAL SITUATION IN EASTERN EUROPE

From the mid-thirteenth to the mid-fifteenth centuries Eastern Europe saw conflict in the north, the east, and the south-east. From the north came the Swedes, who were defeated by Alexander Nevsky in 1240, and the Teutonic Knights, whom he drove back in 1242.

The Lithuanians, too, resisted the Teutonic Knights, thus protecting northwest Rus'. In 1253 the Lithuanian prince Mendovg was baptised, and in the following year he was crowned king. Lithuania expanded steadily to the southeast, taking Rus' lands and eventually reaching the Black Sea.

From the east came the Mongols (Tatars) who, having sacked Kiev in 1240, split into a northern and southern wing. The northern wing routed the Poles and the Teutonic Knights, while the southern wing crushed the Hungarians. However, the Mongols had no plans to establish themselves in these lands and withdrew, content to collect taxes from their Christian vassals. In 1380 the Khanate of the Golden Horde was taken over by the White Horde, which sacked Moscow two years later and maintained a hold over northern Rus' well into the following century. In 1399 the Horde defeated the Lithuanians.

During the second half of the fourteenth century, some kind of union seemed advantageous to the Lithuanians. From 1370 to 1382 they united with the Hungarians. But union with Poland, which had restored its monarchy in 1320 and again flourished under Casimir the Great, expanding into Rus', seemed more advantageous. Such a union was agreed upon at Krevo in 1385 and confirmed when the Lithuanian Grand Prince Jagiello, son of Algirdas, accepted the Catholic Christian faith. He married the Polish princess Jadwiga (Hedwig), and became king.

The union proved strong, and was renewed at Horodlo in 1413, three years after Polish-Lithuanian forces defeated the Teutonic Knights at Tannenberg.

In the Balkans, the Byzantine Empire of Nicaea regained Constantinople in 1261 and part of Greece in 1262. In 1345 King Stephen Dushan of Serbia became emperor of the Serbs and Greeks. The Serbs took the Despotate of Epirus and Macedonia from Byzantium, which shrank to a small portion of the Balkan peninsula. After Dushan's death in 1355, however, his empire split into several principalities. Three years later the Anjou King of Hungary, Louis the Great, expelled the Venetians from Dalmatia and extended his rule over the Wallach, Serb and Bulgar lands. The Byzantine Empire was reduced to Byzantium itself, Salonika, and a bit of the Peloponnesus.

In the midst of this, from 1347 to 1353, the Black Death arrived from Mongolia through the Crimea and into Europe. It killed about a third of the European population.

Towards the end of the fourteenth century yet another invasion struck Eastern Europe, this time from the south-east. The Ottoman Turks advanced from Anatolia, defeating the Serbs at the battle of Kossovo in 1389 and taking Bulgaria in 1396. The Serbs became vassals of the Turks, as did the Bosnians and Wallachians in 1391. After a temporary collapse, the Ottomans continued their onslaught, taking Albania and Salonika in 1430 and, in 1453, the city of Byzantium. By 1457 the lands now constituting Yugoslavia had all fallen to the Turks.

2. THE RELIGIOUS SITUATION IN EUROPE

By the mid-thirteenth century, the Roman Catholic Church, and particularly the Papacy, had reached a pinnacle of power and activity. In the fourteenth and fifteenth centuries, the power of the Church began to decline.

The Roman Catholic Church, organized on the model of the Roman Empire, expanded its activities as European society in general became more complex. The work of its administration became more clearly divided into spiritual and secular functions. The granting of indulgences (remission of temporal punishment for sins already forgiven) increased. New orders and organizations sprang up. Canon law was perfected, and Thomas Aquinas (1225-1274) systematized theology. Church councils became more frequent; among them were the First Council of Lyons (1245), attended by the Rus' Metropolitan Petro Akerovych; the Second Council of Lyons (1274); the Council of Constance (1414-1418), which re-united the Papacy and was attended by the Kievan Metropolitan Hryhoriy Tsamblak; and the Council of Florence (1438-1439), which attempted to bring the Orthodox into union with Rome. The Pope played an increasing role as mediator in international disputes.

At the same time, the Papacy vied with secular rulers. Although in 1278 the German emperor recognized the independence of the central Italian Papal state, the rivalry of emperor and Pope continued. Other secular rulers, originally conceived as the Pope's secular agents, grew assertive and began to compete with him. In 1303 the French King's troops invaded the papal palace at Anagni and kidnapped Pope Boniface VIII. In 1309 the Pope left Italy altogether, remaining in a kind of exile in Avignon until 1377. In 1378, secular forces compelled the Cardinals to elect a Pope not of their choosing; they fled to Avignon and elected their own Pope. During this Great Schism as many as three "Popes" supported by various rulers claimed suzerainty over the Church, and it was not until the Council of Constance that order was restored. Nevertheless, despite this meddling of secular powers in Church affairs, the competition between the two had its limits: ultimately the secular and ecclesiastical hierarchies had enough common interests to maintain a certain solidarity in times of crisis.

The growth of towns and commerce led to new religious currents, including more emotional urban forms of piety. Although the Church had long tended to encourage spiritual innovations, in the fourteenth century it began to condemn new movements. These, however, continued to grow, and the Hussites who, though condemned at Constance, flourished in Bohemia in 1419-1439, foreshadowed the greater crisis of the Reformation a hundred years later.

During this time the Orthodox Patriarchate of Constantinople shared the ill fortune of the Byzantine Empire, which gave way to the Islamic onslaught from the east. However, other Orthodox centers grew up in Eastern Europe. In 1299 the Metropolitan of Kiev moved north to Vladimir-Suzdal. The Muscovite Metropolitanate declared itself autocephalous (self-ruling) in 1448. Thus was founded the Muscovite Orthodox (later Russian Orthodox) Church. In the Balkans, a Serbian Orthodox Patriarchate was set up in 1345.

The Lithuanian Grand Prince Jagiello accepted Catholic faith and married a Polish princess in 1386. As Lithuania and Poland took over the lands of Rus', the rights of the Orthodox Rus' population became restricted, notably in the Union of Horodlo of 1413. Roman Catholicism penetrated eastward; as early as 1375, a Roman Catholic diocese was established at Halych.

During this time a struggle developed between Muscovy and Lithuania over the Kievan Orthodox Metropolitanate. The Patriarchs in Constantinople followed varying policies. In 1303-1304 an Orthodox Metropolitanate was established at Halych, but enjoyed only a brief and fitful existence until its abolition at the beginning of the fifteenth century. Hryhoriy Tsamblak served briefly as Kievan metropolitan, followed later by Isidore. Both continued contacts with the West, Tsamblak attending the Council of Constance and Isidore travelling to Florence. Secular powers, including Muscovy, constantly frustrated attempts to maintain a permanent church organization. In 1458, five years after the fall of Constantinople, the Kievan Metropolitanate was revived once again.

3. THE POLITICAL SITUATION IN UKRAINE*

The mid-thirteenth century saw the zenith of Galicia-Volynia under Danylo, who was confirmed as ruler by the Mongols in 1245 and accepted a papal crown in 1253. However, it was the Mongol Horde, Poland and Lithuania that ruled Ukraine to the mid-fifteenth century, especially after the decline of Galicia-Volynia after 1387.

In 1254 Khan Batu, founder of the Golden Horde (Kipchak Khanate), died. His successors collected tribute from the various Rus' princes. In 1399 the Horde defeated the Lithuanians. In 1430 the Crimean Turks split off from the Khanate.

Baptised in 1253, the Lithuanian prince Mendovg (Mindaugas) was crowned king in the following year. He made peace with Danylo and returned Black Rus' to him. Mendovg united the Lithuanian tribes in their struggle against the Teutonic order. But within several years after his death in 1263, the Lithuanian realm was again falling into disunion. It was not until 1316 that Lithuania was again united by Gediminas (died 1341). He also enlarged the realm by the annexation of Rus' lands.

With the extinction of the Romanovych dynasty in 1340, civil war engulfed Galicia-Volynia. In that year Casimir the Great of Poland attacked and plundered Lviv. By 1349 the Poles had taken Galicia and Kholm. The Lithuanian prince Lyubart took Volynia.

Under Olgierd (Algirdas, died 1377) and Kestutis (died 1381), Lithuania continued to expand to the southeast, reaching the Black Sea towards the end of the century. Vitautas, who took over Lithuania in 1392, fortified the Black Sea coast, but was defeated by the Horde in 1399. He ruled until 1430. After the Union of Horodlo of 1413, the Polish influence in Lithuania grew, alienating the Rus' nobility.

Under Grand Prince Svidrigailo (1430-1435), the Rus' nobility regained influence in Lithuania; this in turn alienated the Poles, whose candidate, Sigismund, succeeded Svidrigailo (1435-1440). Growing Polish influence drove some nobles to seek Muscovite protection. In 1440 Casimir, a son of Jagiello, became Lithuanian grand prince; four years later he took the Polish throne as well. In 1447 the rights of the Rus' nobility were made equal with those of the Lithuanian nobles.

On the whole, the Lithuanians did not impose their culture upon the Rus' lands, but allowed them to maintain their language, religion, and even their laws. The Rus' princes retained considerable autonomy while enjoying Lithuanian protection.

At this time, Transcarpathia came under Hungarian control, while northern Bukovyna and southern Bessarabia passed to Moldavia.

The Black Sea trade flourished during this period. The

Don and Volga rivers, leading to the Caspian Sea and the Silk Route, provided a way to China. The Mongol Horde controlled these routes, trading with the Venetians, Genoese, and Pisans who established colonies in the Crimea and along the northern coast of the Black Sea.

---

* For details of the political situation in Galicia-Volynia from 1199 to 1458, see Chapter IV, Section 3.

4. 13TH-15TH CENTURY RULERS OF KIEVAN RUS' (1240-1458)

UKRAINIAN RULERS

Danylo Romanovych of Galicia 1240
Mykhaylo Vsevolodovych 1241-1246
Yaroslav of the Suzdal dynasty 1246

LITHUANIAN RULERS

Gediminas 1320-1341
Olgierd (Algirdas) 1341-1377
Jagiello 1377-1386
Skirhailo 1386-1392
Vitautas 1392-1430
Svidrigailo 1430-1435
Sigismund 1435-1440
Casimir 1440-1492

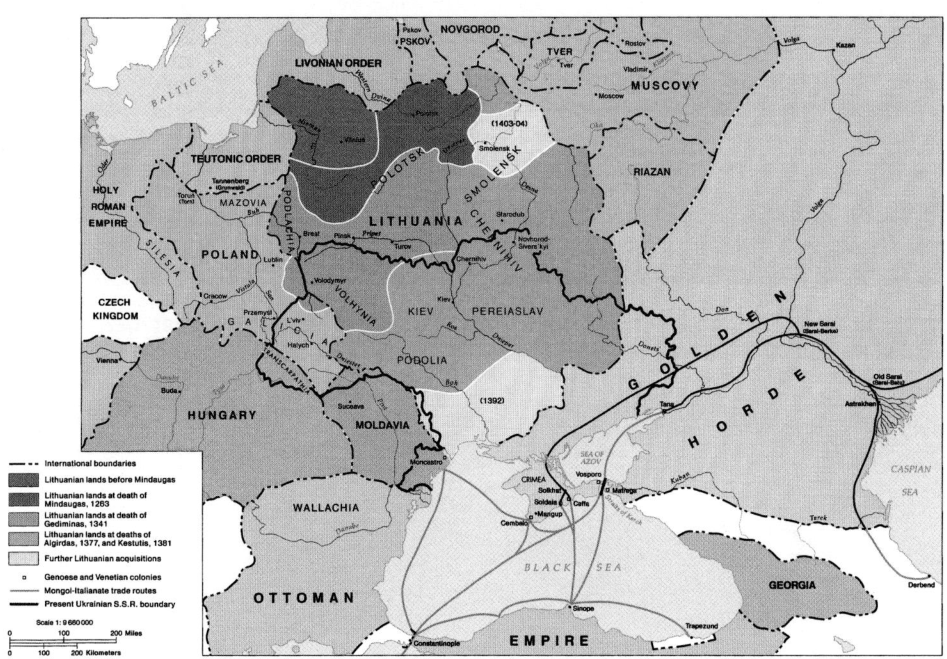

Ukrainian lands in the 14th-15th centuries.

Chronology

1240 — After the Mongols sack Kiev and take the greater part of the Ukrainian lands, the Kievan metropolitan seat is left without a metropolitan and its relations with the Constantinople Patriarchate are temporarily interrupted. Kiev comes under the rule of Danylo Romanovych, Grand Prince of Galicia.

An eyewitness, Serapion, Archimandrite of the Kievan Monastery of the Caves (later Bishop of Vladimir-on-the-Klyazma, 1274-1275) describes the sack of Kiev by the Mongols in one of his epistles:

> God's churches are destroyed, sacred vessels broken, shrines trampled; our bishops have become prey for the sword; the bodies of holy monks are thrown out as food for birds; the blood of our fathers and brothers has nourished the earth like water. The might of our princes and commanders has vanished; our brave people have run away full of fear; many more of our brothers and children were taken into captivity. Our fields are overgrown with grass, our greatness is vanquished; the beauty of our country has perished, our riches have been seized by others and the fruit of our work has been taken by unbelievers. Our land has become the property of foreign people... (Petukhov, p. 17)

After the Mongols conquer the Ukrainian lands, they devise policies aimed at destroying the power of the princes and boyars. But with every passing year the Mongols become more tolerant towards the hierarchs of the Church, and in certain cases even facilitate the development of religious life. Documents and decrees (yarlyky) are distributed to metropolitans and bishops giving them sovereignty over church life.

1240-41 — During the Mongol invasion of Rus'-Ukraine Symon, Bishop of Pereyaslav, dies; Yosyf, Metropolitan of Kiev and the Bishops of Bilhorod, Yuryiv, and Volodymyr-Volynsky disappear without a trace. The Bishops of Chernihiv, Halych, and Peremyshl survive.

24 June 1245 — A Church council is convened in Lyons by Pope Innocent IV. The Council discusses the affairs of the Catholic Church in Europe and the Tatar threat to the Church. According to the English chronicle *Annales Burtonienses,* Archbishop Petro (Akerovych) from Rus' takes part in the Council. He provides the participants with accurate information about the devastated Ukrainian lands.

(Some historians think that Petro was a bishop, while others believe he was a metropolitan. There is no mention of him in Ukrainian chronicles.)

January 1246 — On their way to the Great Khan Kuyuk, emissaries of Pope Innocent IV, led by Joannes Plano de Carpini, stop in Halych. In the absence of Grand Prince Danylo Romanovych, who is in the Tatar capital, the emissaries visit his brother Prince Vasylko and continue to Volodymyr-Volynsky [in his company].

Spring 1246 — Prince Danylo Romanovych returns from the Horde and sends his own ambassadors to the Pope, probably to ask for help in his struggle against the Tatars.

May 1246 — Emissaries from Pope Innocent IV bring Grand Prince Danylo Romanovych of Halych a papal document providing the Prince and his principality with the Pope's protection. Dominican monks arrive with the Papal delegation and remain in Halych. Pope Innocent IV charges the Papal Legate in Prussia with the safekeeping of the Roman Catholic Church in Rus' and authorizes him to appoint Roman Catholic bishops from among Dominican, Franciscan and other monks.

For refusing to participate in Tatar rituals Mykhaylo Vsevolodovych, Prince of Chernihiv, and his boyar, Fedor, are put to death. Later, both martyrs are canonized by the Orthodox Church.

1250 — Danylo Romanovych, Grand Prince of Halych, and his brother, Prince Vasylko, send Kyrylo, their candidate for Kievan-Rus' Metropolitan, to Constantinople to seek the blessing of Patriarch Manuel II. After obtaining the Patriarch's blessing, Metropolitan Kyrylo II returns to Kiev and then visits Chernihiv, Ryazan, Vladimir-on-the-Klyazma, Novgorod and Pereyaslav in Suzdal. The Metropolitan spends most of his term of office outside the Kievan Metropolitanate.

1260 — The eparchies of Pereyaslav and Saray-on-the-Volga, occupied by the Tatar hordes, are united.

1262 — Metropolitan Kyrylo II receives the *Nomocanon* from Bulgaria and incorporates its principles into the organizational structure of the Church. According to the *Nomocanon* the Church in Ukraine should be autonomous in all internal matters; the Metropolitan should hold the authority to ordain new bishops without consulting the Patriarch. The Patriarch retains the authority to select new metropolitans and form new metropolitan sees.

1270 — The Tatar Khan Mengu-Temir issues a decree (yarlyk) whereby those who scorn the Rus' faith, or defile its churches, monasteries, and chapels shall be put to death. The decree also exempts the Church from paying taxes.

1274 — Metropolitan Kyrylo II consecrates Serapion, archimandrite of the Kievan Monastery of the Caves, as Bishop of Vladimir-Suzdal. A synod is convened in Vladimir-on-the-Klyazma, where the rules (pravyla) normalizing ecclesiastical life in the northern part of the Kievan Metropolitanate are established.

1281 — Metropolitan Kyrylo II dies in Pereyaslav-Zalesky in Suzdal.

1283 — Maksym, the new Metropolitan of Kiev and All Rus', arrives in Kiev from Constantinople. In accordance with Tatar laws, he immediately visits Khan Toda-Mangu.

1299 — The Tatars attack Kiev again and sack it completely, but this time do not harm the Metropolitan or clergymen. The northern princes take advantage of the attack and encourage Metropolitan Maksym to flee to the north. The northern rulers have been trying to transfer the seat of the Kievan Metropolitanate to Vladimir-on-the-Klyazma or establish a separate metropolitanate since the 12th century. Falling under their influence and using the pretext of the Tatar attack, Metropolitan Maksym flees north and arrives in Vladimir-on-the-Klyazma on 18 April 1300.

The *Laurentian Chronicle* describes this unauthorized flight from the Metropolitan See:

> Metropolitan Maksym, unable to endure the Tatar violence, left the Metropolitan See, he fled from Kiev and all of Kiev fled. The Metropolitan with all his life [Church administration] went to Bryansk and then to the Suzdal lands.

With the flight of the Metropolitan, Kiev is left without even a bishop; Church matters are dealt with by the Metropolitan's proxy, an archpriest. A battle for the Kievan Metropolitanate ensues. A few decades later the Metropolitanate is divided into the Kievan and Muscovite Metropolitanates.

1301 — Metropolitan Maksym, Teognost, Bishop of Pereyaslav and Saraysk, and probably other bishops from Rus' participate in the Patriarchal Synod in Constantinople.

1303 — Patriarch Athanasius I and Byzantine Emperor Andronicus II Palaeologus issue a decree elevating the Eparchy of Halych to a metropolitanate. The new Metropolitanate is eighty-first on the list of the Constantinople Patriarchate and includes the following Eparchies: Halych, Peremyshl, Volodymyr-Volynsky, Kholm, Lutsk and Turov. Nifont is named the first Metropolitan of Galicia.

1305 — After the death of Metropolitan Maksym, Prince Yuriy Lvovych of Galicia-Volynia sends Hegumen Petro (of the Ratnensky monastery near Lviv) to Patriarch Athanasius as a candidate for metropolitan. At the same time Prince Mikhayil Yaroslavych of Tver in Muscovy sends Hegumen Gerontiy as the candidate from the northern lands. Wishing to preserve the unity of the Kievan Metropolitanate, the Patriarch delays naming a new Metropolitan for three years.

June 1308 — Patriarch Athanasius I appoints Hegumen Petro Metropolitan of Kiev and All Rus'.

1309 — Metropolitan Petro leaves Kiev after barely a year for Vladimir-on-the-Klyazma.

1313 — Metropolitan Petro pays a visit to the Tatar Khan, Uzbek, in order to obtain a yarlyk (decree) allowing him to govern the Kievan Metropolitanate.

1316 — Patriarch John XIII Glykys establishes a Lithuanian Metropolitanate and appoints Theophilus as the first Lithuanian Metropolitan with the seat in Novogrudok.

1320 — Kiev and much of Kievan Rus' comes under the rule of the Lithuanian Grand Prince Gediminas, who governs Ukrainian lands through proxies. Henry, a Dominican monk, is consecrated as the first Roman Catholic Bishop of Kiev and organizes the first Roman Catholic diocese.

1326 — Metropolitan Petro, in residence in Vladimir-on-the-Klyazma transfers the Kievan metropolitan seat to Moscow. Bowing to the demands of the Muscovite grand prince Ivan Kalita, the Metropolitan leaves a testament whereby all future metropolitans shall take up residence in Moscow, which shall henceforth be the new seat of the Kievan Metropolitanate.

May 1328 — The new Metropolitan of All Rus', Teognost, leaves Constantinople and arrives in the Galician-Volynian Principality. Together with the bishops of Peremyshl, Kholm, Lutsk and Turov, the Metropolitan consecrates two new bishops for Halych and Volodymyr-Volynsky. Arriving in Moscow, the Metropolitan attempts to preserve the unity of the Kievan Metropolitanate, whose eparchies are now spread over three separate principalities: Muscovy, Lithuania and Poland. The metropolitan resides in Moscow, in accordance with his predecessor's testament, and contributes to the closing of the Lithuanian Metropolitanate. Illegally, he uses the title of "Metropolitan of Muscovy," and not "Metropolitan of Kiev and All Rus'," as authorized by the Patriarch. He promotes the growth of church life in Moscow and the northern lands and is instrumental in the development of Moscow. In order to increase Moscow's religious and political influence, Metropolitan Teognost, with the approval of Patriarch Isaias, canonize Metropolitan Petro as the first Muscovite saint.

1330 — In Akkerman on the Black Sea Ivan Suchavsky, a merchant from Trebizond, is martyred. He is subsequently proclaimed a saint and in 1400 his relics are moved to the monastery of St. George in Suchava (Suceava). St. Ivan Suchavsky becomes the patron saint of Bukovyna.

1336 — The Galician-Volynian Principality comes under the partial rule of the Polish Principality of Mazovia.

1341 — After the decline of the Galician-Volynian Principality, the Lithuanian Grand Prince Olgierd occupies Ukrainian lands — the regions of Bilhorod, Chernihiv and Podilia — and Byelorussian lands — the regions of Smolensk, Bryansk and Siversk — and in 1362, the Kiev region.

1347 — At the demand of Metropolitan Teognost, the Patriarch of Constantinople informs all northern and southern princes of the dissolution of the Galician Metropolitanate. Teodor, Metropolitan of Galicia, is recalled to Constantinople.

1349 — The Galician Principality falls under the rule of the Polish Kingdom.

1352 — Despite his lack of jurisdiction over the Kievan Metropolitanate, the Bulgarian Patriarch Theodosius II of Trnovo nominates Teodoryt as the new Metropolitan of Kiev.

30 June 1354 — Patriarch Philotheus of Constantinople names a native of Moscow, Bishop Aleksey of Vladimir-on-the-Klyazma, Metropolitan of Kiev and All Rus'. At the request of Metropolitan Aleksey, the Patriarch condemns the appointment of Teodoryt as Metropolitan of Kiev and All Rus' by the Bulgarian Patriarch.

July 1354 — Before leaving Constantinople, Metropolitan Aleksey requests the Patriarchal Synod to permanently relocate the seat of the Kievan Metropolitanate from Kiev to Vladimir-on-the-Klyazma, regardless of the fact that Metropolitan Aleksey's predecessors, Petro and Teognost, had arbitrarily transferred the Metropolitan See from Vladimir-on-the-Klyazma to Moscow. The Patriarch and his Synod describe the situation in a decree:

> His Holiness, together with the most reverend archpriests has examined the matter and has come to the firm conclusion that there is no other place but Vladimir-on-the-Klyazma for the location, sanctuary and retreat of the Holy Metropolitanate of Rus', and that the bishop does not have any means there [in Kiev] to fulfill the most necessary obligations and requirements of his position. Whereas there [in Vladimir-on-the-Klyazma] he can find the necessary safeguards and freedom of rule. Therefore, the present Synod, acting as the will of the Holy Spirit, declares with this decree that the present most Blessed Metropolitan of Rus', and all his successors, shall reside in Vladimir and forever hold Vladimir as their integral and irreplaceable cathedral seat. But let them consider Kiev their own throne and first cathedral of the Metropolitan if it [Kiev] remains standing. After Kiev, and along with Kiev, let the second cathedral and sanctuary for the Metropolitan of Rus' be the most blessed Eparchy of Vladimir. The most Holy Metropolitan of Rus' Kyr Teognost and two of his predecessors, who were Bishops of Kiev, moved there and, in doing so, paid great homage to Kiev... (*Acta Patriarchatus,* pp. 352-352).

1355 — The Lithuanian grand prince Olgierd removes the Kievan metropolitan Teodoryt; on Olgierd's demand Patriarch Callistus I consecrates the monk Roman as Lithuanian Metropolitan, whose seat is to be in Kiev.

A New Metropolitan — Aleksey — arrives in Moscow from Constantinople. According to a decision of Patriarch Callistus I, Metropolitan Aleksey is to take charge of the Kievan Metropolitanate and all eparchies on Ukrainian land under Lithuanian rule.

1356 — Metropolitan Aleksey and Metropolitan Roman are recalled to Constantinople by Patriarch Callistus I for the Patriarchal Synod. After a great dispute between the two metropolitans over the jurisdiction of Kiev, the Synod decides that Kiev will remain part of the Metropolitanate of All Rus' under the jurisdiction of Aleksey, but Ukrainian eparchies under Polish and Lithuanian rule will come under the jurisdiction of Metropolitan Roman.

1358 — Metropolitan Aleksey arrives in Kiev from Moscow. There he is imprisoned by Prince Olgierd but manages to flee to Moscow. Consequently, the battle for the Kievan Metropolitanate intensifies and acquires more of a political rather than a religious ecclesiastical character.

1361 — After the death of Metropolitan Roman, Metropolitan Aleksey succeeds in taking over Ukrainian eparchies in the Polish-Lithuanian kingdom.

1362 — Actively aided by Metropolitan Aleksey, Prince Dmitriy Ivanovich (Donskoy) unites all the northern principalities into one Great Muscovite Principality.

October 1364 — By a decision of the Patriarchal Synod the Lithuanian-Galician Metropolitanate is incorporated into the Metropolitanate of All Rus' with its seat in Vladimir-on-the-Klyazma and Moscow.

2 December 1375 — At the request of the Lithuanian grand prince Olgierd, Patriarch Philotheus appoints the Bulgarian monk-priest Cyprian Metropolitan of Kiev and All Rus'. All eparchies in the Lithuanian-Rus' Principality and, after the death of Metropolitan Aleksey, all eparchies of the southern and northern lands are to come under the rule of Metropolitan Cyprian.

1378 — Metropolitan Aleksey dies in Moscow. Learning of his death, Patriarch Macarius calls archimandrite Mikhail (Mityya) to Constantinople to be appointed Metropolitan, disregarding the fact that Metropolitan Cyprian is ruling in Kiev and is to take over the whole Metropolitanate after the death of Metropolitan Aleksey. On his way to Constantinople, Archimandrite Mikhail dies and the Muscovite emissaries select a new candidate. He is the monk-priest Pimen, who is presented to the Patriarch as the candidate of the Muscovite grand prince Dmitriy Ivanovich.

1379 — Metropolitan Cyprian takes part in the Patriarchal Synod in Constantinople.

June 1380 — Pimen is nominated Metropolitan in Constantinople without the knowledge or consent of the Muscovite grand prince Dmitriy Ivanovich. Upon learning of the nominations, the offended Prince refuses to acknowledge the new Metropolitan and invites Cyprian, Metropolitan of Kiev, to Moscow.

23 May 1381 — Metropolitan Cyprian arrives in Moscow.

December 1381 — As soon as Metropolitan Pimen reaches Muscovy, he and his emissaries are seized and imprisoned by order of the Prince of Muscovy.

Fall 1382 — Guided by political motives and unwilling to have a Kievan Metropolitan in Moscow, Grand Prince Dmitriy Ivanovich expels Metropolitan Cyprian from Moscow, frees Metropolitan Pimen and places him on the metropolitan throne.

Spring 1385 — Patriarch Nilus recalls Metropolitan Pimen and Metropolitan Cyprian to Constantinople to appear before a court to determine the rightful ruler of the Metropolitanate of "All Rus'." Both Metropolitans remain in Constantinople for three years without any decision from the Patriarch.

14 August 1385 — In Krevo in Lithuania, two dynasties are united by the marriage of Lithuanian grand prince Jagiello with the Polish princess Jadwiga. Jagiello converts to Roman Catholicism and becomes King of Poland, thus uniting the territory of Lithuania, Ukraine, Byelorussia and Poland. Jagiello promises to spread Roman Catholicism throughout the lands of his former principality.

St. Michael the Archangel.
15th-century icon from the Elevation of the Cross Church in Drohobych (Lviv oblast).

Mother of God of Eleusis. 15th-16th century icon from the village of Dorosyn (Volynia oblast).

1388 — Ten years after the death of Metropolitan Aleksey, his actions are harshly condemned by the Patriarchal Synod. Expecting such a condemnation, Metropolitan Pimen flees Constantinople. The Patriarchal Synod proclaims Cyprian the rightful Metropolitan of Kiev and All Rus' and defrocks Pimen.

July 1388 — Arriving in Moscow via Turkey, Metropolitan Pimen conceals his defrocking and is greeted with all honors by Grand Prince Dmitriy Ivanovich.

January 1389 — The new Patriarch Antony IV reaffirms the decision of his predecessor, Nilus, and acknowledges Cyprian as Metropolitan of Kiev and All Rus'.

1 October 1389 — Metropolitan Cyprian, Bishop Iona of Volynia and Bishop Mykhayil of Smolensk return from Moscow to Kiev. All the eparchies on Ukrainian, Byelorussian, Lithuanian and Muscovite territory are united into the Kievan Metropolitanate and come under the jurisdiction of Metropolitan Cyprian.

14 February 1390 — After a short stay in Kiev, Metropolitan Cyprian, accompanied by two Greek Metropolitans and six bishops of Rus', arrives in Moscow, chosen by Cyprian as the Metropolitan seat. The monk Toma Izufov remains in Kiev as the Metropolitan's proxy.

2 April 1396 — Metropolitan Cyprian travels to Lithuania and then to Kiev, where he remains for a year and a half.

1404 — Metropolitan Cyprian arrives in Kiev and orders archimandrite Toma Izufov and his administrators to be arrested and taken to Moscow.

1 September 1407 — Patriarch Matthew I nominates Fotiy, a monk from Polotsk, Metropolitan of Kiev and All Rus'.

1407 — A number of schools attached to parishes are founded in Ukraine: in Krasnostav (1407), in Lviv and Peremyshl (1437), and in Kiev and Lutsk (1506).

Fall 1409 — Metropolitan Fotiy, accompanied by emissaries of the Byzantine emperor and of the Patriarch, arrives in Moscow. The Lithuanian grand prince Vitautas agrees to acknowledge Metropolitan Fotiy if the seat of the Metropolitanate of All Rus' is moved to Kiev.

22 March 1410 — Metropolitan Fotiy and the metropolitan administration leave Kiev and move permanently to Moscow where, in Metropolitan Fotiy's own words, his rule is "full of sorrow, tears and sobs."

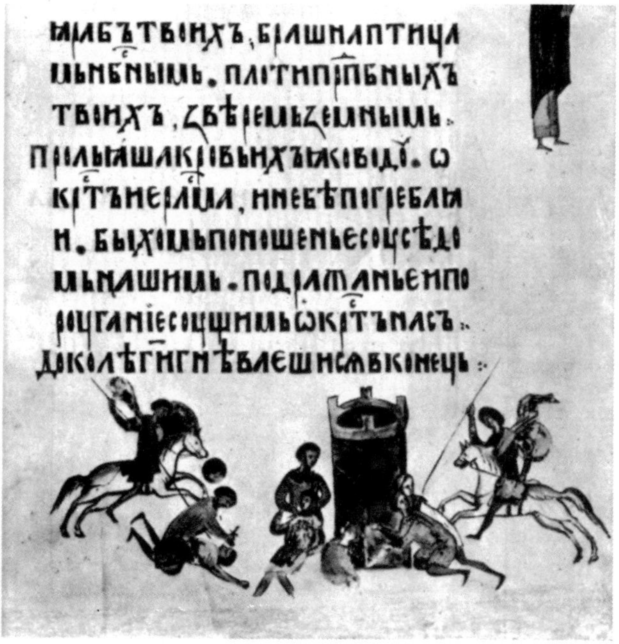

Handwritten edition of the Kievan Psalter. Miniature, 1397.

1414 — Metropolitan Fotiy arrives in the Lithuanian-Rus' principality to collect tribute. He orders precious objects, icons, and church goods to be removed from Ukrainian churches. On the orders of the Metropolitan, the monasteries and churches in Kiev are plundered. Prince Vitautas, indignant at these actions, stops the Metropolitan, takes back the stolen wealth and sends him back to Moscow. All the bishops in Ukrainian and Byelorussian lands send a special document to Prince Vitautas, accusing the Metropolitan of robbing the eparchies and totally ignoring church life in Ukrainian and Byelorussian lands. Prince Vitautas supports the accusations of the bishops, expels the proxy and officials of Metropolitan Fotiy and orders a register prepared of all Church goods in the Metropolitanate as a safeguard against any further plundering by Moscow. At the same time, the bishops send an official letter to Metropolitan Fotiy in which they renounce his authority, anathemize him and demand that he be defrocked.

Summer 1414 — In a letter to Patriarch Euthymius II, the bishops of the Kievan Metropolitanate document all of Metropolitan Fotiy's wrongdoings and petition the Patriarch to appoint Hryhoriy Tsamblak, a relative of Metropolitan Cyprian, as Metropolitan of Kiev. Emissaries of Ukrainian and Byelorussian bishops and of Prince Vitautas arrive in Constantinople at the same time as emissaries of Metropolitan Fotiy and Muscovite Prince Vasiliy Dmitrovich, who is related to the Byzantine emperor Manuel II Palaeologus. Influenced by the Muscovite emissaries and their lavish gifts, the Patriarch not only refuses to appoint Tsamblak but also defrocks him.

March 1415 — The Lithuanian grand prince Vitautas convenes a Synod in Novogrudok attended by all Ukrainian, Byelorussian and Lithuanian bishops and archimandrites. The Synod unanimously passes a resolution supporting the need for a division of the Metropolitanate of "All Rus'," but its participants cannot agree on a candidate for Metropolitan. It is decided to send another delegation to the Patriarch.

August 1415 — The emissaries Havryil and Dosypat, sent by the Patriarch and Emperor, respectively, arrive in Lithuania on their way back from Moscow. They convince Prince Vitautas to postpone the selection of a Metropolitan until November.

15 November 1415 — Receiving no satisfactory response from the Patriarch, Prince Vitautas reconvenes the Synod of Bishops in Novodrudok. The Synod meets in the Church of the Blessed Virgin Mary and is composed of the following: Archbishop Teodosiy of Polotsk, Bishop Isaakiy of Chernihiv, Bishop Dionysiy of Lutsk, Bishop Herasym of Volodymyr-Volynsky, Bishop Helasiy of Peremyshl, Bishop Sevastiyan of Smolensk, Bishop Kharyton of Kholm, Bishop Yevfymiy of Turov, Prince Vitautas, all the princes of the

Lithuanian, Ukrainian, and Byelorussian lands, archimandrites, hegumens, boyars, and many clerics. The Synod renounces Metropolitan Fotiy and elects Hryhoriy Tsamblak Metropolitan of Kiev and All Rus'. The Synod sends a message to the faithful stating that the hierarchs, clergy, and faithful honor the Constantinople Patriarch and together with him "confess the same faith." After the Synod, Metropolitan Hryhoriy moves to Kiev, where he directs the affairs of the Metropolitanate until his death.

After Hryhoriy Tsamblak is named Metropolitan of Kiev and All Rus', the Muscovite metropolitan Fotiy sends a delegation to Patriarch Euthymius II, requesting that he denounce the unlawful election, excommunicate Metropolitan Hryhoriy, and anathemize him at a Patriarchal Church Synod. At the same time Metropolitan Fotiy appeals to all the bishops in the Kievan and Galician Metropolitanates, the princes and the clergy not to recognize Metropolitan Hryhoriy. The Patriarch cedes to Metropolitan Fotiy's demands, and defrocks, excommunicates and lays an anathema on Metropolitan Hryhoriy. The succeeding Patriarch, Joseph II, does the same.

19 February 1418 — Metropolitan Hryhoriy, accompanied by several hundred delegates, arrives at the General Council of Constance (1414-1418). The delegation, arriving at the conclusion of the Council, includes princes, priests, monks and boyars and is greeted by the initiator of the Council, the German King Sigismund.

25 February 1418 — Metropolitan Hryhoriy and his delegation have an audience with Pope Martin V and many cardinals.

1420 — After the death of Hryhoriy, who used the title "Metropolitan of Kiev, Galicia and All Rus'," the Kievan and Galician Metropolitanates come under the jurisdiction of Metropolitan Fotiy as the result of an agreement between the Lithuanian prince Vitautas and Metropolitan Fotiy, who now takes over the title "Metropolitan of Kiev and All Rus'."

1430 — According to the agreement concluded at Vilnius in 1401, the Principality of Lithuania-Rus' was to revert to Poland after Prince Vitautas' death. In contradiction to the agreement the Lithuanian, Ukrainian and Byelorussian boyars proclaim Svidrigailo Grand Prince of Lithuania. Svidrigailo, a Catholic, nevertheless supports Orthodoxy and Ukrainian culture.

1431 — After the death of Metropolitan Fotiy, Prince Svidrigailo sends Bishop Herasym of Smolensk to Patriarch Joseph II as a candidate for Metropolitan of Kiev and All Rus'. The Muscovite Prince Vasiliy Vasilyevich sends his own candidate, Bishop Iona of Ryazan and Murom.

1432 — Patriarch Joseph II selects Herasym to be Metropolitan of All Rus', encompassing the Lithuanian and Muscovite principalities with Kiev as the seat.

Oranta. 14th-century relief. Kievan Monastery of the Caves.

After returning from Constantinople, Metropolitan Herasym first resides in Smolensk and one year later moves to Kiev, the metropolitan seat.

Summer 1434 — The Lithuanian prince Sigismund signs the Charter of Troki, which grants all Ukrainian, Lithuanian and Byelorussian princes and boyars the same rights and privileges, regardless of their faith.

13 November 1434 — Pope Eugene IV sends a missive to Prince Sigismund and Metropolitan Herasym regarding the unification of the Kievan Metropolitanate with the Roman Church. The Prince and the Metropolitan respond favorably.

26 July 1435 — Prince Svidrigailo accuses Metropolitan Herasym of treasonously supporting Sigismund, a pretender to the Lithuanian throne, and puts Herasym to death by burning him at the stake.

Summer 1436 — Patriarch Joseph II nominates Hegumen Isidore (Izydor) Metropolitan of Kiev and All Rus'. Isidore, a Greek philosopher, supports the unification of the Orthodox and Catholic Churches.

2 April 1437 — Metropolitan Isidore, accompanied by Bishop Iona and an emissary of the Byzantine emperor, arrives in Moscow, where he occupies the Metropolitan chair. All Orthodox eparchies on Ukrainian, Byelorussian, Muscovite and Lithuanian territories are under his jurisdiction.

8 September 1437 — After a five-month stay in Moscow, Metropolitan Isidore leaves for Italy to attend the Council of Ferrara-Florence, aimed at unifying the Orthodox and Catholic Churches. The Metropolitan is accompanied by approximately 100 bishops and clergymen. Among them are Bishop Avramiy of Suzdal, archimandrite Vasiyan, the priest Symon, Toma, emissary of the Prince, and boyars. On the journey to Italy, the delegation stops in the cities of Tver, Novgorod, Pskov and Riga, where it is greeted with great honors.

9 April 1438 — The Council of Ferrara, aimed at unifying the Western and Eastern Churches, is officially convened. The meetings of the Council begin on October 8. In January 1439, Pope Eugene IV decides to relocate the Council to Florence.

18 August 1438 — Metropolitan Isidore arrives in Ferrara to find a large delegation from the Patriarchate of Constantinople already present.

15 January 1439 — Metropolitan Isidore is elevated to the rank of Cardinal by Pope Eugene IV. The official decree acknowledging this event is signed September 16, 1439.

5 July 1439 — The unification of the Western and Eastern Churches is officially proclaimed in Florence. One day later the Act of Union is formally signed in the Cathedral of Florence by Pope Eugene IV, Byzantine emperor John VIII Palaeologus, Metropolitan Isidore of Kiev and All Rus', and others.

1439 — The first Brotherhood in Ukraine is founded in Lviv at the Church of the Holy Dormition. In 1586 the Brotherhood obtains the rights of a Holy Cross Society (stavropegia).

March 1440 — On the way back from Florence, Metropolitan Cardinal Isidore stops in Venice and in Buda, Hungary, where he writes an epistle to the faithful, asking them not to make any distinctions between the Greek and Latin rites. Returning to Rus', the Metropolitan finds the Catholic clergy (Lithuanian and Polish) indifferent and in certain places even hostile to the Act of Union. On Ukrainian and Byelorussian lands, the princes and the faithful accept the Union passively, with neither hostility nor enthusiasm. The Muscovite Principality, long isolated from the West as well as from Byzantium, actively resists the Union, thereby further strengthening its political isolation.

1440 — Metropolitan Isidore travels to Poland and then to Lithuania, Byelorussia and Ukraine. He visits Peremyshl, Lviv, Halych, Vilnius, Belz, Hrubeshiv, Kholm, Vlodava, Brest-Litovsk, Vilkaviskis, Troki, Kiev and Smolensk. He proclaims the Union everywhere, but the majority of the faithful does not accept it. The Polish Kingdom, encompassing these lands, does not aid in popularizing the Union, since the Polish rulers, who are in conflict with Pope Eugene IV, do not recognize either him or the anti-Pope Felix V.

19 March 1441 — Metropolitan Isidore arrives in Moscow, where he is greeted as Metropolitan of All Rus', but is not acknowledged as Papal Legate or Cardinal.

23 March 1441 — In Moscow, the Muscovite grand prince Vasiliy II orders Metropolitan Isidore imprisoned. A Synod of Muscovite Bishops convened by the Prince denounces the Metropolitan, proclaims him a heretic and strips him of the metropolitan rank. Metropolitan Isidore is threatened with death unless he renounces the Act of Union. The Synod also repudiates the Union but does not denounce the Byzantine emperor or the Patriarch, who are signatories of the Act.

15 September 1441 — Metropolitan Isidore escapes to Tver, where he is seized and imprisoned once again.

Spring 1442 — As a result of the intercession of Pope Eugene IV, Prince Vasiliy II of Muscovy releases Metropolitan Isidore from imprisonment. After his release he arrives in Lithuania and finally settles in Rome.

15 December 1448 — In Moscow, Prince Vasiliy II convenes a Synod of Muscovite Bishops. The Bishops of Rostov, Suzdal, Kolomna and Perm participate, while the Bishops of Novgorod and Tver send representatives. Without the knowledge or consent of the Patriarch, the Synod names Bishop Iona of Ryazan the first Metropolitan of Moscow.

1449 — After the death of Byzantine emperor John VIII Palaeologus, his brother Constantine XI Palaeologus is put on the throne. An anti-unionist, Constantine deposes the pro-union Patriarch, Gregorio III Mamme, and reinstates Orthodoxy.

31 August 1449 — Casimir, King of Poland and Grand Prince of Lithuania, signs a treaty with Muscovite Grand Prince Vasiliy II proclaiming "eternal brotherhood and love." They send the newly named Metropolitan Iona to the Patriarch requesting his consecration as Metropolitan of all Orthodox eparchies of Lithuania, Ukraine, Byelorussia and Muscovy.

31 January 1450 — Pope Nicholas V gives Metropolitan Isidore the Monastery of St. Basil near Rome, and the Sabine Eparchy in Italy on February 8. The Kievan Metropolitanate still remains under the jurisdiction of Metropolitan Isidore.

31 January 1451 — At the Synod of Vilnius, the Polish king Casimir, ruler of all Ukrainian and Byelorussian lands, transfers the Metropolitan throne of Kiev and All Rus' to Metropolitan Iona of Moscow. Only part of the Galician Metropolitanate remains outside the Metropolitan's jurisdiction.

Spring 1451 — Bishop Daniyil of Volodymyr-Volynsky and Berestya, a supporter of the Union, is named Metropolitan of Kiev and All Rus' by Patriarch

Gregorio III Mamme and Metropolitan Isidore. Upon his return to Kiev, Metropolitan Daniyil is ordered to Moscow by Metropolitan Iona. After being pressured and threatened, Metropolitan Daniyil renounces the Union on October 28. Then he is pardoned and allowed to return to his eparchy.

29 May 1453 — Constantinople is seized by the Turks. The last Byzantine emperor, Constantine XI Palaeologus, dies in the war. With the permission of the Turkish Sultan, Mohammed II, Gennadius II Scholarius, a supporter of Orthodoxy, ascends the Patriarchal throne. After the fall of Constantinople, the union ceases to be a pressing issue, and the Eastern and Western Churches remain divided. Taking advantage of this situation, the Muscovite Church, which formed part of the Kievan Metropolitanate, and which was under the jurisdiction of the Patriarch of Constantinople, separates and declares itself independent of the Patriarchate. Thus, the actual independence of the Muscovite Church from the Constantinople Patriarchs begins during the rule of Metropolitan Iona of Moscow.

The ecclesiastical and administrative division of the heretofore Kievan Metropolitanate into the Metropolitanates of Muscovy and Kiev also dates from this period.

21 July 1458 — At the request of Pope Calixtus III, the former Patriarch Gregorio III Mamme, who accepted the union in 1438, consecrates Hryhoriy, the Bulgarian Abbot of the Monastery of St. Demetrius, Metropolitan of Kiev and All Rus'. The Metropolitan's jurisdiction includes the following Ukrainian and Byelorussian eparchies within the Polish-Lithuanian State: Chernihiv, Polotsk, Smolensk, Turov, Lutsk, Volodymyr-Volynsky, Kholm, Halych and Peremyshl.

All of the above bishops, with the exception of Bishop Yevfymiy of Chernihiv, who departs to Moscow and is appointed Bishop of Suzdal, disregard the numerous appeals and petitions of Metropolitan Iona of Muscovy and continue to acknowledge Metropolitan Hryhoriy.

3 September 1458 — Pope Pius II issues the bull "Decens reputamus" regarding the nomination and consecration of Kievan Metropolitan Hryhoriy. The bull defines the territory of the Kievan Metropolitanate as separate and distinct from the Muscovite Church.

October 1458 — A Synod of Muscovite Bishops proclaims its complete autonomy from the Constantinople Patriarchate, regardless of future Patriarchs' adherence to Orthodoxy or to the union with the Roman Church. After the separation of the Muscovite Church from the Kievan Metropolitanate, the Kievan metropolitans assume the title of "Metropolitan of Kiev and All Rus'."

Principal Ecclesiastical Activities

1. THE KIEVAN METROPOLITANATE DURING THE 13TH-15TH CENTURIES

After the Mongols sack Kievan Rus'-Ukraine in 1240, certain Metropolitans move their seats to the north, at first to Vladimir-on-the-Klyazma and later to Moscow. At first the metropolitans, relocating without the knowledge or approval of the Patriarch, do so for reasons of safety and to protect the financial security of the Metropolitanate. Later this relocation takes on a marked political character.

During this period only one Metropolitan, Hryhoriy Tsamblak, is elected against the will of the Patriarch, by the Episcopal Synod in 1415. Unlike the other metropolitans, Metropolitan Hryhoriy II is named by a Uniate rather than an Orthodox Patriarch, in 1458.

METROPOLITANS OF KIEV (1240-1458)

The following Metropolitans of Kiev and All Rus' retained Kiev as their seat:

Petro Akerovych 1241-1242
Kyrylo II 1250-1281
Teodoryt 1352-1355
Cyprian 1375-1390
Hryhoriy Tsamblak 1415-1419
Herasym 1432-1435
Hryhoriy II 1458-1472

The following Metropolitans of Kiev and All Rus' chose Vladimir-on-the-Klyazma or Moscow as their seat:

Maksym 1283-1305
Petro 1308-1326
Teognost 1328-1353
Aleksey 1354-1378
Cyprian 1390-1406
Fotiy 1407-1414, 1420-1431
Isidore (Izydor) 1436-1442
Iona 1448-1461

2. EPARCHIES IN THE KIEVAN METROPOLITANATE

The following are new eparchies or those mentioned for the first time in the chronicles of this period:

WITHIN THE BORDERS OF PRESENT-DAY UKRAINE:

Lutsk 1284-1288

WITHIN THE BORDERS OF PRESENT-DAY RUSSIA:

Saray 1261
Tver 1274-1285
Suzdal 1347
Kolomna 1353
Perm 1383

The Eparchies of Bilhorod, Yuriyiv and Pereyaslav on the territory of present-day Ukraine are closed. The Eparchy of Pereyaslav is united with the Saray Eparchy, Chernihiv to the Bryansk Eparchy, Bilhorod and Yuriyiv to the Kievan Metropolitan See.

3. SYNODS AND ASSEMBLIES OF BISHOPS IN THE KIEVAN METROPOLITANATE

During the 13th-15th centuries, Synods of the hierarchs of the Kievan Metropolitanate were generally convened in Kiev, other cities and even in Vladimir-on-the-Klyazma and Moscow, since some metropolitans had transferred their seats there.

The following Synods were convened on the territory of present-day Ukraine:

May 1328 — Metropolitan Teognost convenes a Synod to select new bishops. The following participate in the Synod: Bishop Mark of Peremyshl, Bishop Hryhoriy of Kholm, Bishop Teodosiy of Lutsk, Bishop Stefan of Turov. The Synod names the monk-priest Atanasiy Bishop of Volodymyr-Volynsky, and the monk-priest, Fedor, Bishop of Halych.

6 December 1331 — The Synod selecting monk-priest Tryfon for the post of Bishop of Lutsk is composed of the following: Metropolitan Teognost, Bishop Hryhoriy of Kholm, and Bishop Atanasiy of Volodymyr-Volynsky.

April 1332 — The Synod selecting the monk-priest Pavlo as Bishop of Chernihiv is convened.

19 September 1335 — The Synod selecting the monk-priest Ioann Bishop of Chernihiv is convened. The following hierarchs participate: Metropolitan Teognost and the Bishops of Volodymyr-Volynsky, Halych, Kholm, Lutsk and Smolensk.

August 1345 — The Synod selecting the monk-priest Yevfymiy Bishop of Smolensk is convened and includes the following hierarchs: Metropolitan Teognost, Bishop Ioann of Bryansk (Chernihiv), and Bishop Kyrylo of Bilhorod.

15 November 1415 — The Synod to elect Hryhoriy Tsamblak Metropolitan of Kiev and All Rus' is convened in Novogrudok. The following hierarchs participate: Archbishop Teodosiy of Polotsk, Bishop Isaakiy of Chernihiv, Bishop Dionysiy of Lutsk, Bishop Herasym of Volodymyr-Volynsky, Bishop Helasiy of Peremyshl, Bishop Sevastiyan of Smolensk, Bishop Kharyton of Kholm and Bishop Yevfymiy of Turov.

There were probably even more Synods convened during this period of the Kievan Metropolitanate. Unfortunately, no records have been found.

Church and Monastery Construction in the 13th-15th Centuries

During the occupation of Kievan Rus'-Ukraine by the Mongols and Tatars many monasteries and hundreds of churches were ransacked and destroyed. While the building of churches and monasteries had spread to all the principalities during the preceding centuries, the building of monasteries and churches came to a complete halt during the 13th, 14th and 15th centuries, except in Galicia, Volynia, and the Crimea (Krym). The Crimea now belongs to Ukraine, but in the 13th, 14th and 15th centuries its eparchy did not fall under the jurisdiction of the Kievan Metropolitanate. The Crimea was settled by Greek colonists, and since the end of the 13th century by the Genoese.

On the territory of present-day Ukraine (with the exception of Crimea, Galicia and Volynia), only one church and one monastery were built during this period. There are no exact records concerning the building of new churches and monasteries. This standstill was caused by the Mongol-Tatar invasion, but was later perpetuated by the pillaging of eparchies by the metropolitans who had transferred their seat to Vladimir-on-the-Klyazma or to Moscow. Due to the ruin caused by the Mongol-Tatar invasion and the impoverishment of the bishops, clergy, and the faithful, it was impossible to build new churches and monasteries.

In contrast to the situation on Ukrainian territories, in Muscovy 180 monasteries and hundreds of churches were built during this same period (see register of newly-built monasteries and the chapter on church construction in *Istoriya Russkoy Tserkvi (History of the Russian Church)* by Metropolitan Makariy, St. Petersburg, 1891, Vol. 7, pp. 1-104).

CHURCH CONSTRUCTION

CRIMEA OBLAST. Bohate: Church of St. Elias (14th century). ***Feodosia:*** Church of Archangels Michael and Gabriel (1408); Church of St. John the Baptist (1348); Church of St. John the Evangelist (14th century); Church of St. George (14th century); Church of St. Stephen (14th century); Church of St. Sergius (14th-15th century). ***Kudryne:*** Church of the Archangels Michael and Gabriel (1328).

Sudak: Church of the Twelve Apostles (14th-15th century). ***Verkhorichcha:*** Church of St. John the Baptist (14th-15th century).

ODESSA OBLAST. Bilhorod-Dnistrovsky: Armenian Church (14th century); Subterranean church of Iona Suchavsky (14th century).

MONASTERY CONSTRUCTION

CRIMEA OBLAST. Old Crimea: "Surp-Khach" monastery (14th century).

KHARKIV OBLAST. Izyum: Svyatohirsky (Dormition) Monastery, founded by Kievan monks after the sacking of Kiev by the Mongols in 1240.

St. Paraskeva Friday. 15th-century icon from the village Zhohatyn (Poland).

St. Peter the Apostle. Detail from the 15th-century icon "Prayer with Deeds" from the village Vanivka (Lemko region, Poland).

St. Nicholas Monastery on Chernecha Hora in Mukachiv (Transcarpathian oblast), founded in 1360 by Prince Fedir Koryatovych and rebuilt many times. St. Nicholas Church, in a classical style, was built in the monastery in 1789-1804. Baroque-style monks' cells were built by architect D. Rama in 1766-72.

Church of the Protection of the Blessed Virgin Mary in the village of Sutkivtsi (Khmelnytsky oblast), built in the 14th-15th centuries and rebuilt in 1894. Frescos from the 16th century may be found in the church, which was also used as a castle. There is no other church of similar construction in Ukraine.

St. Nicholas Church in the village of Chesnyky (Ivano-Frankivsk oblast). Built in the 14th century, it is a unique example of Ukrainian church architecture of that period.

St. George's Church in Drohobych (Lviv oblast). Built in the village of Nadiyevo in the 15th century, this wooden church was moved to Drohobych in 1670. It was destroyed by the Tatars in 1499 and restored many times.

VI. The Church in Ukrainian Lands in the Polish and Lithuanian States during the 15th-16th Centuries (1458-1596)

General Characteristics of the Period

1. THE POLITICAL SITUATION IN EASTERN EUROPE

The fifteenth and sixteenth centuries in Eastern Europe saw the weakening of the Tatars, the rise of Muscovy, the consolidation of Poland and Lithuania, and the intrusion of the Ottoman Turks.

The Khanates of Kazan and Astrakhan split off from the Khanate of the Golden Horde in 1445 and 1466, respectively, with the Khanate of Kazan eventually becoming a vassal of Muscovy. The Golden Horde itself ceased to exist in 1502.

The Grand Prince of Muscovy conquered Novgorod in 1478 and two years later became effectively free of the "Tatar yoke," ceasing to pay tribute to the Golden Horde. In the early years of the sixteenth century, the monk Philotheus developed the theory that Moscow was the "Third Rome" — the successor to Rome and to Constantinople as the center of (Orthodox) Christendom. Muscovy annexed Ryazan, Tver, and Pskov (1510), pushing back the Poles and Lithuanians, and took Smolensk in 1514. The Lithuanians, however, defeated the army of the Muscovite grand prince Vasily III at Orsha. In 1552 Ivan the Terrible — the first to call himself "Tsar of All Rus'" —conquered Kazan and in 1556 Astrakhan. In 1558 he began a war, fought on Byelorussian land, with Lithuania over Livonia.

In 1466, Poland fought the Teutonic Knights for the last time, defeating them. In the fifteenth century Poland held Moldavia in vassalage and controlled Bohemia. Neighboring Moravia and Lusatia were held by Hungary.

In 1569 the Kingdom of Poland concluded a full union with the Grand Duchy of Lithuania at Lublin: the two states formed a Commonwealth with a common legislature (diet). The new Commonwealth was bordered by the Baltic on the north, Brandenburg on the northwest, Muscovy on the east, the Habsburgs on the southwest, and the Ottomans on the southeast. In the sixteenth century, Poland, like Muscovy, experienced a great increase in population. The Polish-Lithuanian Commonwealth, which became increasingly Polish in character, reached a high point in the reign of King Sigismund III Vasa (1587-1632).

The Ottoman Turks made some advances in Eastern Europe under Mohammed II (1451-1481), taking Bosnia in 1463 and Wallachia, as well as Kaffa (Kefe) in the Crimea, in 1475. Under Bayazid II (1481-1512), however, they made little progress. An army revolt put Bayazid's son Selim the Grim on the throne in 1512. He died in 1520 and his successor Suleiman the Magnificent (1520-1566) pushed onward into Europe, seizing a Hungarian bridgehead at Belgrade in 1521 and crushing Christian forces at Mohacs in 1526. Suleiman's seige of Vienna in 1529, however, was repulsed, as was his invasion of Austria three years later. By the end of the century, the Ottoman sphere of influence included the Crimean Khanate, Moldavia, Transylvania, Hungary, and Wallachia. The Habsburgs of Austria held Silesia, Bohemia and Moravia.

2. THE RELIGIOUS SITUATION IN EUROPE

With the fall of Constantinople and the eclipse of the Orthodox Patriarchate in the mid-fifteenth century, Europe was largely divided between Catholicism and Islam. But the Roman Catholic Church was losing its political influence, as various kings sought to limit the clergy's privileges and the Pope's power. At the same time, corruption and abuses within the Church came under increasing criticism. Continuing calls for reform combined with the growing independence of secular rulers resulted in the formation of Protestant churches in the sixteenth century.

The advent of printing in the fifteenth century made the Bible available to a much larger part of the population. Printed Bibles appeared in Italy (1471), Spain (1478), France (1487), and England (1535). In 1477 the first Dutch printed Old Testament appeared; the first French printed New Testament was published in the same year. The wider availability of Scripture to the literate public made possible the reformationist ideal of individual familiarity with the Bible. It also enabled the laity to form new biblical interpretations, and thus contributed to the development of new religious movements.

The Lateran Council, convened in 1512, sought to implement the reforms so long advocated in the Church. The results, however, proved inadequate. In 1517 Martin Luther produced his 95 Theses, and three years later repudiated papal supremacy, finding protection in the Elector of Saxony. In 1524 the German Anabaptists rose up, suffering bloody repression in the following year. In 1525 the Grand Master of the Teutonic Knights joined Luther's reform and dissolved the Order. Zwingli preached in Zurich, and in the 1530s and 1540s, Calvin carried on the reform in Geneva, publishing his *Institutes* in 1535. Philip Melanchthon promulgated the Augsburg Confession in 1530; it was adopted by various princes and by Hungarian Lutherans in 1545. In 1534 Henry VIII, having defied Rome, set himself up as head of England's Church. Protestantism spread to Poland, where it attracted a part of the aristocracy, as well as to north-east Germany and Scandinavia. In 1559 the reformed church took root in France. In 1566 Unitarianism appeared in Hungary, present-day Romania, and Poland. The Reformation also spread to the Netherlands and Scotland.

Habsburg Austria and Valois France, however, remained within the Catholic Church, as did Spain and Italy. The founding of the Society of Jesus under St. Ignatius Loyola in 1541 heralded the Counter-Reformation. The Jesuits' activity extended into Poland, becoming particularly successful in counter-acting Protestantism in the reign of Sigismund III.

The Congregation of the Universal Inquisition was set up in 1542, and in the following decades Protestants were severely persecuted in France, Spain and elsewhere. The Council of Trent (1545-1563) formulated the Catholic Church's response to the Reformation, and unified Catholic ritual throughout Europe.

In the meantime, the forces of Islam (finally expelled from Spain in 1492) threatened Christian Europe from the southeast. The Serbian Patriarchate was suppressed in 1459. The advances of the Ottoman ruler Suleiman the Magnificent in the 1520s resulted in a mass apostasy of Christians to Islam. Deprived of the support of a Byzantine Emperor, the Orthodox Church lost all political influence. The Orthodox became for the most part a defenseless minority divided between the Muslim Ottomans and the Catholic Poles. Only the rise of Muscovy, described in the early 1500s as the "Third Rome," offered a strong political base for the Orthodox Church. Accordingly, a Patriarchate was established in Moscow in 1589. In view of the rise of Muscovy on the one hand and mass conversions to Roman Catholicism in Poland on the other, the Rus' Orthodox Metropolitanate of Kiev united with the Catholic Church in 1595-1596 subject to the retention of its Eastern liturgical, canonical, and spiritual traditions.

3. THE POLITICAL SITUATION IN UKRAINE

In the fifteenth and sixteenth centuries Ukrainian lands were divided between Poland-Lithuania (with Poland taking by far the greater portion after 1569), the Tatars, and Muscovy. Under Polish-Lithuanian rule, the Ukrainian nobility became polonized. The burghers and peasants encountered various restrictions, and the Kozaks arose as their protectors. Towards the end of the sixteenth century, the term "Ukraine" came to signify a specific territory: the palatinates of Kiev, Bratslav and Chernihiv.

The Khanate of the Golden Horde ruled part of eastern Ukraine until its demise in 1502; the Crimean Khanate under the Girey dynasty eventually came under Ottoman protection and thus presented a threat from the south. The Ottomans took Kaffa (Kefe) from the Genoese in 1475, establishing a foothold in the Crimea. In 1482 Khan Mengli-Girey, acting on instructions of the Muscovite grand prince Ivan III, sacked Kiev. The Tatars continued to make attacks on Ukraine. In the southern steppe, the Nogay Tatars made a living from the slave-trade.

In the reign of Casimir IV (1444-1492), the Ruthenian (Ukrainian) nobility in Poland-Lithuania gained some privileges, but in 1470 Casimir abolished the principalities of Volynia and Kiev. The conspiracy of Olelkovych, involving some Ruthenian nobles, was discovered and suppressed in 1481. In 1501 the dynastic union of Poland and Lithuania was further strengthened. Under Sigismund (1506-1548), the Ruthenian nobility looked to Muscovy for support; thus, the insurgents of the Hlynsky revolt of 1508 fled to Moscow. But while the upper Ruthenian nobility in Lithuania, seeking to protect its privileges, opposed union with Poland, the lesser nobility supported it. Thus, in 1569 the Union of Lublin, uniting the Grand Duchy of Lithuania and the Kingdom of Poland into a Commonwealth, met considerable opposition. Furthermore, it resulted in the transfer of Pidlyashshya, Volynia, Kiev and Podilia from Lithuanian to Polish control. However, it also made the Ukrainian nobility equal in rights to the Polish.

The Union permitted the nobility to acquire land in any part of the Commonwealth. King Sigismund III Vasa distributed vast tracts of vacant Ukrainian land to the Polish nobles. In eastern Ukraine, peasants were attracted with offers of limited periods of use of the land without feudal dues. Rising European demand for grain and the consequent rise in prices encouraged intensive exploitation of the land — and of the peasants.

Muscovy took much of Chernihiv and Siveria in the 1490s. Tsar Ivan III attacked Lithuania in 1500, gaining complete control of Chernihiv.

In the late fifteenth and sixteenth centuries, the military community known as the Kozaks arose in the "no-man's land" of the southern steppes. These frontier warriors often entered the service of the Polish nobility or other employers. However, they posed a threat to the Poles as well, occasionally combining with the discontented peasants and burghers of Ukraine in mass uprisings from the 1590s on.

4. 15TH-16TH CENTURY RULERS OF UKRAINE (1458-1596)

PRINCES AND VICEROYS OF LITHUANIA

The city of Kiev under the rule of the Lithuanian grand prince lost its original significance as the capital of Rus'-Ukraine. At first, it was administered by princes who had been alloted individual territories, and then from 1472 by viceroys of the Lithuanian grand prince. The rulers of the Kievan principality appointed by the Lithuanian grand prince in this period are listed below.

Symon Olelkovych	1455-1472
Martin Hashtold	1472
Ivan Khodkevych	1482
Yuriy Montovtovych	1507-1508
Andriy Nemyrovych	1514-1539
Yuriy Dubrovytsky	1542
Hryhoriy Khodkevych	1554
Konstantyn Konstantynovych Ostrozky	1557-1608

HETMANS OF UKRAINIAN KOZAKS

The hetman's power developed spontaneously in Ukraine. In the 16th-17th centuries (1550-1614) they were chiefs of the Kozaks, an independent military-political force. In the 17th-18th centuries (1614-1775) the hetmans were the rulers of Ukraine as well as the chiefs of Kozak military forces.

The first well-known hetman (chief) of the Kozaks was Dmytro Vyshnevetsky (Bayda), organizer in the 1540s of scattered groups of Kozaks and founder of the Kozak fortress, the Sich, on the Dnieper island of Khortytsya.

Dmytro Vyshnevetsky	ca. 1550-1563
Bohdan Ruzhynsky	1575-1576
Shakh	1576-1577
Samiylo Zborovsky	ca. 1581
Mykhaylo and Kyryk Ruzhynsky	1585
Voytykh Khanovytsky	1590
Khrystofer Kosynsky	1591-1593
Hryhoriy Loboda	1593-1596

Chronology

1458 — Following the division of the Kievan Metropolitanate into separate Kievan and Muscovite jurisdictions, and following the installation of Hryhoriy II as the Metropolitan of Kiev, Metropolitan Iona of Moscow begins a protracted campaign against the Kievan Metropolitanate. In numerous encyclicals to the bishops and clergy of the Kievan Metropolitanate, he calls upon them to reject Metropolitan Hryhoriy II and to side with him. Of ten acting bishops, only one, Bishop Yevtymiy of Chernihiv (Bryansk), leaves his eparchy in 1464 (after Metropolitan Iona's death in 1461), and flees to Moscow. The nine remaining bishops recognize the Metropolitan Hryhoriy II's authority.

13 September 1459 — The bishops of the Northern Muscovite-Vladimir region gather in Moscow beside the grave of Metropolitan Petro to pledge their allegiance to Moscow's Metropolitan Iona. In a joint encyclical, they entreat the Ukrainian and Byelorussian bishops to deny recognition to Metropolitan Hryhoriy II.

1463 — Stepan Droshan', a resident of Lviv, rebuilds the Monastery of St. Onufriy.

1469 — Patriarch Dionysios (1469-1476) gives his blessing to Metropolitan Hryhoriy II and confirms him as Metropolitan of Kiev and All Rus'. He sends viceroys to the Kievan Metropolitanate, as well as to Novgorod and Moscow, enjoining them to recognize the authority of Hryhoriy II as Metropolitan of All Rus', and not that of Metropolitan Iona of Moscow, since the latter had been consecrated as metropolitan without the consent or knowledge of the Patriarch.

Upon the request of the Lviv Brotherhood, King Casimir IV grants the St. Onufriy Monastery to them.

The Tatars invade Galicia and Podilia and take approximately 10,000 prisoners.

1470 — Prince Symon Olelkovych, the Lithuanian viceroy of Kiev, rebuilds the Kievan Monastery of the Caves, destroyed by the Tatars in 1240. He embellishes the monastery and reconstructs the main church with gold, icons, and valuable treasures.

1472 — The last Kievan prince, Symon Olelkovych, dies. He was the great-grandson of the Lithuanian Grand Prince Olgierd. The Polish King Casismir IV changes the Kievan principality to a palatinate and replaces the previous Orthodox viceroy with the Lithuanian Roman Catholic viceroy, Martin Hashtold. Protests against the Roman Catholic palatine by the residents of Kiev have no effect.

1473 — Tatars invade Galicia and Podilia and take approximately 100,000 prisoners.

Bishops of the Kievan Metropolitanate send an epistle to Pope Sixtus IV through the papal legate, Antony.

Metropolitan Hryhoriy II dies in Novogrudok. He was later canonized as a saint.

1475 — During the Novogrudok Synod of bishops, clergy, and faithful, Bishop Mysayil of Smolensk is elected as the new Metropolitan of Kiev and All Rus'.

The nominated Metropolitan was never confirmed by the Patriarch of Constantinople.

14 March 1476 — Metropolitan Mysayil writes an epistle to Pope Sixtus IV, which is considered to be the sole surviving work of Old-Ukrainian ecclesiastical literature of the 15th century. In his epistle, the Metropolitan defends the right of the Ukrainian-Byelorussian Church and faithful to their rites, separate statute, and Eastern faith. He defends the need for unity of Eastern and Western Churches and recognizes the Pope as the Supreme Pontiff. This epistle was signed by the Metropolitan and a number of archimandrites and by laymen of Kiev, Kremenets, and other cities of Volynia.

St. Nicholas Church in the village of Kolodne (Transcarpathian oblast), built of wood in 1470 and rebuilt in the 16th and the 18th centuries. This is one of the oldest churches in Transcarpathia.

1477 — Patriarch Raphael (1474-1477) appoints Spiridon as Metropolitan of Kiev and All Rus'. He is not accepted as Metropolitan in the Kievan Metropolitanate because his appointment took place without its consent, and he was not elected by its bishops. Upon his arrival in the Polish-Lithuanian Kingdom, he is imprisoned but released shortly thereafter. Moving to Moscow, he is incarcerated and dies there. The Moscow Metropolitanate refuses to recognize him because he had been consecrated in Constantinople, which is now in the hands of the "infidel" Turks.

1481 — Patriarch Maximos III (1477-1481) gives his blessing to the nomination of Symon as the Metropolitan of Kiev and All Rus'. Two patriarchal exarchs, Niphontos, Metropolitan of Anea, and Theodore, Bishop of Ipanei, along with the bishops of the Kievan Metropolitanate consecrate the new metropolitan during solemn festivities.

Upon the request of Archimandrite Teodosiy IV and the monks of the Kievan Monastery of the Caves, the Patriarch of Constantinople bestows stauropegial status to the monastery, which thus becomes subject directly to the Patriarch.

1 September 1482 — By mutual agreement with the Grand Prince of Moscow Ivan III, the Crimean Khan Mengli-girey attacks Kiev, destroys the city, burns the Kievan Monastery of the Caves and the Church of the Dormition, and takes captive Archimandrite Teodosiy IV. The Khan gives Ivan III the treasures robbed from the Cathedral of St. Sophia. The Tatars also carry off into captivity the Ukrainian Orthodox palatine of Kiev, Ivan Khodkevych, along with his family.

1482 — King Casimir IV, while agreeing to the consecration of new metropolitans by Patriarchs of Constantinople, issues an *ukaz* (edict) — under pressure from Polish Roman Catholic fanatics — banning the construction of new Ukrainian churches or the restoration of older or damaged ones.

1491 — In Cracow, liturgical books, the Oktoechos (hymnal) and Horologion (Chasoslov or breviary) are printed for the first time in Cyrillic. Somewhat later, the Triodion is also published. The Latins, however, complain and demand the destruction of the books. The government acquiesces by confiscating and burning them.

During their march through Volynia, the Tatars burn all of the churches of Volodymyr-Volynsky. The stone Church of the Mother of God is among those destroyed.

Fall, 1492 — After a four-year vacancy at the Kievan See, Patriarch Maximos IV, upon the request of the Ukrainian and Byelorussian princes, consecrates Archimandrite Iona (Hlezna) of the Polotsk Monastery as the new Metropolitan of Kiev.

1492 — The Lithuanian grand prince Alexander, son of Casimir, grants equal rights and privileges in his principality to the clergy, boyars, and nobility of the Orthodox and Roman Catholic faiths.

1494 — Vassiyan, the Bishop of Volodymyr-Volynsky and Berestya (Brest), rebuilds the fire-ravaged church of the Mother of God, destroyed earlier by the Tatars. He furnishes it with new icons, vestments, vessels, and books.

1495 — At a Synod in Novogrudok, Makariy of

the Holy Trinity Monastery in Vilnius is elected Metropolitan of Kiev and All Rus'. Taking part in the Synod are the bishops Vassiyan of Volodymyr-Volynsky, Luka of Polotsk, Vassiyan of Turov, and Iona of Lutsk.

Fall, 1496 — Patriarch Maximos IV blesses and confirms the new metropolitan.

1 May 1497 — Metropolitan Makariy is killed by the Tatars near Minsk during their invasion of the Byelorussian lands. The Metropolitan was en route to Kiev, where he had hoped to restore the Cathedral of St. Sophia, damaged by the Tatars.

Summer, 1498 — The Lithuanian Grand Prince Alexander appoints Bishop Yosyf (Bolharynovych), a sympathizer of the union with Rome, of Smolensk, as the new Metropolitan of Kiev and All Rus'. The consecration of the new metropolitan takes place on May 10, 1500.

20 August 1500 — Metropolitan Yosyf sends a letter to Pope Alexander VI expressing his desire to unite with the Church of Rome according to the articles of the Council of Florence.

1500 — During their attack on Chernihiv, Muscovite troops capture and carry off to Moscow the local bishop, Iona.

Canon Jan Sacran (Jannis Sacrani) of Cracow writes his work "An Explanation of the Errors of the Ruthenian Rite" (*Elucidarius errorum ritus Ruthenici*) in which he states that of all the Christian nations, the Ruthenians (Ukrainians) are the most adamant about their faith and customs. According to Sacran, they consider themselves the true successors of the apostles and the primary Church.

1500-1502 — Ivan III, Grand Prince of Moscow, attacks the Ukrainian and Byelorussian lands repeatedly. He devastates the territory, burning and destroying many churches as well as some monasteries. Booty from the churches is taken to Moscow. The Kolosh Monastery and the church of SS. Borys and Hlib near Grodno are destroyed.

October 1503 — King Alexander of Poland appoints a strong defender of Orthodoxy, Archimandrite Iona II of the Ascension Monastery in Minsk, as the new Metropolitan of Kiev. Patriarch Pachomius I of Constantinople consecrates Iona II in 1504.

15 March 1504 — Upon the request of the Bishop of Kholm, King Alexander confirms the 1443 statute (hramota) of King Wladyslaw, which granted to the Orthodox clergy the same rights and privileges enjoyed by the Roman Catholic clergy.

12 September 1504 — King Alexander, who through various declarations and statutes granted benefits and privileges to the Orthodox Church, transfers ownership of the Peresopnytsky Monastery near Lutsk to the Princess Maria Czartoryska and subsequently to all her descendants. The grant includes the villages and other property attached to the monastery. The practice of transfering ownership of churches and monasteries to laypersons leads to the impoverishment of the Church, and undermines the authority of the hierarchy.

1505 — During an attack led by the Moscow Prince Ivan III, the Muscovite army takes hostage Senko Kryvy, the son of Metropolitan Iona II, and keeps him imprisoned for many years.

1507 — Prince Konstantyn Ostrozky donates a significant number of church goods to the Derman Monastery and decorates the monastery with gold and silver. In the same year, King Sigismund I gives Prince Ostrozky the St. Nicholas Monastery in Zhydychyn near Lutsk.

December 1507 — According to the will of King Sigismund I, Yosyf II Soltan, Bishop of Smolensk, is selected as the new metropolitan by the Synod of bishops. The nominee for metropolitan is not confirmed by Patriarch Pachomius I until 1509.

1508 — King Sigismund I gives to the Roman Catholic chief magistrate of Halych and Lviv, Stanislav Khodech, the Krylos Orthodox Monastery in Halych with all its goods and riches. The monastery falls fully under his jurisdiction.

15 April 1509 — By decision of King Sigismund I, the Roman Catholic Archbishop of Lviv is to designate viceroys of the Kievan Metropolitanate for the Ukrainian Church in Galicia. However, the Roman Catholic archbishop has no authority to designate priests. Simultaneously, by decision of the King, the Kievan Metropolitan uses the title "Metropolitan of Kiev, Galicia, and All Rus'."

25 December 1509 — Following a long interval, Metropolitan Yosyf II calls a Synod in Vilnius. The bishops Vassiyan of Volodymyr-Volynsky and Berestya, Varsonofiy of Smolensk, Kyrylo of Lutsk and Ostrih, Yevfymiy of Polotsk and Vitebsk, Arseniy of Turov and Pinsk, Antoniy of Peremyshl, Filaret of Kholm, as well as seven archimandrites, six hegumens, and other clergy participate in the Synod. The Synod reviews the unfortunate situation of the Church in Ukraine and Byelorussia and in the Polish-Lithuanian Kingdom. They discuss the strengthening of the people's faith and attempt to normalize church life, producing fifteen resolutions to this effect. The Synod forbids unmarried priests to serve liturgies in the entire Kievan and Galician Metropolitanate.

2 July 1511 — Upon the demand of Metropolitan Yosyf II, Prince Konstantyn Ostrozky, and all the bishops and princes of the Eastern faith, Sigismund I issues a declaration which guarantees the Church and Metropolitan all the rights and privileges that they had from the beginning of their acceptance of Christianity.

1511 — By permission of the King, Prince Konstantyn Ostrozky rebuilds the cathedral of the Dormition of the Most Holy Mother of God in the city of Ostrih on its old foundations.

1514 — Prince Konstantyn Ostrozky is victorious over the Muscovite armies near the city of Orsha. As a sign of his victory over the invaders, he vows to build a series of churches — a vow he later fulfills.

6 March 1516 — Prince Konstantyn Ostrozky gives the Kievan Monastery of the Caves a number of villages and other property. In the course of one year some of the properties are given by Metropolitan Yosyf to the Vydubytsky Monastery, and by King Sigismund I to the Pustynno-Mykolayivsky Monastery in Kiev.

1517 — In Germany, Martin Luther has begun protests against the Pope and the Roman Catholic faith. Luther's and later Calvin's ideas gradually reach Ukraine and Byelorussia via Poland and Lithuania. From 1520 a ban is imposed on bringing Protestant literature into the Polish Kingdom; transgression is severely punished. Lutheranism makes gains in 1524, when five Roman Catholic churches in Danzig convert together with their clergy and many faithful.

1521 — Following the accusations of the Church Brotherhood of Lviv and Prince Konstantyn Ostrozky of repression of the Ukrainian faithful by Polish Roman Catholics, the King issues a decree that limits this repression and gives the Orthodox some rights. They are allowed to make vows in Ukrainian rather than in Roman Catholic churches, and the clergy — fully vested in Eastern-rite vestments — are allowed to visit the sick with the sacraments.

Spring, 1522 — According to the King's wish, the synod of bishops elects the Archbishop of Polotsk, Yosyf III, as the new Metropolitan of Kiev. In the same year, the King designates only one vicar-bishop for the metropolitan for the entire Orthodox Church of Galicia and Podilia. Since 1412 these had been designated by the Polish Roman Catholic Archbishop of Lviv. The vicar, Yatsko Hdashytsky, is responsible for the ecclesiastical territories of Lviv, Halych, Kolomyya, Kamyanets-Podilsky, and Snyatyn. By year's end the King appoints him archimandrite of St. George's Monastery in Lviv. He obtains rights close to those of a bishop or metropolitan. In 1523 the King makes him subject to the Roman Catholic Archbishop of Lviv, Bernard Wilszek, whom Hdashytsky does not recognize as his superior. In 1526 Metropolitan Yosyf III designates him as his vicar for Galicia.

1522-1531 — The Church experiences new repressions and humiliation as the King begins to give away Ukrainian churches and monasteries to laypersons more frequently. Thus, he gives the Church of St. Basil in Volodymyr-Volynsky to Prince Sanguszko (1523) and the churches of St. Nicholas of Mezhyhirsky Monastery, St. Nicholas of the Jordan Monastery, and the Church of the Elevation of the Holy Cross in Kiev to Andriy Dyahylevych (1524). The Monastery of Peresopnytsya near Lutsk goes to Prince Theodore Czartoryski and his successors (1525), while the convent in Ovruch is given to Olexandra Nemyrivna (1531). Simultaneously, a semi-abandoned or ruined monastery such as the Mezhyhirya Monastery of the Holy Savior goes to the Hegumen Mysayil Shcherbyna (1523), while the Golden-domed St. Michael's Monastery, also in Kiev, goes to Hegumen Makariy (1523). By a separate order of the King, neither the metropolitan nor the viceroy has any right to interfere in the life of these monasteries.

1533 — The King takes away a significant portion of the property of the Kholm Orthodox Eparchy and bestows it upon the Polish Roman Catholic bishop of Kholm.

1 March 1534 — Upon the request of the Orthodox princes and boyars, the King names Bishop Makariy of Lutsk and Ostrih as the new Metropolitan of Kiev.

1535 — The Polish Roman Catholic Archbishop of Lviv nominates as the new vicar of the metropolitan Yatsko Sikora, a supporter of the Union. Meanwhile, the Kievan metropolitan nominates the priest Hoshovsky. However, the clergy and Orthodox nobility do not accept either of them. Then the clergy, nobility, and townspeople select Makariy Tuchapsky, whom the King confirms on August 1. Tuchapsky is installed by Lavrentiy, Bishop of Peremyshl, and shortly thereafter becomes archimandrite of St. George's Monastery in Lviv. The Roman Catholic Archbishop of Lviv is angered and demands that Tuchapsky be tried as an illegally appointed vicar. Accompanied by a large number of Orthodox activists from Galicia and Podilia, Tuchapsky travels to Cracow for the trial by the regional parliament. Meanwhile, the King separates the churches of Galicia and Podilia from the Kievan metropolitan and subjects them entirely to the authority of the Polish Roman Catholic Archbishop of Lviv.

22 October 1539 — After an embattled four years and a 72-year absence of Ukrainian bishops from the See of Lviv, King Sigismund I nominates Makariy Tuchapsky as Bishop of Halych, Lviv and Kamyanets-Podilsky. On February 22, 1540, Metropolitan Makariy ordains him as Bishop of Lviv alone and requires of him a promise that he shall never demand the establishment of a separate metropolitanate for Galicia.

November 1539 — Makariy Tuchapsky calls a meeting of the local priests in Lviv and renews the council of canons (krylos) at St. George's Cathedral. These resolutions are finally passed ten years later (January 10, 1549) by Metropolitan Makariy II.

1539 — Abraham Kulva, the first Lutheran preacher in Lithuania, appears. In the same year Lutheranism becomes more widespread among the Orthodox and Roman Catholic population of Volynia and Galicia.

St. Onuphrius Church in Lviv, built in 1550 and transformed into a monastery in 1585. It was damaged by the Turks in 1672 and rebuilt in 1680, with some additions in later years. In 1573 Ivan Fedoriv established Ukraine's first printing establishment here and printed the first books, *The Epistle* and a primer. He was buried at the church in 1583. The monastery was converted into the Ivan Fedoriv Museum in 1974.

1542 — During the regional parliament in Petrivka, the Polish Roman Catholic clergy issue a list of demands to the King, among which are that he annul the creation of the Ukrainian bishopric of Lviv and Halych, that he ban the construction of Ukrainian churches, and that he forbid the Orthodox to ring their church bells and form processions.

18 February 1544 — A Brotherhood is founded at the Church of St. Nicholas in Lviv.

1549 — By permission of the King, Metropolitan Makariy II appoints Marko Balaban, the Galician clergy's candidate, as Bishop of Halych, Lviv, and Kamyanets-Podilsky and as the metropolitan's vicar for Galicia.

1556 — King Sigismund II August appoints the superior of the Holy Trinity Monastery of Vilnius, Sylvester (Stefan Andriy Byelkevych), as the new Metropolitan of Kiev and All Rus'.

1562 — Symon Budny is the first to publish the Calvinist Catechism and the work "On the Justification of Sinful Man before God" in Cyrillic.

1563 — During the regional parliament in Vilnius, King Sigismund II August annuls the Grodno Law of King Jagiello, which banned the Orthodox from holding any governmental or public office. The new statute equalizes the nobility and aristocracy of both Roman Catholic and Eastern Orthodox faiths in their right to occupy all government positions, including senatorial posts.

1564 — The Protestant (anti-trinitarian) preacher Teodosiy Kosoy and his friend Ignatiy flee Moscow via Lithuania to Volynia. They influence a great portion of the Orthodox and Catholic-rite nobility in Volynia with their sermons.

1567 — The theologian and scholar Benedict Herbst raises the issue of union with the Church in Rome in the course of his travels throughout Galicia.

1568 — The King appoints Bishop Iona III Protasovych-Ostrovsky of Pinsk and Turov as the new Metropolitan of Kiev.

25 June 1568 — Heeding the request of the new Metropolitan Iona III, the King decrees that positions in the Church hierarchy (bishops, archimandrites, hegumens, and priests) cannot be filled by laypersons — a common practice for many years. If a layperson should receive such a nomination, he must enter the clerical state within three months or the said position would be filled by a clergyman. The King rejects a

St. Elias Church in the village of Toporivtsi (Chernivtsi oblast), built in 1560. Ukrainian and Moldavian architectural traditions are combined in this church-fortress, one of the oldest remaining churches of Bukovyna.

Dormition Church in the village of Dorohobuzh (Rovno oblast), built in 1577-82 on the site of an 11th-century church. It is a unique example of Volynian church architecture from the 16th and 17th centuries.

request that Orthodox hierarchs be made equal with their Catholic counterparts with regard to their rights and that they be assured of positions in the senate.

1569 — During the regional parliament in Lublin, the final union of the Great Lithuanian Principality with Poland (the Union of Lublin) is realized. Integrated into Poland are those Ukrainian lands (with the exception of Transcarpathia) that have hitherto been under Polish control. In accordance with this union, all royal decrees are to be written simultaneously in the Old Ukrainian language.

The Jesuits arrive in the Polish Kingdom and begin a protracted campaign against Orthodoxy and Protestantism.

15 August 1570 — Metropolitan Iona III, on the recommendation of the King, ordains Ivan Lopatka (previously appointed by the Roman Catholic Archbishop of Lviv to be the metropolitan's vicar) as Bishop of Lviv.

1570-1596 — Approximately 100 Protestant congregations exist in Ukrainian lands under Poland.

1571 — The first Jesuit college on Ukrainian territory is founded in Yaroslav near Peremyshl. Its goal is to spread the Catholic faith among the Orthodox. The college opens missions at the Polish Catholic bishoprics of Lviv and Lutsk.

6 January 1573 — The Warsaw Confederation is declared during the regional parliament in that city. This confederation guarantees the equality of various faiths. Roman Catholic bishops protest against the confederation and refuse to sign the concluding document.

23 September 1576 — Because of old age, Metropolitan Iona III relinquishes his position as Metropolitan. To replace him, the King nominates a layperson, the nobleman Illya Yoakymovych Kucha, as the new metropolitan.

1576 — King Stefan Bathory gives the Mezhyhirsky Monastery in Kiev, as well as the Dermansky and Chernchytsky Monasteries, to laypersons for permanent ownership.

1577 — King Stefan Bathory asks Patriarch Jeremiah II to bless Illya Kucha as Metropolitan of Kiev, Galicia and All Rus'.

The Jesuit canon Piotr Skarga writes an appeal in book form regarding the Union and dedicates it to the most distinguished Orthodox activist of the day, Prince Konstantyn Ostrozky, appealing to him and to all the Orthodox to accept the Union with Rome and the Catholic faith, assuring them that they would be able to retain all their Eastern traditions and rites.

13 January 1577 — St. Athanasius College for students of the Eastern rite is established in Rome, enabling Ukrainians and Byelorussians to study there. The first Ukrainian student to study in the College is the future Uniate Metropolitan Velyamin Rutsky

Dormition of the Mother of God, by Oleksiy, 1547. Icon from the Church of St. Michael the Archangel in the village of Smilnyk (Poland).

The Evangelist. Miniature from the *Peresopnytsky Gospels*, 1556-64.

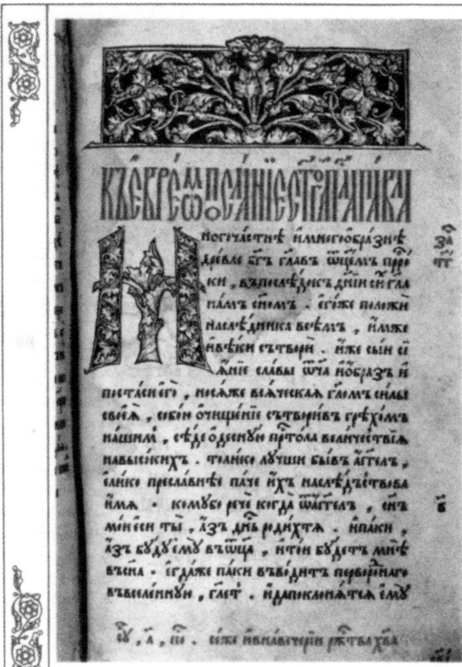

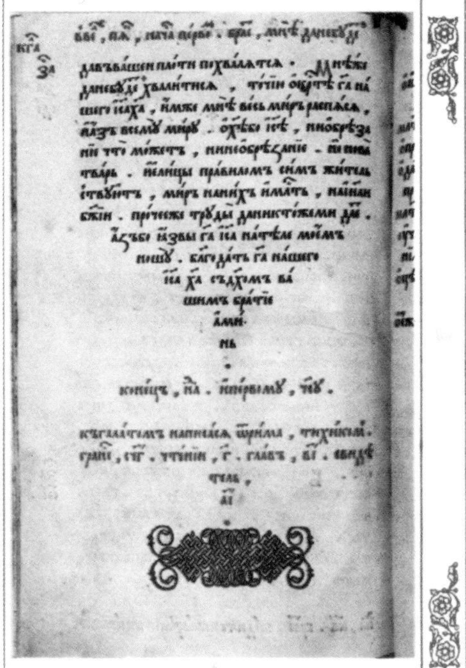

The Epistles, 1574. Title page of the first book printed in Ukraine, by Ivan Fedoriv in Lviv, 1574.

Movchan Monastery of the Nativity of the Mother of God in Putyvl (Sumy oblast), founded in 1579. It was destroyed by the Soviets in the 1930s.

(1601). The College is closed in 1809 and reopened in 1845.

17 February 1579 — By decision of the King and upon the request of Metropolitan Illya Kucha, the Holy Ascension Monastery in Minsk is given to Mykhaylo Rohoza. On November 17, Rohoza is appointed archimandrite of the monastery.

1579 — The King nominates Onysyfor Petrovych Divochka of Galicia as Metropolitan of Kiev, Galicia and All Rus'.

1580 — Prince Konstantyn Ostrozky founds an institute of higher learning in Ostrih, with the blessing of Patriarch Jeremiah II. The first Ukrainian printing press is also opened at the school (later referred to as an academy). The Prince appoints Herasym Smotrytsky as the first rector of the school.

SS. Peter and Paul Church in Kamyanets-Podilsky (Khmelnytsky oblast), built in 1580. Fragments of 16th century frescoes may be found in the church. It is a rare example of Ukrainian church-fortress architecture.

1580-1590 — Through the efforts of Prince Konstantyn Ostrozky, a series of works of various Fathers of the Church against Roman Catholics is published in Ostrih in the Old Ukrainian language. Simultaneously, the Jesuits publish a series of works attacking Orthodoxy, also in Old Ukrainian. Thus begins the publication of the polemical literature that continues to appear during the following centuries.

1581 — Valentyn Nehalevsky translates the Gospels into Slavonic, using the interpretation of Unitarian doctrine.

1581-1583 — The Polish king Stefan Bathory bestows ownership of the following Ukrainian monasteries upon laypersons: the Monastery of the Savior in Volodymyr-Volynsky (1581), the Univ Monastery in Lviv (1581), the Monastery on Lake Nespish near Bratslav (1581), and the convent of the Most Immaculate Virgin (1583).

Church of the Annunciation in Kolomyya (Ivano-Frankivsk oblast), built in 1587. It is one of the finest examples of the wooden church architecture of the Hutsul school.

13 February 1582 — Pope Gregory XIII introduces a new calendar. According to King Stefan Bathory, the Orthodox in the Polish Kingdom are also to be subject to this calendar, in the hope that a common observance of holidays would lead to a closeness of the two faiths. Upon the request of Prince Konstantyn Ostrozky, Patriarch Jeremiah II of Constantinople and Patriarch Sylvester of Alexandria dispatch an epistle in December of that year firmly resolving to adhere to the old calendar.

The Catechism of Peter Canisius appears in Rome in the Old Ukrainian language.

24 December 1583 — As the Ukrainians in Lviv prepare to celebrate Christmas, the Roman Catholic Archbishop of Lviv, Jan-Dmytro Sulikowski orders that all the Eastern-rite church doors remain closed.

9 January 1584 — After protests by Bishop Hedeon Balaban and the Ukrainian clergy, the King allows the Orthodox people to celebrate Christmas according to the old calendar and simultaneously forbids them to work or trade during the new-calendar holiday.

15 February 1585 — The point of open hostility between the Orthodox and Roman-rite Catholics has been reached in almost all regions of Ukraine and Byelorussia. In opposition to the Catholics, the Orthodox proceed to create their own church schools and brotherhoods, and begin to publish religious works in their own language.

In an effort to end the hostility regarding the calendar, Bishop Hedeon Balaban and the Roman Catholic Archbishop of Lviv sign an agreement regarding festal observance. By this agreement, the two churches are not to interfere with each other's holiday observances.

1585 — By permission of the King, Bishop Hedeon Balaban creates new schools, and founds a printing house in the town of Stratyn.

1586 — The Dormition Brotherhood founds the first Theological Seminary in Lviv, which prepares new priests and offers courses in the Church Slavonic and Greek languages. Similar seminaries in Brestya, Rohatyn and Peremyshl are founded by the end of the 16th century.

On a visit to Lviv, Patriarch Joachim of Antioch initiates the opening of a school and printing press. Also by his initiative, the Brotherhood of the Holy Dormition Church is renewed and a new statute accepted. In the summer of this year, the exarch of the Ecumenical Patriarch, Metropolitan Arsenius, comes to Lviv and becomes a teacher in the church brotherhood school.

The Church of the Holy Dormition in Lviv, a center for Ukrainian religious, cultural, and educational activity, burns down.

End of 1587 — For the first time since the acceptance of Christianity in Kievan Rus'-Ukraine, the Ecumenical Patriarch (Jeremiah II) visits Ukrainian and Byelorussian lands, en route to Moscow.

23 January 1588 — During Patriarch Jeremiah II's stay in Moscow, a Patriarchate is established in Muscovy. Metropolitan Iona of Moscow is declared the first patriarch of Moscow.

1588 — The most extensive Orthodox work of the period, the "Sbornik" (678 pages) appears in Ostrih. The author is Vasyliy, a cleric of Ostrih.

1589 — En route from Moscow, Patriarch Jeremiah II (with the permission of King Sigismund III) visits the bishoprics of the Kievan Metropolitanate. He releases Metropolitan Onysyfor from his position for transgressing church law.

(According to other sources, however, the Metropolitan stepped down from the see of his own will due to illness and old age.)

Prince Konstantyn (Vasyl) Ostrozky (1526-1608), voevoda, prominent political, cultural and educational leader, defender of the Orthodox faith, founder of the Ostrih Academy and printing establishment (1577).

St. Nicholas Church in the city of Olevsk (Zhytomyr oblast), built in 1596.

Библїа сирѣчь книгы ветхаго и новаго завѣта, по языку словенску.

The Bible, printed in 1581 by Ivan Fedoriv in the city of Ostrih.

27 July 1589 — Heeding the request of the Orthodox nobility, King Sigismund III designates Archimandrite Mykhaylo Rohoza of the Ascension Monastery in Minsk as the new Metropolitan. On August 1 he is ordained and confirmed in the Cathedral of the Most Immaculate Virgin Mary in Vilnius by Patriarch Jeremiah II.

6 August 1589 — Without the consent or knowledge of the King, Patriarch Jeremiah II designates Bishop Kyrylo Terletsky of Lutsk and Ostrih as the patriarchal exarch for the Kievan Metropolitanate. This is done during the bishops' Synod in Berestya. According to a special document signed by Metropolitan Mykhaylo Rohoza and all the bishops present in Berestya, the newly nominated exarch is to have more rights than a metropolitan. During his stay in the Kievan Metropolitanate, the Patriarch issues a series of contradictory decrees, which he later recalls and annuls.

November 1589 — En route to Constantinople, Patriarch Jeremiah II calls a Synod of bishops in Ternopil to deal with the matter of the Holy Dormition Church Brotherhood in Lviv. The Metropolitan, five bishops, and the Patriarch participate in the Synod. According to the Patriarch's decision, the Brotherhood receives stauropegial status and is to have ownership of a school, printing press, and the St. Onufriy Monastery. These are to be under the direct jurisdiction of the Patriarch or the patriarchal exarch.

20-28 June 1590 — A Synod of bishops is held in Berestya. Metropolitan Mykhaylo Rohoza and five bishops participate. (The bishops of Peremyshl and Polotsk do not attend due to illness.) The Synod reviews the situation of the Church, and her finances, agrees to hold annual synods to better normalize church life, and accepts a resolution to spread the brotherhoods throughout the metropolitanate.

24 June 1590 — Patriarchal exarch Kyrylo Terletsky and three bishops sign a declaration stating their desire to join with the Apostolic See and submit to the Pope. The declaration states:

> We... desire one senior pastor and the true vicar of St. Peter on the Roman throne, the Holy Pope, to recognize him as our pastor, to have him as our head, to submit to him and pledge obedience at all times, by which we hope for a great increase of the glory of God

Church of the Nativity of the Mother of God in the village of Rosokhy (Lviv oblast), built in the 15th-16th centuries.

St. Onufriy Church of the Basilian monastery in the village of Lavriv (Lviv oblast). Built in the 15th-16th centuries, damaged by fire in 1549, it was restored in 1675-1705 in the Baroque style. After restorations in 1860 and 1910-14, it lost its original appearance. Frescoes from the 15th and 16th centuries may be found in the church.

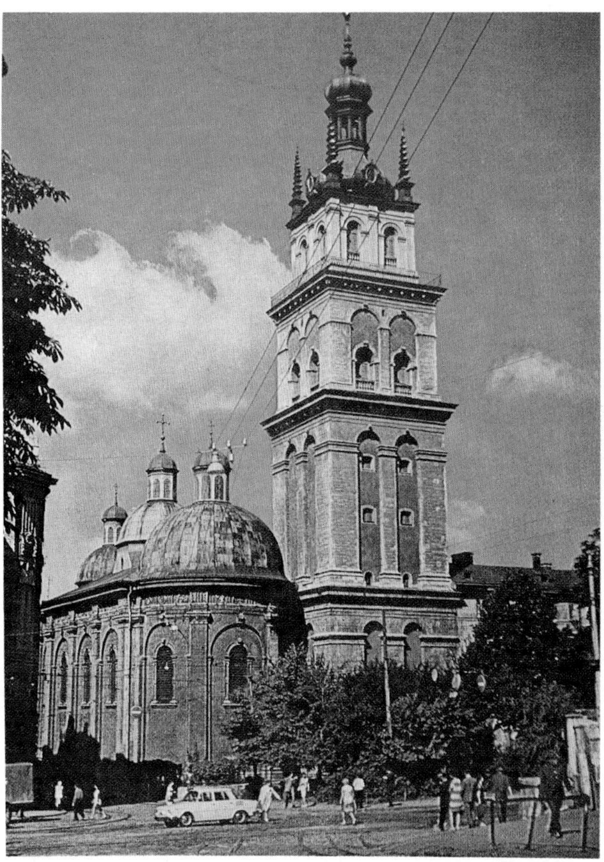

Dormition Church in Lviv, established in 1591 and built under the supervision of P. Rymlyanyn. Petro Kholodny created stained glass windows in the early 20th century. A painting from the 17th century by Ukrainian artists F. Senkovych and N. Petrakhnovych may be found in the church.

St. Peter and the Mother of God, 16th-century icon from the village of Nakonechne (Lviv oblast) (left).

The Transfiguration, 16th-century icon from the village of Yabluniv (Lviv oblast).

"Mother of God," detail of 16th-century icon from St. Nicholas Church in the village of Izky (Transcarpathian oblast).

Holy Trinity Church of the monastery-fortress in the city of Mezhyrich (Rovno oblast), built in the 15th century in the old Ukrainian style, with Gothic and Renaissance elements.

and His Holy Church; and not desiring further division of the Church to be on our consciences, we have inclined our wills and minds as stated above: to pledge obedience to the Most Holy Father, the Pope of Rome, and to submit God's churches to the jurisdiction and benediction of his grace, the Most Holy Pope of Rome, pleading only this, that our rites and all matters such as the Divine Liturgy and all of our ecclesiastical order, which is upheld by the entire Eastern Church from antiquity, remain intact and unchanged by the Most Holy Pope of Rome, and that this order remain intact to the end of time. His majesty the King has guaranteed our freedoms and privileges, and has confirmed the articles that we will propose..." (Hrushevsky, Vol. V. p. 566-567; Makariy, Vol. IX, p. 516-517.)

The declaration is signed by Bishop Kyrylo Terletsky, Bishop Leontiy Pelchytsky, Bishop Hedeon Balaban, and Bishop Dionysiy Zbiruysky.

17 January 1591 — Metropolitan Mykhaylo Rohoza visits the bishoprics of Halych and Peremyshl, something which his predecessors have not done. He is greeted in Lviv with great solemnity by the Brotherhood, clergy, and faithful.

1591 — The Lviv Brotherhood of the Holy Dormition expands and creates chapters in various cities of Galicia. Brotherhoods are created in Horodok, Holohorsk, and Berestya, where a church school is also opened.

January 1592 — Metropolitan Mykhaylo Rohoza visits the bishopric of Halych a second time during the conflict between Bishop Hedeon Balaban and the Holy Dormition Brotherhood. The Metropolitan issues a decree in defense of the Brotherhood and demands from the King that laypersons not interfere in church matters, and that they not be allowed to usurp church and monastery property.

18 June 1592 — In response to the declaration dated June 24, 1590 regarding the desire of union with the Apostolic See by the four bishops, the King issues a decree in which he expresses joy over this decision and guarantees the bishops that after they embrace the Union they will retain their respective sees.

1592 — Chaos and moral decline are in evidence throughout the entire Kievan Metropolitanate. The King continues to bestow churches, monasteries, and their properties upon laypersons. He makes incidental appointments to clerical positions. Both the metropolitan and exarch find themselves helpless in bringing church life to order. In Lviv, Bishop Hedeon Balaban leads a campaign against the Holy Dormition Brotherhood, which results in the closing of the Brotherhood's school and printing press. In two separate letters dated February 6 and September 7 the Brotherhood appeals to the Patriarch for aid. Some hierarchs see acceptance of the Union as a way out of the situation. Following measures taken by the most influential Orthodox provincial administrators, Prince Konstantyn Ostrozky and Teodor Tyshkevych, the King issues a decree on October 15. This decree allows the Holy Dormition

Brotherhood privileges and rights, allows the school and printing press to reopen, and reaffirms the Brotherhood's ownership of St. Onufriy Monastery. On the order of the rector of the St. Christopher Roman Catholic school, angered Polish Roman Catholic residents of Lviv attack the Orthodox. They single out pupils of the Brotherhood's school, beat them and often illegally imprison them.

In Peremyshl, the fourth church school on Ukrainian territory is opened.

February 1593 — A special commission, composed of four Roman Catholics and an Orthodox bishop, reviews the matter of Bishop Hedeon Balaban and his relationship to the Holy Dormition Brotherhood. Contrary to previous resolutions put forth by the Patriarchs and king, the commission decides that the Brotherhood and all its property should come under Bishop Hedeon's jurisdiction. Metropolitan Rohoza, however, does not accept the commission's decision and, on February 15, forbids the Bishop to govern the eparchy. Bishop Hedeon does not accept the Metropolitan's decision. On June 10, 1594, the Synod of bishops bars him from participation in all ecclesiastical matters, and, on September 26 of the same year, the Synod of Novogrudok strips him of his episcopal and ecclesiastical rank. Meddling into church affairs by members of the Roman Catholic rite and secular persons causes confusion and furthers the split between the hierarchy and clergy.

4 March 1593 — Following the death of Meletiy Khreptovych, Bishop of Volodymyr-Volynsky and Berestya, the king appoints Adam Potiy, a senator and castellan of Berestya, as the new bishop. Potiy receives the name Ipatiy and becomes the most active defender of the Union in the Kievan Metropolitanate.

21 June 1593 — Prince Konstantyn Ostrozky, provincial administrator of Kiev and county head of Volodymyr-Volynsky, requests that Bishop Ipatiy Potiy become a mediator in talks between the Kievan Metropolitanate and Rome regarding the unification of the Eastern and Western churches and acceptance of the Union. The Prince suggests eight preconditions. Among these, the most important is that all the Eastern Church, including the Patriarch, reunite with the Apostolic See. Regarding the Kievan Metropolitanate, the preconditions are formulated point by point, among which the most important are the preservation of her Eastern traditions, the equalization of rights and privileges among the Orthodox and Roman Catholic clergy, guaranteed positions in councils and parliaments (Seyms) for hierarchs, and the opening of schools for the education of the clergy.

21 May 1594 — Bishop Kyrylo Terletsky records a letter in the Lutsk archives which contains the following:

> I, Kyrylo Terletsky, by the grace of God exarch and Bishop of Lutsk and Ostrih, and we, the assembly of the cathedral clergy of the cathedral church of St. John the Theologian in Lutsk, publicly reveal to all that by the will and providence of God... the long-awaited truce and unification has ensued, and a brotherly love has arisen between the two Churches of the East and West — so long divided in their faith — and this, with the recognition of the most Holy Pope of Rome as the supreme pastor and apostolic vicar (Makariy, Vol. 9, p. 549).

Holy Trinity Monastery-fortress in the village of Mezhyrich (Rovno oblast), founded in the 15th century. Its cells, belfry and towers were destroyed in 1606-10. It is one of the better-known architectural monuments of Ukraine from the 17th century.

In the same month, King Sigismund III authorizes Bishop Kyrylo Terletsky and Bishop Ipatiy Potiy to lead discussions with Rome regarding the Union.

2 December 1594 — Bishops Kyrylo Terletsky and Ipatiy Potiy compose an edict regarding the Union; this edict is signed by the metropolitan and all the bishops of the Kievan Metropolitanate. An excerpt from the decree reads as follows:

> We, the undersigned, deeply aware of the responsibility laid upon us to lead the lambs of Christ to that unity of faith in which Christ instructed us, and particularly in these miserable times when heresies have become widespread among the people and so many abandon our

St. Nicholas Church in the city of Sokal (Lviv oblast), built in the early 16th century and restored in 1694 after many fires. A rare example of Ukrainian church architecture of the Renaissance period, it was converted into a historical-ethnographic museum by the Soviets in 1975.

Holy Trinity Church in the village of Shchyrets (Lviv oblast). Built in the 16th century, rebuilt in the 19th century, it was restored in the 1970s according to plans prepared by the architect I. Starosolsky. It was converted into an atheist museum in 1977 (left).

Church of the Ascension in Ternopil, built in the 16th century.

Orthodox faith, and mostly because we are not in union with the Romans, children of one and the same Catholic Church, and cannot aid one another. Following our church regulations, we always petition God in our prayers for unity of faith but have never worked toward this in our actions; we have only looked to our elders [the Patriarchs], waiting for them to take care of this. But our hope in them weakens with time, as they find themselves in pagan [Turkish] bondage, and can do nothing, even if they wished to... Thus, not desiring that more mortal souls should perish from such a division, we intend, by the help of God, to unite as previously, with our brothers, the Romans, under one visible supreme shepherd... (Makariy, Vol. 9. pp. 550-551).

The decree is signed by Metropolitan Mykhaylo Rohoza, Archbishop Herman Zagursky of Polotsk and Vitebsk, Bishop Leontiy Pelchytsky of Pinsk and Turov, Bishop Dionysiy Zbiruysky of Kholm and Belz, and Archimandrite Iona Hohol of the Monastery in

St. Nicholas Church in the city of Zolochiv (Lviv oblast), built in the 16th century and restored in 1765.

Kobryn. Missing from the signatures were those of Bishop Mykhaylo Kopystensky of Peremyshl, due to illness, and Bishop Hedeon Balaban.

22 January 1595 — By the efforts of Bishop Hedeon Balaban, a Synod takes place in Lviv with the participation of archimandrites, hegumens, and clergy from other countries. The Synod recognizes the Catholic Church as the one true Church, acknowledges the supremacy of the Pope, and requests that the hierarchy of the Kievan Metropolitanate complete the matter of Union with the Apostolic See. The decree regarding the Union is signed by Bishop Hedeon Balaban, Metropolitan Lucas of Belgrade, Bishop Paisios from Greece, Archimandrite Athanasius of Mt. Athos, Archimandrite Nykyfor Tur of the Kievan Monastery of the Caves, archimandrites of the Suprasl and Derman monasteries, and hegumens of the monasteries in Dubno and Smolnytsya, together with a great number of clergy.

4 March 1595 — At the request of King Sigismund III, Pope Clement VIII issues a papal bull which states that the Kievan Monastery of the Caves would be placed under the Kievan metropolitan's jurisdiction if the Metropolitanate unites with the Apostolic See. On May 5, the king places the monastery under the jurisdiction of Metropolitan Mykhaylo Rohoza.

1 June 1595 — The metropolitan and all the bishops of the Kievan Metropolitanate sign a joint epistle to the Pope regarding acceptance of the Union. An excerpt of the epistle reads thus:

> With the help of God, we have decided to enter into that union, which our forefathers had accepted at the Council of Florence... We have charged our representatives to greet Your Holiness and present our intentions, that Your Holiness would agree to leave us all with our faith, sacraments, and all the ceremonies and rites of the Eastern Church, and not to alter them in any way (Makariy, Vol. 9, pp. 576-577).

The hierarchs outline their pre conditions for accepting the Union in 33 points, contained in the epistle. Among the points are the following demands: priests must not be forced to perform Roman Catholic ceremonies during church feasts; the right of priests to marry must remain unchanged; metropolitans, bishops

The Savior, "Not Made With Human Hands." 15th-16th century icon from the Subcarpathian region.

The Pantocrator with the Apostles, by Dmytriy, 1565. Icon from the Church of the Nativity of the Mother of God in the city of Dolyna (Ivano-Frankivsk oblast) (left).

The Passion of Christ, 1593. Icon from the Church of the Nativity of the Mother of God in the village of Velyke (Lviv oblast).

The Passion of Christ. 15th-16th century icon from the Church of the Protection of the Blessed Virgin Mary in the village of Trushevychi (Lviv oblast) (left).

SS. George and Paraskeva Friday. 15th-16th-century icon from the Church of SS. Cosmas and Damian in the village of Korchyn (Lviv oblast).

and priests must be persons solely of Ruthenian (Ukrainian and Byelorussian) and Greek nationality and faith; bishops (and not Roman Catholic hierarchs) have to consecrate their metropolitans; persons of the Eastern rite cannot change to the Latin rite; abbots of monasteries, and the monasteries themselves, are to be under the jurisdiction of eparchial bishops; all priests and bishops of the Eastern rite are to enjoy the same rights and privileges as their Latin-rite counterparts; monasteries and Eastern-rite churches cannot change to the Latin rite; colleges and church brotherhoods that accept the Union are to remain intact and be placed under the jurisdiction of the metropolitan or bishops; seminaries and schools teaching the Greek and Slavonic languages must be opened for purposes of priestly formation; and printing presses under the supervision of the metropolitan or bishops must be opened for the publication of religious and church books.

When news spreads of the Kievan hierarchs' letter to the Pope, protests are begun by Orthodox mayors, nobility, and clergy. The greatest opposition to the Union is posed by the Holy Trinity Brotherhood in Vilnius, and the provincial administrators, Prince Konstantyn Ostrozky (who had previously advocated the Union of Eastern and Western Churches) and Teodor Skupyna-Tyshkevych.

24 June 1595 — Prince Ostrozky issues an appeal to all the clergy and Orthodox population in the Polish Kingdom. The letter contains the following:

> In our times, by the constant efforts of the most wicked devil, the major leaders of our faith, tempted by the glory of this world and blinded by their desire for riches, our unfaithful pastors, the metropolitan and bishops, have become wolves, and have renounced the one true faith of the Holy Eastern Church, have separated themselves from our ecumenical pastors and teachers, and have gone over to the West... They, the damned ones, secretly agreed among themselves, like Judas the betrayer of Christ had done with the Jews, to break off the pious Christians of this region — without their knowledge — and to drag them down with themselves into iniquity... Many people of our land, particularly the Orthodox, consider me to be the leader of Orthodoxy in this region, although I acknowledge that I am not great, but equal to anyone who is fervently Orthodox. And so, fearing that I might become guilty before God and you, and having learned with certainty of these apostates and open traitors of Christ's Church, I wish to inform you, my dear brothers in Christ, of their actions, and wish to stand together with all of you in a united front against the enemies of our salvation, so that with God's help and your fervent efforts, they might themselves fall into the net that they have secretly prepared for us... As hitherto, throughout the course of my entire life, I have served the immaculate law of the Holy Eastern Church with my work and riches,.. so I promise to serve with all my strength, for the good of my brothers, true-believing Christians, and desire together with all of you of true faith, to stand in piety as long as our strength allows... (Makariy, Vol. 9, pp. 584-586).

End of June 1595 — Bishop Ipatiy Potiy meets with Prince Ostrozky in Lublin. The Prince promises to concentrate all efforts on unification of the Eastern and Western Churches, not only the Kievan Metropolitanate. They agree on a decision to call a general Synod that would decide matters of the Union.

In Vilnius, a book entitled *Unia* (Union) appears in the Slavonic language, signed by the hierarchs of the Kievan Metropolitanate.

1 July 1595 — Under the influence of Prince Konstantyn Ostrozky, Bishop Hedeon Balaban of Lviv retracts his signature from the letter to the Pope of June 12.

13 July 1595 — Protests against the Union spread

St. Nicholas Church in the city of Svalyava (Transcarpathian oblast), built of wood in 1588 (left).

Dormition Church in the village of Krylos (Ivano-Frankivsk oblast), built in the 16th century in the Renaissance style from materials taken from the Dormition Church, destroyed in the 12th century. The Church was destroyed by the Turks and Tatars in 1676. It was rebuilt in 1700, and restored in 1824-25 and again in 1926 by the architect L. Levynsky.

to other and varied segments of the population, particularly in Vilnius. The protest movement is headed by Stefan Zyzaniy, former didascal of the Brotherhood School in Lviv, and later of a similar one in Vilnius.

28 July 1595 — King Sigismund III issues three decrees simultaneously — one to Prince Ostrozky, whom he exhorts to accept the Union; a second to Metropolitan Rohoza, whom he thanks for accepting the Union; and a third to the border authorities, whom he authorizes to deny patriarchal legates permission to enter Poland or Lithuania.

July 1595 — Many members of the Orthodox nobility demand that the King call a council to review matters concerning the Union.

1 August 1595 — The Papal Nuncio in Poland, Germanicus Malaspina, informs Bishops Kyrylo Terletsky and Ipatiy Potiy that the Pope agrees to and is satisfied with all the conditions of June 12 set forth by the hierarchs of the Kievan Metropolitanate; on the following day, the King issues a decree that guarantees adherence to all of the hierarchs' conditions.

Having met with opposition to the Union, Metropolitan Mykhaylo Rohoza makes efforts to call a Synod, but he is indecisive and hesitant.

27 August 1595 — A Synod takes place in Lutsk with the participation of the bishops of Peremyshl, Lviv, Kholm, and Lutsk. The Metropolitan does not participate in the Synod. The bishops proclaim that they have accepted the Union, and that they will not secede from it until death.

1 September 1595 — Metropolitan Mykhaylo Rohoza issues a letter to all the Orthodox clergy and faithful, calming them and stating that "he did not and does not intend to allow his rights and faith to be abused." He exhorts all to stand firm in their faith and to remain loyal to the Eastern Church.

24 September 1595 — On the day of Bishop Kyrylo Terletsky's and Ipatiy Potiy's departure for Rome, the King issues a manifesto to all of the Orthodox population, in which he informs them of the hierarchs' acceptance of the Union and their recognition of papal authority. Prince Konstantyn Ostrozky on his part issues a letter in which he condemns the hierarchs' decision in favor of the Union. In Lviv, the Holy Dormition Brotherhood forcefully protests the Union.

30 September 1595 — Metropolitan Mykhaylo Rohoza bans Stefan Zyzaniy, a defender of Orthodoxy, from preaching.

15 November 1595 — A large delegation of the Kievan Metropolitanate headed by Bishops Kyrylo Terletsky and Ipatiy Potiy arrives in Rome. The delegation is received twice by Pope Clement VIII. Leaders of the delegation give the Pope three documents: a decree by the bishops (dated December 2, 1594) regarding acceptance of the Union; preconditions set forth by the bishops, dated June 1, 1595; and, a joint letter to the Pope dated June 12, 1595. Discussions regarding the preconditions last six weeks.

Church of the Elevation of the Cross in Drohobych (Lviv oblast), built in the early 16th century, with additions in 1661; restored in 1715. In 1972 it was converted by the Soviets into an historical-ethnographic museum.

23 December 1595 — A solemn audience of the delegation from the Kievan Metropolitanate with Pope Clement VIII takes place in Rome. The Pope and the College of Cardinals receive Bishops Kyrylo Terletsky and Ipatiy Potiy in the presence of delegates from France, Poland, and other countries. Church historian Caesar Baronius takes part in the ceremonies. Ipatiy Potiy explains the purpose of the Ruthenian (Ukrainian-Byelorussian) delegation's arrival in Rome. All three documents are read in the Old Ukrainian language by Evstafiy Volovych, a canon of Vilnius, and in Latin by the papal secretary Sylvius Antonius. Following the reading of the documents, Sylvius Antonius, in the Pope's name, states the following:

> Finally, after 150 years, you, the Ruthenian bishops, return to the rock of faith upon which Christ founded His Church, to the Mother and teacher of all churches — the Roman Church. (Makariy, Vol. 9, p. 622).

At his exhortation, both bishops swear an oath on the Gospel and recite the Creed. After pledging the oath, they approach the Pope, who tells them: "I do not desire to rule over you; I wish to take upon myself your burdens." Embracing the bishops, the Pope solemnly proclaims his acceptance of them, Metropolitan Mykhaylo Rohoza, all the bishops, clergy, and all of the Ruthenian faithful into the womb of the Catholic Church and joins them into one body with the Roman Church. That day, the protocol concerning the entire ceremony of unification with the Roman Church is announced, and the Pope issues the bull "Magnus Dominus et laudabilis nimis."

St. George's Church in the city of Lyuboml (Volynia oblast), built in the 16th century (left).

Dormition Church of the Univ Monastery in the village of Mizhhirya (Lviv oblast), built in the 16th century, rebuilt in 1741 and restored in 1904

25 January 1596 — The Synod in Novogrudok excommunicates the Orthodox preacher Stefan Zyzaniy and two of his followers for protesting against the Union; an anathema is imposed on several other laypersons. This date marks the beginning of open conflict between Ukrainian Catholic Uniates and Orthodox, a conflict which continues into the following centuries.

7 February 1596 — Departing from Rome, Bishops Kyrylo Terletsky and Ipatiy Potiy take with them 16 papal letters: one to Metropolitan Mykhaylo Rohoza and the Ruthenian bishops, one to King Sigismund III, and fourteen to the Polish and Lithuanian clergy and laity. In his letter to the Metropolitan, the Pope recommends the convocation of a Synod that publicly proclaims the unification of the Churches.

April 1596 - During the Seym (parliament) in Warsaw, Orthodox delegates from Ukrainian and Byelorussian territories demand that Bishops Kyrylo Terletsky and Ipatiy Potiy be stripped of their clerical rank. They state that they will not recognize these bishops in their provinces.

29 May 1596 — King Sigismund III gives his permission for the convocation of a church Synod.

21 August 1596 — Metropolitan Mykhaylo Rohoza issues a decree regarding the assembly of a church Synod on October 8.

30 August 1596 — Meletius Pigas, Patriarch of Alexandria, sends a letter to Prince Ostrozky, in which he condemns the Union and calls upon the Orthodox population to stand firmly by their faith. The Patriarch sends Cyril Lucaris, protosyncel of the Alexandrian Church and noted theologian, while the Patriarch of Constantinople sends Metropolitan Niphontos, protosyncel of the Patriarchate, to Vilnius.

6-9 October 1596 — The Provincial Church Sobor takes place in Berestya (Brest). This is the greatest Sobor in the history of the Kievan Metropolitanate, both in number of participants, and importance of purpose and resolutions. Representatives of the two opposing sides are present. On the Orthodox side are the two patriarchal exarchs Cyril Lucaris and Metropolitan Niphontos, Metropolitan Luka of Velehrad, Archimandrite Makarios of St. Panteleimon Monastery on Mt. Athos', Bishop Hedeon Balaban of Lviv, Bishop Mykhaylo Kopystensky of Peremyshl, and nine archimandrites of Ukrainian and Byelorussian monasteries — among them Archimandrite Nykyfor Tur of the Kievan Monastery of the Caves. The total is 106 people according to one source, and over 200 according to another. Besides the clerics attending the Sobor, laypersons such as Orthodox government officials, delegates, and provincial administrators (among them Prince Konstantyn Ostrozky) are present.

The following supporters of the Union are present: Metropolitan Mykhaylo Rohoza, the Patriarchal exarch, Bishop Kyrylo Terletsky of Lutsk and Ostrih, Bishop Ipatiy Potiy, Archbishop Herman of Polotsk, Bishop Iona Hohol of Pinsk and Turov, Bishop Dionysiy Zbiruysky of Kholm, and three archimandrites. The Papal legates are the Roman Catholic Archbishop Jan Sulikowski of Lviv, Bishop Bernard Maciejewski of Lutsk, and Bishop Stanislaw Homoliski of Kholm. Also present are the Jesuit preacher Piotr Skarga, Maxim Laterna, chaplain to the late King Stefan Bathory, and others. The King's delegates are the Grand Lithuanian hetman Krzysztof-Nicholas Radziwill, the Lithuanian chancellor Leo Sapieha, and others.

Besides the Orthodox, Catholic, and Uniate delegates, many Protestants attend the Sobor, serving as advisors to the Orthodox.

Prince Ostrozky arrives at the Sobor with a large number of military personnel, for purposes of security and preservation of order.

On Wednesday, October 6, Metropolitan Mykhaylo Rohoza opens the Sobor in St. Nicholas Cathedral, in the presence of the bishops and clergy. Simultaneously, the patriarchal exarch, Metropolitan Niphontos, opens a second Sobor of Orthodox clergy and hierarchs in the Protestant church of the nobleman Raysky. The Orthodox Sobor reviews several issues and comes to the decision that the Sobor cannot accept the Union without the permission of the Ecumenical Patriarchs, that those bishops and priests who accept the Union will be stripped of their spiritual rank and excommunicated, and that the Orthodox dare not accept the new Gregorian calendar.

Meanwhile, the two sides continue their dialogue. Representatives of the Orthodox Sobor reveal that they will accept the Union if all the Eastern Churches — together with their Patriarchs — unite with Rome.

Not having reached a common understanding, on Saturday, October 9, the Metropolitan, all the bishops (with the exception of two — those of Lviv and Peremyshl), and papal and royal legates pass in a procession through the streets of Berestya amid great throngs of people, the ringing of church bells, and the singing of religious hymns, into the Cathedral of St. Nicholas. Following the prayer, Archbishop Herman Zagursky of Polotsk reads the decree issued by the metropolitan and hierarchs regarding the Union and recognition of the Pope as head of the Church. The document is signed on October 8 by Archbishop Mykhyalo Rohoza, Metropolitan of Kiev, Galicia, and All Rus', Bishop Ipatiy Potiy of Volodymyr and Berestya, Bishop Kyrylo Terletsky, exarch and Bishop of Lutsk and Ostrih, Archbishop Herman Zagursky of Polotsk and Bishop of Vitebsk and Mstyslavets', Bishop Dionysiy Zbiruysky of Kholm and Belz, Bishop Iona Hohol of Pinsk and Turov, Archimandrite Bohdan Hodkynsky of Kobryn, Archimandrite Klyment of Bratslav and Grodno, Archimandrite Hedeon Brolnytsky of Lavryshev, and Archimandrite Paisiy of Minsk.

The document also states the following:

> We have sent our legates with the request that the Pope, as the highest pastor of the Universal Catholic Church, accept us into his jurisdiction and release us from subordination to the Patriarch of Constantinople, under the condition, however, that our rite and ceremonies of the Greek-Ruthenian Church remain intact, and that no changes be initiated in our churches, but that all remain true to the tradition of the Holy Greek Fathers for ages unto ages. All this has been truly granted to us by the Holy Father, who has sent us the privileges and documents to that effect, along with instructions that we make a profession of our faith at the assembled Sobor, and pronounce our obedience to the Roman See of St. Peter, to Pope Clement VIII and his successors. We do this today at this Sobor, as proven by our personal signatures, bound by our seals on this document. (Velyky, Vol. IV, pp. 120-121).

All the Sobor's participants proceed from St. Nicholas Cathedral through the streets of the city to the Roman Catholic church of St. Mary, where they sing "Te Deum laudamus." This is how the ceremonies of acceptance of the Union conclude.

On the fourth day of the Orthodox Sobor, a trial of the metropolitan and bishops who have accepted the Union takes place. Their guilt is described in four points. Nykyfor Tur, Archimandrite of the Kievan Monastery of the Caves, pronounces the sentence of the joint trial:

> God's Holy Eastern Church bids us and the present Sobor to strip Metropolitan Mykhaylo [Rohoza] and those bishops named with him of their archiepiscopal titles and office, of episcopal authority, and all spiritual rank. (Makariy, Vol. 9, pp. 671-672).

Following this, a statement is drawn up and signed by all the Sobor clerical participants:

> We pledge an oath of faith, conscience, and honor, for ourselves and our descendants, not to heed those who have been condemned by the Sobor's sentence — that is, the metropolitan and bishops, — not to subject ourselves to their will, not to allow them any authority over us — but on the contrary, to oppose as much as possible their resolutions, acts and orders, and to stand firm in our Holy Faith, and by the true pastors of our Holy Church, particularly our patriarchs, not abandoning our old calendar, meticulously observing the peace guaranteed us by our laws, and opposing all pressures, persecution, and innovations that would interfere with the wholeness and freedom of our divine services, which we practice according to our old customs. We solemnly proclaim this, firstly before Our Lord God, then before all the world, and particularly before all the residents of the Crown, the great Principality of Lithuania and territories belonging to the Crown [The Polish Kingdom]. (Makariy, Vol. 9, pp. 672-673).

St. George's Church in the village of Kasperivtsi (Ternopil oblast), built in the 16th century in the church-fortress style of the Podilia school.

Ruins of the Holy Trinity Monastery in the village of Satanivska Sloboda (Khmelnytsky oblast), built in the 16th century and rebuilt in 1744. It was destroyed by the Soviets in the 1930s (right).

Church of the Nativity of Jesus in the village of Steblivka (Transcarpathian oblast), built in the 16th century. Carvings and paintings by folk artists from the 18th century may be found in this wooden church (left).

Church of the Epiphany in the city of Ostrih (Rovno oblast), built in the 15th-16th centuries and restored in 1887-91.

A similar letter is written and signed by the lay participants of the Orthodox Sobor.

10 October 1596 — Metropolitan Mykhaylo Rohoza, together with the bishops, proclaims a joint provincial decree, excommunicating and divesting of all ecclesiastical rank those persons who did not accept the Union. Among them are: Bishop Hedeon Balaban of Lviv, Bishop Mykhaylo Kopystensky of Peremyshl, Archimandrite Nykyfor Tur of the Kievan Monastery of the Caves, and many others.

On the previous day, the Orthodox Sobor announces the excommunication and divestiture of clerical dignity of the metropolitan, and of all the bishops and priests who accepted the Union. The document is signed by the clerical participants of the Orthodox Sobor; they condemn the Uniate hierarchs and refuse obedience to them.

Both Sobors, their documents, and their reciprocal divestiture of spiritual rank complete the division in a Church that had been united for 608 years. The Sobor of Berestya initiates a new page in the history of the Ukrainian Orthodox and Catholic (Uniate) Churches.

Church of the Transfiguration in the village of Nuyno (Volynia oblast), built of wood in the 16th century.

Principal Ecclesiastical Activities

1. THE KIEVAN METROPOLITANATE DURING THE 15th-16th CENTURIES

Since the time when the Ukrainian territories of the former Kievan-Rus' and Galician-Volynian Principalities came under the authority of the Polish kings, and after the division of the Kievan Metropolitanate into the Kievan and Moscow Metropolitanates (1458), candidates for metropolitan were designated by the Polish king. Following this, they were selected by the synod of bishops and usually confirmed and blessed by the Patriarch of Constantinople.

In the period 1458-1596, the Church underwent almost a total breakdown. Neither metropolitans nor bishops had authority over the monasteries and churches whose ownership was distributed to laypersons, according to the whim and will of the king. Some metropolitans appointed by the king had been laymen directly prior to their designation and had no theological training (for example, Metropolitan Sylvester Byelkevych and Onysyfor Divochka). The same held true for bishops.

All the metropolitans during this period were Orthodox and under the jurisdiction of the Patriarch of Constantinople. Only Metropolitan Hryhoriy II (1458-1472) temporarily accepted the Union and was consecrated by the will of the Pope, while Metropolitan Mysayil (1475-1480) remained only a metropolitan-elect.

Although all the metropolitans held the title of "Metropolitan of Kiev (and sometimes also of Galicia) and All Rus'," nonetheless, the Metropolitan See was not in Kiev, but in the small town of Novogrudok in Byelorussia, which at the time was under the jurisdiction of the Grand Lithuanian princes and later, that of the Polish king.

The following were Metropolitans of Kiev, Galicia and All Rus', whose metropolitan seat was in Novogrudok:

METROPOLITAN OF KIEV, GALICIA AND ALL RUS'

Hryhoriy II 1458-1472
Mysayil Drutsky 1475-1480
Symon 1481-1488
Iona Hlezna 1492-1494
Makariy I 1495-1497
Yosyf I Bolharynovych 1498-1501
Iona II 1503-1507
Yosyf II Soltan............................... 1507-1521
Yosyf III 1522-1534
Makariy II 1534-1556
Sylvester Byelkevych 1556-1567
Iona III Protasovych-Ostrovsky 1568-1576
Illya Kucha 1576-1579
Onysyfor Divochka 1579-1589
Mykhaylo Rohoza............................... 1589-1596

METROPOLITAN VICARS

During the period when there were no bishops in the Galician Metropolitanate, the metropolitans of Kiev appointed their vicars in Lviv. Later, the vicars were appointed by the king and ordained by the metropolitan. From 1509, the vicars were appointed by the Polish Roman Catholic Archbishop of Lviv, and from 1522, were again appointed by the king. Several of the vicars were laymen, and not until 1535 were bishops appointed to the post. This date marks the renewal of the eparchy in Lviv following a long interval. The names of only a few vicars have been preserved in the documents of the period:

Vasyl Pletensky 1510s
Isakiy (Yatsko) Hdashytsky 1522-1535
Yakiv Sikora 1535
Yosyf Hoshovsky.................................... 1535
Makariy Tuchapsky 1535-1548
Arseniy (Mark) Balaban.......................... 1549-1566

2. EPARCHIES IN THE KIEVAN METROPOLITANATE

The Kievan Metropolitanate was first contained within the Great Lithuanian Principality and later, the Polish Kingdom. For this reason, some historians call it the Lithuanian Metropolitanate, regardless of the fact that the metropolitan's title was "Metropolitan of Kiev, Galicia and All Rus'."

The compositon of the Kievan Metropolitanate was constantly changing. In 1503, Moscow conquered Chernihiv and joined the Chernihiv (Bryansk) Eparchy to the Moscow Metropolitanate. In 1514, it was joined to the eparchy of Smolensk, after that city was conquered by Moscow.

The following eparchies belonged to the Kievan Metropolitanate:

WITHIN PRESENT-DAY UKRAINE:

1. Volodymyr-Volynsky and Berestya
2. Lutsk and Ostrih
3. Halych and Lviv (from 1539)
4. Chernihiv-Bryansk (until 1503)
5. Mukachiv.

WITHIN PRESENT-DAY BYELORUSSIA:

1. Novogrudok (the Metropolitans' eparchy)
2. Polotsk
3. Pinsk and Turov
4. Minsk
5. Grodno
6. Slutsk.

WITHIN PRESENT-DAY POLAND:

1. Kholm
2. Peremyshl.

WITHIN PRESENT-DAY LITHUANIA:

1. Vilnius.

BISHOPS OF EPARCHIES WITHIN THE KIEVAN METROPOLITANATE ON UKRAINIAN LANDS

Bishops of the Kievan Metropolitanate were appointed by the Polish king, and some of these, according to the will of the king, were ordained by the metropolitan. Some bishops administered eparchies while remaining laymen. Most of them had no theological training.

Chernihiv *(Bryansk):* Yevtymiy (-1464), Nektariy (-1499), Iona (-1500).

Kholm *(and later also Bilsk):* Hryhoriy Depolnytsky (1446-1467), Sylvester (Sava) (1468-1470), Herasym (Hrytsko Okyshkovych) Bozky (1471-1489), Symeon Buhak (1492-1494), Filaret (Ploshchansky) Oblaznytsky (1507-1533), Iona (Ivashko) Sosnovsky (1504-1507; 1533-1545), Mykhaylo Sosnovsky, bishop elect (1543), Vassiyan (Vasyl) Baka (1546-1552), Teodosiy Lazovsky (1552-1565), Zakharya (Zenko) Illyashevych (1566-1577), Teodor (Terentiy Onnys) Lazovsky, bishop-elect (1566), Leontiy (Levko) Pelchytsky (1577-1585), Dionysiy (Dmytro) Zbiruysky (1585-1603).

Lutsk *(and later, also Ostrih):* Martynyan (1459), Nykyfor I (1490), Iona (1492-1495), Kyrylo (1495-1526), Pafnutiy (1521-1528), Makariy (1528-1534), Arseniy (1540), Teodosiy (1545-1548), Tymotey (1548), Nykyfor II (1564), Marko Zharovnytsky (1564-1567), Kyrylo Terletsky (1585-1596).

In the period 1567-1584 the Lutsk eparchy was administered by Ivan Borzobohaty-Krasensky, a layman.

Lviv: Makariy Tuchapsky (1540-1549), Arseniy (Mark) Balaban (1549-1568), Ivan (Lopata) Ostalovsky (1568-1576), Hedeon (Hryhoriy) Balaban (1576-1594).

Mukachiv: Ivan (1490), Vasyliy (1551), Yevtymiy, Amfilokhiy.

Peremyshl *(and later also Sambir):* Atanasiy (Oleksander) Biretsky (1446-1467), Ioann (Ivan) Biretsky (1467-1476), Yoannikiy (1491-1498), Antoniy Onykiy (1498-1521), Yoakym (1522-1528), Lavrentiy (Arseniy) Terletsky (1528-1549), Antoniy (Yatsko) Radylovsky (1549-1581), Arseniy (Stefan) Brylynsky (1581-1591), Mykhaylo (Matey) Kopystynsky (1591-1596).

Volodymyr-Volynsky *(and later also Berestya):* Nykyfor II (1458), Porfyriy (1470), Teodosiy (1485), Damyan (1487), Vassiyan I (1487-1494), Vassiyan II (1507-1511), Pafnutiy (1513-1521), Iona (1523-1535), Hennadiy (1536-1547), Yosyf (1565), Teodosiy Lazovsky (1565-1579), Meletiy Khrebtovych-Bohurynsky (1580-1593), Ipatiy Potiy (1593-1596).

In the period 1547-1565, the Volodymyr-Volynsky eparchy was administered by Ivan Borzobohaty-Krasensky, a layman.

Church and Monastery Construction during the 15th-16th Centuries

Following the seizure of almost all Ukrainian lands by the Polish kings, the construction of churches and monasteries came to a virtual standstill. Particularly in the eastern Ukrainian territories, contemporary documents hardly noted the building of churches or monasteries. There was some information regarding new churches and monasteries in Galicia and Volynia. However, their construction was curtailed when the king decided that they could be built only by his special permission. To add to the difficulties of religious life, the king bestowed churches and monasteries upon laypersons for their own personal enrichment. Neither churches nor monasteries were under the authority of either metropolitan or bishops.

Below is a listing of churches and monasteries with dates of construction or first reference to them in the chronicles. Places are listed according to their location by present-day oblasts.

CHURCH CONSTRUCTION

CHERNIVTSI OBLAST. Pidvalne: Exaltation of the Cross (1561); ***Toporivtsi:*** St. Elias (1560).

CRIMEAN OBLAST. Feodosia: St. George (15th century).

IVANO-FRANKIVSK OBLAST. Cherche: St. Basil (16th century); ***Kasperivtsi:*** St. George (16th century); ***Kolodne:*** St. Nicholas (1575); ***Kolomyia:*** Annunciation (1587); ***Koshylivtsi:*** church (1564); ***Krylos:*** Holy Dormition (16th century).

LVIV OBLAST. Drohobych: St. George (15th-16th centuries), Holy Cross (16th century); ***Lavriv:*** St. Onufrius (15th-16th centuries); ***Lviv:*** St. Onufrius (1550), Three Hierarchs (1591), financed by the Holy Dormition Brotherhood; ***Mizhhirya:*** Holy Dormition (16th century); ***Nyzhankovychi:*** Holy Trinity (16th century); ***Pisky:*** Nativity of the Mother of God (15th-16th centuries); ***Potelych:*** Holy Spirit (1502); ***Rosokhy:*** Nativity of the Mother of God (15th-16th centuries); ***Shchyrets:*** Holy Trinity (16th century); ***Sokal:*** St. Nicholas (16th century); ***Volya Vysotska:*** St. Nicholas (1598).

ODESSA OBLAST. Kilia: St. Nicholas (1485).

ROVNO OBLAST. Dorohobuzh: Holy Dormition (1577-1582); ***Mezhyrichya:*** Holy Trinity (15th century); ***Ostrih:*** Holy Theophany (15th-16th centuries).

TERNOPIL OBLAST. Bavoriv: St. John the Forerunner (16th century); ***Husyatyn:*** St. Onufrius (16th-17th centuries); ***Terebovlya:*** St. Nicholas (16th century); ***Ternopil:*** Exaltation of the Cross (16th century).

TRANSCARPATHIAN OBLAST. Kolodne: St. Nicholas (1470); ***Oleksandrivka:*** St. Paraskeva (15th century); ***Ruska Dolyna:*** Presentation of Our Lord (15th century); ***Svalyava:*** St. Nicholas (1588).

VOLYNIA OBLAST. Hishyn: St. Demetrius (1567); ***Kovel:*** St. Nicholas (1540, built by Prince Teodor A. Sanguszko); ***Kachyn:*** Holy Dormition (1589); ***Lubomyl:*** St. George (16th century); ***Lutsk:*** Protection of the Mother of God (15th century), Holy Dormition (1495); ***Myltsi:*** St. Nicholas (1542); ***Nuyno:*** Holy Transfiguration (16th century); ***Sukhodoly:*** Exaltation of the Cross and hospital (1577), founded by the Bratslav castellan Vasyl Zavhorodny.

ZHYTOMYR OBLAST. On the Ros' River: Nativity of the Most Holy Mother of God (1582).

MONASTERY CONSTRUCTION

KIEV OBLAST. Bohuslav: St. Nicholas (1575-1586); ***Kiev:*** Mezhyhirsky Transfiguration (16th century), Florivsky Convent of the Ascension (15th century); ***Trekhtymyriv:*** monastery (1576, founded by the Zaporozhian Kozaks).

LVIV OBLAST. Lviv: St. Onufrius (1463), Univsky (15th century).

ROVNO OBLAST. Dubno: Exaltation of the Cross (15th century), founded by the princes Ostrozky, Dermansky (1450), built by Prince Vasyl T. Krasny; ***Maryny:*** monastery (1576), founded by the provincial administrator Horodynsky; ***Mezhyrichya:*** fortress monastery (15th century); ***Novhorod-Volynsky:*** Resurrection (1571), built by Prince Bohush T. Koretsky; ***Ustenske-druhe:*** fortress monastery (15th century).

SUMY OBLAST. Putyvl: Movchansky (1579).

KHMELNYTSKY OBLAST. Holovchyntsi: Transfiguration (1540); ***Satanivka:*** Holy Trinity (16th century).

TERNOPIL OBLAST. Terebovlya: Basilian monastery (16th century).

VINNYTSYA OBLAST. Rozhok: Mykulynsky monastery (16th century).

VOLYNIA OBLAST. Kovel: St. Nicholas (1532), built by the monks of the Verbkivsky settlement; ***Ladyn:*** Protection of the Mother of God (16th century); ***Lutsk:*** Peresopnytsky Mother of God (1490), Zhydychynsky St. Nicholas (1492); ***Olshany:*** St. Nicholas (15th-16th centuries); ***Porytsk:*** Nativity of the Mother of God (1548); ***Volodymyr-Volynsky:*** Our Savior (1500).

ZHYTOMYR OBLAST. Ovruch: SS. Joachim and Anna (1496), Mother of God (1496), Mother of God (Prechystensky), Pustynsky, Savior Immaculate (15th-16th centuries); ***Zhytomyr:*** Tryhorsky Transfiguration (16th century), founded by Prince Volodymyr Zhytomyrsky.

VII. The Division of the Church into Orthodox and Catholic during the 16th-17th Centuries (1596-1686)

General Characteristics of the Period

1. THE POLITICAL SITUATION IN EASTERN EUROPE

During the seventeenth century, the major powers of Eastern Europe were Muscovy and Poland-Lithuania, with the Habsburgs and the Ottomans holding large portions of Slav territory. Sweden also temporarily controlled parts of Eastern Europe. Among the conflicts marking this turbulent period in Eastern and Central Europe were the Thirty Years' War (1618-1648) and the Kozak uprising of Bohdan Khmelnytsky (1648-1654).

Having defeated Ivan the Terrible, the Swedes took Estonia while Poland took Livonia. After Ivan's death, Boris Godunov became regent for Ivan's mentally retarded son, Fyodor. When Fyodor died in 1598, Godunov became Tsar. Upon his death in 1605, Muscovy was plunged into the Time of Troubles, a succession crisis combined with foreign intervention. The Poles took Smolensk in 1611 and Moscow in 1612, placing their Crown Prince on the Tsar's throne; the Swedes took Novgorod in 1613. With the restoration of order and the accession of Mikhail Romanov as Tsar, Muscovy, after taking some eastern Ukrainian and eastern Lithuanian land, and making peace with Sweden in 1617 and Poland in 1618, began its gradual westward and southward advance.

At this time central and eastern Europe entered the long and bloody Thirty Years' War. This began as a Protestant revolt in Bohemia against the Catholic Habsburgs. The Bavarians, allies of the Habsburgs, invaded Bohemia, and in 1620 the Saxons took Silesia and Lusatia. The Swedish Protestant king Gustavus Adolphus took Livonia in 1626, then the eastern Baltic; in 1630 he landed in Pomerania. Allying themselves with the Saxons, the Swedes fought the Austrian Habsburgs and the Spaniards. They raided Bohemia in 1638. After many invasions and battles, negotiations begun in 1644 led to the Peace of Westphalia four years later. Sweden and France profited most from the final arrangements.

No sooner had the Thirty Years' War ended, than the Kozak revolt under Bohdan Khmelnytsky shook the Polish-Lithuanian commonwealth (see section 3). The new Kozak State, seeking to survive between the great powers of Muscovy, Poland, and Turkey, concluded a union with Muscovy at Pereyaslav in 1654.

In 1667 Muscovy and Poland concluded a treaty at Andrusiv which delineated their spheres of influence over Ukraine. Meanwhile, the Turks were pushing northward again, taking parts of Hungary (1664, 1675) and laying siege to Vienna in 1683. A combined European force drove them back, however, and the Ottoman empire began to recede.

2. THE RELIGIOUS SITUATION IN EUROPE

After the sixteenth-century wars of religion, which had been particularly intense in the Netherlands and Germany, there was a tendency towards religious uniformity in Europe, as religious minorities were eliminated. Protestantism grew in northern Europe, while Catholicism reasserted itself in the south.

Although religious allegiance still played a major role in the Thirty Years' War (1618-1648), gradually religious tolerance came to be accepted in Europe. At the same time, the influence of religion in society began to decline. Political rather than religious factors came to dominate international conflicts. The eighteenth century saw a wave of secularism and anti-clericalism.

The French Huguenot king Henry IV converted to Catholicism in 1594 but proclaimed religious tolerance in the Edict of Nantes of 1598. However, the Edict was revoked in 1685, leading to the emigration of 200,000 Huguenots.

In the Netherlands, the religious war ended with an armistice and the creation of a Protestant Dutch Republic in 1607.

The Thirty Years' War began as a Protestant revolt against the Catholic Habsburgs in Bohemia. Yet the Protestant Saxons (as well as the Catholic Bavarians) came to the aid of Catholic Austria.

The 1596 Union of Berestya extended Catholic influence into Ukraine and Byelorussia while preserving the Byzantine rite of the originally Orthodox population. Orthodoxy survived among the peasants, in the urban brotherhoods, and among some noblemen and the Kozaks. It was under the protection of the latter that an Orthodox hierarchy was re-established in Kiev in 1620.

After the death of King Sigismund III in 1632 his successor, Wlasdyslaw IV, declared religious toleration. Both the Uniate and the Orthodox Church were recognized, and Orthodoxy was restored in the central Ukrainian lands. In 1686 the Kievan Metropolitanate was transferred from the jurisdiction of the Patriarch of Constantinople to that of the Moscow Patriarch.

The Orthodox renaissance in seventeenth-century Kiev influenced Muscovite Orthodoxy as well, leading to Patriarch Nikon's reforms in the latter half of the century. These, however, were met with determined opposition from the "Old Believers," primarily on ritual grounds.

3. THE POLITICAL SITUATION IN UKRAINE

At the end of the sixteenth century the Ukrainian lands were divided between Poland-Lithuania, Muscovy, and the Crimean Khanate. During the following century the Hetman (Kozak) state — the first modern Ukrainian state — arose. Although the Ottoman Turks only held Ukrainian territory for a short while, they exerted a strong diplomatic influence on Ukrainian affairs.

The Kozaks, who had arisen in the sixteenth century, played an increasingly important role in European events in the seventeenth. They pursued an independent foreign policy, forming various alliances. They also acted as the protectors of the Orthodox Ruthenian population in the Polish-Lithuanian commonwealth. Revolts and battles in the 1620s and 1630s achieved increases in the number of registered Kozaks permitted by the Poles and in various Kozak privileges. Pavlyuk led a major revolt in 1637; Hunya and Ostryanyn headed another uprising in the following year. The next decade, however, was peaceful.

In 1648 Bohdan Khmelnytsky's quarrel with a Polish neighbor developed into a major Kozak revolt, which sparked a wave of peasant uprisings. Allied with the Crimean Khan, Khmelnytsky won a series of victories against the Poles, advancing as far as Zamosc. The Zboriv treaty of 1649 allowed a Kozak host of 40,000, ruling over Kiev, Bratslav and Chernihiv; a Ukrainian Hetman state was thus effectively recognized. However, conflicts arose among the Kozaks and between landlords and peasants. After the Tatars negotiated a separate peace with the Poles, Khmelnytsky was compelled to form an alliance with Muscovy. The Treaty of Pereyaslav (1654) has been variously interpreted, but its ultimate effect was to permit Russian control over Ukraine.

The 1658 Treaty of Hadyach would have given Ukraine considerable autonomy within the Polish-Lithuanian commonwealth had it been effective. In the following year a Kozak army defeated the Muscovites at Konotop, and in 1660 a Muscovite army was forced to surrender. Subsequently, however, Muscovy gained important rights over left-bank Ukraine, and in 1667 the Polish-Muscovite Treaty of Andrusiv gave Kiev, Chernihiv and Smolensk to Muscovy, Poland retaining Right-Bank Ukraine. Polish-Muscovite peace treaties in 1681 and 1686 sealed the fate of Ukraine.

Between 1672 and 1676 the Ottomans held Podilia. This and other foreign incursions, combined with disorder and dissension in the Kozak ranks and increasing Muscovite strictures, characterized the "Ruin" of late seventeenth-century Ukraine.

4. 16th-17th CENTURY HETMANS IN UKRAINE (1596-1686)

HETMANS OF KOZAKS

Hnat Vasylevych	1596-1597
Samiylo Kishka	1600-1602
Havrylo Krutnevych, Ivan Koziy	1602-1603
Hryhoriy Ivanovych	1606
Hryhoriy Tyshkevych	1610
Petro Sahaydachny	1613-1622
Mykhaylo Doroshenko	1623-1628
Hyrhoriy Chorny	1628-1629
Taras Fedorovych	1629-1630
Ivan Sulyma	1633-1635
Pavlo But	1637-1638
Yakiv Ostryanyn	1638-1641

HETMANS OF UKRAINE

Bohdan Khmelnytsky	1648-1657
Ivan Vyhovsky	1657-1659
Yuriy Khmelnytsky	1659-1663
Pavlo Teterya	1663-1665
Ivan Bryukhovetsky	1663-1668
Petro Doroshenko	1666-1676
Damyan Mnohohrishny	1668-1672
Ivan Samoylovych	1672-1687

Chronology

1596 — In the year following the division in the Church, many polemical works appear against the Union, especially those of Stefan Zyzaniy, and for the Union, such as those of Bishop Ipatiy Potiy.

1597 — Alarmed by the Union of the Kievan Metropolitanate with Apostolic See, Patriarch Meletius Pigas of Constantinople appoints three prominent Orthodox leaders as his deputies for the territories of Ukraine, Byelorussia, and Lithuania in the Polish kingdom: Bishop Hedeon Balaban, of Lviv, Halych and Kamyanets Podilsky, Prince Konstantyn Ostrozky, and his *protosyncel* Cyril Lucaris. The actual function of the deputy is carried out by Bishop Balaban.

1597 — Ivan Vyshensky, a monk in the monastery on Mt. Athos, writes the polemical work *A Letter to the Bishops Who Have Abandoned the Orthodox Faith.* At the same time the Uniates publish a work by Piotr Skarga written in old Ukrainian and Polish, entitled *A Description and Defense of the Ruthenian Council of Berestya.* In response to this work the Orthodox publish a document of the Sobor of Berestya in the Polish language entitled *Ekthesis,* in which it is argued that the Orthodox Sobor in Berestya took place in accordance with church canons.

1598 — The Polish Sejm ratifies the Union of Berestya (Brest).

The Orthodox deputies in the Polish Sejm from Volynia denounce Bishops Kyrylo Terletsky and Ipatiy Potiy for placing the Orthodox Church under the authority of the Pope.

In Lutsk thirty-three of the most prominent Orthodox nobles of Volynia proclaim publicly that they have joined the Uniate Church.

Galician-born Ivan Vyshensky, monk of the Mt. Athos monastery in Greece, writes a series of polemical articles against the Union.

Krzysztof Kazimirski becomes the Polish Roman Catholic bishop of Kiev, where he builds a Roman Catholic Church and the bishop's residence. On the ruins of the church of SS. Borys and Hlib in Vyshhorod, the Dominicans build a monastery. Many Polish missionaries arrive in Kiev with the intention of converting the Ukrainian Orthodox and Uniates to the Latin rite.

1598 — In the city of Ostrih Christophor Philalet publishes *Apokrizis,* the greatest polemical work of the time, written in defense of Orthodoxy. Petro Arkudiy writes the tract *Antirrizis* in defense of the Union. Historians believe that Bishop Ipatiy Potiy is the real author of this work.

Spring 1599 — A conference of all Orthodox and Protestant nobles takes place in Vilnius. Orthodox representatives call upon the Protestants to accept the Orthodox dogmas of faith.

July 1599 — The first Uniate Metropolitan, Mykhaylo Rohoza, dies. On September 21 the king appoints Bishop Ipatiy Potiy as the administrator and candidate to the metropolitan chair.

Pope Clement VIII confirms Potiy as Kievan Metropolitan on November 15, 1600.

1599 — During the transition of the Orthodox hierarchy to the Union, the Kievan Monastery of the Caves, under the leadership of archimandrite Yelysey Pletenetsky, becomes the center of Ukrainian Orthodox cultural and national life.

16 March 1600 — A trial of bishops who went over to the Uniate Church takes place in the Sejm. The bishops claim that they are not subject to the Sejm and that joining the Union with Rome was actually a renewal of the Florentine Union of 1439.

1600s — After ridding itself of the Tatars, Kiev places itself under the protection of the Zaporozhian Kozaks. Kiev is gradually rebuilt and renewed, and

Ecclesiastical divisions in Ukrainian lands in the 16th and 17th centuries.

becomes prominent as the center of Ukrainian religious and national life.

1600-1601 — Patriarch Meletius sends letters to Prince Konstantyn Ostrozky and other distinguished leaders calling on them to defend Orthodoxy. He also writes to the Uniate Metropolitan Ipatiy Potiy and King Sigismund III denouncing the practices of the Roman Catholic Church and the supremacy of the Pope. In his reply, Metropolitan Ipatiy Potiy defends his joining the Catholic Church.

Spring 1603 — Fifty-eight distinguished noblemen of Volynia join the Uniate Church; fifty more princes and noblemen of Lublin follow shortly thereafter.

1605 — For the seventh time, the Polish Sejm looks into the struggle between the Uniates and the Orthodox without adopting any resolutions. In a conciliatory gesture, the King confirms Yelysey Pletenetsky, an Orthodox activist, as the archimandrite of the Kievan Monastery of the Caves. The Monastery is under the jurisdiction of the Uniate Metropolitan Mykhaylo Rohoza until his death. At the same time, the King hands over all churches and monasteries with all their properties, which until then were under the jurisdiction of the Orthodox Metropolitan, to the Uniate Metropolitan Ipatiy Potiy.

A tribunal in Vilnius brings in a verdict in the matter of the Orthodox against the Uniate Metropolitan Ipatiy Potiy: the Union of Berestya was illegal and illegitimate, and the Metropolitan lost his jurisdiction over the Orthodox Church by joining the Catholic Church. King Sigismund III does not confirm the decision of the tribunal.

Ivan Vyshensky, known for his anti-Uniate messages, leaves Mt. Athos and arrives in Ukraine. After a two-year sojourn in the monasteries of Galicia, he returns to Mt. Athos.

1605-06 — *Perestoroha,* an Orthodox polemical work written by Yuriy Rohatynets, is published.

1606 — The Orthodox deputies in the Sejm intensify their struggle for the rights of the Orthodox Church. They demand the removal of the hierarchy that supports the Union, and the return of the Orthodox Church's rights and privileges. Under pressure from the Orthodox and Protestant deputies, the King dissolves the Sejm and does not accept amendments to the constitution on religious matters. Foreign and domestic conflicts bring the Polish Kingdom to a crisis. The Orthodox nobility meets in Lublin and decides to activate the struggle against the Union and in defense of Orthodoxy. This struggle crystallizes the religious, national, and political consciousness of Ukrainians.

Hedeon Balaban (1569-1607), Orthodox Bishop of Lviv, Exarch of the Ecumenical Patriarch for Ukraine after the Union of Berestya, prominent church and educational leader.

Christ in Prison, bas-relief, 17th century. Movchanivsky Monastery in Putyvl (Sumy oblast).

10 February 1607 — Patriarchal exarch Hedeon Balaban dies in the monastery in Univ. He was the acting Orthodox Metropolitan after the Kievan Metropolitanate joined the Catholic Church.

18 June 1607 — During the rebellion of the Voevoda of Cracow Zebrzydowski, King Sigismund III, to earn the goodwill of the Orthodox nobility, issues a proclamation giving the Orthodox the right to have their own bishops and to retain "freely, fully, calmly and without danger, its ancient Greek faith." With this new proclamation, the clergy and faithful of Lviv elect Yevstafiy Tysarovsky as the candidate for bishop. He is confirmed by the King on October 31 as Bishop of Lviv.

1607 — The Uniate Bishop Kyrylo Terletsky dies in Lutsk. Together with Bishop Ipatiy Potiy, he initiated the support of the Orthodox hierarchy for the Union. As his replacement, the King nominates Ostafiy Yelovych-Malynsky as the new Bishop of Lutsk. The Orthodox nobility of Volynia does not recognize him.

13 February 1608 — Prince Konstantyn Ostrozky, Voevoda of Kiev, an ardent defender of Orthodoxy, organizer of Ukrainian religious and educational life, founder of the first academy in Ukraine in the town of Ostrih, and founder of schools, churches, and monasteries, dies in Ostrih.

1608 — Aiming to spread Roman Catholicism on Ukrainian lands, the Polish Jesuits open a series of colleges in Lviv and Lutsk (1608), Kamyanets Podilsky (1612), Ostrih (1623), Berestya (1620), Ovruch (1632),

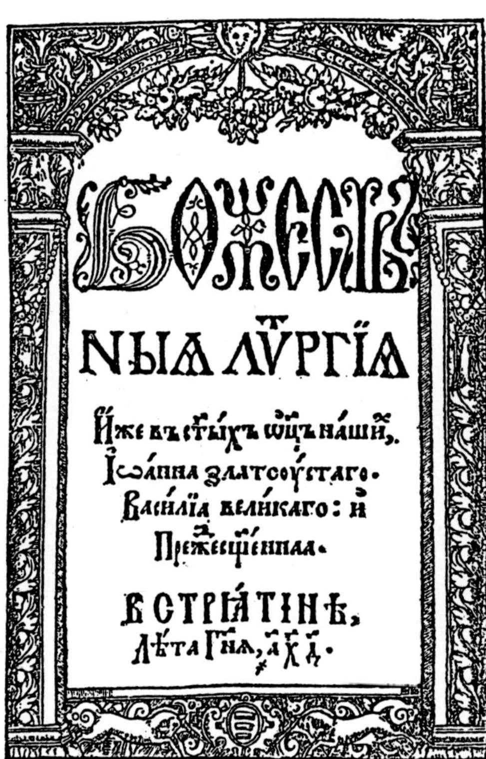

The Peresopnytsky Gospel manuscript, 1556-61 (left).

The Liturgy by Hedeon Balaban. Printed in Stryatyn (1604).

and Kiev (1640), in addition to opening lower-level schools in Lutsk, Vinnytsya, Bar, Peremyshl, Fastiv, and Kiev. During the same period very few Ukrainian Orthodox or Uniate schools are opened.

The nominated Bishop Tysarovsky is consecrated by the Metropolitan of Moldavia. In the same year the Uniate Metropolitan Ipatiy Potiy nominates Yosyf Velyamyn Rutsky as his vicar and Bishop of Lviv.

1609 — After an agreement with the Orthodox, the Uniate Metropolitan Ipatiy Potiy takes under his jurisdiction the Cathedral of St. Sophia in Kiev and appoints Antoniy Hrekovych as the Vicar of the Uniate Metropolitan in Kiev. Hrekovych takes over the Orthodox Vydubytsky Monastery a year later.

Spring 1610 — For the first time in the history of the Church, the Kozaks intervene in the internal affairs of that body. They enter into the city books of Kiev a protest against the appointment of the Uniate vicar Hrekovych in Kiev, and declare their support for the Orthodox faith.

7 May 1610 — Maksym (Meletiy) Smotrytsky's work entitled *Threnos,* in defense of Orthodoxy and against the Union of Berestya, and one of the most important books of the time, appears in Vilnius. King Sigismund III orders the seizure and burning of all copies, the closing of the printing press where the book was published, and the punishment of those responsible for its publication.

1610 — The Orthodox Bishop Mykhayil Kopystensky dies in Peremyshl. The King nominates the Uniate Bishop Atanasiy Krupetsky to replace him. In opposition, the Orthodox clergy and nobles elect Bishop Sylvester Hulevych-Voyutynsky, whom the King does not confirm until 1633. The forty-year struggle between the Orthodox and the Uniates for the Eparchy of Peremyshl and the possession of churches and monasteries often erupts in violence.

After the takeover of the Cathedral of St. Sophia by the Uniates, the Church of the Dormition serves as the cathedral of the Orthodox Metropolitan. From 1620 to 1631, the Cathedral of the Dormition in the Kievan Monastery of the Caves is the See of Metropolitan Yov Boretsky.

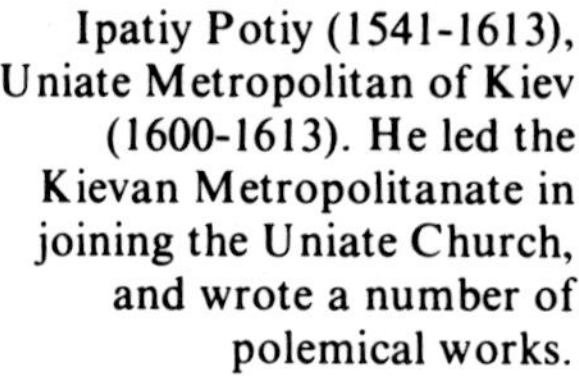

Ipatiy Potiy (1541-1613), Uniate Metropolitan of Kiev (1600-1613). He led the Kievan Metropolitanate in joining the Uniate Church, and wrote a number of polemical works.

Spring 1612 — The Bulgarian Metropolitan Neophitus of Sofia arrives in Kiev. For almost two years he remains in the Monastery of the Caves, where he ordains new Orthodox priests and deacons and consecrates new churches.

Sigismund III hands over the Golden-domed Monastery of St. Michael in Kiev to the Uniate Metropolitan Ipatiy Potiy.

18 July 1613 — Metropolitan Ipatiy Potiy dies in Volodymyr-Volynsky. Together with Bishop Kyrylo Terletsky, he advocated the Union of the Orthodox Church with Rome. He is succeeded by Velyamyn Rutsky, Bishop of Lviv and Halych. He is confirmed by the King in the following month and by Pope Paul V on April 5, 1614. He moves the metropolitan's seat to Vilnius.

1614 — The Uniate Metropolitan Velyamyn Rutsky and Yosafat Kuntsevych, archimandrite of the Uniate monastery of the Holy Trinity in Vilnius, visit Kiev and the Cathedral of St. Sophia; Yosafat Kuntsevych also visits the Kievan Monastery of the Caves.

September 1615 — Velyamyn Rutsky is the first Uniate Metropolitan to visit Rome. He receives permission from the Pope to open Uniate schools with the same rights and privileges as those accorded to the Jesuit schools and procures stipends for free education for the Uniate students in all papal seminaries of Europe. Because of illness the metropolitan does not return to Vilnius until July of 1616.

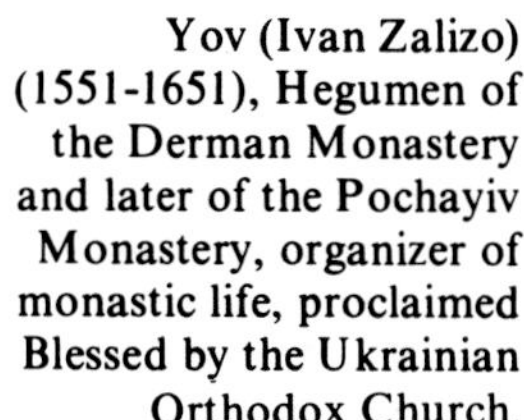

Yov (Ivan Zalizo) (1551-1651), Hegumen of the Derman Monastery and later of the Pochayiv Monastery, organizer of monastic life, proclaimed Blessed by the Ukrainian Orthodox Church.

Velyamyn Rutsky (1574-1637), Uniate Metropolitan of Kiev (1613-37), religious and educational leader, organizer of church life.

December 1615 — Metropolitan Velyamyn Rutsky appeals to the Pope to intercede in the attempts by the Jesuits to draw the Uniates closer to the Roman Catholic Latin rite. This results in Pope Paul V issuing a *Breve* that forbids the Uniates to change their rite.

15 December 1615 — Halshka Hulevychivna bequeaths all her property to the Orthodox monastery of St. Basil, the Orthodox school in Kiev, and Orthodox churches in the Volodymyr-Volynsky and Bratslav regions. Her foundation establishes the religious college and the Brotherhood School at the Holy Theophany Monastery in Kiev.

1615 — Archimandrite Yelysey Pletenetsky opens a printing press at the Kievan Monastery of the Caves. The Monastery becomes the center of church painting, engraving, and illustrations for the whole Slavic world and attracts the most renowned writers, theologians, historians, and polemicists of the day, e.g., Zakhariya Kopystensky, Tarasiy Zemko, Pamvo Berynda, Lavrentiy Zyzaniy, Yov Boretsky, Kasiyan Sakovych, and others. Some of them studied in West European universities and knew Greek, Latin, and Hebrew.

January 1616 — Without the King's knowledge, the Halshka Hulevychivna foundation establishes the first Brotherhood in Kiev, based on the Lviv Brotherhood, and a school whose first rector becomes Yov Boretsky. Among the members of the Brotherhood are the Kozak Hetman Petro Sahaydachny and other prominent Ukrainian Orthodox leaders and scholars.

Ezekiyil Kurtsevych, educated at Padua University, becomes the first archimandrite of the monastery of Terekhtymyriv, between Kiev and Cherkasy, newly renovated by the Zaporozhian Kozaks. Under the protection of the Kozaks, the monastery becomes the center of the Kozaks' council, their arsenal, and an intermediary between Kiev and the Zaporozhian Sich.

1617 — The first book printed at the press of the Kievan Monastery of the Caves appears. It is the *Breviary* prepared by Archimandrite Yelysey Pletenetsky and Archdeacon Zakhariya Kopystensky. In the same year the *Book of the Holy Faith* appears. Two years later the *Anthologion,* a *Mineon* (for the whole year), by Yov Boretsky, Hegumen of the Golden-domed Monastery of St. Michael, is printed.

A conference of all priors and representatives of Uniate monasteries is held in Novohrodovychi at the estate of Metropolitan Velyamyn Rutsky. The Metropolitan reorganizes the Order of St. Basil: all monasteries are freed from the rule of the eparchial bishops, to form an independent community under the name of the Order of St. Basil, headed by a Protoarchimandrite. The conference decides that in the future only members of this order are to be elected as new Uniate bishops.

Through the efforts and funding of Prince Sapieha, the first Uniate missal is published in Vilnius. (The only known extant copy is located in the museum of the memorial church of the Ukrainian Autocephalous Orthodox Church in Bound Brook, New Jersey.)

1 February 1618 — Following the example set by other Orthodox princes and magnates, Princess Rayina Mohylyanka donates her property to the monasteries of Hustyn and Pidhirsk-Ladyn near Pryluky.

23 February 1618 — In the struggle between the Uniates and the Orthodox, Antoniy Hrekovych, the vicar of Uniate Metropolitan Velyamyn Rutsky, dies at the hands of Kozaks; soon thereafter Oklynsky, the representative of the Metropolitan, also dies.

1618 — Needing the Kozaks' assistance in the struggle with Muscovy, the Polish government accepts the Sejm's constitution guaranteeing the Orthodox peace and freedom of religious choice. Roman Catholic deputies in the Sejm pronounce the constitution illegal. At the same time, King Sigismund III transfers, by special order, all churches and monasteries in the eparchy of Polotsk to the Uniate Archbishop Yosafat Kuntsevych, and all churches and monasteries of Mohyliv a year later.

1619 — The Kievan Caves Monastery publishes a monumental work called *Apologion* (1054 pp.) with an introduction written by Yelysey Pletenetsky, the archimandrite of the monastery.

22 March 1620 — Returning from Muscovy, the Patriarch of Jerusalem, Theophanes, stops for a year in Kiev. He has full authority from the Ecumenical Patriarch of Constantinople, Timotheus II, to perform various church functions in the Kievan Metropolitanate. He is met at the border of the Principality of Muscovy and Ukraine by Hetman Petro Sahaydachny and his Kozaks, who escort him to Kiev.

Under the protection of the Ukrainian Kozaks, the Patriarch visits churches and monasteries of Kiev, Mizhhirya, Bila Tserkva, and Terekhtymyriv. Together with the Ecumenical exarch Arsenius, he issues new rights of stauropegia or confirms old ones for the church brotherhoods in Kiev, Lviv, Lutsk, Slutsk, and others.

13 August 1620 — A council at the Kievan Monastery of the Caves of Hetman Petro Sahaydachny and Orthodox representatives from all the lands of Ukraine and Byelorussia appeals to Patriarch Theophanes to establish a new Orthodox hierarchy. Fearing Polish reprisals, they hold all deliberations in great secrecy.

The Homilary Gospel (*Uchytelnoye Yevanheliye*), by Hedeon Balaban, Krylos, 1606 (left).

Printer's mark of the Dormition Brotherhood of Lviv, 1609. From the book *Education of Children* by John Chrysostom.

Holy Mount Dormition Monastery in the city of Slovyanohirsk (Donetsk oblast), built in the early 1600s. It was converted by the Soviets into a rest home in the 1920s, into a sanatorium in the late 1940s and into a historical-architectural monument in 1980 (left).

Church of the Annunciation in the city of Horodok (Lviv oblast), built in 1603. It contains paintings from the 1660s.

6 October 1620 — Patriarch Theophanes, Bulgarian Metropolitan Neophitus, who was the patriarch's representative to the Sobor of Berestya in 1596, and the Greek Bishop Avraamiy consecrate, in great secrecy and without the King's knowledge or approval, a new hierarchy for the Ukrainian-Byelorussian Orthodox Church. The acts of consecration take place at the Brotherhood Church in Kiev. Isaya Kopynsky, Hegumen of the Theophany Monastery, is the first to be consecrated as the Bishop of Peremyshl. On October 9 Yov Boretsky, the rector of the Brotherhood school and Hegumen of the Golden-domed Monastery of St. Michael, is consecrated as the Metropolitan of Kiev, Galicia, and All Rus'. At the beginning of December the following are consecrated: Meletiy Smotrytsky as Archbishop of Polotsk, the Hegumen of Terekhtymyriv Monastery Ezekiyil Kurtsevych as Bishop of Volodymyr-Volynsky, the Hegumen of the Monastery in Bila Tserkva Isaak Boryskovych as Bishop of Lutsk. In February of 1621, the Hegumen of the Miletsky Monastery in Bratslav Paisiy Ipolytovych is consecrated as Bishop of Kholm. The Patriarch appoints the Greek Bishop Avraamiy as Archbishop of Pinsk.

November 1620 — Arriving in Vilnius at the end of December, Archbishop Meletiy Smotrytsky begins a struggle with the Uniate Archbishop Yosafat Kuntsevych for all of Byelorussia. In a very short time a whole series of Byelorussian towns — Vitebsk, Orsha, Mstyslavl, and others — renounce their allegiance to Archbishop Yosafat Kuntsevych and return to the Orthodox fold. Returning from his trip to Warsaw in the Spring of 1621, Yosafat Kuntsevych finds an empty archeparchy. The struggle between the two archbishops for the possession of churches and monasteries encompasses the whole of Byelorussia and is accompanied by intolerance and violence.

1620 — The Uniate leader Sapovych and the Orthodox Meletiy Smotrytsky, before his elevation to the archbishopric, call for peace between the two Churches.

During Patriarch Theophanes' stay in Kiev, the Kievan Brotherhood becomes independent of the local church authorities and becomes directly responsible to the Patriarch of Constantinople.

A descendant of Prince Ostrozky, Anna Eloise Ostrozka, a fanatical Roman Catholic, changes the educational center of Orthodox, the Ostrih Academy, into a Jesuit college.

Many Ukrainian and Byelorussian students who attend Jesuit schools switch to the Latin rite. The Uniate Metropolitan Velyamyn Rutsky demands more schools for the Uniate youth from the Apostolic See.

The first Jesuit missionary arrives in Kiev.

During the first twenty-five years after the Union of Berestya, the populations of over twenty-five towns, especially in Byelorussia, join the Uniates, including three senators, one voevoda, and two castellans. The Uniate Church has seven bishops and twenty monasteries. After the death of Prince Konstantyn Ostrozky, the Orthodox have no senators in the Polish Sejm.

1621 — During the Turkish attack on Poland, the King and the Sejm, wishing to draw the Kozaks to their side, grant no rights or privileges to the Uniate Church. On the status of his Church, the Uniate Metropolitan Velyamyn Rutsky wrote:

> Except for the two [the King and the Apostolic Nuncio] no one was there not only to help, but even to say a kind word to us. In general, they said we were responsible for the discord, they called the Union ill-started and pointed their fingers at us saying we are the disturbers of peace in the country. We were bitter, but God did not let us fall into temptation to use force. (Hrushevsky, Vol. VII, p. 449).

February 1621 — After visiting the regions of Kiev and Bratslav escorted by Hetman Petro Sahaydachny, Patriarch Theophanes leaves the Ukrainian territories and arrives in Moldavia. In the border town of Busha he issues a decree in which he calls upon the Kozaks, under the wrath of God, not to attack Muscovy.

Having discovered the existence of the new hierarchy of the Orthodox Church in Ukraine, Sigismund III threatens Metropolitan Yov Boretsky and Archbishop Meletiy Smotrytsky with imprisonment.

12 March 1621 — Patriarch Theophanes informs Patriarch Filaret of Moscow, that he has left Ukraine, freeing himself from the adversaries of the Moscow Patriarch, and that he is staying in Moldavia.

April 1621 — Bishop Meletiy Smotrytsky's book entitled *Verificatia niewinnosci* (*A Verification of Innocence*) appears in Vilnius; in this work he refutes the accusations of the Uniates in connection with the newly-created Orthodox hierarchy who are considered pretenders. In answer to Smotrytsky's book the Uniate Metropolitan Velyamyn Rutsky publishes a work entitled *Sowita wina* (*Double blame*). Both of these books launch a new wave of polemical literature in Ukraine and Byelorussia.

Spring 1621 — The deputy of Volynia in the Sejm stands up to defend Orthodoxy on Ukrainian and Byelorussian lands and presents a list of names of clergy and faithful persecuted by the Polish authorities. A letter from the Orthodox Brotherhood in Vilnius listing the names of the new Orthodox hierarchy is read in the Sejm. This official announcement to the King and the Polish government is intended to promote recognition of the new hierarchy by the Poles.

28 April 1621 — The new hierarchy of the Orthodox Church announces its first manifesto, in which it explains the foundation upon which the hierarchy was renewed, protests the persecutions of the Orthodox Church by the Polish authorities and declares its recognition of the Zaporozhian Kozaks as representatives of old Kievan Rus' and as the embodiment of Ukrainian sovereignty and national and cultural traditions. The manifesto states:

> This is a tribe [the Zaporozhian Kozaks] of the glorious people of Rus'. These are the descendants of that army which in the days of [Grand Prince] Oleh, the monarch of Rus', waged war by sea and stormed Constantinople. Their ancestors were christened, together with [Grand Prince] Volodymyr, accepted the Christian faith from the Church of Constantinople, and still today continue to be born, are baptized and live in that faith. They live not as pagans, but as Christians; they have priests, learn to write, know God, and have His laws. When they go to sea, they pray first and announce that it is for their Christian faith that they fight the unbelievers [Tatars and Turks]. As their second aim, they declare setting the captives free... They build, construct, and enrich new churches and monasteries.
>
> [We] preach the same faith as our ancestors. We do not step on anybody's life or property. We do not engage in mistreatment, criminal acts, or violence, nor do we call for war on Christians, nor teach to kill. We are not rebels or mutineers but people destined for martyrdom. Let everyone know that, before taking upon ourselves this holy duty, we crowned ourselves with the crown of martyrdom (Hrushevsky, Vol. VII, pp. 391-393, 456).

Bishop Zakhariya Kopystensky (-1627), Orthodox leader, theologian, archimandrite of the Kiev Monastery of the Caves (1624-27), author of theological works.

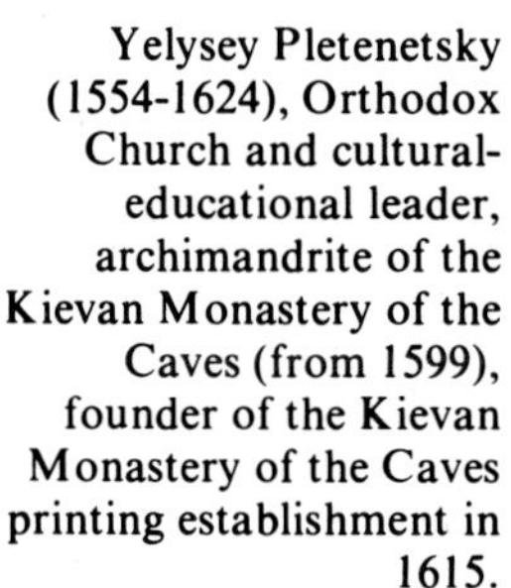

Yelysey Pletenetsky (1554-1624), Orthodox Church and cultural-educational leader, archimandrite of the Kievan Monastery of the Caves (from 1599), founder of the Kievan Monastery of the Caves printing establishment in 1615.

20 May 1621 — The first Synod of the renewed Orthodox hierarchy takes place with many clergy and faithful taking part. A similar Synod takes place later in the year in Zhytomyr.

15-18 June 1621 — The Kozak Council takes place in Sukha Dibrova near Bila Tserkva; present are Metropolitan Yov Boretsky, Bishop Ezekiyil Kurtsevych, 300 priests, 50 monks, and Hetmans Petro Sahaydachny and Yatsko Borodavka.

The Kozaks vow to defend the Orthodox faith to the death, and promise to assist Poland in her war with Turkey, on condition that the King recognize the newly consecrated Orthodox hierarchy, its metropolitan and bishops.

November 1621 — The second Synod of the Orthodox bishops takes place under the title "Council on Piety." The Synod works out and approves 24 rules which are to govern the life of the Church and to provide for the continuity of the hierarchy.

February 1622 — The Kozaks again send their representatives to the King in Warsaw with demands to approve the new Orthodox hierarchy and revoke the Union.

10 April 1622 — Petro Sahaydachny, Hetman of Ukraine dies in Kiev. He was an ardent supporter of Orthodoxy and is also credited with the renewal of the Orthodox hierarchy. He donates all his possessions to churches, monasteries, and Orthodox schools. After

Sahaydachny's death, Metropolitan Yov Boretsky becomes the spiritual leader of the Ukrainian national and religious movement.

December 1622 — Metropolitan Yov Boretsky issues a memorandum to the government, with an addendum from the hierarchy and the Orthodox noblemen, in which the Polish policies towards the Orthodox Church are sharply criticized, charging that these policies are directed toward the denationalization and annihilation of the Ukrainian people, so that "Rus' no longer will be Rus'." He also sharply criticizes the establishment of the Union. At the same time the Kozaks again demand recognition by the King of the Orthodox hierarchy.

At this time Pope Gregory XV sends his Apostolic Nuncio to the Polish Sejm instructing him to defend the Union and the Uniate hierarchy which, due to the political situation, is inconvenient to the Polish government. The Pope appeals to King Sigismund III and the Papal primate in Poland to take under their protection the Uniate Metropolitan Velyamyn Rutsky and the entire Church.

Metropolitan Velyamyn Rutsky prepares a memorandum for the Sejm about the persecutions of Uniates in the Polish Kingdom.

In the Sejm, Polish bishops of the Roman Catholic Church propose to abolish the Union and have all Uniates accept the Latin rite.

1622 — Pope Gregory XV establishes the Congregation for the Propagation of the Faith in Rome. Unsuccessful in obtaining the recognition of the King for the new Orthodox hierarchy and facing new persecutions, a small group of Orthodox clergy decide to seek the support of the Moscow Orthodox Tsar and Orthodox Muscovy. For the first time, a Ukrainian Orthodox bishop, Isaya Kopynsky, sends his representatives to Moscow to ask for the Tsar's help.

January 1623 — Unhappy with the Polish policies of intolerance and persecution of both Churches, Orthodox and Uniate hierarchs, clergy, and noblemen arrive at the Sejm in Warsaw. The King refuses to recognize the new Orthodox hierarchy, believing it to be insubordinate and illegal. The Orthodox demand the annulment of the Union while the Uniates demand safe and free propagation of the Union. Looking for a compromise, the King appoints a mixed commission, headed by the Primate Gembicki, to investigate the religious misunderstandings. Unable to come to an agreement, the Sejm adopts the following resolution on January 23:

> Due to a multitude of issues facing the government, we are postponing the question of appeasing the people of the Greek faith to the next session of the Sejm. Today we promise peace to both sides, to clerical as well as secular individuals of all professions and positions. (Makariy, Vol. XI, p. 301.)

Unable to resolve the religious conflict, the Sejm adopts similar resolutions during its sessions of 1624, 1625, 1626, 1627, 1629 and 1631.

St. Yosafat Kuntsevych (1580-1623), Uniate Archbishop of Polotsk, author of liturgical works. He died a martyr's death in Vitebsk, and was declared a saint of the Catholic Church in 1867.

12 November 1623 — In the struggle between the Orthodox and the Uniates, religious passions and zeal take the upper hand. Agitated residents of Vitebsk in Byelorussia assassinate the Uniate Archbishop of Polotsk, Yosafat Kuntsevych. On the third day after his death his martyred body, is found in the river Dvina. It is eventually taken to Polotsk, Vienna, and after World War II, to the Basilica of St. Peter in Rome. Witnesses described Archbishop Yosafat Kuntsevych's death thus:

> The ringing of cathedral bells and bells of other churches spread. This was the signal and call to insurrection. From all sides of town masses of people — men, women, and children — gathered with stones and attacked the Archbishop's residence. The masses attacked and injured the servants and assistants of the Archbishop, and broke into the room where the Archbishop was alone. One hit him on the head with a stick, another split it with an axe and, when Kuntsevych fell, they started beating him. They looted his house, dragged his body to the plaza, cursed him — even women and children... They dragged him naked through the streets of the city all the way to the hill overlooking the river Dvina. Finally, after tying stones to the dead body, they threw him into the Dvina at its deepest. (Makariy, Vol. XI, p. 307, quotation from Ya. Susha in *Life of Kuntsevych*).

November 1623 — The citizens of Vitebsk are put on trial for the murder of Archbishop Yosafat

Kuntsevych; they are prosecuted by the Grand Chancellor of Lithuania Leo Sapieha.

December 1623 — Fearing persecutions, the Orthodox Archbishop Meletiy Smotrytsky of Polotsk leaves Byelorussia for Kiev, then goes on to visit the Eastern Patriarchs.

30 January 1624 — The Uniate hierarchy meets in Novogrudok. Participants of the Synod appeal to the Pope to canonize Yosafat Kuntsevych.

10 February 1624 — Pope Urban VIII asks that King Sigismund III avenge the death of Yosafat Kuntsevych.

February 1624 — As punishment for the death of Archbishop Yosafat Kuntsevych, two Orthodox churches are destroyed in Vitebsk. At the trial under Sapieha many people are sentenced to death, guilty and innocent alike.

24 August 1624 — Following the martyrdom of Archbishop Yosafat Kuntsevych, persecution of the Orthodox Church spreads with force in Ukraine and Byelorussia. Metropolitan Yov Boretsky sends his emissaries to Krzysztof Radziwill, head of the Lithuanian Protestants, and to the Muscovite Tsar Mikhail Romanov. He asks the Tsar to take the Orthodox Church under his protection.

1624 — The Uniate Metropolitan Velyamyn Rutsky prepares a report to Rome on the status of the Church on Ukrainian and Byelorussian lands. He proposes that a peace be based on the establishment, with the Pope's blessing, of a single Patriarchate with its seat in Kiev. His motto is: "That Rus' not destroy Rus'." With the approval of King Sigismund III, attempts are made to hold a Synod of Uniate and Orthodox representatives concerning the establishment of a patriarchate. The negotiations break down when the Orthodox refuse to acknowledge the Pope's supremacy.

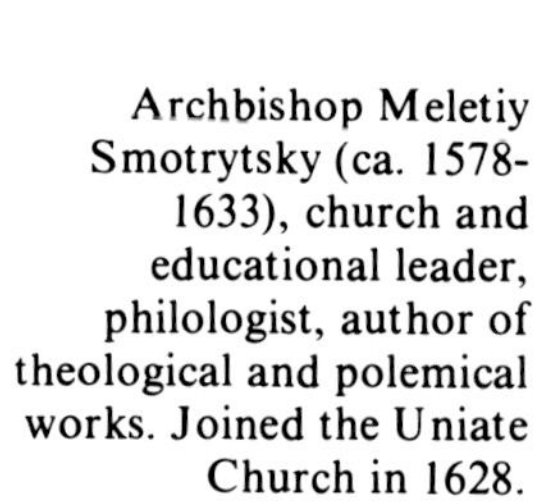

Archbishop Meletiy Smotrytsky (ca. 1578-1633), church and educational leader, philologist, author of theological and polemical works. Joined the Uniate Church in 1628.

Archbishop Meletiy Smotrytsky visits the Patriarchs Cyril I Lucaris of Constantinople and Theophanes of Jerusalem. He familiarizes himself with the theological works of both Patriarchs, and notices a great decline of Orthodoxy and the rise of Roman Catholicism. Upon closer study, he becomes disillusioned with both Patriarchs.

January 1625 — Metropolitan Yov Boretsky takes an active part in the coalition to fight the Turks and to

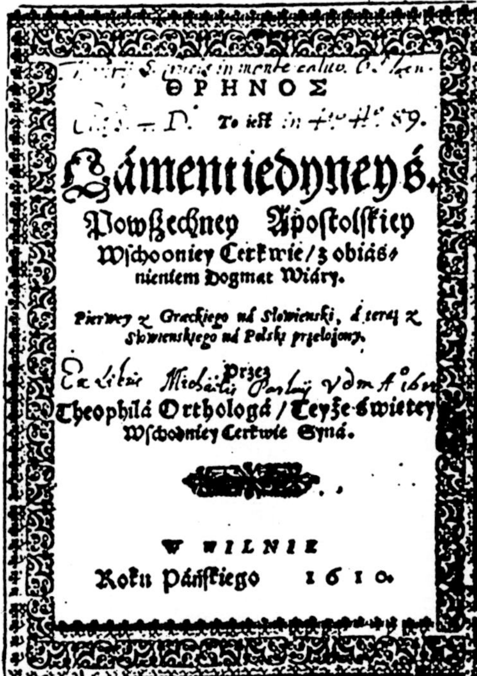

Homilary Gospel (Yevanheliye Uchytelnoye) by Meletiy Smotrytsky, Kiev, 1616 (left).

Threnos, that is the Lament of the One Holy Universal Apostolic Eastern Church (Threnos, to jest Lament jedynej S. Powszechnej Apostolskiey Wschodniej Cerkwie), by Meletiy Smotrytsky, Vilnius, 1610.

The Dormition, by Tymofiy Petrovych. From the book *Discourses of St. John Chrysostom,* Kiev, 1623 (left).

Discourses of St. John Chrysostom (*Besidy Ioanna Zolotoustoho*). Published in 1623 at the Kievan Monastery of the Caves.

renew the Orthodox Church on the lands of the former Byzantine Empire.

20-21 January 1625 — The Poles organize an attack on the Orthodox in Kiev, forcibly taking away and closing their churches. Responding to the appeals of Metropolitan Yov Boretsky, several thousand Kozaks arrive in Kiev. During the disturbances, the Uniate vicar of the Church of St. Basil, Ivan Khodyka, and the magistrate of Kiev, Fedir Khodyka, are killed.

7 February 1625 — To pacify the Orthodox after the fierce repressions, the King confirms a well-known leader, Zakhariya Kopystensky, as Archimandrite of the Kievan Monastery of the Caves.

March 1625 — At the request of Metropolitan Velyamyn Rutsky, Pope Urban VIII grants the Uniate Church the right to hold Synods every four years.

10 December 1625 — Metropolitan Velyamyn Rutsky appoints Rev. Mykola Novak as the first Ukrainian representative of the Kievan Uniate Metropolitanate at the Apostolic See.

December 1625 — Disappointed with the activities of the Eastern Patriarchs, Archbishop Meletiy Smotrytsky returns to Kiev bringing with him the decree issued by the Patriarch of Constantinople, Cyril I Lucaris, regarding subordination of stauropegial brotherhoods and monasteries to the bishops; this angers both brotherhoods and monasteries.

1625 — The continuous struggle between the Orthodox and the Uniates keeps both Churches in turmoil. The Orthodox Church, even though under the protection of the Zaporozhian Kozaks, continues to exist in semi-legal status, with the hierarchy not recognized by the King and in violation of Polish laws. Faced with this difficult situation, Bishop Ezykiyil Kurtsevych of Volodymyr-Volynsky, flees to Moscow, where the Moscow Patriarch appoints him Archbishop of Suzdal. Without protection, the Uniate Church is also on the decline. Finding themselves in a hopeless situation, some Orthodox and Uniate nobles accept Roman Catholicism. The Polish Catholic government rewards them with a whole range of privileges. The nobles are denationalized, becoming Polish. Faced with this critical situation, most moderate leaders of both Churches try to find a way of compromise and reconciliation.

September 1626 — The first Uniate Synod of bishops and clergy since the Sobor of Berestya is held in Kobryn. The following are present: Metropolitan Velyamyn Rutsky and the Bishops of Volodymyr-Volynsky, Lutsk, Polotsk, Smolensk, and Pinsk. Fearing the Tatars, the Bishop of Peremyshl does not participate. The Pope is represented by the Roman Catholic Bishop of Vilnius. The Orthodox bishops, though invited, do not attend the Synod. The Synod takes up issues such as a seminary for the Uniate clergy, the retention of old rites (church customs), the convening of Synods every four years, the marital status of the clergy, and many other current problems. At the Synod the Archimandrite Raphael Korsak of Vilnius is consecrated as Bishop of Lviv. The acts of the Synod are approved by the Apostolic See three years later on December 6, 1629.

December 1626 — The most renowned scholar, theologian, and writer of the time, Meletiy Smotrytsky, secretly joins the Uniate Church.

1626 — Metropolitan Velyamyn Rutsky establishes the first Uniate seminary in Minsk. At that time, Uniate schools existed in three cities: Volodymyr-Volynsky, Kholm, and Novogrudok. Father Mykola Novak becomes the first pastor of the Church of St. Lawrence, the seat of the Uniates in Rome.

January 1627 — After two years of negotiations to reconcile the Uniates and the Orthodox, including consideration of the establishment of a single Patriarchate, the Apostolic See decides that such a Patriarchate can exist only after the Orthodox have recognized the authority of the Pope.

1627 — Petro Mohyla, a voevoda and magnate from Moldavia, is elected Archimandrite of the Kievan Monastery of the Caves. Soon after, he establishes an Orthodox College at the monastery.

3 September 1627 — A Synod of Orthodox bishops and clergy takes place in Kiev with the participation of Metropolitan Yov Boretsky, Archbishop Meletiy Smotrytsky, Archimandrite Petro Mohyla, and others. The Synod, acknowledging the weakened state of both faiths resulting from the struggle, adopts a conciliatory tone and a tolerant attitude towards the Uniates.

20 November 1627 — The Orthodox and Uniate delegates in the Sejm achieve an understanding and agree to a peaceful coexistence.

March 1628 — Public testimony is held in Polotsk and Vitebsk, where eyewitness accounts of the life and martyr's death of Archbishop Yosafat Kuntsevych are taken under oath.

April 1628 — A Synod of Orthodox bishops takes place in Horodok near Rovno in Volynia. The participants are Metropolitan Yov Boretsky, Archbishop Meletiy Smotrytsky, who secretly supports the Union, Bishops Isakiy Boryskovych and Payisiy Ipolytovych, Archimandrite Petro Mohyla, and others. After listening to lectures by Meletiy Smotrytsky, the participants of the Synod conclude that the differences between the two Churches are minor and that they originate from prejudices and not substantive issues. The Synod works on a plan to "unite Rus' with Rus'," the Uniates with the Orthodox.

August 1628 — The most polemical work of the time, the *Apologia* by Meletiy Smotrytsky, appears in Lviv. From the position of an Orthodox theologian, the author criticizes the Orthodox Church and examines her hopeless situation. To escape their tragic predicament, he proposes that the Orthodox accept the Union.

13 August 1628 — A Synod of Orthodox bishops is held in Kiev. Present are Metropolitan Yov Boretsky, seven bishops, archimandrites, hegumens, and many clergy. The most pressing issue is the examination of the *Apologia* of Smotrytsky. On August 15 public denunciation of the *Apologia* takes place, anathema is declared on it, and the book is publicly burned. The participants of the Synod issue a decree proclaiming their unshaken loyalty to the Orthodox faith.

8 December 1628 — Archbishop Meletiy Smotrytsky leaves Kiev for the Dermansky Monastery in Volynia, where he issues his *Protestation* against the Orthodox Synod in Kiev claiming that he renounced the *Apologia* under duress. Shortly thereafter, he openly joins the Uniate Church and proposes the establishment of a Ukrainian-Byelorussian Patriarchate. Concerning the Patriarchate, Smotrytsky writes in his *Protestation:*

> What harm could come to you, Oh Rus', if you were to rid yourself of the protection of the Patriarch of Constantinople? Muscovy has totally repudiated him; Moldavia and Wallachia no longer accept from him their archbishops' consecrations, nor do the archbishops of Cyprus or Armenia, nor the Serbs, nor the Croatians; the Ochridians no longer listen to the Patriarch of Byzantium; they themselves govern their Churches. And what ill effect

St. Onuphrius' Church in the city of Husyatyn (Ternopil oblast), built in the late 16th century in the fortress-church style of the Podilia school of architecture (left).

Church of the Protection of the Blessed Virgin Mary in Lutsk (Volynia oblast), built in 1583 and restored in 1637 and 1873-76.

does it have on them? Yet Rus' did not wish to accept the ordinations of the schismatic leader Michael Cerularius in 1051 for her Metropolitan Ilarion. In 1146 Klym [Smolyatych] and in 1417 Hryhoriy Tsamblak were consecrated as bishops, and Hryhoriy, the monk of Constantinople, was ordained by the Roman Pope Pius II. And what harm was done? The same would happen if Rus' were to establish a separate archbishopric or patriarchate. (Velyky, Vol. V, p. 41.)

February 1629 — The Uniate and Orthodox deputies in the Polish Sejm agree to call a Uniate-Orthodox Synod to settle their religious differences, to be preceded by separate synods of both Churches.

28 February 1629 — King Sigismund III calls for a joint Synod of Uniates and Orthodox to be held on October 28 in Lviv. Shortly thereafter, Metropolitan Yov Boretsky issues a proclamation calling for participation of the Orthodox in the Synod "to reconcile religious affairs"; strong opposition comes from some Orthodox and Protestant nobility.

July 1629 — The Uniate Synod takes place in Volodymyr-Volynsky to discuss the unification of both Churches. The Metropolitan, four bishops, and their deputies participate. The Synod proposes Petro Mohyla as candidate for the first Patriarch of Ukraine and Byelorussia.

29 July 1629 — The Orthodox Synod concerning unification of both Churches takes place in Kiev. Participating are the Metropolitan, bishops, the Kievan voevoda Adam Kysil, representatives of the Zaporozhian Kozaks and nearly 500 priests. The Synod discusses the idea of unification of the Churches with a Patriarch at their head, united with the Ecumenical Patriarch, who in his turn was to recognize the supremacy of the Pope. Metropolitan Yov Boretsky, Petro Mohyla, and a large group of participants declare their willingness to participate in a joint Synod in Lviv; strong opposition to such an idea is expressed by the representatives of the Zaporozhian Kozaks and by part of the clergy. The majority votes not to participate in the Synod.

September 1629 — The Apostolic See forbids the Uniate hierarchy to participate in a Synod with the Orthodox in Lviv. The Uniate Metropolitan and bishops arrive defiantly in Lviv to take part in the joint Synod, but the Orthodox hierarchy is absent. Notwithstanding the wishes of the Orthodox as well as the Uniate hierarchies, all measures on religious compromise come to naught as a result of the Apostolic See's interdiction on one side and the strong opposition from the Zaporozhian Kozaks on the other.

1630 — Mykola Dyletsky, a composer of religious choir music and the author of the theoretical works *Muzychna hramatyka* (1677) and *Muzyka* (1681) is born; he dies in 1690.

Winter 1630 — Metropolitan Velyamyn Rutsky visits towns in Volynia and also Kiev. In the town of Stepaniv an attempt is made on his life.

Petro Mohyla (1596-1647), Metropolitan of Kiev (1633-47), Archimandrite of the Kievan Monastery of the Caves (from 1627), prominent Ukrainian church, political, cultural and educational leader, author of many theological works, founder of the Kiev Mohyla College (1632).

1630s — The Polish army enters eastern Ukraine in great numbers and begins a reign of terror against the Orthodox. The main defenders of Orthodoxy are the Zaporozhian Kozaks, who issue a proclamation to the populace calling it to a holy war with Catholic Poland.

12 March 1631 — One of the most renowned leaders of the Ukrainian Orthodox Church, Metropolitan Yov Boretsky, dies in Kiev.

June 1631 — The Orthodox bishops and clergy elect the Bishop of Peremyshl and founder of monasteries in Lubny, Isaya Kopynsky, as the new Metropolitan. In the autumn of the same year, Patriarch Cyril I confirms the election.

15 June 1631 — The Archimandrite of the Kievan Monastery of the Caves, Petro Mohyla, issues in Lviv a declaration concerning the spreading of education and the opening of new Orthodox schools.

1631 — At the request of the Uniate hierarchy, Pope Urban VIII issues a decree unifying all monasteries and monastics under one Basilian Order to be headed by a protoarchimandrite.

March 1632 — After an interval of several years, the Zaporozhian Kozaks address the Sejm with a renewed demand to confirm the Orthodox hierarchy.

20 April 1632 — Poland's King Sigismund III dies. During his reign the Ukrainian-Byelorussian Church became divided into Uniate and Orthodox.

Spring 1632 — In the regional sejms in Volynia, Bratslav and Kiev, issues concerning the legalization of the Orthodox Church including the confirmation by the King of her hierarchy, are brought up. The Kozak council in Pryluky adopts a resolution demanding that the Sejm annul the Union.

June 1632 — A long debate takes place in the Sejm regarding the coexistence of the two Churches. The Uniates are represented by Metropolitan Velyamyn Rutsky and the Orthodox by the deputy of Bratslav, Mykhaylo Kropyvnytsky.

September-October 1632 — During the Sejm session devoted to the election of a new King, the Muscovite army attacks Poland. The Sejm and the candidate to the throne Wladyslaw IV change their policy towards the Orthodox Church, hoping that the defenders of Orthodoxy, the Ukrainian Kozaks, will join their side. Reacting to the strong demands of the Orthodox deputies Lavrentiy Drevynsky of Volynia and the Kievan voevoda Adam Kysil, the nominated King and the Sejm are compelled to agree to almost all their demands.

30 October 1632 — After long debates and negotiations, the Sejm adopts articles granting rights and privileges to the Orthodox Church similar to those enjoyed by the Uniates in the Polish Kingdom. According to the new law, the Metropolitan and bishops will be elected by the Orthodox clergy and nobility, confirmed by the King and blessed by the Patriarch of Constantinople. Many churches and monasteries will be returned to the Orthodox Church, including the historic cathedral of St. Sophia in Kiev, which King Sigismund III had turned over to the Uniate Metropolitan. At the same time, to the detriment of the Uniate Church, much of her property is confiscated.

The new law legalizes the Orthodox Church and its renewed hierarchy for the first time since the Sobor of Berestya in 1596, without recognizing the previous hierarchy established by the Patriarch of Jerusalem Theophanes in 1620. Ignoring the protests of the Uniate hierarchs and of the Pope's legate, the King-candidate approves the new law on November 1. A week later, the Roman Catholic hierarchy and some deputies in the Sejm launch a strong protest.

3 November 1632 — In accordance with the new law, the Orthodox clergy and noblemen present at the session of the Sejm in Warsaw elect two candidates for Metropolitan, Archimandrite Petro Mohyla of the Kievan Monastery of the Caves and Mykhaylo Lozka, the vice-governor of Vinnytsya. Even before his election to the throne on November 10, Wladyslaw IV confirms Petro Mohyla as Metropolitan of Kiev, Galicia and All Rus', and on November 12 the King sends emissaries to the Patriarch asking him to bestow his blessings on Mohyla. On November 15 Yosyf Bobrykovych is nominated Bishop of Mstyslav in Byelorussia, and Oleksander Puzyna is nominated Bishop of Lutsk.

1632 — The Kievan Brotherhood School, established in 1615, and the Lavra School of the Kievan Monastery of the Caves, established by Petro Mohyla in 1631, are united into the Kiev Mohyla College. The first rector of the College is a doctor of theology, Isaya Kozlovsky (1632-1638), and the prefect is Sylvester Kosiv. The Kiev Mohyla College becomes the religious center for the entire Orthodox world of Ukraine, Byelorussia, Poland, Lithuania, and later Muscovy.

The new law regarding religious affairs and the legalization of the Orthodox Church brings uncertainty into the Uniate Church. In some Uniate circles, rumors about a nullification of the Union are spread. The Roman Catholic Church refuses to reconcile itself to separate Uniate Church rites or to a Uniate Church as a second Catholic Church in the Polish Kingdom. Metropolitan Velyamyn Rutsky sends his emissary, Raphael Korsak, to Rome with an appeal to Pope Urban VIII asking him to intercede on behalf of the Uniate Church.

The Kiev Mohyla Academy, 18th-century engraving (left).

"The Printing Establishment of the Kievan Monastery of the Caves", engraving of 1758.

1 January 1633 — Pope Urban VIII appeals to King Wladyslaw IV and to other Catholic dignitaries in Poland to repeal the law on religious affairs, or at least not to enforce it.

12 March 1633 — In a special decree Wladyslaw IV transfers the entire Kievan Metropolitanate to Petro Mohyla.

15 March 1633 — King Wladyslaw signs all laws pertaining to religious affairs, issues decrees to the newly elected bishops and, against the wishes of the Metropolitan, nominates Ivan Popil as Bishop of Peremyshl, giving him three monasteries. At the same time, the King issues a certificate to all Orthodox faithful in his kingdom, in which he states:

> We confirm to the Orthodox, in accordance with ancient rights and constitutions, the freedom to celebrate Divine Services in all cities, towns, and monasteries of the Kingdom and in the Great Principality of Lithuania. Also all brotherhoods, schools, seminaries, typographical institutions, and hospitals are to be under Orthodox administrations. We restore all privileges they had from our predecessors and from the King of blessed memory, our father. (Makariy, Vol. XI, p. 451.)

28 April 1633 — In a solemn ceremony at the Brotherhood Church in Lviv, Petro Mohyla is consecrated as Metropolitan of Kiev, Galicia, and All Rus'. The act of consecration is performed by Bishop Yeremiya Tysarovsky, Bishop of Lviv and patriarchal exarch in Ukraine and Byelorussia, together with Bishop Isaakiy Boryskovych of Lutsk, and Bishop Paisiy Ipolytovych of Kholm, Bishop Avraamiy of Turov and Pinsk, with many archimandrites, hegumens, clergy, noblemen, and faithful present. The Patriarch's blessing arrives in the same month.

7 July 1633 — Metropolitan Petro Mohyla returns in great triumph to Kiev, where he is met by many thousands of faithful and hundreds of clergy.

The Gift of Petro Mohyla, fresco from a Church of the Kievan Monastery of the Caves (1643).

12 July 1633 — Metropolitan Petro Mohyla takes over the cathedral of St. Sophia from the Uniate Metropolitan Raphael Korsak. Petro Mohyla also takes over the churches of St. Simeon, St. Nicholas and St. Basil.

Summer 1633 — Metropolitan Isaiya Kopynsky, elected in 1631, renounces his position and becomes hegumen of the St. Michael Golden-domed Monastery. Later he is appointed Archbishop of Novhorod-Siversky and Zadniprovia.

1633 — According to the new religious laws, a whole series of churches and monasteries on Ukrainian and Byelorussian lands are transferred from Uniate to Orthodox.

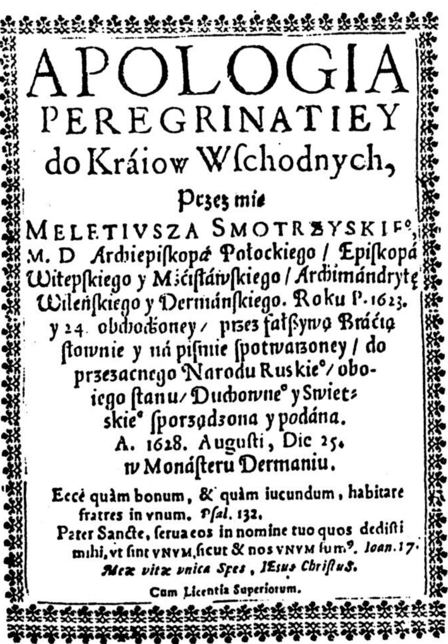

APOLOGIA
PEREGRINATIEY
do Kráiow Wschodnych,
Przez mię
MELETIVSZA SMOTRZYSKIEº,
M. D Archiepiskopá Połockiego / Episkopá
Witepskiego y Mścisłáwskiego / Archimándrytę
Wileńskiego y Dermáńskiego. Roku P. 1623.
y 24. obchodzoney / przez fałszywą Bráciq
słownie y ná pismie spotwarzoney / do
przezacnego Narodu Ruskieº / obo-
iego stanu / Duchowneº y Swiet-
skieº sporządzona y podána.
A. 1628. Augusti, Die 25.
w Monásteru Dermaniu.
Ecce quàm bonum, & quàm iucundum, habitare
fratres in vnum. Psal. 132.
Pater Sancte, serua eos in nomine tuo quos dedisti
mihi, vt sint VNVM, sicut & nos VNVM sum⁹. Ioan. 17.
Meæ vitæ vnica Spes, IEsus ChristuS.
Cum Licentia Superiorum.

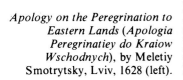

Apology on the Peregrination to Eastern Lands (*Apologia Peregrinatiey do Kraiow Wschodnych*), by Meletiy Smotrytsky, Lviv, 1628 (left).

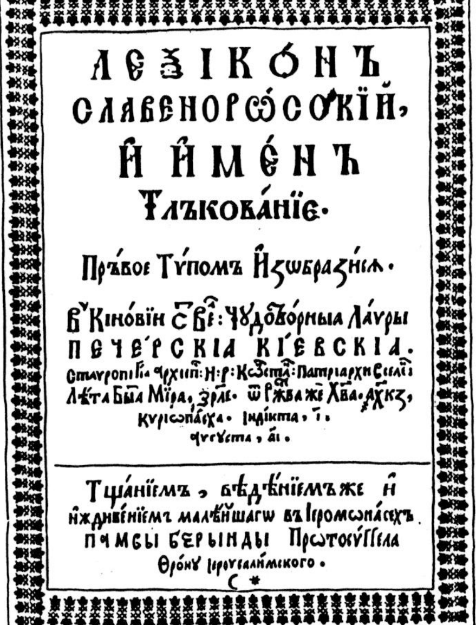

ЛЕѮІКОНЪ
СЛАВЕНОРωССКІЙ,
И ИМЕНЪ
ТЛЪКОВАНІЕ.
Прьвое Тυпомъ Изωбраженіа.
В Кіновіи С҃тыѧ: Чудотворныа Лаvры
ПЕЧЕРСКІА КІЕВСКІА.
Тщаніемъ, вѣдѣніемъ же и
иждивеніемъ малѣйшагω въ Іеромонасєхъ
Памвы Берынды Прωтосvггела
Θрόнꙋ Іерꙋсалимского.

The Lexicon of the Slavonic-Rus' Language and Explanation of Names (*Leksykon Slovenorosky i imen tolkovaniye*) by Pamvo Berynda, 1627, published at the Kievan Monastery of the Caves.

The Kievan Monastery of the Caves: Holy Trinity Church Above-the-Gate, the Dormition Cathedral and the wooden belfry. Engraving of 1677.

1633 — Bishop Raphael Korsak becomes the representative of the Kievan Metropolitanate at the Apostolic See.

Autumn 1634 — King Wladyslaw IV directs Metropolitan Petro Mohyla to close the Roman Catholic press in Kiev and the Roman Catholic schools in Kiev and Vinnytsia, and to allow only the existence of Ukrainian schools in these cities.

14 March 1635 — Protests of the Uniate hierarchy and laymen in the Sejm force the King to issue two circulars in which he guarantees them rights and privileges equal to those of the Orthodox. In a circular of March 14 the King writes:

> We witness in our benevolent disposition to those people who find themselves in union with the Roman Church, we reserve to them the Metropolitanate and estates, which belong to her in perpetuity; to the Uniates are to belong forever the Archbishopric of Polotsk, the Bishoprics of Volodymyr-Volynsky, Pinsk, Kholm and Smolensk with monasteries, churches, and their land holdings. In Vitebsk, Polotsk, and Novogrudok non-Uniates are never to establish any churches. We take upon ourselves and our successors the responsibility that those bishoprics, archimandries, and hegumenates will not be given to anyone, except well-deserving monks of the Order of St. Basil, who will be selected from those proposed to us and our successors by the current Uniate Metropolitan and his successors. (Makariy, Vol. XI, p. 476.)

On the same day the King issues a circular to the Orthodox hierarchy, transferring to them the Vydubytsky Monastery in Kiev, and forbidding any opening of Uniate churches. The King allows the teaching of Latin and Greek in the Orthodox schools of Kiev and Vilnius but forbids the teaching of philosophy and theology.

1 June 1635 — Two commissions composed of equal numbers of Uniates and Orthodox begin to divide churches and monasteries, prorating them according to the number of faithful.

1635 — Metropolitan Petro Mohyla begins to rebuild the churches and monasteries in Kiev that fell into ruin and dilapidation in the last centuries and decades. During the reconstruction of the Church of the Tithes, the relics of St. Volodymyr the Great are discovered and moved in solemn ceremony to the Cathedral of St. Sophia.

Through the efforts of Metropolitan Petro Mohyla the Polish-language *Kievan Patericon* about the saints of the Ukrainian Church appears in a new edition by Sylvester Kosiv. In 1638 Atanasiy Kalnofoysky's work *Teratourgema,* a book of stories about the miracles and events that have taken place in the Kievan Caves Monastery is published.

June 1636 — All the Uniate bishops, archimandrites, hegumens and representatives of monasteries assemble in Vilnius. The Synod, under the leadership of Metropolitan Velyamyn Rutsky, works out rules to normalize the life of monks in the Uniate Church.

5 September 1636 — King Wladyslaw IV addresses the Orthodox and Uniate hierarchs in regard to establishing a Patriarchate in the Polish Kingdom. He writes:

> The animosity in Rus' between those in the Union and those outside it brings much disagreement to the Polish land. We know that the most important question between you and them [the Uniates] is your obedience to the Patriarch of Constantinople. But if you consider what has happened with that patriarchal throne and what is happening today, you can easily understand that without breaking any patriarchal rules, you could follow the example of Muscovy and other states to have at home that which you are seeking elsewhere. Do a good deed to God, a useful one to Poland, and a needed one for the people of Rus'. (Hrushevsky, Vol. VIII, p. 105; Makariy, Vol. XI, p. 481.)

The King negotiates with both sides proposing a joint patriarchate, independent of Constantinople, but acknowledging the Pope's superiority in the affairs of the Church. The King proposes Metropolitan Petro Mohyla as the first Patriarch. The King's project is met with great oppostion from the Congregation for the Propagation of the Faith in Rome.

1637 — Metropolitan Petro Mohyla solemnly consecrates the main altar of the restored Cathedral of St. Sophia in Kiev, placing a silver ark with saints' relics on it.

5 February 1637 — In the Dermansky Monastery in Volynia, the Uniate Metropolitan Velyamyn Rutsky dies. He is called the "Atlas of Unity" for his advocacy of unification of the Churches. At the request of the Uniate hierarchs, King Wladyslaw IV confirms the Bishop of Lviv and Halych, Raphael Korsak, as the new Metropolitan.

Spring 1637 — Believing false rumors about a union with the Catholics, spread especially by Muscovy, a group of Orthodox monks and nuns from the monasteries of Hustyn and Ladyn leave for Muscovy with the approval of Tsar Mikhail Romanov. These were the first emigrants from Ukraine that settled in the distant monasteries in Muscovy.

July 1638 — The Congregation for the Propagation of the Faith in Rome forbids the Uniate Metropolitan Raphael Korsak to participate in a joint Synod with the Orthodox, approved by the King, to discuss the establishment of a Patriarchate. At the same time the Pope and the Congregation send letters to Metropolitan Petro Mohyla and the Orthodox voevoda of Kiev Adam Kysil attempting to persuade them to join the Uniate Church.

12 May 1639 — The Apostolic See transfers in perpetuity the Church of SS. Sergius and Bacchus with its adjoining buildings to the Uniate Church.

1639 — Metropolitan Petro Mohyla transfers the Orthodox college from Vinnytsa to the town of Hosha in Volynia. He appoints Ihnatiy Starushych as its first rector.

28 August 1640 — The Uniate Metropolitan Raphael Korsak dies in Rome and is buried in the Church of SS. Sergius and Bacchus.

8-18 September 1640 — The first Synod of the new Orthodox bishops, established in accordance with the laws of 1632, takes place in Kiev. Taking part in the Synod are Metropolitan Petro Mohyla, the former Bishop Isakiy Boryskovych of Lutsk, the former Bishop Avraamiy of Pinsk, hegumens, and Orthodox theologians. The Synod examines Church rites and customs and the normalization of life in the Church. The most important question that the Synod takes up is a new catechism. In planning the new catechism, Metropolitan Petro Mohyla attempts to return to the Ecumenical Orthodox Church its primary meaning and importance, before it found itself in crisis. The new catechism entitled *The Orthodox Confession of Faith* is written by a group of theologians headed by Isaya Kozlovsky, hegumen of the Monastery of St. Nicholas in Kiev. This catechism is later approved by four Eastern Patriarchs, thus making it an important contribution to the Ecumenical Orthodox Church.

October 1640 — The former Metropolitan Isaya Kopynsky dies in Kiev.

Raphael Korsak (ca. 1600-1640), Uniate Metropolitan of Kiev (1637-45).

Holy Trinity Church of the Basilian monastery in Nesterov (Lviv oblast), built in 1612. The interior was painted by Y. Butsmanyuk in the early 20th century (left).

Brotherhood Church of the Elevation of the Cross in Lutsk (Volynia oblast), built in 1619-22.

1640 — Bishop Vasyl Tarasovych of Mukachiv (Transcarpathia) accepts Catholicism of the Eastern rite in Vienna, but shortly thereafter returns to Orthodoxy.

After a relative calm on the religious front, Jesuits and Dominicans again begin aggressively to convert the populace to Roman Catholicism. The Jesuits open their first college in Kiev, and the Dominicans build the monastery of St. Nicholas.

1640-1646 — Religious struggles continue in Ukraine and Byelorussia often leading to violence and bloodshed. The struggle centers around the taking over of churches and monasteries.

March 1641 — Pope Urban VIII appoints Archbishop Antin Selyava of Polotsk as the new Uniate Metropolitan.

3 November 1643 — Pope Urban VIII writes to Metropolitan Petro Mohyla to persuade him to join the Union. The same month he sends 22 letters to the King, to the Orthodox bishops and to highly placed government officials, in which he discusses propagation of the Union in the Polish-Lithuanian Kingdom.

1643 — A Council of the Roman Catholic clergy in the diocese of Kholm demands the annulment of the rights and privileges enjoyed by the Uniate bishops and clergy.

12 November 1644 — In Rome, in a solemn ceremony with the participation of Cardinal Antonio Barberini, Archbishop Yosafat Kuntsevych is pronounced "Blessed." Similar ceremonies are held in Polotsk with Metropolitan Antin Selyava and in Vilnius in the presence of King Wladyslaw IV.

1644 — An anonymous, extensive work on reconciliation and unification of the Orthodox and Uniate Churches appears in Ukraine. It is ascribed to Metropolitan Petro Mohyla. On March 16, 1645 the Congregation for the Propagation of the Faith secretly accepts his project; for its realization, they hand it over to the Papal Nuncio in Poland, Jan Torres. The death of Metropolitan Petro Mohyla and the uprising of Bohdan Khmelnytsky in 1648 put an end to these attempts.

Metropolitan Antin Selyava sends a message to the Congregation for the Propagation of the Faith protesting new persecutions of the Uniate Church by the Polish Catholic bishops.

The great polemical work *Lithos,* written by Metropolitan Petro Mohyla's colleagues, is published in Kiev. The work focuses on the character of Orthodox rites and is used as a liturgical work. In 1646 a *Trebnyk,* a third work written by Metropolitan Petro Mohyla's colleagues, is published; it is the most complete liturgical work in the entire history of the Ukrainian Orthodox Church.

1645 — A condensed version of the catechism *The Orthodox Confession of Faith* appears in Kiev, first in Polish and later in Old Ukrainian. This edition is reissued in Lviv in 1646, and in Moscow in 1649, in Old Church Slavonic.

24 April 1646 — A Synod of the Orthodox clergy with 63 priests is held in Uzhhorod, Transcarpathia. All the participants join the Union at the initiative of Father Parteniy Petrovych, a monk of the Order of St. Basil. The Apostolic See orders the new Uniate Eparchy of Mukachiv to subordinate itself to the Roman Catholic bishop of Eger in Hungary.

1 January 1647 — Petro Mohyla, the greatest Metropolitan of the Ukrainian Orthodox Church, dies in Kiev. He was highly regarded as a theologian, scholar, author of many works, organizer of the renewed

Holy Trinity Church of the Holy Trinity Monastery in Korets, built in 1620.

The Church of the Nativity of Jesus in Ternopil, built in 1602-08 by Leontiy. Rebuilt many times. It is one of the better examples of stone church architecture of the Podilia school.

Coat of arms of Metropolitan Petro Mohyla, by Illya, 1646. From the Great Missal (left).

Engraving from a panegyric in honor of Metropolitan Petro Mohyla, *Helicon or the Orchard of First Knowledge* (*Helikon, to yest sad umiyetnosty Pervyj*), printed at the Kievan Monastery of the Caves, 1632.

Ukrainian Orthodox Church, and preeminent organizer of schools. In his will, Metropolitan Petro Mohyla wrote:

> As soon as God saw fit to make me the Archbishop of the Kievan Metropolitanate and before that the archimandrite of the Kievan Monastery of the Caves, noting that the decline of faith and mercy in the Rus' people were the results of a total lack of education and schools, I gave my word to God, that all my wordly possessions I would donate to rebuild God's ruined sanctuaries, which were left in wretched ruin, to establish schools in Kiev, and to consolidate the rights and liberties of the people of Rus'. (Makariy, Vol. XI. p. 612.)

25 February 1647 — A Synod of bishops and clergy in Kiev elects Bishop Sylvester Kosiv of Mstyslavl and Byelorussia, rector of the Kiev Mohyla College, as the new Metropolitan.

7 December 1647 — Bohdan Khmelnytsky, captain of a Kozak regiment in Chyhyryn, flees to Zaporizhzhya. There he starts an insurrection against Poland. His motto becomes "struggle for freedom and the Orthodox Faith."

May 1648 — Led by Hetman Bohdan Khmelnytsky, an insurrection against Poland erupts on the lands of Ukraine. This insurrection forever changes the political and religious status of Eastern Europe, especially Ukraine. On the arena appear the Zaporozhian Kozaks, who influence political, social, national, and religious life.

Autumn 1648 — The Orthodox deputies of Kiev and Volynia in the Sejm demand the annulment of the Union but agree to the existence of the Roman Catholic religion on Ukrainian territory.

5 September 1648 — Hegumen Atanasiy Fylypovych (Beresteysky) of the St. Simeon Monastery dies a martyr's death, at Polish hands, in Berestya. On August 20, 1666, he is proclaimed a saint of the Orthodox Church.

September 1648 — Patriarch Paisius of Jerusalem arrives in Ukraine accompanied by Syluyan Muzhylovsky, Hetman Khmelnytsky's representative; a month later, he comes to Kiev.

23 December 1648 — After winning several battles against Poland, Hetman Khmelnytsky enters Kiev in triumph. He is met by thousands of residents and is received by Patriarch Paisius and Metropolitan Sylvester Kosiv. The Patriarch celebrates the liturgy with the Hetman and his commanders in attendance. During the many meetings with the Hetman, the Patriarch advances the idea of establishing a State of Rus'-Ukraine in close unity with the hospodars of Wallachia and the Tsars of Muscovy. The Patriarch proposes that Khmelnytsky recognize the authority of the Tsar of Muscovy in the name of the unification of the entire Orthodox world and the liberation of Christ's Tomb in Jerusalem.

January 1649 — After his victory over Poland, Hetman Khmelnytsky puts a set of demands to the Polish government, the first being religious. Khmelnytsky demands annulment of the Union, and a seat in the Polish Senate for the Metropolitan, and agrees to the existence of the Polish Roman Catholic Church in Ukraine.

14 May 1649 — Tsar Aleksey Mikhailovich asks Metropolitan Sylvester Kosiv to send him scholars, theologians, and teachers, which Moscow lacks. The Metropolitan sends to Moscow the first Ukrainian scholars, experts in Latin and Greek: Arseniy Satanovsky, Teodosiy Safonovych and Epifaniy Slavenytsky, and nearly 30 learned monks. A special monastery is built in Moscow to house them. There they translate the Bible into Old Church Slavonic and teach grammar, rhetoric, and philosophy to the children of eminent boyars. Some boyars see heresy in education, and oppose the spreading of learning by these Ukrainian scholars.

18 August 1649 — Hetman Khmelnytsky wins a battle near Zboriv, but the Tatars' betrayal forces him to sign the Treaty of Zboriv. Thirteen of the eighteen points deal with religion. After the negotiations, the King issues the "Zboriv Manifesto," in which only four points deal with religious matters: the annulment of the Union is to be decided at the next session of the Sejm and after negotiations with the Metropolitan; in the provinces of Kiev, Bratslav, and Chernihiv the King will appoint only nobles of the Orthodox faith to various positions; the Polish Jesuit schools and other institutions in Kiev and other cities on Ukrainian and Byelorussian territories are to be closed; only Orthodox institutions are to exist in those cities.

December 1649 — After meeting with Metropolitan Sylvester Kosiv and the Kiev voevoda Adam Kysil, Hetman Khmelnytsky decides not to ask for annulment of the Union at the next session of the Sejm in Warsaw but to demand the return to the Orthodox Church of all her properties taken over by the Uniate Church.

1649 — Patriarch Paisius of Jerusalem arrives in Moscow accompanied by Hetman Khmelnytsky's representative. There, in the name of the Orthodox Faith, he negotiates with the Tsar for the freeing of the Orthodox in Poland, and asks the Tsar to take Ukraine under his protection.

January 1650 — Bishops of the Orthodox and Uniate Churches arrive in Warsaw for the session of the Sejm. Among those arriving are Metropolitan Sylvester Kosiv, the representative of the ailing Uniate Metropolitan, Bishop Pakhomiy Oransky of Pinsk, many bishops, heads of monasteries and a delegation from Hetman Khmelnytsky. The main business in the Sejm is discussion of religious matters. On January 12, the Sejm ratifies the Zboriv Treaty, adopts the new amendments to the constitution on the division of churches and monasteries, and postpones the questions of annulment of the Union and a seat in the Senate for the Orthodox Metropolitan to the next session. On February 12, King Jan Casimir orders the transfer of additional churches and properties in the city of Lviv to the Orthodox, but cancels the order after Khmelnytsky loses the battle of Berestechko.

December 1650 — The Corinthian Metropolitan Joasaph becomes the chaplain and intimate counselor of Khmelnytsky. He dies in the Battle of Berestechko on June 20, 1651.

1650 — Patriarch Parthenius II of Constantinople sends his emissary to Khmelnytsky with precious gifts. At the same time the Patriarch of Jerusalem also sends his representative, Bishop Gabriel of Nazareth. They dissuade him from going to war with Muscovy, under threat of anathema. They try to convince him to put Ukraine and the Zaporozhian army under the protection of the Muscovite Tsar in the name of Orthodoxy, for he is "the only Christian ruler under the sun." Although no assistance comes from the Tsar in 1649, under the influence of the Patriarchs and their emissaries Khmelnytsky changes his political course and asks Tsar Aleksey Mikhailovich to take Ukraine under his protection. Khmelnytsky's decision is taken without the knowledge or agreement of the Kievan Metropolitan or any other Orthodox bishop.

8 March 1651 — The Holy Synod of the Orthodox Church of Muscovy takes place in Moscow with the participation of Patriarch Nikon of Moscow, metropolitans, bishops and boyars. The Synod bestows its blessings on Tsar Alexey Mikhailovich's efforts to take Ukraine, Hetman Khmelnytsky, and the Zaporozhian Kozaks under his protection. The blessing is issued in the name of Orthodoxy, seemingly for the defense of Ukraine against Turkey and Poland. On March 10, the Tsar breaks the treaty of 1637 with Poland.

St. Sophia Cathedral in Kiev, as depicted in an architectural drawing by A. Kalnofoysky in 1638.

14 July 1651 — Polish and Lithuanian armies surround Kiev. Metropolitan Sylvester Kosiv and the clergy issue an appeal to the commanders to show their mercy and not to ruin the monasteries and churches of Kiev.

3-4 August 1651 — Polish-Lithuanian armies under the command of Radziwill capture Kiev. With this storming of Kiev a legend is born about the icon of the Blessed Virgin, which saves the city from ruin in the first few days of capture. Radziwill is welcomed in the Cathedral of St. Sophia by the Metropolitan and clergy. After a few days of calm, the occupying forces start pillaging the city, including churches and monasteries. To add to the destruction and looting, fire erupts in Kiev on August 17. The Poles burn the Church of the Holy Mother of God, loot the treasures and destroy the icons in the churches of the Kievan Monastery of the Caves, St. Sophia, Mezhyhirsky Monastery, Golden-domed St. Michael the Archangel, St. Nicholas of the Desert, St. Cyril, and Vydubytsky Monastery. The churches of St. Nicholas the Good, St. Nicholas on the River Bend, St. Basil, St. Elijah, and the Theophany are burned.

31 August 1651 — King Jan Casimir orders his armies not to ruin the churches, monasteries, or any other church properties of Kiev.

16 September 1651 — Bohdan Khmelnytksy signs a treaty with Poland in Bila Tserkva. Of the eleven points, only six deal with religious matters:

> The Greek religion, which is the confessional faith of his majesty's Zaporozhian army, and also cathedrals, churches, monasteries and the Kiev College are to enjoy their former liberties and privileges. If during previous upheavals a person has acquired for himself some property that belonged to a church or clergy, then the right of ownership is to be revoked. (Hrushevsky, Vol. IX-1, p. 366.)

1651 — The Synod of the Mukachiv Eparchy elects a new Uniate bishop, Father Parteniy Petrovych. He is not confirmed by the Austrian Emperor Leopold I until 1659.

20 February 1652 — After Bohdan Khmelnytsky's defeat near Berestechko, and the capture of Kiev and a large portion of Ukraine and Byelorussia by the Lithuanian Hetman Radziwill, King Jan Casimir issues a new order, returning to the Uniate Church all churches, monasteries, and properties earlier turned over to the Orthodox Church in the Treaty of Zboriv of 1649.

1652 — At the initiative of Bishop Parteniy Petrovych Rotoshynsky, a large group of clergy joins the Uniate Church.

22 February 1653 — The Tsar's Duma in Moscow decides to take Ukraine under its protection, justifying this as a matter of religious defense and struggle against the Union.

22 June 1653 — The Tsar of Muscovy notifies Khmelnytsky that he is putting the Zaporozhian army under his authority. The Tsar's decision forever changes the history of Eastern Europe. For centuries thereafter, Ukraine is subjugated to Moscow.

3-17 August 1653 — Negotiations take place near Lviv between Muscovite and Polish representatives. Under the guise of being defenders of Orthodoxy, the Muscovites demand cancellation of the Union.

October 1653 — Tsar Aleksey calls the next Synod, in which Patriarch Nikon, metropolitans, hierarchs, and clergy participate. The Synod blesses Moscow's break of relations with, and declaration of war on Poland "in the name of the Orthodox and Greek faith," and blesses the "protection," under the Tsar's authority, of the Zaporozhian army as an "act of mercy."

2 November 1653 — After a meeting with Patriarch Nikon in Moscow's Cathedral of the Assumption, the Tsar announces war against Poland.

18 January 1654 — An assembly takes place in Pereyaslav during which Ukraine comes under the protection of Muscovy. Taking part in the Pereyaslav Council is Hetman Bohdan Khmelnytsky, Kozak chieftains and a massive Muscovite representation. The bishops of the Kievan Metropolitanate do not take part in the ceremony and do not swear an oath of allegiance to the Tsar.

26 January 1654 — Moscow's voevodas arrive in

St. Nicholas Church in the village of Okhlopiv (Volynia oblast), built in 1638 (left).

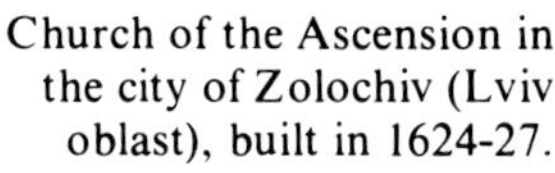

Church of the Ascension in the city of Zolochiv (Lviv oblast), built in 1624-27.

Kiev, and garrison the city. The hierarchy of the Orthodox Church at first shows its independence from Moscow by refusing to allow the Muscovites to build fortifications on church lands and forbidding the clergy to pledge loyalty to the Tsar.

Spring 1654 — Patriarch Nikon of Moscow sends his priests and deacons to Ukraine. Under threat of deportation to Moscow, he orders the reconsecration of churches, and for clergy to take the oath of loyalty to the Tsar without the necessary approval from the Metropolitan.

16 March 1654 — Dissatisfaction of the clergy and laity with the Moscow Patriarch and his interference in the internal affairs of the Kievan Metropolitanate spreads in Ukraine. An Orthodox nobleman, writing to the Kozak Colonel Bohun, notes the following:

> Great sorrow descends upon us and all our brothers, who are of the same blood with us and who recognize the same Eastern Church as their mother, when we hear that the Moscow Patriarch demands from our clergy and all the faithful an oath of allegiance to himself, and demands that we distance ourselves from the most venerable father, His Holiness the Patriarch of Constantinople, in whose dominion our churches were given by the Holy Fathers and by our ancestors; for this reason, we did not want to accept the Union with the Roman Church, so that we would not have to oppose our Oldest Pastor, given to us by God. (Makariy, Vol. VII, p. 71.)

21 March 1654 — After meeting with representatives of Hetman Khmelnytsky, Tsar Aleksey issues a decree, consisting of eleven points, which is considered a treaty between Ukraine and Muscovy. On the question of religious affairs the decree notes the following:

> The Kievan Metropolitan, as well as all other religious people of Little Rus', are to be under the blessing of the blessed Patriarch of Moscow and of all Great, Little and White Rus'; regarding ecclesiastical matters, the blessed Patriarch will not interfere. (Makariy, Vol. XII, p. 71.)

At the same time, the Tsar demands that Khmelnytsky send Metropolitan Sylvester Kosiv to Moscow with repentance for having insulted the Muscovite voevodas in Kiev. The Hetman refuses.

24 March 1654 — Hetman Bohdan Khmelnytsky, disappointed in the union with Moscow, sends a protest to the Tsar. Among the 23 points under dispute, two deal with religious affairs. In the 13th point the Hetman insists that "rights given by princes and kings from time immemorial to people of the cloth and laymen not be violated in any way."

1654-1655 — In towns occupied by the Muscovite army and voevodas, forced public swearings of loyalty to the Tsar take place.

5 April 1654 — Athanasius III Patellaros, former Patriarch of Constantinople (1634, 1652), dies in the Mharsky Monastery near Lubny. He is the only Patriarch to die on Ukrainian soil.

April 1654 — The entire population of the Byelorussian territory occupied by the Muscovite army takes an oath of loyalty to the Tsar. All Uniate churches and monasteries are taken away by force, and those who refuse to accept Muscovite Orthodoxy are either punished or banished.

12 May 1654 — In the Hetman's capital of Chyhyryn, Metropolitan Sylvester Kosiv and representatives of Kievan monasteries confer with the Hetman and his chieftains on religious matters. On May 25, 27, and 29 the Hetman and his general secretary Ivan Vyhovsky write letters to the Tsar and Patriarch Nikon of Moscow in which they defend the independence of the Ukrainian Church and the rights of the hierarchs and clergy.

After the Muscovite army occupies Byelorussia, the Moscow Patriarch for the first time starts using the title of "Patriarch of Moscow and All Great (Muscovite), Little (Ukraine) and White (Byelorussia) Russia."

Dormition Cathedral of Holy Mount (Svyatohirsky) Monastery in Slovyanohirsk, founded in 1624 (left).

St. Michael's Church in the village of Hoshcha (Rovno oblast), built in 1639. It is a rare example of stone church construction of the Volynia school of architecture.

10 June — 20 July 1954 — On his way to Moscow, Patriarch Makarios of Antioch, stops on Ukrainian soil. He meets with Hetman Bohdan Khmelnytsky and Metropolitan Sylvester Kosiv, visits churches and monasteries, and blesses the Kozaks in their struggle with Poland.

28 July 1954 — Responding to the continuous demands of the Tsar of Metropolitan Sylvester Kosiv to visit Moscow in penitence, the Metropolitan sends his emissaries to negotiate with the Tsar. He sends hegumens of Kievan monasteries — Innokentiy Gizel of St. Nicholas and Klymentiy Starushych of Vydubytsky — and representatives of the Brotherhood, St. Sophia, and of the Kievan Monastery of the Caves. The Ukrainian delegation meets the Tsar near Smolensk and delivers a letter from the Metropolitan in which he asks the Tsar to confirm all rights, privileges, and freedoms for the Ukrainian Orthodox Church. The Metropolitan requests that the Church remain under the jurisdiction of the Patriarch of Constantinople, that the Tsar not send anyone to control or administer the affairs of the Church, that the Orthodox who live in Ukraine and Lithuania remain under the Kievan Metropolitan, and that no clergy be removed to Muscovy. During the talks the head of the delegation, Hegumen Innokentiy Gizel, requests the following in writing:

> The Metropolitan joins us in asking for all freedoms and rights. And above all for the first freedom, which is the root of all rights and liberties — obedience to our Highest Pastor in Constantinople, to whom we were united through God's laws, the first-summoned Apostle St. Andrew, and the canons of the Holy Fathers. [The Metropolitan] knows that which was established and legalized by the Ecumenical Council cannot be changed by anyone, except the Council itself; and that the Ecumenical Council can take place only with the approval of all the Patriarchs and their local councils. Therefore, the Metropolitan together with us requests to leave us with our Pastor, for on this basis are built all our liberties. (Hrushevsky, Vol. IX-I, p. 862; Makariy, Vol. XII, p. 79.)

The wearisome demands of the Tsar to accept the authority of the Moscow Patriarch are met by strong opposition from the Ukrainian church representatives. The Tsar sends the representatives away without having reached any agreement. But with the traditional Muscovite bribery, he sends gifts to the metropolitan and other clergy.

11 August 1654 — Marching into Poland, the Tsar issues an appeal to the clergy and populace of Volynia and Galicia to submit to the Tsar "in the name of the Orthodox Faith."

15 September 1654 — After occupying large parts of Byelorussia and Lithuania, Tsar Alexey issues the first decree on religious affairs, thus violating and totally negating the church authority of the Kievan Metropolitan existing on those lands since 988. In the decree to the people and clergy of Mohyliv he writes as follows:

Innokentiy Gizel (ca. 1600-83), Orthodox Church and educational leader, historian, rector of the Kiev Mohyla College (from 1656), Archimandrite of the Kievan Monastery of the Caves (from 1656), author of historical and theological works.

> The Bishop of Mohyliv and all other successive bishops are to be consecrated and protected by God and our Tsar of the city of Moscow and of All Russia by Our Father, the Pious and Most Holy Nikon, Patriarch of Moscow and of All Russia; the Bishop of Mohyliv and the entire eparchy of Mohyliv are to remain under the blessing of the Holiest Patriarch of Moscow and of All Russia. (Makariy, Vol. XII, p. 88.)

With this decree, the Muscovite Tsar willfully takes a portion of the Kievan Metropolitanate from the jurisdiction of the Ecumenical Patriachate of Constantinople and transfers it to the jurisdiction of the Patriarchate of Moscow.

24 September 1654 — After the capture of Smolensk, the Tsar forces all Uniate and Roman Catholic clergy and their faithful out of the city; he transfers their churches and monasteries to the jurisdiction of Lavrentiy, Archbishop of Tver.

The Uniate Metropolitan Antin Selyava leaves Polotsk, fleeing before the advancing Muscovite army. He takes with him the relics of Archbishop Yosafat Kuntsevych, placing them in the Zhyrovytsky Monastery, whence they are later transferred to Zamostya.

1654 — Having conquered Byelorussia, the Tsar arbitrarily puts three eparchies of the Kievan Metropolitanate — Smolensk, Polotsk, and Turov — under the rule of the Moscow Patriarch.

As a result of the strong protests and demands of Metropolitan Sylvester Kosiv, the Muscovite voevodas of Kiev release the Metropolitan's representatives, the monastic priest Makariy Krynytsky and the monk Teofan, from imprisonment.

January 1655 — In the name of the Tsar, the Muscovite representative Artemon Matveyev protests to Khmelnytsky that the Ukrainian clergy do not pray during the Divine Services for the Tsar's family, but only for the Hetman himself.

Winter 1655 — The hegumen of St. Michael's Monastery, Teodosiy Vasylevych, flees Kiev and becomes Archbishop-exarch of the Kievan Metropolitanate on Ukrainian and Byelorussian territories remaining under Poland.

19 May 1655 — The Tsar demands again that

Khmelnytsky send Metropolitan Sylvester Kosiv to Moscow to repent.

2 June 1655 — Hetman Bohdan Khmelnytsky approves Teodosiy Safonovych as the newly elected Archimandrite of St. Michael's Golden-domed Monastery in Kiev with the blessings of Metropolitan Sylvester Kosiv. This is the first time since the Pereyaslav treaty of 1654 that a new archimandrite is elected without the knowledge or approval of the Tsar or the Patriarch.

1655 — The Uniate Metropolitan Antin Selyava dies in the village of Tykotsyn in Pidlyashshya.

13 March 1656 — On his own initiative Patriarch Nikon of Moscow appoints Bishop Filaret of Suzdal as Bishop of Smolensk, a city belonging to the Kievan Metropolitanate. At the same time, he appoints Hegumen Kalist Ritoraysky of the Vitebsk Monastery as his vicar for the Polotsk Eparchy. A year later, breaking the canons of the Ecumenical Orthodox Church, he consecrates him in Moscow as bishop, and charges the bishop to come only to him, and not to the Metropolitan of Kiev, in all affairs.

20 May 1656 — In a letter to Metropolitan Sylvester Kosiv, Patriarch Nikon admonishes the Ukrainian clergy to live in agreement with Moscow's voevodas in Kiev and to execute every wish of the Tsar without reservations.

14 June — 15 August 1656 — Returning from Moscow, Patriarch Makarios of Antioch stops for a longer period in Ukraine. Describing his trip, his son, Archdeacon Paul of Aleppo in Syria, notes the differences in the religious life of Muscovy and Ukraine. He describes the church in Muscovy in these words:

> Experienced people told us that whoever wants to shorten his life by fifteen years should go to the land of the Muscovites and live there like a hermit, continuously restricting himself, reading prayers, and rising at midnight. He should stop all jests, laughter and liberties, for the Muscovites place guards by the hierarchs and at monasteries who watch all visitors day and night; through cracks in the door they observe whether the visitors pass their time humbly in silence, fasting and prayer, or whether they drink, play, joke, smile, or quarrel. The minute they notice someone behaving improperly, be it in a small or large way, he is immediately sent to the land of darkness, from where one cannot escape, nor return, nor be rescued; they send him to Siberia — there to procure sable, grey squirrels, black fox, and ermine.

Paul of Aleppo writes thus of what he saw with his father the Patriarch in Ukraine, in contrast to Muscovy:

> What a blessed people! What a blessed country this is! Her great worth lies in that she has no other religion than the true believers of Orthodoxy, faithful and pious! Happy are our eyes for what they saw, our ears for what

St. Paraskeva-Friday Church in Lviv, built in 1643-45 as a fortress. It retains elements of Gothic and late Renaissance styles and contains gold-plated carvings and paintings by artists of the Senkovych circle of the 17th century (left).

St. Basil Church in Kiev. Built in 1183 and rebuilt in the 17th century. It was destroyed by the Soviets in 1935.

they heard, and our hearts for that joy and exultation that they experienced. Having been in captivity, the Kozaks live in joy, happiness and freedom. They have erected many churches. They have produced icons, iconostases, and cross-shaped banners. As we mentioned earlier, one church is prettier than the next; iconostases, frames, and icons, each one prettier than the previous one; even in the villages, beautiful churches exist one after another. People openly praise their religion. With the greatest enthusiasm they began to study, read, and raise their voices in singing beautiful prayers. And they are worthy of this happiness. (Hrushevsky, Vol. IX-2, p. 969-970.)

Bishop Lazar Baranovych (1620-93), Orthodox Church and political leader, writer, rector of the Kiev Mohyla Collegium (from 1650), founder of the printing establishment in Novhorod-Siversky (1674), author of theological works.

September 1656 — The Lithuanian hetman Radziwill frees Byelorussian lands from Moscow. Metropolitan Sylvester Kosiv sends his pastoral letter to the clergy and the faithful of the liberated land, thanking them for their loyalty to their traditional Church.

November 1656 — At the peace talks in Vilnius between Poland and Muscovy, the Muscovite representatives agree to the existence of the Roman Catholic Church but forcefully demand annulment of the Union of Berestya on the territory of the Polish Kingdom.

18 March 1657 — Elected Bishop of Chernihiv, the Rector of the Kievan Mohyla College Lazar Baranovych is instructed by Metropolitan Sylvester Kosiv to travel to Moldavia, not Moscow, for the consecration ceremony. At the request of the ailing Metropolitan Sylvester Kosiv, Lazar Baranovych is consecrated by Metropolitan Hedeon of Suceava and two bishops. On April 22, a few days before his death, Metropolitan Sylvester Kosiv himself blesses Lazar Baranovych as Bishop of Chernihiv.

25 April 1657 — Metropolitan Sylvester Kosiv dies in Kiev. He was an ardent defender of the Orthodox Church in Ukraine and of her independence from the Muscovite Patriarchate. After his death, Hetman Bohdan Khmelnytsky nominates Bishop Lazar Baranovych of Chernihiv as vicar of the Kievan Metropolitanate, the only bishop in Ukraine under Muscovite rule. At the same time the Hetman invites the bishops of Lutsk, Lviv, and Peremyshl (of the Ukrainian and Byelorussian eparchies on territories under Polish rule) to a Synod in Kiev for the election of a new Kievan Metropolitan. The Hetman notifies neither the Tsar nor the Patriarch of Metropolitan Sylvester Kosiv's death, of Bishop Lazar Baranovych's nomination, or of the forthcoming Synod.

6 August 1657 — Hetman Bohdan Khmelnytsky, during whose reign of constant wars the Ukrainian people gained social, religious, and political freedoms, dies in Chernihiv. Finding himself without a trusted ally and without achieving any agreement with Poland, especially in religious affairs, he delivered Ukraine to the protection of Muscovy. The Orthodox Church freed itself and became the dominant Church in Khmelnytsky's Kozak State. The Polish nobility was replaced by Ukrainian and Byelorussian Orthodox nobles, who historically stood alongside the Kozaks, the defenders of the Church, faith, and education. Bohdan Khmelnytsky was the first ruler in Ukraine since her ruin at the hands of the Tatars in 1240 to appoint and nominate candidates for metropolitan and bishop, a right

Dormition Church in the village of Nyzkynychi (Volynia oblast), built in 1653. It contains frescos from the 17th century, sculptures and a portrait of the Kievan voevoda Adam Kysil (left).

Dormition Church in the city of Pidhaytsi (Ternopil oblast), built in 1650. It is a unique exception to the prevailing style of Ukrainian churches.

that had been exercised up to then by the King of Poland.

14 August 1657 — The new Hetman, Ivan Vyhovsky, calls for the Synod to take place in accordance with the wishes of the deceased Bohdan Khmelnytsky, ignoring the protests of the Muscovite voevoda in Kiev, Buturlin. When Buturlin tries to deny passage to bishops from Polish territory without the Tsar's approval or the Muscovite Patriarch's blessing, Vyhovsky answers him thus on August 23:

> Rights and ancient traditions allow (the bishops) to attend the synods for the election of metropolitans with the Hetman's letter. (Makariy, Vol. XII, p. 589.)

6 December 1657 — The Synod to elect a new Metropolitan takes place in the Cathedral of St. Sophia. Participating in the Synod is Pavlo Teterya, the representative of Hetman Ivan Vyhovsky, Bishop Lazar Baranovych of Chyhyryn, Bishop Dionysiy Balaban of Lutsk, Archimandrite Yosyf Tukalsky, many clergy, representatives of the Orthodox nobility, and Kozaks. The Synod is held without the Tsar's approval or knowledge, and the Muscovite voevodas in Ukraine do not take part in it. Bishop Dionysiy Balaban is elected the new Metropolitan.

28 February 1658 — Patriarch Parthenius IV of Constantinople gives his blessing to the new Metropolitan.

24 March 1658 — The Turkish Sultan Mohammed IV sentences Parthenius III, Patriarch of Constantinople, to death, believing him to be in treasonable contact with the Ukrainian Kozaks.

June 1658 — Metropolitan Dionysiy Balaban flees Kiev from the repressions of the Muscovite voevodas to the Hetman's capital of Chyhyryn, and later to the monastery in Slutsk in Byelorussia.

St. Elias Cathedral in Subotiv (Cherkasy oblast), built in the early Ukrainian Baroque style by Bohdan Khmelnytsky, Hetman of Ukraine. Bohdan Khmelnytsky was buried here.

14 July 1658 — The Uniate bishops Yakiv Susha of Kholm and Havryil Kolenda of Polotsk and on August 3 the entire Uniate clergy, appeal to the Pope to defend the Uniate Church on the lands occupied by the Muscovite forces. They ask the Pope to use his influence with the King, so that the King would also stand up for the rights of the Uniate Church during his talks with Moscow.

16 September 1658 — In Hadyach, Hetman Ivan Vyhovsky signs a peace treaty with Poland, in accordance with which Ukraine with its regions of Kiev, Bratslav and Chernihiv is united with Poland and Lithuania. The treaty is ratified by the Sejm on May 22, 1659. Many points deal with religious issues. According to the treaty, the Union is forbidden in the three regions constituting the Ukrainian duchy and is legalized with all rights and privileges on all other

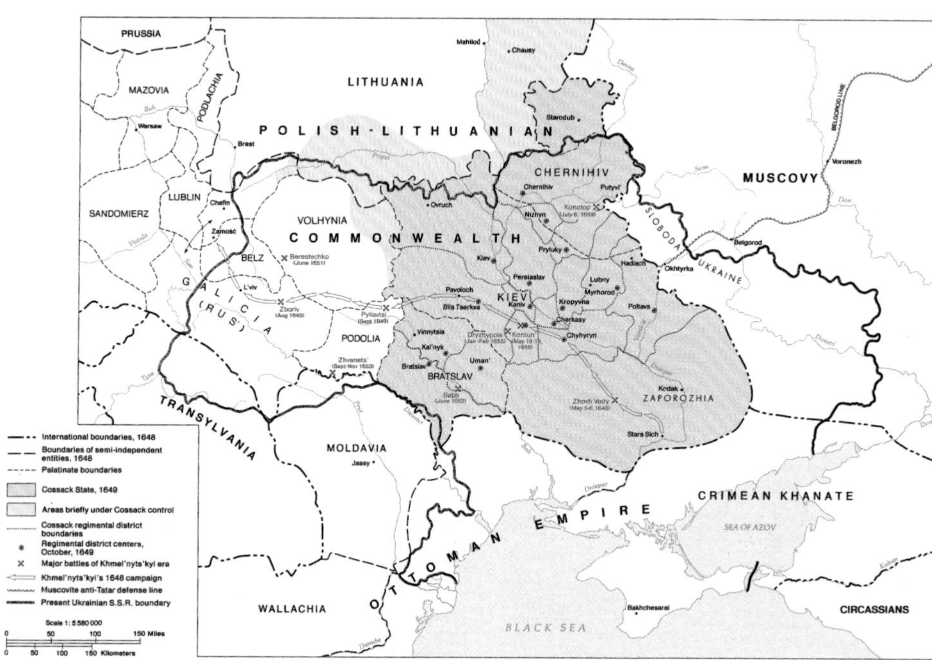

The Kozak Ukrainian State in the 17th century.

St. Michael the Archangel, 17th century. Detail from an icon in the Church of St. Theodosius of the Caves in Kiev.

The Crucifixion, 16th-century icon from the village of Vovche (Lviv oblast).

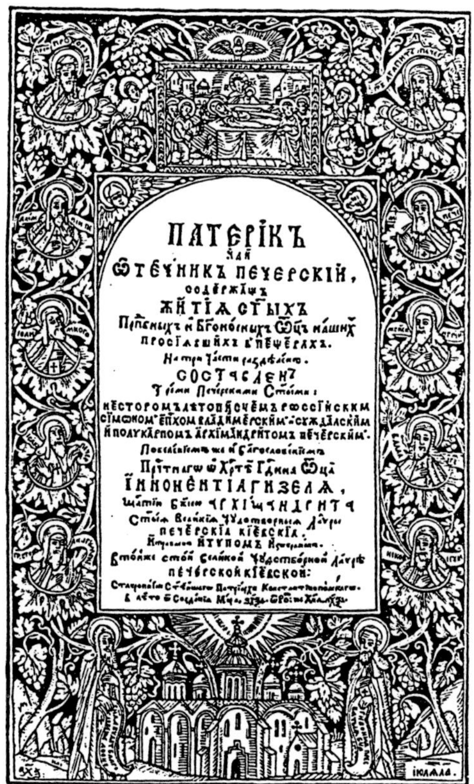

ПАТЕРІКЪ
или
ОТЕЧНИКЪ ПЕЧЕРСКІЙ,
содержащъ
ЖИТІА СТЫХЪ
Прпбныхъ и Бгоносныхъ Отцъ нашихъ
просіавшихъ в пещерахъ.
На три части раздѣленъ.
СОСТАВЛЕНЪ
древними Печерскими Стыми:
НЕСТОРОМЪ ЛѢТОПИСЦЕМЪ РОССІЙСКИМ
СІМОНОМ ЕПКОМ ВЛАДИМЕРСКИМ И СУЖДАЛСКИМ
И ПОЛУКАРПОМЪ АРХІМАНДРИТОМЪ ПЕЧЕРСКИМ.
Повелѣніемъ же и благословеніемъ
Пресвятагω ω Хрстѣ Гдина Отца
ІННОКЕНТІА ГИЗЕЛА,
Милостію Божіею АРХІМАНДРИТА
Стыя Великія Чудотворныя Лавры
ПЕЧЕРСКІА КІЕВСКІА.
В тойже Стой Великой Чудотворной Лаврѣ
ПЕЧЕРСКОЙ КІЕВСКОЙ:

The Kievan Monastery of the Caves Patericon, 1661, published at the Kievan Monastery of the Caves (left).

Detail of the iconostasis of the Friday Church in Lviv. 17th century.

Churches and monasteries of 17th-century Kiev. Drawing by Westerfeld, 1651.

Ukrainian and Byelorussian lands. Churches and their properties are again transferred to the Orthodox; the Orthodox bishops have seats in the Sejm on equal terms with the Roman Catholic bishops. In addition, the treaty guarantees to the Orthodox Church all her former rights and privileges.

1658 — A new Muscovite voevoda, Vasiliy Sheremetyev, arrives in Kiev. Persecutions immediately begin, primarily of the clergy. The disobedient are taken en masse to Moscow. To break the opposition and to earn the goodwill of the Patriarch of Moscow, the Tsar instructs his voevoda to use bribes; the dociles ones are to be rewarded with sables, money, or estates.

1659 — Following Metropolitan Dionysiy Balaban's escape, the commander-in-chief of the Muscovite army in Ukraine appoints Bishop Lazar Baranovych of Chernihiv as vicar of the Kievan Metropolitanate.

25 January 1660 — During the negotiations in Minsk between Poland and Muscovy, the Tsar's representative demands the annulment of the Union of Berestya.

13 March 1660 — The new Hetman, Yuriy Khmelnytsky, calls for Metropolitan Dionysiy Balaban to return to Kiev.

23 October 1660 — The Muscovite forces in Ukraine lose new battles with Poland and agree to capitulate and pull their forces out of all Ukrainian lands.

2 May 1661 — Metropolitan Dionysiy Balaban consecrates Yosyf Nelyubovych-Tukalsky as Bishop of Mstyslavl and Orsha.

4 May 1661 — In violation of the church canons, against the will of the Hetman of Ukraine, and against the wishes of the Metropolitan of Kiev, but at the command of the Tsar, Archbishop Pitirim and the Synod of the Muscovite Church consecrate the Moscow-oriented presbyter Metodiy Filimonov of Nizhyn as Bishop of Mstyslavl and Orsha, and appoint him vicar of the Kievan Metropolitanate. The new bishop does not receive the blessing of the Patriarch of Constantinople and fails to receive the recognition of the Kievan clergy. Arriving in Kiev, the new bishop takes over the Cathedral of St. Sophia from Bishop Lazar Baranovych and spends most of his time on political matters.

1661 — Contrary to the Treaty of Hadyach, the Polish Sejm does not admit the Orthodox and Uniate bishops to its session.

1662 — The Greek edition of the catechism *The Orthodox Confession of Faith* by Metropolitan Petro Mohyla and a group of Kievan theologians appears in Amsterdam. The book also appears in Ukrainian in Kiev.

Dionysius III, Patriarch of Constantinople, excommunicates Bishop Metodiy Filimonov, newly consecrated by Moscow.

10 May 1663 — Metropolitan Dionysiy Balaban dies in Korsun. A struggle for the Kievan Metropolitanate begins between Poland and Muscovy.

19 November 1663 — The Synod to elect the new Metropolitan takes place in Korsun. The participants are Hetman Pavlo Teterya of Right-Bank Ukraine, and Bishops Lazar Baranovych of Chernihiv, Yosyf Tukalsky of Mohyliv, Hedeon Chetvertynsky of Lutsk, Arseniy Zheliborsky of Lviv, and Antin Vynnytsky of Peremyshl. According to the rules, the Synod elects two candidates: Bishop Antoniy Vynnytsky and Bishop Yosyf Tukalsky. On November 24, the King confirms Bishop Yosyf Tukalsky, who remains in Korsun. Irritated by this election, the Muscovite Tsar forbids Metropolitan Yosyf Tukalsky to move to Kiev. Backed by the new Muscovite voevoda of Kiev, Prince Veliki-Gagin, Bishop Metodiy Filimonov remains the vicar of the Kievan Metropolitanate, in spite of protests from the archimandrite of the Kievan Monastery of the Caves and the hegumens of all the monasteries in Kiev.

March 1664 — Under the pretext that he is guilty of treason to the King, Metropolitan Yosyf Tukalsky is taken to Warsaw and thrown into the Marienburg prison for two years. The King appoints Bishop Arseniy Zheliborsky of Lviv as administrator of the Kievan Metropolitanate, which consists of the territory of the Right-Bank Ukraine. Bishop Metodiy Filimonov remains church administrator for the Left Bank, under the rule of Moscow.

22 April 1665 — The Roman Catholic Archbishop of Vilnius, Havryil Kolenda, who joined the Uniate Church ten years earlier, is appointed by the Apostolic See as the new Kievan Metropolitan.

1665 — The newly elected Hetman of Ukraine, Ivan Bryukhovetsky, arrives in Moscow to swear the oath of allegiance to the Tsar. He is the first Ukrainian Hetman to take such action. The Tsar notifies the Hetman that the Church in Ukraine is to be administered by a Metropolitan sent by Moscow. The clergy in Kiev oppose this decision, as does Bishop Metodiy Filimonov.

22 February 1666 — Bishop Metodiy Filimonov, Archbishop Innokentiy Gizel, the hegumens of all the monasteries, and the clergy of Kiev protest the Tsar's decision to send a Metropolitan from Moscow to rule in Kiev. They write thus to the Tsar:

> If by your will we are to have a Muscovite Metropolitan not selected by us, than let the Tsar punish us by death, for we will not agree to such a decision. When a Metropolitan from Moscow arrives in Kiev, we will lock ourselves in the monasteries, and only if we are dragged out by our feet and necks, only then will there be a Muscovite Metropolitan in Kiev. Today Archbishop Filaret sits in Smolensk; he took away all the rights from the clergy, he calls them of foreign faith, and yet they are Orthodox Christians; thus will a Muscovite Metropolitan call all residents of Kiev and Little Rus'. We would rather accept death than see a Muscovite Metropolitan in Kiev. (Makariy, Vol. XII, p. 589.)

13 January 1667 — Negotiations between Poland and Muscovy in Andrusiv near Smolensk, result in the division of Ukraine into the Right Bank, transferred to Poland, and the Left Bank, remaining under Muscovy.

23 July 1667 — The Congregation for the Propagation of the Faith sends out thirteen letters to Ukraine, including letters to Hetman Pavlo Teterya and all the Orthodox bishops and prominent noblemen attempting to induce them to join the Union.

Yosyf Nelyubovych-Tukalsky, Ukrainian Orthodox Metropolitan of Kiev (1663-75), defender of the independence of the Ukrainian Church.

Dionisiy Balaban, Orthodox Metropolitan of Kiev (1658-63), defender of the Ukrainian Church against Moscow.

1667 — After the death of Atanasiy Zheliborsky, who was the administrator of the Kievan Metropolitanate for the Right Bank, the Synod in Lviv elects Bishop Antoniy Vynnytsky as the new Orthodox Metropolitan. He is immediately confirmed by the King. Unable to move to Kiev, he administers the Metropolitanate from Peremyshl.

The Great Synod of the Muscovite Church establishes the new Eparchy of Bilhorod as a new Metropolitanate, thus breaking the canons of the Church. The new Metropolitanate consists of cities that previously had been part of the Kievan Metropolitanate: Kharkiv, Ostrih, and Chyhyryn. The newly elected Metropolitan Teodosiy (1667-1671) has 38 cities with 542 churches in his jurisdiction.

16 March 1668 — The Patriarch of Constantinople, Methodius III, confirms Yosyf Tukalsky as the Metropolitan of Kiev; unrecognized by Moscow, he cannot move to Kiev.

1669 — The city of Baturyn becomes the capital of Hetman Ukraine. Ukrainian Hetmans reside there until 1708, when it is destroyed by the Russian armies of Tsar Peter I.

12 March 1669 — The new Hetman of Ukraine, Petro Doroshenko, signs a treaty with the Turks in Korsun in which they agree to wage war against Moscow. Religious issues are taken up in the treaty as follows:

> Upon entering Ukraine, Turkish and Tatar armies will not build mosques, will not ruin or pillage Ukrainian churches or turn them into mosques. The Ukrainian clergy will remain under the jurisdiction of the Patriarch of Constantinople but will be administered by the Kievan Metropolitan, who will be confirmed by the Hetman. No one can take away the Hetman's power of governing until his death. (Ohiyenko, p. 129.)

Spring 1669 — The new Polish King Michal Wisniowiecki asks the Sejm to establish a new commission

Cyprian Zhokhovsky, Uniate Metropolitan of Kiev (1674-93), author of church works. Portrait by O. Tarasevych.

to review religious issues, as proposed by Hetman Petro Doroshenko and the Uniate hierarchy.

1670 — The monk Cyprian Zhokhovsky prepares an extensive proposal of "general means to unite the Greek and Roman churches," in which he raises the possibility of the Uniate Church coming under the jurisdiction of the Patriarch of Constantinople, provided the latter were to recognize the authority of the Pope.

1672 — In a report to the Apostolic See by the Uniate Metropolitan Havryil Kolenda the status of the Orthodox and Uniate Metropolitanate in the Ukrainian lands under Poland and Muscovy is described.

The Orthodox Church has the following eparchies and parishes:
1. The Metropolitan eparchy of Kiev (8,000 parishes), 2. Polotsk (7,000), 3. Lutsk (5,000), 4. Lviv (6,000), 5. Peremyshl (5,000), 6. Novhorod-Siversky (2,000).

The Uniate Church has the following eparchies and parishes:
1. Polotsk (Archeparchy), 2. Vitebsk, 3. Mohyliv, 4. Mstyslavl. The eparchies have a total of close to 4,000 churches, 17 archimandrites, 14 monasteries, and 10 nunneries.

A Synod of the Orthodox Church called by the Patriarch of Jerusalem Dositheus II recommends the use of the catechism published by Metropolitan Petro Mohyla, *The Orthodox Confession of Faith,* by all Ecumenical Orthodox churches. The book appeared in Greek, Latin, German, old Church Slavonic, and other languages, and was in use as a textbook in all Orthodox seminaries until 1867.

18 February 1674 — After the death of Metropolitan Havryil Kolenda, the Apostolic See appoints Bishop Cyprian Zhokhovsky of Vitebsk as the new Metropolitan.

1674 — Archbishop Lazar Baranovych establishes a printing press in Novhorod-Siversky, which he transfers to Chernihiv in 1679. After Kiev and Lviv, Chernihiv becomes the largest religious and educational center in Ukraine.

22 July 1675 — The Pochayiv monastery in Volynia miraculously escapes an attack by Turks and Tatars. The miracle is ascribed to Hegumen Yov (Zalizo) who, after his death in 1651, was canonized a saint on August 28, 1659 by Metropolitan Dionysiy Balaban.

26 August 1675 — Yosyf Tukalsky, the last Ukrainian Metropolitan independent of Muscovy, dies in Chyhyryn. After his death, the Patriarch of Moscow appoints the Archbishop of Novhorod-Siversky, Lazar Baranovych, as the administrator for the Kievan Metropolitanate.

1675 — The Turks and Tatars leave Ukraine, which is again occupied by Muscovite troops.

1676 — The Apostolic See appoints Metropolitan Theophanes Mavrocordato to the see of the Eparchy of Mukachiv.

The Tatars burn and destroy two Orthodox monasteries in Galicia — Skyt Manyavsky and the Uhornytsky Monastery. During the attack almost all the monks in Skyt Manyavsky perish.

The Polish government forbids all contacts with the Eastern Patriarchs under threat of death.

7 March 1677 — Bishop Yosyf Shumlyansky of Lviv secretly joins the Uniate Church.

11 August 1677 — Muscovite troops conquer the Ukrainian Hetman's capital of Chyhyryn and destroy the city, including many churches.

7 September 1678 — Archimandrite Makariy of the Kaniv Monastery suffers a martyr's death at the hands of the Turks. Later he becomes a saint in the Ukrainian Orthodox Church.

26 November 1679 — The Ukrainian Orthodox Metropolitan Antoniy Vynnytsky dies in Peremyshl.

24 January 1680 — A joint Synod of Orthodox and Uniate Churches takes place in Lublin. Because of canonical obstacles, it is merely called the "Lublin

Havryil Kolenda, Uniate Metropolitan of Kiev (1665-74).

St. Nicholas Church of the Kievan Monastery of the Caves, built in the 17th century on the site of a 12th-century wooden church; restored in 1718 after a fire. It was converted by the Soviets into a conference hall.

St. Catherine Church in Chernihiv, built in 1715 and rebuilt in 1837 after sustaining damage in a fire. A fine example of Ukrainian stone architecture of the 17th-18th centuries, it was partially destroyed by the Soviets in the 1930s.

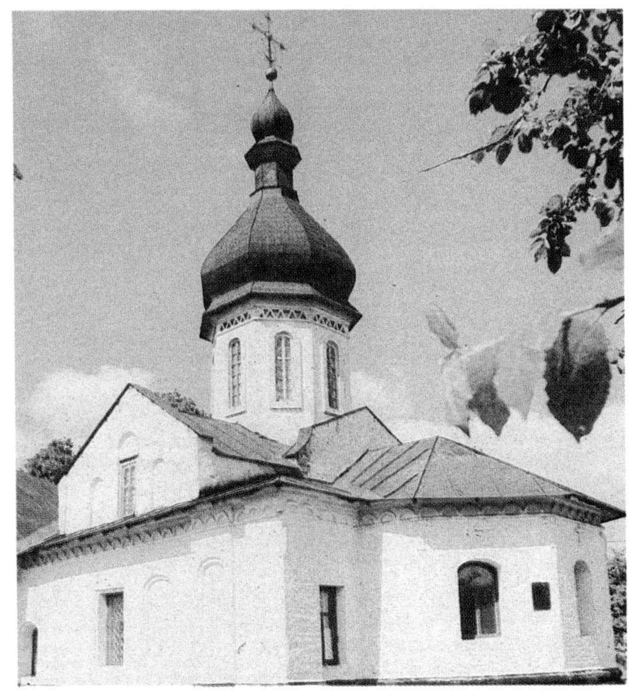

The Church of SS. Peter and Paul of the Holy Savior-Transfiguration Monastery in Novhorod-Siversky (Chernihiv oblast), built in the 17th century. It is a fine example of the original stone church architecture of that period.

The Presentation of the Virgin Mary at the Temple, 17th-century icon from the Church of the Transfiguration in the village of Velyki Sorochyntsi (Poltava oblast).

talks." The Orthodox side is represented by Bishop Yosyf Shumlyansky of Lviv, Bishop Innokentiy Vynnytsky of Peremyshl, Bishop Hedeon Chetvertynsky of Lutsk, deacon Sylvester Vyshyatsky of the Byelorussian Mohyliv eparchy, and 17 hegumens, archimandrites, and laymen. The Uniate Church is represented by Metropolitan Cyprian Zhokhovsky, Bishop Ivan Malakhovsky of Peremyshl, Bishop Yakiv Susha of Kholm, Bishop Lev Zalensky of Volodymyr-Volynsky, Mytrofan Drutsky, Maryan Bilozor, archimandrites, and clergy. The Synod, called to discuss the possible unification of both Churches, opens with a joint Liturgy celebrated by hierarchs of both Churches. On the eve of the talks, the Apostolic See's emissary in Poland and King Jan Sobieski demand the closing of the Synod. Thus the Synod does not continue.

26 March 1681 — At the Sejm in Warsaw, Bishop Yosyf Shumlyansky of Lviv and Bishop Innokentiy Vynnytsky of Peremyshl publicly announce their joining the Uniate Church. In the King's palace, in the presence of Roman Catholic Bishop Stanislaw Witwicki of Kiev, they accept the Catholic creed.

August 1681 — The Patriarch of Constantinople Jacobus I appoints Bishop Pankratiy of Kamyanets-Podilsky as his exarch and as Metropolitan of Galicia and Kamyanets-Podilsky on Ukrainian territories under the Turks.

13 December 1681 — The priest Ivan Lypnytsky becomes the administrator of the Uniate Eparchy of Mukachiv. From 1683, he and Father Porfyriy Kulchytsky become vicars of the Eparchy.

June 1683 — Pope Innocent XI finances a corps of Kozaks to fight with other units of European armies against the Turks outside Vienna. He also finances the Kozaks to fight the Crimean Tatars.

13 November 1683 — Archimandrite Innokentiy Gizel of the Kievan Monastery of the Caves dies. He defended the independence of the Ukrainian Church

St. Nicholas Cathedral in the city of Nizhyn (Chernihiv oblast), built in 1658. Though partially destroyed by the Soviets in the 1930s, it remains one of the better examples of the Ukrainian Baroque style in Left-Bank Ukraine (left).

Holy Trinity Cathedral of the Hustyn Monastery (Chernihiv oblast), built in 1672-76 in the Ukrainian Baroque style. It was destroyed by the Soviets in the 1930s.

from the Moscow Patriarchate. Shortly before his death, he was nominated by the Patriarch of Constantinople, Dionysius IV, to be Metropolitan of Kiev.

May 1684 — The Papal Nuncio in Poland, Franciscus Bonesana, visits Kozak units in Nemyriv on the Dniester. He thanks them in the name of the Pope for their participation in the battle against the Turks and Tatars. In response, the Kozaks send a letter to the Pope, dated August 5 and signed by Otaman Andriy Mohyla and other chieftains, in which they assure the Pope that they are always ready to fight against the enemies of Christ.

1684 — The candidates for the Metropolitan See, Archbishop Lazar Baranovych and Archimandrite Varlaam Yasynsky, refuse to accept the authority of the Patriarch of Moscow.

February 1685 — Hetman Ivan Samoylovych is directed by Moscow to select a candidate for Metropolitan who would accept the authority of the Moscow Patriarch.

29 June 1685 — At the request of Hetman Ivan Samoylovych, Archbishop Lazar Baranovych calls a Synod to elect a new Metropolitan. Learning that the new Metropolitan can only be a person who would accept the Moscow Patriarch as his superior, the bishops and clergy refuse to come to the Synod. The Synod, composed mainly of laymen, elects as its new Metropolitan Bishop Hedeon Chetvertynsky of Lutsk, who a year earlier had notified the Moscow Patriarch Yoakim of his willingness to accept the Patriarch's

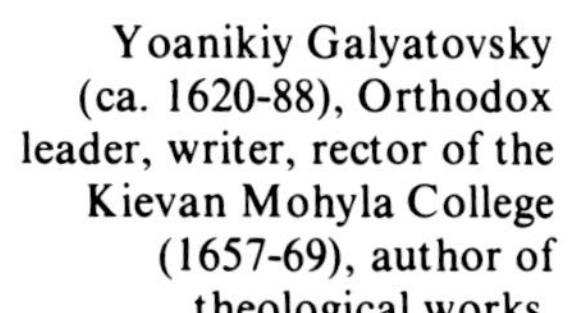

Yoanikiy Galyatovsky (ca. 1620-88), Orthodox leader, writer, rector of the Kievan Mohyla College (1657-69), author of theological works.

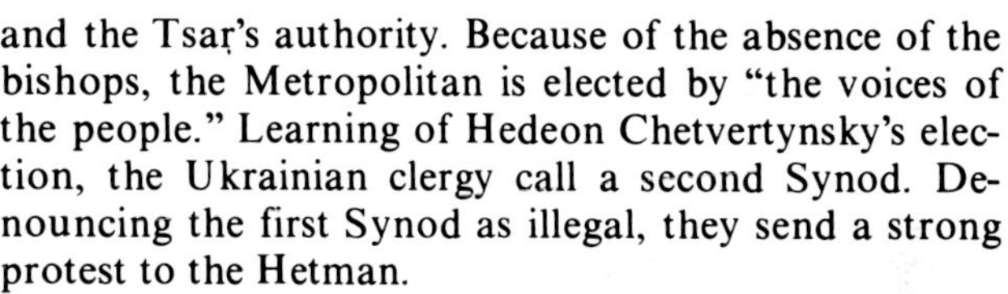

and the Tsar's authority. Because of the absence of the bishops, the Metropolitan is elected by "the voices of the people." Learning of Hedeon Chetvertynsky's election, the Ukrainian clergy call a second Synod. Denouncing the first Synod as illegal, they send a strong protest to the Hetman.

8 October 1685 — The newly elected Metropolitan Hedeon Chetvertynsky arrives in Moscow to be consecrated by the Patriarch and to swear the oath of loyalty. With these actions the Ukrainian Orthodox Church leaves the fold of the Constantinople Patriarchate, in whose jurisdiction she was for 697 years. Gradually she loses all her rights, privileges, and freedoms. Through a series of uncanonical, illegal, and violent acts she is incorporated into the Muscovite Church. The ceremony of consecration of Chetvertynsky in Moscow's Cathedral of the Assumption ends the independence of the Ukrainian Orthodox Church.

Title page of *The Key to Understanding,* by Yoannikiy Galyatovsky, 1659. Published at the Kievan Monastery of the Caves (left).

Dormition Cathedral in Kiev in the 17th century, by the artist Illya. From the *Kievan Monastery of the Caves Patericon,* Kiev, 1661.

11 December 1685 — Through the Greek Zakhar Sofir, the Muscovite Tsar sends a message to the Patriarch of Constantinople Jacobus I, along with 40 sables and 200 red (golden) coins requesting the Patriarch to transfer the Kievan Metropolitanate to the Moscow Patriarchate. The Moscow Patriarch Yoakim sends his representative cantor, Nikita Alekseyev, accompanied by Hetman Ivan Samoylovych's representative Ivan Lysytsya to Constantinople. Learning the purpose of the Muscovite delegation, the Patriarch of Jerusalem Dositheus II sends them an angry letter, in which he points out the illegality of their request and accuses them of trying to acquire a Metropolitanate by means of bribes of money and gifts. After prolonged negotiations, the new Patriarch of Constantinople, Dionysius IV, does not agree to hand over the Kievan Metropolitanate. Then Moscow's representative appeals to the Turkish Vizier. At that time, the Ottomans were preparing for war with Poland, Austria, and Venice, with Moscow still uncommitted. Under threat, the Vizier orders the Patriarch Dionysius IV to hand over the Kievan Metropolitanate to Moscow.

May 1686 — In a general decree, Dionysius IV hands over the Kievan Metropolitanate to the Muscovite Patriarchate. He issues six separate decrees: two to the Tsars, and one each to the Patriarch of Moscow, the Metropolitan of Kiev, Hetman Ivan Samoylovych, and the Ukrainian people. The rights of the Kievan Metropolitanate are spelled out in three points: 1. The candidate to the metropolitan's seat is to be elected freely, according to the ancient traditions; 2. The new Metropolitan is not required to go to Moscow for his consecration; 3. During the Divine Services, the Metropolitan is to pray for and mention first the Patriarch of Constantinople and then the Patriarch of Moscow.

All these messages Dionysius IV delivers to Moscow's representative Alekseyev, who returns to Muscovy. Shortly thereafter, the Tsar declares war on the Turks. Having negotiated with Moscow, Patriarch Dionysius IV is in a difficult position. The Eastern clergy call a Patriarchal Synod for the end of the year, during which they deprive Dionysius IV of his office and cancel all his decrees connected with the transfer of the Kievan Metropolitanate to the jurisdiction of the Patriarchate of Moscow. After an unsuccessful campaign against the Turks, the Tsar blames the whole incident on Hetman Ivan Samoylovych. The Hetman and his son are taken to Moscow and all their estates are confiscated. He dies in prison a year later, and his son is put to death.

St. Nicholas Church in the city of Terebovlya (Ternopil oblast), built in the 16th-17th centuries in the fortress-church architectural style of the Podilia school. Rebuilt in 1734 (left).

Holy Trinity Cathedral of the Holy Trinity-St. Elias Monastery in Chernihiv, built in 1679-95 under the direction of I. Batist. It was damaged by fire in 1731 and 1808, but rebuilt.

Principal Ecclesiastical Activities

1. THE KIEVAN ORTHODOX AND EASTERN-RITE CATHOLIC (UNIATE) METROPOLITANATES DURING THE 16th-17th CENTURIES

The entire Kievan Metropolitanate, except for the Bishops of Lviv and Peremyshl, joined the Union at Berestya in 1596. Prior to 1620, when the Patriarch of Jerusalem consecrated a new Orthodox hierarchy, only the Uniate Kievan Metropolitanate existed on Ukrainian and Byelorussian territories in the Polish Kingdom. The seats of the Uniate Metropolitanate were Vilnius and Novogrudok. After the renewal of the Orthodox hierarchy, Kiev again became the seat of the Kievan Metropolitanate. From 1620, two independent metropolitanates existed on the territories of Ukraine and Byelorussia. The Uniate Metropolitanate was within the jurisdiction of the Apostolic See, and the Orthodox within the jurisdiction of the Ecumenical Patriarch of Constantinople. There were Uniate Metropolitans chosen by a Synod of bishops, approved by the King and confirmed by the Pope. The Metropolitan could be consecrated by Uniate bishops or Papal representatives. The Metropolitan had the right to select and consecrate bishops, ordain priests, and appoint them to eparchies and parishes.

Beginning in 1632, the Metropolitan of the Orthodox Church was elected by a Sobor of bishops, clergy, and faithful, was confirmed by the King, and was blessed by the Patriarch of Constantinople. The Metropolitan had the right to select and consecrate bishops and ordain priests, and to appoint them to eparchies and parishes respectively. From 1620 to 1657, the seat of the Kievan Metropolitan, after a 320-year interval, was again Kiev. From 1658, the seat was the Hetman's capital of Chyhyryn or Korsun.

2. ORTHODOX METROPOLITANS OF KIEV, HALYCH, AND ALL RUS' (1620-1686)

Yov Boretsky 1620-1631
Isaya Kopynsky 1631-1633
Petro Mohyla 1633-1647
Sylvester Kosiv 1647-1657
Dionysiy Balaban 1657-1663
Yosyf Nelyubovych-Tukalsky 1663-1675
Antoniy Vynnytsky 1677-1679
Hedeon Svyatopolk Chetvertynsky 1685-1690

BISHOPS OF EPARCHIES IN THE KIEVAN ORTHODOX METROPOLITANATE (1596-1686)

Chernihiv, Smolensk and Siversk: Isaya Kopynsky (1633-1640), Zosym Prokopovych (1650-1657), Lazar Baranovych (1657-1693).

Kholm: Payisiy Ipolytovych (1621-1633), Dionysiy Balaban (1650-1657).

Lutsk: Isaakiy Boryskovych (1620-1633), Afanasiy (Oleksander) Puzyna (1632-1650), Yosyf Chaplych (1650-1654), Dionysiy Balaban (1654-1657), Hedeon (Svyatopolk) Chetvertynsky (1663-1689), Atanasiy Shumlyansky (1685-1694).

Lviv: Hedeon Balaban (1568-1607), Yeremiya (Yevstakhiy) Tysarovsky (1606-1641), Zheliborsky (1641-1658), Atanasiy Zheliborsky (1658-1667), Yevstakhiy (Yeremiya) Svystelnytsky (1667-1676), Yosyf (Ivan) Shumlyansky (1676-1681).

Mohyliv, Vitebsk, Mstyslavl, and Orsha: Yosyf Bobrykovych (1632-1635), Sylvester Kosiv (1635-1647), Yosyf Horbatsky (1650-1653), Yosyf Nelyubovych-Tukalsky (1661-1663), Teodosiy Vasylevych (1677-1678).

Peremyshl: Mykhayil Kopystensky (1591-1610), Ivan Khlopetsky (1610-1611), Isaya Kopynsky (1620-1631), Ivan Popel (1633-1635), Sylvester (Semen) Hulevych-Voyutynsky (1633-1645), Antoniy Vynnytsky (1650-1679), Yuriy Hoshovsky (1667-1679), Innokentiy Vynnytsky (1679-1681).

Pinsk: Avraamiy Strahonsky (1621-1633).

Polotsk: Meletiy Smotrytsky (1620-1623).

Volodymyr-Volynsky: Ezekiyil Kurtsevych (1620-1625).

ORTHODOX BISHOPS OF EPARCHIES OUTSIDE THE JURISDICTION OF THE KIEVAN METROPOLITANATE

Bilhorod *(Metropolitanate under the jurisdiction of the Moscow Patriarchate):* Teodosiy Smyelich (1667-1671).

Kamyanets-Podilsky and Halych *(under the jurisdiction of the Metropolitan of Moldavia):* Pankratiy (1679-).

Mukachiv: Amfiloniy (1596-1606), Serhiy (1601-1616), Sofroniy Yuska (1614-1648), Yevtymiy (1618), Sofroniy Rechko (1620), Petroniy (1623-1627), Ivan Hryhorovych (1627-1633), Vasyl Tarasovych (1633-1646), Yoanykiy Zeykan (1651-1686), Yosyf Voloshynovsky (1667-1675), Metodiy Rakovetsky (1686-1688).

3. UNIATE (EASTERN-RITE CATHOLIC) METROPOLITANS OF KIEV AND ALL RUS' (1596-1686)

Mykhaylo Rohoza 1596-1599
Ipatiy Potiy 1600-1613
Velyamyn (Yosyf) Rutsky 1614-1637
Raphael Korsak 1637-1640
Antin Selyava 1641-1655
Havryyil Kolenda 1665-1674
Cyprian Zhokhovsky 1674-1693

BISHOPS OF EPARCHIES IN THE KIEVAN UNIATE METROPOLITANATE (1596-1686)

Kholm and Belz: Dionysiy Zbiruysky (1596-1604), Arseniy Andriyevsky (1605-1619), Atanasiy Pakosta (1619-1625), Teodor Meleshko (1626), Metodiy Terletsky (1629-1649), Andriy Furs (1649), Yakiv Susha (1652-1686).

Lutsk and Ostrih: Kyrylo Terletsky (1596-1607), Ostafiy Yelovych-Malynsky (1607-1621), Yeremiya Pochapovsky (1621-1636), Nykyfor Lasovsky (1637), Prokopiy Khmelyovsky (1660), Antoniy Terlecky (1662-1666), Havryyil Kolenda (1666-1674), Cyprian Zhokhovsky (1693).

Lviv and Halych: Makariy Tuchansky (1605-1608), Yosyf Velyamyn Rutsky (1608-1613), Raphael Korsak (1626-1632), Yosyf (Ivan) Shumlyansky (1681-1708).

Mukachiv *(under the jurisdiction of the Hungarian Roman Catholic Bishop of Eger):* Vasyl Tarasovych (1646-1648), Parteniy Petrovych Rostoshynsky (1652-1665), Yosyf Voloshynovych (1674), Theophanes Mavrocordato (1676-1678), Porfyriy Kulchytsky (1683).

Peremyshl, Sambir and Syanok: Atanasiy Krupetsky (1610-1652), Pavlo Ovluchynsky (1637-1649), Prokopiy Khmilevsky (1652-1664), Antoniy Terletsky (1664-1669), Yakiv Susha (1667-1669), Ivan Malakhovsky (1669-1691), Innokentiy Vynnytsky (1681-1700).

Pinsk and Turov: Yona Hohol (1596-1603), Payisiy Sakhovsky (1603-1626), Hryhoriy Mykhalovych (1626-1632), Raphael Korsak (1632-1637), Pakhomiy Oransky (1637-1653), Andriy Kvasnynsky-Zloty (1654-1665), Markiyan Bilozor (1666-1697).

Polotsk, Vitebsk, Mstyslavl, and Mohyliv: Hryhoriy Khrebtovych (1596-1601), Hedeon Brolnytsky (1601-1617), Josafat Kuntsevych (1617-1623), Antoniy Selyava (1624-1655), Havryyil Kolenda (1655-1674), Cyprian Zhokhovsky (1674-1693).

Smolensk: Lev Krevza (1625-1639), Andriy Kvasnynsky Zloty (1640-1654), Varlaam Kosynsky (1655), Mykhayil Pashkovsky (1666-1670), Mytrofan Drutsky-Sokolynsky (1680), Heorhiy Maleyevsky (1690).

Volodymyr-Volynsky and Berestya: Ipatiy Potiy (1596-1613), Yoakym (Atanasiy) Morokhovsky (1613-1631), Yosyf Bakovetsky (1632-1650), Ivan (Mykhaylo) Potiy (1655-1666), Benedykt Hlynsky (1667-1678), Lev Zalensky (1678-1708).

Church and Monastery Construction in the 16th-17th Centuries

CHURCH CONSTRUCTION

Many churches and monasteries were built on Ukrainian territories in the Polish Kingdom between 1596 and 1686. Below are listed only those churches built during this period that are of architectural or historical significance and have survived to our days. Years given in parentheses denote when the church was built or first mentioned in documents.

The list of monasteries is complete. All of them, except the monastery of Krekhiv, were Orthodox. Only a few remain. Most were destroyed or converted to secular uses by the Soviet authorities in the 1930s.

Churches and monasteries are listed according to the present-day administrative divisions of Ukraine.

KIEV OBLAST. Kiev: Brotherhood Church (1625), built by the Kievan Brotherhood; Mizhhirya Monastery — SS. Peter and Paul, Refectory, and Transfiguration (1612), built by Hegumen Atanasiy; the Church of the Theophany in the Brotherhood Monastery (1620), built by Hetman Petro Sahaydachny. ***Sulymivka:*** Protection of the Blessed Virgin Mary (1622), built by Hetman Ivan Sulyma.

CHERKASY OBLAST. Chyhyryn: Elijah (1646); Holy Trinity (1679). ***Subotiv:*** Elijah (1653), built by Hetman Bohdan Khmelnytsky.

CHERNIHIV OBLAST. Chernihiv: Presentation, in the Temple-Elijah Monastery (1677). ***Hustyn:*** Cathedral of the Holy Trinity in the Hustyn Monastery (1674), built by Hetman Ivan Samoylovych. ***Nizhyn:*** Cathedral of St. Nicholas (1658). ***Novhorod-Siversky:*** Dormition Cathedral (1671).

CHERNIVTSI OBLAST. Bayraky: Nativity of the Virgin Mary (1646). ***Chernivtsi:*** Resurrection (17th century); St. Nicholas (1607). ***Dubivtsi:*** Dormition (17th century). ***Mohylivka:*** Dormition (17th century). ***Petrashivka:*** Archangel (1663). ***Plyana:*** St. Nicholas (1618). ***Selyatyn:*** Nativity of the Virgin Mary (17th century). ***Yaseny:*** Protection of the Blessed Virgin Mary (17th century).

DONETSK OBLAST. Slovyansk: the Church of St. Nicholas in the Svyatohirsk Dormition Monastery (17th century).

IVANO-FRANKIVSK OBLAST. Manyava: Elevation of the Cross in the Manyava Hermitage (1619). ***Rohatyn:*** Holy Spirit (1598). ***Yaremche:*** St. Michael (17th century).

KHARKIV OBLAST. Izyum: Transfiguration of our Lord (1684). ***Kharkiv:*** Cathedral of the Protection of the Blessed Virgin Mary (1686), built by Hetman Ivan Samoylovych.

KHMELNYTSKY OBLAST. Letychiv: St. Michael (17th century). ***Satanivska Slobidka:*** Trinity (17th century).

St. Michael's Church in the village of Kraynykovo (Transcarpathian oblast), built of wood in 1668. It contains carvings and paintings from the 17th and 18th centuries (left).

Dormition Church in the village of Novoselytsya (Transcarpathian oblast), built in the 17th century. Wall paintings and paintings by Western Ukrainian and Transcarpatian artists from the 17th and 18th centuries are found in this church, which is the most famous monuments of Ukrainian wooden church construction.

LVIV OBLAST. ***Belz:*** Holy Friday (17th century). ***Brody:*** St. George (1625). ***Bukhovychi:*** SS. Borys and Hlib (17th century). ***Buniv:*** St. Paraskeva (1676). ***Busk:*** St. Onuphrius (1680). ***Derniv:*** St. Nicetas (1666). ***Dmytrovychi:*** St. Nicholas (1653). ***Isayiv:*** St. Michael (1663). ***Kaminka Buska:*** St. Nicholas (17th century). ***Kletsko:*** Dormition (1603). ***Krasnoseltsi:*** Elevation of the Cross (17th century). ***Krekhiv:*** SS. Peter and Paul, Protection of the Blessed Virgin Mary; Transfiguration; St. Nicholas; Trinity, in the Uniate Monastery of the Basilian Order (17th century). ***Lviv:*** St. Paraskeva (1643-1645); Trinity (17th century). ***Mala Belyna:*** St. Paraskeva (17th century). ***Mala Horozhanka:*** St. Nicholas (1688). ***Medenytsya:*** Dormition (1644). ***Muzhylovychi:*** St. Michael (1600). ***Popely:*** Protection of the Blessed Virgin Mary (17th century). ***Sasiv:*** St. Nicholas (17th century). ***Sereda:*** Presentation (1680). ***Skolye:*** St. Paraskeva (17th century). ***Stara Sil:*** Resurrection (17th century). ***Stary Yavoriv:*** St. Paraskeva (17th century). ***Strilkiv:*** St. Nicholas (17th century). ***Velytsia Derevlyanska:*** Ascension (1680). ***Voroblyachyn:*** Transfiguration (1622). ***Yavoriv:*** Nativity of the Virgin Mary (1670); Dormition (1670). ***Zarayske:*** Nativity of the Virgin Mary (1634). ***Zhovkva (now Nesterov):*** Trinity (1612). ***Zolochiv:*** Resurrection (1624-1627).

POLTAVA OBLAST. ***Hadyach:*** Theophany (1666), built by Hetman Ivan Bryukhovetsky. ***Mhar:*** Cathedral of the Transfiguration in the Mhar Monastery (1684-1692). ***Poltava:*** Redeemer (17th century).

ROVNO OBLAST. ***Hoshcha:*** St. Michael (1639). ***Plyashcheva:*** St. Michael (1650).

SUMY OBLAST. ***Putyvl:*** Cathedral of the Transfiguration of Our Lord (1617); Nativity of the Virgin Mary in the Movchanivsky Monastery (1630-1636).

TERNOPIL OBLAST. ***Buchach:*** St. Nicholas (1610). ***Chortkiv:*** Dormition (1635). ***Kopychyntsi:*** Elevation of the Cross (17th century). ***Kozyna:*** St. Paraskeva (17th century). ***Nahoryanka:*** Dormition (17th century). ***Nahoryany:*** St. Nicholas (17th century). ***Pidhaytsi:*** Dormition (1650-1653). ***Pochayiv:*** Protection of the Blessed Virgin Mary (1643). ***Skoryky:*** St. John the Divine (17th century). ***Ternopil:*** Nativity of Christ (1602-1608). ***Volytsya:*** St. Anne of the Conception (17th century). ***Zaluzhzhya:*** Transfiguration (1600).

VOLYNIA OBLAST. ***Bilostok:*** St. Michael (1636). ***Chetvertnya:*** Transfiguration (1600-1604). ***Ivanivka:*** SS. Peter and Paul (1629). ***Kremenets:*** Theophany (1633), established by Lavrentiy Drevynsky and Danylo Elamalynsky. ***Ludyn:*** St. Nicholas (1601). ***Lutsk:*** Elevation of the Cross (1619-1622). ***Novosilky:*** Nativity of Virgin Mary (1676). ***Nyzhkynychi:*** Dormition (17th century). ***Okhlopiv:*** St. Nicholas (1638). ***Zhorany:*** St. Demetrius (1624).

ZAKARPATSKA OBLAST. ***Bukovtsevo:*** St. Anne (17th century). ***Husny:*** St. Nicholas (1655). ***Ivashkovytsya:*** St. Michael (1658). ***Kraynykovo:*** St. Michael (1668). ***Lykytsary:*** St. Basil (17th century). ***Novoselytsya:*** Dormition (17th century). ***Serednye Vodyane (Nyzhne):*** St. Nicholas (17th century). ***Uzhhorod:*** Cathedral of the Elevation of the Cross (1644).

ZHYTOMYR OBLAST. ***Olevsk:*** St. Michael (1596). ***Zhubrovychi:*** Nativity of the Virgin Mary (17th century).

MONASTERY CONSTRUCTION

KIEV OBLAST. ***Kiev:*** Brotherhood of the Theophany (1615), founded by Halshka (Anna) Hulevychivna; Holosiyiv Hermitage, established by Metropolitan Petro Mohyla; Kytayiv Hermitage (17th century).

CHERKASY OBLAST. ***Cherkasy:*** Moshnohorsky Resurrection (17th century). ***Chyhyryn:*** Medvydovsky St. Nicholas (17th century); Holy Trinity (17th century). ***Korsun-Shevchenkivsky:*** St. Onuphrius Hulyanytsky (17th century), established by the chieftain of the Zaporozhian Kozaks Hryhoriy Hulyanytsky.

CHERNIHIV OBLAST. ***Kozelets:*** St. George (1654), established by monks. ***Maksaky:*** Trinity (1642) established by Adam Kysil.

DNIPROPETROVSK OBLAST. ***Novomoskovsk:*** St. Michael Pustynno-Samarsky (17th century), established by the Zaporozhian Kozaks.

IVANO-FRANKIVSK OBLAST. ***Uhornyky:*** Velyky Skyt (1603), established by the monk Yov Knyahynynsky.

KHARKIV OBLAST. ***Kuryazh:*** Transfiguration (1663), established by the Kharkiv Sloboda Kozak Regiment.

POLTAVA OBLAST. ***Chernechy Yar:*** convent, Transfiguration (17th century). ***Hustynets:*** Trinity (1614) established by the monk Yoasaf of the Mt. Athos Monastery. ***Lubny, Mhar:*** Mhar Monastery (1618), established by Princess Rayina Mohylyanka; Transfiguration of Our Lord (1624), established by Bishop Isaya Kopynsky of Peremyshl. ***Poltava:*** Elevation of the Cross (1650), built with the blessings of Metropolitan Sylvester Kosiv by the nobles of Poltava Martyn Pushkar, Ivan Iskra and Ivan Kramar. ***Pryluky:*** convent, Pidhirsko-Ladynsky (1617), founded by Bishop Isaya Kopynsky of Peremyshl. ***Zolotonosha:*** Krasnohirsky St. John the Divine (17th century).

SUMY OBLAST. ***Kaminske:*** Dormition (1681), established by the monk Yona Bolkhovsky and Hetman Ivan Mazepa. ***Krolevets:*** St. Nicholas (1666). ***Okhtyrka:*** Trinity (1654), established by Hegumen Yoanikiy.

TERNOPIL OBLAST. ***Zahaytsi:*** St. John (1637), established by the noblewoman Iryna Yarmolynska.

VINNYTSYA OBLAST. ***Bar:*** Protection of the Blessed Virgin Mary (1616). ***Bershad:*** Transfiguration (1616). ***Brayiliv:*** convent of the Trinity (1636), built by the Polish Senator Michal Kropiwnicki.

VOLYNIA OBLAST. ***Kremenets:*** Theophany (1636), founded by Danylo Malynovsky and Lavrentiy Drevynsky. ***Novhorod Volynsky:*** St. George (1666), founded by Prince Lyubarsky. ***Richytsya:*** Annunciation Monastery and nunnery (1609), endowed by Adam and Oleksa Vyshnevetsky. ***Rzhyshchiv:*** Transfiguration (17th century).

ZAKARPATSKA OBLAST. ***On the river Batorsa:*** Life-Giving Cross (1612), established by the monk Yov Knyahynynsky.

Holy Savior-Transfiguration Cathedral in the city of Izyum (Kharkiv oblast), built in the Ukrainian Baroque style in 1684. Restored many times and rebuilt, this is one of the oldest churches still-standing in the Kharkiv oblast (left).

Dormition Church in the village of Lyutenky (Poltava oblast), built in 1686.

VIII. The Church under the Muscovite and Polish Occupations during the 17th-18th Centuries (1686-1795)

General Characteristics of the Period

1. THE POLITICAL SITUATION IN EASTERN EUROPE

In the late seventeenth and eighteenth centuries the Turks were gradually pushed out of the Balkans. After their siege of Vienna had been overcome by a combined European army (including the Polish king Jan Sobieski and Kozak troops) in 1683, they were roundly defeated by an Austrian army at the battle of Mohacs in 1687. Supported by Venice and the Papacy, the Austrians liberated Belgrade in 1688. Although the Turks rallied, taking Transylvania, they were again pushed back and made peace in 1699. The Austrians again defeated the Turks at Peterwardein in 1718. Despite the Turkish capture of Azov (1711) and the Peloponnesus (1714), and a new offensive in Europe in 1737-1739, their empire was on the wane.

Swedish King Charles XII began a war in 1700 against the Poles, Danes and Muscovites, whom he defeated at the Narva. In the following year he pushed the Poles back from the Dvina, and took Warsaw in 1702. Charles' protegé Stanislaw Leszczynski received the Polish crown. In 1708 Charles marched against Muscovy: in the following year, having swung south into Ukraine, he allied himself with the Ukrainian hetman Ivan Mazepa. They confronted the army of Tsar Peter I at Poltava, and were defeated.

In the peace treaties of 1719-1721 ending the Great Northern War, Sweden was left with only Finland, Wismar and a small part of Pomerania. Expanding Muscovy (renamed "Russia" in 1713) took the Baltic provinces, but most of Pomerania went to Prussia.

Tsar Peter established his capital at the new city of St. Petersburg, built as a "window to the West" with naval access to the Baltic. Following western models, he modernized Russia's bureaucracy and army and introduced western customs. After his death in 1725, the Empire continued to expand. Catherine II, who acceded to the throne in 1762, promoted "enlightened despotism." The system of serfdom was strengthened (1783); monastic lands were confiscated by the State (1786).

During the War of the Polish Succession (1731-1735) the Poles elected Stanislaw Leszczynski as their King, but in 1734 the invading Russians succeeded in again placing their Saxon candidate on the Polish throne. Russian domination of the Polish-Lithuanian Commonwealth continued, as peasant uprisings in Right-Bank Ukraine provided a pretext for Russian military intervention. Finally, Poland was segmented by Russia, Austria and Prussia in 1772, 1793 and 1795.

Prussia took Silesia from Austria in 1740 and Bohemia in 1757. Though driven back from Bohemia by the Austrians, Prussia kept Silesia after the Seven Years' War ended in 1763.

In 1774 Russia defeated the Ottomans after a five-year war. The Russo-Turkish wars continued, with the Crimea and Azov allocated to Russia in 1783.

In the first partition of Poland (1772), Galicia went to Austria (which took Bukovyna from the Turks in 1774-5), and Pomerania to Prussia. Russia took all Polish or Polish-held lands east of the Dvina and Dnieper. In 1783 Russian control in Ukraine was secured by abolition of the Hetman State.

2. THE RELIGIOUS SITUATION IN EUROPE

In the eighteenth century, the population of the Catholic countries grew by 50% on the average, while the Protestant states' population increased by 75% (on the average).In the Catholic countries, secular rulers succeeded in curbing Church influence. The Jesuit order was suppressed in Portugal (1759), France (1764), and in Spain and Italy (1767). Pope Clement XIV finally dissolved the order in 1773.

Secular rulers also sought to make the Church a part of the State bureaucracy, fulfilling state needs. In France, as in other countries, the Catholic Church grew increasingly independent of Rome, but more and more controlled by the state. The Church could no longer adequately fulfill its role in health and education. Furthermore, conflicts developed between the bishops (who were drawn largely from the aristocracy), and the parish clergy.

In France, the Church also came under attack from the *philosophes*, who saw logic in conflict with, and preferable to, faith. In England, however, philosophers demonstrated the inadequacy of rationalism.

The French Revolution of 1789 initially brought a declaration of religious liberty, the separation of the Church from the State, and a new Constitution of the Clergy. Only later would it unleash major anti-clerical and anti-religious forces.

In Austria, Emperor Joseph II issued an Edict of Toleration in 1780. Although he introduced secularizing reforms, he favored the Greek-Catholic (Uniate) Church, which was given equal status with the Latin-rite Catholic Church.

In Muscovy, Peter I imitated the secularizing trends of western Europe. He sought to weaken the influence of the Russian Orthodox Church, making it an arm of the state. In 1721 the Patriarchate of Moscow was abolished and replaced with a Holy Synod, consisting of eleven bishops but presided over by a lay Procurator.

Despite the abolition of the Moscow Patriarchate, Russia remained the prime political support for the Orthodox faith. The Russian Orthodox Church extended its influence as the Muscovite (and from 1713 "Russian") state expanded to the west and south in the seventeenth and eighteenth centuries. By the end of the eighteenth century, the Uniate (Catholic) Church was either liquidated or under threat in the Byelorussian and Ukrainian lands acquired by Russia; it remained secure only in Austrian-ruled Galicia and Transcarpathia.

During the eighteenth century large numbers of Jews were expelled from Russia. At the same time, Dutch and German Mennonites and Serbian and other Orthodox were invited to settle the newly conquered lands in southern Ukraine.

By 1715, Islamic domination in Europe was largely confined to the Crimea and the tip of the Balkans. Islamic minorities did, however, remain in the lands formerly held by the Ottomans, particularly in the Balkans.

During the eighteenth century, various new religious movements appeared in Europe. In Germany, Pietism competed with Lutheranism. England saw an Evangelical Revival and the rise of Methodism. In France, Jansenism continued to challenge traditional Catholic doctrines and particularly the teachings of the Jesuits.

3. THE POLITICAL SITUATION IN UKRAINE

In 1709 the Hetman of Ukraine Ivan Mazepa (1687-1709) allied himself with Charles XII of Sweden against Tsar Peter I of Muscovy. Mazepa's defeat at the battle of Poltava presaged the end of Ukrainian autonomy.

Hlukhiv became the capital of the Hetman state, officially called Malorossia (Little Russia). During the tenure of Mazepa's successor, Hetman Ivan Skoropadsky (1709-1722), the Russian regime sought to control the Kozaks more closely. A resident general was given supervisory powers over the Hetmanate, and Tsar Peter I began to appoint the colonels himself. Various Russian officials were brought into Ukraine. In 1722 a Little Russian College was set up to administer the country, but soon disbanded. The Tsarist regime also stirred up the lower Kozak class against its superiors. After the death of Hetman Danylo Apostol in 1734, the post was left vacant for a number of years.

In 1750 the post of Hetman, revived by Empress Elizabeth, was assumed by Kyrylo Rozumovsky. However, he was forced to resign in 1764. In that year a new Little Russian College was formed. In 1781 the Tsarist regime abolished the regimental system of the Kozak Hetman state, and by 1783 the state was virtually defunct. The Hetmanate was divided into the imperial provinces of Kiev, Chernihiv and Novhorod Siversky, reunited in 1796 into the Little Russian province.

Apart from the Kozaks of the Hetman State, Kozak communities developed in Slobidska Ukrayina (near present-day Kharkiv), and in Zaporizhzhya ("beyond the rapids" of the Dnieper River). Slobidska Ukraine, named after the free settlements (*slobody*) formed along the southern frontier of Muscovite-held territory for purposes of defense against the Tatars, consisted of five Kozak regiments. These were disbanded in 1765, when the area became an imperial province.

After the Battle of Poltava, many Zaporozhian Kozaks who had sided with Mazepa and consequently had their Old (*Stara*) Sich destroyed, emigrated to the Ottoman territory and settled at Oleshky (1711-1734), near the mouth of the Dnieper. However, in 1734 several thousand Zaporozhians were allowed to return to Ukraine and establish themselves at New (*Nova*) Sich.

In the 1750s, foreigners were settled along the northern edge of Zaporizhzhya, forming New Serbia and Slavic Serbia. In 1775 a Russian army forced Nova Sich, the last independent Kozak stronghold, to disband. Thousands of Kozaks fled to Turkish territory. New Serbia and Slavic Serbia were combined with the rest of Zaporizhzhya and the Sloboda Regiment into the province of New Russia.

Russian campaigns against the Turks fought over Ukrainian land helped strengthen Russian domination of the country. During the reign of Catherine II (1762-1796), more foreigners, including Germans, were invited to settle the southern Ukrainian steppe newly won from the Turks in 1774 and 1791. Large private estates were granted to state officials. The Black Sea littoral was settled and the port of Odessa was founded.

In Polish-Lithuanian territory (Right-bank Ukraine), the Kozak-led peasant revolts of the *haydamaky* in 1734, 1750 and especially in 1768 (the "Koliyivshchyna") further weakened the Polish state and provided Russia with pretexts for military intervention. Poland-Lithuania was increasingly influenced by Russia.

With the first partition of Poland in 1772, the western Ukrainian province of Galicia was taken over by Austria. A few years later, the Habsburgs gained Bukovyna from the Ottomans.

The partitions of Poland of 1793 and 1795 gave the Russian Empire the Ukrainian lands known as the Southwestern Territory and consisted of the provinces of Volynia, Kiev and Podilia.

4. 17th-18th-CENTURY HETMANS OF UKRAINE (1686-1795)

Ivan Mazepa 1687-1709
Ivan Skoropadsky 1709-1722
Pylyp Orlyk (in Exile) 1710-1742
Danylo Apostol 1727-1734
Kyrylo Rozumovsky 1750-1764

Chronology

1686 — With annexation of the Kievan Metropolitan Archeparchy by the Moscow Patriarchate, the Ukrainian eparchies of Lviv, Lutsk and Peremyshl and the Byelorussian eparchies of Mohyliv and Mstyslav remain under Poland. The Metropolitan Archeparchy of Kiev and the Eparchy of Chernihiv fall under the Moscow Patriarchate's jurisdiction, as does the Eparchy of Bilhorod.

As a result of the "Eternal Peace" treaty between Poland and Muscovy, Ukraine is divided into "Left Bank" (the Dnieper) Ukraine, under Muscovy and "Right Bank" Ukraine, under Poland. All the eparchies of Ukraine and Byelorussia continue under the ecclesiastical authority of the Metropolitan of Kiev. Article 9 of the treaty guarantees to the Orthodox clergy the freedom to conduct religious services, and to the Metropolitan Archeparchy the right to administer the eparchies and church holdings.

1687-1709 — Ivan Mazepa, Hetman of Ukraine, becomes the most distinguished church patron in the history of Ukraine. During his reign, he builds the following churches: the Church of St. Nicholas on Pechersk in Kiev (1687); the Brotherhood Church of St. Nicholas in the Podil (1687); the Church of All Saints in the Kievan Caves Monastery (1696-98); the Church of the Dormition in Pereyaslav, the Cathedral at the Mharsky Monastery (1687-88); the Church of Our Savior at the Mharsky Monastery. At the same time, Hetman Mazepa funds the re-building of the following churches: in Kiev, the Cathedral of St. Sophia (1690-97), the Golden-domed Monastery of St. Michael, the Church of the Dormition of the Blessed Virgin Mary (1695-96), the Holy Trinity Church (1698) in the Kievan Caves Monastery, the Church of Our Savior at the Mezhyhirsky Monastery, St. Michael's Church at the Vydubytsky Monastery, the Holy Spirit Church at the Brotherhood Monastery and the Church of St. Mary the Protectress in the village of Dekhtyarivka.

22 February 1687 — Patriarch Yoakim of Moscow grants stauropegial status to the Mezhyhirsky Monastery of Kiev, thus releasing it from the jurisdiction of the Metropolitan of Kiev and placing it under the direct control of the Patriarch.

2 January 1688 — Ioannikiy Galyatovsky, the author of many church works, and the archimandrite of the Yeletsky Monastery, dies in Chernihiv; he was one of the most prominent Ukrainian theologians and church activists.

6 March 1688 — Patriarch Yoakim directs the Kievan Metropolitan Hedeon Chetvertynsky, who is in Moscow, to change his title from "Metropolitan of Kiev, Galicia and All Rus'" to "Metropolitan of Kiev, Galicia and Little Rus'."

10 April 1688 — By decree of Tsar Ivan V Romanov, the Archeparchy of Chernihiv is separated from the Kievan Metropolitanate and placed under the direct control of the Moscow Patriarchate. The archbishop of Chernihiv and all hegumens of Chernihiv monasteries are henceforth appointed by Moscow and not by Kiev.

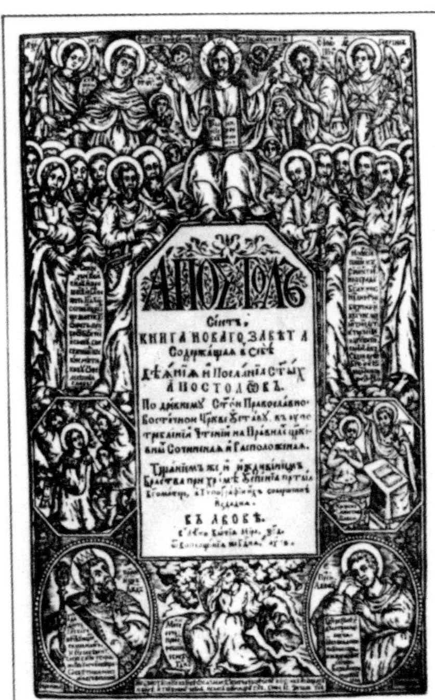

The Epistles (*Apostol*), 1696. Nikodym Zubrytsky, engraver. Printed by the Dormition Brotherhood in Lviv (left).

Title page of a panegyric in honor of Metropolitan Varlaam Yasynsky, by O. Tarasevych, 1690, Kiev.

Ivan Mazepa, Hetman of Ukraine (1687-1709) and patron of the Church. He funded magnificent churches and protected the Ukrainian Orthodox Church from incursions by the Moscow Patriarchate. From *Die Europaeische Fama,* Vol. XXV, Leipzig, 1706.

18 April 1688 — Patriarch Yoakim grants stauropegial status to the Kievan Monastery of the Caves and places it under the direct control of Moscow. The Tsar approves this action on May 31, thus barring the Metropolitan of Kiev from exercising control over the monastery.

1689 — Theological courses open at the Kiev Mohyla College.

Cathedral of the Ascension of the Ascension Monastery in the city of Pereyaslav-Khmelnytsky (Kiev oblast), built in 1695-1700.

During the printing of "Chetya-Mineya" (Lives of the Saints) at the Kievan Monastery of the Caves, Patriarch Yoakim forbids the printing of any other books without his permission and approval.

An Apostolic Vicariate is created in Mukachiv. The first vicar is Bishop Joseph de Camelis.

22 October 1689 — Patriarch Yoakim proposes the creation of a separate Archbishopric of Lviv (without the consent of the Tsars of Moscow and the Kings of Poland) to be directly subordinated to the Patriarch of Moscow and not to the Metropolitan of Kiev.

1690 — The Synod of the Muscovite Church condemns many Ukrainian church books, among them the Great Missal and Small Cathechism of Petro Mohyla.

2 June 1690 — By direction of Hetman Ivan Mazepa, a Church Synod is held in Kiev where Archimandrite Varlaam Yasynsky, rector of the Kiev Mohyla College, is elected Metropolitan. Contrary to the agreement of 1686, his consecration is held in Moscow by demand of the Patriarch and the Tsar.

1690-1693 — Hetman Ivan Mazepa builds the main church of the Kiev Mohyla College in the Monastery of the Holy Theophany Friars. The Church was destroyed by the Soviet authorities in 1936.

1691 — Hetman Ivan Mazepa and Metropolitan Varlaam Yasynsky send envoys, headed by the Prefect of the Kiev Mohyla College, the monk Fr. Ozersky, to Moscow asking the Tsar to grant the College the status of a higher school or Academy. The Rector of the College, Yoakym Krokovsky, goes to Moscow in June 1693 with a similar plea.

23 June 1691 — Bishop Innokentiy Vynnytsky and the whole Eparchy of Peremyshl with 800 churches join the Uniate Church.

1692 — The Muscovite Patriarch Adrian forbids the import and dissemination of Ukrainian books in Moscow.

23 June 1692 — Emperor Leopold grants the Uniate clergy in Transcarpathia equal rights with Roman Catholic clergymen.

August 1692 — Patriarch Dositheus II of Jerusalem counsels the Patriarch of Moscow Adrian to appoint bishops for Ukraine from the Muscovy.

3 September 1693 — Archbishop Lazar Baranovych dies in Chernihiv. He was the first bishop to be removed from the Kievan Metropolitanate and subjugated directly by the Patriarchate of Moscow.

26 October 1693 — The Uniate Metropolitan Cyprian Zhokhovsky dies. The Bishop of Volodymyr-Volynsky, Lev Slyubych-Zalensky, is named by the Papal Nuncio in Warsaw as administrator of the Metropolitanate and the Archeparchy of Polotsk.

1694 — The Kiev Mohyla College assumes all responsibilities of a higher school. In addition to poetics and rhetoric, philosophy and theology are now included in the curriculum.

St. Andrew's Cathedral in Kiev, built in the Baroque style by B. Rastrelli in 1747-53. World-renowned for its interior, it was painted by some of the finest artists of the 18th century.

The great belfry of the Kievan Monastery of the Caves, built in 1718 according to plans by Johann Schadel, on the site of a wooden belfry destroyed by fire. The dome is gold-plated. The belfry is the tallest structure in Ukraine (96.52 m). In the 1920s and 30s, the Soviets took away its ten largest bells, leaving only three.

All Saints Church of the Kievan Monastery of the Caves, built in 1696-98 in the Ukrainian Baroque style and restored in 1718-27 after being damaged by fire. A wooden carved and gold-plated iconostasis was added in the 18th century. The interior was painted in the early 20th century under the direction of I. Yizhakevych.

Churches founded by Ivan Mazepa, Hetman of Ukraine. Engraving by I. Myhura, 1706. From left: St. Nicholas Church, Holy Trinity Church and Dormition Cathedral, all at the Kievan Monastery of the Caves; Epiphany Church in Podil in Kiev; All Saints Church of the Kievan Monastery of the Caves; Church of the Ascension in Pereyaslav.

January 1694 — Patriarch Adrian of Moscow reaffirms the jurisdiction of the Kievan Metropolitan over the Lithuanian-Byelorussian clergy. After a break of 40 years, the Metropolitan of Kiev Varlaam Yasynsky consecrates Serapion Polsky as bishop of Mohyliv and Mstyslav, and names him as a vicar of the Kievan Metropolitanate in Byelorussia.

April 1694 — A Synod of Uniate bishops in Volodymyr-Volynsky elects Lev Zalensky as the new Metropolitan. Pope Innocent XII confirms him on 22 September 1695.

16 December 1694 — An assembly of representatives of Orthodox monasteries, fraternal religious organizations, nobility and clergy takes place in Lviv. Also taking part are the Uniate Bishop of Peremyshl Innokentiy Vynnytsky and representatives of the King and the Papal Nuncio. The majority expresses views against the Union. Disenchanted, Bishop Yosyf Shumlansky shortly afterwards writes a letter to the Kievan Metropolitan Varlaam Yasynsky expressing his fidelity to Orthodoxy.

1700 — Archbishop Ioan Maksymovych establishes a theological college in Chernihiv.

1700s — Not heeding the Treaty of 1686, which subordinated the Metropolitanate of Kiev to the Patriarch of Moscow with the provision that the former "would continue to exercise old rights and privileges," the Tsars and Patriarchs liquidate the Kievan Metropolitanate. Within fifteen years of the treaty, they change the Kievan Metropolitanate's status to that of an eparchy, demote metropolitans to bishops without the right to elect new metropolitans and leave the bishops without Sees.

April 1700 — Hetman Ivan Mazepa and Metropolitan Varlaam Yasynsky send two candidates for the post of Bishop of Pereyaslav to Moscow. The Tsar and the Patriarch retain one of the candidates, Hegumen Stefan Yavorsky, in Moscow. The Patriarch consecrates him Bishop of the city of Ryazan in Muscovy.

18 May 1700 — The Bishop of Lviv Yosyf Shumlansky professes the Catholic faith in the Polish Sejm; he does the same publicly in the church of the Capuchin Fathers on June 6. On May 29 the Sejm accepts all his preconditions to enable the Eparchy of Lviv to join the Uniate Church. On June 15, King Augustus II issues a universal proclamation on the protection of the Eastern-rite Catholics in Galicia, granting church positions only to the Uniate nobility and to the members of the Order of St. Basil the Great, and granting rights and privileges equal to those of the Latin-rite Catholic nobility to the Uniate nobility. Bishop Shumlansky's demand to create a Uniate metropolitanate in Galicia and a seat in the Sejm for the metropolitan remains unanswered.

11 July 1700 — In the Brotherhood Dormition Church, Bishop Yosyf Shumlansky proclaims that the Eparchy of Lviv joined to the Uniate Church. This declaration is repeated in all churches of the eparchy. In a year's time, 1186 churches of the Lviv Eparchy join the Uniate Church. There is generally no great resistance to such acts. The Orthodox faith is retained only by the stauropegial Brotherhood in Lviv, St. Nicholas Monastery in Krekhiv, and a few other institutions.

1701 — The Kiev Mohyla College receives the juridical rights and the title of an Academy.

4 March 1702 — Hetman Ivan Mazepa issues a decree on the status of the Eparchy of Pereyaslav. Bishops of this eparchy are to be consecrated by the Metropolitan of Kiev with the blessings of the Patriarch, and subordinated to the Metropolitan.

1703-04 — Hetman Ivan Mazepa builds an entire new complex for the Kiev Mohyla Academy.

1704 — After the death of Bishop de Camelis, the Apostolic Vicar in Mukachiv, a ten-year struggle between the Apostolic See and the Austrian emperor, with both political and religious implications, begins in Transcarpathia.

1705 — Bishop Yosyf Shumlansky opens an Uniate

printing press at St. George's Cathedral in Lviv.

11-12 July 1705 — Tsar Peter I occupies part of Byelorussia while on his way to aid Polish King Augustus II in his war against Sweden. On his orders, Muscovite soldiers destroy all the icons of St. Yosafat Kuntsevych in Vitebsk. He personally leads his soldiers in a raid on the Uniate Cathedral in Polotsk. The monks of the Basilian Order Teofan Kolbechynsky, Yosafat Ankurovych and Rev. Konstantyn Zayachkivsky die by his hand. The priests Klyment Rozhnyatovsky, Yakiv Knyshevych, Yakiv Kizikivsky, and others are also killed in the Basilian Monastery. After the sack of the Basilian Monastery, his soldiers plunder the Uniate Cathedral in Polotsk and hand it over to the Orthodox population. When the latter refuse to accept it, the church is closed.

1707 — A Synod of Bishops in Kiev elects Yosyf Krokovsky as the new Orthodox Metropolitan.

Bishop Yuriy Vynnytsky's foundation in Lviv is transformed into a theological seminary of the Theatine Order.

1708 — On orders of Peter I, the Muscovite army apprehends Uniate Bishop Dionysiy Zhabokrytsky in Volynia and deports him to Moscow. He is later imprisoned on the Solovky Islands where he dies in 1715.

2 May 1708 — The Lviv Brotherhood, the last and oldest Orthodox association in Galicia, joins the Uniate Church.

16 June 1708 — The Bishop of Lviv, Yosyf Shumlansky, dies. He was instrumental in bringing the Lviv Eparchy into the Uniate Church.

21 July 1708 — The Uniate Metropolitan Lev Zalensky dies in Volodymyr-Volynsky. The Uniate bishops elect Yuriy Vynnytsky, Bishop of Peremyshl, Sambir and Syanok, the new Metropolitan. Because of the change on the royal throne, he is confirmed only in 1710 by Pope Clement XI and King Friedrich August.

Fall 1708 — Hoping to achieve independence for Ukraine, the Hetman of Ukraine Ivan Mazepa signs a treaty with Charles XII, King of Sweden, to aid the latter in his war against Peter I, Tsar of Muscovy.

8 November 1708 — By order of Peter I and under threat of imprisonment, the Kievan Metropolitan Yosyf Krokovsky, Bishop Ioan Maksymovych of Chernihiv and Bishop Zakhariy Kornylovych of Pereyaslav, excommunicate Hetman Ivan Mazepa.

1708-09 — Locked in bloody battle, the armies of Muscovy, Sweden and Poland pillage Ukraine, bringing great desolation to the Ukrainian population of both faiths. Muscovite Orthodox and Swedish Protestant troops are especially harsh in their treatment of the Ukrainian and Byelorussian Uniate faithful; Polish Catholics treat the Orthodox faithful in like manner. Many churches of both faiths are destroyed, and institutions brought to ruin by innumerable levies.

Apotheosis of Ivan Mazepa, Hetman of Ukraine, by I. Myhura, 1706. The engraving shows churches built or restored by Mazepa (left).

Thesis in Honor of Prokop Kalachynsky, by I. Shyrsky, 1690, Kiev.

Yuriy Vynnytsky (1660-1713), Uniate Metropolitan of Kiev (from 1708).

Early 1709 — When Tsar Peter I continues to curtail Ukraine's autonomous rights in an effort to completely liquidate the Ukrainian population as a distinct national and political entity Hetman Ivan Mazepa chooses to liberate Ukraine from Muscovite rule. Mazepa's struggle in union with the Swedish King Charles XII becomes a war for national, religious and political liberation from the rule of Muscovy.

5 April 1709 — Pope Clement XI grants the status of stauropegion to the Dormition Brotherhood in Lviv. It joined the Uniate Church in 1708.

8 July 1709 — A battle between the Muscovite armies of Peter I and the Swedish-Ukrainian armies of Charles XII and Hetman Ivan Mazepa takes place near Poltava. The Muscovite victory seals the fate of the Ukrainian nation and Church for a long time to come.

2 March 1711 — Peter I establishes the Holy Synod in Moscow, to which he subordinates all clergy who were, at that time, under the Patriarch.

22 September 1713 — The Uniate Metropolitan Yuriy Vynnytsky dies. The Synod of Bishops elects Lev (Luka) Kishka, Bishop of Volodymyr-Volynsky, as the new Metropolitan. Pope Clement XI confirms his election in September 1714.

1713 — The name Muscovy is changed by Tsar Peter I to Russia.

Monastery of the Protection of the Blessed Virgin Mary in Kharkiv, built in 1689. The oldest building in the city, it was partially destroyed by the Soviets in the 1930s.

"The Life of St. Barbara," icon painted in 1703 in Rybotychi, now in the delapidated church of St. Paraskeva in Brusno Nove near Lubachiv (Lubaczow, Poland).

1715 — Bishop Dionysiy Zhabokrytsky of Lutsk, who accepted the Union for his eparchy, and was imprisoned by Tsar Peter I in 1709, dies in a Russian prison.

3 September 1716 — The Polish Sejm promulgates a resolution that forbids building new Orthodox churches and repairing old ones on the territories of Ukraine and Byelorussia within the Kingdom of Poland.

1718 — On orders of Peter I, the Kievan Metropolitan Yoakym Krokovsky, suspected of treason, is taken for interrogation to St. Petersburg. He dies in transit under suspicious circumstances. The Kievan Metropolitanate remains vacant for the next four years. By direction of the Moscow Holy Synod, Kyrylo Shumlansky, Bishop of Pereyaslav, administers the Metropolitanate.

26 August — 17 September 1720 — A Synod of the Uniate Church takes place in Zamostya. Taking part are Papal Nuncio Hieronymus Grimaldi and the following Uniate hierarchs: Lev Kishka, Metropolitan of Kiev and All Rus'; Bishop Florian Hrebnytsky of Volodymyr-Volynsky and Berestya; Archbishop Lavrentiy Drutsky-Sokolnytsky of Polotsk, Vitebsk, Mstyslav and Mohyliv; Archbishop Yosyf Vyhovsky of Smolensk; Bishop Yosyf Levytsky of Lutsk and Ostrih; Bishop Atanasiy Sheptytsky of Kholm and Belz; Bishop Yeronim Ustrytsky of Halych, Lviv and Kamyanets Podilsky; Bishop Teofil Godebsky of Peremyshl, Syanok and Sambir; Bishop-designate Antin Zavadsky of Pinsk and Turov. Proto-archimandrite of the Order of St. Basil the Great. In addition, eight archimandrites of Basilian monasteries and 129 representatives of the clergy take part in the Synod. The Synod opens in the Church of the Protection of the Blessed Virgin Mary with the reading of a series of documents. All present profess and subscribe to the Creed of the Catholic Faith in the presence of the Papal Nuncio Hieronymus Grimaldi. The Synod holds discussions about important Church matters during the plenary sessions of August 26, September 1, and September 17. During the last session it

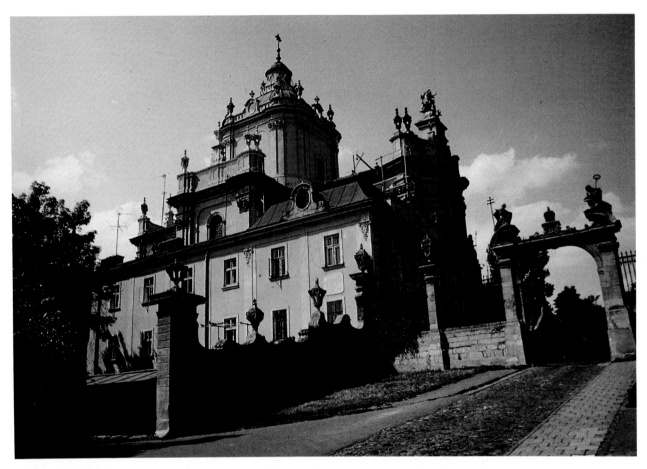

St. George's Cathedral in Lviv, built in 1744-70 on the site of a 14th-century wooden church of the same name. A bell remaining from the old church, cast in 1341, is the oldest bell in Ukraine. Construction began under the direction of B. Meretyn and continued after 1759 under the direction of Fessinger. The interior was painted by Yu. Radzivilovsky, F. Smuhlevych, and L. Dolynsky. The sculptures are by Pinsel. The cathedral was restored in 1905-11 and again in 1933. It was the seat of the metropolitans of Galicia and an important center of Ukrainian religious, national and cultural-educational life. Metropolitan Andrey Sheptytsky is buried there.

Church of the Mother of God the Protectress, built in 1792 in the village of Ploske (Transcarpathian oblast). In 1920 it was moved to the village of Kanora, and in 1969 to its present site at the outdoor Museum of Folk Architecture and Customs of the Ukrainian S.S.R.

Church of the Resurrection in the city of Sumy, built in 1702 in the defensive style of church architecture. The Soviets converted it into a museum of applied folk art.

Lev Kishka (1663-1728), Uniate Metropolitan of Kiev (1714-28), author of works on history and canon law.

adopts a number of decisions that are formulated in 19 paragraphs, and pertain to the following: the Catholic Faith, preaching the Word of God, Holy Sacraments, standardization of services, Metropolitans, bishops, officials, secretaries-notaries, protopresbyters, pastors, faithful, seminaries, monasteries and the life of the religious, churches and their properties, simony, fasts, feast days, relics of the saints and pay for the delegates. For the first time since accepting the Union of Berestya in 1596, the Synod normalize the life of the Uniate Church, reorganizes her structure and brings uniformity into the Church's traditional Eastern rite. Some of the privileges given in Berestya to the Uniate Church are taken over by the Apostolic See or the Papal Nuncio (e.g., permission to publish religious books). The decisions of the Zamostya Synod, approved by Pope Benedict XIII only in 1724, become the basis of the operation and life of the Church for the next two centuries.

1721 — The Pochayiv Monastery joins the Uniate Church and becomes a monastery of the Basilian Order.

The last Orthodox eparchy under Poland, Lutsk, joins the Uniate Church.

Persecuted by the Polish authorities, Orthodox Bishop Kyrylo Shumlansky of Lutsk flees to Kiev.

Muscovite occupation forces in Ukraine arrest and deport into exile Hedeon Odorsky, Archimandrite of the Hetman's capital Baturyn, and Ivan Rohachevsky, Archpriest of Lokhvytsya.

21 January 1721 — By order of Tsar Peter I, the Patriarchate of Moscow ceases to exist and is replaced by the Holy Synod of the Russian Orthodox Church. The Tsar promulgates the "Spiritual Regulations" (Constitution of the Church) in which there is no mention of either the autonomous rights of the Metropolitan of Kiev, or other rights and privileges of the Metropolitan. The Kievan Metropolitanate becomes the Kiev Eparchy of the Russian State Church headed by the Tsar and the Synod.

21 August 1721 — Peter I subordinates both Ukrainian printing establishments, in Kiev and Chernihiv, to the Synod of the Russian Orthodox Church in St. Petersburg. They are forbidden to print any books without the consent and approval of the Holy Synod.

1722 — The Polish king Augustus II grants a special privilege to the Orthodox Church on Ukrainian and Byelorussian territories for the preservation of everything that was given to the Orthodox by preceding kings and the State. This privilege notwithstanding, the Orthodox Church continues to be persecuted under Poland.

Bishop Yepifaniy Tykhorsky of Bilhorod establishes a religious school in Bilhorod, which is moved to Kharkiv in 1726 and is granted collegial status.

April 1722 — Peter I abolishes Ukraine's autono-

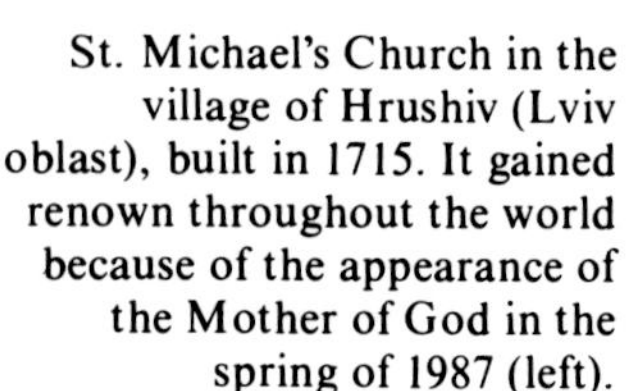

St. Michael's Church in the village of Hrushiv (Lviv oblast), built in 1715. It gained renown throughout the world because of the appearance of the Mother of God in the spring of 1987 (left).

Belfry of St. Michael's Church in Hrushiv.

mous right to be ruled by a Hetman, and establishes an administrative body for Ukraine, the "Little Russian College." After the death of Hetman Ivan Skoropadsky in July of that year, he forbids the election of a new Hetman.

14 May 1722 — The Archimandrite Varlaam Vonatovych of Tikhvin Monastery of the Novgorod Eparchy, a Ukrainian, is appointed by Peter I and consecrated Archbishop of Kiev, but without the title of "Metropolitan of Kiev and All Little Rus'."

1723 — Peter I liquidates the autonomous government of Ukraine, imprisons acting Hetman Pavlo Polubotok and the whole Kozak officer's corps, and deports them to St. Petersburg, where they are sentenced to life imprisonment. Polubotok dies in prison a year later.

1724 — The Synod of the Russian Church punishes the Ukrainian printing establishment in Chernihiv for breaking censorship regulations and carts its properties off to Moscow.

1727 — The Synod of the Russian Church for the first time appoints a Russian, the Archimandrite of Tambov Yoakim Strukov, as bishop of the Ukrainian city of Pereyaslav. He is consecrated bishop not in Kiev but in St. Petersburg.

1728 — During the reign of the new Tsar Peter II, the Archbishop of Kiev Varlaam Vonatovych demands the return of old rights and privileges to the Metropolitanate, but without success.

The Uniate Metropolitan Lev Kishka dies, and the Papal Nuncio in Poland appoints the Bishop of Lviv Atanasiy Sheptytsky as administrator of the Metropolitanate. Bishop Atanasiy Sheptytsky is thereafter elected Metropolitan by the Synod of Bishops, and the election is confirmed by the Pope on August 17, 1729. With the election of Atanasiy Sheptytsky as the Metropolitan of Kiev, Galicia and All Rus', the center of the Uniate Church moves from Byelorussia to Western Ukraine.

St. Michael the Archangel, 1720.
Icon from the Holy Trinity Church of the Basilian monastery in Zhovkva (Lviv oblast).

Siege of the Pochayiv Monastery by the Turks in 1675, by N. Zubrytsky, Pochayiv, 1704. According to legend, thanks to the miraculous intercession by the Mother of God, the Turks retreated from the monastery after a three-day siege (left).

Adoration of the Magi. Altar trim, silver and gold-plating, 18th century. Kievan Monastery of the Caves.

The Byelorussian Bishop Sylvester Svyatopolk Chetvertynsky demands independence for the Byelorussian Church from both the Kievan Metropolitanate and the Muscovite Holy Synod.

1729 — Andriy Rachynsky, a composer and Kapellmeister at the palace of Hetman Kyrylo Rozumovsky in Hlukhiv, is born. He organizes the largest music library in Eastern Europe; these works still exist today.

1730 — For his demands of Metropolitan rights for Kiev, the Russian occupation authorities in Ukraine arrest Archbishop Varlaam Vonatovych. He and the whole Consistory of Kiev are deported to Moscow.

Varlaam Vonatovych is stripped of his position as archbishop and jailed in the Kyrylo-Bilozersky Monastery. He remains there until 1740, when he is released with the advent of the new Tsar Ivan VI.

1730s — The spokesman for the clergy who demand an independent Ukrainian Church, the monk Yepyfaniy Revutsky, repeatedly petitions the Synod of the Russian Church to reestablish the Kievan Metropolitanate with its former rights. Instead of producing positive results, his demands bring about even greater oppression of the Orthodox Church in Ukraine.

A Consistory of the Uniate Church opens in Radomyshl, Kiev Region, and the Uniate movement begins to spread anew in Right-Bank Ukraine.

1731 — After the imprisonment of the Archbishop of Kiev Varlaam Vonatovych in 1730, the Russian authorities forbid the election of a new Metropolitan. Instead of a Metropolitan, the Russian Synod appoints Raphael Zaborovsky Archbishop of Kiev, and Tsarina Anna Ivanovna confirms him. Of Ukrainian origin, Archbishop Raphael Zaborovsky was the Archimandrite of the Klyazynsky Monastery in the Tver Eparchy, and a member of the Synod.

1732 — According to the decisions of the Synod of Zamostya of 1720, Metropolitan Atanasiy Sheptytsky prepares and publishes a *Liturgikon* (Missal) and two years later, a *Chasoslov* (Breviary).

19 February 1733 — The Synod of the Russian Church subordinates the Ukrainian Eparchy of Pereyaslav, which prior to this was part of the Kievan Metropolitanate, to itself.

27 April 1733 — The electoral Sejm, during which Augustus III is elected the new King of Poland, takes away all political rights from the Protestants and considers the Orthodox Church on Byelorussian and Ukrainian territories as nonexistent. Remnants of the Orthodox clergy and faithful are cruelly persecuted by the Polish authorities.

1734 — Polish and Russian armies quell a popular uprising of the "Haydamaky" on the Ukrainian territories under Poland. The "Haydamaky" fought against social injustice and religious oppression perpetrated by Polish Catholic fanatics.

1738 — An Orthodox theological seminary opens in Pereyaslav.

1739 — A Uniate Council of representatives of monasteries on Ukrainian territories — Galicia, Volynia, Kholmshchyna and Pidlashshya — unites all Ukrainian monasteries into the Basilian Congregation of the Rus' Province. Patrykiy Zhyravsky is elected Proto-archimandrite.

Belfry of the Cathedral of the Transfiguration at the Mhar Monastery (Poltava oblast), founded in 1624 by Bishop Isaya of Peremyshl. Most of the monastery, in which Patriarch Atanasius III Patellaros of Constantinople was buried in 1654, was destroyed by the Soviets in the 1930s. The belfry still stands (left).

Holy Savior-Transfiguration Cathedral in the city of Pryluky (Chernihiv oblast), built in 1710-20 in the Ukrainian Baroque style. Damaged by fire, it was rebuilt in the mid-19th century.

Atanasiy Sheptytsky (1686-1746), Uniate Metropolitan of Kiev (from 1729), organizer of Church and educational life.

1740-47 — In the Kozak Hetmanate of Ukraine there are 866 parish schools in 1099 settlements.

12 August 1742 — The Archbishop of Kiev Raphael Zaborovsky petitions the new Russian Tsarina Elizabeth to return the rights of a metropolitanate to Kiev, and the title of metropolitan to the Kievan archbishop. Shortly thereafter, the Tsarina promulgates an "Ukase" "for Kiev to be the Metropolitanate it once was," and gives the Archbishop the title of Metropolitan. Tsarina Elizabeth's decision raises among the Ukrainian clergy hopes of a renewal of the Ukrainian Church with her former rights and privileges, which she had before her subordination to the Moscow Patriarchate in 1686.

1743 — An Assembly in Dubno combines the two Basilian Provinces — Rus' (Ukrainian) and Byelorussian — into one Basilian Order.

1744 — The construction of St. George's Cathedral in Lviv begins.

10 April 1744 — Pope Benedict XIV condemns persecution of the Uniate Church on Ukrainian and Byelorussian territories under Poland.

13 December 1746 — The Uniate Metropolitan Atanasiy Sheptytsky dies in Lviv. In accord with the decision of the Synod of Zamostya, the Archbishop of Polotsk, Floriyan Hrebnytsky, a Byelorussian, succeeds him and is confirmed by Pope Benedict XIV, but not until 1748.

1747 — Tsarina Elizabeth secretly marries Oleksiy Rozumovsky, a Ukrainian. Influenced by him, she reestablishes the Hetmanate and partially returns autonomous rights to Ukraine.

22 October 1747 — The Ukrainian Orthodox Metropolitan Rafayil Zaborovsky dies in Kiev.

1748 — The Archbishopric of Polotsk returns again to the Kievan Uniate Metropolitanate.

6 March 1748 — With Tsarina Elizabeth's permission, the Archimandrite of the Kievan Monastery of the Caves, Tymofiy Shcherbatsky, is consecrated Orthodox Metropolitan of Kiev, Lviv and Little Rus'.

1750s — Having declared the Orthodox Church on Ukrainian and Byelorussian territories under Poland as nonexistent, Polish Catholic fanatics begin cruel persecution of the Uniate Church. The Uniates undergo the same persecution that the Orthodox underwent previously.

1751 — Irakliy Lisovsky becomes Proto-archimandrite of all the Basilian provinces — Ukraine, Byelorussia and Lithuania.

23 February 1752 — The Hetman of Ukraine, Kyrylo Rozumovsky, by agreement with the Kievan Metropolitan Tymofiy Shcherbatsky, but without the knowledge or approval of Tsarina Elizabeth or of the Russian Synod, orders the election of a new Bishop of Pereyaslav. The Synod does not approve any of the three Ukrainian candidates, reproves the Metropolitan, and appoints Archimandrite Ivan Kozlovich, rector of the Moscow Theological Seminary, as the new Bishop of Pereyaslav a year later.

St. Catherine's Church in Chernihiv, built in 1715 in the Baroque style, rebuilt many times, and partially destroyed by the Soviets in the 1930s. The structure is a typical example of stone church architecture of the 17th and 18th-century Left-Bank Ukraine (left).

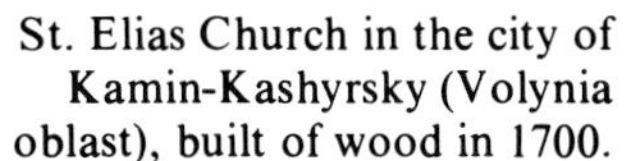

St. Elias Church in the city of Kamin-Kashyrsky (Volynia oblast), built of wood in 1700.

Floriyan Hrebnytsky (-1762), Uniate Metropolitan of Kiev (1748-62).

5 June 1752 — In reply to numerous demands of the Kievan metropolitan Tymofiy Shcherbatsky, the Russian Synod declines to return the See of Pereyaslav and the Mezhhirsky Monastery near Kiev, to the Kievan Metropolitanate. It also declines to permit the publishing of church books in Kiev.

March 1753 — Metropolitan Floriyan Hrebnytsky and the Uniate Bishops demand that King Augustus III forbid by law the aggressive transfer of Uniates to Latin-rite.

5 April 1753 — By decree of Pope Benedict XIV, the Latin-rite Catholic Theological College in Vilnius becomes a seminary for Ukrainian and Byelorussian Eastern-rite clergy. Simultaneously, the Pope sets the number of students for the two existing seminaries in Lviv and Vilnius.

18 September 1755 — Pope Benedict XIV promulgates an encyclical stating that, by the will of the Apostolic See, the faithful of the Eastern rite are to remain in that rite, and to keep it pure. At the same time, he instructs his missionaries in Eastern Europe that the wish of the Apostolic See is that all people be Catholic but not necessarily of the Latin rite.

1757 — In contravention of the treaty of 1686 regarding the subordination of the Kievan Metropolitanate to the Moscow Patriarchate, according to which the elected Kievan Metropolitan was to retain the See for life, the Russian authorities order the removal from office of the Kievan Metropolitan Tymofiy Shcherbatsky and against his will assign him the Bishopric of Moscow. Forbidding an election of a new Metropolitan, Tsarina Elizabeth appoints Arseniy Mohylyansky, Bishop of Pereyaslav-Zalisky in Muscovy, the new Metropolitan of Kiev.

1760 — A movement against the Union, and against dependence on the Roman Catholic bishop of Eger, spreads in Transcarpathia.

31 January 1760 — On orders of the Russian Synod, the Bishop of Zaporizhzhya Anatoliy Melas, independent of both the Kievan Metropolitanate and the Russian Synod, is arrested, and the Metropolitan appoints his own vicar. The clergy of the Zaporizhzhya Host (Sich), selected by their parishes, commemorate only the leader of the Host in their services.

1762 — The Uniate Metropolitan Floriyan Hrebnytsky dies. According to the order of succession, the Bishop of Volodymyr-Volynsky, Pylyp Volodkovych, becomes the new Metropolitan.

1763 — The Hetman of Ukraine Kyrylo Rozumovsky demands in St. Petersburg that the Kiev Mohyla Academy be upgraded to a university status with four faculties, one of which is to be a theological faculty.

The Kievan Church Consistory protests attempts by the Russian government to take away properties of churches and monasteries.

August 1764 — A conference of Uniate Bishops in preparation for the next Synod takes place in Berestya. The participants send a protest to King Stanislaw Poniatowski, which attacks the practice of degrading sons of Uniate priests to serf status.

St. Paraskeva Church in the village of Pluhiv (Lviv oblast), built in 1715. It is one of the better examples of wooden church architecture of the Galician school (left).

Holy Spirit Church in the village of Konyukhy (Ternopil oblast), built in 1700 in the style of wooden church architecture of the Galician school.

10 November 1764 — The new Russian Tsarina Catherine II liquidates the Hetmanate of Ukraine and all forms of Ukrainian autonomous status.

The Bishop of Mukachiv, Manuyil Olshevsky, convokes a Synod of clergy at which they decide to continue to struggle to free themselves from the authority of the Latin-rite Catholic Bishop of Eger.

26 August 1765 — All the Uniate Bishops arrive in Berestya for the first Synod to be convoked after 40 years. King Stanislaw Poniatowski closes the Synod, demanding that the agenda and all decisions be first agreed upon with him.

30 June 1767 — The Kievan Metropolitan Arseniy Mohylyansky and the clergy of Ukraine send a number of demands to the Commission for the Preparation of the New Code and State Laws in St. Petersburg: to codify election of the Metropolitan of Kiev and the Archimandrite of the Kiev Monastery of the Caves; not to subordinate the Metropolitan to the Russian Holy Synod; to give the Metropolitan the title of "Metropolitan of Little Rus'"; to grant appropriate privileges to the Kiev Mohyla Academy and the Chernihiv Theological Seminary; and to allow the printing of books in Kiev and the free distribution of these books. The Commission later rejects all these demands.

Summer 1767 — The Poles execute the sexton of the Orthodox Church in Zhabotyn, Danylo Kushnir, and Captain Kharko by firing squad. News of their deaths spreads like wildfire throughout Ukraine and leads to anti-Polish and anti-Catholic uprisings, known as the "Koliyivshchyna," in 1768.

Archbishop Yuriy Konysky (1717-95), rector of the Kiev Mohyla Academy (from 1752), author of theological works.

The Russians capture the Polish Latin-rite Bishops of Cracow and Kiev and deport them into exile in Muscovy. News spreads among the people that Catholics of both Latin and Eastern rites will be caught and deported to Muscovy if they do not return to Orthodoxy. Either from conviction or from fright, a great number of Uniates in the Smila and Chyhyryn regions convert back to Orthodoxy in a short time. An important part in this conversion is played by the Hegumen

The Liturgicon or Missal (Leiturhikon si yest sluzhebnyk). Ivan Fylypovych, Nikodym Zubrytsky, Heorhiy Vyshlovsky, engravers. Printed in 1759 by the Dormition Brotherhood, Lviv (left).

Liturgicon or Missal (Leiturhikon si yest sluzhebnyk), 1744. Andriy Holota, engraver. Printed at the Pochayiv Monastery.

Protection of the Blessed Virgin Mary 17th-18th centuries. Icon from the Church of St. John the Theologian in the village of Fusiv (Lviv oblast).

of the Motryn Monastery, Melkhisedek Znachko-Yavorsky.

15 November 1767 — The Polish Sejm grants a number of rights and privileges to the Orthodox Church in the Polish Kingdom. The Bishop of Mohyliv, Yuriy Konysky, becomes vicar for the Orthodox Church on Ukrainian and Byelorussian territories under Poland.

10 June 1768 — During the popular uprising known as the "Koliyivshchyna," the hegumen of the Uniate Monastery Irakliy Kostetsky and his deputy Levytsky perish in Uman. The Basilian school is destroyed, its rector, Rev. Ivan Volkovytsky, and many teachers and students are killed. About 300 Uniate priests perish during the uprisings on the Right-Bank territories.

20 June 1768 — Fearing that the "Koliyivshchyna" is growing into a struggle for the independence of Ukraine, the Russian Tsarina Catherine II sends her armies, together with Polish troops, to quell the uprising. Polish troops execute the captured leader Ivan Gonta and the Russians execute Maksym Zaliznyak. Having occupied the Right-Bank territories of Ukraine, the Poles cruelly persecute both Uniate and Orthodox clergy.

1769 — The Russian Synod forbids the Kiev Monastery of the Caves to publish the *Primer* and orders the destruction of all copies already printed and distributed.

1770 — Catherine II and the Russian Synod appoint a Ukrainian of Russian orientation and a spokesman of Russian centralized church politics, Havryil (Hryhory) Kremyanetsky, a member of the Russian Synod, as the new Metropolitan of Kiev. During his rule, Russians are appointed as hegumens of Ukrainian monasteries for the first time.

18 March 1770 — The Russian Synod and Catherine II forbid the Metropolitan of Kiev to use the title of "Metropolitan of Kiev, Galicia and Little Rus'." "Little Rus'" is deleted from the title, thus narrowing his authority to the Kiev Eparchy only. Once again the Metropolitan ceases to be the head of the Ukrainian Church.

19 September 1771 — By a bull, Pope Clement XIV establishes an independent Eparchy of Mukachiv in Transcarpathia that is directly subordinated to the Apostolic See, and nominates Ivan Bradach as its first bishop.

7 November 1771 — On orders of Catherine II, the Field Marshal of the Russian forces in Right-Bank Ukraine begins mass arrests of the Uniate clergy who refuse to join Russian Orthodoxy. In a short time, 1,200 churches are taken away from the Uniates in the Kiev region.

1772 — As a result of Russian church policy, which was directed towards liquidation of the Kievan Metropolitanate, only one eparchy — the Metropolitan Eparchy of Kiev — remains under its jurisdiction; six eparchies were under it at the time of its subordination to the Moscow Patriarchate in 1686.

The Uniate Eparchy of Peremyshl has 1,253 parishes, nine monasteries and six convents of the Basilian Order at the time of its annexation by the Austrian Empire.

28 February 1772 — The Metropolitan of Tobolsk, Arseniy Matsiyevych, dies in prison in Revel (Tallinn). He was stripped of his metropolitancy in 1763 and sentenced to life imprisonment in 1767 for his protests against confiscation of church properties by the Russian government.

5 August 1772 — As a result of the division of the Polish Kingdom between Russia, Prussia and Austria, Eastern Byelorussia with the Eparchies of Polotsk, Vitebsk, Orsha, Mohyliv and Smolensk of the Kievan Uniate Metropolitanate, and the Orthodox Eparchy of Mohyliv with Bishop Yuriy Konysky, fall under Russian rule. Four Uniate eparchies — Peremyshl, Lviv, Kholm, and Mukachiv — almost all the lands of

Western Ukraine — pass to the Habsburg Empire. Austria then becomes the defender of the Ukrainian Uniate Church against Russian Orthodoxy and Polish Catholicism. The hierarchy of the Uniate Church now maintains contact with Rome through the Papal Nuncio in Vienna.

1773 — By decree of Pope Clement XIV, the Jesuit Order is disbanded; on orders of Catherine II, however, Jesuits may remain in the Russian Empire as before.

1773-74 — By direction of Joseph Garampi, the Papal Nuncio in Poland, the Uniate Bishop of Kholm Maksymilyan Ryllo makes a tour of the Right-bank territories of Ukraine. He is arrested by the Russians and spends six months in prison.

1773-96 — On orders of Catherine II, 145 Uniate Basilian monasteries on Ukrainian territories under Russian rule are closed. Some of them are transferred to the Orthodox Church.

1775 — On orders of Catherine II, Russian armies raze the Zaporizhzhya Sich, the last bulwark of Ukrainian independence and Ukrainian Orthodoxy. They also raze almost all of the 70 Orthodox churches of the Sich.

At the same time the Russians capture and imprison Petro Kalnyshevsky, the last Hetman of the Zaporozhian Kozaks. He dies in prison on the Solovky Islands in 1801.

7 May 1775 — The Russian Synod directs the Kievan Monastery of the Caves to publish only books identical to Muscovite books.

1778 — As a result of a treaty between Russia and Poland, all parishes that joined the Uniate Church in 1717 are to return to Orthodoxy. Clergy who refuse to accept Orthodoxy are arrested and deported to Russia.

A Uniate Theological Seminary, which exists until the Soviet authorities close it in 1947, opens in Uzhhorod.

13 February 1778 — The Uniate Metropolitan Pylyp Volodkovych dies in Radomyshl. Bishop Lev Sheptytsky of Lviv succeeds him.

13 May 1779 — The Uniate Metropolitan Lev Sheptytsky dies in Radomyshl. The Archbishop of Polotsk, Yason Smogozhevsky, who lives on Russian-occupied lands, succeeds him as an ex-officio administrator. He is elected Metropolitan by the Synod of Bishops on February 26, 1780.

August 1779 — The Provincial Government of Galicia petitions Austrian Empress Maria Theresa for the creation of a separate Metropolitanate of Galicia to which all Uniate eparchies within the Austro-Hungarian Empire would be subordinated.

1780 — Instead of a coadjutor for Metropolitan Yason Smogozhevsky, Catherine II appoints a consistory of three priests who are to administer the Uniate Metropolitanate in the event of the Metropolitan's death.

A building of the Theological College in Chernihiv, established in the latter part of the 16th century, and One of the oldest institutions of learning in Ukraine. Additions were made in the 17th, 18th and 19th centuries. Elements of the Baroque style are evident.

The Austrian emperor Joseph II introduces church reforms (known as the Josephine Reforms) in his empire, which grant the Uniate Church parity in rights and privileges with the Latin-rite Church and introduce for the first time two new terms: "Roman Catholic Church" (Latin-rite) and "Greek Catholic Church" (Uniate or Eastern-rite). State law forbids the Uniates to join the Latin rite. These new reforms benefit the normalization of Ukrainian culture and literature, as well as the national consciousness of the population.

Because of the new political situation and changes in the occupants of Ukrainian and Byelorussian territories, the Basilian Order is divided into two separate provinces: the Holy Savior Province of Galicia, and St. Nicholas Province of Byelorussia.

Bishop Maksymilyan Ryllo opens an Eparchial Theological Seminary in Peremyshl, which is closed three years later by decree of the Austrian emperor Joseph II.

Pope Pius VI appeals to Catherine II in defense of the Ukrainian-Byelorussian Catholic Church.

1781 — For the first time in the history of the Catholic Church, the Apostolic See cannot confirm the Uniate Metropolitan, Yason Smogozhevsky, who at the time is Archbishop of Polotsk, and resides under Russian occupation. To confirm a Metropolitan, the Apostolic See needs the consent of three powers — Russia, Poland and Austria — because his authority would extend to parts of each. The Russian government agrees to Yason Smogozhevsky's confirmation if the seat of the Metropolitanate is moved from Polotsk to Warsaw. Shortly thereafter, the Metropolitan moves to Warsaw, organizes the first Uniate church and administers the Metropolitanate from there.

Catherine II annexes the Hetmanate of Ukraine to Russia and makes the territory an integral part of the empire. She also introduces serfdom in Left-Bank Ukraine.

1781-82 — As a result of the church reforms of Joseph II, the Apostolic See cannot issue any instructions without the knowledge and agreement of the Emperor. Many churches and monasteries are closed and their properties are turned over to the civilian authorities.

24 April 1781 — On the instructions of Emperor Joseph II, the Orthodox Church of Bukovyna is transferred to the jurisdiction of Dositheus Khereskula, Bishop of Radivtsi, who moves his seat to Chernivtsi on December 12. The Orthodox Church of Bukovyna remains under the jurisdiction of the Patriarch of Constantinople.

13 October 1781 — Joseph II decrees religious tolerance for three faiths: Protestant, Lutheran and Orthodox.

1782 — Joseph II gives equal status to the three Catholic Rites in Galicia: Latin, Armenian and Greek. Religious intolerance becomes a crime.

1783 — With the consent of the Apostolic See, Catherine II nominates the Archbishop Irakliy Lisovsky of Polotsk, to be the first Uniate Metropolitan in the Russian Empire. At the same time, she appoints Bishop Samuyil Myslavsky, a Russified Ukrainian who spent a 15-year apprenticeship serving in different Russian bishoprics, as the Orthodox Metropolitan of Kiev.

Catherine II introduces the Imperial Russian system of government in the occupied territories of Ukraine.

4 July 1783 — Emperor Joseph II subordinates the Orthodox Eparchy of Bukovyna to the Serbian Metropolitanate in Karlovci (Croatia): it remains a part of this Metropolitanate for 90 years.

November 1783 — By decree of Joseph II, the teaching of theology and philosophy is curtailed in the monasteries, and these subjects are now taught in the universities.

1784 — By decree of Catherine II, children of Ukrainian clergy not studying in the theological seminaries are drafted into the army or into the civil service.

21 October 1784 — By decree of Joseph II, the first university on Ukrainian territories opens in Lviv. At almost the same time, a Major Seminary with the Old-Ukrainian language of instruction opens in Lviv for the Ukrainian Catholics of Galicia, Transcarpathia and Bukovyna.

1785 — The Austrian government closes the only existing Orthodox monastery in Galicia, Skyt Manyavsky.

31 March 1785 — Catherine II appoints the Bishop of Pereyaslav Viktor Sadkovsky as Orthodox Bishop of Volynia, Pidlashshya and Podilia. He swears allegiance to the Tsarina and the Polish King Stanislaw Poniatowski. In two years, 206 churches on the territory of his eparchy return to Orthodoxy due to his efforts. Bishop Viktor Sadkovsky, whose see is in Slutsk, becomes administrator of the Orthodox Church on territories under Poland.

1786 — The Ukrainian language becomes a State language in Galicia and the language of instruction at the University and the Major Theological Seminary. After the death of Joseph II in 1790, theology and philosophy are taught in Latin.

The Polish Latin-rite clergy introduces in the Sejm a project to disband the Ukrainian Uniate Church and to subordinate her to the hierarchy of the Latin-rite. At the same time, persecution of the Uniates intensifies on Ukrainian and Byelorussian territories under Poland.

Holy Spirit Cathedral in the city of Romny (Sumy oblast), built in 1742-46 in the Ukrainian Baroque style (left).

Church of the Protection of the Blessed Virgin Mary in the village of Piddubtsi (Volynia oblast), built in 1745 in the late Baroque style.

St. Nicholas Church in the village of Danyliv (Transcarpathian oblast), built of wood in 1799 (left).

Belfry of the Kievan Monastery of the Caves in the Farther Caves in Kiev, built by S. V. Kovnir in 1754-61 in the Ukrainian Baroque style.

By decree of Catherine II, the Ukrainian clergy is placed on a par with the Russian, through secularization of church and monastery properties, which are forcibly taken away by the State.

10 April 1786 — On orders of the Tsarina's officials, the Theophany Brotherhood Monastery in Kiev is closed and trasformed into a hospital. All properties of the monastery and of the Kiev Mohyla Academy are taken over by the Russian State. The Russian government begins a forced Russification of the Academy by assigning teachers from Moscow and by introducing new subjects into its curriculum. The Academy begins to gradually lose its status as a Ukrainian cultural-educational center.

1787 —. A theological-philosophical department for Ukrainians opens at the University of Lviv.

1788 — The Uniate Metropolitan, Yason Smogozhevsky, dies. His successor is Bishop Teodosiy Rostotsky of Kholm, whose seat is in Vilnius and Warsaw.

1789-90 — With the introduction of the religious reforms of Joseph II, thirty-eight Ukrainian Uniate monasteries are closed in Galicia and twenty-four in Bukovyna. Fifty four Latin-rite Catholic monasteries are closed. In addition to monasteries, hundreds of churches are closed and converted into jails, schools, warehouses or military buildings. Houses of study for monks and educational foundations for children cease operating. The remaining open monasteries are removed from the jurisdiction of the Proto-archimandrite of the Basilian Order and subordinated to eparchial bishops.

24 April 1789 — Accusing Orthodox Bishop Viktor Sadkovsky of planning an uprising, the Polish authorities incarcerate him for three years.

1790 — The Ukrainian Catholic hierarchs in Galicia petition the new Austrian emperor Leopold II to establish a Metropolitanate for Galicia.

13 April 1790 — The four-year Polish Sejm passes a universal proclamation of religious freedom, guaranteeing to the Protestant and Orthodox Churches the protection of the State while at the same time forbidding patronage or help from Churches outside Poland. It also proclaims renewal of an Orthodox hierarchy independent from the Russian Holy Synod but within the canonical jurisdiction of the Patriarch of Constantinople.

November 1790 — After a centuries-long interval, the Patriarch of Constantinople sends a pastoral letter to the Orthodox Church in Poland.

3 May 1791 — The Polish Sejm proclaims a new constitution, stating that the Catholic Faith of both rites — Latin and Greek (Eastern) — takes precedence in the Polish Kingdom; transfering from one rite to the other is considered State treason; the Uniate Metropolitan acquires a seat in the Senate; and the Protestant and Orthodox Faiths are given guarantees of full freedom. Shortly after adoption of the new document it is declared null and void by the Russian government through the "Confederation of Targowica," (1792), and then by Prussia.

15 June — 8 July 1791 — After almost 200 years, the first Synod of the Orthodox Church takes place in Pinsk, by order and with the permission of the Polish King Stanislaw Poniatowski. Ninety-six delegates take part in the Synod including representatives from the clergy, monasteries, parishes and Orthodox nobility, as well as two Uniate Bishops — Yoakym Dashkevych-Horbatsky of Pinsk and Yuriy Bulhak of Turov. Chaired by the Archimandrite of the Motronsky Monastery Irynakh Balanovsky, at its plenary session of 2 July the Synod swears allegiance to the law and obligates itself not to seek foreign dependency. The Synod adopts rules about the organization of the Orthodox Church in Poland in 11 paragraphs as follows: the Orthodox Church in Poland is within the jurisdiction of the Patriarch of Constantinople, who is to appoint a new Church hierarchy; the Synod is to assemble every four years and elect new archbishops, bishops, archimandrites and other governing organs of the Church; matters of faith and rite are decided by the clergy based on the seven Ecumenical Councils: the Church is governed by the Synod composed of an Archbishop with the rights of a Metropolitan and three bishops, with the help of the General Consistory; eparchies are governed by bishops with help from eparchial consistories, and they (the eparchies) are divided into deaneries (protopresbyteries); every parish is to have a religious school. At its conclusion, the

St. Nicholas Church, built in 1763 in the village of Kryvky (Lviv oblast). Damaged in 1916 during World War I, it was restored by T. Dzhuryn and P. Demkiv and moved to Lviv in 1930. It is a masterpiece of church architecture of the Boyko school. It has been converted by the Soviets into a museum.

Synod decides that a General Consistory will administer the Church until the new hierarchy is appointed. The hegumen of the Bilsk Monastery in Pidlyashshya, Sava Palmovsky, is elected the first assessor of the General Consistory. On July 8, the Synod proclaims a Manifesto on the renewal of the Ukrainian-Byelorussian Orthodox Church in Poland, which in fact acquires the rights of autocephaly.

May 1792 — The second partition of Poland takes place. Russian forces occupy the whole Kiev voevodeship, Podilia, Volynia and a large part of Lithuania and Byelorussia with the cities of Vilnius and Minsk.

1793 — The Russian Synod annuls the decisions of the Synod of the Ukrainian-Byelorussian Orthodox

Church of St. Michael the Archangel, built in 1777 in the village of Shelestovo and moved in 1927 to the city of Mukachiv (Transcarpathian oblast) (left).

Belfry of St. Michael's Church in the village of Yasenytsya-Zamkova (Lviv oblast), built in 1790. It is a masterpiece of church architecture of the Galician school.

Dormition Cathedral of the Pochayiv Monastery, built in 1771-83. Construction was started according to plans by H. Hofman and finished according to plans by Petro Poleyevsky in the style of the transitional period from Baroque to Classical.

Church in Pinsk and subordinates the elected General Consistory to itself.

13 July 1793 — The treaty of Grodno, which sanctions the second partition of Poland, makes the following statements on religious matters:

Roman Catholics of both rites (Latin and Greek-Eastern), who by the force of Article II of this treaty find themselves under the rule of Her Imperial Majesty the Tsarina of All the Russias, shall have in the whole of the Russian Empire not only the right of full and free exercise of their beliefs according to the governing system of toleration of religion, but they shall also retain their traditional properties in the provinces described by this treaty. Her Imperial Majesty the Tsarina of All the Russias confirms and bases on this, in an irrevocable way, in her own name and in the name of her heirs and successors, the protection of said Catholics of both rites in all their privileges, properties and churches, in free exercise of their beliefs, and in her own name and in the name of her successors declares that she will not ever or in any way exploit her sovereign powers to the detriment of the Roman Catholic Faith of both rites in the provinces that come under her rule by the force of this treaty. (Velyky, Vol. VII, p. 121-122.)

Fall 1793 — A secret council of Church dignitaries of the Russian Empire takes place in St. Petersburg. The Council adopts a project of Bishop Yevgeny Bulgaris, counsel on Church matters to Catherine II, for the liquidation of the Uniate and Roman Catholic Churches on the occupied Russian territories. The Council creates a "private" Missionary Orthodox Institute which, with the help of Russian military garrisons, is to spread Russian State Orthodoxy.

1795 — In contravention of the treaty of Grodno of July 13, 1793, and with the help of Russian military garrisons and the Russian Missionary Institute, in the span of two years 2,300 churches, 2 monasteries and 1032 Uniate clergy, some under force and duress and some willingly, revert to Orthodoxy on the Ukrainian territories acquired by Russia.

After more than 450 years of being part of the Polish Kingdom, all the central territories of Ukraine fall under Russian rule; the western territories

Dormition Cathedral in Kharkiv, built in 1771-77 in the Baroque style (left).

Church of the Presentation at the Temple in the village of Artemivka (Dnipropetrovsk oblast), built in 1761 by Yakym Pohribnyak, a master of folk architecture. Considered a classic example of Ukrainian wooden church architecture, it was destroyed by the Soviets in the 1930s.

Dmytro Bortnyansky (1751-1825), born in Hlukhiv, Ukraine's greatest composer of church music. For many years he was director of the imperial court choir in St. Petersburg.

(Galicia, Bukovyna and Transcarpathia) remain with the Habsburg Empire.

In contravention of the treaty of Grodno of 1793, Catherine II decrees the liquidation of four Uniate eparchies — Podilia, Volynia, Byelorussia and Lithuania. All properties of the Uniate bishops are confiscated and given to Russian generals and governors. The Uniate Metropolitan Teodosiy Rostotsky, whose see was the Archeparchy of Polotsk, is arrested by the Russians and deported to St. Petersburg, where he is confined and forbidden to exercise any duties of the Metropolitan on the territories of the Russian Empire. Matters pertaining to the Metropolitanate in Galicia are to be handled through diplomatic channels between Vienna and St. Petersburg.

The third partition of Poland takes place. The Polish Kingdom ceases to exist, and all its lands come under the rule of Russia, Prussia and Austria.

27 March 1795 — The Russian Synod creates an Orthodox bishopric on the Ukrainian and Byelorussian territories of the former Polish Kingdom and appoints Bishop Viktor Sadkovsky vicar of the Kievan Metropolitanate on these territories.

18th Century — Under the rule of the Russian Tsars, Ukraine suffers more and more losses and, treaties notwithstanding, the liquidation of the Ukrainian Orthodox Church. From the start, the Patriarchs of Moscow, and later the Russian Holy Synod, extract from Ukraine the ablest Ukrainian academics, theologians, archimandrites and hegumens and bring them to Russia, thus "decapitating" the Ukrainian Church and making it impossible for her to exist on Ukrainian territories.

Three prominent composers of Ukrainian church music live in this century — Maksym Berezovsky (1745-1777), Dmytro Bortnyansky (1751-1825) and Artem Vedel (1767-1806).

Holy Trinity Cathedral in the city of Novomoskovsk (Dnipropetrovsk oblast), built of wood in 1775-78 by Yakym Pohribnyak, a master of folk wooden architecture, and partially rebuilt in 1888 by the architect Kharmansky. The Soviets converted it into a museum of applied arts. An attempt to destroy this church inspired Oles Honchar to write the novel *The Cathedral*, which was banned in the U.S.S.R. for twenty years.

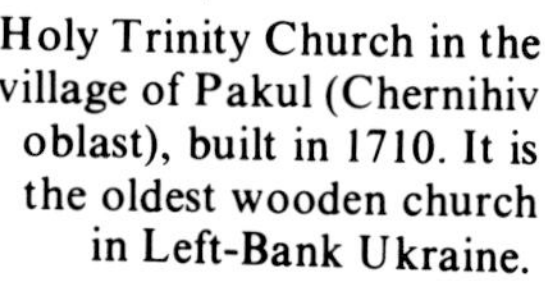

Holy Trinity Church in the village of Pakul (Chernihiv oblast), built in 1710. It is the oldest wooden church in Left-Bank Ukraine.

Principal Ecclesiastical Activities

1. THE KIEVAN ORTHODOX AND CATHOLIC (EASTERN-RITE) METROPOLITANATES DURING THE 17TH-18TH CENTURIES

THE ORTHODOX METROPOLITANATE OF KIEV, GALICIA AND ALL RUS' (1686-1795)

After its subordination to the Moscow Patriarchate in 1686, the Metropolitanate of Kiev gradually loses its rights and privileges. Only the Metropolitan Eparchy of Kiev remains under the jurisdiction of the Metropolitanate, while all other eparchies are placed under direct control of the Moscow Patriarchate. As decreed by the Tsar of Muscovy and the Patriarch, the title of the Metropolitan undergoes changes. In 1688 the words "and of All Rus'" are changed to "and of Little Rus'." With the creation of the Synod of the Russian Orthodox Church in 1721, the Metropolitanate of Kiev ceases to exist. The Metropolitan of Kiev loses his title and becomes Archbishop of Kiev. The title of metropolitan is returned in 1742 with some broadening of his powers — but this is rescinded shortly thereafter.

UKRAINIAN ORTHODOX METROPOLITANS

Varlaam Yasynsky 1690-1707
Yoakym Krokovsky 1707-1718
Rafayil Zaborovsky 1742-1747
Tymotey Shcherbatsky 1748-1757
Arseniy Mohylyansky 1757-1770
Havryyil Kremyanetsky 1770-1783
Samuyil Myslavsky 1783-1796

ARCHBISHOPS OF KIEV

Varlaam Vonatovych 1722-1730
Rafayil Zaborovsky 1731-1742

ORTHODOX BISHOPS OF EPARCHIES ON THE TERRITORIES OF UKRAINE

Bilhorod: Epyfaniy Tykhorsky (1722-1731).

Chernihiv (and Novhorod Siversky): Lazar Baranovych (1657-1693), Teodosiy Uhlytsky (1693-1696), Ioan Maksymovych (1697-1712).

Lutsk (and Ostrih): Atanasiy Shumlansky (1687-169?), Kyrylo Shumlansky (1710-1712).

Lviv: Yosyf Shumlansky (1677-1700).

Peremyshl: Innokentiy Vynnytsky (1680-1691).

Pereyaslav: Zakhariy Kornylovych (1701-1716), Kyrylo Shumlansky (1716-1726), Ioakym Strukov (1727-1730), Varlaam Lenytsky (1730-1731), Arseniy Berlo (1733-1744), Nikodym Skryabnytsky (1745-1751), Ivan Kozlovych (1753-1757), Hevrasiy Lyntsevsky (1757-1769), Yov Bazylevych (1770-1776), Ilarion Kondratovsky (1776-1785), Viktor Sadkovsky (1785-1793), Dmytro Ustynovych (1793-1795).

Slovyano-Kherson: Yevheniy Bulharyn (1775-1779), Nykyfor Feotoky (1779-1786), Amvroziy Serebrenikov (1786-1793), Havryyil Banulesko-Bodoni (1793-1799).

Zaporizhzhya Host: Anatoliy Melas (1754-1760).

THE CATHOLIC (EASTERN-RITE) METROPOLITANATE OF KIEV, GALICIA AND ALL RUS' (1686-1795)

CATHOLIC (EASTERN-RITE) METROPOLITANS

Cyprian Zhokhovsky 1674-1693
Lev Zalensky-Slyubych 1694-1708
Yuriy Vynnytsky 1708-1713
Lev Kishka 1714-1728
Atanasiy Sheptytsky 1729-1746
Florian Hrebnytsky 1746-1762
Pylyp Volodkovych 1762-1778
Lev Sheptytsky 1778-1779
Yason Smogozhevsky 1780-1788
Teodosiy Rostotsky 1788-1805

CATHOLIC (EASTERN-RITE) BISHOPS UKRAINIAN TERRITORIES

Kholm and Belz: Oleksander Lodzyata (1685-1691), Ivan Malakhovsky (1691-1692), Hedeon Oransky-Voyna (1693-1709), Yosyf Levytsky (1711-1730), Pylyp Volodkovych (1730-1758), Maksymilian Ryllo (1759-1785), Teodosiy Rostotsky (1785-1790), Porfyriy Vazhynsky (1790-1804).

Lutsk and Ostrih: Lev Zalensky-Slyubych (1700), Dionysiy Zhabokrytsky (1702-1715), Yosyf Vyhovsky (1716-1730), Teodosiy Rudnytsky (1731-1751), Sylvester Rudnytsky (1752-1777), Cyprian Stetsky (1778-1782), Mykhayil Stadnytsky (1783-1787), Stefan Levynsky (1787-1809).

Lviv, Halych and Kamyanets Podilsky: Yosyf Shumlansky (1700-1708), Varlaam Sheptytsky (1709-1715), Atanasiy Sheptytsky (1715-1746), Lev Sheptytsky (1749-1779), Petro Byelansky (1780-1798).

Mukachiv *(within the jurisdiction of the Hungarian Latin-rite Catholic Bishop of Eger, and from 1771 directly under the jurisdiction of the Apostolic See):* Metodiy Rakovetsky (1687), Rafayil Habryelovych (1687-1688), Joseph de Camelis (1689-1706), Yuriy Vynnytsky (1706), Ioan Hodermarsky (designate) (1707), Polikarp Fylypovych (designate) (1710), Yuriy Bizantsiy (1716-1733), Symon Olshavsky (1734-1737), Habriyel Blazhovsky (1737-1742), Manuyil Olshavsky (1743-

1767), Ivan Bradach (1767-1772), Andriy Bachynsky (1772-1809).

Peremyshl, Sambir and Syanok: Ivan Malakhovsky (1669-1691), Innokentiy (Ioan) Vynnytsky (1691-1700), Yuriy (Havryyil) Vynnytsky (1700-1713), Yeronim (Yuriy) Ustrytsky (1715-1746), Onufriy (Yosyf) Shumlansky (1746-1762), Maksymilian Ryllo (1785-1793).

Volodymyr-Volynsky and Berestya: Lev Zalensky-Slyubych (1679-1708), Lev Kishka (1711-1728), Kornel Lebetsky (1729-1730), Teofil Godebsky (1730-1756), Pylyp Volodkovych (1758-1778), Antoniy Mlodovsky (1778), Symon Mlotsky (1778).

BYELORUSSIAN TERRITORIES

Pinsk and Turov: Antoniy Zholkyevsky (1697-1702), Porfyriy Kulchytsky (1703-1716), Yoakhym Tsyekhanovsky (1716-1719), Teofil Godebsky (1720-1730), Yuriy Bulhak (1730-1769), Hedeon Horbatsky (1769-1784), Yoakhym Horbatsky (1785-1795), Yosafat Bulhak (1795).

In 1795 the eparchy was liquidated on orders of the Russian Tsarina Catherine II and the Russian Synod.

Polotsk, Vitebsk, Mstyslav and Mohyliv: Cyprian Zhokhovsky (1674-1693), Markiyan Bilozor (1697-1707), Sylvester Pyeshkevych (1709-1719), Floriyan Hrebnytsky (1720-1762), Yason (Yunosha) Smogozhevsky (1762-1780), Irakliy Lisovsky (1784-1809).

Smolensk: Heorhiy Maleyevsky (1690), Yosafat Hutorovych (1697), Hedeon Shumlansky (1703), Mykhaylo Tarnavsky (1708), Lavrentiy Drutsky-Sokolynsky (1709-1727), Antoniy Tomulovych (1736-1745), Polikarp Myhunevych (1747), Tsezariy Stebnovsky (1756-1762), Herakliy Lisansky (1763-1771), Yosyf Lepkovsky (1771-1778).

Church and Monastery Construction during the 17th-18th Centuries

During the period 1686-1795, a great number of churches were built in the Ukrainian Hetmanate State. Ukrainian hetmans, especially Ivan Mazepa, contributed greatly with their benevolence. Many churches were also built on the territories originally under Poland and later under the Austrian-Hungarian Empire during period of religious toleration.

The listing below provides a roster of only those churches and monasteries that were built during this period, have historic-architectural significance, have survived to our times and are protected by the laws of the Ukrainian Soviet Socialist Republic. Thousands of churches were destroyed or converted to other uses by the Soviet Government during 1920-1940 and during World War II.

The listing is organized according to the present administrative organization of Ukraine. Dates of construction or funding of the church or monastery are shown in parentheses.

CHURCH CONSTRUCTION

KIEV OBLAST. Kiev: In the Monastery of the Caves — Birth of the Mother of God (1696), All Saints (1696-1698), Elevation of the Cross (1700); in the Vydubytsky Monastery — St. George Cathedral (1696-1701), Refectory Church (1696-1701); St. Andrew (1747-1753); Resurrection (1698); St. Demetrius (1757-1865); St. Elias (1692); St. Nicholas Naberezhny (1772-1775); Protection of the Blessed Virgin Mary (1766-1772); Prytysko-Mykilska (1695-1707); Refectory Church (1722); Refectory Church in the St. Michael Goldendomed Monastery (1713); Holy Trinity (1763-1767); Teodosiy of the Caves (1698-1700); Elevation of the Cross in the Florovsky Monastery (1722-1732. ***Antonivka:*** Birth of the Mother of God (1777). ***Bila Tserkva:*** St. Nicholas (1706-1852). ***Bushevo:*** Holy Trinity (1750). ***Chayky:*** St. Nicholas (1758). ***Dubivka:*** St. Alexander Nevsky (1748). ***Fastiv:*** Pro-

St. Michael's Church in the city of Voronezh (Sumy oblast), built in 1776-81 in the Ukrainian Baroque style (left).

St. Nicholas Church in Novhorod-Siversky (Chernihiv oblast), built in 1720. It is one of the better examples of Ukrainian wooden church architecture of the Chernihiv school.

Church of St. John the Theologian in the city of Nizhyn (Chernihiv oblast), built in 1752. This is one of the better examples of the Ukrainian Baroque style (left).

Church of the Nativity of the Mother of God in Horech, a suburb of Chernivtsi, built in 1767 in the Baroque style. It is a typical example of 18th-century Ukrainian church architecture in Bukovyna.

tection of the Blessed Virgin Mary (1779-1781). ***Kozhanka:*** Protection of the Blessed Virgin Mary (1758). ***Krenychi:*** Protection of the Blessed Virgin Mary (1761). ***Lypovy Skytok:*** St. Onuphrius (1705). ***Ostriv:*** Archangel Michael (1740). ***Pereyaslav-Khmelnytsky:*** Cathedral of Resurrection in the Resurrection Monastery (1695-1700). ***Pidhirtsi:*** St. Michael (1742). ***Rosova:*** St. Nicholas (1752). ***Shkarivka:*** Pentecost (1750). ***Tovsty Lis:*** Resurrection (1760). ***Tulyntsi:*** Birth of the Mother of God (1784). ***Vasylkiv:*** Cathedral of SS. Anthoniy and Theodosius (1756-1758), St. Nicholas (1792). ***Zhytni Hory:*** St. Joseph (1766).

CHERKASY OBLAST. ***Drabivtsi:*** St. Nicholas (18th century), Trinity (1794), St. Demetrius (1773). ***Dumantsi:*** St. Nicholas (1789). ***Kirovo:*** Transfiguration (1738). ***Puhachivka:*** Trinity (1761). ***Zolotonosha:*** Transfiguration (1767-1771).

CHERNIHIV OBLAST. ***Behach:*** Holy Trinity (1787). ***Chernihiv:*** Resurrection (1772-1799), St. Catherine (1715). ***Danivka:*** St. George (1741-1756). ***Horodyshche:*** St. Nicholas (1726). ***Hustynya:*** Resurrection Church of the Hustyn Monastery (1695), St. Nicholas Over the Gate church-belfry (1693-1708). ***Korop:*** Ascension (1764), St. Elias (18th century). ***Kozelets:*** St. Nicholas (1784), Birth of the Mother of God (1752-1763). ***Lemeshi:*** Three Holy Hierarchs (1755). ***Nizhyn:*** Annunciation Cathedral (1702-1716), Presentation at the Temple Cathedral (1788), St. John the Evangelist (1752), St. Nicholas (18th century), Protection of the Blessed Virgin Mary (1765), Savior-Transfiguration (1757), Holy Trinity (1733). ***Novhorod-Siversky:*** St. Nicholas (1720), Savior-Transfiguration Cathedral of the Savior-Transfiguration Monastery (1791-1806). ***Novy Bilous:*** Holy Trinity (173?). ***Petrivske:*** St. Michael (1782-1796). ***Polonky:*** St. Michael (18th century). ***Pryluky:*** Savior-Transfiguration (1710-1720). ***Sedniv:*** St. George (1747), Birth of the Mother of God (1690). ***Stolne:*** St. Andrew (1782). ***Synyavka:*** Protection of the Blessed Virgin Mary (1706). ***Voloskivtsi:*** Dormition (1765). ***Vyshenky:*** Dormition (1787).

CHERNIVTSI OBLAST. ***Berehomet:*** St. Nicholas (1786). ***Bila Krynytsya:*** SS. Cosmas and Damian (18th-19th centuries). ***Bilousivka:*** St. Demetrius (1794). ***Bukivka:*** St. Demetrius (18th century). ***Chernivtsi:*** Birth of the Mother of God (1767), St. Spiridon (1715), Dormition (1783). ***Hlynytsya:*** Dormition (1786). ***Ivankivtsi:*** Birth of the Mother of God (1794). ***Khreshchatyn:*** St. John the Evangelist (1765-1768). ***Konyatyn:*** St. Basil (1790). ***Krypyanske:*** Annunciation (1772). ***Kulevtsi:*** Dormition (1779). ***Lukovytsya:*** St. Demetrius (1757). ***Nyzhni Stanovtsi:*** St. Nicholas (1794). ***Oshykhliby:*** St. Constantine (1779). ***Turyatka:*** Dormition (1718). ***Valyava:*** Dormition (1778). ***Velyka Buda:*** Dormition (1794). ***Verenchanka:*** Dormition (1794). ***Verkhni Synivtsi:*** Elevation of the Cross (1790). ***Voloka:*** St. Nicholas (1784). ***Vyzhenka:*** St. John of Suceava (1792). ***Zvenyachyn:*** Birth of the Mother of God (1797).

CRIMEA OBLAST. Not a single church of architectural-historical significance remains from this period in the whole oblast.

DNIPROPETROVSK OBLAST. ***Kytayhorod:*** St. Nicholas (1757), Dormition (1754), St. Barbara (1756). ***Novomoskovsk:*** St. Nicholas Church of the Samarsky Monastery (18th century), Trinity Cathedral (1775-1780).

IVANO-FRANKIVSK (formerly STANYSLAVIV) OBLAST. ***Bili Oslavy:*** Immaculate Conception (1746). ***Brusturiv:*** Ascension (1785). ***Delyatyn:*** Birth of the Mother of God (1785). ***Hvizd:*** Dormition (1739). ***Ivano-Frankivsk (formerly Stanyslaviv):*** Cathedral (1753-1763). ***Krementsi:*** St. Demetrius (18th century). ***Rohatyn:*** St. Nicholas (1729). ***Slyvky:*** St. Nicholas (1760). ***Tysmenytsya:*** Birth of the Mother of God (1736). ***Uyizd:*** St. Nicholas (1775). ***Vorokhta:*** Nativity of Jesus (18th century). ***Yaremche:*** St. John the Charitable (18th century). ***Zahirya:*** Elevation of the Cross (18th century). ***Zalaniv:*** St. Demetrius (1724).

KHARKIV OBLAST. ***Ivanivka:*** St. John the Baptist

(1776). ***Kharkiv:*** Cathedral of the Protection of the Blessed Virgin Mary (1689), Dormition Cathedral (1771-1777).

KHERSON OBLAST. Beryslav: Presentation at the Temple (1726). ***Kherson:*** St. Catherine (1782-1787).

KHMELNYTSKA OBLAST. Adamivka: Protection of the Blessed Virgin Mary (1773). ***Karvasary:*** Elevation of the Cross (1799-1801). ***Samchyky:*** St. Paraskeva Friday (1772). ***Stary Kryvyn:*** Resurrection (1763). ***Zaluchchya:*** St. Demetrius (1738). ***Zapadyntsi:*** St. Michael (1733). ***Zinkiv:*** St. Michael (1769).

KIROVOHRAD (formerly YELYSAVETHRAD) OBLAST. Novomyrhorod: St. Elias (1786).

LVIV OBLAST. Artasiv: St. Paraskeva (1748). ***Batsiv:*** Theophany (1738). ***Batyatychi:*** St. George (1759). ***Berezhnytsya:*** Birth of the Mother of God (1724). ***Bryukhovychi:*** Birth of the Mother of God (1735). ***Budkiv:*** Elevation of the Cross (1781). ***Busk:*** St. Paraskeva (1708). ***Busovysko:*** Birth of the Mother of God (1780). ***Bybshany:*** Birth of the Mother of God (1739). ***Cherpyn:*** Presentation of Christ at the Temple (1758). ***Chervonohrad:*** St. George (1771-1776). ***Chyzhiv:*** Birth of the Mother of God (1702). ***Dmytrovychi:*** St. Michael (1765). ***Dobrivlyany:*** Elevation of the Cross (18th century). ***Frusiv:*** St. John the Evangelist (1782). ***Hlynyany:*** Dormition (1749). ***Hodyny:*** Elevation of the Cross (1729). ***Horbachi:*** St. Ignatius (1712). ***Horodok:*** St. John (1755). ***Hostyntsevo:*** Mother of God (1690). ***Hrabova:*** Holy Birth of Christ (1778). ***Hromne:*** Transfiguration (1777). ***Hrushiv:*** St. Michael (1715). ***Hryniv:*** St. George (1781). ***Karpatske:*** St Michael (1772). ***Knyazhe:*** St. Nicholas (1782). ***Komarno:*** St. Michael (1754). ***Koropets:*** Holy Spirit (1760). ***Kosheliv:*** Presentation at the Temple (1708). ***Kotsuriv:*** St. Simeon on the Pillar (1729). ***Krasne:*** St. Elias (1750). ***Krekhiv:*** St. Paraskeva (1724). ***Krupske:*** Birth of the Mother of God (1750). ***Kryvko:*** St. Nicholas (176?). ***Kuchayiv:*** Theophany (1693). ***Kuty:*** Mother of God (1750), St. Michael (1697). ***Lelekhivka:*** Dormition (1739). ***Leshnya:*** St. Elias (1698). ***Loni:*** Mother of God (1724). ***Lukavets:*** Protection of the Blessed Virgin Mary (1740). ***Lviv:*** Cathedral of St. George (1744-1770). ***Makhnivtsi:*** SS. Cosmas and Damian (1697). ***Mala Olshanka:*** St. Michael (1704). ***Nadyby:*** Dormition (1732). ***Nesterov (formerly Zhovkva):*** Birth of the Mother of God (1705), Holy Trinity (1720). ***Novy Kropyvnyk:*** St. Michael (1695). ***Novy Vytkiv:*** Transfiguration (1738). ***Novy Yar:*** St. Paraskeva (1748). ***Ohladiv:*** Dormition (18th century). ***Peredelnytsya:*** St. Nicholas (1736). ***Perevolochna:*** Presentation at the Temple (1754). ***Pidhirtsi:*** St. Michael (1720), St. Onuphrius of the Basilian monastery (18th century). ***Pidlissya:*** Transfiguration (1735). ***Pluhiv:*** St. Paraskeva (1715). ***Polove:*** Holy Spirit (1727). ***Pomeryany:*** Mother of God (1690). ***Prybylchi:*** Mother of God (1741). ***Pykulovychi:*** Mother of God (1792). ***Radvantsi:*** Birth of the Mother of God (1700). ***Rakovo:*** Theophany (1779). ***Semenivka:*** St. Michael (1718). ***Semerivka:*** St. John the Evangelist (1718). ***Shklo:*** St. Paraskeva (1732). ***Silets:*** Mother of God (1700). ***Stare Selo:*** St. John (1742). ***Stybyrivka:*** Mother of God (1702). ***Troytsya:*** Holy Trinity (1760). ***Tsetula:*** St. Nicholas (1745). ***Turka:*** St. Nicholas (1739), Dormition (1750). ***Uzlove:*** Protection of the Blessed Virgin Mary (1724). ***Velykopole:*** Mother of God (1781). ***Verkhnya Yablonska:*** Mother of God (1791). ***Verkhnye Vysotske:*** Birth of the Mother of God (18th century). ***Vilshanytsya:*** St. George (1715). ***Vodnyky:*** St. Nicholas (1729). ***Voloshchyna:*** Ascension (1794). ***Volya Homuletska:*** Holy Trinity (1756). ***Vydniv:*** Birth of the Mother of God (1738). ***Vysloboky:*** Immaculate Conception (1762). ***Zabolottsi:*** Mother of God (1746). ***Zamochok:*** St. Demetrius (1790). ***Zarudtsi:*** Elevation of the Cross (1787). ***Zavereshchytsya:*** Presentation at the Temple (1693). ***Zhyrivka:*** St. Michael (1770). ***Zvertiv:*** St. Simeon (1776).

MYKOLAIV OBLAST. Kateryna: St. Catherine (end of 18th — beginning of 19th century).

ODESSA OBLAST. Not a single church of architectural-historical significance remains from this period in the whole oblast.

POLTAVA OBLAST. Dykanka: St. Nicholas (1794), Trinity (1780). ***Poltava:*** Cathedral of the Elevation of the Cross (1699-1709). ***Peryatyn:*** Nativity of Jesus (1781). ***Velyki Sorochyntsi:*** Savior-Transfiguration (1732). ***Vyshnyaky:*** Trinity (1794-1799).

ROVNO OBLAST. Dorotychi: Trinity (1725). ***Dubno:*** St.

St. George's Church in the village of Danivka (Chernihiv oblast), built in 1741-56. Damaged by fire, it was rebuilt in the Baroque style in 1770. It is one of the better examples of Ukrainian architecture of the Baroque period (left).

St. Nicholas Church in the city of Vasylkiv (Kiev oblast), built in 1792.

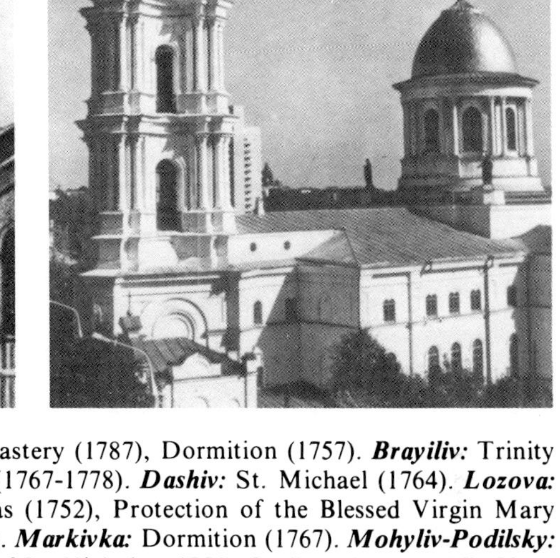

Church of the Annunciation in the city of Trostyanets (Sumy oblast), built in 1750 in the early Classical style with Baroque elements (left).

Holy Savior-Transfiguration Cathedral in Sumy, built in 1776 on the site of an old wooden church and completely rebuilt in 1882-92.

George (1709), St. Demetrius (18th century). ***Horodok:*** St. Nicholas (1740). ***Hrabiv:*** St. George (1775). ***Klevan:*** Nativity of Jesus (1777). ***Kornyn:*** St. Nicholas (18th century). ***Korytne:*** Birth of the Mother of God (18th century). ***Mykhalkivtsi:*** Trinity (1740). ***Mylyatyn:*** St. Michael (18th century). ***Mytnytsya:*** Protection of the Blessed Virgin Mary (18th century). ***Obariv:*** Protection of the Blessed Virgin Mary (1781). ***Orzhiv:*** Transfiguration (1770). ***Remchytsi:*** Birth of the Mother of God (1766). ***Rovno:*** Dormition (1756). ***Rozvazh:*** SS. Cosmas and Damian (1781). ***Siyantsi:*** St. George (1743). ***Stepan:*** Trinity (1759). ***Svitanok:*** Protection of the Blessed Virgin Mary (18th century). ***Velyky Stydyn:*** Protection of the Blessed Virgin Mary (1768).

SUMY OBLAST. ***Hamaliyivka:*** Cathedral of the Birth of the Mother of God (1735). ***Hlukhiv:*** St. Nicholas (1693), Savior-Transfiguration (1765). ***Lebedyn:*** Resurrection (1748). ***Okhtyrka:*** Presentation at the Temple (1783), Cathedral of the Protection of the Blessed Virgin Mary (1753-1762). ***Pyrohivka:*** St. John the Evangelist (18th century). ***Putyvl:*** St. Nicholas of the Kozaks (1735-1737). ***Romny:*** Holy Spirit Cathedral (1742-1746), St. Basil Cathedral (18th-19th centuries). ***Sumy:*** Resurrection (1702). ***Trostyanets:*** Annunciation (1750). ***Voronezh:*** St. Michael (1781-1776). ***Yunakivka:*** St. Nicholas (1793-1806).

TERNOPIL OBLAST. ***Berezhany:*** St. Nicholas (1691), Trinity Cathedral (1768). ***Buchach:*** Elevation of the Cross (1753-1770), Protection of the Blessed Virgin Mary (1764). ***Butsniv:*** SS. Peter and Paul (1744). ***Chortkiv:*** Ascension (1738). ***Ivane-Puste:*** St. John the Evangelist (1775). ***Konyukhy:*** Holy Spirit (1700). ***Krohulets:*** St. Paraskeva (18th century). ***Mizhhirya:*** Elevation of the Cross (18th century). ***Pidhaytsi:*** Savior (1772). ***Pochayiv:*** All Saints (1773-1775), Dormition Cathedral of the Pochayiv Monastery (1771-1783). ***Sapohiv:*** St. Nicholas (1777). ***Shumlyany:*** SS. Borys and Hlib (1711-1772). ***Shumske:*** Transfiguration (1715). ***Urman:*** SS. Peter and Paul (1688). ***Vysichka:*** St. Nicholas (1763). ***Zalozhtsi:*** Protection of the Blessed Virgin Mary (1740).

VINNYTSYA OBLAST. ***Bar:*** Protection of the Blessed Virgin Mary Church, of the Protection of the Blessed Virgin Mary Monastery (1787), Dormition (1757). ***Brayiliv:*** Trinity Cathedral (1767-1778). ***Dashiv:*** St. Michael (1764). ***Lozova:*** St. Nicholas (1752), Protection of the Blessed Virgin Mary (1700-1702). ***Markivka:*** Dormition (1767). ***Mohyliv-Podilsky:*** Cathedral of St. Nicholas (1754), St. Paraskeva (1775). ***Nova Hreblya:*** St. Michael (1701). ***Sloboda-Sharhorodska:*** Birth of the Mother of God (1750). ***Tulchyn:*** Dormition (1789). ***Ulaniv:*** Ascension (1777). ***Vinnytsya:*** St. Nicholas (1746). ***Voronovytsya:*** St. Michael (1752).

VOROSHYLOVHRAD (formerly LUHANSK) OBLAST. ***Mykhaylivka:*** Archangel Michael (1787). ***Stary Aydar:*** St. Michael (1787).

VOLYNIA OBLAST. ***Borky:*** St. Joseph (1769). ***Borochyche:*** St. Nicholas (1757). ***Brany:*** Protection of the Blessed Virgin Mary (1725). ***Buzhkovychi:*** Mother of God (1766). ***Dorosyny:*** St. Luke (18th century). ***Dorotyshche:*** Dormition (1767). ***Drozdny:*** St. Michael (1710). ***Holoby:*** St. George (1783). ***Horodyny:*** Protection of the Blessed Virgin Mary (1762). ***Hrudky:*** St. Michael (1771). ***Kamin-Kashyrsky:*** St. Elias (1700), Birth of the Mother of God (1723). ***Karasyn:*** St. Michael (1691). ***Khmeliv:*** St. Michael (1770). ***Khoteshiv:*** St. Michael (1790). ***Kolona:*** Elevation of the Cross (1779). ***Korshiv:*** Elevation of the Cross (17??). ***Krasiv:*** Transfiguration (1765). ***Kutriv:*** St. George (1761). ***Kysylyn:*** St. Michael (1777). ***Lukiv:*** St. Paraskeva (1723). ***Lypno:*** St. Michael (1770). ***Makarevychi:*** St. Michael (1776). ***Mylyatyn:*** St. Paraskeva (1778). ***Myltsi:*** St. Onuphrius (1723). ***Nesvich:*** St. Michael (1778). ***Novosilky:*** SS. Peter and Paul (1783). ***Osa:*** St. Michael (1772). ***Osivtsi:*** St. Paraskeva (1774). ***Piddubtsi:*** Protection of the Blessed Virgin Mary (1745). ***Pozharky:*** St. Stephen (1761). ***Rudka-Kozynska:*** Trinity (1786). ***Rzhyshchiv:*** St. Michael (1779). ***Shchuryn:*** St. Michael (1767). ***Shepel:*** Dormition (1780). ***Shtun:*** St. John the Evangelist (1777). ***Smolyava:*** St. Michael (1783). ***Smolyhiv:*** St. Nicholas (1743). ***Sokil:*** Dormition (18th century). ***Stary Porytsk:*** Dormition (1784). ***Syrnychky:*** St. Luke (1788). ***Troyanivka:*** Birth of the Mother of God (1772). ***Tur:*** St. Nicholas (1778). ***Turopyn:*** Elevation of the Cross (1777). ***Usychi:*** St. Stephen (1795). ***Zabolottya:*** Elevation of the Cross (1794). ***Zalisoche:*** Presentation of Christ at the Temple (1784). ***Zalisy:*** St. Paraskeva (1794). ***Zapruddya:*** Dormition (1795). ***Zhydychyn:*** St. Nicholas Church of the St. Nicholas Monastery (1723). ***Velyka Hrusha:*** Dormition (1779). ***Velyky Okorsk:*** St. Michael (1787). ***Verkhy:*** St. Michael (1742). ***Vilkhivka:*** Elevation of the Cross (1782). ***Volodymyr-Volynsky:*** St. Nicholas (1780). ***Vorotniv:*** Birth of the Mother of God (1785). ***Vyderta:*** Birth of the Mother of God (1738).

ZAKARPATSKA OBLAST (formerly Carpatho-Ukraine). ***Chetovo:*** Reformation (1753). ***Danylove:*** St. Nicholas (1779). ***Deshkovytsya:*** Protection of the Blessed Virgin Mary (18th century). ***Dibrova:*** St. Nicholas (18th century). ***Dilove:*** Dormition (1750). ***Huklyvy:*** Holy Spirit (18th century). ***Imstychevo:*** St. Michael Church of the St. Michael Monastery (18th century). ***Kobyletska Polyana:*** Ascension (18th century). ***Lazeshchyna:*** SS. Peter and Paul (1780). ***Lokot:*** Presentation at the Temple (1734). ***Nehrovets:*** St. Michael (18th century). ***Pylypets:*** Birth of the Mother of God (1780). ***Repynne:*** St. Demetrius (1780). ***Shelestovo:*** St. Michael (1777). ***Sol:*** St. Basil (1703). ***Sukhe:*** St. John the Baptist (1700). ***Uzhok:*** St. Michael (1745). ***Volovets:*** Protection of the Blessed Virgin Mary (1792). ***Vyshka:*** St. Michael (1700).

ZAPORIZHZHYA OBLAST. Not a single church of architectural-historical significance remains from this period in the whole oblast. All other churches were either razed or transformed into buildings for other uses by the Soviet authorities during the years 1920-40, and 1946-86.

MONASTERY CONSTRUCTION

Buildings of only four monasteries of that period remain as architectural-historical monuments:

KIEV OBLAST. ***Pereyaslav-Khmelnytsky:*** Ascension (1695-1700).

SUMY OBLAST. ***Hamaliyivka:*** Birth of the Mother of God (1702), founded by Hetman Ivan Skoropadsky.

VINNYTSYA OBLAST. ***Sharhorod:*** St. Nicholas (1717), founded by the Basilian Order.

ZAKARPATSKA OBLAST. ***Imstychevo:*** St. Michael (18th century).

Twelve monasteries built during the period 1686-1795 were razed or transformed into buildings for other uses by the Soviet authorities during 1920-40 and after World War II:

CHERKASY OBLAST. ***Vynohrad:*** Dormition (18th century). ***Zhabotyn:*** Zhabotyn Monastery (18th century).

CHERNIHIV OBLAST. ***Domnytsya:*** Birth of the Mother of God (1696), founded by Hetman Ivan Mazepa. ***Nizhyn:*** Annunciation (1716), founded by Metropolitan Stefan Yavorsky; Presentation at the Temple Convent (18th century), founded by Anna Braslavska.

IVANO-FRANKIVSK OBLAST. ***Ulashkivtsi:*** St. John (1738).

KHERSON OBLAST. ***Beryslav:*** St. Gregory the New Theologian (1783).

KHMELNYTSKY OBLAST. ***Korshovtsi:*** Birth of the Mother of God (1742).

LVIV OBLAST. ***Drohobych:*** Holy Trinity (1775). ***Nesterov:*** Nativity of Jesus (18th century). ***Zolochiv:*** Ascension (18th century).

ZAKARPATSKA OBLAST. ***Bukova Hirka:*** Elevation of the Cross (1742).

Cathedral in Ivano-Frankivsk, built in 1753-63 according to plans by the architect S. Pototsky, restored in 1885 (left).

Holy Trinity Church in Berezhany, built in 1768 and rebuilt in 1893 and 1903.

IX. The Ukrainian Churches in the Russian and Austro-Hungarian Empires during the 19th-20th Centuries (1795-1917)

General Characteristics of the Period

1. THE POLITICAL SITUATION IN EASTERN EUROPE

From the end of the eighteenth century to World War I, the major powers in Eastern Europe were Austria, Russia, Prussia and the Ottoman Empire. All were imperial powers which ruled over subject Slavic peoples.

In the 1790s Russia continued to take land from the Turks along the Black Sea. During the nineteenth century the Ottomans gradually were pushed out of the Balkans.

In May 1791 the Poles, whose country had been partitioned by Austria, Prussia and Russia in 1772, proclaimed a Constitution. In 1793 Russia and Prussia occupied more of Poland, taking half its lands. A revolt followed; in 1795 a third partition brought the Polish state to an end. Until 1918 it would remain divided among Austria, Prussia and Russia. For a while a French protectorate was established over the Duchy of Warsaw, and the Congress Kingdom enjoyed some autonomy under Russian authority from 1815 to 1861; however, the Poles would not effectively rule themselves until after World War I.

Polish uprisings against Russia in 1830-1831 and in 1863 led to massive emigrations, notably to France, and to severe repressions at home. A revolt of the Polish nobility in Austrian-ruled western Galicia in 1846 was easily suppressed after the authorities instigated a peasant massacre of their landlords.

The Napoleonic wars brought a period of French rule and influence to other countries as well. But after Napoleon's march to Moscow in 1812, he was forced to retreat, and in 1814-1815 the Congress of Vienna rearranged the map of Europe.

In 1812 the Ottoman Sultan scored a temporary gain by recovering Moldavia and Wallachia (except for Bessarabia); in the following year he suppressed a Serbian revolt. But the Greeks rose successfully in 1821, and ten years later a settlement was reached regarding Greece, Moldavia and Wallachia.

The revolutions of 1848 had only a limited effect in Eastern Europe. The Hungarian uprising was suppressed with Russian help. In 1849 an Austrian assembly at Kromeriz approved a federal system that would have given the Slavic lands considerable autonomy, but Emperor Franz Josef put an end to these plans and a period of centralization set in . In 1860 Austria issued a liberal constitution (the October Diploma); however, it was modified in the following year and centralism was revived. Austria's crushing defeat by Prussia in 1866 led to a reform in the following year creating a dual monarchy: from 1867 the Empire was known as Austria-Hungary. The Hungarians, however, imposed cultural assimilation (Magyarization) upon their Slavic subject peoples, the Ruthenians (Ukrainians), Slovaks and Croatians. In the 1870s and later, the Poles and Czechs began to participate actively in the Austrian Parliament and provincial diets, working to better their own positions in the Empire.

In the meantime, Russia's defeat in the Crimean War (1853-1856) led to internal reforms, especially the abolition of serfdom in 1861. However, the unsuccessful Polish revolt in 1863 brought about severe repressions in Russian-ruled Poland. After the assassination of the "Tsar-liberator" Alexander II in 1881, a period of reaction set in . Military defeat in the Russo-Japanese War of 1904-1905, and a revolution in 1905-1906, led to the granting of constitutional liberties and a parliament (*Duma*). However, the *Duma* was later dissolved, and a period of reaction set in again.

The latter half of the nineteenth century saw the emergence of new Balkan states in the wake of the receding Ottomans. The Balkans became the complex and restive "powder keg of Europe." Turkish massacres of Bulgarians led to the Russo-Turkish war of 1877-1878 and the partition of Bulgaria at the 1878 Congress of Berlin. In that year Austria occupied Bosnia-Herzegovina and the Sanjak of Novipazar. It returned the latter territory to Turkey in 1908, but in the same year formally made Bosnia-Herzegovina a regular Austrian province, inflaming Serbian nationalism. In the First and Second Balkan Wars (1912-1913) Serbia, Greece, Bulgaria and Montenegro pushed the Ottomans almost to Istanbul, then quarrelled among themselves. Albania became independent in 1913, blocking Serbian access to the Adriatic.

In June 1914 the Austrian Archduke Franz Ferdinand was assassinated by a Serbian nationalist on a visit to Bosnia-Herzegovina. Austria seized the opportunity to declare war on Serbia, triggering the European system of alliances and thus precipitating a World War in which many Slavs fought in opposing armies. By March 1917, when revolution broke out in Russia, Eastern Europe was ripe for the formation of new national states.

2. THE RELIGIOUS SITUATION IN EUROPE

From the end of the eighteenth century, the territorial pattern of religion in Europe remained generally stable. The major changes in the religious situation involved adjustments in church-state relations and revival or reform of existing churches and religious groups rather than their relative extent. The various churches' overseas missions, however, did compete in expanding their influence. In Eastern Europe, religion often combined with nascent nationalism.

The French occupation of the Papal states in 1798 was the first of a series of blows to the Roman Catholic Church's temporal power. The movement for Italian unification threatened the Papal states in 1849 and, in 1870, brought them under secular national control. Deprived of state power and driven from the city of Rome, the Pope confined himself to the Vatican as a purely spiritual leader. In 1870s Germany, Bismarck's *Kulturkampf* assailed Catholic political influence.

It was not the Church's temporal authority alone, however, that was being challenged in Europe. Secular philosophy, in particular Marxist socialism, attacked the very idea of religion.

At the same time, the long Papacy of the charismatic Pius IX, though ultimately disappointing the hopes of many liberals, saw the proclamation of important doctrines (the Immaculate Conception, 1854; Papal infallibility, 1870) as well as the convocation of the Vatican Council in 1869-1870. Indeed, there were other signs that the tide of secularism was turning. The Jesuits were revived in 1814, and in the following century Roman Catholic orders and congregations multiplied. Lourdes became a famous pilgrimage center after the apparition of the Virgin Mary in 1858. The Catholic Action movement began in Bologna in 1868. Catholic theology experienced a renaissance, primarily at Tubingen.

Evangelical revivals took place as well in France, Germany, Switzerland, and the Low Countries. Despite apparent challenges to religion from the natural sciences and literary criticism, theology blossomed in Protestant Germany under the leadership of F.D.E. Schleiermacher (1763-1834).

In England, Catholics and Nonconformists were allowed to participate in government from the late 1820s. The Free Churches grew, while within the Church of England both Evangelical and High Anglican societies flourished. The Oxford Movement brought many prominent Anglicans into the Roman Catholic Church.

In France, a Concordat between Church and State was signed in 1801, and the country returned to official Catholicism when Napoleon was crowned Emperor in 1804. The revolution of July 1830, however, had a distinctly anticlerical tenor. But by paying priestly salaries the State gained some control over the Church, as had been the case in the previous century. Some leaders of the Ultramontane movement, which sought to tie the Gallican Church more closely to Rome and thus free it of state control, came to support the liberal Catholic notions of popular sovereignty (rejecting the divine right of kings), freedom of conscience, and separation of Church from State (formally declared in 1905). Although in 1832 the Pope had condemned liberalism, it did tend to free the Church of its dependence on the state. This made possible an understanding, after 1848, between Catholic and democratic forces.

The debate in France between Catholic conservatives, who rejected modern ideas, and liberals, who accepted them selectively, became a concern of the Catholic Church as a whole. Pope Leo XIII (1878-1903) advanced Catholic social teaching as an alternative to secular notions of social justice. Modernism, an attempt to adjust religious beliefs to scientific theories which arose in the 1890s, was condemned by Pope Pius X in 1907. But his successor Benedict XV tempered the Church's position; as a result, dogma was permitted to evolve rather than remain static.

A number of new ideas affected all Christian denominations in this period. Christian Socialism developed in England and France. The International Eucharistic Congress (Lille, 1881) and the International Missionary Conference (Edinburgh, 1910) heralded an era of ecumenism, while the first Velehrad congress of 1907 was a harbinger of closer relations between Christians of East and West.

In Eastern Europe, churches continued to be buffeted by the winds of political change. For example, the depolonization campaign that followed the unsuccessful Polish rising against Russia in 1863 involved an attack on the Roman Catholic Church as well as on the Uniates, who had already suffered persecution and formal liquidation in 1839. The Union was abolished in Kholm in 1875. Polish Catholicism was also a target of the German regime.

The Russian Orthodox Church remained a State church closely tied to government policy, particularly during the tenure of the influential Over-Procurator of the Holy Synod Pobedonostsev. Evangelicals and Baptists were persecuted. In the Balkans, where the Orthodox had long been subject to the authority of a Patriarch politically subservient to his Ottoman masters, independence from the Turks resulted in the creation of autocephalous (self-governing) national Churches. Both Orthodoxy and Catholicism at times combined with nationalist movements.

3. THE POLITICAL SITUATION IN UKRAINE

Between the late eighteenth century and 1917, Ukraine remained divided between two empires which, however, differed considerably in their character and development.

By the 1830s Russian-held Ukraine, known as Little Russia, was governed by governors-general for the Left Bank (eastern Ukraine), Right Bank and "New Russia." Later the Little Russian general governorships were abolished. The Kholm region became part of Congress Poland, administered by Russia, but in 1913 became a separate *guberniya* (province).

The settlement of the southern Ukrainian steppe by Russian military land-owners and their serfs, as well as by free colonists, continued into the nineteenth century, although the military settlements were abolished under Nicholas I (1825-1855). Centralization continued: cities were deprived of the rights of the Magdeburg Law in the 1830s, and the Lithuanian Statute was repealed in 1842. The Ukrainian nobility became equal in rights with the Russian nobility, but at the same time it was Russified. In Kharkiv in the early 1800s, however, it was the Ukrainian nobility which began the first phase of the Ukrainian national revival, centered around the new university founded in that city. Later the focus of the Ukrainian movement moved to Kiev, where a university was founded in 1832.

Social and political unrest was marked by the uprisings led by Ustym Karmalyuk in Right-Bank Ukraine in the 1820s and 1830s, as well as in the revolt of the Chernihiv regiment fifteen days after the Russian Decembrist uprising of December 1825. The Polish revolt of 1830 found support among Poles in Right-Bank Ukraine, but the Ukrainian peasantry aided in its suppression. From 1845 the Ukrainian Brotherhood of SS. Cyril and Methodius, including the Ukrainian national poet Taras Shevchenko (1814-1861), met secretly until its members were discovered and arrested in 1847.

It was Russia's defeat in the Crimean War, however, which was the main spur to reform. Tsar Alexander II liberated the serfs in 1861; reforms of the court system (1864) and municipal government (1870) followed, and the *zemstvo* (rural council) system brought in a measure of local self-government in Left-Bank and Steppe Ukraine in the late 1860s.

In the new atmosphere of reform, Ukrainian intellectuals living in St. Petersburg founded the journal *Osnova* (1861-1862), and in the 1870s the *Hromada* groups were active in Kiev and elsewhere. However, the Valuyev decree of 1863 and the Ems decree of 1876, forbidding publishing in the Ukrainian language, arrested the development of the Ukrainian cultural revival, which shifted to Austrian-ruled Western Ukraine (see below). Despite a period of reaction in the 1870s and particularly after the assassination of Tsar Alexander II (1881), Populism flourished in Eastern Ukraine along with Socialism. A Revolutionary Ukrainian Party was founded in Kharkiv in 1899-1900, and Ukrainians sought to make the most of the temporary reforms following the 1905 revolution. They participated in the Dumas of 1905-1906, and benefited from the introduction of the *zemstvo* to Right-Bank Ukraine in 1911. The Russified Ukrainian nobility, however, generally took a conservative line.

Austrian-ruled Western Ukraine consisted of eastern Galicia and Bukovyna, which after 1861 had provincial diets in Lviv and Chernivtsi, respectively; and Transcarpathia, which in 1867 was divided into several counties coming under the Hungarian half of the Dual Monarchy. In these lands, the Galician Ruthenian cultural revival of the first half of the nineteenth century (led largely by country priests) grew into a full-fledged Ukrainian national movement. At that time, the imperial government favored the loyal Ruthenians as a counterweight to the restless Poles. In the wake of the European "Spring of Nations" (1848), a "Chief Ruthenian Council" loyal to the Emperor was formed in May. In the same year, serfdom was abolished in Galicia. The constitutional reforms of 1860-1861 provided for provincial diets; the Galician diet, in Lviv, gave the Ruthenians (Ukrainians) some voice in their affairs.

In the 1860s and 1870s, many Ruthenians looked to Russia as cultural guide and eventual political savior from Polish aristocratic control. In fact, after 1867 the Austrian government began to favor the Galician Poles more and more. The Ruthenian (later consciously Ukrainian) populists, however, identified, and sought contact, with eastern Ukraine. In the 1880s they were influenced by socialist, radical and anti-clerical views, expressed by Drahomanov. Both Russophiles and Radicals agreed, however, in their opposition to the Polish-Ukrainian accord being sought by some of the more moderate Ukrainian populists in the 1890s. In 1899 the influential National-Democratic Party was formed. In 1902 a major agricultural strike nearly paralyzed the province.

Efforts to educate the impoverished and illiterate peasantry, were headed by the Greek-Catholic (Uniate) clergy, and resulted in the founding of the "Prosvita" (Enlightenment) Society in 1868. A Literary Shevchenko Scientific Society was founded in Lviv in 1873.

Conflicts between the Ukrainians (who in 1910 constituted 63% of the eastern Galician population) and the Poles, who dominated the landowning and middle classes, centered on the questions of electoral reform and a Ukrainian university. In 1908 a Ukrainian assassinated the Galician viceroy, Count Potocki; in 1910 student unrest in defense of the Ukrainian language resulted in the death of a Ukrainian student. Throughout this time the Ukrainian cause in Austria-Hungary was most effectively represented by the moderate but charismatic Metropolitan Andrey Sheptytsky, head of the Ukrainian Greek-Catholic Church.

Thus, Ukrainians fared differently in the two empires. Those under Russian rule were materially better off, but suffered from the political strangulation of absolutism. Those in Austria-Hungary were poorer, but enjoyed broader political opportunities and consequently developed a greater degree of national and political consciousness.

Ukrainians of the two empires encountered each other with the outbreak of war in 1914 and the Russian occupation of Galicia. Less than five years later they would join forces in a Ukrainian state.

Chronology

6 October 1795 — Russian Tsarina Catherine II closes all Uniate eparchies in the empire — the archeparchy of Polotsk, and eparchies of Pinsk, Lutsk and Berestya.

14 May 1796 — An Orthodox theological seminary for students from Volynia is opened at the Divine Transfiguration Monastery in Ostrih.

1797 — An Orthodox Theological Seminary is opened at the former Jesuit monastery in Sharhorod. In 1806 the Seminary is moved to Kamyanets-Podilsky and replaced by a theological school.

22 June 1797 — Tsar Paul I proposes that the title of "Metropolitan of Kiev" be changed to "Uniate Metropolitan" or "Metropolitan of Vilnius" in Russia. Caught without a primate between Latin-rite Catholicism on the one hand and Russian Orthodoxy on the other, a number of Ukrainian and Byelorussian Catholics accept the Latin rite or convert to Russian Orthodoxy.

1798 — Tsar Paul I restores six Roman Catholic and two Uniate eparchies that were eliminated by his predecessor Catherine II, including the Berestya Eparchy of the Byelorussian and Lithuanian provinces and the Lutsk Eparchy for the provinces of Volynia, Podilia and Kiev.

1799 — The last Ukrainian Orthodox Metropolitan, Yerofey Malytsky of Kiev, dies. In his place Tsar Paul I and the Russian Synod appoint Havryil Banulesko-Bodoni, a Rumanian, as the new Metropolitan. The new Metropolitan announces as his mission the elimination of all differences between the Ukrainian and Russian Churches. With this pronouncement, the Ukrainian church, as an autonomous institution, ceases to exist in Ukraine and becomes a part of the Russian church. All subsequent metropolitans appointed by the Russian Tsars and Synods until 1917, are Russians.

Upon the decision of the Russian Synod, the Bilhorod Eparchy, established in 1667, is converted into the Slobidsko-Ukrainian and Kharkiv Eparchy.

As a result of the ecclesiastical reforms of Emperor Joseph II, 33 monasteries of the Basilian Order in Transcarpathia are closed.

1803 — The Polish Roman Catholic bishops who after the division of Poland find themselves under Austrian rule demand that, upon the death of the Ukrainian Uniate bishops in Galicia, the Uniate Church be subjugated to the Polish Roman Catholic hierarchy. After these demands, the Ukrainian hierarchs in Galicia send Vicar Mykhaylo Harasevych of the Lviv Eparchy as a representative to Vienna, to appeal to Emperor Francis I and the Papal Nuncio Severoli for the establishment of a Metropolitanate of Galicia as the successor of of the Ukrainian Uniate Metropolitanate of Kiev and Galicia, which was eliminated by the Russians.

Tsar Alexander I forbids Uniate Metropolitan Teodosiy Rostotsky of Kiev, Galicia and All "Little Rus'," who was confined in St. Petersburg, to appoint a successor for Galicia.

13 November 1803 — The Russian Synod does not permit the restoration of the Kievan Uniate Metropolitanate.

December 1803 — Thomas Arezzo, a Papal legate, conducts talks with Tsar Alexander I in connection with the restoration of the Kievan Uniate Metropolitanate.

15 July 1804 — By edict of Alexander I, the Ecclesiastical College in St. Petersburg, which governs all Catholic Church matters in the Russian Empire, is divided into two departments — one for the Latin rite and the other for the Eastern or Uniate rite. The Tsar appoints the Bishop of the Lutsk Eparchy, Stefan Levynsky, as the first head of the Eastern-rite department; later, he appoints as his successors Bishop Yosafat Bulhak of Berestya and, on September 8, 1805, Archbishop Irakliy Lisovsky of Polotsk.

25 January 1805 — Teodosiy Rostotsky, the last Uniate Metropolitan of Kiev, who is imprisoned by the Russian authorities, dies in St. Petersburg. The existence of the Kievan Uniate Metropolitanate comes to an end with the death of the Metropolitan, although the Metropolitanate is never liquidated.

30 April 1805 — The Austrian Government appoints Andrey Tseisel, an opponent of the establishment of the Metropolitanate of Galicia, as representative for church matters in Galicia.

August 1805 — After the deaths of the Bishops of Lviv and Kholm, only one Uniate Bishop, Antin Anhelovych, is left in Galicia. He becomes the administrator of the entire Galician province. In Rome the Procurator of the Basilian Order, Yordan Mitskevych, takes steps before the Apostolic See toward the establishment of the Metropolitanate of Galicia and the appointment of bishops for the vacated eparchies. As a result of the negotiations of the Papal Nuncio with the Austrian government and in accordance with the Synod of Zamostya, a decision is made to appoint bishops of Lviv and Kholm prior to the establishment of the metropolitanate. The Metropolitanate is to be established by the Synod of bishops. In Rome, the entire College of Cardinals declares its support for the establishment of a separate Metropolitanate of Galicia.

1805 — The Ukrainian Orthodox Bishop Varlaam Shyshatsky of Volynia moves to the eparchy of Mohyliv in Byelorussia where, in 1808, he is elevated to the rank of archbishop.

July 1806 — Tsar Alexander I restores the Kievan Uniate Metropolitanate under the name of "The Metropolitanate of the Uniate Churches in Russia" and appoints Archbishop Irakliy Lisovsky of Polotsk as the first Metropolitan. The Apostolic See refuses to con-

Church of the Protection of the Blessed Virgin Mary in Kiev, built in 1766-72, restored in the early 19th century (left).

Church of the Holy Trinity of the Yonovsky Monastery in Kiev. Built in 1871-72.

firm Archbishop Lisovsky and states as the reason for its refusal its unwillingness to divide the Uniate Church into two metropolitanates.

17 July 1806 — The Austrian authorities adopt a resolution regarding the establishment of the Metropolitanate of Galicia and nominate Bishop Antoniy Anhelovych of Peremyshl as the first candidate for metropolitan. Emperor Francis II confirms the resolution on September 11, 1806. Simultaneously the Austrian government proposes that the Apostolic See grant the metropolitans of Galicia the same rights and privileges as were previously granted by Pope Clement VIII to the Kievan metropolitans in 1596 at the time of the Union of Berestya.

1807 — Pope Pius VII agrees with the establishment of the Metropolitanate of Galicia. The Apostolic See specifies that the Metropolitanate of Galicia should consist of three eparchies — the Metropolitan archeparchy of Lviv (Halych and Kamyanets Podilsky), and the eparchies of Peremyshl (Sambir and Syanok) and Kholm (and Belz).

August 1808 — The Austrian emperor Francis II confirms the bull issued by Pope Pius VII regarding the establishment of the Metropolitanate of Galicia. In accordance with the Papal bull, the new Metropolitanate is excluded from any allegiance to the Kievan Uniate Metropolitanate, and is divided into three eparchies with its metropolitan nominated by the Austrian emperor and confirmed by the Pope. Bishop Antoniy Anhelovych of Peremyshl becomes the first Metropolitan of Galicia and is given the title "Metropolitan of Lviv and Galicia." The Apostolic See extends to the Metropolitan the right to appoint, confirm and ordain new bishops nominated by the emperor. Metropolitans of Galicia receive rights equal to those of patriarchs, as were previously available to the Kievan metropolitans who owed only nominal allegiance to the Patriarch of Constantinople.

1809 — As a result of the treaty between Napoleon and the Austrian emperor Francis II, Austria agrees to cede Kholm and part of the Peremyshl region, with the Ukrainian Uniate eparchy of Kholm and the theological seminary, to the newly-created Polish Duchy of Warsaw. Metropolitan Antin Anhelovych of Galicia ordains Bishop Ferdinand Tsyekhanovsky to head the Kholm Eparchy and all Uniate parishes in the Polish principality. The new bishop receives a senatorial seat in the Polish Sejm, which previously was available only to a metropolitan.

Irakliy Lisovsky, the first metropolitan of the Uniate church in Russia, dies. Tsar Alexander I appoints his co-adjutor, Bishop Hryhoriy Kokhanovych of Lutsk, as the new metropolitan. The new metropolitan is not permitted to have any ties with the Apostolic See. As with his predecessor, the Apostolic See refuses to confirm him as metropolitan.

January 1811 — Without the knowledge and agreement of the Apostolic See, Metropolitan Hryhoriy Kokhanovych, with the assistance of Roman Catholic bishops, ordains the new bishops Ioann Krasovsky, Adriyan Holovnya and Lev Yavorovsky, who were nominated by Alexander I for the Uniate eparchies in Russia.

Antin Anhelovych (1756-1814), the first Ukrainian Catholic Metropolitan of Galicia (1808-14), historian, rector of the Theological Seminary in Lviv.

July 1812 — With the occupation of Byelorussia by French armies, the Orthodox Archbishop of Mohyliv, the former Ukrainian Bishop of Volynia Varlaam Shyshatsky, along with the clergy, swears allegiance to Napoleon and conducts services for a French victory over Russia. After the retreat of the French armies, the Archbishop is tried by the Russian Synod, relieved of his religious rank and imprisoned at the monastery in Novhorod-Siversky where he dies in 1820.

1813 — After their victory over Napoleon, the Russian armies occupy the Kholm region. They ruin and plunder Ukrainian churches and monasteries.

Metropolitan Hryhoriy Kokhanovych of the Uniate Church in Russia dies in Polotsk.

9 August 1814 — The first Metropolitan of Galicia, Antin Anhelovych, dies in Lviv. One year later, on August 17, 1815, Emperor Francis II nominates Bishop Mykhaylo Levytsky of Peremyshl as the new Archbishop of Lviv and Metropolitan of Galicia.

Church of the Elevation of the Cross in the city of Kamyanets-Podilsky (Khmelnytsky oblast), built in 1799-1801. It is a typical example of the Podilia school of wooden church architecture.

1816 — The Pope establishes the Congregation of Extraordinary Ecclesiastical Affairs in Rome. The congregation is entrusted with all matters relating to the Uniate Church in the Austrian and Russian empires.

1816-1819 — Through the efforts of Metropolitan Mykhaylo Levytsky, 383 new parochial schools are opened in Galicia.

6 July 1817 — Tsar Alexander I appoints Bishop Yosafat Bulhak of Berestya as the new metropolitan for the Uniate church in Russia without designating the location of the Metropolitanate. The Apostolic See refuses to confirm the new metropolitan but issues a decree temporarily appointing Metropolitan Yosafat Bulhak as the administrator of the Apostolic See in Russia and grants him all the rights and privileges of a metropolitan.

Spring 1818 — By decision of the Apostolic See and with the agreement of the Austrian government, a new eparchy is created at Pryashiv (Presov) from the former Mukachiv Eparchy. The new eparchy, confirmed by Pope Pius VII on September 22, includes 193 parochial churches. The Pryashiv Eparchy, like the Mukachiv Eparchy, remains under the jurisdiction of the Roman Catholic Esztergom Archeparchy. The bishops for the eparchy are nominated by the Austrian emperor.

July 1818 — Emperor Francis II appoints Hryhoriy Tarkovych the first Bishop of Pryashiv. Because of various political and ecclesiastical complications and health problems, Hryhoriy Tarkovych is not consecrated as bishop until 1821.

1818 — Religious instruction of Ukrainian students in Galicia and Bukovyna is introduced in the Ukrainian native language.

The first institute for the training of deacons and parochial school teachers is opened in Peremyshl.

1819 — The Kiev Theological Academy is established on the basis of the Kiev Mohyla Academy, which has been disbanded by the Tsarist government.

1824 — A Theological Institute is opened in Chernivtsi. In 1875, this institute becomes the Theological faculty of the University of Chernivtsi.

1825 — With the accession of the new Russian Tsar, Nicholas I, an added emphasis is placed by the Russian authorities aligning all that is Russian with Orthodoxy and all that is Orthodox with Russia. These two concepts become unified within the Russian Empire. The Russian government begins to use this conceptual unification and the Church as tools in its efforts to russify and denationalize non-Russian nationalities within the Russian Empire.

The Kievan Metropolitan Yevheniy Bolkhovitinov writes two important works on the history of the Ukrainian church — *Description of the St. Sophia Cathedral in Kiev* and *Description of the Kievan Monastery of the Caves.*

In Ukrainian and Byelorussian territories under Russia, the faithful who convert from the Uniate Church to Orthodoxy are demeaned, and their churches exist in terrible poverty. The Theological Seminary in the town of Annopole is located in a stable on the estate of Prince Yablonsky. Roman Catholicism remains the faith of privilege. With the permission of Alexander I, the principal Catholic theological semi-

Dormition Ukrainian Orthodox Cathedral in the city of Hrubeshiv (now in Poland), built in 1873 (left).

Church of St. John the Theologian and belfry in the village of Shtun (Volynia oblast), built in 1777.

nary in the Latin-rite eparchy is opened in Vilnius and a small number of Uniate students are permitted to study there. A theological lyceum is established in the Ukrainian town of Kremenets in Volynia, which becomes the center for the spread of Roman Catholicism and Polish culture on Ukrainian territory.

1826 — Tsar Nicholas I forbids the sale and distribution of Ukrainian Catholic prayer books and other religious literature.

1827 — With the agreement of the Russian Imperial Minister of Internal Affairs Bludov, the Uniate archpriest Yosyf Syemashko of Lutsk, a member of the Catholic College of the Eastern rite in St. Petersburg, prepares a nine-point plan for the gradual and imperceptible unification of the Uniate Church in Russia with the Russian Orthodox Church.

22 April 1828 — In accordance with Yosyf Syemashko's plan for liquidation of the Uniate Church, Tsar Nicholas I pronounces a Decree (Ukase) regarding the full reorganization of the Uniate Church. The Metropolitanate of the Uniate Church in Russia on Ukrainian and Byelorussian territories is divided into two metropolitanates — the Byelorussian with its seat in Polotsk and the Lithuanian with its seat in Zhyrovytsi. A Theological Academy is established in Polotsk and a Seminary in Zhyrovytsi. Both schools are staffed with instructors trained in Russian Orthodoxy. Both metropolitanates are controlled by the Catholic College in St. Petersburg, members of which are appointed only by the Tsar. As a result of this Decree, the Uniate eparchy in Lutsk is liquidated. Metropolitan Yosafat Bulhak and Bishop Kyrylo Syrotynsky of Pinsk are transferred to St. Petersburg and relieved of any connections with the Church. Metropolitan Yosafat Bulhak's two auxiliary bishops, Lev Yavorovsky and Adriyan Holovnya, are relieved of their episcopal ranks and relocated in monasteries.

1829 — Bishop Ivan Snihursky of Peremyshl organizes a publishing group in that town which attracts Ukrainian clergy and cultural leaders — Yosyf Levytsky, Antin Dobryansky, Ivan Mohylnytsky, and Ivan Lavrivsky among others. Peremyshl becomes a religious-cultural center which plays a significant role in the national self-awareness of the Ukrainians in Western Ukraine.

3 February 1830 — As a consequence of the Russian government's opposition, in order that the eparchy of Kholm and Belz remain under the jurisdiction of the Metropolitanate of Galicia, Pope Pius VII subordinates the eparchy to the Apostolic See. This decision is confirmed by Emperor Francis II on May 4.

November 1830 — An anti-Russian uprising erupts in the Polish Congress kingdom. Accusing the Ukrainian Uniate clergy and faithful of participating in this uprising, Tsar Nicholas I begins forcible liquidation of the Uniate Church under Russian rule.

1831 — The Russian government takes control of the Pochayiv Monastery, which for over 110 years was the seat of the Basilian Order, and turns it over to the Orthodox Church. In 1833 the monastery is designated a Lavra and becomes the seat of the Bishop of Volynia, who in that year is granted the title of archbishop.

Mykhaylo Levytsky (1774-1858), Ukrainian Catholic Metropolitan of Galicia from 1816, church, cultural and educational leader, first Ukrainian Cardinal (1856).

The Archpriest I. Skvortsov, at the behest of the Russian Synod, undertakes an accounting of the Orthodox churches and clergy in the Podilia Eparchy under Russian rule. His accounting shows that neither the Russian Synod nor the Russian government cared about the condition of churches in Ukraine — out of a total of 1839 churches, 774 were completely destroyed and incapable of being used, one-third of the clergy were uneducated, and a mere one-seventh of the clergy had completed theological seminaries.

Tsar Nicholas I issues five decrees directed at the liquidation of the Uniate Church under Russian rule: all Uniate theological seminaries are to be closed; the Eastern-rite section of the Catholic Church College in St. Petersburg is included in the Russian Synod as one of its sections; under threat of severe penalties, any relation between the Roman Catholic and Uniate faithful is forbidden; children of mixed marriages are thereafter to be raised only in the Orthodox faith; and the Roman Catholic clergy are forbidden to give communion to Uniate faithful.

17 July 1832 — Tsar Nicholas I disbands the Basilian Order in the Russian Empire, and all Basilian

РУСАЛКА

ДНѢСТРОВАЯ.

Ruthenische Volks-Lieder.

У БУДИМѢ

Письмом Корол. Всеучилища Пештанского.

1837.

The Dniester Waternymph, Buda, 1837. Published by the "Ruthenian Triad" — Markiyan Shashkevych and Yakiv Holovatsky (Ukrainian Catholic priests) and Ivan Vahylevych.

property is confiscated by the state and in part turned over to the Russian Orthodox Church.

1833 — The Uniate Bishops Yakiv Martusevych and Lev Yavorovsky die under Russian rule. Tsar Nicholas I and the Ecclesiastical College in St. Petersburg appoint Yosyf Syemashko as the Metropolitan in Lithuania. Antoniy Zubko and Vasyl Luzhynsky, both of whom were educated in theological seminaries established by the Russian authorities for the training of candidate bishops and rigidly maintained a Russian direction in the Church, are appointed as his auxiliary bishops. The Tsar orders Metropolitan Yosafat Bulhak, who throughout this period remains in St. Petersburg, to return to Polotsk as the Byelorussian Metropolitan. Through the efforts of the Minister of Internal Affairs Bludov, clergy appointed to the Consistories of Bishops support the liquidation of the Uniate Church. Secret supporters of the liquidation plan are remunerated and given privileges.

1833-34 — During the famine in Byelorussia, all persons willing to convert to Russian Orthodoxy are promised food subsidies. Serfs willing to convert are promised freedom.

1834 — In Ukrainian and Byelorussian territories, with the assistance of Russian troops, the faithful are dispossessed of Uniate churches, priests are driven out, and Orthodox priests are appointed in their place.

2 April 1834 — 54 Uniate priests located in Ukrainian and Byelorussian territories protest before Metropolitan Yosyf Syemashko against the introduction of Russian books, rituals and liturgical texts published in St. Petersburg. By order of Metropolitan Syemashko, all priests who participated in the protest are punished by a sentence of one year's penance in monasteries. After their release, the unrepentant priests Plavsky, Mytsevych and .others are sent with their families to Siberia or imprisoned in local prisons.

1835 The Theological Seminary and School for Volynia is opened in the building previously occupied by the Roman Catholic Lyceum in Kremenets. The new institution is under the direct control of the Russian Synod.

1837 — Markiyan Shashkevych and Yakiv Holovatsky, two Ukrainian priests, and Ivan Vahylevych, who call themselves the "Ruthenian Triad," publish the *Rusalka Dnistrova,* the first Ukrainian-language anthology to appear in Galicia. This publication launches the Ukrainian national renaissance in the Church and the literature of Western Ukraine.

1837 — Metropolitan Yosyf Syemashko demands that the Uniate clergy sign agreements for the transfer of Uniate parishes to priests of the Russian Church. Many priests refuse to sign such agreements; among them is Metropolitan Yosyf Syemashko's own father, a Uniate priest.

1838 — At the Polotsk Synod, the Lithuanian

Holy Trinity Church of the Motronyn Monastery in the village of Melnyky (Cherkasy oblast), built in 1804 in the Baroque style. The monastery was founded in 1568; it became the center of the Kozak struggle against Poland. It was destroyed by the Soviets in the 1930s (left).

Church of the Presentation at the Temple in the village of Torun (Transcarpathian oblast), built of wood in 1809.

Metropolitan Yosyf Syemashko and his assistants, Bishop Vasyl Luzhynsky of Orsha, and Bishop Antoniy Zubko of the Byelorussian Eparchy, prepare a document called "A Synodal Act of Unification" of the Uniate Church with the Russian Orthodox Church. Disregarding the demands of Tsar Nicholas I and Minister of Internal Affairs Bludov, Metropolitan Yosafat Bulhak refuses to sign this Act. Under intense pressure to sign, he dies in St. Petersburg. Upon his death, the Tsar announces that prior to his death, Metropolitan Bulhak had agreed to convert to Russian Orthodoxy, and orders an elaborate funeral and interment of his earthly remains at the Alexander Nevsky Monastery beside various Moscow metropolitans. These efforts are intended to create confusion among the Uniates and encourage their conversion to Russian Orthodoxy.

Yosafat Bulhak (1758-1838), last Uniate Metropolitan in the Russian Empire (from 1817).

Over 160 Uniate priests along with their families are banished to Siberia for their refusal to convert to Russian Orthodoxy. Many others die in Russian prisons.

12-23 February 1839 — The Uniate Metropolitan Yosyf Syemashko convenes a Synod in Polotsk which is attended by Bishops Vasyl Luzhynsky and Antoniy Zubko, 21 Uniate priests, 19 members of the Consistory and other Uniate officials. They sign the "Synodal Act of Unification with Orthodoxy." The Act is not signed by any Uniate parish priest, deacon or member of the congregation. On the same day, Yosyf Syemashko requests Tsar Nicholas I to accept the Uniate Church into the Russian Orthodox Church. The Tsar, as head of the Russian Orthodox Church, signs the request with the words "I thank God and accept."

Researchers explain that the conversion of a large portion of the Uniate faithful to Orthodoxy resulted from constant persecution and oppression of the Uniate Church. The Russian government conveniently and cynically used the situation existing on Ukrainian and Byelorussian territories for its own goals. After the submission of the Lithuanian and Byelorussian Metropolitanates to the Russian Orthodox Church, only the Kholm Uniate Eparchy, which was part of the Polish Congress Kingdom, remained in the Russian Empire.

22 June 1839 — Pope Gregory XVI, in a speech before the College of Cardinals, harshly denounces the unification of the Uniate Church with the Russian Orthodox Church. His speech elicits wide-ranging responses in Europe.

16 December 1839 — Nicholas I announces a series of decrees for limiting church construction and sets up new controls of religious life by civilian officials.

1839 — The Russian government closes 22 Uniate monasteries and 3 convents in the Lutsk Eparchy.

Martyrdom of Ukrainian Catholics in the Kholm Region. 19th-century painting depicting Russian persecution of Ukrainian Catholics.

Yosyf Sembratovych (1821-1900), Ukrainian Catholic Metropolitan of Galicia (1870-82).

The Secretary of State of the Apostolic See prepares a "White Book" on the forced unification of the Uniate Church to Russian Orthodoxy.

20 January 1840 — Tsar Nicholas I begins to use the term "Greek Uniate Church" and announces this Church as non-existing.

18 February 1840 — The Uniate Metropolitan Mykhaylo Levytsky of Galicia issues a message in which he summarizes the history of the Ukrainian Church from the oldest times and bitterly condemns the unification of the Uniate Church with the Russian Orthodox Church.

1840 — Tsar Nicholas I appoints Yosyf Syemashko the Orthodox Archbishop of Lithuania and in 1852 he is given the title of Metropolitan.

10 March 1841 — The Ukrainian Metropolitan Mykhaylo Levytsky of Galicia issues a message "To the Faithful of Uniate Rus'" in which he condemns the "Synodal Act of Unification of the Uniate Church" with the Russian Church.

17 December 1841 — By Decree of Tsar Nicholas I, all properties of the former Uniate churches and monasteries become possessions of the Russian government.

1841 — The Russian Minister of Internal Affairs Uvarov postulates the ideological foundation of the Russian Empire with the slogan "autocracy, Orthodoxy, nationality." "Nationality," in his way of thinking, is synonymous with pan-Russianism, which involves the merger of the Ukrainian and Byelorussian nationalities with the Russians, with the help of the Russian Orthodox Church.

1843 — A temporary Commission for the Review of Ancient Acts is formed at the Kiev, Volynia and Podilia General-Governorship. As a result of the efforts of this Commission, four volumes of documents on the history of the Ukrainian Church are published under the title *Monuments:* on the Lutsk Brotherhood of the Elevation of the Holy Cross, on the Kiev Brotherhood of the Theophany (1615-1787), on the Lviv Brotherhood (1586-1637), and a volume on smaller brotherhoods and monasteries. In the second half of the 19th century and at the beginning of the 20th century, this Commission, under the editorship of Volodymyr Antonovych, publishes 12 volumes entitled *Acts on the History of the Orthodox Church in South-Western Russia.*

1845 — On the initiative of the Ukrainian historian Mykola Kostomarov, the Brotherhood of SS. Cyril and Methodius is founded in Kiev. Its aim is to reconstruct society on the foundations of the Christian teachings of justice, liberty, equality and fraternity by means of a number of reforms: the abolition of serfdom, the granting of equal rights to all nations and the creation of a federation of equal Slavic States. In 1847 the Russian police uncover the existence of the Brotherhood and its members are sentenced to varying terms of imprisonment. Among them is the Ukrainian poet Taras Shevchenko, who is sentenced to ten years' hard labor.

The Greek College in Rome is renamed the Pontifical Greek and Ruthenian College.

A Theological Seminary is opened in Peremyshl. One hundred years later, in 1945, this Seminary is closed by the Polish communist regime.

16 April 1848 — Under the slogans of freedom generated throughout Europe by the French Revolution, protests and revolts occur in the Austro-Hungarian Empire. As a result of these events the Austrian government abolishes serfdom. On May 5, the first Ukrainian political party, the Supreme Ruthenian Council (Holovna Ruska Rada), is established in Western Ukraine and is headed by the Uniate Bishop Hryhoriy Yakhymovych. The Council demands the

Cathedral of the Elevation of the Cross in Poltava, built in 1699-1709. The only church in Ukraine with seven domes (cupolas) (left).

Former church in the village of Chornobay (Cherkasy oblast), built in 1808. Churches of this architectural type were the most common in Ukraine in the 19th century.

separation of Galicia, Bukovyna and Trascarpathia into a separate kingdom. Even though this political turmoil, given the name "Spring of Nations," is suppressed by the Austrian authorities, it leaves an indelible impact on the further development of Ukrainian church, religious and cultural life. The first appeal of the Ruthenian Council concerns the matter of the Church. The appeal asserts:

> Our first assignment is to protect the faith and to place our traditions and the rights of our priests and the Church at the level attained by other denominations. (Velyky, Vol. VIII, p. 118).

October 1848 — Under the initiative of the Rev. Mykola Ustyanovych, the First Congress of Ukrainian intellectuals takes place in Lviv. Out of the 118 participants of this Congress 106 are members of the clergy. Among other matters, the Convocation focuses its attention on theological matters and the introduction of the Ukrainian language into the Liturgy.

1849 — Opposing the will of the Russian Synod, Archpriest Vasyl Hrychulevych publishes the first collection of sermons in Ukrainian. Similar collections are prepared and published by Revs. Ivan Babchenko and Stepan Opanovych.

Bukovyna becomes a separate province with its own government.

20 January 1850 — The Rev. Ippolit Terletsky opens the first Ukrainian Uniate Seminary and church in Paris.

May 1850 — As a result of Metropolitan Levytsky's efforts, the Eparchy of Stanyslaviv (now Ivano-Frankivsk) is established in Galicia. Its establishment is confirmed by the Apostolic See on September 22, 1850 and it opens officially in 1885.

23 December 1853 — Polish Roman Catholic bishops and Ukrainian Eastern-rite bishops agree to a proposal of understanding between the two Churches. This proposal, entitled the "Concordia," is finally confirmed by Pope Pius IX on July 17, 1863.

16 June 1856 — Pope Pius IX nominates Metropolitan Mykhaylo Levytsky of Galicia as the first Ukrainian cardinal.

2 January 1858 — Metropolitan Mykhaylo Levytsky of Galicia dies in Univ. Bishop Spyrydon Lytvynovych becomes the administrator of the Metropolitanate.

Hryhoriy Yakhymovych (1792-1863), Ukrainian Catholic Metropolitan of Galicia (from 1860), rector of the Theological Seminary in Lviv, cultural and educational leader.

September 1859 — Emperor Franz Josef I nominates Bishop Hryhoriy Yakhymovych of Peremyshl as Metropolitan of Galicia. Bishop Yakhymovych is confirmed by Pope Pius IX on March 23, 1860 and ascends to the metropolitan throne on November 13, 1860.

1860 — *The Works of the Kiev Theological Academy,* devoted mainly to the history of the Church in Ukraine, begin appearing in Kiev.

In the Chernihiv province, which experienced widespread cultural and educational growth during the reign of the Ukrainian hetmans, the closing of numerous parochial schools is the culmination of over a hundred years of Russian rule. In the entire province only 70 students out of 2290 are left. During the course of several decades, after the elimination of serfdom in 1861, the number of parochial schools in the province increases to 850, with 17,000 students. In 1900, there are 1812 parochial schools in the Kiev province, 1600 in Volynia and 2045 in Podilia. These schools, in addition to fulfilling educational functions, become the means of russification and denationalization of the Ukrainian populace.

1860s — As a result of the reformist polemic con-

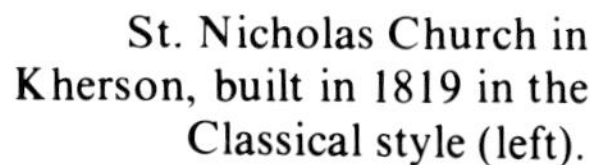

St. Nicholas Church in Kherson, built in 1819 in the Classical style (left).

Church of the Protection of the Blessed Virgin Mary in the city of Pervomaysk (Mykolayiv oblast), built in 1805 in the Classical style.

cerning ritual and Liturgy begun by the Rev. Ivan Naumovych and the monk Ippolit Terletsky in Galicia, in 1862 Pope Pius IX establishes the Eastern department of the Congregation for the Propagation of the Faith for the purpose of reviewing the reasons for the polemic, and of the correction of liturgical books. Simultaneously, Metropolitan Hryhoriy Yakhymovych of Galicia issues a message to the faithful in which he asks for the cessation of the polemics concerning ritual reform and Liturgy. The two responsible priests are punished. The Rev. Ivan Naumovych is removed from the Metropolitanate. In the 1880's he returns to Galicia and along with his parish convert to Orthodoxy.

1861 — The Synod of the Orthodox clergy in Chernivtsi, chaired by Bishop Yevhen Hakman, demands the establishment of a separate Metropolitanate of Bukovyna.

November 1861 — Under the new reforms, Bishop Spyrydon Lytvynovych of Lviv becomes deputy to the president of the Austrian Parliament.

29 April 1863 — Metropolitan Hryhoriy Yakhymovych of Galicia dies in Lviv. In June, Emperor Franz-Josef I nominates Bishop Spyrydon Lytvynovych as the new Metropolitan. Bishop Lytvynovych is confirmed by the Pope on September 17 and assumes his post on May 5, 1864.

17 July 1863 — Pope Pius IX issues a decree concerning understanding and normalization of relations between the Latin and Eastern-rite Churches in Galicia. The decree, entitled the "Concordia," is published on October 6. In accordance with this decree, conversion from one rite to the other is forbidden without the prior approval of the Apostolic See. Furthermore, priests of one rite are forbidden to christen children of the other rite. This decree becomes operational on January 23, 1864.

18 July 1863 — By a special circular, the Russian Minister of Internal Affairs Valuyev bans the use of the Ukrainian language on the Ukrainian lands under Russian domination.

August 1863 — The Russian government rejects the recommendation of the Academy of Sciences in St. Petersburg to publish the *New Testament* and the *Acts of the Apostles* in Ukrainian, arguing that such publications could weaken Ukrainian ties to Russia.

1863 — After an unsuccessful Polish uprising, the Russian government, which controlled the Ukrainian Catholic Eparchy of Kholm as part of the Polish Congress Kingdom, begins mass persecution of Catholics of both rites. Having completely russified the Uniate Theological Seminary, the government appoints Russian-oriented priests to the parishes. Bishop Ivan Kalinsky, newly-nominated by the Apostolic See, is forbidden by the Russians to be consecrated in Galicia. In return, he refuses to commemorate the tsar during the Liturgy and to recognize Russian Church reforms.

12 July 1864 — Pope Pius IX confirms the Lviv Krylos, which was previously confirmed by Emperor Francis II in 1813. The Peremyshl Krylos was confirmed by the emperor in 1816.

1864 — By order of the Russian government all Uniate monasteries in the Kholm Eparchy are closed.

1865 — The Russian government confiscates numerous Uniate churches in the Kholm Eparchy and forces clergy to convert to Russian Orthodoxy. This causes an exodus of Uniate clergy to Galicia and a return of "Russophiles" to Kholm.

The Bukovyna Eparchy is joined to the Rumanian Metropolitanate of Transylvania.

2 September 1866 — The Ukrainian Uniate Bishop-nominee Ivan Kalinsky is arrested by the Russian occupation authorities in Kholm. For his refusal to convert to Russian Orthodoxy, he is imprisoned and banished to Vyatka in Russia where he dies on October 19. In his place, without consultation or approval by the Apostolic See, Tsar Alexander II appoints Russian-oriented bishop Yosyf Voytsitsky. Bishop Voytsitsky, disregarding clerical opposition, institutes Russian Orthodox reforms in the Church.

29 June 1867 — In Rome, at the time of the commemoration of the 1800th anniversary of the martyrdom of the Apostles SS. Peter and Paul, the Catholic Church announces the canonization of Archbishop Yosafat Kuntsevych of Polotsk, who died a martyr's death in Vitebsk in 1623. Metropolitan Spyrydon Lytvynovych of Galicia, accompanied by a

Church of the Ascension in the village of Matusiv (Cherkasy oblast), built in 1812-18 in the late Classical style (left).

Holy Trinity Church in the village of Kotelva (Poltava oblast), built in 1812. It includes elements of the Classical style.

Annunciation Church in Kharkiv, 19th century (left).

Belfry of the Church of St. John the Theologian in the villge of Nekrasivka (Odessa oblast), built in 1823.

sizeable Ukrainian delegation, participates in the canonization ritual and celebration along with Cardinals and over 500 Bishops from all over the world. On July 6, 1867, the Cardinals of the Catholic Church sign a document entitled "The Shining Light of the Eastern Church" about St. Yosafat.

The canonization of Archbishop Yosafat Kuntsevych was prepared by a special commission convened by Pope Pius IX and composed of Vicar Patrici of Rome, Hegumen Contieri of Grottaferrata, former Protohegumen of the Ukrainian Basilian Order Mykhaylo Dobryansky and auxiliary Bishop Yosyf Sembratovych of Peremyshl.

Celebrations comparable to those conducted in Rome take place in Lviv and are attended by Ukrainian Eastern-rite, Polish Latin-rite and Armenian Catholic hierarchs. Saint Yosafat is commemorated by the entire Catholic Church on November 12.

Fall 1867 — Pope Pius IX issues an encyclical condemning the activism of Bishop-nominee Yosyf Voytsitsky of Kholm and the persecution of the Uniate Church by the Russians.

1867 — The Habsburg Empire is divided into the dual state of Austria-Hungary.

22 June 1868 — The Apostolic See, with the concurrence of Tsar Alexander II, nominates the Priest Mykhaylo Kuzemsky of Lviv as Bishop of Kholm. Bishop Kuzemsky is consecrated in Lviv on August 23 by the Metropolitan Spyrydon Lytvynovych of Galicia.

8 December 1868 — The Rev. Stepan Kachala establishes the cultural-educational society "Prosvita" in Lviv. It plays an important role in the spread of national self-awareness among the population of Western Ukraine. For many years thereafter, the society is headed by members of the clergy.

Metropolitan Yosyf Syemashko, who completed the annexation of the Uniate Church to the Russian Orthodox Church in Ukrainian and Byelorussian territories under Russian rule, dies.

4 June 1869 — Metropolitan Spyrydon Lytvynovych dies in Lviv. On June 26, 1870, Emperor Franz-Josef I nominates Bishop Yosyf Sembratovych of Peremyshl as the new Metropolitan. Shortly thereafter, Bishop Sembratovych's nomination is confirmed by Pope Pius IX and he assumes his duties on August 7, 1870.

1869 — The Ukrainian authors Panteleymon Kulish, Ivan Puluy and Pylyp Morachevsky work on the first translation of the *Bible* into Ukrainian. Panteleymon Kulish's translation of a part of the *Bible* appears in Lviv, and two years later his translation of the *New Testament* is published.

1870 — In Chernivtsi, at the initiative of Orthodox Bishop Hakman, the Rev. Vasyl Prodan and Deacon Vasyl Dron, the "Ruthenian Discourse" ("Ruska Besida") society is formed for the purpose of engendering national self-awareness among Ukrainians in Bukovyna. Later, two other organizations are formed for the purpose of pursuing the same goal — the "Association

Churches of Lviv in the early 19th century. Lithography of a painting by A. Lange, 1826.

of Ukrainian Orthodox Priests" and the "Orthodox Academy," which unites theological students.

Ukrainian researcher Pavlo Chubynsky, with the assistance of clergy and students of theological seminaries, collects ethnographic records from different regions of Ukraine. These documents show that despite the intense pressure for russification and conversion to Russian Orthodoxy, Orthodox Ukrainians manage to retain Ukrainian national rituals, traditions and beliefs that differ from those of Russia.

28 March 1871 — Under pressure and demand from the Russian government, Bishop Mykhaylo Kuzemsky of Kholm resigns. In his place Tsar Alexander II appoints, without the knowledge or approval of the Apostolic See, the Russian-oriented Bishop Markyl Popel of Kholm.

1872 — In Warsaw, the Russian authorities close the last Ukrainian Basilian monastery.

1873 — Emperor Franz Josef I elevates the Bukovyna Orthodox Eparchy to a Metropolitanate consisting of three eparchies — one for Bukovyna and two for Dalmatia.

Yevheniy Hakman becomes the first Metropolitan.

13 May 1874 — As a result of Russian reforms put into operation by Bishop Markyl Popel of Kholm, Pope Pius IX censures Bishop Popel's conduct by issuing a special apostolic letter. The Russian authorities reject the papal letter as alien to the Eastern-rite Church.

1875 — A Theological faculty is founded at the University of Chernivtsi; it is closed down by the Soviet authorities in 1940.

2 May 1875 — After many years of Russian preparation, the Kholm Uniate Eparchy is subordinated to the Russian Orthodox Church. Tsar Alexander II appoints Uniate bishop Markyl Popel, who converts to Russian Orthodoxy, as the Orthodox bishop of Lublin and an auxiliary of the Kholm and Warsaw eparchies. Russian troops in the Kholm province commence terrorist activities in an effort to convert the "stubborn" faithful to Russian Orthodoxy. The priests Klementiy Vitoshynsky, Ihnatiy Bukovytsky, Severy Voynovsky, Antoniy Zatkalyk, Ivan Kharlampovych, Mykola Nazarevych and Yakiv Zatkalyk are sentenced to march on foot to Siberia. Within three years, 18 priests die in jails or under persecution. The entire village of Pratulyn in Pidlyashshya is destroyed by the Russians and the inhabitants executed. Other villages — Rossoshi, Lomazy and Lukivka — having refused to convert to Russian Orthodoxy, are severely punished.

30 May 1876 — Tsar Alexander II issues the Ems

St. Nicholas Church in the city of Mykolayiv, built in 1813-17. The structure is remarkable for the Classical elements in its architectural style (left).

St. Nicholas Cathedral of St. Nicholas Monastery in Sharhorod (Vinnytsya oblast), built in 1829 by the architect Feofan.

St. Nicholas Church in the city of Izmayil (Odessa oblast), built in 1833 (left).

Cathedral of the Transfiguration in Katerynoslav (now Dnipropetrovsk), built in 1830-35.

Ukase, which forbids the use of the Ukrainian language under Russian rule and pronounces Ukrainian a non-existent language. In the Ukrainian territories within Austro-Hungary, this decree elicits further Ukrainian religious, cultural and intellectual activity, led mostly by the clergy.

1876 — Metropolitan Yosyf Sembratovych of Galicia issues a message to the faithful entitled "Concerning the Great Dignity of Man," which addresses the need for moral and physical healing and improvement of the life of the population. This episcopal message evokes bitter opposition from wealthy Polish landowners in Galicia.

1878 — A society named after the great chronicler Nestor is formed at Kiev University and publishes *Readings* (*Chteniya*) containing historical materials on the Ukrainian Church and culture.

1880s — Ukrainian Catholic immigrants in the United States are joined by the first priests — Ivan Volyansky from Galicia and Stepan Dzubay from Transcarpathia. In the following decade the number of immigrant priests increases to ten.

1881 — A Theological Seminary is opened in Pryashiv which survives until 1950, when it is closed by the Czechoslovak communist authorities.

12 May 1882 — Pope Leo XIII issues an apostolic letter entitled "A Separate Bastion" concerning reform of the Basilian Order in Galicia. This letter removes the Order from the control of the metropolitan and entrusts the institution of the reforms to the Polish Jesuits. The reforms are started in the monastery at Dobromyl and therefore are named the Dobromyl Reforms. The involvement of the Polish Jesuits in reforming a Ukrainian monastic order is protested throughout Galicia and results in the resignation of Metropolitan Yosyf Sembratovych. In his place the Pope appoints auxiliary Bishop Sylvester Sembratovych as administrator of the Metropolitanate. On March 26, 1885, Bishop Sylvester Sembratovych finally is nominated as Metropolitan by the Apostolic See. He assumes the duties of metropolitan on May 5, 1885.

1882 — As a result of the "Russophile" movement in Galicia, the Uniate parish of Father Ivan Naumovych in the village of Hnylychky is the first to convert to Orthodoxy. In Transcarpathia, Father Ivan Rakovsky champions the cause of Russian Orthodoxy. The Russophile movement is transferred by emigrants from Transcarpathia to the United States, where in the 1890's they establish the "Carpathian Orthodox Greek Catholic Church."

1883-84 — The Ukrainian Catholic priests Stepan Kachala, Danylo Tanyakevych and, later, the brothers Yulyan and Toma Dutkevych, begin the cooperative, economic and agricultural reawakening and establish numerous civic, cultural and educational organizations and publications.

19 December 1884 — Rev. Ivan Volyansky, the first Ukrainian Catholic priest in America, serves the first Ukrainian Liturgy in Shenandoah, Pennsylvania.

25 March 1885 — With the agreement of Emperor Franz Josef I and Pope Leo XIII, the Stanyslaviv Eparchy is officially opened.

5 December 1888 — Metropolitan Sylvester Sembratovych of Galicia pleads with the Pope for permission to convene a Synod of the Ukrainian Catholic Church.

1890s — Anti-Russian secret student groups are started at the Kiev Theological Academy and in other

Yuliyan Pelesh (1845-96), Ukrainian Catholic Bishop of Stanyslaviv, and later Peremyshl, prominent historian of the Ukrainian Church.

theological seminaries throughout Ukraine. Members of these groups later play a significant role in the rebirth of the Ukrainian Orthodox Church in 1921.

24 September — 8 October 1891 — With the permission of Pope Leo XIII, a Synod of the Ukrainian Catholic Church takes place in Lviv. Since the establishment of the Metropolitanate, the Uniate Church has become the Ukrainian national Catholic Church in Galicia. Thus, only Ukrainians are participants at the Lviv Synod, unlike the Synod of Zamostya in 1720, which was attended by Ukrainian and Byelorussian bishops and priests. The Synod is attended by Metropolitan Sylvester Sembratovych, Archbishop of Lviv and Bishop of Kamyanets-Podilsky, and also by Bishop Yuliyan Pelesh of Peremyshl, Sambir and Syanok, Bishop Yuliyan Kuyilovsky of Stanyslaviv, the Apostolic delegate, Protohegumen of the Basilian Order Klyment Sarnytsky, the rector of the Lviv Major Theological Seminary Oleksander Bachynsky, the rector of the Theological Seminary in Vienna Teofil Sembratovych, the Hegumen of the Hoshiv Monastery Father Meletiy Tybinka, the Hegumen of the Zolochiv Monastery Father Pavlo Pylynsky, the Pidhortsi Hegumen Father Lonhyn Karpovych, the Buchach Hegumen Father Yeron Ostroverkha and 148 priests and instructors from Lviv University and from the theological seminaries in Lviv and Vienna. The Synod functions through three working committees and conducts four plenary sessions on September 27 and October 1, 4, and 8. The Synod adopts numerous decrees and acts which are formulated on the basis of 15 principles concerning the Catholic faith; the Holy Sacraments and communion; ordination and consecration; universal worship of God; the holy Liturgy; consecration of churches for worship; the church hierarchy; theological seminaries; priests; monks; fasts; memorial services for the dead; church trials; synods; and church property.

The Lviv Synod confirms its Catholic faith and reorganizes Church activity and liturgical matters in accordance with the demands of present-day life. Two points of view are repeated during the deliberations of the Synod: the conservative and the reformist. The Synod decides that Uniate priests can continue to marry, but recommends celibacy. The Julian calendar remains obligatory in the Ukrainian Catholic Church.

1892 — A new female monastic order, the Society of the Sisters Servants of Mary Immaculate, is established in Galicia.

1891-1913 — As a result of continuous misunderstandings with Roman Catholic priests and bishops in the United States and because of the enforcement of celibacy, a group of Ukrainian Catholic priests and faithful converts to Orthodoxy.

29 May 1893 — Metropolitan Sylvester Sembratovych and a large group of pilgrims take part in celebrating the 50th anniversary of Pope Leo XIII in Rome.

1895 — On the 300th anniversary of the Union of Berestya, Pope Leo XIII names Metropolitan Sylvester Sembratovych a Cardinal. The new Cardinal arrives in Lviv on December 12.

22 April 1896 — Bishop Yuliyan Pelesh, Ukrainian intellectual, theologian, historian of the Ukrainian

Church of St. John the Theologian in the village of Makiv (Khmelnytsky oblast), built in 1839 (left).

Church of the Transfiguration in the village of Moshny (Cherkasy oblast), built in 1830-40 according to plans by Toricelli. Many styles are intermixed in this structure.

Church, author of the *History of the Union, Pastoral Theology* and *Handbook of the Christian Faith,* dies in Peremyshl.

1896 — A political party called the "Catholic Ruthenian People's Union" is formed in Lviv and headed by Oleksander Barvinsky.

18 December 1897 — In Rome, at the request of Metropolitan Sylvester Sembratovych, Pope Leo XIII establishes the St. Josafat Papal Seminary, but under the leadership of the Jesuit order. From 1904 the Seminary is operated by the Ukrainian Basilian Order.

4 August 1898 — Metropolitan Sylvester Cardinal Sembratovych of Galicia dies in Lviv. In his place, Emperor Franz Josef I nominates Bishop Yuliyan Sas-Kuyilovsky of Stanislaviv as the new Metropolitan. He is confirmed by the Pope on August 30, 1899.

1898 — Ukrainian clergy in Galicia actively participate in celebrating the 100th anniversary of the publication of Ivan Kotlyarevsky's "Eneida" and the Ukrainian cultural rebirth, as well as the 50th anniversary of the abolition of serfdom. These celebrations are pivotal in accepting the use of the names "Ukraine" and "Ukrainian" instead of "Malorossiya," "Rus'," "Ruthenia," and "Rusyn."

The First Assembly of Ukrainian Catholic clergy in the United States takes place. The Assembly elects the Rev. N. Khanat first vicar for Ukrainian Catholic immigrants in this country.

4 May 1900 — Metropolitan Yulian Sas-Kuyilovsky dies in Lviv. On December 17, the Pope nominates Bishop Andrey Roman Graf Sheptytsky of Stanyslaviv as the new Metropolitan. Bishop Andrey Sheptytsky assumes the throne of the Metropolitanate on January 17, 1901.

23 October 1900 — Former Metropolitan Yosyf Sembratovych of Galicia dies in Rome.

19th century — Ukrainian territories under Russian rule have no self-government, and are a part of the Russian empire as the separate provinces of Kiev, Poltava, Chernihiv, Kharkiv, Podilia, Volynia, Katerynoslav (now Dnipropetrovsk), Kherson, and Tavria. Each province is governed by a Russian governor.

Second half of 19th century — Numerous professors and students at the Kiev Theological Academy focus, in their dissertations and research, on the history of the Ukrainian Church. Their efforts appear in anthologies published by the Academy.

Sylvester Sembratovych (1836-98), Ukrainian Catholic Metropolitan of Galicia (1885-98), prominent church, cultural and educational leader, appointed cardinal, 1895.

Beginning of the 1900s — The Russian Archbishop Antoniy Khrapovytsky of Volynia takes the first steps in disseminating Russian Orthodoxy in Transcarpathia. In the absence of a Patriarch in Russia, he is appointed the Exarch of Galicia and Transcarpathia by the Patriarch of Constantinople.

1903 — The British Bible Society publishes the first complete translation of the Holy Bible — both the Old and New Testaments — by Panteleymon Kulish, Ivan Nechuy-Levytsky and Ivan Puluy. This publication is available for distribution in Ukraine only after the 1905 revolution.

SS. Peter and Paul Church in the village of Kosmach (Ivano-Frankivsk oblast), built in 1904-05 (left).

St. Michael's Church in the village of Ustye (Ivano-Frankivsk oblast), built of wood in 1853.

1904 — The first Ukrainian Protestant groups in the United States are formed in the Dakotas.

12 March 1905 — Bishop Parfeniy Levytsky of Kamyanets-Podilsky organizes the first Ukrainian Commission for translation of theological books into the Ukrainian language. This Commission consists of theologians from the Kiev Theological Academy — Y. Sitsinsky, K. Starynkevych, A. Neselovsky, N. Bychkovsky, M. Savkevych, and S. Ivanytsky. Ukrainian intellectuals and Russian members of the Academy of Sciences in St. Petersburg headed by the academician A. Shakhmatov, also work on translations.

March 1905 — After a struggle of many years, the Russian Synod permits the publication of a Ukrainian-language *New Testament* translated by P. Morachevsky, P. Kulish, and M. Lobodovsky and edited by Bishop Parfeniy Levytsky.

17 April 1905 — Tsar Nicholas II announces a manifesto concerning religious tolerance in the Russian Empire. Shortly thereafter, 200,000 faithful return to Catholicism in the Kholm and Pidlyashshya provinces.

1905 — Metropolitan Andrey Sheptytsky establishes the Ukrainian National Museum in Lviv. The museum collection consists of numerous icons, documents, old graphics and manuscripts concerning the history of the Ukrainian Church. In 1945, the Soviets plunder the museum's collection and remove many exhibits to Russia.

The Ukrainian priests and members of the Russian parliament (the Duma) A. Hrynevych, M. Senderko, K. Volkov, V. Solukha, and O. Trehubov play an active role in this forum and thus protect Ukrainian national interests.

Metropolitan Andrey Sheptytsky renews ancient eastern monasticism, modeled on that of the Kievan Monastery of the Caves of the 11th-13th centuries, and founds the Studite Order in Sknyliv near Lviv and develops its charter.

5-29 September 1906 — Metropolitan Andrey Sheptytsky organizes a pilgrimage to the Holy Land under the slogan "As Rus' Followed in the Footsteps of Danylo" ("Yak Rus' Khodyla Slidamy Danyla"). Five hundred five pilgrims, including 100 priests, participate in the pilgrimage.

1906 — The General Convocation of the Basilian Order takes place in Krystynopil (now Chervonohrad). The Convocation has a new charter in accordance with the monastic rule of 1901. This Basilian charter is confirmed by Pope Pius X on July 26, 1909 and continues to be obligatory until 1954.

26 January 1907 — An anti-Russian protest by students at the Theological Seminary in Zhytomyr is suppressed by police and the army.

4 July 1907 — Through the efforts of Metropolitan Andrey Sheptytsky and with the approval of the Austrian emperor, the Apostolic See nominates Father Soter S. Ortynsky first Ukrainian Catholic Bishop in the United States. As vicar, he must remain under the jurisdiction of the Roman Catholic bishop.

12 October 1907 — Under the influence of the slogans of the 1905 revolution, Bishop Parfeniy Levytsky and the eparchial convocation in Podilia decide to institute Ukrainian as the instructional language in parochial schools. The Bishop and numerous priests first preach in their native language. Shortly afterwards, the Russian Synod transfers the Bishop to Tula in Russia and forbids the use of Ukrainian in parochial schools.

St. Anastasia's Church in the city of Hlukhiv (Sumy oblast), built in 1885-86 in the neo-Byzantine style, according to plans by Academician A. Hun. The interior was painted by the brothers A. and P. Svidomsky (left).

Church of the Protection of the Blessed Virgin Mary in the village of Pleshyvets (Poltava oblast), built in 1902-06 by the architect P.S. Kuznetsov. This is a smaller copy of the 18th-century Holy Trinity Cathedral in Novomoskovsk.

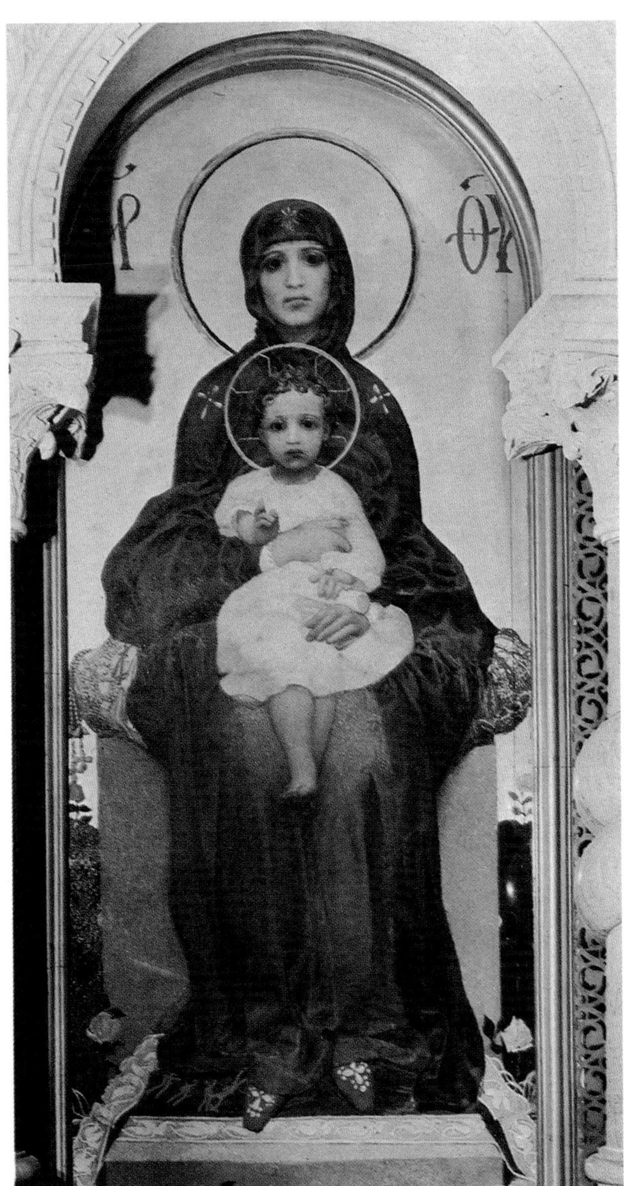

The Mother of God, by M. Vrubel, 1884. St. Cyril Church in Kiev.

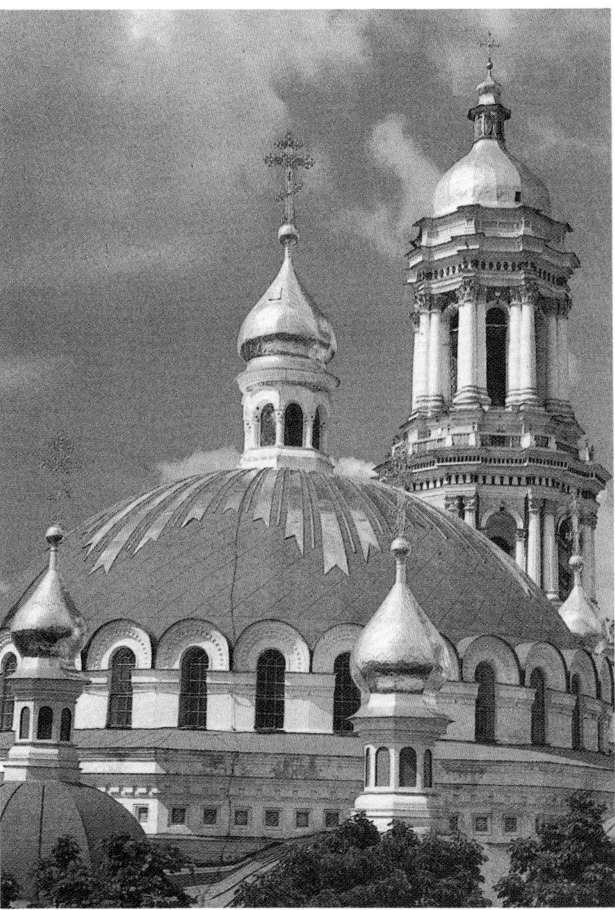

Church of SS. Anthony and Theodosius of the Kievan Monastery of the Caves, built in 1893-95. In 1980 it was converted by the Soviets into the Museum of Christianity and Atheism in Ukraine and a concert hall.

Cathedral of the Transfiguration in Zhytomyr, built in 1864.

1907 — A Ukrainian Catholic Theological Seminary is opened in Stanyslaviv. The first rector of the seminary, Father Yeremiya Lomnytsky, is deported by the Russians to Siberia in 1917. The Seminary is closed by the Soviet authorities in 1945.

The Russian Synod orders the opening of a Kholm Eparchy.

In pursuit of the goal of rapprochment between Orthodox and Catholic faithful in the Slavic nations, Metropolitan Andrey Sheptytsky organizes a congress in Velehrad in Moravia (now Czechoslovakia), which is attended by theologians from both faiths. These congresses take place in 1909 and 1911 as well.

1908 — On the 1500th anniversary of the death of St. John Chrysostom, Metropolitan Andrey Sheptytsky issues an epistle entitled "Approaching Times" on the subject of the unification of the Catholic and Orthodox Churches.

By the order of the Russian Archbishop Antoniy Khrapovytsky of Volynia, the Kiev Theological Academy is purged of the renowned Ukrainian educators and scholars M. I. Petrov, Rozov, Volodymyr Zavitnevych, V. Ekzemplyarsky, Skabalanovych, V. P. Rybynsky and others — for their Ukrainophile activities or their liberalism. Their academic posts are filled by Russians.

1910 — Metropolitan Andrey Sheptytsky visits Canada.

Metropolitan Andrey Sheptytsky founds the Eastern-rite Redemptorist Order.

1911 — In the United States, 11,800 Orthodox Ukrainians from Galicia and 6,400 from Bukovyna pray under the jurisdiction of the Russian Orthodox Church.

After many years of disputes, protests and demands, the Russian Synod in Moscow publishes the full *New Testament* in the Ukrainian and Slavonic languages.

In Rome, Metropolitan Andrey Sheptytsky founds the "Ruthenian Historical Mission," whose purpose is locating in the Roman archives materials on the history of the Church in Ukraine. Ten volumes of these materials in the original languages are finally published in the 1970's by the Ukrainian Catholic University in Rome.

1912 The "Provydinnya" (Providence) Union of Ukrainian Catholics is founded in New York.

15 July 1912 — Pope Pius X appoints Father Nykyta Budka as the first Ukrainian Catholic Bishop for 80 Canadian parishes and 80,000 faithful. In October, Father Budka is consecrated by Metropolitan Andrey Sheptytsky and in December he arrives in Canada and assumes his post in Winnipeg.

1913 — Pope Pius X establishes an Exarchate in Philadelphia for Ukrainian Catholic immigrants from Galicia and Transcarpathia.

The first Ukrainian Redemptorist province is established and the first monastery of the Redemptorist Order is built in Yorkton, Canada.

28 July 1914 — World War I begins. European countries divide themselves into two blocks: the Grand Alliance nations (Austria and Germany) and the Entente (Russia, France, Great Britain and others). Russian troops quickly defeat the Austro-Hungarian armies, occupy Galicia and, in 1915, advance as far as Peremyshl. Later that year, under pressure from the armies of the Grand Alliance, the Russians retreat and leave Ukrainian territory. A year later, the Russians reoccupy Ukrainian territories they had vacated.

1 August 1914 — The Ukrainian General Council (Holovna Ukrayinska Rada) is formed in Western

Tepla Church of the Mhar Monastery (Poltava oblast), built in the late 19th century in a pseudo-Byzantine style (left).

A wooden church in the village of Kotelnytsya (Transcarpathian oblast), built in the late 19th century.

Church of the Protection of the Blessed Virgin Mary in Yelysavethrad (now Kirovohrad), built in 1850 in a military settlement (left).

Church of the Protection of the Blessed Virgin Mary in Kamyanets-Podilsky, built in 1845-61 in an eclectic style by architects A. Ostrovsky and N. Kulakovsky.

Ukraine. The goal of the Council is to create an independent Ukrainian state.

24 August 1914 — Russian troops occupy Lviv. One week later, the Russian Synod orders the Russian Archbishop Yevlogiy Georgiyevsky of Volynia to start preliminary efforts to subjugate the Ukrainian Catholic Church in Galicia to the Russian Orthodox Church. On September 7, Archbishop Yevlogiy, accompanied by a group of Russian theologians, arrives in Galicia. After a brief stay among Ukrainian Catholics, he reports to the Russian Synod that the population is fervently loyal to the Union, fiercely opposes the Russians and the Russian Orthodox Church, and supports the independence of Ukraine.

19 September 1914 — Russians arrest Metropolitan Andrey Sheptytsky in Lviv and deport him to Russia. He is imprisoned in Kursk, Suzdal and Yaroslavl. The Apostolic See, the King of Spain, the Austrian and German governments and numerous other prominent nobility and leaders of European countries speak out in the Metropolitan's defense.

1914 — The First Assembly of Ukrainian Catholic clergy, whose purpose is to normalize the life of the Church, is convened in Canada. At this time the Ukrainian Catholic Church in Canada consists of 299 parishes and 49 priests.

November 1914 — The highest ranking officer of the Russian army in Western Ukraine, Prince Nikolay Nikolayevich, fearing disturbances among the population at the rear of the Russian armies, rejects the demands of Archbishop Yevlogiy regarding the immediate subjugation of the Ukrainian Catholics and forbids their forced subordination to the Russian Church.

Spring 1915 — Russian troops, having occupied Galicia, pronounce themselves "liberators of their Russian brothers from German and Catholic imprisonment." Archbishop Yevlogiy Georgiyevsky, appointed by the Russian Synod to Galicia, demands the establishment of a Russian Orthodox Eparchy of Lviv and the transfer of St. George's Ukrainian Catholic Cathedral and the Dormition and Divine Transfiguration churches along with all church property to the Russian Orthodox Church. Archbishop Yevlogiy also demands the closing of all Basilian monasteries and the transfer of these properties to the Russian authorities. G. A. Bobrynsky, the Russian governor of Lviv, convinces the Russian government in St. Petersburg that "the organizational unification of Galicia with Russia will occur only when Galicia becomes unified with Russia in faith" (Vlasovsky, Vol. III, p. 248). In Galicia, the Russian authorities close all Ukrainian newspapers, publishing houses and organizations. They forbid the use of Ukrainian in schools, courts and government offices, and start mass arrests of Ukrainian clergy and intelligentsia. Many of those arrested are deported to Siberia.

28 April 1915 — Bishop Konstantyn Chekhovych dies during the Russian occupation of Peremyshl.

1915 — Austrian troops, having returned to Galicia, start a campaign of mass terror against clergy and intellectuals, based on false Polish and Hungarian denunciations as Russian sympathizers. Thousands are imprisoned in concentration camps; hundreds are publicly shot or hanged.

24 March 1916 — The first Ukrainian Catholic Bishop in the United States, Soter Ortynsky, dies in Philadelphia. During the following eight years the

Exarchate is governed by vicars general: for immigrants from Galicia, Father Petro Ponyatyshyn, and for immigrants from Transcarpathia, Father H. Martynyak.

23 October 1916 — The nations of the Grand Alliance, Austria and Germany, pronounce the establishment of a Polish kingdom in the Polish territories captured from Russia and in the Ukrainian territory of Galicia.

1916 — Father S. Dzyubay is consecrated as the first Ukrainian Orthodox Bishop in the United States.

Principal Ecclesiastical Activities

1. ORTHODOX METROPOLITANATES, 1795-1917

ORTHODOX METROPOLITANATES OF KIEV, GALICIA AND LITTLE RUS'

The Metropolitanates of Kiev, Galicia and Little Rus' cease to exist with the death of the last Ukrainian Metropolitan Yerofey Malytsky in 1799. All subsequent metropolitans, with the exception of the Rumanian Havryil Banulesko-Bodoni (1799-1803), are Russian, appointed and sent to Ukraine by the Russian Tsar.

The Russian Orthodox Church, including the Orthodox Church in Ukraine as a subordinate and integral part, is headed by the Tsar and governed by the All-Russian Holy Synod, which is headed by a layman as Over-Procurator.

UKRAINIAN ORTHODOX METROPOLITAN OF KIEV, GALICIA AND LITTLE RUS'

Yerofey Malytsky 1796-1799

RUSSIAN METROPOLITANS OF KIEV AND GALICIA

Havryil Banulesko-Bodoni 1799-1803
Serapion Aleksandrovsky 1803-1819
Yevgeniy Bolkhovitinov 1822-1837
Filaret Amfiteatrov 1839-1857
Isidor Nikolsky 1858
Arseniy Moskvin
Vladimir Bogoyavlensky 1915-1918

ORTHODOX METROPOLITANATES OF BUKOVYNA AND DALMATIA

In 1781, the Radovytsi Eparchy in the Bukovyna territory of Ukraine is reorganized into three eparchies — one for Bukovyna and two for Dalmatia. In 1873, these three eparchies are changed to a Bukovyna Metropolitanate.

METROPOLITANS OF BUKOVYNA AND DALMATIA

Yevheniy Hakman 1873
Sylvester Andriyevych-Morar 1880-1895
Volodymyr Repta 1902-1925

BISHOPS OF ORTHODOX EPARCHIES

Volynia: Varlaam Shyshatsky (1799-1805)

Bukovyna and Dalmatia: Danylo Blakhovych (1789-1822), Yevhen Hakman (1835-1873).

2. THE CATHOLIC (UNIATE) METROPOLITANATE OF KIEV, GALICIA AND ALL RUS', 1795-1917

In 1806, by decision of the Russian Tsar Alexander I, the Kievan Uniate Metropolitanate is restored under Russian control. The Metropolitanate is given a new name, "the Metropolitanate of the Uniate churches in Russia." The Tsar, not the Apostolic See, appoints the metropolitans. In 1828, by resolution of Tsar Nicholas I, this Metropolitanate is divided into two — the Byelorussian Metropolitanate with its seat in Polotsk and the Lithuanian Metropolitanate with its seat in Zhyrovytsi. These Metropolitanates exist until 1839, when they are forcefully joined to the Russian Orthodox Church.

METROPOLITANS OF THE UNIATE CHURCH IN RUSSIA

Irakliy Lisovsky 1806-1809
Hryhoriy Kokhanovych 1809-1813
Yosafat Bulhak 1817-1828

METROPOLITANS OF THE BYELORUSSIAN UNIATE METROPOLITANATE IN RUSSIA

Yosafat Bulhak 1828-1838
Antoniy Zubko (administrator) 1838-1839

METROPOLITANS OF THE LITHUANIAN UNIATE METROPOLITANATE IN RUSSIA

Yosyf Syemashko 1833-1839

3. UKRAINIAN CATHOLIC (UNIATE) METROPOLITANATE OF GALICIA

By decree of Pope Pius VII, the Metropolitanate of Galicia is established with three eparchies — Lviv (Halych and Kamyanets Podilsky), Peremyshl (Sambir and Sianok) and Kholm (and Belz).

Antin Anhelovych 1807-1814
Mykhaylo Levytsky 1818-1858
Hryhoriy Yakhymovych 1860-1863
Spyrydon Lytvynovych 1863-1869
Yosyf Sembratovych 1870-1882
Sylvester Sembratovych 1885-1898

Yuliyan Sas-Kuyilovsky 1899-1900
Andrey Sheptytsky 1900-1944

UKRAINIAN CATHOLIC CARDINALS

Mykhaylo Levytsky .... nominated in 1856
Sylvester Sembratovych .... nominated in 1895

PARISHES IN UKRAINIAN CATHOLIC EPARCHIES

Lviv Eparchy: 1850 — 1167 parishes, 1885 — 742, 1900 — 725.

Peremyshl Eparchy: 1915 — 630 parishes.

Stanyslaviv Eparchy: 1885 — 425 parishes.

UKRAINIAN (UNIATE) BISHOPS
ON UKRAINIAN TERRITORIES

Lviv Eparchy (and of Halych and Kamyanets Podilsky): Mykola Skorodynsky (1798-1805), Antin Anhelovych (1807-1814).

Auxiliary Bishops to the Metropolitan of Galicia: Hryhoriy Yakhymovych (1841-1848), Ivan Bokhensky (1850-1857), Spyrydon Lytvynovych (1857-1859), Sylvester Sembratovych (1878-1885).

Peremyshl Eparchy (and of Sambir and Syanok): Antin Anhelovych (1796-1807), Mykhaylo Levytsky (1813-1816), Ivan Snihursky (1818-1847), Hryhoriy Yakhymovych (1849-1859), Toma Polyansky (1860-1869), Yosyf Sembratovych (1869-1872), Ivan Stupnytsky (1872-1890), Yulyan Sas-Kuyilovsky (1890-1891), Yuliyan Pelesh (1891-1896), Konstantyn Chekhovych (1896-1915), Yosafat Kotsylovsky (1916-1947).

Lutsk Eparchy (and of Ostrih): Stefan Levynsky (1798-1807), Hryhoriy Kokhanovych (1807-1813), Floryan Korsak (1810-1811), Yakiv Martusevych (1817-1826), Ivan Krasovsky (1826). Closed by Tsar Nicholas I in 1839.

In 1820, the Lutsk Eparchy included 160 parish churches, 460 priests, 22 Basilian monasteries and two convents. The Uniates of Podilia, Volynia and Kiev with their 549 parish churches and 675 priests were also within its jurisdiction.

Kholm Eparchy (and of Belz): Ferdinand Tsyekhanovsky (1809-1828), Felitsyan Shumborsky (1828-1851), Ivan Terashkevych (1851-1863), Ivan Kalinsky (1863-1866), Yosyf Voytsitsky (1866-1868), Mykhaylo Kuzemsky (1868-1871), Markyl Popel (1871-1875).

In 1825, the Kholm Eparchy consisted of 817 parishes. There were 400 parish priests, 5 Basilian monasteries and one convent. Tsar Nicholas I closed this eparchy in 1828.

Stanyslaviv Eparchy: Yuliyan Pelesh (1885-1891), Yuliyan Sas-Kuyilovsky (1891-1899), Andrey Sheptytsky (1899-1900), Hryhoriy Khomyshyn (1904-1945).

Mukachiv Eparchy: Andriy Bachynsky (1773-1809), Mykhaylo Bradach (1809-1814), Oleksiy Povchiy (1815-1831), Vasyl Popovych (1837-1864), Stepan Pankovych (1867-1874), Ivan Pasteliy (1875-1891), Yuriy Firtsak (1891-1912), Antoniy Pap (1912-1924).

In 1818, 193 parishes from the Mukacheve Eparchy were formed into the Pryashiv (Presov) Eparchy. In 1823, 52 parishes from Mukacheve were added to the Rumanian Eparchy in Oradea Mare. In 1853, 94 parishes were added to the Rumanian eparchy in Gherla. In 1913, 33 parishes were added to the Hungarian vicarate in Hajdudorog.

Pryashiv Eparchy: Hryhoriy Tarkovych (1818-1841), Yosyf Hahanets (1843-1875), Mykola Tovt (1876-1882), Ivan Valiy (1882-1911), Stepan Novak (1913-1920).

UKRAINIAN CATHOLIC EXARCHATE
IN THE UNITED STATES

Philadelphia Exarchate: Soter Ortynsky (1907-1916).

UKRAINIAN CATHOLIC EXARCHATE IN CANADA

Winnipeg Exarchate: Nykyta Budka (1912-1927).

Church and Monastery Construction in Ukraine during the 19th-20th Centuries

CHURCH CONSTRUCTION

Listed below are the churches and monasteries that were built during this period and have survived to the present day as architectural-historical monuments. Many of these churches are now museums or other facilities. Only a few of them are open for worship.

The list is organized in accordance with the present-day administrative division of Ukraine. The date of construction or foundation of the church or monastery is provided in parentheses.

KIEV OBLAST. Kiev: St. Volodymyr Cathedral (1862-1886), SS. Anthony and Theodosius at the Kiev Monastery of the Caves (1893-1895), Annunciation (1905), Holy Trinity at the Trinity Monastery (1871-1872), Resurrection Convent (1824). ***Bila Tserkva:*** Divine Transfiguration Cathedral (1833-1839). ***Bohuslav:*** Holy Trinity (1862). ***Borodany:*** Ascension (1800). ***Demivshchyna:*** Mary the Protectress (1823). ***Olkhivets:*** Dormition (1850s). ***Parkhomivka:*** Mary the Protectress (1903-1906). ***Pereyaslav-Khmelnytsky:*** SS. Borys and Hlib (1839). ***Pivni:*** St. John Chrysostom (1850s). ***Pyatyhory:*** Dormition (1821). ***Romashky:*** Mary the Protectress (1843). ***Roskopantsi:*** St. John (1884). ***Rosyshky:*** Archangel Michael (1905). ***Rude Selo:*** Holy Trinity (1841). ***Rzhyshchiv:*** Holy Trinity (1853-1860). ***Shamrayivka:*** St. Spiridon (1849). ***Skybentsi:*** Mary the Protectress (1825). ***Sloboda:*** Dormition of St. Anne (1852). ***Sukholisy:*** Divine Transfiguration (1849).

CHERKASY OBLAST. Burty: Mary the Protectress (1819-1829). ***Helmyaziv:*** Holy Trinity (1841). ***Heronimka:*** Transfiguration (1840). ***Horodyshche:*** St. Michael (1844). ***Lebedyn:*** Divine Transfiguration (1826). ***Matusiv:*** Ascension (1812-1818). ***Melnyky:*** Holy Trinity at Motrynsky Monastery (1804). ***Moiseyivka:*** SS. Peter and Paul (1808). ***Moshny:*** Divine Transfiguration. ***Zhabotyn:*** Holy Trinity (1801), Assumption (1851).

CHERNIHIV OBLAST. Baturyn: Resurrection (1803). ***Bezuhlivka:*** St. Michael (1805-1835). ***Dyahova:*** Mary the Protectress (1896). ***Kachanivka:*** St. Gregory (1817-1828). ***Kozelets:*** Ascension (1866-1874). ***Lyubech:*** Resurrection (1817).

Obolonnya: Nativity (1800). ***Pryluky:*** Nativity of the Blessed Virgin (1806). ***Rayhorodok:*** Divine Transfiguration (1825-1840). ***Vyshenky:*** Dormition (18th century). ***Yablonivka:*** Divine Transfiguration (1841).

CHERNIVTSI OBLAST. Bila Krynytsya: Church-Rotunda of St. Mary Magdalene (mid-19th century), Dormition Cathedral (1900-1908). ***Dykhtynets:*** St. Demetrius (1871). ***Hertsa:*** St. Spiridon (1807). ***Mahala:*** Holy Trinity (1818). ***Mala Buda:*** All Saints (1818). ***Orshivtsi:*** Dormition (1850). ***Putyla:*** St. Michael (1885). ***Rostoky:*** Dormition (1846). ***Shepot:*** St. Elias (1898). ***Shypyntsi:*** Nativity (1812). ***Ternavka:*** St. Demetrius (1811). ***Turyatka:*** Archangel (1796). ***Ust-Putyla:*** St. Paraskeva. ***Vasyliv:*** Nativity of the Blessed Virgin (1835). ***Vikno:*** St. John (1826).

CRIMEA OBLAST. Livadiya: Holy Cross (1864). ***Oreanda:*** Mary the Protectress (1885). ***Sanatorne:*** Resurrection (1892). ***Sevastopol:*** St. Volodymyr Cathedral (1859-1866), St. Michael (1848), St. Michael Pyramid (1857-1870), SS. Peter and Paul (1848).

DNIPROPETROVSK OBLAST. Dnipropetrovsk: Church of Bryansk (1913), St. Michael in Kodaky (1807), St. Nicholas (mid-19th century), Transfiguration Cathedral (1830-1835). ***Dniprodzerzhynsk:*** St. Michael Cathedral (1894). ***Nikopol:*** Nativity in Sulytsk (1812-1820). ***Novomoskovsk:*** Holy Trinity Cathedral (19th century). ***Petrivka:*** Nativity (begin. 19th century). ***Semenivka:*** Ascension (1823).

DONETSK OBLAST. Druzhivka: St. John (1898-1900). ***Slovyanohirsk:*** St. Nicholas (18th century). ***Slovyansk:*** Dormition Cathedral at the Holy Mountain Dormition Monastery (1859-1860).

IVANO-FRANKIVSK OBLAST. Babyn: Ascension (1896). ***Barvinkiv:*** St. Michael (1867). ***Bili Oslavy:*** St. Demetrius (1835). ***Biloberizka:*** Mary the Protectress (1849). ***Bystrets:*** Dormition of St. Anne (1872). ***Cheremoshna:*** St. Michael (1872). ***Cherhanivka:*** St. John (1842). ***Dovhopole:*** St. Michael (1872). ***Horod:*** St. Stephen (1866). ***Khlibychyn:*** Dormition (1854). ***Kosiv:*** St. Basil (1895). ***Kosmach:*** SS. Peter and Paul (1904-1905). ***Krasnoyiliv:*** SS. Peter and Paul (1843). ***Krivorivna:*** Nativity of the Blessed Virgin (1818). ***Lyucha:*** Ascension (1844). ***Lyuchky:*** St. Michael (19th century). ***Maly Rozhyn:*** Nativity of St. John the Baptist (1860). ***Mykulychyn:*** Holy Trinity (1868). ***Mykytyntsi:*** Holy Cross (1859). ***Nazavyziv:*** St. John Chrysostom (1820). ***Pidhirya:*** Nativity of Christ (1832). ***Pistyn:*** Dormition of St. Barbara (1858). ***Prokurava:*** Holy Virgin Cathedral (1889). ***Sheshory:*** St. Paraskeva (1874). ***Smodna:*** SS. Joachim and Anna (1841). ***Sokolivka:*** Holy Spirit (1866). ***Stari Kryty:*** Divine Transfiguration (1868). ***Ustya:*** St. Michael (1853). ***Velyky Rozhyn:*** St. Demetrius (1895). ***Verbovets:*** Annunciation (1850). ***Verkhniy Yasyniv:*** Holy Trinity (1882). ***Zelena:*** Beheading of St. John the Baptist (1846).

KHARKIV OBLAST. Chuhuyiv: Cathedral of the Protection of the Blessed Virgin Mary (1824-1834). ***Izyum:*** Ascension (1819-1826), St. Michael (1808-1823). ***Lyubotyn:*** St. Michael (1843). ***Parkhomivka:*** Protection of the Blessed Virgin Mary (1808). ***Rakytne:*** St. Michael (1805). ***Volodymyrivka:*** Divine Transfiguration (1911-1913).

KHERSON OBLAST. Kherson: St. Michael (1819), Holy Spirit Cathedral (1804-1836).

KHMELNYTSKY OBLAST. Kamyanets-Podilsky: Elevation of the Cross (1799-1801), St. Gregory (1851-1861), Mary the Protectress (1845-1861). ***Makiv:*** St. John Chrysostom (1839-1862). ***Stary Ostropil:*** Divine Transfiguration (1840). ***Velyka Radohosh:*** St. Michael (1799).

KIROVOHRAD OBLAST. Kirovohrad: Mary the Protectress (1850). ***Rozumivka:*** Holy Cross (1833-1855).

LVIV OBLAST. Besidy: Dormition (1835). ***Derevnya:*** Nativity of the Blessed Virgin Mary (1848). ***Hrabovets:*** St. Basil (1894). ***Ivan Franko Village:*** St. Nicholas (1801). ***Kalne:*** Ascension (1820). ***Khashchovane:*** St. John (1846). ***Komarynky:*** St. Michael (1817). ***Korostiv:*** St. Paraskeva (1874). ***Krushelnytsi:*** Holy Trinity (1842). ***Lavochne:*** St. Michael (1908). ***Lesnevychi:*** St. Simeon of the Pillar (1828). ***Lyublyana:*** St. Elias (1809). ***Lybokhora:*** Holy Virgin (1798). ***Matkiv:*** Nativity of the Blessed Virgin (1838). ***Mytulyn:*** Mary the Protectress (1863). ***Nyzhnye:*** Holy Virgin Cathedral (1870). ***Nyzhnye Husyne:*** Holy Trinity (19th century). ***Nyzhnye Vysotske:*** Holy Spirit (1814). ***Nyzhnye Synevidne:*** Dormition (1803). ***Oporets:*** Holy Cross (1844). ***Oryavchyk:*** St. Luke (1862). ***Pidhirtsi:*** Holy Spirit (1810). ***Plave:*** St. Michael (1888). ***Pryslip:*** Holy Virgin Cathedral (1895). ***Rava Ruska:*** St. George (1846). ***Rykiv:*** St. Basil (1810). ***Smozhe:*** St. Michael (1901). ***Tukholka:*** Dormition (1858). ***Tyshytsya:*** Dormition (1881). ***Velyki Peredrymykhy:*** St. Michael (1891). ***Verkhnya Rozhanka:*** Holy Spirit (1804). ***Volosyanka:*** Divine Transfiguration (1804-1824). ***Vybranivka:*** Presentation of the Blessed Virgin Mary (1800). ***Vyshnya:*** SS. Cosmas and Damian (1805). ***Yalynkovate:*** Protection of the Blessed Virgin Mary (1868). ***Zavydovychi:*** St. Michael (1810).

MYKOLAYIV OBLAST. Mykolayiv: St. Nicholas (1813-1817). ***Katerynka:*** St. Catherine (18th century). ***Ochakiv:*** St. Michael (1804). ***Pervomaysk:*** Protection of the Blessed Virgin Mary (1805).

ODESSA OBLAST. Odessa: Holy Trinity (1808). ***Bolhrad:***

Church of the Transfiguration of the Holy Trinity Monastery in the village of Tryhirya (Zhytomyr oblast), built in 1854-73 (left).

Church of the Nativity of the Mother of God in the village of Kodnya (Zhytomyr oblast), built in 1841.

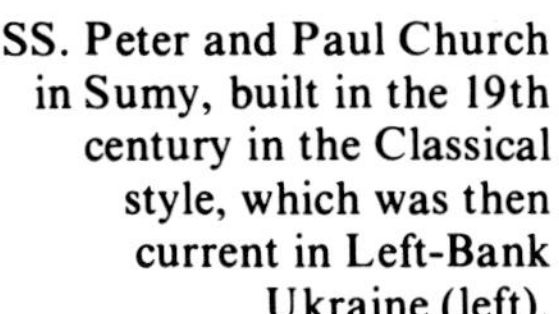
SS. Peter and Paul Church in Sumy, built in the 19th century in the Classical style, which was then current in Left-Bank Ukraine (left).

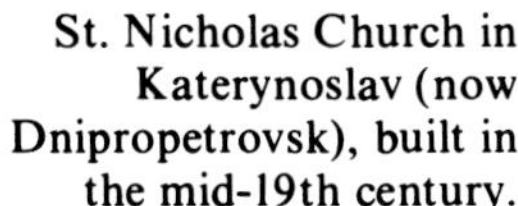
St. Nicholas Church in Katerynoslav (now Dnipropetrovsk), built in the mid-19th century.

Transfiguration Cathedral (1833-1838), St. Michael (1871). ***Izmayl:*** St. Nicholas (1852), Protection of the Blessed Virgin Mary Cathedral (1822-1836), Nativity (1823), St. Nicholas (1833), Dormition (1841). ***Kyrnychky:*** Dormition (1841). ***Lypetske:*** St. Michael (1807). ***Nerubayske:*** Ascension (1826). ***Nova Nekrasivka:*** Presentation of the Blessed Virgin (19th century). ***Usatove:*** Nativity (1822).

POLTAVA OBLAST. Hadyach: All Saints (1836). ***Fedorivka:*** Annunciation (1828). ***Kotelva:*** Holy Trinity (1812). ***Mhar:*** Tepla Church of the Mhar Monastery (19th century). ***Pisky:*** Dormition (19th century). ***Pleshyvets:*** Mary the Protectress (1902-1906). ***Snityn:*** Resurrection (1805). ***Vepryk:*** St. Michael (1823), Dormition (1821). ***Verhuny:*** Nativity (1801-1807).

ROVNO OBLAST. Dubrovytsya: Nativity of the Blessed Virgin (1861). ***Korets:*** St. Michael (1834). ***Marynyn:*** Divine Transfiguration (1801). ***Mlyniv:*** Mary the Protectress (1830-1840). ***Plyashiv:*** St. Gregory Mausoleum (1910-1914). ***Stara Rafalivka:*** St. Michael (18th century). ***Velyki Mezhyrichi:*** SS. Peter and Paul (1848).

SUMY OBLAST. Sumy: St. Elias (1851), St. Panteleimon (1911), SS. Peter and Paul (19th century), Divine Transfiguration of Christ (18th century), Holy Trinity (1901-1914). ***Bakyrivka:*** Holy Friday (19th century). ***Hlukhiv:*** St. Anastasia Cathedral (1885-1886). ***Okhtyrka:*** Archangel Michael (1884), Holy Cross (1825). ***Pustoviytivka:*** St. Michael (1900-1906). ***Romny:*** Ascension (1801). ***Slavhorod:*** Holy Trinity (1808). ***Trostyanets:*** Ascension (1913). ***Velyky Bobryk:*** Resurrection (1808).

TERNOPIL OBLAST. Dzvenyhorod: Dormition (1801). ***Novostav:*** St. Michael (1865). ***Pidhaytsi:*** Elevation of the Cross (19th century). ***Pochayiv:*** Holy Trinity Cathedral at Pochaiv Lavra (1906-1912).

VINNYTSYA OBLAST. Kukavka: St. Demetrius (1806). ***Nova Pryluka:*** St. Paraskeva (begin. 19th century). ***Sharhorod:*** St. Michael Cathedral at St. Nicholas Monastery (1829). ***Tyshkivska Sloboda:*** Dormition Cathedral at the Hranovsky Monastery (1867).

VOLYNIA OBLAST. Holovno: Holy Trinity (1841). ***Metelene:*** Mary the Protectress (1810). ***Obenyzhi:*** Holy Cross (1821). ***Pishcha:*** Church of Kazan (1801). ***Stara Vyzhivka:*** Divine Transfiguration (1869). ***Svityaz:*** SS. Peter and Paul (1846). ***Zamshany:*** St. Michael (1809).

VOROSHYLOVHRAD OBLAST. Osynovo: Dormition (1802).

ZAKARPATSKA OBLAST. Bukovets: Presentation of the Blessed Virgin (1808). ***Izky:*** St. Nicholas (1798). ***Kolochava:*** Holy Spirit (1795). ***Kotelnytsya:*** Church (19th century). ***Neresnytsya:*** St. Michael (1813). Nyzhniy Studeny: Annunciation (1820). ***Pryslop*** St. Nicholas (1797). ***Synevyrska Polyana:*** Mary the Protectress (1817). ***Torun:*** Presentation of the Blessed Virgin (1809). ***Tyshiv:*** Ascension (1898). ***Verkhniy Studeny:*** St. Nicholas (1804). ***Yalove:*** Ascension (19th century). ***Yasinya:*** Ascension (1824). ***Zadelske:*** St. Basil (begin. 19th century).

ZAPORIZHZHYA OBLAST. Prymorsk: Holy Trinity (1838).

ZHYTOMYR OBLAST. Zhytomyr: Divine Transfiguration Cathedral (1864). ***Kodnya:*** Nativity of the Blessed Virgin (1841). ***Tryhirya:*** Divine Transfiguration of the Holy Trinity Monastery (1854-1873).

MONASTERY CONSTRUCTION

In 1825, the following Uniate monasteries of the Basilian order existed on Ukrainian territories: in the Metropolitanate of Galicia, 14 men's and 2 women's; in the Lutsk Eparchy, 22 men's and 3 women's; in the Kholm Eparchy, 5 men's; and in the Mukachiv Eparchy, 8 men's monasteries.

The list below identifies the Ukrainian monasteries constructed during the years 1795-1917. All these monasteries were destroyed by the Soviet authorities or converted to other uses, and have not survived in their original state to the present day.

MONASTERIES DESTROYED OR CONVERTED TO OTHER USES BY THE SOVIETS, 1921-1941

KIEV OBLAST. Kiev: Trinity Monastery (1868), Theophany Ascetic Monastery (1861), Presentation of the Blessed Virgin Convent (1898), Mary the Protectress Monastery (1889).

CRIMEA OBLAST. Chatyrdah: SS. Cosmas and Damian Convent (1856). ***Kerch:*** St. Gregory Convent (1857). ***Sevastopol:*** St. Volodymyr Monastery in Kherson (1850), St. Clement Monastery in Inkerman (1852). ***Sudak:*** St. Paraskeva Convent (1858).

DNIPROPETROVSK OBLAST. Dnipropetrovsk: Tykhvynsky Convent (1866). ***Novomoskovsk:*** St. Joseph Monastery (1873). ***Pavlohrad:*** Holy Trinity Monastery (1885), founded by Rafail Verbovsky.

KHARKIV OBLAST. Bohodukhiv: Holy Trinity Monastery (1889). ***At the Kharkiv River:*** St. Nicholas Monastery Convent (1845). ***Ryasne:*** St. Demetrius Monastery (1867). ***Starobilsk:*** All Sorrows Monastery (1886). ***Zmiyiv:*** Kazan Monastery (1886).

KHERSON OBLAST. Kherson: Annunciation Convent (1866).

KIROVOHRAD OBLAST. Dushenkevycheve: St. John the Baptist Monastery (1870). ***Olesky:*** Dormition Convent (1896). ***Tahanrih:*** Jerusalem Monastery of the Holy Trinity (1814).

LVIV OBLAST. Mykhaylivtsi: St. Basil Monastery (1896), founded by Ivan and Karolyna Dashkevych.

ODESSA OBLAST. Odessa: Dormition Monastery (1824), Archangel Michael Convent (1844).

POLTAVA OBLAST. Kobelyaky: Nativity of the Blessed Virgin Convent (1886).

VINNYTSYA OBLAST. Bar: Mary the Protectress Monastery (1838).

ZAKARPATSKA OBLAST. Uzhhorod: St. Basil Monastery (1911).

ZHYTOMYR OBLAST. Zhytomyr: Theophany Monastery (1898).

Dormition Church in the village of Rostoky (Chernivtsi oblast), built in 1846 (left).

Church of the Protection of the Blessed Virgin Mary in the village of Yalynkovate (Lviv oblast), built of wood in 1868.

X. The Churches in Ukrainian Lands and in the Ukrainian Diaspora during the 20th Century (1917-1988)

General Characteristics of the Period

1. THE POLITICAL SITUATION IN EASTERN EUROPE

In 1917 the two great European alliances, the western Entente and the Central Powers, were locked in combat. In Eastern Europe, Germany, Austria, Turkey and Bulgaria fought Russia, Serbia, Montenegro and Romania.

In March the Russian Tsar abdicated, and a liberal-democratic Provisional Government took over the weakened Russian war effort. In November the Bolshevik party staged a coup d'etat and concluded an armistice with the Central Powers; early in the next year the Bolsheviks signed a peace at Brest-Litovsk, giving up considerable territory.

Despite Russia's pulling out of the war, the Central Powers began to crumble, and when the war came formally to an end in November 1918 both Germany and Austria were in near-chaos. New Slav states emerged: Poland, struggling with the Western Ukrainians in 1918-1919 and with the Russian Bolsheviks in 1920; Czechoslovakia and Ukraine; and the Kingdom of Serbs, Croats and Slovenes (later Yugoslavia). As the Versailles Conference re-drew the map of Europe during 1919, Hungary emerged as an independent state, while an expanded Romania and a somewhat diminished Bulgaria preserved independent status. In the north, the Baltic states of Estonia, Latvia and Lithuania emerged from the ruins of the Russian empire, though the inclusion of Vilnius (Wilno) in Poland displeased the Lithuanians.

As Tomas Masaryk was a prime architect of Czechoslovakia, so Jozef Pilsudski did much to unite the formerly Austrian, Prussian and Russian lands of Poland. However, the inclusion of eastern Galicia in the country's borders — confirmed by the Council of Ambassadors in 1923 — alienated the Ukrainians, who along with the Byelorussian, Jewish, and Lithuanian minorities made up close to a third of the country's population. Marshal Pilsudski, virtual dictator from May 1926 until his death in 1935, was succeeded by a group of colonels who ruled until the German invasion of 1939.

In 1922 the Bolsheviks, having defeated the Russian White Armies and various independence movements and thus consolidating their hold on Russia and a good part of her colonies, formed the Union of Soviet Socialist Republics. At the same time they made a temporary retreat on the economic front through Lenin's New Economic Policy. Peasants were thus given the land they had been promised, and normal economic life helped repair the ravages of war. But in 1928-1929 the newly-emerged dictator Stalin inaugurated the First Five-Year Plan of breakneck industrialization and agricultural collectivization. This was accompanied by the liquidation of the most productive sector of the peasantry (the *kulaks*) and by a man-made famine centered in Ukraine. Simultaneously, waves of police terror decimated the ranks of the Party and intelligentsia, virtually paralyzing the population with fear.

The world-wide depression beginning in 1929 hurt the still unsteady new states of Eastern Europe. Throughout the 1930s, the threats of the U.S.S.R. and (after 1933) Nazi Germany forced the Eastern European states into a series of shifting alliances. In some cases, right-wing parties came to the fore. In September 1938 Hitler, having annexed Austria in March, secured western acquiescence in his annexation of part of Czechoslovakia. In the following year he took the rest of Bohemia and Moravia, leaving Slovakia with a separate but pro-German government. At the same time Poland, with verbal support from Britain and France and avoiding an alliance with the Soviet Union, defied Hitler. Germany and the U.S.S.R. then concluded a secret pact dividing Poland and the Baltic states between them. On September 1, 1939 Germany invaded Poland, precipitating World War II; on the 17th the U.S.S.R. occupied Poland's eastern territories with their mainly Byelorussian and Ukrainian population.

In the ensuing war, Eastern Europe was again devastated. The U.S.S.R. took the Baltic States, Northern Bukovyna and Bessarabia in 1940. Later that year Germany invaded the Balkans, Slovakia, Hungary, Romania, Bulgaria and Croatia sided with the Germans. When in June 1941 Germany invaded the U.S.S.R., Byelorussia and Ukraine took the brunt of the attack and occupation.

As the Red Army rolled back the Germans after Stalingrad, it ran over most of Eastern Europe. Communist regimes were installed in Hungary, Romania, Bulgaria and Yugoslavia — though the latter left the pro-Soviet camp in 1949. Communist take-overs in Poland (1946) and Czechoslovakia (1948) consolidated Soviet control in Eastern Europe.

After Stalin's death in 1953, unrest became evident in the Soviet satellites. The Polish crisis and the unsuccessful Hungarian revolution of 1956 did force a partial thaw, as a limited "de-Stalinization" proceeded in the U.S.S.R. under Premier Nikita Khrushchev. Post-Stalinist regimes were led by Gomulka in Poland, Novotny in Czechoslovakia, and Kadar in Hungary. After 1964 Khrushchev's successor Leonid Brezhnev led the U.S.S.R. into a period of economic stagnation, but in Hungary and Romania a certain liberalization of the economy was permitted. In Czechoslovakia, liberal Communist currents brought about Dubcek's "Prague Spring" of 1968, stopped by a Soviet invasion in August of that year.

In the 1970s, Husak's Czechoslovakia and Ceausescu's Romania were among the most repressive of regimes, despite the latter's relative political and economic independence of the Soviet Union. Hungary and Yugoslavia enjoyed relative economic liberalization and some prosperity, though the latter country's ethnic conflicts (particularly between Serbs and Croats) did not disappear. Under Edward Gierek, Poland suffered continued economic troubles.

The era of detente and the Helsinki Final Act of 1975 brought human rights violations in Eastern Europe to international attention. Helsinki Groups were formed in Russia, Ukraine, Lithuania, Georgia and Armenia — and almost immediately repressed. In Czechoslovakia, the Charter 77 group was formed. In Poland, amidst worsening economic conditions, an independent workers' movement called "Solidarity" received Church and intelligentsia support in the early 1980s, in the face of a military government.

Far-reaching reforms and a virtual transformation of society were promised by Soviet General Secretary Mikhail Gorbachev upon his accession in March 1985. The U.S.S.R.'s economic ills, like those of Poland and Romania, appeared to call for major changes, the political consequences of which could only be guessed.

2. THE RELIGIOUS SITUATION IN EUROPE

In the wake of the Russian Tsar's abdication and the formation of a Provisional Government, the Russian Orthodox Church, freed of state control, convoked a Church Council (*Sobor*) in 1917. The Sobor re-established the Moscow Patriarchate.

After taking power, the Bolsheviks declared the separation of the Church from the state and the school. They then began an attack on the Russian Orthodox Church. Throughout the Civil War and the 1920s, hierarchs and countless clergy and laity were persecuted, exiled, jailed, sent to labor-camps, or shot. At the same time, the Bolsheviks supported the competing Renovationist Church. For a few years they also tolerated the Ukrainian Autocephalous Orthodox Church.

In the 1920s the Bolsheviks persecuted Catholics of both the Latin and Eastern rites. But they tolerated and even encouraged the Protestants, Evangelicals and Baptists, who had been persecuted under the Tsars.

After the death of Russian Orthodox Patriarch Tikhon in 1925, his post remained vacant. Metropolitan Sergey's 1927 declaration of loyalty to the Soviet state did not end the persecutions. Indeed, in the 1930s they only increased, so that by 1939 the Russian Orthodox Church was almost extinct. The Renovationist and Ukrainian Autocephalous Orthodox Churches were liquidated as well. Similarly, in the 1930s the Bolsheviks turned against the non-Orthodox Protestant and Evangelical denominations.

The 1929 Law on Religious Associations called on religious groups to register with the authorities and severely restricted their activities. At the same time, the League of Militant Atheists and Party activists wrecked churches and harassed believers. No religion was spared in the general onslaught.

In the rest of Eastern Europe and in Western Europe, where religious tolerance generally prevailed in the inter-war period, the Roman Catholic Church continued to exert political influence. In Poland, where it was accorded certain rights under the 1925 Concordat, the Church was perceived as supporting the more conservative elements in society. (At the same time, the government discriminated against Eastern-rite Catholics and persecuted the Orthodox outright.) In Spain, where the Catholic Church was seen as a supporter of conservative forces, it was persecuted under the Republic and, during the Civil War of 1936-1939, was attacked by communists and anarchists. Indeed, Pope Pius XI (1922-1939) condemned communism in the 1937 encyclical *Divini Redemptoris.* The Church condemned the Nazis as well in *Mit brennender Sorge.*

During World War II it became clear that both totalitarian systems, Nazi and communist, abhorred religion. Clergymen died in both Nazi and Soviet concentration camps. For political reasons, however, the German occupation authorities in formerly Soviet territories permitted some revival of Orthodoxy and Catholicism. In response, Stalin revived the Patriarchate of the Russian Orthodox Church in 1943, enlisting the newly elected Sergey's help in the war effort. He also permitted the formation of the All-Union Council of Evangelical Christians and Baptists. But in Western Ukraine, the government found it expedient to suppress the Ukrainian Greek-Catholic Church and stage its "return" to the Russian Orthodox Church in 1945-1949.

The suppression of the Ukrainian Catholics was echoed in the brutal liquidation of the Uniate Church in Romania in 1948 and of the Greek-Catholic Church in Czechoslovakia in 1950. Indeed, Catholics of both rites suffered under the new communist regimes. In Poland and Hungary, Cardinals Wyszynski and Mindszenty came to be revered as heroes and martyrs.

At the same time, loyal Orthodox churches in Poland and Czechoslovakia enjoyed government support as counter weights to the larger Catholic communities, while in Romania and Bulgaria, where Orthodoxy was the traditional national faith, these churches became valuable partners of the new regimes. In Yugoslavia, Croatian and Slovenian Catholicism was balanced with Serbian Orthodoxy and Islam in the south.

The partial thaw after 1956 improved the situation of many of the churches of Eastern Europe. In 1968, the liberal communist Dubcek regime in Czechoslovakia permitted the revival of the Greek-Catholic Church; even Soviet intervention and the harsh Husak regime did not reverse this act.

In Western Europe, the election of Pope John XXIII in 1958 heralded great changes in the Roman Catholic Church. The Second Vatican Council (1962-1965) re-defined Church teaching on a number of issues, including ecumenical relations. From about 1960, the Church sought contact with the Russian Orthodox Church and with the Soviet government, and Pope Paul VI (1963-1978) continued his predecessor's Eastern policy. The Russian Orthodox hierarchy, which under Patriarch Aleksey (1945-1970) enjoyed government toleration in return for public support of Soviet foreign policy, welcomed the Vatican initiative. It also joined the World Council of Churches, since 1948 a focus of world ecumenism.

Yet at the same time, the Soviet government was waging a fierce anti-religious campaign (1959-1964). Soviet restrictions resulted in the formation in 1965 of the Council of Churches of Evangelical Christians-Baptists, which defied what it regarded as anti-Christian laws and regulations. An Orthodox dissident movement criticizing Soviet religious policy and the hierarchy's subservience to the regime, as well as an Orthodox revival among urban intellectuals, continued under Patriarch Pimen (1971-). In both Soviet-ruled Lithuania and Western Ukraine, Catholics participated in dissident movements in the 1970s and 1980s.

The election of a Polish Cardinal, Karol Wojtyla, as Pope John Paul II in 1978 turned the attention of the world to Eastern Europe. In Poland, Cardinal Wyszynski continued to make his Church a mainstay for the Polish people in the face of an unpopular regime. In Czechoslovakia and Hungary, a more pliant Catholic hierarchy sometimes bent to government wishes, thus securing greater toleration for the Church. In Hungary as in Protestant East Germany, churches were able to obtain freedom of action in providing social services for their people. Religion was weakest in Albania, which was declared a totally atheist state.

In the Soviet Union, a number of Orthodox dissidents were arrested in 1980, though many were released in 1987. Preparations for the 1988 official Russian Orthodox celebrations of the Millennium of state Christianity in Kievan Rus' went ahead amidst rumors of new laws on religion and a new religious policy.

3. THE POLITICAL SITUATION IN UKRAINE

With the collapse of the Tsarist government in 1917, Ukrainians formed a Central Council (*Rada*), composed mostly of moderate socialists who supported Ukrainian autonomy or independence. Understanding with either the Provisional Government or the Bolsheviks, who seized power in November, proved impossible. In January 1918 Ukrainian independence was proclaimed, as Bolshevik troops supporting a rival "Ukrainian" regime marched on Kiev. The *Rada's* representation at Brest-Litovsk secured recognition of the Ukrainian National (People's) Republic (U.N.R.). Soon a government under Hetman Skoropadsky was erected, but was toppled by Petlyura's nationalist forces at the end of 1918. After joining forces with the newly formed Western Ukrainian Republic in January 1919, Ukrainian governments sought to survive in the face of Bolshevik, "White" Russian, and Polish onslaughts in 1919-1920. Cooperation with the Poles in 1920 could not save the Ukrainian cause, which was met with indifference or hostility by the Allies. By the end of the year, Eastern Ukraine was under Bolshevik control, and the 1921 Polish-Soviet Treaty of Riga left most of Western Ukraine with Poland; this was approved by the Council of Ambassadors in 1923. Transcarpathian Ukraine passed to Czechoslovakia, while Bukovyna came under Romanian rule.

Courageous Ukrainian resistance to Bolshevism, and the persistence of patriotic Ukrainian elements even among the Bolsheviks, made at least temporary concessions necessary. In the 1920s, a policy of "Ukrainization" combined with the New Economic Policy to allow Ukrainians considerable freedom to build their cultural and economic life in Soviet Ukraine. In Western Ukraine, by contrast, poverty in the villages combined with assimilationist and discriminatory Polish government policies to stunt Ukrainian life. Nevertheless, attempts were made to continue the educational, cultural and economic activities that had flourished under Austrian rule.

By 1930, Ukrainization had ended in Soviet Ukraine. Mass deportation of the "kulaks" (*kurkuli*), collectivization of farms, and the man-made famine of 1932-1933 resulted in millions of deaths and permanently crippled Ukrainian agriculture. At the same time, terror campaigns against the Ukrainian cultural and scholarly intelligentsia, against the Church, and even against Party cadres killed countless Ukrainians and threatened to destroy the nation once and for all.

In Polish-ruled Ukraine conditions were far milder, but conflict between the Ukrainian national movement and the government escalated. The moderate Ukrainian National-Democratic Party sought in vain to reach an acceptable compromise with the increasingly militaristic Polish regime. The violent "pacification" of 1930 sparked a response by the Organization of Ukrainian Nationalists, including sabotage and assassination. The Ukrainian Orthodox were the targets of a government-inspired assault in 1938.

Ukrainian cultural life developed in the inter-war period in Romanian-held Bukovyna and in Transcarpathia, which enjoyed democratic Czechoslovak rule and a measure of autonomy. In 1938, German seizure and partition of Czechoslovakia provided an opportunity for the creation of a Carpatho-Ukrainian state under Msgr. Avhustyn Voloshyn. But within a few months Hitler allowed the Hungarians to occupy the land, crushing the short-lived republic.

In September 1939, under the secret terms of the Molotov-Ribbentrop Pact, Galicia was occupied by Soviet forces, and was officially annexed to the Ukrainian Soviet Socialist Republic. A cautious Sovietization followed, accompanied by a limited Ukrainization. Abroad, the leadership of the Organization of Ukrainian Nationalists split in 1940.

The German attack on the U.S.S.R. in June 1941 provided the opportunity for the declaration of a revived Ukrainian state in Lviv, but within weeks key Ukrainian nationalist leaders were arrested and imprisoned.

Administratively, Western Ukraine became part of the *Generalgouvernement;* Eastern Ukraine became a *Reichskommissariat.* The German occupation, which lasted from 1941 to 1944, was brutal. Nazi racial theories about the "inferior" Slavs dictated discriminatory treatment of Ukrainians. Prisoners of war were starved en masse; peasants were recruited for forced labor; food and supplies were requisitioned; villages were burned. There were mass executions; at Babyn Yar near Kiev, tens of thousands of Jews as well as Ukrainians, Russians, Poles and others were shot.

A Ukrainian insurgent movement formed in Volynia in 1942 became the seed of the Ukrainian Insurgent Army, which fought both German and Soviet forces. In 1943 the German authorities permitted the formation of the "Galicia" SS combat division, which Ukrainian leaders regarded as the nucleus of an independent Ukrainian army.

Soviet re-annexation of Western Ukraine at the end of the war met with resistance from the Ukrainian Insurgent Army, with considerable popular support, until about 1950. In the meantime, collectivization caused famine conditions in the region. The annexation of Galicia, Transcarpathia and Bukovyna to the Ukrainian S.S.R. did, however, permit greater contact among the conscious Ukrainians of all regions.

After Stalin's death in 1953, and with the return of many prisoners from labor camps after Khrushchev's "de-Stalinization" of 1956, Ukrainian life revived somewhat. In the 1960s a literary and artistic movement flourished briefly with the apparent approval of Petro Shelest, First Secretary of the Communist Party of Ukraine. The *Ukrainian Herald,* an organ of the new civil liberties movement, appeared in 1968. Ukrainian intellectuals denounced Russification of their country.

After Shelest was removed and replaced by the hardliner Volodymyr Shcherbytsky, arrests increased, particularly from 1972. Nevertheless, the 1970s saw a second wave of cultural activity, joined by a growing human rights movement and from 1976 by the Ukrainian Helsinki Monitoring Group. Yet by the mid-1980s the Group had been virtually destroyed; over a sixteen-month period four Ukrainian human-rights activists died in a single labor camp in Perm. Yet after General Secretary Mikhail Gorbachev announced his policies of *glasnost* ("openness") and *perestroika* ("rebuilding") in 1985, some Ukrainian Communists, particularly within the Writers' Union, began to demand greater cultural and linguistic rights for their people.

Ukraine (Ukrainian S.S.R.) since 1945.

Kievan Rus'-Ukraine in the 10th-13th centuries.

Ukrainian lands under Poland and Lithuania in the 16th century.

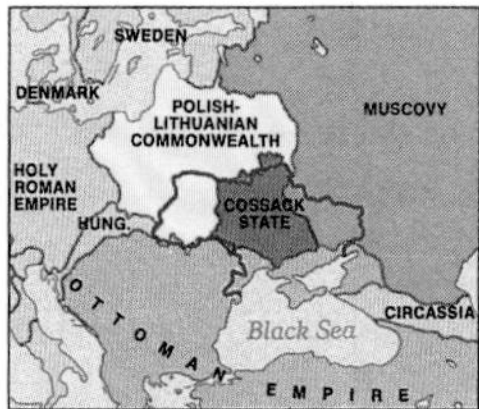

The Ukrainian Hetman (Kozak) State in the 17th-18th centuries.

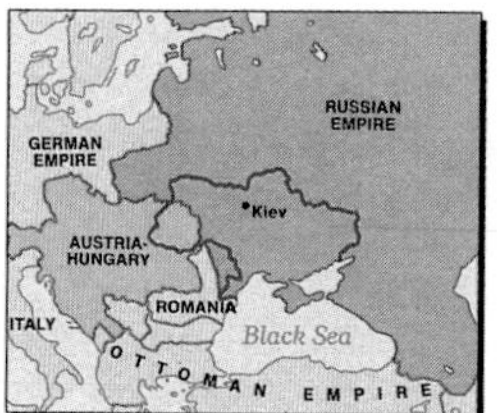

Ukrainian lands divided by the Russian and Austro-Hungarian Empires in the 19th-20th centuries.

Ukraine (Ukrainian S.S.R.) since 1945.

Chronology

The Ukrainian Orthodox Church

8 March 1917 — In the Russian Empire a revolution erupts, which topples the old regime and leads to the establishment of an independent Ukraine and the resumption of new church life.

March 1917 — Numerous church synods take place in Ukraine, during which the participants begin demanding that the Ukrainian Church become independent from Moscow and that the Ukrainian language be introduced into religious services. The priests Nestor Sharayivsky, D. Khodzitsky and H. Chernyavsky are elected to the Ukrainian Parliament — the Ukrainian Central Council. Rev. Vasyl Lypkivsky begins to play an important role in the church movement; since the Revolution of 1905, he has been the head of the Kievan Eparchial Congress.

14-19 April 1917 — The Volynia Eparchial Congress during which de-Russification and the Ukrainization of the church are the main topics of discussion, takes place in Zhytomyr.

Easter 1917 — The Kiev Eparchial Congress passes a resolution calling for the organization of an All-Ukrainian Church Sobor. Bishop Dmytriy Verbytsky of Uman heads the organizing committee.

April 1917 — Speaking to mass gatherings in Kiev, Mykola Mikhnovsky, the ideologist of the Ukrainian national renaissance, raises the idea of the autocephaly of the Ukrainian Church, headed by a patriarch.

26 May 1917 — After a speech given by Archpriest Feofil Buldovsky at the Poltava Eparchial Congress, a resolution is passed concerning the introduction of the Ukrainian language into church services, the reinstatement of Ukrainian monastic orders, rites and traditions, and the Ukrainization of the Kiev Theological Academy and the de-Russification of the Church. The Eparchial Congress in Podilia passes similar resolutions.

Summer 1917 — The Russian Metropolitan of Kiev, Vladimir Bogoyavlensky, publishes a declaration denouncing the Ukrainian church movement.

7 November 1917 — The Bolshevik Revolution erupts in St. Petersburg, bringing the Bolsheviks to power. On November 8 the All-Russian Congress of Soviets publishes a decree on the confiscation of monastic and church lands and their transfer to the state. Later this decree comes into force in Ukraine as well.

18 November 1917 — At the All-Russian Church Sobor in Moscow Tikhon Belavin is elected Patriarch of Moscow.

20 November 1917 — In Kiev the Third Universal of the Ukrainian Central Council proclaims the establishment of the Ukrainian National Republic.

On the initiative of Rev. Vasyl Lypkivsky the "Brotherhood of the Resurrection" is founded in Kiev to help gain autocephaly for the Orthodox Church in Ukraine.

6 December 1917 — The Organizing Committee for the All-Ukrainian Church Sobor is renamed the Temporary All-Ukrainian Orthodox Church Council, and elects Rev. Oleksander Marychiv the head of the Council and Archbishop Oleksander Dorodnytsyn as honorary head. The Council is declared the temporary administration of the Orthodox Church in Ukraine.

24 December 1917 — The Bolshevik government deprives the Orthodox Church of the right to have a say in the affairs of general-education schools, and a decree issued on December 31 forbids the clergy to conduct marriages and birth and death registrations.

December 1917 — At the Congress of the Ukrainian party of Independentists-Socialists a resolution is passed concerning the independence of the Ukrainian Church from Moscow and the introduction of the Ukrainian language in religious services.

19 January 1918 — The Council of the Russian Episcopate in Ukraine bars Archbishop Oleksander Dorodnytsyn from performing religious duties for agreeing to be the honorary head of the All-Ukrainian Orthodox Church Council.

20 January — 1 February 1918 — The first session of the All-Ukrainian Church Sobor takes place in Kiev with the participation of 279 delegates representing the clergy and laity. The Sobor elects the membership of six committees, which hold meetings daily. The Committee for the Ukrainization of the Church is headed by a Ukrainophobe, the Russian Archbishop of Volynia, Yevlogiy Georgiyevsky. The Ukrainian delegates to the Sobor, who are in the minority, demand autocephaly for the Church in Ukraine and its separation from the Moscow Patriarchate. Influenced by the declaration of the Fourth Universal of the Ukrainian Central Council concerning the establishment of the full independence of Ukraine, the delegates to the Sobor agree to hear a speech given by Prof. Ivan Ohiyenko entitled "The Rebirth of the Ukrainian Church," in which he sketches the plan for the Ukrainization of the Church. On February 2, after the Bolsheviks capture Kiev, the Sobor interrupts its meetings and destroys all its documents.

22 January 1918 — The Ukrainian Central Council proclaims the Fourth Universal, establishing the complete independence of Ukraine. The first president of the Ukrainian National Republic is Prof. Mykhaylo Hrushevsky, an eminent Ukrainian historian.

26 January 1918 — The Bolsheviks capture Kiev and murder Metropolitan Vladimir Bogoyavlensky.

9 February 1918 — The Ukrainian government

Oleksander Lototsky (1870-1939), Minister of Religion in the government of the Ukrainian People's Republic (1918-19), church and political leader, scholar, author of numerous works on Ukrainian church history.

signs a treaty in Berestya (Brest-Litovsk) with the Central Powers. They recognize the independence of Ukraine and establish diplomatic relations. In exchange for Ukrainian grain, they are obliged to give Ukraine military aid in its struggle against Bolshevik Russia.

February 1918 — The government of the Russian S.F.S.R. publishes a decree about the separation of the Church from the state and schools from the Church. After the Bolsheviks overrun Ukraine this decree comes into force.

The Germans arrive in Ukraine. Under pressure from the Ukrainian and German armies the Bolsheviks are forced to abandon Ukraine.

29 April 1918 — As a result of a coup, Hetman Pavlo Skoropadsky comes to power in Ukraine.

20 June — 11 July 1918 — The summer session of the All-Ukrainian Church Sobor convenes in Kiev. The sessions are dominated by delegates of Russian orientation and are transformed into a distinct anti-Ukrainian gathering. The Church in Ukraine is in Russian hands and is used for activities hostile to Ukrainian national interests. During the sessions the majority of the delegates veto the voting rights of all the Ukrainian delegates, eliciting a protest from the Minister of Religious Confessions of Ukraine, Prof. Vasyl Zinkivsky. On July 6, members of the Sobor pay a visit to Hetman Pavlo Skoropadsky, who declares that all Ukrainian Church affairs must be resolved in Ukraine without the interference of the Moscow Patriarchate. At the conclusion of the Sobor on July 9, a ceremony is held marking the acceptance of a statute of the Supreme Church Administration, according to which the Orthodox Church in Ukraine becomes an autonomous institution, but under the jurisdiction of the Moscow Patriarchate. On the basis of this new statute the members of the Supreme Church Council, none of whom is a Ukrainian clergymen or lay person, are later elected. This selection makes official the great rift between the Russian hierarchy of the Orthodox Church in Ukraine and the Ukrainian church activists who advocate autocephaly and independence.

June 1918 — The Kholm Theological College is established in Kiev to oversee religious-ecclesiastical affairs in Kholm, Pidlyashshya, Volynia and Polissya.

10 July 1918 — At the Cathedral of St. Sophia in Kiev, festivities dedicated to Hetman Ivan Mazepa of Ukraine take place. Since the Russian Tsar Peter I rule, Mazepa has been anathematized in churches. The participants of the celebration decide to move the body of Ivan Mazepa to Ukraine and to bury him in the Cathedral of St. Sophia, next to the Ukrainian prince Yaroslav the Wise.

18 July 1918 — The Ukrainian Greek-Orthodox Church in Canada is established during a convention in Saskatoon.

Summer 1918 — The Ministry of Religious Confessions of Ukraine begins publishing a bi-weekly journal, *Faith and the State.*

13 August 1918 — The Ministry of Religious Confessions of Ukraine passes a temporary charter for the Kiev Theological Academy, grants it independence from Moscow, subordinates its administration to the Ministry of Religious Confessions and places it under the jurisdiction of the Kievan Metropolitanate.

26 September 1918 — The Moscow Patriarch, Tikhon, approves the temporary statute of the Orthodox Church in Ukraine, curtails its independence and expands the control of the Russian Church over the Church in Ukraine.

Autumn 1918 — A Ukrainian university is established in Kamyanets-Podilsky, with a theological faculty, the dean of which is Prof. Vasyl Bidnov. A special commission in charge of the translation of books for religious services into the Ukrainian language is organized at the university. Prof. Ivan Ohiyenko becomes rector of the University.

November 1918 — The Polish government liquidates the Kholm Orthodox Eparchy and attaches it to the Warsaw Eparchy.

14 December 1918 — After an anti-government insurrection Hetman Pavlo Skoropadsky steps down from his post. The Directorate of the Ukrainian National Republic headed by Volodymyr Vynnychenko, followed by Symon Petlyura, comes to power in Ukraine. On December 19 the new government of Ukraine arrives triumphantly in Kiev and the Archbishop of Katerynoslav, Ahapyt Vyshnevsky, greets the government on the square of the Cathedral of St. Sophia, together with the Ukrainian clergy. After the armies of the Russian general Denikin overrun Ukraine, the Russian hierarchy divests the Archbishop of his post and deports him from Ukraine.

1918 — The Polish government forcibly takes over the Orthodox Cathedral of the Birth of the Blessed Virgin Mary in Kholm, built in the 13th century by King Danylo Romanovych, who is buried there. The church is transferred to the Polish Catholic Church.

The Russian authorities issue a special decree

whereby all churches, synagogues and other houses of worship are confiscated and may be given to the so-called committees of "twenty" for an appropriate fee.

26 December 1918 — The government of the Directorate of the Ukrainian National Republic is headed by the eminent church activist Volodymyr Chekhivsky.

1919 — The first parishes of the Ukrainian Orthodox Church are founded in the U.S.

1 January 1919 — The government of Ukraine proclaims a law concerning the autocephaly of the Ukrainian Orthodox Church, grants it independence from the Moscow Patriarchate and establishes its ruling body — the Ukrainian Church Synod.

The law includes the following points:

Article 1. The supreme ecclesiastical legislative, judicial and administrative authority in Ukraine is held by the All-Ukrainian Church Sobor, whose resolutions are subject to examination and approval by the legislative bodies.

Article 2. The Ukrainian Church Synod is created for the management of the affairs of the Ukrainian Autocephalous Orthodox Church.

Article 6. The Ukrainian Autocephalous Orthodox Church and its Synod and spiritual hierarchy are in no way subordinate to the Russian Patriarch.

Article 7. The Ukrainian Church Synod, for the purposes of conducting its activities and for the convening of a Church Sobor, formulates orders which become law after approval by the Ukrainian Republican government. (Martyrology, Vol. 1, pp. 50-51.)

22 January 1919 — The unification of the two Ukrainian republics — the Eastern (Dnieper) Ukraine and the Western (Galician) Ukraine into one Ukrainian National Republic takes place in Kiev on the square of the Cathedral of St. Sophia. The event is attended by a large number of clergymen, and bells ring in all the churches of Kiev.

5 February 1919 — The Bolsheviks capture Kiev.

February-March 1919 — A Ukrainian delegation headed by Prof. Oleksander Lototsky, ambassador extraordinary to the Turkish government, begins talks in Constantinople with the Ecumenical Patriarchate concerning the recognition of the autocephaly of the Ukrainian Orthodox Church.

17 March 1919 — In Zvenyhorod the Bolsheviks destroy the relics of St. Sava.

April 1919 — In Kiev the All-Ukrainian Orthodox Church Council is re-established and is headed by Mykhaylo Moroz. The vice-chairman is Archpriest Vasyl Lypkivsky and the secretary is Ivan Tarasenko.

Spring 1919 — The first Ukrainian Orthodox parish in Kiev obtains the Church of St. Nicholas on Pechersk for its own use. The church was built in the 17th century by Hetman Ivan Mazepa. On May 22, the first Ukrainian Holy Liturgy is served by Archpriest Vasyl Lypkivsky. Shortly thereafter, a second Ukrainian parish is founded in Kiev, and the Church of St. Andrew is given to the parish.

16 June 1919 — By a special order the Polish government forcibly takes over a number of Ukrainian Orthodox churches in the Kholm and Lublin regions.

July 1919 — A third Ukrainian parish is founded at the Cathedral of St. Sophia in Kiev, whose pastor is Archpriest Vasyl Lypkivsky.

12 July 1919 — The first Ukrainian Liturgy is celebrated in the Cathedral of St. Sophia in Kiev.

6 August 1919 — The Bolsheviks kill 17 monks, among them Hegumen Amvrosiy of the Spaso-Preobrazhensky Monastery near Lubny.

19 August 1919 — The Patriarch of Moscow, Tikhon, calls on the Ukrainian clergy to loyally fulfill the directives of the Russian episcopate in Ukraine.

31 August 1919 — The Ukrainian armies wrest Kiev from the Bolsheviks. Archpriest Vasyl Lypkivsky and many clergymen, in a solemn procession from the Cathedral of St. Sophia, meet Symon Petlyura as he enters Kiev. That same day the armies of the Russian general Denikin capture Kiev. Arriving with them is Metropolitan Antoniy Khrapovytsky. The Metropolitan defrocks all the Ukrainian priests, and puts Rev. Vasyl Lypkivsky on trial. He directs all the churches to be taken away from the Ukrainians.

Autumn 1919 — Fleeing from the Bolsheviks, and later from Denikin's armies, many Ukrainian church activists settle temporarily in Kamyanets-Podilsky, where they continue their work aimed at the rebirth of the Ukrainian Church.

16 December 1919 — Metropolitan Antoniy Khrapovytsky flees Kiev together with the retreating armies of Denikin. Once again the Russian Bolsheviks occupy large parts of Ukraine. In the village of Danivka they murder the hegumen of the Monastery of St. George; they turn the church of the theological seminary in Kharkiv into a club with a stage; in Poltava, the Church of the Cadet Corps is turned into a reading-room and icons and religious books are burned.

December 1919 — Two other parishes are established in Kiev — at the Church of St. Elias and the Church of SS. Peter and Paul.

January 1920 — The honorary head of the first All-Ukrainian Orthodox Church Council, Archbishop Oleksiy Dorodnytsyn, dies in the monastery in Novorossiysk.

Spring 1920 — Ukrainian parishes are established in various cities and villages in the Kiev region and are joined in a Union of Ukrainian Parishes. After registering its statute with the Soviet authorities, the Union gains legal status in Soviet Ukraine.

In Lubny the Soviet authorities close a boys' seminary and an eparchial school for girls, and imprison several teachers.

5 May 1920 — The All-Ukrainian Orthodox Church Council proclaims the autocephaly of the Ukrainian

Orthodox Church and on May 30 holds its first congress of Ukrainian parishes in Kiev.

6 June 1920 — The church congress of clergymen and lay people in Volodymyr-Volynsky obtains approval for the Ukrainization of church life on Ukrainian lands under Polish rule.

12 June 1920 — The Red Army captures Kiev and almost all Ukrainian lands east of the river Zbruch. These lands remain under Russian occupation until World War II. The Soviet Ukrainian government, which proclaims Kharkiv the capital of the Ukrainian S.S.R., arrives with the Red Army.

June 1920 — In Kiev the first book for religious services to appear since the end of World War I is published. It is the Liturgy of St. John Chrysostom, translated into Ukrainian by Rev. Vasyl Lypkivsky.

Summer-Autumn 1920 — Ukrainian parishes are established in all the large cities, towns, and villages of Ukraine. They take over churches from the Russian clergy and Ukrainize church life.

29-30 December 1920 — The Ukrainian Orthodox Church in the U.S. is established during a congress in Newark: it is placed under the jurisdiction of Metropolitan Hermanos, the exarch of Antioch in the U.S.

1920 — During the two years of the occupation of Ukrainian lands, the Polish government forcibly closes numerous Ukrainian Orthodox churches in the regions of Kholm, Polissya and Volynia. The government transfers many churches to Polish Roman Catholics.

The Mukachiv-Pryashiv Orthodox Eparchy, under the jurisdiction of the Serbian Orthodox Church, is established in Transcarpathia.

23 January 1921 — Mykola Leontovych, a composer of liturgical songs and church music, dies under mysterious circumstances.

January 1921 — Patriarch Tikhon appoints Archbishop Mikhail Yermakov, a Ukrainophobe, Exarch of the Russian Church in Ukraine.

February 1921 — The Synod of the Russian episcopate in Kiev defrocks all the priests in Ukrainian parishes and orders the dissolution of the All-Ukrainian Orthodox Church Council and the Union of Ukrainian Parishes. During a congress one month later, the Ukrainian clergy rejects the directives of the Russian hierarchy in Ukraine.

18 March 1921 — As a result of the treaty signed by Poland and Soviet Russia in Riga, the Ukrainian lands of Western Volynia, Polissya, Kholm, Pidlyashshya and Galicia fall under Polish rule. A total of 1411 Orthodox parishes falls under Polish occupation: 760 parishes in the Volynia Eparchy, 298 parishes in the Eparchy of Polissya, and 65 parishes in the Warsaw-Kholm Eparchy. The majority of the population in these eparchies is Ukrainian.

May 1921 — The Kiev Provincial Church Synod attended by 400 delegates confirms the autocephaly of the Ukrainian Orthodox Church and decides not to recognize Metropolitan Mikhail Yermakov, the Exarch of the Moscow Patriarchate in Ukraine. The Synod decides to convene an All-Ukrainian Church Sobor in Kiev on October 14.

13 June 1921 — The All-Russian Central Executive Committee publishes a decree banning the teaching of religion in churches, restricting sermons and governing the conditions of the use of churches and shrines.

28 September 1921 — With the agreement of the Polish government, Patriarch Tikhon appoints a Ukrainian, Archbishop Yuriy Yaroshevsky, as Patriarchal Exarch in Poland. The new exarch creates the Supreme Church Directorship on the basis of broad autonomy and dissolves the Russian Church Council in Poland, which aimed to take full control of the Church.

Participants of the First All-Ukrainian Orthodox Church Council, October 1921, St. Sophia Cathedral in Kiev.

Vasyl Lypkivsky (1864-1938), first Metropolitan of the Ukrainian Autocephalous Orthodox Church (1921-1927). He died in a Soviet concentration camp.

30 September 1921 — The *Religious-Scholarly Herald,* edited by Rev. Petro Bilon, begins appearing in a Ukrainian prisoner-of-war camp in Aleksandrow-Kujawski in Poland; the editorial board recognizes the leadership of the Ukrainian Autocephalous Orthodox Church in Kiev.

3-10 October 1921 — The Eparchial Congress of the clergy and laity of Volynia convenes in Pochayiv. The participants elect Bishop Dionysiy Valedynsky honorary head and Archpriest Nikanor Abramovych the acting head. During the Congress, Archpriest Nikanor serves the first Holy Liturgy in the Pochayiv Lavra in the Ukrainian language, without mentioning the Moscow Patriarch. The Congress approves the Ukrainization of the Church and the publication of Ukrainian-language books for religious services.

14-30 October 1921 — The First All-Ukrainian Orthodox Church Sobor convenes in the Cathedral of St. Sophia in Kiev, attended by 472 delegates. The Sobor, headed by Mykhaylo Moroz, consists of plenary sessions and meetings of separate committees. Since Kievan Metropolitan Mikhail Yermakov has refused to consecrate bishops for the Ukrainian Church and not a single bishop takes part in the Sobor, the sessions focus on the problem of the canonical status and the need for bishops for the Ukrainian Church. After Prof. Volodymyr Chekhivsky's speech, in which he determines the canonical status of the Sobor, the participants take a vote by secret balloting. By a sweeping majority of votes it is decided to hold a general consecration of bishops by means of the laying on of hands by presbyters, in accordance with an old practice of the Alexandrine Church. The first to be elected and consecrated in St. Sophia's Cathedral is Archpriest Vasyl Lypkivsky, who becomes Metropolitan of the Ukrainian Autocephalous Orthodox Church. The following are consecrated bishops: Archpriest Nestor Sharayivsky, Rev. Ivan Teodorovych, Oleksander Yaroshenko, Rev. Yuriy Mikhnovksy, and Archpriest Stepan Orlyk. The Sobor denounces as amoral

Consecration of Vasyl Lypkivsky as first Metropolitan of the Ukrainian Autocephalous Orthodox Church, October 23, 1921, St. Sophia Cathedral in Kiev.

Nestor Sharayivsky (1865-1929), UAOC Archbishop of Kiev (left). Volodymyr Chekhivsky (1876-1938), prominent church and political leader, ideologue of the UAOC.

and uncanonical the subordination of the Ukrainian Church to the Moscow Patriarchate, cancels all the resolutions of the Sobor of 1918, approves the autocephaly of the Ukrainian Orthodox Church and its apolitical nature, approves the use of the Ukrainian language in church services, and confirms the canons and structure of the Ukrainian Autocephalous Orthodox Church. Shortly after the Sobor, the Russian episcopate in Ukraine, headed by Metropolitan Mikhail Yermakov, calls the Sobor uncanonical and first uses the term "self-consecrated clergy," which continues to be used by the enemies of the Ukrainian Autocephalous Orthodox Church.

17 November 1921 — Patriarch Tikhon forbids the use of any language but Church Slavonic in church services.

Autumn 1921 — Metropolitan Vasyl Lypkivsky of the Ukrainian Autocephalous Orthodox Church journies throughout Ukraine and visits more than 500 Ukrainian parishes. After the Sobor the following new bishops are consecrated: Rev. Ivan Pavlovsky, Hryhoriy Storozhenko and Rev. Volodymyr Brzhosnyovsky.

24-28 January 1922 — The first Synod of Orthodox bishops on Polish territory convenes in Warsaw. Among the participants are Metropolitan Yuriy Yaroshevsky and the following bishops: Dionysiy Valedynsky, Panteleymon Ruzhanovsky and Volodymyr Tykhonitsky. The bishops cannot concur in the matter of the legal status of the Orthodox Church in Poland.

30 January 1922 — The Polish government issues "Temporary Rules concerning the relations between the government of the Polish Republic and the Orthodox Church in Poland," which in effect control the life and organization of the Church until November 18, 1938, when they are replaced by a special decree of the president of Poland. According to these Rules, the legal representative of the Orthodox Church in Poland is the Council of Bishops, under whose jurisdiction are more than four million people of the Orthodox faith: 2.7 million Ukrainians, 1.3 million Byelorussians, 700,000 Czechs and a small number of Russians. The Orthodox Church is divided into four eparchies: the Warsaw Eparchy with 40 parishes, the Grodno Eparchy with 150 parishes, the Pinsk-Novogrudok Eparchy with 200 parishes and the Volynia Eparchy with 700 parishes.

January 1922 — In Kremenets in Volynia the first Ukrainian Orthodox journal entitled *Orthodox Volynia* begins appearing.

February 1922 — In Ukraine four new bishops of the Ukrainian Autocephalous Orthodox Church are

Metropolitan Vasyl Lypkivsky preaching in Chokolivka near Kiev, 1923.

consecrated: Yukhym Kalishevsky, Konon Bey, Konstantyn Malyushkevych and Mykola Boretsky.

8 March 1922 — The All-Ukrainian Central Executive Committee publishes a decree entitled "On the Transfer of Treasures to the Aid Fund for the Hungry." This decree becomes the pretext for the plunder of churches and monasteries. Thefts from the Kievan Caves Monastery and the Cathedral of St. Sophia are carried out by the assistant to the Peoples' Commissar of Internal Affairs of the U.S.S.R., Serafimov. The accusation of "hiding church and monastic treasures" is used to arrest many hegumens, monks and priests in Ukraine.

May 1922 — On the initiative of the Soviet authorities a pro-government "Living Church" is established in Moscow; in a short time this church begins to expand throughout Ukraine.

14-15 June 1922 — At a Church Synod in Warsaw, a majority of bishops supports the autocephaly of the Orthodox Church in Poland.

August 1922 — In Balta, the Soviet authorities sentence 70 priests to five years' imprisonment each. A mass trial of clergymen takes place in Korolivka in the Chernihiv region: two monks are executed by firing squad and many are sentenced to varying terms of imprisonment. In Kiev the Bolsheviks execute the secretary of the All-Ukrainian Orthodox Church Council, Ivan Tarasenko, his daughter, Marusia, and 43 other activists of the Ukrainian Autocephalous Orthodox Church.

22-29 October 1922 — The Great Pokrova (the feast of St. Mary the Protectress) Meeting of the All-Ukrainian Orthodox Church Council takes place in Kiev; the meeting is attended by 167 people, including Metropolitan Vasyl Lypkivsky, 16 bishops, 61 priests, 7 deacons and 82 lay people. The participants reject an attempt by the GPU, the Soviet secret police, to destroy the Church from within, and draw up a declaration about the separation of the Church from all political activity.

1922 — The following are consecrated bishops of the Ukrainian Autocephalous Orthodox Church in Ukraine: Mykola Shyryay, Yuriy Zhevchenko and Yosyp Oksiyuk. According to data compiled by the researcher M. Polsky, during a period of three years the following numbers of clergy are tortured to death and executed: 98 in the Kharkiv Eparchy in Ukraine; in the Odessa-Kherson Eparchy — 191; in the Poltava Eparchy — 124; in the Katerynoslav Eparchy — 92; in the Chernihiv Eparchy — 78. Information about other eparchies is unavailable.

The renewal of the Ukrainian Church and the First All-Ukrainian Orthodox Church Sobor excites all of Ukraine. Pilgrims from many villages and cities arrive in great numbers at the Cathedral of St. Sophia in Kiev to see the Ukrainian bishops and hear Liturgies conducted in the Ukrainian language. These pilgrimages take place despite persecution and various obstacles placed by the Bolsheviks. More than 700 parishes belonging to the Ukrainian Autocephalous Orthodox Church in Ukraine are organized in one year.

Yuriy Yaroshevsky (1872-1923), first Ukrainian Metropolitan of the Orthodox Church in Poland, assassinated by a Russian Orthodox fanatic.

The Orthodox Church in Bosnia (Yugoslavia) acknowledges the leadership of the Ukrainian Autocephalous Orthodox Church and of Metropolitan Vasyl Lypkivsky.

January 1923 — According to official Soviet statistics, from November 7, 1917 to January 1, 1923, 38 Orthodox bishops and 1275 priests are executed in the U.S.S.R.

8 February 1923 — Archimandrite Smarahd (Pavlo Lyatyshenko), the former rector of the Kholm Theological Seminary and a fanatical activist in the Russian Church, murders the Ukrainian Metropolitan of the Orthodox Church in Poland, Yuriy Yaroshevsky, in Warsaw. The pretext for the murder is allegedly the attempt of the Metropolitan to establish autocephaly and the separation of the Church from the Moscow Patriarchate.

20-25 February 1923 — At a Synod of bishops Dionysiy Valedynsky, Bishop of Kremenets is elected the new Metropolitan of the Orthodox Church in Poland. He requests a blessing from the Ecumenical Patriarch of Constantinople rather than from the Moscow Patriarch.

9 January 1924 — Ioann Teodorovych, Archbishop of the Ukrainian Autocephalous Orthodox Church, leaves Ukraine for the United States in order to organize the Ukrainian Orthodox Church in the United States and Canada.

3 September 1924 — The Synod of the Orthodox Church in Poland allows the use of the Ukrainian, Byelorussian, Polish and Czech languages in religious services.

1923-1924 — At the initiative and under the protection of the GPU, many splinter groups of the Orthodox Church, the "Renovationist Church," the "Living Church," the "Active Church of Christ" and many brotherhoods are founded in Ukraine. They attempt to weaken the influence of the Ukrainian Autocephalous Orthodox Church and destroy it from with-

Episcopate of the Ukrainian Autocephalous Orthodox Church (1921-26). In the center is Metropolitan Vasyl Lypkivsky.

in. At the same time, attacks on the Ukrainian Autocephalous Orthodox Church increase in the Soviet press, and public religious disputes take place during which bishops and leading priests take a stand against atheism and in support of the Ukrainian Autocephalous Orthodox Church.

13 November 1924 — The Ecumenical Patriarch and the Synod of the Constantinople Patriarchate announce a Tomos (Charter) concerning the autocephaly of the Orthodox Church in Poland and its independence from the Moscow Patriarchate.

1924 — The All-Ukrainian Orthodox Church Council begins to organize parishes and groups of supporters of the Ukrainian Autocephalous Orthodox Church in China, in the Zeleny Klyn region, the Kuban and in various places of Ukrainian settlement in the Russian Republic and Kazakhstan. The Ukrainian Autocephalous Orthodox Church movement expands among Ukrainian emigres in Czechoslovakia, Switzerland, France, the United States and Canada.

8 February 1925 — An Orthodox theological department is established at Warsaw State University, and its staff includes the Ukrainian intellectuals Ivan Ohiyenko, Dmytro Doroshenko, Vasyl Bidnov, Pavlo Zaytsev, Oleksander Lototsky, Roman Smal-Stotsky, and Bishop Oleksiy Hromadsky. Volodymyr Vyshnevsky organizes the library.

16-19 September 1925 — Ceremonies marking the establishment of autocephaly of the Orthodox Church in Poland are held in Warsaw. Metropolitans of the Constantinople Patriarchate Joachimus of Chalcedon and Germanos of Sardica, Metropolitan Nektariy of Bukovyna and the representative of the Rumanian Patriarchate, many foreign representatives, the entire hierarchy of the Orthodox Church in Poland, many clergymen and lay people, as well as representatives of the Polish government take part in these ceremonies. During the ceremonies the patriarchal Tomos dated November 13, 1924 is read out in the Polish, Ukrainian and Russian languages and given to Metropolitan Dionysiy Valedynsky, the head of the Orthodox Church in Poland.

1925 — Inspired by the GPU, the "Living Church" in Ukraine proclaims itself, with the approval of the Soviet authorities, the legal heir of the Ukrainian Autocephalous Orthodox Church and takes over parishes and churches from the clergy of the Church with the aid of the Soviet secret police. At the same time a number of articles attacking the Ukrainian Autocephalous Orthodox Church and its hierarchs appear in *Pravda, Komunist* (Kharkiv) and in Russian newspapers abroad.

The Union of Militant Atheists, an anti-religious organization, is founded in Ukraine. During its existence, until 1941, its members publish the propaganda journal *Bezvirnyk* (Atheist) and the newspaper *Voyovnychy bezvirnyk* (Militant Atheist).

January 1926 — New arrests of priests take place in Ukraine. More than 100 priests are incarcerated by the GPU in Kiev.

1 April 1926 — Archbishop Oleksander Yareshchenko of the Ukrainian Autocephalous Orthodox Church is arrested in Kharkiv. He is deported to Moscow and later exiled to Tashkent. Approximately at the same time V. Dolenko, the head of the District Church Council, is arrested. On June 6 Archdeacon

Oleksander Yareshchenko (1890-1938), UAOC Archbishop of Kharkiv. He died in a Soviet concentration camp (left). Yuriy Zhevchenko (1885-1938), UAOC Archbishop of Odesa. He died in a Soviet concentration camp.

Vasyl Potiyenko, the head of the All-Ukrainian Orthodox Church Council, is arrested; on July 30, Metropolitan Vasyl Lypkivsky is arrested, but released on September 18. At the same time the GPU shuts down the Kiev office of the All-Ukrainian Orthodox Church Council, confiscates all its documents, and forbids its members to conduct any kind of meetings.

1-3 September 1926 — The Soviet authorities in Kiev order a meeting of Bishops and representatives of the All-Ukrainian Orthodox Church Council to be held. During the meeting, the ouster of Metropolitan Vasyl Lypkivsky from the Ukrainian Autocephalous Orthodox Church is discussed. The Soviet authorities put forward this demand, and the existence of the Ukrainian Church is endangered. During the meeting, at the insistence of the GPU, the alleged political and anti-Soviet speeches of Metropolitan Vasyl Lypkivsky, Archbishop Oleksander Yareshchenko, Archdeacon Vasyl Potiyenko and the entire membership of the All-Ukrainian Orthodox Church Council are criticized. This criticism lays the foundation for the gradual liquidation of the Ukrainian Autocephalous Orthodox Church and is the prelude to the mass imprisonment of the hierarchy and clergy in Ukraine. In order to augment the internal ferment within the Ukrainian Autocephalous Orthodox Church, the authorities demand the creation of the so-called "All-Ukrainian Commission for Normalizing the Life of the Ukrainian Autocephalous Orthodox Church."

25-30 October 1926 — The Soviet authorities permit the Great Pokrova (the feast of St. Mary the Protectress) Meeting of the All-Ukrainian Orthodox Church Council to take place. At the demands of the GPU, the activities of Metropolitan Vasyl Lypkivsky and other leaders of the Ukrainian Autocephalous Orthodox Church are criticized. The participants draw up a declaration of loyalty to the Soviet authorities, elect Bishop Petro Romodanov to be the new head of the All-Ukrainian Orthodox Church Sobor and decide to hold the second All-Ukrainian Church Sobor in one year's time.

1926 — By a decision of the Soviet authorities, the Kievan Caves Monastery is changed to the "Ukrainian Museum Town."

The All-Ukrainian Orthodox Church Council (1924-25). In the center of the first row is Archdeacon Vasyl Potiyenko, President of the Council. Metropolitan Vasyl Lypkivsky is in the center of the lower row.

Mykola Boretsky (1879-1936), Metropolitan of the Ukrainian Autocephalous Orthodox Church (1927-30). He died in a Soviet concentration camp.

15 January 1927 — A short-lived period of tolerance by the Soviet authorities toward the Ukrainian Autocephalous Orthodox Church begins. The Church obtains permission to publish its own organ, *Church and Life.* Metropolitan Vasyl Lypkivsky becomes the head of the editorial board.

January 1927 — The so-called "Active Church of Christ" liquidates itself in Ukraine, and its bishops and clergy join the Ukrainian Autocephalous Orthodox Church.

March 1927 — At the demand of the Soviet authorities, Metropolitan Vasyl Lypkivsky draws up a declaration of loyalty to the Soviet state.

Spring 1927 — The St. Elias, Jordan (Epiphany) and Protection (Intercession) churches in Kiev, the Cathedral of the Protection in Odessa, the Cathedral of SS. Borys and Hlib in Chernihiv and the Trinity Church in Poltava are given to the Ukrainian Autocephalous Orthodox Church.

2 June 1927 — An open campaign for the ouster of Metropolitan Vasyl Lypkivsky from the leadership of the Ukrainian Autocephalous Orthodox Church begins. Under pressure from the GPU, this campaign spreads to various places in Ukraine. Some church leaders are convinced that the Church may be saved from persecution by Metropolitan Vasyl Lypkivsky's ouster.

5-6 June 1927 — A congress of the Ukrainian National-religious Movement of the Orthodox Church in Poland takes place in Lutsk, with the participation of 565 representatives. Eight Ukrainian members of the Polish Sejm and Senate, as well as delegates from all Ukrainian lands under Polish rule, take part in the congress. The means of de-russifying the Church, making it independent from the Russian hierarchs and the question of obtaining a Ukrainian bishop are discussed during the congress. In order to achieve these goals the congress establishes a Ukrainian Church Committee. A counter-meeting of priests and religious activists of Russian orientation, among them Metropolitan Dionysiy Valedynsky, is held. The participants of this congress appeal to the Polish government to ban the activities of the Ukrainian Church Committee.

17-30 October 1927 — The Second All-Ukrainian Church Sobor, under the leadership of Volodymyr Chekhivsky, takes place in Kiev. On the day the Sobor convenes, the GPU demands that Chekhivsky make the ouster of Metropolitan Vasyl Lypkivsky from the Church the first point of order. If not, the Metropolitan and Chekhivsky are to be imprisoned and the Sobor dissolved. In an atmoshpere of confusion and uncertainty and the presence of agents of the GPU, the Sobor "removes the burden of service as metropolitan from Metropolitan Vasyl Lypkivsky for objec-

Participants of the Second All-Ukrainian Orthodox Church Sobor, October 17-30, 1927, St. Sophia Cathedral in Kiev.

tive reasons." In his place Mykola Boretsky is elected as the new Metropolitan and Archpriest Leontiy Yunakiv is elected the new head of the All-Ukrainian Orthodox Church Council. The ouster of Metropolitan Vasyl Lypkivsky from the Ukrainian Church concludes the first period of the activities of the Church, which comprises of 22 eparchies and more than 2000 parishes. The Church begins publishing the journal *Church and Life* at this most precarious time. Besides the journal, a number of religious books, including the Holy Gospels, the Liturgy of St. John Chrysostom, the *Psaltyr* (Psalter), *Chasoslovets* (Breviary), *Trebnyk* (Sacramentary), and *Akafyst* (Acathist) are published in the Ukrainian language.

29 May — 1 June 1928 — The Great Mykilsky (Feast of St. Nicholas) Meeting takes place in Kiev with the participation of Metropolitan Mykola Boretsky, 19 bishops and representatives of the clergy and lay people. The participants discuss the possibility of uniting the Orthodox Church in Ukraine, and elect a separate commission headed by Archbishop Yosyp Oksiyuk to look into this question.

Summer 1928 — The Polish government bans the activities of the Ukrainian Church Committee.

December 1928 — Soviet authorities ban the publication of the Ukrainian Autocephalous Orthodox Church organ *Church and Life.* They enlist 50,000 new members of the Union of Militant Atheists in the struggle against the Ukrainian Church and religion in Ukraine.

1928 — In the Bukovyna Metropolitanate under Rumanian rule, where 60% of the population is Ukrainian, the Rumanian authorities deprive the Ukrainians the right to have their own parishes and to participate in decisions affecting the Church.

1927-1930 — Under pressure from the GPU and by means of constant repression and persecution in Ukraine, during the years 1927-28, 179 priests leave the priesthood, during the years 1928-29 — 439, and in 1929-30 — 2000.

Stepan Orlyk (1891-1939), UAOC Archbishop of Volynia and Zhytomyr. He died in a Soviet prison (left). Yosyp Oksiyuk (1894-1961), UAOC Archbishop of Poltava. He spent fifteen years in a Soviet concentration camp.

March 1929 — Metropolitan Sergey (Stragorodsky), the vicar of the Moscow Patriarchate, concludes a secret agreement with the Soviet authorities concerning the creation of a single church leadership for all Orthodox Churches in the U.S.S.R. According to this agreement, all the parishes of the Ukrainian Autocephalous Orthodox Church and other churches in Ukraine are to become part of the Russian Orthodox Church and come under the jurisdiction of the Moscow Patriarchate.

17 March 1929 — The Russian Metropolitan of Kiev, Mikhail Yermakov, the exarch of the Moscow Patriarchate in Ukraine and an ardent foe of the Ukrainian Autocephalous Orthodox Church, dies in Kiev. After his death, the Moscow Patriarchate does not appoint any more exarchs for Ukraine until 1939.

9 April 1929 — The first parish of the Ukrainian Orthodox Church in the U.S., placed under the jurisdiction of the Ecumenical Patriarch of Constantinople, is founded during a congress in Allentown, Pennsylvania. The first bishop of this Church is Rev. Yosyf

Publications of the Ukrainian Autocephalous Orthodox Church in the 1920s. From left to right: *Chasoslovets (Breviary)* (1925), *Mineya (Mineon)* (1927), the journal *Tserkva i Zhyttya (Church and Life),* forbidden in 1928.

Feodosiy Serhiyiv (1890-1938), UAOC Archbishop of Pereyaslav. He died in a Soviet concentration camp (left). Yakiv Chulayivsky (1889-1930s), UAOC Bishop of Berdychiv. He died in a Soviet concentration camp.

Zhuk, who is consecrated by the bishops of the Syrian Orthodox Church in the U.S.

Summer 1929 — The Polish Catholic Episcopate begins to make appeals calling for the transfer of Orthodox churches and monasteries to the Polish Catholic Church. Some 724 such appeals are made in a short period of time.

29 July 1929 — Volodymyr Chekhivsky, one of the most prominent Ukrainian Orthodox activists and the author of many scholarly works, is arrested in Kiev.

29 October 1929 — Archbishop Nestor Sharayivsky of the Ukrainian Autocephalous Orthodox Church, deputy to the Metropolitan during the years 1921-27, dies in Kiev.

1929-30 — Hundreds of priests in Ukraine are sentenced to varying terms of imprisonment for alleged counter-revolutionary activities. In addition, 347 churches, 136 synagogues and 50 prayer buildings are closed, destroyed or converted for other purposes.

1 January 1930 — During the period of Soviet rule until January 1, 1930, 31 bishops, 1600 priests and 7000 monks are murdered in the U.S.S.R. By 1930 48 bishops, 3700 priests and 8000 monks and nuns are incarcerated in prisons and labor camps.

28-29 January 1930 — At the demand of the GPU an "extraordinary sobor" of the Ukrainian Autocephalous Orthodox Church is convened in Kiev. The Sobor declares the Church a counter-revolutionary organization and an integral part of the clandestine "Union for the Liberation of Ukraine." Through GPU pressure and blackmail the Sobor announces the liquidation of the Ukrainian Autocephalous Orthodox Church. The Soviet press depicts this "Sobor" as the "self-liquidation" of the Church.

12 February 1930 — The Polish government bans the convening of the Regional Synod of the Orthodox Church in Poland.

9 March — 19 May 1930 — A trial of 45 members of the so-called "Union for the Liberation of Ukraine" takes place in Kharkiv. Among the defendants are three eminent activists of the Ukrainian Autocephalous Orthodox Church: Volodymyr Chekhivsky, his brother, Mykola, and Kost Tovkach from Poltava. They are accused of counter-revolutionary activities, and planning a rebellion in Ukraine and its secession from the U.S.S.R. Volodymyr Chekhivsky is given the death sentence. His sentence is commuted to ten years' imprisonment. His brother, Mykola, is sentenced to three years' imprisonment, and Kost Tovkach is sentenced to five years' imprisonment. All three of them perish in Soviet concentration camps.

April 1930 — An anti-religious museum is opened in the Cathedral of St. Volodymyr in Kiev.

The All-Ukrainian Orthodox Church Council, elected in 1927. In the first row from the left: Archdeacon Leontiy Yunakiv (Head), Archbishop Yosyp Oksiyuk, Metropolitan Mykola Boretsky, Archbishop Konstantyn Malyushkevych, Bishop Yuriy Mikhnovsky. Standing: Rev. Yakiv Chulayivsky, Volodymyr Chekhivsky, Archdeacon Leonid Karpov, Stepan Kobzyar.

Spring 1930 — Almost all bells from Ukrainian churches and monasteries in Kiev are removed for remelting. Twenty tons are removed from St. Volodymyr's Cathedral; from the Tithes church — 34 tons; from St. Michael's Golden-domed Cathedral — 12 tons; from the Florivsky convent — 12.7 tons; from the monastery of St. Jonas — 30 tons.

June 1930 — Metropolitan Mykola Boretsky of the Ukrainian Autocephalous Orthodox Church is arrested in Ukraine, together with Bishops Yukhym Kalishevsky, Yuriy Teslenko, Maksym Zadvirnyak and Yakiv Chulayivsky.

1 October 1930 — The number of members of the Union of Militant Atheists grows to 523,000 in Ukraine.

9-12 December 1930 — At the behest of the Soviet regime, the second "extraordinary sobor" of the Ukrainian Orthodox Church is held in Kiev. The Sobor elects Ivan Pavlovsky Metropolitan and bestows the title of "Metropolitan of Kharkiv and All Ukraine" on him. The word "autocephalous" is removed from the name of the Church. The Metropolitan's seat is transferred from Kiev to the capital of Ukraine, Kharkiv. At this time only 300 parishes of the Ukrainian Church remain active out of more than 2000; these are divided into seven eparchies-districts.

December 1930 — In a period of six months, 800 priests and deacons of the Ukrainian Autocephalous Orthodox Church are arrested in Ukraine.

1930 — On the orders of the GPU all churches of the Christian faith are closed in Kherson, and converted into movie theaters, stores, workers' clubs, or are destroyed. After World War II a few churches in Kherson are converted into museums, and have been preserved as historical-architectural monuments. Kherson becomes the first large city in Ukraine without a functioning church. The Mezhyhirsky Spaso-Preobrazhensky (Transfiguration) Monastery near Kiev, built in 988, and the Troyitsky (Trinity) Monastery in the village of Demydivka in the Poltava region are destroyed.

January 1931 — The GPU arrests the bishops of the Ukrainian Autocephalous Orthodox Church Volodymyr Dakhivnyk-Dakhivsky, Kost Krotevych and Antin Hrynevych.

1 May 1931 — The number of members of the Union of Militant Atheists has grown to 1.5 million in Ukraine, and the membership of the Young Militant Atheists has grown to 600,000.

16 June 1931 — The Metropolitan Petro Mohyla Society, headed by Senator Serhiy Tymoshenko, is founded in Lutsk in Volynia. Its goal is to work for the Ukrainian religious-national renaissance.

1931 — Due to pressure, repressions and blackmail exerted by the GPU, bishops Petro Tarnavsky, Hryhoriy Mozolevsky, Petro Romodanov and Mykhaylo Malyarevsky leave the Ukrainian Church. The GPU forbids bishops Feodosiy Serhiyev and Mykola Shyryay to serve Liturgy and be involved in church affairs.

Yuriy Mikhnovsky (1868-1937), UAOC Archbishop of Chernihiv. He died in a Soviet concentration camp (left). Ivan Pavlovsky (1890-1938), Metropolitan of the Ukrainian Orthodox Church (1930-36). He died in a Soviet concentration camp.

10 April 1932 — Archimandrite Polikarp Sikorsky is consecrated Bishop of Lutsk in the Cathedral of St. Mary Magdalen in Warsaw. During World War II he becomes Metropolitan of the Ukrainian Autocephalous Orthodox Church on Ukrainian lands under German occupation.

September 1932 — Joseph Stalin proclaims a "five-year-plan for atheism" in the U.S.S.R., according to which all religious confessions and various external manifestations of religious cults are to be eradicated by 1937.

5 June 1933 — The Polish press launches an organized campaign against the Orthodox Church in Poland and its head, Metropolitan Dionysiy Valedynsky.

10 September 1933 — The Ukrainian Parliamentary Representation in Poland organizes a massive demonstration in Pochayiv. The participants of the demonstration demand the Ukrainization of the Church, the

Volodymyr Samborsky (1882-1935), UAOC Archbishop of Vinnytsya, executed by the Soviet authorities (left). Hryhoriy Mozolevsky (1876-1938), UAOC Bishop of Konotop. He died in a Soviet concentration camp.

Konstantyn Malyushkevych (1890-1937), UAOC Archbishop of Kiev. He died in Soviet imprisonment (left). Yukhym Kalishevsky (1892-1930s), UAOC Bishop of Odessa. He died in a Soviet concentration camp.

introduction of the Ukrainian language into church services and the appointment of a Ukrainian bishop for the Volynia Eparchy.

1933 — Despite the ban forbidding starving peasants to enter churches, Metropolitan Ivan Pavlovsky and many priests in various places in Ukraine organize aid to the starving.

The Soviet regime closes four Ukrainian parishes in Kiev: St. Sophia, Trukhaniv, Pokrova (Protection) and Demiyiv.

Only three bishops remain in their chairs: Bishop Karabinevych in Uman, Bishop Chervinsky in Vinnytsya and Metropolitan Pavlovsky in Kharkiv.

February 1934 — Due to international outcry and protests, the Cathedral of St. Sophia in Kiev is saved from destruction and is converted into a museum. Ukraine is engulfed by a wave of closures, conversion and wholesale destruction of churches and monasteries of great architectural and cultural value. The Pokrova (Protection) Church and its historical cemetery in Kharkiv, and the Golden-domed Cathedral of St. Michael and monastery built by Grand Prince Svyatoslav Izyaslavych in 1108-13 in Kiev, are destroyed by the communist regime.

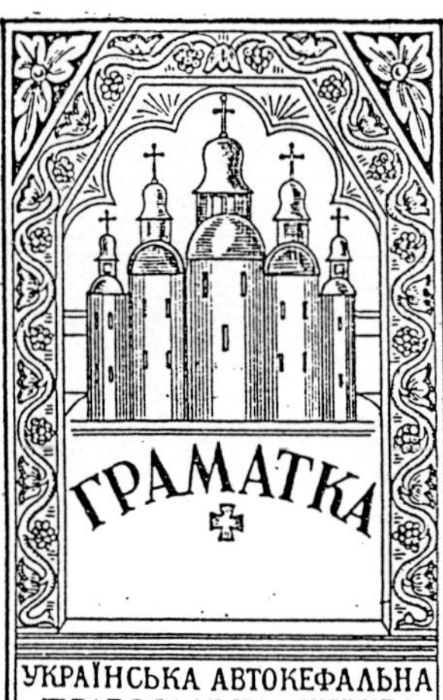

Hramatka (Grammar), a publication of the UAOC.

Spring 1934 — At the Soviet regime's behest, Metropolitan Ivan Pavlovsky moves to Kiev, where the capital of Ukraine has been transferred.

29-30 January 1935 — An eparchial conference headed by Archbishop Oleksiy Hromadsky convenes in Volynia. Representatives of parishes, monasteries, delegates of lay people and Volynian deputies and senators attend in great numbers. The participants decide to continue the struggle for the Ukrainization of the Church, to publish the journal *Church and the People* and to demand the opening of the Orthodox Theological Lyceum in Kremenets.

January 1935 — In Tyachev, in Transcarpathia a church congress takes place. The participants decide to cancel their juridical dependence on the Serbian Orthodox Church, which is under the control of Russian emigres; to establish a Ukrainian Orthodox Church under the jurisdiction of the Ecumenical Patriarch; and to introduce the use of the Ukrainian language into church services.

29-30 January 1935 — The Volynia Consistory adopts the use of the Ukrainian language.

15 March 1935 — The journal *Church and the People,* under the editorship of Prof. Ivan Vlasovsky, begins appearing in Volynia.

June 1935 — The Soviet regime closes the cathedral of Metropolitan Ivan Pavlovsky in Kiev and deprives him of the right to fulfill his spiritual duties. The Metropolitan is forced to leave Kiev. He moves to Cherkasy, where he works as a bookkeeper.

1935 — A Mass in the Ukrainian language is served for the first time in Kremenets and in Dubno in Volynia.

23 January 1936 — A trial of activists of the Ukrainian Autocephalous Orthodox Church takes place in Kharkiv. The defendants are Rev. Andriy Kukharenko, archpriests Mykyta Kokhno, Ivan Harashchenko and Drobytsky. They are sentenced to 3-4 years' imprisonment. Except for Ivan Harashchenko, they perish in Soviet labor camps. In February a second trial of activists of the Ukrainian Orthodox Church takes place. The defendants are Mykyta Vlasenko, Ivan Kocherkevych, Vasyl Lapa and Antin Tupchiy. All of them perish in Soviet prisons.

25 February — 1 March 1936 — A Polish trial of 19 Orthodox Ukrainians takes place in Kremenets in Volynia. They are tried for defending the church in Vyshhorod, which the Poles have been trying to take over forcibly. All the defendants are sentenced to varying terms of imprisonment; a few are amnestied after the trial.

May 1936 — Metropolitan Ivan Pavlovsky of the Ukrainian Orthodox Church is arrested in Cherkasy and deported to Kazakhstan, where he perishes. After his arrest the Ukrainian Orthodox Church practically ceases to exist.

Summer 1936 — The following hierarchs of the Ukrainian Autocephalous Orthodox Church, who are no longer fulfilling their duties in the Church, are arrested in Ukraine: Archbishop Feodosiy Serhiyiv and bishops Mykhayil Malyarevsky, Mykola Shyryay and Hryhoriy Mozolevsky. With the exception of bishop Malyarevsky, all perish in Soviet labor camps.

1936 — The four remaining parishes of the Ukrainian Autocephalous Orthodox Church are closed in Ukraine: the parish of Kvitka-Osnovyanenko's church in Kharkiv, and parishes in the villages of Vilshana, Solonytsivka and Merefa.

The Polish government closes the Orthodox Theological Seminaries in Kremenets and Vilnius, despite the protests of the Orthodox hierarchy.

1936-37 — The following bishops of the Ukrainian Autocephalous Orthodox Church are arrested in Ukraine: Yuriy Mikhnovsky, Volodymyr Samborsky, and Volodymyr Brzhosnyovsky. All of them perish in Soviet labor camps.

27 February 1937 — The Synod of the Orthodox Church in Poland, under pressure exerted by Russian church activists, changes the resolution of September 3, 1924 concerning the use of the living language in church services. This change elicits mass protests on the part of the Orthodox Ukrainians in all of Poland.

28 April 1937 — The Rumanian language is introduced into church services and school teaching in Bukovyna. The Eparchial Council of Bukovyna forbids Ukrainian priests to use the Ukrainian language in church services and for teaching in schools. This action elicits a wave of protests on the part of the Ukrainian Orthodox population and its leaders.

October 1937 — The Polish authorities and the Roman Catholic clergy begin the forcible conversion of Orthodox Ukrainians to Polish Roman Catholicism. Examples of such conversions in the village of Hrynky elicit a wave of protests in the Polish Sejm and from all over the world.

1937 — By a decision of the Soviet government all Orthodox Churches under various jurisdictions are officially liquidated in Ukraine. The Soviet government orders the dismantling and destruction of 2900 churches and 63 monasteries in the U.S.S.R. The Scottish Bible Society publishes a report on the destruction, closures and the conversion to other uses of 70,000 churches in the Soviet Union by the year 1937. By 1937 the following churches and monasteries in Kiev are partially or completely destroyed: the Yonivsky and Vydubytsky monasteries; and the Desyatynna (Tithes), St. Basil, Three Hierarchs, Ascension, Iron, St. Elias, Evangelist, Trinity, and St. Nicholas Church on Askold's burial mound. The following monasteries are converted to other uses: the Bratsky Monastery — to a textile workers' village; the Pokrovsky Monastery — to a turners' village; the Mykolayivsky Monastery — to residential buildings. The following churches are turned into museums: the Cathedrals of St. Sophia and St. Andrew; the St. Cyril Church; the Kiev Caves Monastery; and the Cathedrals of St. Volodymyr and St. Nicholas (Great Nicholas). A similar fate befalls thousands of churches and more than one hundred monasteries throughout Ukraine.

Konon Bey (1884-1930s), UAOC Bishop of Cherkasy. He died in a Soviet concentration camp (left). Yuriy Teslenko (1849-1943), UAOC Bishop of Bila Tserkva. He spent ten years in a Soviet concentration camp.

1938 — The Carpatho-Ruthenian Greek Catholic

Red Army Soldiers destroying a church in Ukraine in the 1930s.

Volodymyr Dakhivnyk-Dakhivsky (1893-1930s), UAOC Bishop of Tulchyn. He died in a Soviet concentration camp (left). Oleksander Chervinsky (1886-1930s), UAOC Bishop of Vinnytsya. He died in a Soviet concentration camp.

Orthodox Church, within the jurisdiction of the Constantinople Patriarch, is made into a separate eparchy in the U.S.

15 January 1938 — The Department of Cults of the NKVD issues a directive about the closing of churches throughout the Soviet Union. In a period of one year more than 8000 churches are destroyed, closed down or converted to other uses.

February 1938 — Ukrainian members of the Polish Sejm Stepan Skrypnyk, Serhiy Tymoshenko, Stepan Baran and Archpriest Martyn Volkov come forward in defense of the Orthodox Church and issue protests against the forcible conversion of Orthodox Ukrainians to Roman Catholicism.

The Metropolitan of the Ukrainian Autocephalous Orthodox Church in the years 1921-27, Vasyl Lypkivsky, is arrested near Kiev. He is imprisoned in a labor camp on the Solovky Islands, where he dies shortly thereafter.

Spring 1938 — The Polish government launches a campaign of massive destruction of Ukrainian Orthodox churches in the Kholm and Pidlyashshya regions. These actions on the part of the Polish Catholic government elicit a wave of new protests from Ukrainian members of the Polish Sejm and the international community. In July the Ukrainian representatives in the Sejm — Dr. Stepan Baran, Stepan Skrypnyk, Archpriest Martyn Volkov, Martyn Maslov, Ostap Lutsky, and the Polish representative J. Hofman give speeches in the Polish Sejm and the Senate.

16 July 1938 — The Council of Bishops of the Orthodox Church in Poland issues a memorandum protesting the destruction of Orthodox churches and the persecution of the faithful. The Polish authorities confiscate this declaration, and it is only published abroad. Priests who read this declaration publicly in church are arrested. On August 2, the Ukrainian Catholic Metropolitan Andrey Sheptytsky and Archbishop Ioann Teodorovych in the United States issue similar memoranda and on October 5, Hetman Pavlo Skoropadsky issues a declaration. In the memorandum issued by the Orthodox hierarchy, which is signed by Metropolitan Dionysiy Valedynsky, three archbishops and three bishops, the following is stated:

> The history of all peoples, particularly that of the Poles, provides convincing proof that violence and brutality will never achieve the goals set by people who have lost a feeling for the truth... We have seen the strength of spirit of those thousands of Orthodox faithful in the

The last letter of Metropolitan Vasyl Lypkivsky before his arrest, received by Father Petro Mayevsky in Canada.

Lublin region from whom the Church of the Living God has been taken. However, they themselves have not ceased to be living temples. The groans and bitter tears of an oppressed people, who see with their own eyes the destruction of their churches, these tears flow to us and are ready to drown us. And in sharing the grief of our faithful, we, the archpastors of the Orthodox Church in Poland, today join our sorrow and pain with the pain of our people, which will pass into the history of this ill-fated year of 1938, that, as the jubilee year of our Christianization, should be a happy and joyful one for us. (Martyrology, Vol. 1, p. 565).

In his message Metropolitan Andrey Sheptytsky writes:

> Approximately one hundred churches have been dismantled and torn down. Many have been shut down. Some have been burned by unknown criminals. In the closed churches and chapels Liturgies have been banned, both in them and outside of them. Among the churches destroyed are precious monuments of ancient church architecture. Sacramental objects have been destroyed in many cases. People have been forced, often by violent means, to accept the Catholic faith of the Latin rite... The events in the Kholm region are destroying in the souls of our disunited Orthodox brothers the very idea of the possibility of unity; they show the Ecumenical [Catholic] Church as hostile and dangerous to the Orthodox people. In the eyes of the Orthodox population of Poland, numbering several million, the Apostolic See is represented as co-participant in the act of destruction. A new chasm is opening between the Eastern and Western Churches. (*Martyrology,* Vol. 1, p. 571).

August-October 1938 — The 950th anniversary of the Christianization of Rus'-Ukraine is solemnly observed in the cities and in almost all the villages in the Ukrainian lands under Polish rule. All the commemoration are organized by a special Executive Committee. The largest festivities take place on August 12-14 in Volodymyr-Volynsky in Volynia.

October 1938 — Yezhov, the NKVD Commissar, declares that in the first nine months of this year 238 priests have been sentenced to varying terms of imprisonment and other types of punishment.

As a result of protests organized throughout the world by the Orthodox population on the Ukrainian and Byelorussian lands under Poland, the Polish government halts the destruction of Orthodox churches and allows those people who have been forcibly converted to Roman Catholicism to return to the Orthodox faith. Simultaneously with the change in Polish church policies, a three-year Orthodox Theological Lyceum is opened in Warsaw.

The Polish language is introduced into the Orthodox Church, and Liturgies must be conducted in this language. The first issue of the official organ of the Orthodox Church, *Wiadomosci Metropoliji Prawoslawnej w Polsce,* begins appearing in Warsaw in the Polish language.

The Synod of the Orthodox Church in Romania passes a resolution allowing Liturgies to be conducted in the Orthodox churches in Bukovyna in the Church Slavonic language, instead of exclusively in Romanian.

Metropolitan Vasyl Lypkivsky before his arrest.

In Chernihiv the Preobrazhensky (Transfiguration) Cathedral, built in the 11th century, and the resting-place of Prince Ihor, is converted into a warehouse. The Church of the Holy Trinity is converted into a food store and the church of SS. Borys and Hlib is converted into a warehouse for drying vegetables.

19 November 1938 — By decree of the President of Poland, Ignacy Moscicki, the name of the Orthodox Autocephalous Church in Poland is changed to the Polish Autocephalous Orthodox Church.

15 December 1938 — The Polish government bans the further publication of the Ukrainian Orthodox journal *Church and the People,* which has been appearing since 1935 in Kremenets.

January 1939 — Not a single Orthodox bishop remains on the entire territory of Ukraine. In Russia only four have remained in office: the vicar of the patriarchal throne, the Moscow Metropolitan Sergey Stragorodsky, the Leningrad Metropolitan Aleksey Simansky; Archbishop Sergey Voskresensky; and the Ukrainian archbishop Mykolay Yarushevych. All the others throughout the U.S.S.R. have been executed, imprisoned, or exiled. Those who have not withstood the constant repression have left religious life.

Mykola Karabinevych (1888-1934), UAOC bishop of Uman, executed by the Soviet authorities (left). Maksym Zadvirnyak (1882-1930s), UAOC Bishop of Proskuriv. He died in a Soviet concentration camp.

A monument to Metropolitan Vasyl Lypkivsky at the site of the Memorial Church of St. Andrew the Apostle in South Bound Brook, N.J., by Petro Kapshuchenko, 1983.

15 March 1939 — Hungary occupies a part of Carpathian Ukraine, including the Ukrainian cities of Uzhhorod and Mukachiv. The Mukachiv Orthodox Eparchy headed by Bishop Volodymyr Rayich comes under Hungarian rule.

Spring 1939 — The first Altar Gospel is published in the Ukrainian language in Warsaw.

23 June 1939 — Due to public opinion, the Polish government passes a law regulating the life and activities of the Orthodox Church, and recognizes the confiscation and destruction of churches as an illegal act.

Konstantyn Krotevych (1872-1930s), UAOC Archbishop of Vinnytsya. He died in Soviet imprisonment (left). Hryhoriy Storozhenko (1889-1938), UAOC Bishop of the Kiev oblast. He died in a Soviet prison.

1 September 1939 — Without first declaring war the German armies attack Poland and begin penetrating the country. Two days later Great Britain and France declare war on Germany. World War II begins.

17 September 1939 — As a result of the pact signed between Nazi Germany and Soviet Russia, the Soviet armies occupy Western Ukraine and Western Byelorussia. The four Orthodox eparchies of Volynia, Polissya, Grodno-Novogrudok and Vilnius fall under Soviet occupation, while the Eparchy of Warsaw-Kholm becomes part of the General-Gouvernement under Germany. Metropolitan Dionysiy Valedynsky and Bishop Tymotey Shretter come under German occupation while Archbishops Feodosiy Fedoseyev, Oleksander Inozẹmtsev and Oleksiy Hromadsky and Bishops Polikarp Sikorsky, and Symon Ivanovsky come under Soviet jurisdiction. Bishop Savva Sovyetov flees to England.

During the bombing of Warsaw the Library of the Orthodox Theological Faculty, containing many rare documents and manuscripts, burns down.

5 November 1939 — A Church Council is founded in Kholm, headed by Rev. Illya Levchuk, the administrator of Orthodox parishes in the Kholm and Pidlyashshya regions.

23 November 1939 — Under pressure and at the demand of the German occupation authorities Metropolitan Dionysiy is forced to abdicate his duties as Metropolitan and passes them to the Berlin Archbishop Serafym Lade, who is under the jurisdiction of the Russian Orthodox Church.

December 1939 — Metropolitan Sergey of Moscow Patriarchate appoints Archbishop Mykolay Yarushevych Exarch of the Russian Orthodox Church for Western Ukraine and Byelorussia.

The Germans place Metropolitan Dionysiy under house arrest for one year.

The museum of the Kievan Caves Monastery is plundered. Ancient icons, including that of St. Demetrius of Thessalonika, vestments and gifts of the Ukrainian Hetmans, and precious jewels from the 16th, 17th and 18th centuries are stolen.

Mosaics from the 11th-12th centuries are taken from the Golden-domed Monastery of St. Michael and transported to Moscow.

19 May 1940 — The Cathedral of the Blessed Virgin Mary, built in the 13th century by King Danylo Romanovych and forcibly taken by the Polish Catholics in 1918, is returned to the Orthodox Church in Kholm.

Spring 1940 — Through the efforts of the Ukrainian

Central Committee in the General-Gouvernement, 40 churches are returned to the Ukrainian Orthodox Church after being forcibly confiscated by the Poles between 1918-1938. One hundred and nine Orthodox churches remain in the hands of Polish Catholics.

June 1940 — The Archbishop of Volynia and Kremenets Oleksiy Hromadsky arrives in Moscow and recognizes the juridical authority of the Moscow Patriarchate.

24 September 1940 — Due to the efforts of the Ukrainian community, Metropolitan Dionysiy once again heads the Orthodox Church on the territory of Poland now under German occupation.

30 September 1940 — The Council of Bishops of the Autocephalous Orthodox Church in the General-Gouvernement establishes an Orthodox Metropolitanate, which comprises three eparchies: the Ukrainian-Russian Warsaw-Radom Eparchy and two Ukrainian eparchies — the Kholm-Pidlyashshya and the Cracow-Lemko eparchies. On October 20 the consecration of Archimandrite Ilarion (Prof. Ivan Ohiyenko) takes place. He is consecrated Bishop of Kholm and Pidlyashshya with the title of Archbishop. On February 9, 1941 Archimandrite Palladiy Vydybida-Rudenko is consecrated Archbishop of Cracow and the Lemko region.

March 1941 — The vicar of the Moscow Patriarchate, Metropolitan Sergey Stragorodsky, appoints Archbishop Mykolay Yarushevych Metropolitan of Volynia with a seat in Lutsk. The newly created Eparchy of Kremenets is taken over by Archbishop Oleksiy Hromadsky. The Metropolitan deprives Bishop Polikarp Sikorsky of his throne in Lutsk; he is appointed bishop-vicar of Volodymyr-Volynsky against his wishes.

The Metropolitan divests Oleksander Inozemtsev, Archbishop of Polissya, of his eparchy.

April 1941 — At the demand of the Moscow Metropolitan, Sergey, twelve Orthodox bishops arrive in Moscow from Western Ukraine, Byelorussia, Lithuania, Estonia and Bukovyna, which are under Soviet occupation. They sign an act of subordination to the Moscow Patriarchate. Only Bishop Polikarp Sikorsky of Lutsk and Archbishop Oleksander Inozemtsev of Polissya refuse to go to Moscow to recognize the authority of the Moscow Patriarchate. The chirotony of Archimandrite Panteleymon Rudyk, a Russophile

Polikarp Sikorsky (1875-1953), Metropolitan of the Ukrainian Autocephalous Orthodox Church in Ukraine and in the diaspora (1942-1953).

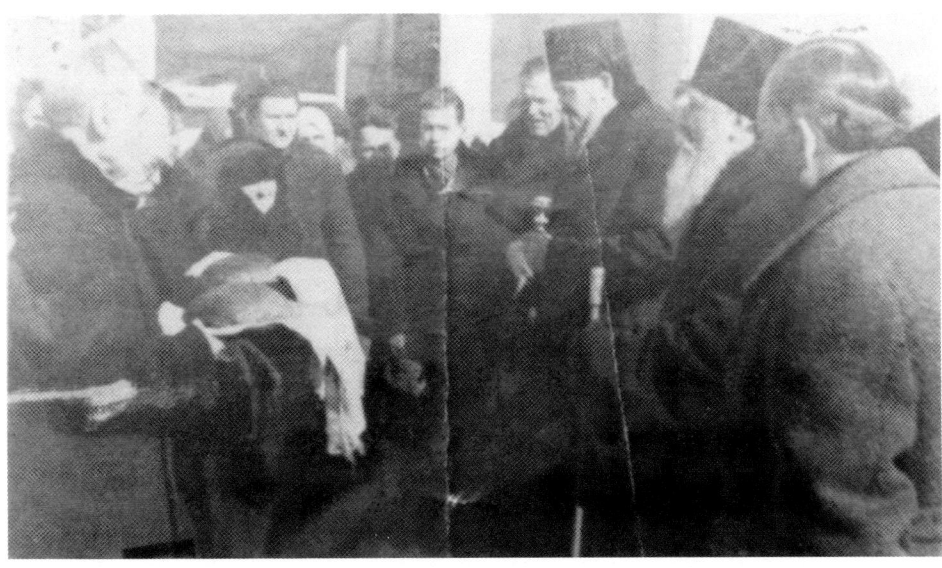

Ukrainian Orthodox faithful greeting the first Bishops of the renewed Ukrainian Autocephalous Orthodox Church, Nikanor Abramovych and Ihor Huba, upon their arrival in Kiev, February 1942.

Participants of the First Synod of the renewed Ukrainian Autocephalous Orthodox Church, in Lutsk (Volynia), 1942. In the first row, on the left are Metropolitan Polikarp Sikorsky and Archbishop Oleksander Inozemtsev.

and the abbot of the Pochayiv Lavra, also takes place in Moscow. He is consecrated Bishop of Lviv.

1940-41 — Arrests of the Orthodox clergy take place in Volynia and Polissya. The Soviet authorities deport many of them, together with their families, to Siberia. Bishop Polikarp organizes aid to prisoners and those deported with their families.

22 June 1941 — Without declaring war, the German armies invade the Soviet Union and immediately begin penetrating the interior of the country. In the next three months they occupy most Ukrainian territories.

18 August 1941 — Archbishop Oleksiy Hromadsky convenes a secret Synod together with three like-minded bishops in the Pochayiv Lavra, without the knowledge of the Ukrainian clergy, which is seeking ways to effect the rebirth of the Ukrainian Orthodox Church. The participants of this Synod of Russian orientation decide to keep the Ukrainian Church under the Germans in canonical dependence of the Moscow Patriarchate; they declare Archbishop Oleksiy Metropolitan. The Synod lays the foundations for the schism within the Orthodox Church on Ukrainian lands during World War II. The Church, headed by Metropolitan Oleksiy, receives the popular title of the "Autonomous Church." Other bishops and clergymen who have survived the Soviet terror re-establish the Ukrainian Autocephalous Orthodox Church in Ukraine as an independent Church.

29 September 1941 — A group of priests and activists of the Ukrainian Autocephalous Orthodox Church who have survived Soviet repressions re-establish the Ukrainian Autocephalous Orthodox Church in Kiev.

10 October 1941 — The first Ukrainian-language Divine Liturgy after a long interval is celebrated in the Cathedral of St. Andrew in Kiev.

3 November 1941 — Mines placed by the Soviets before their retreat from Kiev underneath the main church of the Kievan Caves Monastery — the church of the Dormition of the Blessed Virgin Mary — explode. The whole church is in ruins. Only a bell-tower from the 18th century is preserved.

Autumn 1941 — After the Soviet retreat Metropolitan Feofil Buldovsky, having survived the persecutions, joins the Ukrainian Autocephalous Orthodox Church. The head of the district Church Council of the Kharkiv region is the former head of the All-Ukrainian Orthodox Church Council — Archdeacon Vasyl Potiyenko. The rebirth of church life, in which former priests and activists of the Church play a major role, is launched in various cities and villages of Ukraine.

24 December 1941 — Metropolitan Dionysiy appoints Bishop Polikarp Sikorsky temporary Administrator of the Orthodox Autocephalous Church on Ukrainian lands under German occupation, and bestows the title of Archbishop of Lutsk and Kovel on him.

December 1941 — Bishop Panteleymon Rudyk of the Autonomous Church arrives in Kiev; he has been assigned to subordinate church life to the Moscow Patriarchate.

5 February 1942 — The Patriarchal vicar, Metropolitan Sergey, publishes a declaration in Moscow entitled "To the Orthodox Faithful of Ukraine" directed against Archbishop Polikarp, the Administrator of the Ukrainian Orthodox Church in Ukraine. Moscow radio and Soviet partisans spread the declaration, urging the faithful in Ukraine not to recognize the authority of Archbishop Polikarp.

9-10 February 1942 — A Synod of the Orthodox Church takes place in Pinsk, with the blessing of Metropolitan Dionysiy, during which the Archbishop of Pinsk and Polissya Oleksander Inozemtsev, Archbishop of Lutsk and Kovel Polikarp Sikorsky and Bishop of Berestya Yuriy Korenistov consecrate the new bishops for the Ukrainian Autocephalous Orthodox Church, Archimandrite Nikanor Abramovych and Archimandrite Ihor (archpriest Ivan Huba). They are designated vicars with a seat in Kiev by Archbishop Polikarp. After the consecration of the new bishops, all the hierarchs convene the First Synod of Bishops of the Ukrainian Autocephalous Orthodox Church, which restores the Ukrainian Church's canonical ties and complete unity with the Ecumenical Orthodox Church, of which it is an integral part.

11 February 1942 — The German authorities in Kiev dissolve the All-Ukrainian Orthodox Church Council and ban all its activities; the SS and the police are issued directives "to create as many obstacles as possible to prevent the creation of a general Ukrainian Autocephalous Church under the leadership of a metropolitan."

13 March 1942 — The first Ukrainian bishops of the Ukrainian Autocephalous Orthodox Church Nikanor Abramovych and Ihor Huba arrive in Kiev. On March 15 they conduct a Liturgy in the Cathedral of St. Andrew with a great number of faithful in attendance.

28 March 1942 — Metropolitan Sergey, the vicar of the Moscow Patriarchate, and the Council of Russian bishops publish another declaration in Moscow directed against Archbishop Polikarp and the Ukrainian Autocephalous Orthodox Church.

1 April 1942 — Bishop Nikanor establishes the Supreme Church Leadership in Kiev.

9-17 May 1942 — The chirotony of the following new bishops of the renewed Ukrainian Autocephalous Orthodox Church takes place in the Cathedral of St. Andrew in Kiev without the knowledge or consent of the German occupation authorities: Fotiy Tymoshchuk Bishop of Nizhyn and Vinnytsya; Mykhayil Khoroshy Bishop of Yelysavethrad; Mstyslav Skrypnyk Bishop of Pereyaslav; Sylvester Hayevsky Bishop of Lubny; Hryhoriy Ohiychuk Bishop of Zhytomyr. After the chirotony, the Second Synod of bishops of the Ukrainian Autocephalous Orthodox Church takes place, and elevates Archbishops Polikarp Sikorsky and Oleksander Inozemtsev to the rank of Metropolitans, and Metropolitan Dionysiy Valedynsky to that of vicar of the Kievan Metropolitan throne until the convening of an All-Ukrainian Church Sobor. The Synod appoints Nikanor Abramovych Archbishop of Kiev and Chyhyryn, and Ihor Huba Archbishop of Poltava, and decides to dissociate itself from the activities of the Autonomous Church. Soon after, Archbishops Polikarp and Oleksander, and Metropolitan Dionysiy approve all the resolutions of the Synod.

26 May 1942 — The German occupation authorities ban the consecration of new bishops for the Ukrainian Autocephalous Orthodox Church without their knowledge or consent. Soon after, favoring the Autonomous Church within the jurisdiction of the Moscow Patriarchate, the occupation authorities confiscate the Metropolitan's palace, which is the residence of Archbishop Nikanor, in Kiev and the offices of the Supreme Church Leadership. On September 7 the German General-Commissar of Kiev forbids Archbishop Nikanor to use the title of vice-administrator of the Ukrainian Autocephalous Orthodox Church on Eastern Ukrainian lands, and restricts his activities to Kiev.

Metropolitan Polikarp Sikorsky (left) and Metropolitan Dionysiy Valedynsky, head of the Orthodox Church in Poland.

1 June 1942 — The Reichskommissar of Ukraine Erich Koch issues "Directives on the Legal Relations among the Religious Organizations in Ukraine," guaranteeing religious freedom. At the same time Koch establishes strict control over all churches, faiths, and religious organizations.

22 September 1942 — The German occupation authorities forbid Bishop Mstyslav Skrypnyk to live in Kiev, the Kiev district and the lands west of the Dnieper river.

1942 — During this year the following Ukrainian bishops are consecrated: Hennadiy Shyprykevych, Bishop of Dnipropetrovsk; Volodymyr Malets, Bishop of Cherkasy; Platon Artymyuk, Bishop of Rovno; Vyacheslav Lisytsky, Bishop of Dubno. The Metropolitan of Kharkiv and Poltava, Feofil Buldovsky, becomes the head of the Ukrainian Autocephalous Orthodox Church in Left-Bank Ukraine.

September 1942 — Despite the persecution and the many obstables created by the German occupation authorities, the Ukrainian Autocephalous Orthodox Church spontaneously regenerates itself. In a short period 698 new parishes are established: 298 in the Kiev Eparchy; 150 in the Poltava Eparchy; 150 in the Dnipropetrovsk Eparchy; and 100 in the Mykolayiv-Kirovohrad Eparchy. Hundreds of new priests are ordained for the newly-created parishes; they join church life together with those priests who have survived Soviet persecution and imprisonment.

25 September 1942 — The German occupation authorities arrest Bishop Hryhoriy Ohiychuk in Zhytomyr. He spends eight months in prison.

4-6 October 1942 — Despite the ban issued by the Germans, the Third Synod of Bishops of the Ukrainian Autocephalous Orthodox Church convenes in Lutsk under the leadership of Metropolitan Oleksander Inozemtsev. The Synod decides to unite the Ukrainian Autocephalous and the Autonomous Church.

8 October 1942 — Representatives of the Ukrainian Autocephalous Orthodox Church — Archbishop Nikanor and Bishop Mstyslav — and the head of the Autonomous Church, Metropolitan Oleksiy Hromadsky, sign an Act of Union in the Pochayiv Lavra joining the two Churches into one Ukrainian Autocephalous Orthodox Church. Under pressure from the German occupation authorities and pro-Russian bishops of the Autonomous Church, Metropolitan Oleksiy removes his signature from the Act of Union. Thus the Orthodox Church in Ukraine remains divided until the end of World War II.

October 1942 — The German occupation authorities arrest Bishop Mstyslav Skrypnyk and he spends seven months in prisons in Chernihiv, Pryluky and Kiev.

1942 — Yuriy Teslenko, former Bishop of Bila Tserkva, consecrated in 1921, dies in Kiev. After completing his term in Soviet labor camps he returned to Kiev after the retreat of the Soviet armies.

11 January 1943 — According to the new directives of Reichskommissar Erich Koch, the rights and activities of the Church are further restricted. Metropolitan Polikarp can only function in Volynia and Podilia. It is forbidden to convene synods of bishops and ordain priests for parishes without the knowledge and consent of the German authorities.

4 May 1943 — An Orthodox Theological Seminary opens in Warsaw.

7 May 1943 — Metropolitan Oleksiy Hromadsky of the Autonomous Church is shot to death by insurgents in Volynia and on May 12, Metropolitan Polikarp, the administrator of the Ukrainian Autocephalous Orthodox Church, issues a declaration in which he denounces the murder of Metropolitan Oleksiy.

15-16 July 1943 — In the cities of Volynia the Germans conduct mass arrests of Ukrainian intellectuals and clergy of the Ukrainian Autocephalous Orthodox Church. Many are shot.

4 September 1943 — On the orders of Joseph Stalin, Metropolitan Sergey Stragorodsky is proclaimed Patriarch of Moscow. He has been the vicar of the Moscow Patriarchate since the death of his predecessor, Patriarch Tikhon, in 1925. Stalin, whom the Russian Orthodox Church supports in the war against the Nazis, also agrees to the consecration of new bishops and the renewal of Church activities.

15 October 1943 — In Rovno the Germans execute Rev. Mykola Malyuzhynsky, Metropolitan Polikarp's secretary and Rev. Volodymyr Mysechko, a member of the Church Leadership under Bishop Platon. In Volynia the Germans burn down churches filled with the faithful in the villages of Malyn, Velyka Horodnytsya, Hubkiv, Kortelisy in Polissya and others. In Yugoslavia the Ukrainian Orthodox priests Rev.

Kiev, 1944. After returning to Kiev, the Soviet authorities forced the monks to pose for foreign correspondents in front of the Kievan Monastery of the Caves. In the 1960s, the Monastery was closed, and the monks were persecuted or imprisoned.

Kryzhanivsky and Rev. Moyseyenko, are executed. In the regions of Kholm, Pidlyashshya and the Lemko region, Polish communist partisans wage terror against Ukrainian Orthodox and Catholic priests and their families. Approximately 200 priests are murdered together with their families.

The Council for Russian Orthodox Church Affairs is created in Moscow.

January 1944 — The hierarchs of the Ukrainian Autocephalous Orthodox Church flee Ukrainian lands before the invading Soviet armies and arrive in Warsaw.

February 1944 — The Moscow Patriarchate appoints a Russian, Ioann Sokolov, Metropolitan of Kiev and Exarch of the Russian Orthodox Church in Ukraine.

11 March — 8 April 1944 — In Warsaw the Synod of Bishops of the Ukrainian Autocephalous Orthodox Church convenes under the leadership of Metropolitan Polikarp Sikorsky. The Synod approves a temporary charter for the Ukrainian Church and creates a Holy Synod, the executive body of the Church.

25 April 1944 — Before their departure to the West, the Synod of Bishops of the Ukrainian Autocephalous Orthodox Church in Bratislava, Czechoslovakia, publishes a message to the Ukrainian people. Metropolitan Polikarp Sikorsky, the Administrator of the Ukrainian Autocephalous Orthodox Church, three archbishops and six bishops sign the message.

1944 — The entire hierarchy of the Ukrainian Autocephalous Orthodox Church leaves for the West before the arrival of the Soviet armies. The following hierarchs flee Ukraine: Metropolitan Polikarp Sikorsky, Metropolitan Oleksander Inozemtsev, Archbishop Nikanor Abramovych, Archbishop Ihor Huba, Archbishop Hennadiy Shyprykevych, Archbishop Mykhayil Khoroshy; Bishops Mstyslav Skrypnyk, Hryhoriy Ohiychuk, Platon Artymyuk, Volodymyr Malets, Sylvester Hayevsky and Vyacheslav Lisytsky. Only the Metropolitan of Kharkiv Feofil Buldovsky, seriously ill, remains under Soviet occupation. The following bishops of the Autonomous Church under the jurisdiction of the Moscow Patriarchate remain in Ukraine: Archbishop Symon Ivanovsky, and Bishops Yov Kresovych, Pankratiy Hladkov, Venyamin Novytsky, and Nikodym. Archbishop Antoniy Martsenko and Bishop Ivan Lavrynenko remain in Czechoslovakia and recognize the jurisdiction of the Moscow Patriarchate. The Byelorussian Bishop of Berestya, Yuriy Korenistov remains in Poland. Metropolitan Dionysiy Valedynsky first settles in Vienna, where he is captured by the Soviet authorities who deport him to Warsaw. He lives under house arrest until his death in 1960, despite having been forced to recognize the authority of the Moscow Patriarch.

1945 — The Germans forbid the bishops and priests of the Ukrainian Autocephalous Orthodox Church who have come to Germany to serve the needs of the Orthodox faithful.

After communist rule is established in Poland, the Polish Catholic Church authorities in Kholm forcibly confiscate the Cathedral of the Blessed Virgin Mary from the Ukrainian Orthodox faithful.

1 November 1945 — After the Soviet armies occupy Ukrainian lands, a Theological Seminary is opened in Lutsk. In 1948 a similar seminary is opened in Kiev.

Many priests of the Ukrainian Autocephalous Orthodox Church are deprived of their parishes and are deported to Siberia.

8-10 March 1946 — At a pseudo-synod in Lviv the Ukrainian Catholic Church is forcibly joined to the Russian Orthodox Church.

14-17 March 1946 — In Esslingen, West Germany, the first Synod of bishops of the Ukrainian Autocephalous Orthodox Church since the end of World War II is convened. The types of activities of the

Participants of the first Synod of the Ukrainian Authocephalous Orthodox Church after World War II. In the center is Metropolitan Polikarp Sikorsky. Esslingen, West Germany, 1946.

Nikanor Abramovych (1883-1969), Metropolitan of the Ukrainian Autocephalous Orthodox Church in the diaspora (1953-69), author of theological works.

Church in new conditions are drawn up to guide the work of the bishops.

1946 — After Carpathian Ukraine is ceded to the Ukrainian S.S.R., the Mukachiv-Pryashiv Orthodox Eparchy, which has been under the jurisdiction of the Serbian Patriarchate, is subordinated to the Moscow Patriarch.

The Ukrainian Orthodox Theological Academy is established in Munich for the preparation of spiritual cadres.

The communist government of Poland conducts mass deportations of the Ukrainian population of Kholm, Pidlyashshya and the Lemko region to Western Poland. The authorities destroy or transfer to the Polish Catholic Church both Orthodox and Ukrainian Catholic churches.

13 September 1946 — Metropolitan Polikarp (Sikorsky) and the Holy Synod of the Ukrainian Autocephalous Orthodox Church present a memorandum to the United Nations on the state and the persecution of the Ukrainian Church during the German occupation and the state of the Church and religion under the Soviet regime.

25-26 August 1947 — During a congress in Aschaffenburg, West Germany, a part of the clergy and faithful split off from the Ukrainian Autocephalous Orthodox Church and create the Conciliar (Sobornopravna) Ukrainian Autocephalous Orthodox Church. The head of the Church becomes Bishop Hryhoriy Ohiychuk. Chicago becomes the center of the Church from 1960.

9 February 1948 — Oleksander Inozemtsev, Metropolitan of Pinsk and Polissya, dies in Munich.

Summer 1948 — A German colonist from Volynia, Archbishop Tymofiy Shretter becomes the head of the Orthodox Church in Poland. Besides him, the Russian bishop Mikhail Kedrov and the Byelorussian Yuriy Korenistov belong to the episcopate of the Church.

1949 — The Moscow Patriarchate and the Russian Orthodox Church in the West publish articles in the press attacking the Ukrainian Autocephalous Orthodox Church and Archbishop Mstyslav Skrypnyk in particular.

14 October 1950 — During a congress in New York the American-Ukrainian Orthodox Church and the Ukrainian Orthodox Church are joined to form a Ukrainian Orthodox Church in the U.S. Archbishop Ioann Teodorovych of Philadelphia, heads the Metropolitanate of this Church and Archbishop Mstyslav Skrypnyk becomes his deputy and the councillor of the Metropolitanate.

July 1951 — The Moscow Patriarchate appoints Makariy Oksiyuk, the Archbishop of Lviv and Ternopil, as head of the Orthodox Church in Poland. However, the Ecumenical Patriarch does not recognize him.

23 November 1951 — The Moscow Patriarch Aleksey Simansky signs the act granting autocephaly the Orthodox Church in Czechoslovakia, which is headed by the Russian Metropolitan Elevferiy Vorontsov, Exarch of the Moscow Patriarchate.

1951 — The Metropolitanate of the Ukrainian Orthodox Church in the U.S. transfers its seat to Bound Brook, New Jersey, where a memorial church is built, a museum and archival library are founded and a central Ukrainian cemetery is created.

Archbishop Palladiy Vydybida-Rudenko establishes the Ukrainian Autocephalous Orthodox Church in Exile in the U.S. Since 1954 the Church is under the jurisdiction of the Patriarch of Constantinople.

The Ukrainian Greek-Orthodox Church in Canada becomes a Metropolitanate, and its first metropolitan is Ilarion Ohiyenko.

22 October 1953 — Metropolitan Polikarp Sikorsky dies in Paris; he was the head of the Ukrainian Autocephalous Orthodox Church during World War II and after the war, in the diaspora. His successor is Metropolitan Nikanor Abramovych.

7 October 1954 — Archbishop Mstyslav Skrypnyk of the Ukrainian Orthodox Church in the United States testifies before the House Select Committee (the Kersten Committee) in New York on the destruction of the Ukrainian Autocephalous Orthodox Church by the Soviet regime and the persecution of believers in the U.S.S.R.

Archbishop Antoniy Martsenko, one of the leaders of the Autonomous Church during the War, perishes in Tula under mysterious circumstances. Having come under Soviet occupation, Antoniy was deported to Tula and deprived of the right to return to Ukraine.

1956 — The Synod of the Ukrainian Autocephalous Orthodox Church is convened in Karlsruhe, West Germany, under the leadership of Metropolitan Nikanor Abramovych.

1959 — In Ukraine the last remaining monasteries are closed. Young people are forbidden to attend Liturgies under threat of punishment.

15 March 1960 — Metropolitan Dionysiy Valedynsky, the former head of the Orthodox Church in Poland, dies in Warsaw.

28 April — 1 May 1960 — A conference of three Ukrainian Orthodox metropolitanates — the Ukrainian Greek-Orthodox Church in Canada, the Ukrainian Orthodox Church in the U.S. and the Ukrainian Autocephalous Orthodox Church in the diaspora — is convened in Winnipeg by Metropolitan Ilarion Ohiyenko. The conference asserts that one Ukrainian Orthodox Church, consisting of three administratively independent metropolitanates which constitute one spiritual unity, exists in the Ukrainian settlements in the diaspora.

1961 — A campaign of persecution is launched against the monks of the Pochayiv Lavra. A number of monks are imprisoned in psychiatric hospitals for their religious convictions and their refusal to cooperate with the Soviet authorities. The militia burns down St. Nicholas Church, located at the Lavra cemetery.

In Irkutsk the trial of Archbishop Veniamin Novytsky is held. During World War II he acknowledged the jurisdiction of the Autonomous Church.

In the Odessa oblast 68 church communities are liquidated and 75 churches are converted into clubs and libraries.

During the years 1958-62, in the Dnipropetrovsk oblast 140 parishes out of 180 are closed and 180 churches in the Volynia oblast are shut down. Approximately half the functioning churches in Ukraine have been closed.

8 March 1962 — The KGB arrests Archimandrite Sevastiyan of the Pochayiv Lavra, and confiscates many materials and documents.

1962 — In Kiev the Theological Seminary is closed and the publication of the only Orthodox journal in the Ukrainian language, *The Orthodox Herald,* is stopped.

20 May 1962 — Metropolitan Tymofiy Shretter of Warsaw and All Poland dies in Warsaw and Archbishop Yuriy Korenistov becomes the new Metropolitan.

11 July 1963 — The Soviet secret police conduct a pogrom of the residents of Pochayiv for their friendly relations with pilgrims visiting the Pochayiv Lavra and for extending aid to them. The militia smashes the windows of private homes, breaks down doors, confiscates religious books and beats the inhabitants up.

Pilgrims deprived of lodging, sleeping in their clothes in a church of the Pochayiv Lavra, 1960s.

Ilarion Ohiyenko (1882-1972), Minister of Education in the government of the Ukrainian People's Republic in 1918, Metropolitan of the Ukrainian Greek Orthodox Church in Canada (1952-72), author of works on church history, canon law, philology and Slavistics.

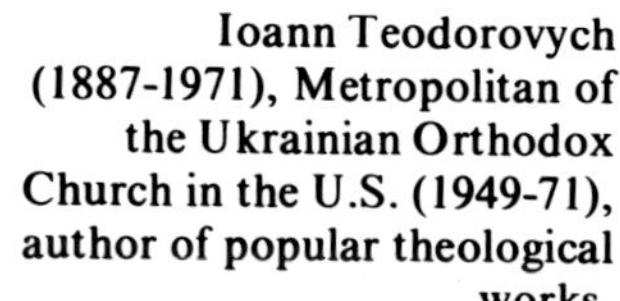

Ioann Teodorovych (1887-1971), Metropolitan of the Ukrainian Orthodox Church in the U.S. (1949-71), author of popular theological works.

9-12 July 1963 — On the eve and the feastday of St. Yov, Soviet police surround Pochayiv in order to stop pilgrims from visiting.

1963 — Once again the Kievan Caves Monastery is converted into a state museum. Monks had resided there during World War II through 1961.

30 March 1964 — The Moscow Patriarchate appoints a Russian, Ioasaf Lelyukhin as the new Metropolitan of Kiev and Exarch of the Russian Orthodox Church in Ukraine.

В Організацію Об'єднаних
Націй
від жителів м. Почаїв і
богомольців

Скарга

Ми жителі м. Почаїв і приїзні богомольці,
любимо Почаївську Лавру і бажаємо завжди
в ній молитися, але зустрічаємо зі сторо[ни]
влади багато приниженнь і насильства.
Всі знаємо, що Радянський Союз бореться
за права людини, но це тільки на словах,
а насправді вони грубо і безбожно попирають
і нарушають права віруючої людини.
Напр.: в Почаївській Лаврі вони відняли
всю землю і даже огород з садом, який входи[в]
в охоронну зону архітектурного пам'ятника
відрізали біля стін Лаври і передали в розпо[ря]
дження лікарні і міської Ради, які знищили в
це Будинок Лаври, бувший архієрейський
будинок, який знаходиться на території

An appeal of the monks of the Pochayiv Lavra to the United Nations, 1963.

23-25 October 1964 — The Fifth Synod of the Ukrainian Orthodox Church in the U.S. convenes in Chester, Pennsylvania, under the leadership of Metropolitan Ioann Teodorovych.

20 December 1964 — The Soviet police stage another pogrom of the Pochayiv Lavra and the residents of the city.

1964 — In the post-war years 29 out of a total of 38 active monasteries in Ukraine have been closed. In the Poltava oblast, only 52 churches out of a total of 340 in 1958 remain open.

April 1965 — The Theological Seminary in Lutsk is closed.

15-16 July 1965 — The Soviet police organize another pogrom against pilgrims visiting Pochayiv.

10 October 1965 — A church erected in memory of the millions of victims of the great famine in Ukraine during 1932-33 is blessed at St. Andrew the Apostle Orthodox Center in Bound Brook, New Jersey.

1965 — The Council for Russian Orthodox Church Affairs and the Council for Religious Cults are joined into the Council for Religious Affairs at the Council of Ministers of the U.S.S.R. In every Soviet republic there are officials responsible for religious affairs attached to the Council of Ministers.

In the space of a few years, hundreds of parishes are closed in Ukraine. In the Odessa Eparchy 210 out of 400 parishes are shut down; in the Volynia Eparchy — 180; in the Zhytomyr Eparchy — 68; in the Poltava Eparchy — 43; in the Cherkasy Eparchy — 40; in the Kiev Eparchy — 17 out of 25; and in Odessa 14 out of 23 parishes are shut down.

1966 — For the first time the Moscow Patriarchate appoints a Ukrainian, Filaret Denysenko, as Exarch of the Russian Orthodox Church in Ukraine, and Metropolitan.

12 April 1968 — Metropolitan Ioann Teodorovych of the Ukrainian Orthodox Church in the U.S. and the Council of Bishops send a memorandum to the International Human Rights Conference in Teheran in

The Church of St. Michael the Archangel, built in Ghent, Belgium in 1987 to commemorate the Millennium of Christianity in Ukraine.

"Christ the Teacher," a mosaic by Petro Kholodny in the Memorial Church of St. Andrew the Apostle in South Bound Brook, New Jersey.

Monument at the site of the baptism of Ukraine in 988 in Kiev, destroyed by the Soviets in the 1930s.

A memorial to the victims of the artificial famine in Ukraine in 1932-1933 orchestrated by the Soviets, founded by Metropolitan Mstyslav Skrypnyk of the Ukrainian Autocephalous Orthodox Church.

Ukrainian Orthodox Church in Washington, built in 1987 to commemorate the victims of Chornobyl.

Mykhayil Khoroshy (1883-1975), Metropolitan of the Ukrainian Greek Orthodox Church in Canada (1972-75), composer and author of theological works (left). Andrey Metyuk (1898-1983), Metropolitan of the Ukrainian Greek Orthodox Church in Canada (1975-83), author of theological works.

connection with the persecution of the Church and religion in the Soviet Ukraine and the U.S.S.R. Archbishop Mstyslav Skrypnyk, the spokesman for the Ukrainian Orthodox Church, takes part in the conference.

May 1968 — As a result of protests on the part of Ukrainian and international scholars, writers and believers, the Kiev Mohyla Academy is saved from destruction. It is converted into a museum.

1969 — Metropolitan Nikanor Abramovych of the Ukrainian Autocephalous Orthodox Church dies in West Germany. Archbishop Mstyslav Skrypnyk becomes the new Metropolitan of the UAOC.

1970 — Only one church in Chernihiv remains open.

1971 — Metropolitan Ioann Teodorovych of the Ukrainian Orthodox Church in the U.S. dies in Philadelphia. Archbishop Mstyslav Skrypnyk takes his place.

Mstyslav Skrypnyk, Archbishop of the Ukrainian Orthodox Church in the U.S. (left), and archpriest Bohdan Zhelikhivsky (right) with the Ecumenical Patriarch Athenagoras in Istanbul.

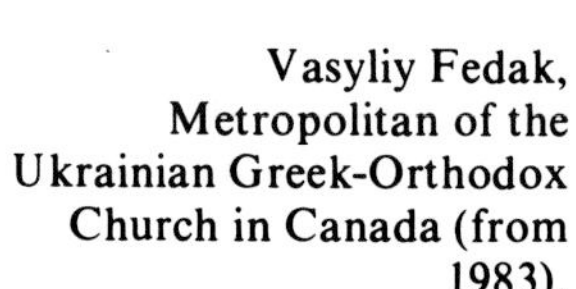

Vasyliy Fedak, Metropolitan of the Ukrainian Greek-Orthodox Church in Canada (from 1983).

December 1971 — The Conciliar (Sobornopravna) Ukrainian Autocephalous Orthodox Church becomes a Metropolitanate.

1972 — Metropolitan Ilarion Ohienko of the Ukrainian Greek-Orthodox Church dies in Winnipeg. Archbishop Mykhayil Khoroshy of Toronto becomes the new Metropolitan.

1975 — Metropolitan Mykhayil Khoroshy of the Ukrainian Greek-Orthodox Church in Canada dies in Toronto. Archbishop Andriy Metyuk of Western Canada becomes the new Metropolitan.

7 September 1975 — St. Sophia's Theological Seminary opens in the Ukrainian Orthodox center in Bound Brook, New Jersey.

26 October 1977 — Bishop Teodosiy Dykun of Poltava and Kremenchuk appeals to Leonid Brezhnev in connection with the persecutions of his Eparchy. For this appeal he is transferred by the Moscow Patriarch to the Astrakhan Eparchy in the Asian part of the U.S.S.R.

Autumn 1977 — In a letter to Mstyslav Skrypnyk,

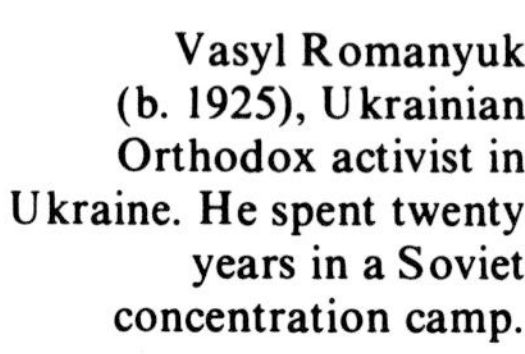

Vasyl Romanyuk (b. 1925), Ukrainian Orthodox activist in Ukraine. He spent twenty years in a Soviet concentration camp.

Ivan Vlasovsky, Ukrainian Orthodox scholar, church leader, author of works on Ukrainian church history.

the Metropolitan of the Ukrainian Orthodox Church in the U.S., Rev. Vasyl Romanyuk, a Ukrainian political prisoner, states that he considers himself a member of the Ukrainian Autocephalous Orthodox Church and asks for help in his defense.

November 1980 — The KGB and militia surround the building of the Ukrainian Exarch, Metropolitan Filaret, in Kiev and conduct a thorough search of the building.

13-15 March 1981 — A second conference of the three Ukrainian Orthodox metropolitanates — the Ukrainian Greek-Orthodox Church in Canada, the Ukrainian Orthodox Church in the U.S. and the Ukrainian Autocephalous Orthodox Church in the diaspora — takes place in Winnipeg.

August 1981 — The Soviet police banish Hegumen Allipiy and a number of monks from the Pochayiv Lavra.

1983 — Metropolitan Andrey Metyuk of the Ukrainian Greek-Orthodox Church in Canada dies in Winnipeg. Bishop Vasyliy Fedak of Central Canada becomes the new Metropolitan.

4 June 1986 — The Orthodox activist Pavlo Protsenko is arrested in Kiev. During a search of his house an appeal demanding the opening of the Kievan Caves Monastery on the occasion of the millennium of the Christianization of Kievan Rus' is confiscated together with the manuscript *The Catacomb Church in Ukraine* and many religious books.

13-16 August 1987 — The Ukrainian Greek-Orthodox Church begins celebrating the millennium of the Christianization of Rus'-Ukraine in Canada; a large gathering of the faithful is held and the blessing of a monument to St. Volodymyr the Great takes place in Saskatoon.

16 August 1987 — Celebrations marking the millennium of the Christianization of Rus'-Ukraine begin in the U.S. with a large gathering of the faithful at the Orthodox center in Bound Brook, New Jersey and the consecration of a monument to St. Olha, Princess of Kievan Rus'.

Mstyslav Skrypnyk (b. 1898), Metropolitan of the Ukrainian Autocephalous Orthodox Church in the diaspora (from 1969), Metropolitan of the Ukrainian Orthodox Church in the U.S. (from 1971), organizer of Ukrainian churches, cultural, and educational life.

January 1988 — Oles Shevchenko, a former Ukrainian political prisoner, and a group of his associates send an appeal to Mikhail Gorbachev requesting the restoration of the Ukrainian Autocephalous Orthodox Church on the occasion of the millennium of the Christianization of Rus'-Ukraine.

Archbishop Teodosiy Dykun of Astrakhan, in the Asian part of the U.S.S.R., sends an appeal to Mikhail Gorbachev to open the Kievan Caves Monastery on the occasion of the millennium of the Christianization of Rus'-Ukraine.

The Ukrainian Catholic Church

1917 — After a lengthy struggle on the part of Ukrainian believers, the Austrian government divides the Metropolitanate of Bukovyna into Ukrainian and Romanian vicariates with their own consistories. The first bishop of the Ukrainian vicariate is Tyt Tyminsky, while Ipolit Vorobkevych is assigned to the Romanian vicariate.

Pope Benedict XV founds the Congregation for Eastern Churches in Rome, renews the Ruthenian College and lays the foundation for the creation of an Eastern Institute.

March 1917 — As a result of a democratic revolution in Russia, the Tsarist government falls and Alexander Kerensky establishes a Provisional Government in St. Petersburg.

At the request of the Orthodox bishop Nikon, Kerensky's Provisional Government releases Metropolitan Andrey Sheptytsky from prison. On his way home the Metropolitan stops in St. Petersburg, where he convenes a Synod of Russian Catholics and appoints Leonid Fedorov Exarch in Russia. In Kiev the Metropolitan founds a Ukrainian Catholic parish and on September 10, 1917 he returns to Lviv.

17 March 1917 — The Ukrainian Central Council is set up in Kiev and is headed by the historian Prof. Mykhaylo Hrushevsky. The Council aims to establish independence for Ukraine.

7 November 1917 — The "October" Revolution organized by the Bolsheviks erupts in the former Russian Empire.

20 November 1917 — The Ukrainian Central Council proclaims the Third Universal, which establishes the Ukrainian National Republic.

December 1917 — The first parish priest in the Ukrainian Catholic church in Kiev is Rev. Mykola Shchepanyuk.

21 February 1918 — The hierarchy of the Ukrainian Catholic Church issues an epistle to the clergy and the faithful in Galicia and Bukovyna.

1 November 1918 — Ukrainians take power by arms in the Western Ukrainian lands of Galicia and Bukovyna, and proclaim independence.

1919 — The Polish armies, aided by the Entente countries, occupy all of Western Ukraine.

After the occupation of Eastern Galicia, Kholm, Volynia and the Lemko regions, the Polish authorities arrest and deport to concentration camps more than 200 Ukrainian Catholic and Orthodox priests.

25 May 1919 — Count Mykhaylo Tyshkevych becomes the first ambassador of the Ukrainian National Republic to the Apostolic See in Rome. After his arrival in Rome he has an audience with Pope Benedict XV. On June 16 the Apostolic See recognizes the Ukrainian National Republic.

26 August 1919 — The hierarchy of the Ukrainian Catholic Church gathered in Peremyshl issues an epistle in which the following is stated:

> It seems as though the entire nation is fated for annihilation. Many murders and robberies have gone unpunished [on Ukrainian lands]. Five priests have been murdered, while hundreds have been imprisoned or deported. Many churches and the most important monasteries have been plundered. Many parishes have been deprived of their pastors. (*Velyky,* Vol. 9, p. 128.)

1920 — Celibacy is introduced in the Eparchy of Stanyslaviv; it is introduced in the Eparchy of Peremyshl in 1925.

September 1920 — Through the intervention of the Apostolic Nuncio Achille Ratti, the Theological Seminary in Lviv, which was closed during the war years, is re-opened. The rector of the seminary under the leadership of the Basilians is Rev. Teodosiy Tyt Halushchynsky.

1920-22 — As a result of a long-term internal religious struggle in Transcarpathia, more than 100,000 Ukrainian Catholics convert to Orthodoxy.

March 1921 — After a long interval the Ruthenian Theological College is re-opened in Rome.

18 March 1921 — As a result of a treaty signed by Poland and Soviet Russia, the Ukrainian lands of Volynia and Galicia fall under Polish rule.

1921-22 — Metropolitan Andrey Sheptytsky of Galicia visits Ukrainian settlements in North and South America.

1923 — The Theological Scientific Society (Bohoslovske Naukove Tovarystvo) is established in Lviv and comprises four sections: Biblical, philosophical-dogmatic, historical-juridical, and pastoral-theological. The Society publishes a scholarly journal entitled *Theology* (Bohosloviye) and *Works.* It lasts until 1939 and is re-established after World War II in Rome in 1963.

1924 — *The Annals of the Basilian Order,* devoted to religious-historical questions in Eastern Europe, begin publication in Zhovkva (present-day Nesterov).

8 May 1924 — By a decision of Pope Pius XI the Ukrainian Catholic exarchate in the U.S. is divided into two exarchates: an exarchate in Philadephia for Ukrainian emigres from Galicia and Bukovyna, and an exarchate in Homestead, near Pittsburgh, for Ukrainians from Transcarpathia, Hungarians and Yugoslavs.

10 February 1925 — The Apostolic See and Poland sign a Concordat which normalizes the life, organization and rights of the three Catholic rites in Poland: the Polish Latin rite, the Ukrainian Eastern rite and the Armenian rite. According to the Concordat, five Latin-rite Church provinces, one Ukrainian and one Armenian are established in Poland. Christian education in the Eastern rite in schools is safeguarded for Ukrainian youth as well as the preparation of clerics in the minor and major seminaries.

29 November — 7 December 1927 — The first post-war conference of Ukrainian Catholic hierarchs convenes in Lviv under the aegis of Metropolitan Andrey Sheptytsky. The hierarchs gather from all Ukrainian lands under Poland and Czechoslovakia, as well as from Canada and the United States. The participants of the conference discuss matters of ritual, the publication of religious books, establishing canon law, organizational methods and methods for servicing the spiritual needs of the faithful, and the expansion of the Apostolate of SS. Cyril and Methodius. Similar conferences are convened in Rome on 21-29 October 1929, and in 1932.

1928 — Metropolitan Andrey Sheptytsky founds a Theological Academy, modeled as a university, in Lviv. It has two faculties, theological and philosophical. The first rector of the Academy is Rev. Yosyf Slipyj. Ten seminars are offered at the Academy: dogma, Biblical studies, law, the history of the Union, homiletics, catechism, the history of Ukraine, art, sociology, and the Church Slavonic language. During the years 1928-39, 2750 students attend the Academy, which publishes 22 volumes of its *Works.*

7 July 1929 — As a result of the Concordat signed between the Apostolic See and Rumania, the Ukrainian Catholic Vicariate of Bukovyna is established at the Rumanian Catholic Episcopate of the Eastern rite; it is headed by Rev. Mykhaylo Simovych, who has 17 parishes under his jurisdiction.

1930 — On the initiative and under the leadership of Bishop Ivan Buchko, a branch of Catholic Action — the Ukrainian Catholic organization called "The Rock" — is established in Lviv. Shortly thereafter the Catholic Action spreads in Canada through the creation of the Brotherhood of Ukrainian Catholics in 1932, the Ukrainian Catholic Youth in 1938, and the League of Ukrainian Catholic Women in 1943. In 1933 the organization Ukrainian Catholic Youth is established in the U.S.; in 1962 the organization is renamed the League of Ukrainian Catholics. The Catholic Action spreads among Ukrainian Catholics in Brazil in 1940 and in European countries in 1949.

1930-37 — With the aim of conducting missionary work among the Orthodox population, Polish Catholic bishops hold six conferences in Pinsk. Ukrainian Catholic scholars, particularly the professors of the Theological Academy in Lviv, take part in the conferences. The first conference takes place in April 1930.

1931 — Metropolitan Andrey Sheptytsky appoints Bishop Mykola Charnetsky the head of the Ukrainian Catholic mission in Volynia.

The Ukrainian Minor Theological Seminary of St. Volodymyr the Great is founded in Stamford, Ct., U.S.

1932 — The Ukrainian order of the Salesian Fathers is founded.

December 1932 — The Pontificio Seminario di San Giosafat in Urbe — a new building of the St. Josaphat Ukrainian College, is opened in Rome. Metropolitan Andrey Sheptytsky is the founder of the new building.

The "Eagles" Ukrainian Catholic Youth Association is founded in Lviv.

6-7 May 1933 — At the initiative of Metropolitan Andrey Sheptytsky a large gathering convenes in Lviv on the occasion of the 1900th anniversary of Christ's death. The gathering is called "Ukrainian Youth for Christ," and more than 100,000 young people from Galicia take part in it. Accompanied by the sound of bells ringing from all the Ukrainian churches in Lviv a solemn Liturgy is conducted in St. George's Cathedral, where Bishop Ivan Buchko gives a homily to the gathering. The following day a march before Metropolitan Andrey Sheptytsky takes place. At the conclusion of the gathering the participants take an oath: "Christ the Redeemer! On the 1900th anniversary of Your Death and Resurection, we pledge you eternal loyalty. So help us, Christ."

10 February 1934 — The congregation of Eastern Churches establishes the Lemko Apostolic Administration comprising 121 parishes with a total of 127,000 faithful; former Lemko parishes were part of the Metropolitanate of Galicia.

1934 — In Kiev the first Ukrainian Catholic Church, built in 1917 and designed by Ivan Levynsky, is destroyed.

3 August 1936 — Metropolitan Andrei Sheptytsky issues a pastoral letter condemning communism.

22-25 December 1936 — On the 300th anniversary of the death of Metropolitan Yosyf Velyamin Rutsky, the first Ukrainian Uniate Congress is held under the auspices of the Theological Academy headed by Rev. Yosyf Slipyj. The aim of the congress is to verify and establish the views of Ukrainian Catholics with respect to the Union, to define the situation of Ukrainian Catholics vis-a-vis the Orthodox East, to draw up methods for future work among the Orthodox, and to awaken interest in the matter of the Union. In point 4 of the conclusions and resolutions, the Congress puts forward the need to create a Ukrainian Patriarchate.

19 March 1937 — Pope Pius XI publishes an encyclical on Godless communism. In the encyclical it is stated:

> Communism deprives a person of his freedom, which is simultaneously the spiritual principle of his behavior in life; it also deprives a person of his dignity, and in the moral sphere — of all restraint. [Communism] is a world

Ukrainian Catholic Church in Kiev, destroyed by the Soviets in 1936.

perception that is full of lies and deceit, which opposes the truths of God's revelation and of man's wisdom; it is a world perception which destroys the social order, ruining its foundation... it contradicts and deprives a person of his rights, dignity and freedom. Communism could not and cannot attain its goals on the purely economic plane, for there are morals even in the sphere of economics and a certain moral feeling of responsibility, and a materialistic system alone, the communism, cannot provide this...

The Pope states the following about the peoples of the U.S.S.R.:

> We have no intention of making general criticisms of the peoples of the Soviet Republics; on the contrary: we embrace them with a warm fatherly love. We know very well that many of them have experienced the burden of unjust rule of people who are completely uninterested in the good of these people, and many of them have been misled by deceitful promises. First and foremost we criticize the very system and its creators and advocates, who have chosen these peoples for their terrain of operations, on which they might put into practice the long-devised system and expand it from there all over the world. (*Velyky,* Vol. 9, pp. 203-5.)

On May 14, 1937 the Pope issues a second encyclical, condemning the falsity of pagan, totalitarian Nazism.

1938 — Due to the cruel religious persecutions in Ukraine under Russian domination, the 950th anniversary of the Ukrainian Church is not commemorated. At that time, Ukrainian Orthodox Bishops and thousands of priests and faithful were in Soviet concentration camps.

12 July 1938 — On the 950th anniversary of the Christianization of Rus'-Ukraine the Ukrainian Catholic hierarchy of the Galician Metropolitanate issues a declaration in which the following is stated:

> If the sign of the cross is shining over [our] ruin, which has lasted for centuries, then this disease [ruin] is not intended for death, but so that the glory of God can appear in it or through it. Therefore, despite the horrible circumstances in which our people find themselves, shattered and scattered in all the corners of the world, in inviting them today to our festive celebrations of the 950th anniversary of the Christianization of our ancestors in St. Volodymyr's time, we do this not in sad hopelessness for tomorrow's day, but on the contrary: with the strong conviction that our people will be able, despite the circumstances in which God's Providence has placed us, to answer God's call in the history of mankind... May the Lord give us first and foremost that which brings us closer to unity, to unity of spirit, unity of peace, unity of love, to that unity which all, despite the varying confessions and membership in various churches, must consider the greatest good in the Christian faith, the heritage of St. Volodymyr. (*Velyky,* Vol. 9, pp. 13-15.)

The message of the hierarchy begins the jubilee celebrations and festivities of Ukrainian Catholics in all Ukrainian settlements outside the U.S.S.R. The Committee for the "Feast of Christian Ukraine" organizes and directs all the celebrations. It prepares a special Liturgy entitled "A Light from Heaven," materials for the celebrations called "God is With Us," and stories about the early Christians in Ukraine called *The First Rays.* Memorial crosses are erected in the villages and cities during the time of celebrations.

October 1938 — The Ukrainian Catholic priest Avhustyn Voloshyn becomes the prime minister of Carpathian Ukraine.

14 March 1939 — The independence of Carpathian Ukraine is proclaimed in Khust, and one day later the Sejm elects Rev. Avhustyn Voloshyn, its first president. After heavy fighting against overwhelming forces, Carpathian Ukraine is occupied by Hungary.

15 May 1939 — Ukrainian Catholics conclude the celebrations marking the 950th anniversary of the Christianization of Rus'-Ukraine with a separate celebration devoted to the sons of St. Volodymyr, the martyrs SS. Borys and Hlib.

21 May 1939 — The celebrations of the 950th anniversary of the Christianization of Rus'-Ukraine take place in St. Peter's Basilica in Rome with a Solemn Liturgy served by bishops and with the blessing of Pope Pius XII.

1 September 1939 — Germany attacks Poland and on September 17, as a result of a pact signed by the Soviet Union and Nazi Germany, Soviet armies occupy Western Byelorussia and the Ukrainian lands of Galicia, Volynia and Polissya. The Kholm and Lemko regions are occupied by Germany. The Pryashiv region becomes part of the Slovak state. The administrator of the Ukrainian Catholics in the Lemko region is Rev. Oleksander Malynovsky, while Bishop Hryhoriy Lakota directs the affairs of part of the Peremyshl Eparchy.

15 September 1939 — During the bombing of Lviv

the church and the building housing the Theological Seminary, together with the library and archives of the Theological Scientific Society, are destroyed.

9 October 1939 — Metropolitan Andrey Sheptytsky appoints four exarchs for large sections of the U.S.S.R. Bishop Mykola Charnetsky heads the Exarchate of Volynia, Polissya, Pidlyashshya and Kholm; Rev. Antoniy Nyemancewicz heads the Exarchate of Byelorussia; Rev. Klyment Sheptytsky heads the Exarchate of Russia and Siberia; and Archbishop Yosyf Slipyj heads the Exarchate of Ukraine.

26 October 1939 — Volynia, Polissya and Western Ukraine are annexed to the Ukrainian S.S.R. The Orthodox Church on these lands is subordinated to the Moscow Patriarchate. All the church wealth is confiscated. The teaching of religion, and all religious rituals and crosses are removed from schools.

Autumn 1939 — The Soviet occupation authorities close the Theological Academy in Western Ukraine and the theological seminaries in Lviv, Peremyshl, and Stanyslaviv. All monastic orders and religious institutions are banned. Catholic publishing houses are shut down and their equipment confiscated. In the "Biblos" printing house in Lviv all printed books and journals are destroyed.

22 December 1939 — Together with Bishop Nykyta Budka, Bishop Mykolay Charnetsky and the canons of the Metropolitan Council, Metropolitan Andrey Sheptytsky consecrates the rector of the Theological Academy, Rev. Yosyf Slipyj, as his co-adjutor with the right of succession.

1939 — The Soviet authorities murder the brother of Metropolitan Sheptytsky, Count Lev Sheptytsky and his wife.

1 April 1940 — Metropolitan Andrey Sheptytsky publishes a pastoral letter concerning atheists. He writes the following about them:

> Their throats are an open grave. They use their language for betrayal. The venom of vipers is beneath their lips. Ruination and death lie on their path. (*Martyrology*, Vol. 2, p. 61.)

19 April — 30 August 1940 — An Archepiscopal Synod takes place in St. George's Cathedral in Lviv; bishops and 80 priests take part in it. The Synod discusses the methods of the Church's work under the new Soviet conditions. After the conclusion of the Synod 14 of its participants are arrested.

30 May 1940 — The Secretary of State of the Apostolic See A. Mallone informs Metropolitan Andrey Sheptytsky about Pope Pius XII's decision to forbid the Metropolitan from naming exarchs for the territory of Russia, a right given to him by Pope Pius X in 1907.

2 July 1940 — The Ukrainian lands of Bukovyna and a part of Bessarabia are annexed to the Ukrainian S.S.R. as a result of a Soviet military advance on Rumania.

Andrey Sheptytsky (1865-1944), Ukrainian Catholic Metropolitan of Galicia (1900-1944), organizer of church, educational, cultural and scholarly life, founder of Ukrainian Catholic organizations and publications, author of theological works, benefactor of youth, declared Blessed by the Catholic Church. He was imprisoned by the Russian government in 1914-1917.

18-19 September 1940 — A secret Synod of exarchs for Soviet lands takes place in Lviv; it plans mission work in the Soviet Union and passes 10 resolutions in this matter.

1940 — The Soviet occupation authorities forbid priests to visit the sick in hospitals. Metropolitan Andrey Sheptytsky protests against this ban. In his protest petition it is stated:

> In Soviet hospitals the dying are treated worse than people sentenced to death in European prisons where, in general, they do not reject the granting of a last wish.

He directs his priests to visit the sick dressed in secular clothing:

> Bring the sick Holy Communion secretly and administer it in such a way that even the closest neighbor of the sick person will not notice anything. (*Martyrology*, Vol. 2, p. 63.)

1941 — Representatives of the Soviet regime make the first attempts to persuade Rev. Havryil Kostelnyk to lead a campaign against the Union with Rome. When he refuses, the NKVD arrests and executes his son, 17-year-old Bohdan.

24 January 1941 — All four exarchs — Bishop Mykolay Charnetsky, Rev. Archimandrite Klyment Sheptytsky, Rev. Antoniy Nyemancewicz and Archbishop Yosyf Slipyj write a long secret letter to the Apostolic See in which they explain the need to establish exarchates for the Soviet lands.

16 August 1941 — Metropolitan Andrey Sheptytsky notifies the Apostolic See after the Soviet retreat from Western Ukraine that during the second occupation, the Soviet authorities have deported 250,000 people to Siberia, while 6000 people have been found murdered in prisons during their retreat. On November 7 the Metropolitan informs the Apostolic See that during the occupation the Soviet authorities murdered 32 Ukrainian Catholic priests and deported 33 to Siberia.

November 1941 — Pope Pius XII changes his original decision and approves the four exarchs named by Metropolitan Andrey Sheptytsky for the territories of the U.S.S.R.

30 December 1941 — Metropolitan Andrey Sheptytsky writes a separate letter to the Ukrainian Orthodox bishops, appealing to them for religious unity. He addresses the Orthodox intelligentsia with a similar letter on March 3, 1942. He promises that the entire Ukrainian Catholic hierarchy will subordinate itself to the Kievan Metropolitan in union with Rome.

9-15 June 1942 — Under the leadership of Metropolitan Andrey Sheptytsky, the Second Synod of Exarchs convenes in Lviv and passes a number of decrees concerning missionary activities on those territories occupied by the Germans.

1942 — In Kiev the Ukrainian Catholic parish liquidated by the Soviet authorities in 1934 is renewed.

1943 — Metropolitan Andrey Sheptytsky protests against the policies of Nazi Germany in Ukraine many times. He lodges a protest with Himmler against the murder of Jews, and directs his faithful to hide them in St. George's Cathedral and in monasteries and nunneries.

Summer 1944 — Soviet armies occupy all of Western Ukraine for the second time. On July 27 they capture Lviv and on October 27 they claim Uzhhorod. As a result of this occupation the entire Galician Metropolitanate — the Archeparchy of Lviv, and the eparchies of Peremyshl, Stanyslaviv, and Mukachiv, the Apostolic administration of the Lemko region and Volynia, fall under Soviet rule. The entire Lemko region and a part of the Peremyshl region fall under Polish communist rule as a result of the new borders established between the U.S.S.R. and Poland. The Pryashiv region falls under Czechoslovakia.

24 September 1944 — Rev. Teodor Romzha is consecrated Bishop of Uzhhorod-Mukachiv in Carpathian Ukraine.

1 November 1944 — The Galician Metropolitan Andrey Sheptytsky dies in Lviv. On November 5 the Metropolitan's funeral takes place. The new Metropolitan, Yosyf Slipyj, serves the funeral Liturgy, together with Bishops Yosyf Kotsylovsky, Nykyta Budka, Mykola Charnetsky, Hryhoriy Lakota, the Protohegumen of the Basilian Order, Rev. Hradyuk, the Protohegumen of the Redemptorists, Rev. De Voght, the hegumen of the Studite Order, Rev. Klyment Sheptytsky, and many priests. The funeral procession, including thousands of mourners, passes through the streets of Lviv and returns to St. George's Cathedral, where the remains of the Metropolitan are laid to rest.

By way of succession Yosyf Slipyj becomes the Metropolitan of the Ukrainian Catholic Church.

November 1944 — The commander of the 4th Ukrainian Front, the Soviet general I. Yu. Petrov and the political commissar, General Mekhlis, demand that the bishop of Uzhhorod-Mukachiv, Teodor Romzha, break relations with the Apostolic See and convert to Russian Orthodoxy.

Representatives of the Russian Orthodox Church forcibly take over 15 Ukrainian Catholic churches in Transcarpathia and disperse the priests. Church books are destroyed and burned in the churches of Uzhhorod-Tsehelnya, Ploskiv and Radvantsi. The Soviet colonel Tyulpanov directs the liquidation of the Ukrainian Catholic Church in Carpathian Ukraine. In December, churches in 29 villages are forcibly taken away from Ukrainian Catholics.

December 1944 — A delegation from the Ukrainian Catholic Church consisting of Rev. Havryil Kostelnyk, Archimandrite Klyment Sheptytsky, Rev. Hryhoriy Budzinsky and Rev. Ivan Kotiv, on instructions from Metropolitan Yosyf Slipyj, visits the Soviet government in Moscow and expresses willingness for co-existence with the Soviet regime. The demand of the Soviet government that the Ukrainian Catholic Church actively participate in the struggle against the Ukrainian Insurgent Army is rejected by the delegation.

In the Lemko and Peremyshl regions, so-called "peasant battalions" created by Soviet and Polish Communists are actively carrying out the murder of Ukrainian Catholic priests, and the Ukrainian intelligentsia and the destruction of Ukrainian churches.

The Soviet newpapers *Pravda* and *Izvestia,* and Radio Moscow, launch an indiscriminate campaign against the Apostolic See and the Ukrainian Catholic Church and its hierarchs, unjustifiably accusing them of cooperating with the Nazis.

January 1945 — Patriarch Aleksey of Moscow appeals to the Ukrainian Catholic hierarchy to break relations with the Vatican and subordinate itself to the Russian Orthodox Church.

2 February 1945 — A Sobor of the Russian Orthodox Church in Moscow criticizes the Apostolic See and the entire Catholic Church.

3 March 1945 — In the village of Skopiv in the Lemko region Polish communist partisans murder the Ukrainian Catholic priests Rev. S. Konkolyovsky, Rev. I. Demyanchuk and five members of his family, and 82 parishoners in the village.

24 March 1945 — The Soviet Peoples' Council in Carpathian Ukraine publishes a decree stating that Ukrainian Catholic priests, their widows and orphaned children are hereby deprived of all social insurance whatsoever and the estates of the Ukrainian Catholic Church are confiscated, and transferred to the Russian Orthodox Church.

March 1945 — Communist partisans murder Rev. Lenets, the parish priest in the village of Pavlokoma in the Lemko region, and more than 300 Ukrainian Catholics. In the village of Vilshana in the Peremyshl region the partisans murder the wife and two daughters of Rev. Stepan Kopystyansky, and seven believers.

March-April 1945 — Bishop Teodor Romzha visits a number of villages in Carpathian Ukraine where he appeals to the people to adhere to their faith and to persevere under the difficult new conditions.

11 April 1945 — In Western Ukraine five Ukrainian Catholic hierarchs are arrested: Metropolitan Yosyf Slipyj; Nykyta Budka, the vicar of the Lviv Metropolitanate; Mykola Charnetsky, the Apostolic Administrator in Volynia; Hryhoriy Khomyshyn, Bishop of Stanyslaviv; and Ivan Lyatyshevsky, the auxiliary Bishop of Stanyslaviv. These arrests take place after the hierarchs refuse to convert to Russian Orthodoxy. The arrests of more than 500 Ukrainian Catholic priests occur simultaneously.

April 1945 — At the beginning of the month Patriarch Aleksey of Moscow dispatches Makariy Oksiyuk, as the Russian Bishop of Lviv and Ternopil.

Mykola Charnetsky (1884-1959), Ukrainian Catholic Bishop, Apostolic Administrator of Volynia, Polissya and Pidlyashshya (from 1939). He spent ten years in Soviet concentration camps and exile (left). Nykyta Budka (1877-1949), Ukrainian Catholic Bishop in Canada (1912-28). He died in a Soviet concentration camp.

Yosyf Slipyj, Metropolitan of the Ukrainian Catholic Church, in Siberia in the 1950s.

The Soviet occupation authorities create the "Initiative Group for the Reunification of the Greek (Eastern-rite) Catholic Church with the Orthodox Church" in Lviv. Its members include Rev. Havryil Kostelnyk (Lviv), Rev. Mykhaylo Melnyk (Drohobych) and Rev. Antoniy Pelvetsky (Stanyslaviv). The authorities proclaim this group the administrator of the Ukrainian Catholic Church on the lands of Western Ukraine; the group is responsible for arranging all juridical matters concerning the submission of the Ukrainian Catholic Church to the Russian Orthodox Church. The group must prepare lists of names of all those priests who have refused to submit to the group and send them to the plenipotentiary for the Russian Orthodox Church of the Council of Peoples' Commissars of the Ukrainian S.S.R.

Spring 1945 — In response to uninterrupted repressions directed against Ukrainian Catholics in Carpathian Ukraine, a large number of Orthodox parishes convert to the Ukrainian Catholic Church. New parishes are established in 18 villages.

4 May 1945 — The leaders of the Armenian Catholic Archdiocese in Lviv are arrested: Rev. Dionysiy Kayetanovych, the Council Vicar; Rev. Viktor Kvapinsky; Rev. Kazymyr Romoskano; Rev. Stanislav Dobryta, and all the Armenian priests in the city.

21 May 1945 — Rev. Avhustyn Voloshyn is arrested in Prague, Czechoslovakia; he is an eminent church activist from Carpathian Ukraine and its president in 1939.

25-26 May 1945 — All the prominent activists of the Ukrainian Catholic Church are arrested in Western Ukraine.

28 May 1945 — The "Initiative Group" is forced by the NKVD to appeal to the Council of Peoples' Commissars and to Joseph Stalin with a request to join the Ukrainian Catholic Church with the Russian Orthodox Church.

1 July 1945 — Three hundred Ukrainian Catholic priests write a letter of protest to the head of the Council of Peoples' Commissars, Vyacheslav Molotov, concerning the illegality of the activities of the "Initi-

Rev. Avhustyn Voloshyn (1874-1945), President of Carpathian Ukraine (1939), organizer of church, educational and cultural life, executed by the Russians in Moscow in 1945.

ative Group" and the persecution of the Ukrainian Catholic Church, its priests and faithful.

11 July 1945 — Rev. Avhustyn Voloshyn, the eminent church activist in Transcarpathia and the former president of Carpathian Ukraine, is tortured to death in Lefortovo Prison in Moscow.

July 1945 — In Uzhhorod Bishop Teodor Romzha secretly consecrates Rev. Oleksander Khira bishop.

Summer-Autumn 1945 — Searches lasting many days take place in St. George's Cathedral in Lviv and the bishop's palace in Stanyslaviv. During the searches archival materials and church documents are confiscated.

21 September 1945 — In Peremyshl the Ukrainian Catholic bishop, Yosafat Kotsylovsky, is arrested by the Polish communist authorities, and the Minor and Major Theological Seminaries are closed.

For their refusal to convert to Russian Orthodoxy more than 500 priests from the Lviv oblast and from the Ternopil oblast are deported to Siberia. At the same time almost all the members of the bishop's consistories and the lecturers of the theological seminaries of Lviv, Stanyslaviv and Peremyshl and a large number of monks and nuns are arrested.

Ivan Lyatyshevsky (1879-1957), Ukrainian Catholic Auxiliary Bishop of Stanyslaviv. He spent ten years in Soviet concentration camps (left). Hryhoriy Khomyshyn (1867-1947), Ukrainian Catholic Bishop of Stanyslaviv, murdered in a Soviet prison.

September 1945 — The Polish communist government begins a mass persecution campaign against Ukrainian Catholics in the Lemko and Peremyshl regions. Frequent searches of the bishop's palace in Peremyshl and the Basilian monastery are conducted.

1946 — Pope Pius XII names Bishop Ivan Buchko Archbishop and Apostolic Administrator for Ukrainian Catholics in Western Europe.

8 February 1946 — A Ukrainian Catholic Theological Seminary is opened in Hirshberg, West Germany. Its first rector is Rev. Vasyl Laba.

24-25 February 1946 — Metropolitan Ioan Sokolov of the Russian Orthodox Church secretly consecrates Rev. Antoniy Pelvetsky a bishop of the Russian Orthodox Church and Rev. Mykhaylo Melnyk the Russian Orthodox bishop of Drohobych and Sambir.

1 March 1946 — The Procurator's Office of the Ukrainian S.S.R. issues an indictment against the hierarchs of the Ukrainian Catholic Church, and in the summer of 1946 they are sentenced to long terms of imprisonment: Metropolitan Yosyf Slipyj is sentenced to 8 years' imprisonment; Bishop Nykyta Budka to 8 years; Rev. Petro Verhun, the Apostolic Administrator for Germany to 8 years; Bishop Ivan Lyatyshevsky to 10 years; and Bishop Mykola Charnetsky to 6 years' imprisonment and 5 years' exile. Bishop Hryhoriy Khomyshyn is tortured to death during interrogations in the Kiev prison.

8-10 March 1946 — The illegal pseudo-synod takes place in St. George's Cathedral in Lviv. Neither the Metropolitan of the Ukrainian Catholic Church nor a single bishop takes part in this pseudo-synod. According to official sources, 216 priests (out of an approximate total of 2950 priests on the lands of Western Ukraine) and 19 lay "delegates" take part in the "synod." The "synod" "voids" the Union of 1596 and subordinates the Ukrainian Catholic Church to the Russian Orthodox Church. The leaders of the "synod" are Rev. Hryhoriy Kostelnyk, Bishop Mykhaylo Melnyk and Bishop Antoniy Pelvetsky. At the conclusion of the "synod" a "solemn service" takes place in which the representatives of the Russian Orthodox Church, Metropolitan Ioann (Kiev), and Bishop Makariy (Lviv) participate. Telegrams containing greetings are sent to Patriarch Aleksey of Moscow, the Ecumenical Patriarch of Constantinople, Joseph Stalin, and the head of the Council of Ministers of the Ukrainian S.S.R.; "greetings" are also sent to the faithful and the clergy of Western Ukraine. The "synod" establishes the illegal status of the Ukrainian Catholic Church in the U.S.S.R.

According to the *Journal of the Moscow Patriarchate,* during 1945-46 1,111 Ukrainian Catholic priests submit to Russian Orthodoxy. Among them are 532 from the Lviv Eparchy, 203 from the Peremyshl Eparchy, 277 from the Stanyslaviv Eparchy,

Teodor Romzha (1911-1947), Ukrainian Catholic Bishop of Mukachiv, poisoned by the Soviets.

Yosafat Kotsylovsky (1876-1947), Ukrainian Catholic Bishop of Peremyshl. He died in a Soviet concentration camp.

and 99 others. At the same time approximately 1600 priests are imprisoned and several hundred go underground.

7 June 1946 — The Polish government arrests Bishop Yosafat Kotsylovsky of Peremyshl and extradites him to the Soviet Union. After his arrest a mob of Polish fanatics plunders the bishop's palace for three days.

9 June 1946 — The Polish government arrests Bishop Hryhoriy Lakota, Auxiliary Bishop of Peremyshl, and extradites him to the Soviet Union.

22 October 1946 — Bishop Nestor, appointed for the Uzhhorod-Mukachiv Eparchy by Patriarch Aleksey of Moscow, arrives in Carpathian Ukraine.

Autumn 1946 — In Peremyshl, which is under Polish communist rule, the bishop's palace has been converted into a museum, Roman Catholic Carmelites occupy the Cathedral, the army occupies the building formerly housing the Theological Seminary, and nuns of the Polish Josephite order occupy the Basilian monastery and church. At the same time the bishop's library and archives are plundered and transferred to libraries of the Universities of Warsaw, Cracow and Lublin. All the documents of the bishop's consistory are destroyed. In many villages in the Lemko region Polish Catholics, with the help of the authorities, confiscate Ukrainian Catholic churches.

The Soviet secret police organize so-called small regional councils of priests and faithful in all the cities and villages of Western Ukraine. During these councils the Apostolic See and the Union of 1596 are attacked by the communists.

17 January 1947 — Hryhoriy Khomyshyn, Bishop of Stanyslaviv, is tortured to death in a Kiev prison during interrogations.

26 January 1947 — The Polish communist authorities liquidate the Ukrainian Catholic Chapter clergy (Capitula) of Peremyshl.

24 March 1947 — The Soviet police surround the Basilian Monastery in Mukachiv, takes it by force and transfer it to the Russian Orthodox Church. The protohegumen of the Order of Basilians in Transcarpathia, Rev. Antoniy Mondyk, hegumen Ivan Satmariy and 28 monks are transported to a small monastery in Imstychiv and later deported to Siberia.

1 April 1947 — The Polish Cardinal Hlond names Rev. Vasyl Hrynyk the vicar-general of the Ukrainian Greek-Catholics in the Peremyshl Eparchy.

11 May 1947 — The festive consecration of Rev. Vasyl Hopko as Auxiliary Bishop takes place in Pryashiv.

Spring 1947 — The Polish communist authorities arrest and extradite to the Soviet Union the last five Ukrainian priests in Peremyshl.

On the Feast of the Dormition of the Blessed Virgin Mary the Soviet authorities attempt to proclaim the reunification of the Ukrainian Catholic Church in Transcarpathia with the Russian Orthodox Church. On Monk's Hill (Chernecha Hora) near Mukachiv some 80,000 faithful gather and are joined by representatives of the Russian Orthodox Church. But neighboring churches begin tolling an alarm, the thousands of believers leave Monk's Hill, and the act of reunification never takes place. Afterwards, mass arrests of Ukrainian Catholics take place in Transcarpathia.

Klyment Sheptytsky (1869-1958), Ukrainian Catholic Archimandrite of the Studite Order. He died in a Soviet prison (left). Hryhoriy Lakota (1883-1950), Ukrainian Catholic Auxiliary Bishop of Peremyshl. He died in a Soviet concentration camp.

Pavlo Goydych (1888-1960), Ukrainian Catholic Bishop of Pryashiv. He died in a Czechoslovak communist prison (left). Vasyl Hopko (1904-1976), Ukrainian Catholic Auxiliary Bishop in Pryashiv. He spent fourteen years in Czechoslovak communist prisons.

After the visit of Patriarch Aleksey to Rumania, a campaign of persecution of Ukrainian Catholics begins there.

Summer 1947 — The Soviet authorities place Bishop Teodor Romzha of Uzhhorod-Mukachiv under house arrest.

27 October 1947 — On the Mukachiv-Uzhhorod highway Soviet soldiers attack Bishop Teodor Romzha and beat him unconscious.

1 November 1947 — Bishop Teodor Romzha of Uzhhorod-Mukachiv dies in Mukachiv after being poisoned by the Soviets.

17 November 1947 — Bishop Yosafat Kotsylovsky of Peremyshl dies in Soviet imprisonment.

1947 — The Basilian Order is banned in Transcarpathia. The Basilian Order is also banned in other communist countries: in Rumania in 1948; in Czechoslovakia in 1949-50; in Hungary in 1951.

February 1948 — After the communist coup in Czechoslovakia the new government refuses to register the Greek Catholic Church due to pressure exerted by the Soviet government. The Church is outlawed.

3 March 1948 — By a decision of the Apostolic See, the Ukrainian Catholic Church in Canada is divided into three Exarchates: Winnipeg, Edmonton and Toronto.

Summer 1948 — At a meeting of government representatives from Czechoslovakia and the U.S.S.R., the Soviet minister of Foreign Affairs, Andrey Vishinsky, proposes that the Ukrainian Catholic Church in Czechoslovakia be liquidated. It is decided that Archbishop Yelevferiy Vorontsov of the Russian Orthodox Church direct the liquidation of the Church from the Soviet side.

August 1948 — The arrests of Ukrainian Catholic priests, monks and nuns originally from Western Ukraine begin taking place in Czechoslovakia. Some clerics are imprisoned in local labor camps, and some nuns are extradited to Poland.

21 September 1948 — The former head of the "Initiative Group," Rev. Havryil Kostelnyk, whose activities led to the subordination of the Ukrainian Catholic Church to the Russian Orthodox Church, is killed in Lviv. His murder, although attributed to the Soviet secret police, becomes the pretext for mass arrests of Ukrainian priests and nationalists. A few years later, another member of the initiative group, Mykhaylo Melnyk, who had become a bishop of the Russian Orthodox Church, is poisoned en route from Moscow to Lviv.

1 October 1948 — The communist government of Romania convenes a congress of Eastern-rite Catholic priests and by means of threats, blackmail and force persuades them to sign a declaration voiding the Union of 1700 and approving reunification with the Rumanian Orthodox Church.

13-18 December 1948 — The first trial of Ukrainian Catholic priests in Czechoslovakia opens in Prague; the defendants are Rev. P. Huchko and Rev. S. Sabol,

Ukrainian faithful and a priest in a Soviet labor camp in the Krasnoyarsk region in the 1950s.

the latter being absent from the trial. They are accused of having contacts with the Organization of Ukrainian Nationalists and the Ukrainian Insurgent Army.

1948 — Vasyl Velychkovsky, the hegumen of the Redemptorist monastery in Ternopil, is sentenced to death; in 1949 the sentence is commuted to 10 years' imprisonment.

January 1949 — The "Committee for the Conversion of Greek [Eastern-rite] Catholics to Orthodoxy" is established in Pryashiv.

10 February 1949 — Bishop Oleksander Khira is arrested in Mukachiv, Transcarpathia, and sentenced to 25 years' imprisonment.

16 February 1949 — The Soviet police forcibly occupy the bishop's residence in Uzhhorod and transfer it to Archbishop Makariy Oksiyuk of the Russian Orthodox Church. All Ukrainian Catholic churches are closed and priests are forbidden to fulfill their spiritual duties. Rev. Iryney Kondratovych heads the regime's movement for liquidating the Ukrainian Catholic Church in Transcarpathia. At the same time many priests and intellectuals are arrested.

28 August 1949 — Rev. Iryney Kondratovych, the head of the pro-government group of priests advocating the conversion of Ukrainian Catholics to Russian Orthodoxy, Archbishop Makariy of the Russian Orthodox Church, and two Catholic priests purportedly void the Union of Uzhhorod of 1646 and proclaim the "reunification" of the Ukrainian Catholic Church of Transcarpathia with the Russian Orthodox Church. Eventually, 35 priests are forced to submit to Russian Orthodoxy.

6 October 1949 — Bishop Nykyta Budka dies in a Soviet labor camp.

1949 — In Transcarpathia, 18 priests are tortured to death during interrogations; 147 priests are deported to Siberia, and 40 of them perish in labor camps.

28 April 1950 — A so-called "Peace Congress" is convened in Pryashiv, obligating every village to send a parish priest to the congress with church banners. Anyone who refuses is branded a "war agitator" and arrested. In the hall of the Black Eagle under the protection of the Czechoslovak communist gendarmerie, the "delegates" are greeted by groups of communist youth shouting slogans as "The Orthodox faith is a guarantee of peace." Shortly after, the "peace congress" is transformed into a "Congress of Greek [Eastern-rite] Catholic clergy and lay people," and is forced to proclaim the nullification of the Union of Uzhhorod of 1646, the breaking of relations with the Apostolic See, and the subordination of the Eastern-rite Catholic Church to the Moscow Patriarch, Aleksey. When Bishop Pavlo Goydych refuses to transfer the cathedral and bishop's residence to the Russian Orthodox Church, a communist mob breaks down the gates of the cathedral and occupies it, while the militia arrests the Bishop. The Russian bishops Yelevferiy Vorontsov and Aleksey Dekhteryev enter the cathedral and conduct a "thanksgiving service" as a sign of victory over the Uniates. That same day the Auxiliary Bishop, Vasyl Hopko, is arrested.

Bishop Yosafat Kotsylovsky a few weeks before his death in a Soviet concentration camp (left). Oleksander Khira (1897-1983), bishop of the Ukrainian Catacomb Catholic Church. He spent seven years in a Soviet concentration camp and died in exile in Khazakhstan.

27 May 1950 — The Czechoslovak government publishes a decree on the liquidation of the Eastern-rite Catholic Church (Ukrainian and Slovak) and the transfer of all its estates to the Russian Orthodox Church. Eighty priests who have refused to convert to Russian Orthodoxy are imprisoned in labor camps and 200 priests, together with their families, are exiled to forced labor in the Czech part of the republic.

12 November 1950 — The Auxiliary bishop Hryhoriy Lakota of Peremyshl dies in a Soviet labor camp.

11 January 1951 — Bishop Pavlo Goydych is sentenced to death in Bratislava; his sentence is later commuted to life imprisonment.

10 March 1951 — The Ukrainian Catholic Eparchy of Saskatoon is established in Canada.

Archimandrite Klymentiy Sheptytsky in a Soviet prison (a drawing by an unknown political prisoner) (left). Bishop Mykola Charnetsky in a Soviet concentration camp in the 1950s.

Metropolitan Yosyf Slipyj in Siberia in the early 1960s.

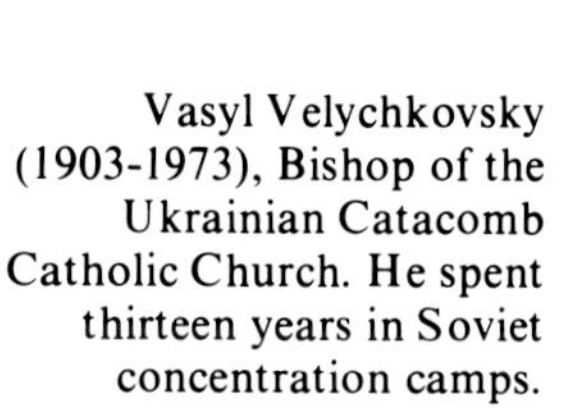

Vasyl Velychkovsky (1903-1973), Bishop of the Ukrainian Catacomb Catholic Church. He spent thirteen years in Soviet concentration camps.

29 June 1952 — The St. Josaphat Ukrainian Minor Seminary is opened in Loury, France. In 1956 it is transferred to Castelgandolfo, and in 1959 to new buildings near Rome. The Salesian Fathers direct the Seminary. In 1963 the Papal title is bestowed on the Seminary.

15 December 1952 — Pope Pius XII issues an encyclical in defense of imprisoned hierarchs in the communist countries of Eastern Europe. In the encyclical it is stated:

> At the present time We are stricken in a most particular way; We turn to another nation, one that is most dear to Us, that is to the people of Ukraine, among whom a large number of Christians look with the greatest grief and limitless love toward Rome and considers the Apostolic See the center of the Christian faith, since this originates from Christ's teachings, as the infallible teacher of truth... In particular we wish to mention those bishops of the Eastern rite who were the first to suffer so many sacrifices, suffering and humiliation in the defense of the faith: they have been transported to the capital city of Kiev where they have been tried and sentenced to various kinds of punishment — in that capital city of Kiev, which, as we have said, once shone with Christian teachings and was the center of the expansion of Christianity throughout all the neighboring lands. (*Martyrology*, Vol. 2, pp. 743-44.)

1953 — Metropolitan Yosyf Slipyj is sentenced to an indefinite term of exile after completing his sentence.

20 December 1954 — An apparition of the Virgin Mary is reported in the village of Seredne, Ivano-Frankivsk oblast. This and subsequent apparitions, as well as the Virgin's reported message that victims of Communism would be spared in the coming catastrophe, gives rise to many pilgrimages and to the sect of the "Penitents," who refuse all cooperation or contact with the Soviet authorities.

1954 — The Ukrainian Christian Movement, headed by Prof. Volodymyr Yaniv, is founded in France. Shortly afterwards, the movement spreads to other countries of Ukrainian settlement.

20 July 1956 — The Ukrainian Catholic Exarchate of Stamford, Conn., U.S.A., is established.

3 November 1956 — The first Metropolitanate of the Ukrainian Catholic Church in Canada is established in Winnipeg. The Apostolic See appoints Maksym Hermanyuk as the first Metropolitan.

The Apostolic See bestows the status of eparchy on Ukrainian Catholic exarchates in Toronto and Edmonton.

1956-57 — As the result of an amnesty following Stalin's death some priests are released from imprisonment and exile.

February 1957 — On the occasion of the installation of Metropolitan Maksym Hermanyuk, the First Conference of Ukrainian Catholic bishops from all Ukrainian settlements in the Western world convenes in Winnipeg.

27 November 1957 — Auxiliary Bishop Ivan Lyatyshevsky dies in Stanyslaviv (now Ivano-Frankivsk). The bishop had returned there after completing a ten-year sentence in Soviet labor camps.

1957 — Metropolitan Yosyf Slipyj is sentenced to an additional 7 years' imprisonment.

12 August 1958 — The first Ukrainian Catholic Metropolitanate with a seat in Philadelphia is established in the U.S. Pope Pius XII names Bishop Konstantyn Bohachevsky the first Metropolitan. At the same time the Stamford exarchate is granted the status of an eparchy.

2-3 November 1958 — On the occasion of the installation of Metropolitan Konstantyn Bohachevsky in Philadelphia, the Second Conference of Ukrainian Catholic bishops takes place.

2 April 1959 — The Apostolic Administrator for Volynia, Pidlyashshya and Polissya, Bishop Mykola Charnetsky, dies in Lviv, where he returned after serving 6 years' imprisonment and 5 years' exile.

12-14 October 1959 — The Third Conference of Ukrainian Catholic bishops takes place in Rome. During the conference it is decided to use the official title — "Ukrainian Catholic Church." Succeeding conferences take place in the following years: the Fourth in Munich in 1961; the Fifth does not take place; during the Sixth conference in Winnipeg on 2-3

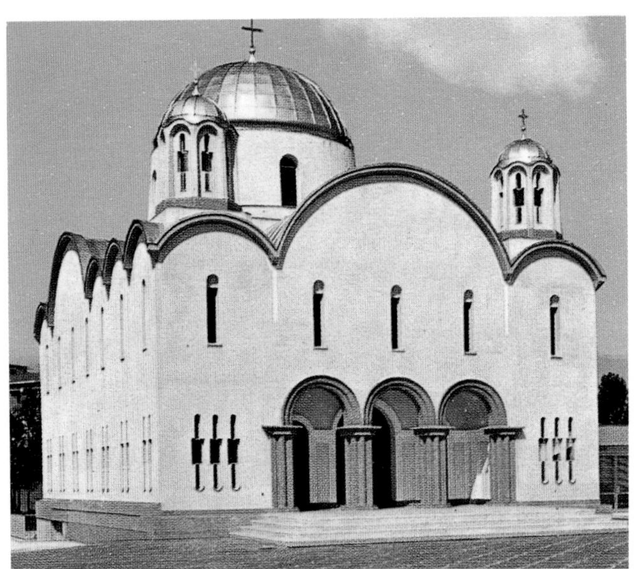

St. Sophia Cathedral in Rome, founded by Patriarch Yosyf Slipyj.

"On the Mount of Olives," by Mykhaylo Dmytrenko, 1984. Polychrome, St. George's Church, New York.

St. Nicholas Ukrainian Catholic Cathedral in Chicago, built in 1913-15 according to plans by I. G. Steinbach.

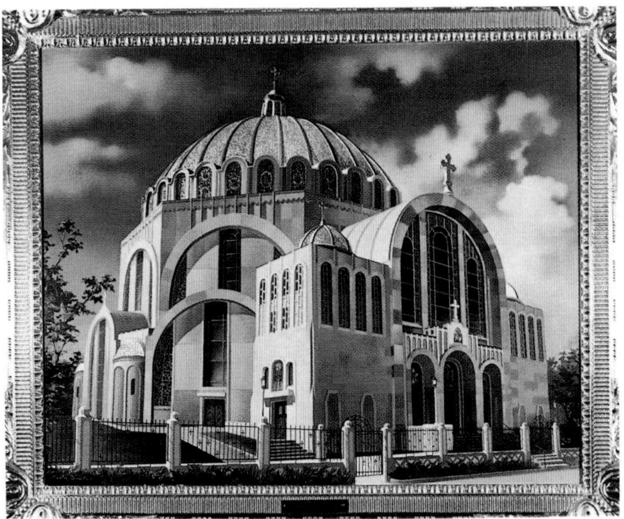

Cathedral of the Immaculate Conception in Philadelphia, seat of the metropolitan of the Ukrainian Catholic Church in the U.S.

Konstantyn Bohachevsky (1884-1961), Metropolitan of the Ukrainian Catholic Church in the U.S. (1958-61), organizer of Ukrainian cultural and educational life.

Ambrose Senyshyn (1903-1976), Metropolitan of the Ukrainian Catholic Church in the U.S. (1961-76).

July 1962, the statute and the following name for the conference are approved: "The Conference of Catholic Bishops of the Ukrainian Rite." The Apostolic delegate, Monsignor Sebastiano Baggio, takes part in a Conference of Ukrainian bishops for the first time. Metropolitan Maksym Hermanyuk is elected the permanent head of the Conference. According to the charter the Conference is not a Synod; it does not take place with the Pope's blessing, and its decisions do not have the force of law.

1959 — The former hegumen Vasyl Velychkovsky is secretly nominated Bishop of the Ukrainian Catacomb Catholic Church. In 1963 he is secretly consecrated bishop of Lutsk by Metropolitan Yosyf Slipyj.

Spring 1960 — Three catacomb convents are discovered in Lviv: the Sister's Servants of Mary Immaculate, St. Vincent's and the Basilian nunneries. Almost all the nuns work as nurses, but live according to their vows.

17 July 1960 — Pavlo Goydych, Bishop of Pryashiv, dies in Leopoldovo prison in Czechoslovakia.

14 August 1961 — The Ukrainian Catholic Eparchy of Chicago is founded.

1961 — 528 formerly Ukrainian Catholic churches in the jurisdiction of the Russian Orthodox Church remain open in the Lviv oblast; 672 have been destroyed, closed or converted to other uses.

1962 — According to a new Polish law concerning the preservation of historical monuments, some Ukrainian churches are saved from destruction.

11 October — 8 December 1962 — The first session of the Second Vatican Council takes place in Rome; Ukrainian bishops are among the participants.

27 January 1963 — After 18 years' imprisonment and exile Metropolitan Yosyf Slipyj is released thanks to the insistent efforts of Pope John XXIII and U.S. President John F. Kennedy and journalist Norman Cousins. On the day of his departure to the West, the Metropolitan consecrates the former hegumen of the Basilian monastery in Ternopil, Vasyl Velychkovsky, bishop of the Ukrainian Catholic Church in the catacombs.

28 September 1963 — The Seventh Conference of Ukrainian Catholic Bishops takes place in Rome with the participation of Metropolitan Yosyf Slipyj and 16 bishops. By a decision taken by all the bishops, the Conference is changed to a Synod, and all decisions on Church matters adopted by two-thirds of the bishops' votes become binding. Other Synods take place on September 13-14 and November 5-19, 1964. During the Synod held on September 13-30 and November 7-28, 1965, the question of the beatification of martyred Ukrainian bishops and the participation of Ukrainian Orthodox bishops in the capacity of observers at the Second Vatican Council are discussed.

11 October 1963 — At the Second Vatican Council Metropolitan Yosyf Slipyj makes a motion to elevate the Kievan-Galician Metropolitanate to the status of Patriarchate. The motion was accepted by all the Ukrainian Catholic bishops.

October 1963 — The Apostolic See declares Metropolitan Yosyf Slipyj the Archbishop Major of the Ukrainian Catholic Church.

28 November 1963 — Metropolitan Yosyf Slipyj establishes the Ukrainian Catholic University of St. Clement in Rome.

23 December 1963 — The Apostolic See appoints Metropolitan Yosyf Slipyj a member of the Sacred Congregation for the Eastern Churches.

1963 — The Ukrainian Press Bureau, which publishes *News from Rome,* is established in Rome.

21 November 1964 — The Second Vatican Council issues a decree on the Eastern Catholic Churches, granting them greater rights of autonomy. The publication of this decree is the inspiration for the creation of the Ukrainian patriarchal movement, which aims to establish a patriarchate for the Ukrainian Catholic Church.

21 January 1965 — Pope Paul VI names Metro-

Ivan Buchko (1891-1974), Archbishop, Apostolic Administrator for Ukrainian Catholics in Western Europe (1945-74), organizer of Ukrainian church, cultural and scholarly life.

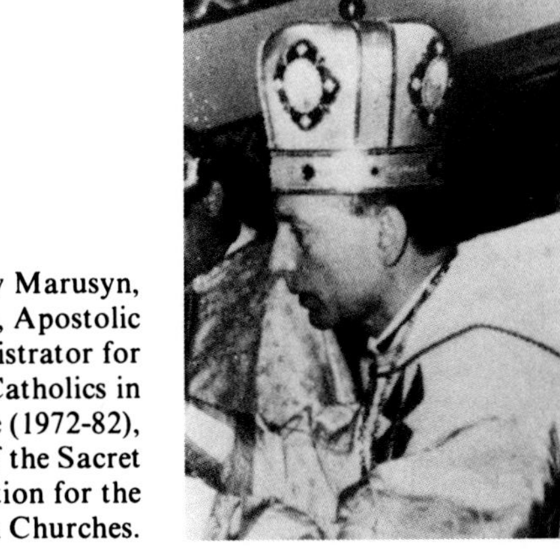

Myroslav Marusyn, Archbishop, Apostolic Administrator for Ukrainian Catholics in Western Europe (1972-82), Secretary of the Sacret Congregation for the Eastern Churches.

politan Yosyf Slipyj a cardinal and on February 25 the festive investiture takes place in Rome.

7-28 November 1965 — A Synod of Ukrainian Catholic bishops in Rome decides to adopt the use of the Ukrainian language in all liturgical services.

January 1967 — In the Lemko region under Polish rule, 180 Ukrainian churches out of a total 514 (before 1939) remain. Between 1939 and 1956 164 churches were destroyed in this region.

1967 — On the 20th anniversary of the forcible liquidation of the Ukrainian Catholic Church, the Ukrainian Catholic hierarchy in the Western world circulates a special appeal to the hierarchs of the entire Catholic Church, protesting against the violence being perpetrated against the Ukrainian Church and refuting the legitimacy of the so-called "Lviv Synod" of 1946.

10 April 1968 — 113 Ukrainian and Slovak priests gather in Kosice in Czechoslovakia. They establish an Executive Committee headed by Bishop Vasyl Hopko for the restoration of the rights of the Eastern-rite Catholic Church in Czechoslovakia. On April 29 Bishop Hopko presents a special memorandum about the re-establishment of the Eastern rite Catholic Church to the Czechoslovak government and the Slovak National Council.

13 June 1968 — The government of Alexander Dubcek permits the legalization of the Eastern-rite Catholic Church in Czechoslovakia and the re-establishment of the Pryashiv Eparchy.

Spring-Summer 1968 — As a result of a plebiscite conducted in 205 parishes forcibly incorporated into the Russian Orthodox Church in Czechoslovakia, these parishes revert to the Eastern-rite Catholic Church. On July 7 the Cathedral of St. John the Baptist is returned to Ukrainian and Slovak Catholics.

18 October 1968 — A search is conducted in the homes of 13 Ukrainian Catholic priests in Lviv. All church and religious publications and religious objects are confiscated from them.

30 October 1968 — The remains of Bishop Pavlo Goydych, who is buried in the Leopoldovo prison cemetery, are transferred to the Cathedral of St. John the Baptist in Pryashiv.

October 1968 — A Czechoslovak court in Bratislava rehabilitates Bishop Vasyl Hopko.

1968 — The Soviet police intensify the persecution of Ukrainian catacomb priests in all parts of Western Ukraine. Many of them are beaten, fined or imprisoned.

January 1969 — The catacomb bishop, Vasyl Velychkovsky, is arrested in Lviv and sentenced to three years' imprisonment.

21 February 1969 — The Apostolic See establishes a Metropolitanate for the Carpathian-Ruthenians in the U.S. with a seat in Munhall; on March 11, 1977 it is transferred to Pittsburgh. The Eparchy of Passaic, established July 6, 1963 and the Eparchy of Parma, established February 21, 1969, are included in the metropolitanate. Stepan Kocisco becomes the first Metropolitan.

Metropolitan Yosyf Slipyj with Pope John XXIII after his arrival in Rome in 1963.

Maksym Hermanyuk (1911-), first Metropolitan of the Ukrainian Catholic Church in Canada (from 1956), author of scholarly books on the Bible.

Stepan Sulyk (1924-), Metropolitan of the Ukrainian Catholic Church in the U.S. (from 1981).

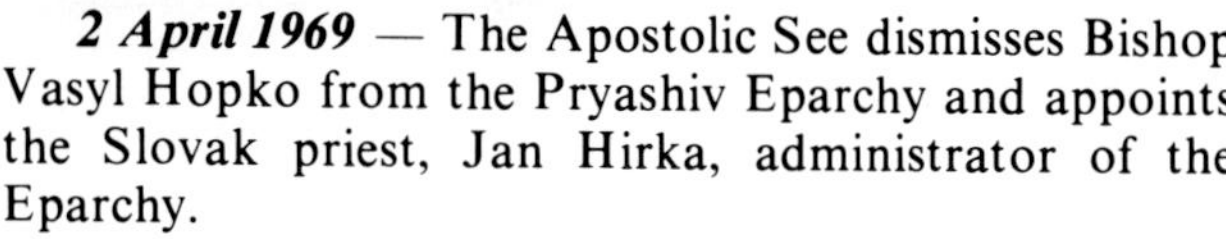

2 April 1969 — The Apostolic See dismisses Bishop Vasyl Hopko from the Pryashiv Eparchy and appoints the Slovak priest, Jan Hirka, administrator of the Eparchy.

3 June 1969 — The Eastern-rite Catholic Church in Czechoslovakia becomes a legal religious institution.

27-28 September 1969 — The solemn consecration of the Cathedral of St. Sophia in Rome takes place. A Synod is convened from September 29 to October 4, with the participation of 17 Ukrainian bishops.

23 October 1969 — On the initiative of Yosyf Slipyj, the Archbishop Major, a meeting of representatives of Eastern Catholic Churches takes place in Rome. The following patriarchs take part: Paulus Petrus Meouchi, the Maronite Patriarch of Antioch; Stephanos I Sidarouss, the Coptic Patriarch of Alexandria; Maximos V Hakim, the Melchite Patriarch of Antioch; the Syrian Patriarch Ignatius Antonius Hayek of Antioch; Patriarch Paulus II Cheikho of Chaldea; the Babylonian Patriarch of Chaldea; Ignatius Petrus XVI Batanian, Patriarch of the Armenians, and the hierarchs of India, Ethiopia, Bulgaria and Ukraine in exile. Archbishop Yosyf Slipyj proposes the establishment of a permanent Ecumenical Conference of Eastern Churches.

November 1969 — The Soviet police invade the historic Ukrainian church of the Holy Dormition in Lviv, remove ancient church books from it and burn them.

December 1969 — A thousand copies of the "Prayer-book for the Ukrainian People" are published clandestinely in Lviv.

30 May — 2 June 1971 — A Synod of the Russian Orthodox Church convenes in Zagorsk, near Moscow. The Synod approves the nullification of the Union of Berestya of 1596 and the Union of Uzhhorod of 1646, and approves the subordination of the Ukrainian Catholic Church to the Russian Orthodox Church.

16 August 1971 — The Ukrainian dissident Vyacheslav Chornovil protests against the destruction of the graves of Ukrainian soldiers at the Yaniv cemetery in Lviv. Within a period of several years, the monuments are completely destroyed.

November 1971 — Archbishop Major Yosyf Slipyj, speaks in defense of the Ukrainian Catholic Church at the Papal Synod of the Catholic Church.

31 October — 5 November 1971 — A Synod of the Ukrainian Catholic Church takes place in Rome

Ukrainian Catholic Bishops with Pope John Paul II during the 1987 Synod. From left: Bishops Platon Kornylyak, Vasyl Filevych, Ivan Prashko, Yefrem Kryvy, and Basil Losten, Metropolitans Stefan Sulyk, and Myroslav Lubachivsky, Pope John Paul II, Metropolitan Maksym Hermanyuk, Bishops Innokentiy Lototsky, Avhustyn Hornyak, Robert Moskal, Andriy Sepalyak, and Slavomir Miklovsh

Ukrainian Catholic Cathedral of SS. Volodymyr and Olha in Chicago, built in 1971-73 in the Ukrainian-Byzantine style of the 11th-13th centuries.

Roadside cross in Soviet Ukraine, one of the few remaining, 1980. The faithful still decorate them with flowers.

A *samvydav* postcard issued in Ukraine for the millennium of the Baptism of Kievan Rus'-Ukraine.

Interior of a church in Soviet Ukraine, 1980. Despite religious persecution, the faithful continue to decorate churches with traditional Ukrainian embroidery and carvings.

Volodymyr Yaniv, head of the Ukrainian Christian Movement, church leader, scholar, author of works on church history.

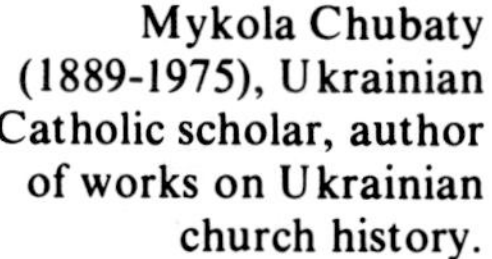

Mykola Chubaty (1889-1975), Ukrainian Catholic scholar, author of works on Ukrainian church history.

with the participation of 16 bishops. At the Synod the Constitution of the Ukrainian Catholic Church, entitled "The Patriarchal Organization of the Particular *(Pomisna)* Ukrainian Catholic Church" is approved, and a Permanent Synod of the Ukrainian Catholic Church is established. The Permanent Synod consists of Archbishop Major Yosyf Slipyj (head), Archbishop Ivan Buchko, Metropolitans Ambrose Senyshyn and Maksym Hermanyuk, and Bishop Andriy Sapelyak.

6 December 1971 — The Byzantine-Ruthenian Metropolitanate of the U.S. draws up a protest statement against the nullification of the Unions of Berestya and Uzhhorod by the Russian Orthodox Church.

1972 — Bishop Vasyl Velychkovsky of the catacomb Ukrainian Catholic Church leaves the Soviet Union for the West.

The Soviet authorities destroy the graves of Ukrainian soldiers in Ivano-Frankivsk, Ternopil, Zolochiv and Horodok.

4-8 June 1972 — The assembly of the Permanent Synod takes place in Rome with the participation of Bishop Vasyl Velychkovsky of the catacomb Ukrainian Catholic Church, who has arrived in the West. The Synod decides to intensify the campaign in defense of the persecuted Ukrainian Catholic Church in the Soviet Union. The following Synod takes place on the occasion of the 350th anniversary of the martyrdom of St. Yosafat, on November 18-23, 1973. During the Synod on July 14, 1975 the financial corporation of the St. Sophia Association is established; the Association becomes the owner of new Ukrainian property in Rome.

30 June 1973 — Bishop Vasyl Velychkovsky dies in Canada.

15 July 1973 — The KGB uncovers an underground publishing house of Ukrainian Catholic literature in Western Ukraine.

December 1973 — The Soviet authorities destroy numerous wayside crosses on many roads in Western

Patriarch Yosyp Slipyj with President Gerald Ford, Bishop Ivan Prashko (left) and Bishop Basil Losten. Washington, D.C., September 18, 1976.

Ukraine. Some of them were erected in 1848 when serfdom was abolished and some in 1938 to commemorate 950 years of the Christianization of Kievan Rus'-Ukraine.

1973 — In Lviv, Ivano-Frankivsk and Kolomyya a number of people are arrested and later sentenced for publishing underground Catholic literature.

During a period of ten years, 974 former Ukrainian Catholic churches in the Lviv oblast are closed, destroyed, burned down or converted to other uses. Only 287 churches remain open in the entire oblast, in the jurisdiction of the Russian Orthodox Church.

27 June 1974 — A Ukrainian Catholic Eparchy is founded in New Westminster, British Columbia, in Canada.

3 October 1974 — At the Papal Synod of the Catholic Church in Rome Cardinal Yosyf Slipyj speaks in defense of the Ukrainian Catholic Church. He states that the Ukrainian Church has sacrificed "mountains of bodies and rivers of blood."

1975 — The first Ukrainian Catholic priests since the end of World War II are ordained in Poland.

Spring 1975 — After over a decade of urgent petitions by concerned bishops, clergy and faithful from all over the world, Archbishop Major Yosyf Slipyj accepts the title of Patriarch, taking into consideration that unity in the Patriarchate will unify and strengthen the Ukrainian Catholic Church.

23 July 1976 — Bishop Vasyl Hopko of Pryashiv dies in Czechoslovakia.

11 September 1976 — Metropolitan Ambrose Senyshyn of the Ukrainian Catholic Church in the U.S. dies in Philadelphia. Auxiliary Bishop Yosyf Shmondyuk becomes the new Metropolitan in 1977.

27 November 1977 — Patriarch Yosyp Slipyj speaks in defense of the Ukrainian Catholic Church in Soviet Ukraine at the International Sakharov Hearings in Rome.

20 August 1978 — Patriarch Yosyf Slipyj appeals to the entire Catholic world to come to the defense of the persecuted Ukrainian Catholic Church in the Soviet Union.

17-18 November 1978 — The Synod of the Ukrainian Catholic Bishops decides to start the preparations for the jubilee celebrations of the millennium of the Christianization of Rus'-Ukraine. A memorandum concerning the difficult situation of the Ukrainian Catholic Church is sent to Pope John-Paul II.

15 January 1979 — Rev. M. Muraniy, the administrator of the catacomb Ukrainian Catholic Church in Transcarpathia, dies.

19 March 1979 — Pope John Paul II publishes a letter on the occasion of the millennium of the Christianization of Kievan Rus'-Ukraine.

28 December 1979 — Bishop Yosafat Fedoryk of the catacomb Ukrainian Catholic Church dies prematurely in Ukraine.

Yosyf Slipyj (1892-1984), Patriarch of the Ukrainian Catholic Church, Metropolitan of Galicia (1944-84), Cardinal from 1965, founder of the Ukrainian Catholic University in Rome, organizer of church, educational and scholarly life, imprisoned by the Soviets 1945-63.

1979 — Believers in the villages of Mshany and Zavadiv in the Lviv oblast demand the legalization of Ukrainian Catholic parishes in their villages.

26-27 February 1980 — The priest Anatoliy Gurgula and his wife are burned alive by communists in the village of Tomashivtsi in the Ivano-Frankivsk oblast.

23 March 1980 — A Synod of the Ukrainian Catholic Church is convened by Pope John-Paul II in Rome. The Pope directs the Synod himself. Three candidates for the co-adjutor of the Archbishop Major with the right of succession are selected during the Synod. On March 27 the Pope names Metropolitan Myroslav Lubachivsky the co-adjutor.

25 November — 2 December 1980 — A second Synod of the Ukrainian Catholic Church is convened in Rome with the blessing of Pope John-Paul II. Patriarch Yosyf Cardinal Slipyj directs the Synod, in which 18 hierarchs take part. The Synod solemnly denounces the legality of the so-called Lviv Synod of 1946, during which the Ukrainian Catholic Church

Myroslav Ivan Lyubachivsky (1914-), Archbishop Major of the Ukrainian Catholic Church (from 1984), Cardinal from 1985.

was subordinated to the Moscow Patriarchate. The Apostolic See bans the publication of the Synod's epistle to the Ukrainian people.

21 January 1981 — Rev. Ihnatiy Soltys, the head of the Ukrainian Catholic Penitents, is arrested; Rev. Soltys was imprisoned during the years 1958-65 and exiled from 1965-72. He is sentenced to five years' imprisonment and five years' exile. In March Rev. Roman Yesyp and Rev. Vasyl Kavatsiv are arrested.

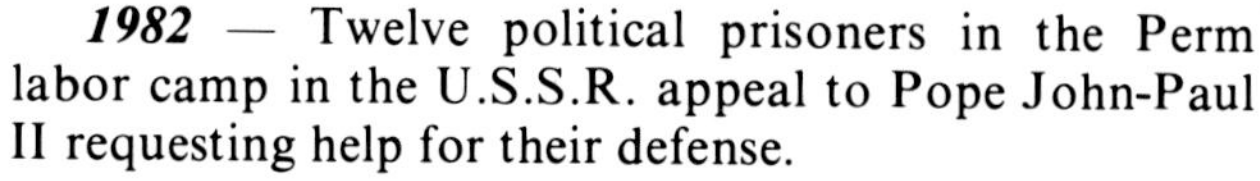

1982 — Twelve political prisoners in the Perm labor camp in the U.S.S.R. appeal to Pope John-Paul II requesting help for their defense.

Archbishop Myroslav Marusyn becomes the Secretary of the Congregation for the Eastern Churches.

9 September 1982 — The "Initiative Group for the Defense of the Rights of Believers and the Church" is formed in Ukraine, with Yosyp Terelya as its head. The goal of the group is the legalization of the Ukrainian Catholic Church in the U.S.S.R. and defense of her rights.

19 September 1982 — The Apostolic See elevates the Ukrainian Catholic Exarchate of Australia and New Zealand to an Eparchy.

30 January — 12 February 1983 — The Third Synod of the Ukrainian Catholic Church takes place in Rome. The participants approve a statute for the Synod, which is confirmed with some changes by the Apostolic See on February 25, 1984. The Apostolic See forbids the publication of the decisions concerning the Ukrainian Catholic Church in the Soviet Union.

26 May 1983 — Bishop Oleksander Khira of the Mukachiv Eparchy dies in Kazakhstan, having served 33 years in Soviet imprisonment and exile.

6 March 1984 — Ukrainian Catholics in Poland write a letter to the Bishops' Conference in Poland demanding their legal rights and equality with Polish Catholics of the Latin rite.

7 September 1984 — Patriarch and Cardinal Yosyf Slipyj dies in Rome. His co-adjutor, Metropolitan Myroslav Lubachivsky, becomes the head of the Ukrainian Catholic Church.

22 September — 5 October 1985 — A Synod of the Ukrainian Catholic Church, directed by the new Archbishop Major, Myroslav Lubachivsky, is convened in Rome.

21-30 September 1987 — The Synod of 1987 of the Ukrainian Catholic Church convenes in Rome, officially launching the celebrations marking the millennium of the Christianization of Kievan Rus'-Ukraine.

Lychakiv cemetery in Lviv, destroyed by the Soviets in the 1970s.

Ukrainian Protestant Churches

Communities of Evangelical Christian-Baptists, Pentecostals, Adventists and, to a lesser degree, Jehovah's Witnesses are spread throughout Ukraine.

The evangelical movement begins to spread through Ukraine during the period of expansion of various Protestant faiths in Western Europe. As they come into being in the West, they also make their way into Ukraine, although some years later. After a period of decline, the history of the Protestant Churches starts anew about mid-19th century.

1852 — Ivan Onyshchenko from the village of Osnova, Kherson oblast, founds the Evangelical-Baptist Church in Ukraine.

1869 — The first Baptist preachers Ivan Onyshchenko, Mykhaylo Ratushny, Yukhym Tsymbal and Ivan Ryaboshapka spread the Baptist movement on Ukrainian territories under Russia. Ryaboshapka, Tsymbal and Khlystun spend time in Russian prison for proselytizing. After completing his term in prison, Ryaboshapka is exiled and dies in 1900 in Bulgaria.

30 April — 1 May 1884 — The first secret congress of Ukrainian Baptists in Novo-Vasylivka, in Tavriya province, takes place.

1889 — Kharyton Savarovych, the first Ukrainian Baptist from the Kiev region, arrives in the United States.

1891 — Ivan Onyshchenko, founder of the Evangelical-Baptist movement in Ukraine, dies in Osnova.

1900 — The first group of Baptists from Ukraine arrives in Canada.

1904 — Ivan Kolesnykiv organizes the first Ukrainian Evangelical Church in Scranton, Pennsylvania.

1905 — The Russian tsar proclaims a law concerning religious tolerance in Russia; Protestant Churches begin to flourish anew.

1915 — Ukrainian Baptist communities are formed in a number of cities in the United States and Canada.

1-8 October 1918 — The first official congress of Baptists of Ukraine takes place in Kiev. During the period of the Ukrainian National Republic, Baptists have full and unlimited freedom of religion. 130 delegates of this congress establish a Ukrainian Baptist Church under the name of the All-Ukrainian Federation of Christians-Baptists.

A Ukrainian Presbyterian Church in Newark, New Jersey, in the 1930's.

Ukrainian Evangelical preachers in Volynia. From left to right: Volodymyr Borovsky, P. Krat and T. Dovhalyuk, 1932.

May 1921 — The Second All-Ukrainian Congress of Baptists of Ukraine takes place in Yelysavethrad (now Kirovohrad). The name is changed to the All-Ukrainian Union of Baptist Congregations of Ukraine. The Congress approves the decision to publish the journal *Baptist of Ukraine.*

1921 — The Baptist movement expands on Ukrainian territories under Poland and Czechoslovakia.

1922 — The Third All-Ukrainian Congress takes place in Kiev. The All-Ukrainian Union self-liquidates in answer to an appeal by the Russian Union of Baptists.

14-16 March 1922 — At the Council of Ukrainian Baptists in Rochester, New York, the Ukrainian Evangelical Union of North America is founded with Vasyl Kuziv, a preacher, as the head. The Council decides to spread the Evangelical movement on Ukrainian territories under Poland.

1923 — The Union of Slavic Baptists is founded in Poland. It includes Ukrainian Baptists who form a separate national group with its own rules and rights.

1924 — According to a decision of the Council of Ukrainian Baptists, Pastor P. Krat arrives in Poland to conduct missionary work. Vasyl Kuziv follows him a year later.

1925 — The Ukrainian Evangelical-Reformed Church and the Ukrainian Lutheran Church are founded almost simultaneously on the Ukrainian territories under Poland.

12-17 May 1925 — The Fourth Baptists' Congress

Vasyl Kuziv (1887-1958), Bishop of the Ukrainian Evangelical Reformed Church in Western Ukraine, later in the U.S. (left). Hryhoriy Domashovets, Baptist preacher and leader in Ukraine and the U.S., head of the Ukrainian Evangelical Baptist Brotherhood in the diaspora (from 1959).

convenes in Kharkiv. 333 delegates from all parts of Ukraine take part. The All-Ukrainian Baptist Union is re-established under A. P. Kostyukiv's leadership. The minutes of the Congress show that, in addition to the pastors of the congregation, there are 400 preachers-missionaries supported by the Union.

1926 — The journal *Baptist of Ukraine* begins appearing in Ukraine. There are 60,000 members of the All-Ukrainian Baptist Union in Ukraine. They are organized in 1,000 communities served by 400 preachers.

Summer 1927 — Vasyl Kuziv, head of the Ukrainian Evangelical Union in the United States, visits Soviet Ukraine. He meets in Kiev with Metropolitan Vasyl Lypkivsky of the Ukrainian Autocephalous Orthodox Church, with Volodymyr Chekhivsky, the ideologue of Ukrainian Orthodoxy, and with the historian Mykhaylo Hrushevsky.

Ukrainian Evangelical preachers from Canada and the U.S. at a conference in Toronto. From left to right: O. Bachynsky, D. Shumylo, L. Standret, P. Krat, I. Danylchuk, Y. Korsakov, and I. Bodrug.

10-13 May 1928 — The Sixth (last) All-Ukrainian Congress of Christians-Baptists convenes in Kharkiv with the NKVD's permission. 390 delegates and 476 representatives of Baptist communities take part. This is the largest and last congress before the great persecution of Ukrainian Baptists, which starts the following year and lasts until 1939, by which time all pastors and missionaries are shot, exiled or imprisoned. Some faithful remain undercover.

26-27 January 1932 — The Bukovyna Union of Baptists is founded during the Congress of Ukrainian Baptists of Rumania.

1934 — The Church of Christian-Baptists of Galicia comprises 27 communities and approximately 2,000 members.

15 September 1935 — Vasyl Kuziv is consecrated the first Ukrainian Evangelical Bishop in Kolomyya, the center of the Ukrainian Evangelical movement in Galicia.

1939 — The Ukrainian Evangelical-Reformed Church on Ukrainian territories under Poland comprises of 35 church communities, 15 preachers and approximately 5,000 members.

1942 — The German occupation authorities in Ukraine ban publication and distribution of Baptist editions of the *New Testament* and the *Gospels* translated into Ukrainian by Professor Ivan Ohiyenko. Many pastors, preachers and missionaries of the Ukrainian Baptist Church find themselves in Germany during and after World War II. Many of them migrate to the United States, Canada, England, South America and Australia after the war.

18-20 July 1943 — The (Seventh) All-Ukrainian Congress of Baptists convenes in Dnipropetrovsk. It is decided to renew and revitalize the Baptist Church, destroyed by the Soviets. It is reported that there are 713 Baptist communities with 32,000 members in Ukraine. Pastor Danylo D. Shapovaliv heads the reborn Ukrainian Baptist Church.

1944 — The Soviets liquidate the All-Ukrainian Union of Baptist Congregations of Ukraine. Pastor Shapovaliv is sentenced to 15 years imprisonment. He serves 12 years in Siberia, returns to Ukraine and dies in 1972.

The Baptist Church in the U.S.S.R. is renewed under one name and with one base — Moscow. The new name is the All-Russian Union of Evangelical Christian-Baptists.

1945 — The Ukrainian Missionary-Bible Society is established in the United States and headed by Ya. Homynyuk and from 1949 by Pavlo Bartkiv.

15-16 January 1947 — The Ukrainian Evangelical-Baptist Union is founded during the First Congress of the Ukrainian Baptist-Emigrants. S. Nyshnyk is elected head and H. Domashovets secretary.

12-14 July 1947 — The Second Congress of the Union takes place.

Volodymyr Borovsky (1907-1987), Evangelical Reformed preacher and leader in Ukraine and in the U.S.

3-6 December 1948 — The Congress of the Ukrainian Evangelical Union takes place in Oshawa, Ontario.

May 1950 — The Ukrainian Evangelical Baptist Brotherhood in the United States and Canada is founded during the Congress in Cleveland, Ohio. Pastor Petro Kindrat of Winnipeg, Manitoba, is elected head.

1951 — The Ukrainian Missionary-Bible Society begins publishing the journal *The Messenger of Truth.*

30 May — 1 June 1952 — The First Jubilee Congress of the Ukrainian Evangelical Baptist Brotherhood takes place in Hamilton, Ontario, on the centenary of the founding of the Evangelical-Baptist movement in Ukraine.

20 September 1953 — S. Tymtsiv becomes the head of the Ukrainian Evangelical-Baptist Church.

15-17 October 1955 — The Ukrainian Union of Evangelical Christians and Baptists and the Ukrainian Bible Institute, headed by Mykhaylo Bakhor, are founded in Argentina.

1958 — The Union of Ukrainian Evangelical-Baptist Churches, headed by Pastor Oleksa Harbuzyuk, is established as the central organization of Ukrainian Baptist Churches in the diaspora.

27-31 May 1959 — H. Domashovets is elected head of the Ukrainian Evangelical Baptist Brotherhood during its Second Congress.

1961 — A large number of Baptists in the Soviet Union who wish to function outside the control of the state split off from the All-Russian Union (later the All-Union Council) of Evangelical Christians-Baptists. In 1965 they group together in the unregistered Council of Churches whose general secretary is the Baptist Pastor Heorhiy Vins from Kiev.

November 1966 — Heorhiy Vins is sentenced to three years' imprisonment for his religious activities. He is again sentenced to five years imprisonment and five years exile in 1975. In 1978 he is released and emigrates with his family to the United States.

August 1985 — Vasyl Boyechko, Bishop of the Evangelical Pentecostal Church, is sentenced to three years' imprisonment in Lviv for his religious activities.

Oleksa Harbuzyuk (b. 1920), head of the All-Ukrainian Evangelical-Baptist Church in the diaspora (from 1972).

Beginning in 1950, congresses of the All-Ukrainian Evangelical-Baptist Brotherhood — Ukrainian Baptist Church are held every five years. There are also special conventions, conventions of pastors, etc.

HEADS OF THE ALL-UKRAINIAN EVANGELICAL-BAPTIST CHURCH

Pastor Petro Kindrat	1950-1965
Pastor Dr. L. Zhabko-Potapovych	1965-1973
Pastor Oleksa R. Harbuzyuk	1972-

The All-Ukrainian Evangelical-Baptist Brotherhood — Ukrainian Baptist Church includes Churches in the United States, Canada, South America, England and Australia. The Following organizations also belong:

Ukrainian Missionary-Bible Society of the United States and Canada; publishers of *Doroha Pravdy* (*The Way of the Truth*); radio broadcasting *Holos Yevanheliyi v Ukrayinu* (*Voice of the Gospel into Ukraine*); world-wide All-Ukrainian Youth Federation; world-wide All-Ukrainian Sisters' (Women's) Federation; local church and youth communities; Ukrainian Bible Homestead (17 buildings and 200 acres of land). *Pislanets Pravdy* (*Messenger of Truth*) is the official organ of the All-Ukrainian Evangelical-Baptist Brotherhood.

Principal Ecclesiastical Activities

Ukrainian Orthodox Church

At the outset of the revolution in 1917, there occurs in the Ukraine a rebirth of the Ukrainian Orthodox Church, which in 1799 was deprived of all its rights and privileges and became part of the Russian Orthodox Church. In 1919 the government of the Ukrainian National Republic proclaims the independence of the Ukrainian Orthodox Church. In 1921 the First All-Ukrainian Orthodox Sobor elects a metropolitan of Kiev and All Ukraine, and creates the Ukrainian Autocephalous Orthodox Church, juridically independent from the patriarch of Moscow. Other Orthodox churches, however, still continue to exist in Ukraine. In January 1930 the Soviet government liquidates the Ukrainian Autocephalous Orthodox Church (UAOC) and in December of that same year grants permission for the renewal of the Ukrainian Orthodox Church, which lasts until 1936; in that year the entire hierarchy of the Church is arrested and imprisoned.

During World War II the UAOC, headed by Metropolitan Polikarp Sikorsky is reborn. With the departure of its entire hierarchy to the West in 1944, the Soviet government forcibly incorporates all its parishes into the Russian Orthodox Church; however, church life continues to flourish among the Ukrainian immigrants, with new eparchies being created.

1. THE UKRAINIAN AUTOCEPHALOUS ORTHODOX CHURCH (UAOC) IN UKRAINE 1921-1936

METROPOLITANS OF KIEV AND ALL UKRAINE

Vasyl Lypkivsky 1921-1927
Mykola Boretsky 1927-1930

METROPOLITAN OF KHARKIV AND ALL UKRAINE

Ivan Pavlovsky 1930-1936

ARCHBISHOPS: Anton Hrynevych of Balta (1923-30); Konstantyn Krotevych of Poltava (1922-24), of Vinnytsia (1924-30); Konstantyn Malyushkevych of Uman (1922-27), of Kiev (1927-34); Yuriy Mikhnovsky of Chernihiv (1921-22); Stepan Orlyk of Volynia and Zhytomyr (1921-23), Berdychiv and Shepetivka (1925-27); Yosyp Oksiyuk of Kamyanets-Podilsky, Lubny, Poltava and Myrhorod (1922-29); Mykola Pyvovariv in various church districts (1922-26), Kamyanets-Podilsky (1927-29); Volodymyr Samborsky of Kaniv, Konotop and Bila-Tserkva (1923-27), Hlukhiv (1928-29), Vinnytsya (1930-32); Nestor Sharayivsky of the Kievan villages district (1921-27), assistant to the metropolitan (1927-29); Teodosiy Serhiyiv of Pereyaslav (1924-28), Berdychiv (1928-30); Ioann Teodorovych of Podilia and Vinnytsya (1921-24); Oleksander Yareshchenko of Lubny (1921-23), Kharkiv (1923-26); Yuriy Zhevchenko of Skvyr (1922-24), of Poltava (1924-27), of Odessa (1928-29).

BISHOPS: Konon Bey of Bohuslav, Pryluky and Romny (1922-24), Cherkasy (1928); Volodymyr Brzhosnyovsky of Bila-Tserkva (1921-24), Dnipropetrovsk (1928-30); Pylyp Buchylo of Mykolayiv (1922-23); Oleksander Chervinsky of Konotop and Hlukhiv (1925-26), Chernihiv and Nizhyn (1927-30), Vinnytsya (1932-34); Yakiv Chulayivsky of Berdychiv (1928-31); Volodymyr Dakhivnyk-Dakhivsky of Pereyaslav and Kamyanets-Podilsky (1922-27), Tulchyn (1927-30); Marko Hrushevsky of Konotop and Tarashcha (1922-26); Yukhym Kalishevsky of Zvenyhorod and Cherkasy (1922-29), Odessa (1929-30); Mykola Karabinevych of Mohyliv and Podilia (1922-28), Uman (1928-30); Mykhaylo Malyarevsky; Hryhoriy Mozolevsky of Konotop (1924-26); Yuriy Prokopovych of Luhansk (1926); Petro Romodaniv of Lokhvytsya (1923-26); Mykola Shyryay of Nizhyn (1922-24), Romny (1928-30); Hryhoriiy Storozhenko; Petro Tarnavsky; Yuriy Teslenko of Bila Tserkva (1925-30); Maksym Zadvirnyak of Proskuriv (1923-30).

EPARCHIES OF THE UAOC IN 1926

1.Balta, 2. Bila Tserkva, 3. Berdychiv, 4. Cherkasy, 5. Chernihiv, 6. Dnipropetrovsk, 7. Kamyanets-Podilsky, 8. Kharkiv, 9. Kiev (city), 10. Kiev (villages), 11. Konotop, 12. Lubny, 13. Odessa, 14. Poltava, 15. Proskuriv, 16. Romny, 17. Tulchyn, 18. Uman, 19. Vinnytsia, 20. Volynia.

TABLE OF EPARCHIES AND PARISHES OF THE UAOC, 1924, 1926, 1927

1924 Eparchies	Parishes	1926 Eparchies	Parishes	1927 Eparchies	Parishes
1. Berdychiv	25	1. Berdychiv	23	1. Berdychiv-Shepetivka	51
2. Bila-Tserkva	69	2. Bila-Tserkva	70	2. Bila-Tserkva	104
3. Cherkasy	44	3. Bohuslav	28	3. Cherkasy	107
4. Chernihiv	6	4. Bratslav	27	4. Chernihiv-Nizhyn	52
5. Hluhiv	16	5. Cherkasy	110	5. Dnipropetrovsk-Zaporizhzhya	29
6. Katerynoslav-Zaporizhzhya	25	6. Chernihiv	6	6. Kamyanets	35
7. Kharkiv (with Donetsk)	2	7. Hlukhiv	16	7. Kharkiv	12
8. Kiev	117	8. Haysyn	27	8. Kiev (city)	10
9. Konotop	36	9. Katerynoslav-Zaporizhzhya	30	9. Kiev (villages)	108
10. Lubny	60	10. Kharkiv (with Donetsk)	24	10. Konotop-Hlukhiv	48
11. Lypovets	20	11. Kiev (city)	10	11. Korosten	10
12. Nizhyn	50	12. Kiev (villages)	114	12. Lubny	62
13. Odessa-Mykolayiv	5	13. Konotop	32	13. Odessa-Mykolayiv-Kherson	6
14. Pereyaslav	21	14. Lubny	62	14. Pereyaslav	17
15. Podilia	247	15. Mykolayiv	4	15. Poltava	50
16. Poltava	40	16. Nizhyn	30	16. Proskuriv	31
17. Radomyshl	14	17. Odessa	4	17. Pryluky	17
18. Shevchenkivsky	90	18. Poltava	50	18. Romny	22
19. Skvyr	39	19. Proskuriv	34	19. Tulchyn	41
20. Tarashcha	27	20. Pryluky	14	20. Uman	114
21. Uman	53	21. Romny	16	21. Vinnytsya	100
22. Volynia	56	22. Shepetivka	40	22. Zhytomyr-Volynia	13
23. Zolotonosha	11	23. Tulchyn	24		
		24. Uman	125		
		25. Vinnytsya	104		
		26. Volynia	14		
Total	1073	Total	1038	Total	1039

ORTHODOX CHURCHES AND PRIESTS IN UKRAINE
1914 and 1932

	1914	1932
Churches	14,371	8,000
Priests	24,665	9,200

2. THE UAOC IN UKRAINE DURING WORLD WAR II 1941-1945

COMPOSITION OF EPARCHIES IN 1942

Administrator of the UAOC: Archbishop Polikarp Sikorsky with the seat at Lutsk.

Representative of the Administrator of the UAOC in the Eastern lands of Ukraine: Bishop Nikanor Abramovych with the seat in Kiev.

Eparchy of Dnipropetrovsk and Sicheslav: Bishop Hennadiy Shyprykevych.

Eparchy of Lutsk and Kovel: Archbishop Polikarp Sikorsky; Bishops Platon (Artymyuk) of Rivne; Vyacheslav Lisytsky of Dubno.

Eparchy of Mykolayiv and Kherson: Bishops Mykhayil (Fedir) Khoroshy of Kirovohrad; Volodymyr (Vasyl) Malets of Cherkasy.

Eparchy of Polissya: Archbishop Oleksander Inozemtsev.

Eparchy of Uman and Poltava: Archbishop Ihor Huba.

Bishops: Fotiy Tymoshchuk of Nizyn and Vinnytsya; Hryhoriy Ohiychuk of Zhytomyr; Sylvester Hayevsky of Lubny; Metropolitan Teofil Buldovky of Kharkiv; Mstyslav (Stepan) Skrypnyk of Pereyaslav.

3. AUTOCEPHALOUS ORTHODOX CHURCHES IN COUNTRIES WITH UKRAINIAN POPULATIONS

In Poland and Czechoslovakia Ukrainians constitute a majority in the Autocephalous Orthodox Churches. In 1921 in Poland, out of 2,846,639 Orthodox, Ukrainians numbered 1,676,060, i.e. 58.9%. The center of the Orthodox Church in Poland until World War II was Volynia, where 70% of the inhabitants were Ukrainians.

The Orthodox Churches before and after World War II included a large number of Ukrainian bishops and priests. The national composition of the members of the Orthodox Churches in unknown. Both Churches (of Poland and Czechoslovakia) are under the jurisdiction of the Moscow Patriarchate, but are autocephalous.

THE POLISH AUTOCEPHALOUS ORTHODOX CHURCH

COMPOSITION OF THE HIERARCHY IN 1938

Metropolitan of Warsaw and All Poland — Dionysiy Valedynsky.

Archbishops: Oleksander Inozemtsev of Polissya and Pinsk, Oleksiy* Hromadsky of Volyn and Kremenets, Teodosiy Feodoseyev of Vilnius and Lodz.

Bishops: Matviy Semashko of Wroclaw, Savva Sovyetov of Grodno and Novogrudok, Tymofiy Shretter of Lublin, Polikarp* Sikorsky of Lutsk, Symon Ivanovsky of Ostrih.

* Bishops of Ukrainian nationality.

CHURCH STATISTICS FOR 1938

Eparchies	5
Deaneries	126
Parishes	1624
Sacramental buildings	2016
Church buildings	2968
Monasteries: Men	9
Women	5

Schools: Department of Orthodox Theology at Warsaw University. Two seminaries (Vilnius and Kremenets). School for deacons and psalm readers at the monastery in Yablochyn. Theological school in Pochayiv.

COMPOSITION OF THE HIERARCHY IN 1986

Metropolitan of Warsaw and All Poland — Vasyliy (Volodymyr) Doroshkevych.

Eparchy of Warsaw and Bielsk: Metropolitan Vasyliy Doroshkevych.

Eparchy of Bialystok and Gdansk: Bishop Sava (Mykhaylo) Hrytsunyak.

Eparchy of Wroclaw and Szczecin: Bishop Yeremiya (Jan) Ankhimyuk.

Eparchy of Lodz and Poznan: Bishop Symon Romanchuk.

Eparchy of Peremyshl (Przemysl) and Novy Sancz: Bishop Adam (Oleksander) Dubets.

CHURCH STATISTICS FOR 1964 AND 1984

	1964	1984
Archbishops	2	2
Bishops	1	4
Eparchies	4	5
Deaneries	20	21
Parishes	206	217
Priests	145	214
Churches	N.A.	227
Monasteries: Men	1	1
Women	1	1
Theological Seminaries	1	1
Theological Academies	1	1

THE AUTOCEPHALOUS ORTHODOX CHURCH IN CZECHOSLOVAKIA

COMPOSITION OF THE EPARCHY IN 1986

Metropolitan of Prague and All Czechoslovakia: Dorofey (Fylyp).

Eparchy of Prague: Metropolitan Dorofey (Fylyp).

Eparchy of Michalovce: Bishop Jan Golonich.

Eparchy of Olomouc: Bishop Nikanor Yukhymyuk.

Eparchy of Pryashiv (Presov): Bishop Mykola Kotsvar.

4. THE UKRAINIAN ORTHODOX CHURCH IN THE DIASPORA

After the end of World War II almost the entire hierarchy of the Ukrainian Orthodox Church finds itself in West Germany. In the years following, they migrate, like the rest of the Ukrainian population, to the United States, Canada, South America and Australia. However, some remain in Europe: in West Germany, France, England and Belgium. They found new parishes, eparchies and metropolitanates, in most cases as separate church organizations.

Under the jurisdiction of the UAOC are Orthodox Ukrainians in the countries of Western Europe, Australia, New Zealand and South America.

HIERARCHY OF THE UKRAINIAN AUTOCEPHALOUS ORTHODOX CHURCH IN WESTERN EUROPE 1945

Metropolitans: Polikarp Sikorsky — Head of the Holy Synod of Bishops of the UOAC, Oleksander Inosemtsev — Archbishop of Polissya (died 1948).

Archbishops: Nikanor Abramovych of Chyhyryn, Mykhayil Khoroshy of Kirovohrad, Ihor Huba of Uman and Poltava, Hennadiy Shyprykevych of Dnipropetrovsk.

Bishops: Volodymyr Malets of Cherkasy, Vyacheslav

Lysytsky of Dubno, Sylvester Hayevsky of Lubny, Serhiy Orhotenko of Melitopol, Mstyslav Skrypnyk of Pereyaslav, Platon Artemyuk of Rovno, Hryhoriy Ohiychuk of Zhytomyr.

HIERARCHY OF THE UKRAINIAN AUTOCEPHALOUS CHURCH IN THE DIASPORA

Polikarp Sikorsky 1945-58
Nikanor Abramovych 1953-69
Mstyslav Skrypnyk 1969-

Archbishops: Sylvester Hayevsky (1949-1975) of Australia and New Zealand; Varlaam Soloviy (1957-66), Donat Burtan (1963-70) of Australia; Orest Evanyuk (1970-80), Anatoliy Dublyansky (1982-) of Western Europe; Mykola Soloviy (1952-53), Yov Skakalsky (1970-74) of South America; Volodymyr Didovych (1986-1988) of London.

Bishops: Ivan Danylyuk (1952-54) of Australia and New Zealand; Oleksiy Pylypenko (1952-69) of South America; Volodymyr Didovych (1984-86) of London.

Statistics for 1980 (not including the United States): Eparchies — 3, Bishops — 3, Parishes — 68, Priests — 31, Faithful — 16,000.

5. METROPOLITANATE OF THE UKRAINIAN ORTHODOX CHURCH IN THE UNITED STATES

The Ukrainian Orthodox Church in the United States is organized in 1919. In 1950 it becomes a metropolitanate. Orthodox Ukrainians in South America are under the jurisdiction of the UOC.

METROPOLITANS OF THE UKRAINIAN ORTHODOX CHURCH IN THE UNITED STATES

Ioann Teodorovych 1950-71
Mstyslav Skrypnyk 1971-

Archbishops: Ioann Teodorovych (1924-71), Mstyslav Skrypnyk (1950-71) of Philadelphia; Hennadiy Shyprykevych (1950-61), Konstantyn Bagan (1979-83) of Chicago; Volodymyr Malets (1950-66) of Detroit; Mstyslav Skrypnyk (1950-1970), Marko Hundyak (1970-84) of New York; Iov Skakalsky (1970-74) of South America.

Bishops: Oleksander Novytsky (1965-70), Kostyantyn Bagan (1972-79) of Chicago; Antoniy Sharba (1986-) of New York; Volodymyr Gay (1974-77) of South America.

Statistics for 1980: Eparchies — 3, Bishops — 3, Parishes — 93, Priests — 94, Faithful — 100,000.

6. METROPOLITANATE OF THE UKRAINIAN GREEK ORTHODOX CHURCH IN CANADA

Founded in 1918 in Saskatchewan and until 1924 is under the jurisdiction of Metropolitan Hermanos, Exarch of the Patriarchate of Antioch. The UGOC spreads throughout Canada and, in 1951, becomes a metropolitanate consisting of three eparchies — Eastern Canada (Ontario and Quebec, with Toronto as the seat), Central Canada (Manitoba and Saskatchewan, with Winnipeg as the seat), and Western Canada (Alberta and British Columbia, with Edmonton as the seat).

METROPOLITANS OF THE UKRAINIAN GREEK ORTHODOX CHURCH (UGOC)

Hermanos 1919-24
Ilarion Ohiyenko 1951-72
Mykhayil Khoroshy 1972-75
Andriy Metyuk 1975-83
Vasyliy Fedak................................. 1983-

Archbishops: Ioann Teodorovych (1924-1947), Mstyslav Skrypnyk (1947-1949), Ilarion Ohiyenko (1949-1951).

Eparchy of Eastern Canada: Archbishop Mykhayil Khoroshy (1952-1977), Bishop Mykolay Debryn (1977-1981).

Eparchy of Central Canada: Archbishop Borys Yakovkevych (1963-1983), Bishop Vasyliy Fedak (1978-1983).

Eparchy of Western Canada: Archbishop Andriy Metyuk (1959-1975), Bishop Ivan Stinka (1984-).

Statistics of the UGOC in Canada. **1924:** Orthodox communities — 70, Priests — 12. **1955:** Orthodox communities — 200, Priests — 70. **1980:** Eparchies — 3, Bishops — 4, Parishes — 315, Priests — 93, Faithful — 120,000.

7. CONCILIAR UKRAINIAN AUTOCEPHALOUS ORTHODOX CHURCH (SOBORNOPRAVNA)

Formed in 1947 at Ashaffenburg (West Germany), the Conciliar UAOC has jurisdiction over various Orthodox communities in different countries of Ukrainian settlement. Since 1960, the seat has been Chicago.

Metropolitan: Hryhoriy Ohiychuk (1971-1985).

Archbishops: Hryhoriy Ohiychuk (1947-71), Hennadiy Shyprykevych (1961-72), Varlaam Dzyuba (1973-82), Oleksiy Pylypenko (1975-77).

Bishops: England — Ivan Hrytsenko (1969-85), Ivan Burma (1981); Australia — Donat Burtan (1955-63); Winnipeg — Mykola Urbanovych (1954-56); Western Europe — Yevhen Bachynsky (1955-83); South America — Oleksiy Pylypenko (1969-73); Chicago — Petro Kolesnyk (1975-); San Francisco — Izyaslav Honchariv (1981-).

Statistics for 1987: Eparchies — 2, Bishops — 3, Parishes — 21, Priests — 20, Faithful — 3000.

8. UKRAINIAN ORTHODOX CHURCH IN THE UNITED STATES AND CANADA

The UOC in the U.S. and Canada was founded in Allentown (USA) in 1928 and falls under the jurisdiction of the Patriarch of Constantinople.

Bishops: Yosyf Zhuk (1932-37), Bohdan Shpylka (1937-63), Metropolitan Andriy Kushchak (1967-86), Vsevolod Maydansky (1987-).

Statistics for 1980. In the USA: Eparchies — 1, Bishops — 1, Parishes — 26. In Canada: Parishes — 8, Priests — 35. Total number of Faithful — about 80,000.

9. UKRAINIAN AUTOCEPHALOUS ORTHODOX CHURCH IN EXILE

The UAOC in Exile was founded in 1951. From 1954 it was under the jurisdiction of the Patriarch of Constantinople. In 1980 the majority of the faithful became members of the Ukrainian Orthodox Church of the United States, with one parish falling under the jurisdiction of the Greek-Orthodox Church of the United States.

Archbishops: Palladiy Vydybida-Rudenko (1951-71), Ihor Huba (1951-67).

Samvydav postcards from Ukraine commemorating "A Thousand Years of the Ukrainian Church."

Ukrainian Catholic Church

The Ukrainian Catholic Church is a Church of the Eastern Byzantine rite, under the jurisdiction of the Pope since 1596. At first it is known as the Uniate Church, then from the late 18th century, as the Ruthenian Greek-Catholic Church and in the 1930s as the Ukrainian Greek-Catholic Church. After World War II the name Ukrainian Catholic Church is adopted. Since the 1960s the Apostolic See uses this terminology in all its official documents.

1. UKRAINIAN CATHOLIC CHURCH IN UKRAINE

METROPOLITANATE OF GALICIA

METROPOLITANS OF GALICIA, ARCHBISHOPS OF LVIV AND BISHOPS OF KAMYANETS-PODILSKY

Andrey Sheptytsky 1900-44
Yosyf Slipyj 1944-84
Myroslav Ivan Lubachivsky 1984-

Archeparchy of Lviv: Archbishop — Andrey Sheptytsky (1900-44); Auxiliary Bishops: Yosyf Botsyan (1924-26), Nykyta Budka (1928-49), Ivan Buchko (1929-40), Yosyf Slipyj (1939-44).

Apostolic Administrator of Volynia, Polissya and Pidlyashshya: Bishop Mykola Charnetsky (1931-59).

Eparchy of Lutsk: Bishop Yosyf Botsyan (1914-1924), Bishop Vasyl Velychkovsky (1963-73).

Eparchy of Peremyshl, Sambir and Sianok: Bishop Yosafat Kotsylovsky (1917-47); Auxiliary Bishop Hryhoriy Lakota (1926-51).

Eparchy of Stanyslaviv *(now Ivano-Frankivsk):* Bishop Hryhoriy Khomyshyn (1904-47); Auxiliary Bishop Ivan Lyatyshevsky (1929-57).

Apostolic Administration of Lemkivshchyna *(Apostolic Exarchate):* Rev. Vasyliy Mastsyuk (1934-36), Rev. Yakiv Medvedsky (1936-41), Rev. Oleksander Malynovsky (1941-45).

Apostolic Exarchs: Ukraine — Archbishop Yosyf Slipyj (1939-84); Volynia, Polissya and Pidlyashshya — Bishop Mykola Charnetsky (1939-59).

Eparchy of Mukachiv *(under direct jurisdiction of the Apostolic See):* Bishops: Oleksander Stoyka (1932-43); Apostolic Administrator: Dionysiy Nyaradi (1938-39), Mykola Dudash (1944), Bishop Teodor Romzha (1944-47).

Eparchy of Pryashiv (Presov) *(under direct jurisdiction of the Apostolic See):* Apostolic Administrators — Bishop Dionysiy Nyaradi (1922-27), Bishop Pavlo Goydych (1927-40); Bishop of Pryashiv — Pavlo Goydych (1940-60); Auxiliary Bishop Vasyl Hopko (1947-76); Administrator — Rev. Jan Hirka (1969-).

Bishops of the Catacomb Ukrainian Catholic Church: Oleksander Khira (1945-83), Vasyl Velychkovsky (1963-73).

Poland: Cardinal Jozef Glemp — Delegate of the Apostolic See for the Eastern-rite Catholic Faithful (1981-).

Bukovyna: Rev. Mykhaylo Simovych — Vicar-general of Marmarosh, Bishop for Eastern-rite Catholics (1930-43).

UKRAINIAN CATHOLIC CHURCH IN UKRAINE
1944*

	Bishops	Parishes	Churches	Priests	Seminaries	Faithful in Thousands	Monks
Archeparchy of Lviv	4	1,267	1,308	1,067	2	1,300	53
Eparchy of Peremyshl	2	640	1,268	715	1	1,160	66
Eparchy of Stanyslaviv	2	455	866	531	1	1,000	68
Apostolic Administration of Lemkivshchyna	—	129	198	135	—	128	—
Apostolic Administration of Volynia	1	28	—	41	—	35	—
Eparchy of Mukachiv	1	281	459	367	1	462	8
Eparchy of Pryashiv (Presov)	1	150	298	247	1	321	8
Eparchy of Marmarosh and Bukovyna	1	35	48	35	—	55	—
Total	12	2,985	4,445	3,138	6	4,461	203

* After the occupation of Ukraine by the Soviet Union the Ukrainian Catholic Church was forcibly liquidated in 1946. Ukrainian Catholic parishes exist legally only in two Eastern-bloc Communist countries, Poland and Czechoslovakia. The Eparchy of Pryashiv in Czechoslovakia is composed of 200 parishes, 232 priests and about 286,000 faithful (Ukrainians and Slovaks).

In 1987, there were 59 Ukrainian Catholic priests active in Poland. Ukrainian Catholics had 71 pastoral centers. These comprised 49 Latin-rite churches available for Ukrainian-rite services, and 22 Ukrainian-rite churches. There were approximately 350,000 Ukrainian Catholic faithful in Poland.

2. THE UKRAINIAN CATHOLIC CHURCH IN THE DIASPORA

After World War II the Ukrainian exarchates and eparchies abroad are under the direct jurisdiction of the Apostolic See. In 1963 the Apostolic See recognizes Metropolitan Yosyf Slipyj as Archbishop Major of the Ukrainian Catholic Church in the diaspora. In 1980 the Holy See grants permission to hold Synods of Ukrainian Catholic Hierarchs.

ARCHBISHOPS MAJOR OF THE UKRAINIAN CATHOLIC CHURCH

Metropolitan Yosyf Slipyj 1963-84
Metropolitan Myroslav Lubachivsky 1984-

3. METROPOLITANATE OF THE UKRAINIAN CATHOLIC CHURCH IN THE UNITED STATES

In 1907 the Apostolic See nominated the first Bishop for Ukrainian Catholics in the U.S. In 1913 the Apostolic See established an Exarchate, with the seat in Philadelphia. In 1958 the Exarchate was given the status of a Metropolitanate, and the Exarchate of Stamford (created in 1956) was raised to an eparchy. A third Ukrainian eparchy was established in 1961 in Chicago (St. Nicholas) and in 1983 a fourth in Parma, Ohio, (St. Josaphat).

METROPOLITANS OF THE UKRAINIAN CATHOLIC CHURCH IN THE UNITED STATES

Konstantyn Bohachevsky 1958-61
Ambrose Senyshyn 1961-76
Yosyf Shmondyuk 1976-79
Myroslav Lubachivsky 1979-80
Stefan Sulyk 1981-

Eparchy of Philadelphia (Exarchate until 1958): Bishop Konstantyn Bohachevsky (1924-58); Auxiliary Bishops: Ambrose Senyshyn (1942-56), Yosyf Shmondyuk (1956-61), Ivan Stakh (1971-72), Vasyl Losten (1971-77), Robert Moskal (1981-83), Mykhaylo Kuchmyak (1988-).

Eparchy of Stamford (Exarchate until 1958): Bishops Amvrosiy Senyshyn (1956-61), Yosyf Shmondyuk (1961-76), Vasyl Losten (1977-).

Eparchy of St. Nicholas in Chicago: Bishops Yaroslav Gabro (1961-80), Innokentiy Lototsky (1981-).

Eparchy of St. Josaphat in Parma: Robert Moskal (1983-).

Statistics for 1987: Bishops — 4, Parishes — 205, Priests — 239, Theological seminaries — 2, Faithful — 255,000.

4. METROPOLITANATE OF THE UKRAINIAN CATHOLIC CHURCH IN CANADA

In 1912 the Apostolic See nominates the first Bishop for the Ukrainian Catholic Church in Canada. In 1956 the Exarchate of Winnipeg is elevated to a Metropolitanate, with three eparchies — Toronto, Edmonton and Saskatoon. In 1974 a fourth eparchy, New Westminster, is created.

METROPOLITANS OF THE UKRAINIAN CATHOLIC CHURCH IN CANADA

Maksym Hermanyuk 1956

Eparchy of Winnipeg (Exarchate until 1956): Bishops Nykyta Budka (1912-28), Vasyl Ladyka (1929-56), Archbishop Maksym Hermanyuk (1956-); Auxiliary Bishops — Nil Savaryn (1943-48), Andriy Roboretsky (1948-51), Maksym Hermanyuk (1951-56), Myron Datsyuk (1982-).

Eparchy of Toronto (Exarchate until 1956): Bishop Isydor Boretsky (1948-).

Eparchy of Edmonton (Exarchate until 1956): Bishop Nil Savaryn (1948-86); Auxiliary Bishop Dmytro Greshchuk (1974-86), Bishop Dmytro Greshchuk (1986-).

Eparchy of Saskatoon (Exarchate until 1956): Bishops — Andriy Roboretsky (1951-82), Vasyl Filevych (1984-).

Eparchy of New Westminster: Bishop Yeronim Khymiy (1974-).

Statistics for 1987: Bishops — 6, Parishes — 187, Priests — 187, Theological Seminaries — 1, Faithful — 226,000.

5. APOSTOLIC ADMINISTRATION FOR UKRAINIAN CATHOLICS IN THE DIASPORA 1945-1988

APOSTOLIC EXARCHATES AND EPARCHIES IN WESTERN EUROPE

Bishop Ivan Buchko 1945-53
Archbishop Ivan Buchko 1953-72
Rev. Myroslav Marusyn 1972-74
Bishop Myroslav Marusyn 1974-82

Statistics for 1987: Bishops — 2, Parishes — 10, Priests — 12, Faithful — 5,000.

Germany: The Apostolic Administrator — Rev. Petro Verhun — (1940-45), Bishop Platon Kornylyak — Exarch (1959-).

Statistics for 1987: Bishops — 1, Parishes — 21, Priests — 26, Faithful — 29,000.

France: Exarchs — Bishops Volodymyr Malanchuk (1960-82), Mykhyalo Hrynchyshyn (1982-).
Statistics for 1987: Bishops — 1, Parishes — 12, Priests — 14, Faithful — 5,000.

Great Britain: Bishop Avhustyn Hornyak (1961-87), Apostolic Administrator — Bishop Mykhaylo Hrynchyshyn (1987-).
Statistics for 1987: Bishops — 1, Parishes — 15, Priests — 16, Faithful — 25,000.

Argentina: Bishop Andriy Sapelak — Apostolic Administrator (1961-68), Apostolic Exarch (1968-78), Bishop of Buenos Aires Eparchy (1978-).
Statistics for 1987: Bishops — 1, Parishes — 12, Priests — 20, Faithful — 115,000.

Brazil: Yosyf Martynets — Auxiliary Bishop (1958-62), Apostolic Exarch (1962-71), Bishop of Curitiba Eparchy (1971-78), Bishop Yefrem Kryvy (1978-).
Statistics for 1987: Bishops — 1, Parishes — 18, Priests — 48, Faithful — 88,000.

Australia: Bishop Ivan Prashko — Exarch (1958-82), Bishop of Melbourne Eparchy (1982-).
Statistics for 1987: Bishops — 1, Parishes — 10, Priests — 12, Faithful — 30,000.

Eparchy of Krizevci (Yugoslavia): Bishop Dionysiy Nyaradi — Apostolic Administrator (1914-20), Bishop of Krizevci (1920-40); Rev. Janko Shimrak — Apostolic Administrator (1941—42), Bishop of Krizevci (1942-46); Rev. Havryil Bukatko — Apostolic Administrator (1950-52), Bishop (1952-60), Bishop of Krizevci (1960-61), Archbishop of Krizevci (1961-81); Auxiliary Bishop Ioakim Segedi (1963-84), Bishop Ioakim Segedi — Apostolic Administrator (1981-83); Bishop Slavomir Miklovsh (1983-).
Statistics for 1987: Bishops — 2, Parishes — 57, Priests — 56, Theological seminaries — 1, Faithful — 48,000.

Apostolic Administration of Bosnia and Herzegovina: Rev. Oleksander Bazyuk — Apostolic Administrator (1914-24).

Destruction of Churches and Monasteries on Ukrainian Territories (1917-1988)

DESTRUCTION OF CHURCHES

According to Soviet data*, on the territories of Ukraine which became part of the U.S.S.R., 6,371 churches (out of 14,371 in 1914) were destroyed or changed into structures for other uses (jails, schools, clubs, warehouses) during the period 1917-1932. Only a relatively small number of churches of historical architectural significance was preserved. All church communities in Ukraine (as well as in the whole U.S.S.R.) and all churches of different faiths were liquidated by 1937.

Several churches were reopened and restored during World War II. However, 1,670 Orthodox churches, 237 Catholic churches, 69 chapels, 532 synagogues and 258 religious buildings were destroyed during this time.**

Having occupied all Ukrainian territories in 1945, the Soviet government now had 3,961 Ukrainian Catholic churches under its rule. The Ukrainian Catholic Church was forcibly liquidated by the Soviets in 1946, and all Catholic churches were given over to the Russian Orthodox Church.

According to the best estimates of researchers, in 1987 there were about 4,000 churches still open in the Ukrainian S.S.R. while 14,332 churches had been either destroyed or converted to other uses. Only 842 church structures were preserved because of their historical-architectural significance.

Compiled below is a partial list of Ukrainian churches destroyed or converted to other uses. This listing was compiled based on the Soviet periodical press, the work of researchers, and eyewitness accounts.***

Most of the churches destroyed by the Soviets were those built during the period of statehood of Kievan Rus' (10th-13th centuries) and of the Kozak Ukrainian Hetman State (17th-18th centuries). Churches built in more recent years, especially those of stone, were converted to other uses.

The listing is compiled according to the present administrative division of the Ukrainian S.S.R. The date of construction or funding of the church, if known, is given in parentheses.

* *Bezvirnyk*, No. 19-20, Kharkiv, October 1932, pg. 10.

** *News from Ukraine*, No. 47, Kiev, November 1986.

*** Mostly based on the Rev. Mytrofan Yavdas archives at the Ukrainian Academy of Arts and Sciences in the United States.

CHURCHES DESTROYED BY THE SOVIETS 1928-1941

KIEV OBLAST. Kiev: Dormition Cathedral of the Kiev Monastery of the Caves (1073-1089), St. Basil (Three Holy Hierarchs) (12th century), Tithes (10th century), Irene, St. Elias, Annunciation, Holy Trinity, St. Nicholas on Askold's grave, Refectory of the St. Michael (St. Demetrius) Monastery (12th century), St. Olha (19th century), Cathedral of St. Nicholas (Military) (1690-1696), SS. Peter and Paul (17th century), Dormition (12th century), St. Irene (11th century), Theophany Cathedral (1696), St. Nicholas the Good (19th century), Nativity (1814), Presentation of Christ at the Temple, Mary the Sorrowful (1861), St. George (11th century), Cathedral of the Brotherhood Monastery (18th century), Ascension Cathedral of the Florivsky Monastery (1732), Nativity of the Mother of God of the Florivsky Monastery (1857), Refectory Church of the Florivsky Convent, Protection of the Blessed Virgin Mary, St. John the Baptist, Transfiguration, All Saints in Shchekavytsya, Ascension in Podil, SS. Constantine and Helen in Podil, Resurrection in Podil, Elevation of the Cross in Podil, Presentation of the Blessed Virgin Mary into the Temple, SS. Borys and Hlib in Podil, Holy Trinity of the Holy Trinity Monastery (1868), St. Barbara in Pechersk, St. John Chrysostom on the Jewish Plaza, Ascension in Lukyanivka, St. Demetrius of Thessalonika in Lukyanivka, Protection of the Blessed Virgin Mary in Lukyanivka, St. Theodore of Tyre in Lukyanivka, Resurrection on Lviv Street, St. Alexander in Lypky, SS. Cosmas and Damian in Lypky, Holy Trinity in Kytayiv Monastery (1767), St. John the Theologian in Kytayiv Monastery (1835), Trasfiguration in Holosiyivsky Monastery, Nativity of the Mother of God in Feofaniya, Holy Trinity on the Vasylkivska Street, St. Elizabeth on Trukhanov Island, Protection of the Blessed Virgin Mary in Darnytsya, St. Michael the Archangel in Demyyivka, St. Nicholas in Syrets, St. Nicholas Prytysko (1631) (damaged in 1984). RUINED CEMETERIES: On Askold's Grave, St. Cyril, Zviryn, Military, Shchekavytsya in the Florivsky Monastery.

Baryshivka: Annunciation (18th century), Protection of the Blessed Virgin Mary (19th century); ***Dmytrenky:*** Protection of the Blessed Virgin Mary (1723-1727); ***Khodosiyivka:*** 17th century church; church in ***Kolovetsk; Lypskytok:*** Dormition (17th century); ***Medvyn:*** St. Nicholas (18th century), Dormition (1756-1762); ***Ostriyky:*** 17th century church; ***Pereyaslav-Khmelnytsky:*** Ascension (1688-1691), Protection of the Blessed Virgin Mary (17th century), SS. Borys and Hlib (18th century), Dormition (11th century), Nativity of the Mother of God, St. Andrew the Apostle, St. Theodore the Martyr; in the villages of ***Popruzhna*** and ***Rohizna; Synyava:*** Kozak church (18th century).

Six churches from the 11th-16th centuries and 24 from the 17th-19th centuries remain in Kiev, and 40 churches from the 17th-19th centuries remain in the Kiev Oblast (city excluded).

CHERKASY OBLAST. Cherkasy: St. John the Theologian (18th century), Dormition Cathedral (19th century), Protection of the Blessed Virgin Mary (19th century); ***Moysivka:*** SS. Peter and Paul (1712); church in ***Mykhaylivka; Okhmativ:*** St. John the Theologian (17th century); ***Poludnya:*** Most Holy Mother of God (1749-1752); ***Sloboda Tekucha:*** St. John the Theologian (18th century); ***Stebliv:*** Transfiguration (19th century); ***Subotiv:*** St. Elias (1648-1651); ***Synyava:*** Protection of the Blessed Virgin Mary (17th century); ***Trakhtymyriv:*** Holy Trinity (1855); ***Uman:*** Regimental Cathedral; ***Zhabotyn:*** Dormition (1850-1852), St. Nicholas (1845-1949); ***Zhornoklovy:*** SS. Peter and Paul (1890).

CHURCHES CONVERTED TO OTHER USES

Church in ***Byrlivka; Cherkasy:*** Cathedral, church in Kazbet; church in ***Drendelevo;*** church in ***Nekhayky; Uman:*** Cathedral.

One church from the 12th century and 18 churches from the 17th-19th centuries remain in the oblast.

CHERNIHIV OBLAST. Chernihiv: Cathedral of the Holy Trinity Monastery (17th century) (interior destroyed), Church of the Theological Seminary.

During the 1950-60s, St. Cyril Church was destroyed. ***Altynivka:*** Protection of the Blessed Virgin Mary (18th century), Transfiguration (19th century); ***Baturyn:*** Resurrection (18th century); ***Borzna:*** St. Nicholas Cathedral (18th century); ***Klymivka:*** Nativity of the Mother of God (19th century); ***Konotop:*** Cathedral of the Holy Trinity (18th century), St. George the Victor (18th century); ***Kozelets:*** Cathedral of the Nativity of the Mother of God, St. John the Baptist (18th century); ***Luchnyky:*** St. John the Theologian (18th century); ***Lyubech:*** Dormition (16th century), Resurrection (17th century), SS. Peter and Paul (17th century), St. Anthony of the Caves (18th century); ***Lyubytiv:*** Holy Trinity (18th century); ***Nizhyn:*** SS. Peter and Paul (17th century), Dormition (18th century), Resurrection (18th century); ***Novhorod-Siversky:*** Refectory Church of the Presentation at the Temple (17th century), Holy Trinity Cathedral (18th century); ***Oster:*** St. George Temple (11th century), Holy Prophet Elias (18th century), Nativity of the Mother of God (18th century), Ascension (18th century); ***Ozarychi:*** St. Nicholas (19th century); ***Pryluky:*** Cathedral of the Protection of the Blessed Virgin Mary (18th century); ***Ripky:*** St. John the Theologian (18th century); ***Sedniv:*** St. George the Victor (17th century), Protection of the Blessed Virgin Mary (1711-1715); ***Zhaldaky:*** SS. Peter and Paul (20th century); Churches in ***Didivka, Rudivka*** and ***Yankivtsi.***

CHURCHES CONVERTED TO OTHER USES

Baturyn: St. Michael the Archangel; ***Borzna:*** Annunciation (18th century); ***Lyubech:*** Annunciation (17th century); ***Nizhyn:*** St. Nicholas (18th century); ***Novhorod-Siversky:*** Transfiguration (17th century), Dormition (17th century); ***Novi Mlyny:*** St. George; ***Pryluky:*** Holy Trinity (18th century), Annunciation (18th century); ***Zamistya:*** St. Elias the Prophet (19th century); Churches in ***Hnylytsya, Mazhosivka*** and ***Vitovtsi.***

Six churches from the 11th-16th centuries and 47 from the 17th-19th centuries remain in the oblast.

CHERNIVTSI OBLAST. Three churches from the 15th-16th centuries and 51 from the 17th-19th centuries remain in the oblast.

CRIMEA OBLAST. 17 churches from the 3rd-16th centuries and 7 from the 17th-19th centuries remain in the oblast.

DNIPROPETROVSK OBLAST. Chervonohryhorivka: SS. Borys and Hlib; ***Danylivka:*** Annunciation (19th century); ***Dniprodzerzhynsk:*** St. George the Victor (19th century); ***Dniprokamyanka:*** Dormition (18th century), St. Nicholas of Myra (19th century); Church in ***Komyshuvata:*** SS. Peter and Paul (19th century), Protection of the Blessed Virgin Mary (19th century); ***Krasnosilka:*** St. Simon the Apostle (18th century); ***Kryvyy Rih:*** St. Nicholas (19th century), Ascension (19th century), Protection of the Blessed Virgin Mary (19th century); ***Mala Mykhaylivka:*** Elevation of the Cross (19th century); ***Mushyryn Rih:*** SS. Peter and Paul (19th century); ***Nikopol:*** Zaporizhzhya Cathedral, Holy Trinity (17th century); church in ***Novoivanivka; Novomoskovsk:*** Zaporizhzhya Cathedral (1745-48); ***Petrivka:*** SS. Peter and Paul (19th century); churches in ***Novomykolayivka*** and ***Novopavlivka; Petrykivka:*** St. George (1674); church in ***Pokrovka; Romankove:*** Elevation of the Cross (18th century), Dormition (19th century); ***Verkhnyodniprovsk:*** Protection of the Blessed Virgin Mary (19th century); ***Voznesenske:*** Theophany Cathedral; ***Zhdanivka:*** St. Michael the Archangel (19th century).

CHURCHES CONVERTED TO OTHER USES

Dnipropetrovsk: Annunciation Cathedral, Bryansk church, St. Nicholas; ***Chervonohryhorivka:*** Holy Savior-Transfiguration; ***Dniprodzerzhynsk:*** Holy Trinity (19th century); ***Krasnosilka:*** Protection of the Blessed Virgin Mary (19th century); ***Nikopol:*** Protection of the Blessed Virgin Mary, Holy Savior-Transfiguration Cathedral; Church in ***Pokrovsk; Voznesenske:*** Resurrection (19th century).

13 churches from the 17th-19th centuries remain in the oblast.

DONETSK OBLAST. Donetsk: Ascension (19th century); ***Makiyivka:*** St. Demetrius of Thessaloniha (19th century); ***Mariyinske:*** Protection of the Blessed Virgin Mary (18th century), Holy Trinity (19th century); ***Pidhorodne:*** Dormition (19th century); ***Znamenka:*** Protection of the Blessed Virgin Mary (19th century).

CHURCHES CONVERTED TO OTHER USES

Bakhmut: St. Nicholas (18th century); church in ***Kramatorsk; Makiyivka:*** Dormition (19th century); ***Slovyansk:*** Ascension (19th century).

Four churches from the 17th-20th centuries remain in the oblast; the following are museums or architectural monuments:

Artemivsk: Holy Trinity Cathedral (1746); ***Slovyanohirsk:*** St. Nicholas (18th century).

IVANO-FRANKIVSK OBLAST. Churches destroyed by the Soviets in 1950-1975 — ***Ivano-Frankivsk:*** Most Holy Mother of God; ***Kobaky:*** Holy Cross (1852); ***Volodkiv:*** St. George (1876); ***Kolomyya:*** Annunciation (1587); ***Rybne:*** Resurrection (1870).

CHURCHES CONVERTED TO OTHER USES

Horodenka: St. Nicholas (1879); ***Pavelche:*** (1912); ***Pidhaychyky:*** Annunciation (1854).

Nine churches from the 12th-16th centuries and 53 churches from the 17th-19th centuries remain in the oblast.

KHARKIV OBLAST. Kharkiv: St. Nicholas Cathedral (19th century), Myrrh-Bearing Women (19th century), St. Michael the Archangel, Holy Spirit (19th century), St. Demetrius of Thesalonika (19th century), Holy Trinity (20th century), Resurrection (19th century), SS. Cyril and Methodius (together with the cemetery), Kapluniv church, churches of the Vocational School, High School #1, Commercial School, dormitory and Theological Seminary; ***Barvinkove:*** Protection of the Blessed Virgin Mary (19th century); ***Bohodukhiv:*** Holy Trinity (18th century), Presentation of Christ at the Temple (19th century); ***Borove:*** Elevation of the Cross (18th century); ***Derhachi:*** St. Nicholas; ***Derkachi:*** St. Nicholas (19th century); ***Dudivka:*** Nativity of the Mother of God (19th century); ***Husarivka:*** St. Michael the Archangel (19th century); ***Izyum:*** Nativity (19th century), St. Nicholas (19th century), Ascension (19th century); ***Krasnokutsk:*** SS. Peter and Paul (1671-1675), Dormition Cathedral (17th century); ***Vala Komyshvakha:*** St. Demetrius of Thessalonika (18th century); ***Pashkove:*** Nativity of the Mother of God (19th century); church in ***Ryasne; Sanzhary:*** Dormition, St. Nicholas, St. Alexander Nevsky; ***Semenivka:*** St. Demetrius of Thessalonika (19th century); ***Sloboda Velyka:*** St. Nicholas (19th century), Nativity of the Mother of God (19th century); ***Zmiyiv:*** St. George the Victor, St. Nicholas Cathedral (1665-1668).

CHURCHES CONVERTED TO OTHER USES

Kharkiv: Annunciation Cathedral, Ozeryanska Church; St. Panteleymon, St. Andrew, Nativity; church in ***Birky; Bohodukhiv:*** Resurrection (19th century); ***Derhachi:*** SS. Peter and Paul (19th century); ***Krasnokutsk:*** Resurrection (1690-1700), Protection of the Blessed Virgin Mary (19th century); ***Pohozhivka:*** St. George the Victor (18th century); ***Snizhkiv:*** St. George the Victor.

13 Churches from the 17th-19th centuries remain in the oblast.

KHERSON OBLAST. Kherson: Holy Savior-Transfiguration Cathedral (19th century), Dormition (19th century).

Only four churches from the 17th-19th centuries remain in the oblast.

KHMELNYTSKA OBLAST. Kamyanets-Podilsky: Dormition Cathedral (19th century), St. John the Baptist (16th century), St. George the Victor (18th century), St. Nicholas (16th century), Protection of the Blessed Virgin Mary (17th century), St. John the Theologian at the Theological Seminary; ***Hryshky:*** Nativity; ***Mezhybizh:*** Dormition (17th century) (destroyed in 1960); ***Nova Hreblya:*** St. Michael the Archangel (1697-1701), Mother of God (19th century).

Only five churches from the 13th-16th centuries and 14 from the 17th-19th centuries remain in the oblast.

KIROVOHRAD OBLAST. Church in Delfynivka; ***Krasnosillya:*** Protection of the Blessed Virgin Mary, St. Simeon; ***Osota:*** St. John the Baptist; church in ***Semyduby.***

Only three churches from the 17th-19th centuries remain and none as an architectural monument.

LVIV OBLAST. Churches destroyed or converted to other uses by the Soviets in 1960-1984 — ***Korosno:*** Nativity of the Blessed Virgin Mary Cathedral (1865); ***Lavochne:*** St. Michael (1908); ***Mezhyrichcha:*** Ascension (1812); ***Mshana:*** Presentation of the Blessed Virgin Mary (1799); ***Oporets:*** Holy Cross (1844); ***Pidlisky:*** St. Paraskeviya (1912); ***Rozhanka Nyzhnya:*** Theophany (1909); church in ***Rozhanka;*** church in ***Vyzhnya,*** (1804), Divine Transfiguration (1892); church in ***Skolye; Smilno:*** St. Nicholas (1912); ***Tysovets:*** St. Michael (1863).

18 churches from the 11th-16th centuries and 158 from the 17th-19th centuries remain in the oblast.

MYKOLAYIV OBLAST. Mykolayiv: St. Nicholas Cathedral (19th century), Resurrection (19th century).

Only four churches from the 17th-19th centuries remain in the oblast.

ODESSA OBLAST. Odessa: St. Demetrius Cathedral (1896), Military Cathedral of Archdeacon St. Stephen (1912), St. Alexis (1888), St. Michael the Archangel (1820), Ascension (1896), Ascension in Romanivka, Italo-Jerusalem (1858), Kazan (1846), Elevation of the Cross (1859), St. Nicholas (1887), St. Nicholas at the Port (1862), St. Nicholas Peresypska, St. Demetrius (1896), SS. Peter and Paul (1939), Protection of the Blessed Virgin Mary (1812), Nativity of the Mother of God (1858), Presentation of Christ at the Temple (1842), All Saints (1829), Dormition (1855), churches of the monasteries of St. Panteleymon (1895), of St. Andrew (1887) and of St. Elias (1896), Bishop's of the Holy Cross, St. Michael the Archangel of the nunnery (1826), St. Demetrius of the bishop's residence, Nativity by the city hospital (1814), Transfiguration Cathedral (1795) (destroyed in the 1960s); ***Andriyivka:*** St. Panteleymon; ***Dalnyk:*** St. George (1817), Elevation of the Cross; ***Fontanka:*** Resurrection (1846), SS. Constantine and Helen; ***Hnylyakovo:*** Protection of the Blessed Virgin Mary; ***Kryva Balka:*** Holy Trinity; ***Tatarka:*** Dormition (1816); ***Usatove:*** Nativity of the Mother of God (1822).

Some of the masonry churches in Odessa were converted to other uses. Two churches from the 14th-15th centuries and 12 from the 17th-19th centuries remain in the oblast.

POLTAVA OBLAST. Poltava: Dormition Cathedral (1700-1703), Resurrection Cathedral (1722-1725), Presentation of Christ at the Temple (18th century), Nativity of the Mother of God (19th century), Ascension (19th century), Holy Trinity (1850-1863), St. Nicholas (18th century), Protection of the Blessed Virgin Mary (1771-1772), All Saints (19th century), Transfiguration, Holy Savior, Kladbyshchenska Church, Pavlenkivska church, Bazarna church, Horbanivska, St. Macarius, the Church on the Swedish Tomb, St. George, Transfiguration, Prophet Elijah; ***Abazivka:*** Dormition, St. John the Theologian (19th century); ***Andriyashivka:*** St. Nicholas (19th century); ***Bilsk:*** St. Michael the Archangel (18th century); ***Cherkasivka:*** Holy Trinity; ***Chernykhy:*** Elevation of the Cross (18th century), Protection of the Blessed Virgin Mary (19th century); ***Chutove:*** Elevation of the Cross (19th century); ***Dekalivka:*** Holy Trinity (1830-1832); ***Deymanivka:*** St. Nicholas; in ***Dovhalivka*** and ***Drabynivka:*** 2 churches; ***Fedorivka:*** Nativity of the Mother of God; ***Hadyach:*** Dormition Cathedral (18th century), St. George the Victor (19th century), St. John the Theologian (19th century); ***Hlynske:*** Dormition (18th century), Protection of the Blessed Virgin Mary (19th century); ***Horbanivka:*** Nativity of the Mother of God (18th century); ***Kaplunivka:*** Dormition (19th century), St. John the Theologian (19th century); ***Khorol:*** Cathedral of the Nativity of the Mother of God (18th century), St. Nicholas (18th century), Protection of the Blessed

Virgin Mary (19th century), Resurrection (19th century), SS. Peter and Paul (19th century), All Saints (19th century); ***Klymivka:*** Most Holy Virgin Mary; ***Klyushnykivka:*** Mother of God; ***Kobelyaky:*** Nativity of the Mother of God (18th century), SS. Peter and Paul (18th century), Dormition (19th century); ***Konstyantynohrad:*** St. George the Victor (18th century), Ascension (19th century); ***Koshmanivka:*** (16th century); ***Kotelva:*** Transfiguration Cathedral (18th century), Protection of the Blessed Virgin Mary (18th century), Elevation of the Cross (19th century), Nativity of the Mother of God (19th century), St. Nicholas (19th century), All Saints (19th century), Myrrh-Bearing Women (19th century); ***Kremenchuk:*** Dormition Cathedral (18th century), Holy Trinity (18th century), Transfiguration (19th century), Protection of the Blessed Virgin Mary (19th century); churches in ***Kruta Balka, Kustolove*** and ***Kustolovo-Sukhodilka; Kylyberda:*** Protection of the Blessed Virgin Mary (16th century); ***Lokhvytsya:*** Holy Trinity Cathedral (18th century), St. John the Baptist; ***Lubny:*** Savior Cathedral at the Savior-Transfiguration Monastery (1615-1619), Holy Spirit Refectory (19th century), Holy Spirit Fraternal (17th century), St. John the Theologian (18th century); church in ***Luky; Lyutenski Budyshcha:*** Protection of the Blessed Virgin Mary (18th century); ***Muchakhy:*** Dormition (19th century), St. Michael the Archangel (1890), Protection of the Blessed Virgin Mary; churches in ***Mala Pereshchepyna*** and ***Malyy Kobelyachok; Maryivka:*** Dormition (19th century); ***Matyashivka:*** St. Nicholas; ***Melekhy:*** Three Holy Hierarchs, Dormition (1907); ***Mhar:*** Transfiguration Cathedral of the Mhar Monastery (1682-1694); church in ***Mykhaylivka; Mykolske:*** Transfiguration; ***Myrhorod:*** Holy Trinity (18th century), St. John the Theologian (18th century), Resurrection (19th century), Dormition Cathedral (19th century), All Saints (17th century); ***Nastasivka:*** Elevation of the Cross (19th century); ***Novi Sanzhary:*** Elevation of the Cross (18th century), Dormition, St. Nicholas, St. Michael, St. Alexander Nevsky, Holy Trinity, St. George; ***Opishnya:*** Dormition (19th century), Transfiguration, St. Michael the Archangel (18th century), Holy Trinity (17th century); ***Ostapye:*** St. Nicholas (19th century); ***Paraskoviyivka:*** St. Barbara the Martyr (18th century); ***Perekopivka:*** Nativity of the Mother of God (19th century); ***Petrivka:*** St. Nicholas the Miracle-Worker; ***Pisky:*** Protection of the Blessed Virgin Mary (19th century); churches in ***Poluzirya, Popivka*** and ***Popove; Povstyn:*** St. Michael (18th century); ***Prokofiyivka:*** St. Nicholas; ***Pushkarivka:*** Ascension (16th century); ***Pyryatyn:*** Cathedral of the Protection of the Blessed Virgin Mary (18th century), St. Michael the Archangel (18th century), Dormition (19th century), Holy Trinity Cathedral; ***Reshetylivka:*** Holy Trinity (19th century), Elevation of the Cross (19th century); ***Romodan:*** St. Demetrius of Thesslonika (19th century); ***Ruda:*** Holy Savior, Ascension (1903), Transfiguration (1900-1903); ***Runivshchyna:*** Elevation of the Cross (18th century), St. George; ***Sencha:*** Dormition (17th century), St. Nicholas (18th century); church in ***Suprotyvna Balka; Takhtaulove:*** Protection of the Blessed Virgin Mary (18th century); ***Tarandyntsi:*** St. George the Victor (19th century); church in ***Turbayi; Ustymivka:*** St. Michael, Dormition; ***Vasylivka:*** St. Michael the Archangel (18th century); ***Velyki Budyshcha:*** Protection of the Blessed Virgin Mary (18th century); church in ***Velyki Solontsi; Velyki Sorochyntsi:*** Elevation of the Cross (18th century), St. John the Theologian (18th century), Dormition (1723-1726); two churches in ***Velyky Kobelyachok; Vesely Podil:*** Dormition (18th century); ***Voronky:*** Nativity of the Mother of God (18th century); ***Vovcha:*** Transfiguration of the Mother of God (18th century); ***Vovcha:*** Transfiguration Cathedral (1810-1814), St. Nicholas (19th century); ***Yabluchne:*** St. Demetrius of Thessalonika (18th century); ***Zinkiv:*** Holy Trinity Cathedral (17th century), Resurrection (17th century), Holy Spirit (19th century), Annunciation (19th century), St. Nicholas (19th century), Protection of the Blessed Virgin Mary (19th century).

Only 18 churches from the 17th-19th centuries remain in the oblast.

ROVNO OBLAST. Churches in ***Khynochi*** and ***Znosychi.***

Two churches from the 15th-16th centuries and 32 from the 17th-19th centuries remain in the oblast.

SUMY OBLAST. Altynivka: Transfiguration, Protection of the Blessed Virgin Mary; ***Bobryk:*** Protection of the Blessed Virgin Mary (18th century), Ascension (19th century); ***Dubovychi:*** Mother of God of Dubovychi (1776), Kochubeyivska Church, Cemetery church; ***Esman:*** St. Gregory (1851); ***Hlukhiv:*** SS. Peter and Paul Cathedral of the Hlukhiv Monastery (17th century), Nativity of the Mother of God; ***Konotop:*** Dormition, Holy Trinity and all other churches; church in ***Kozatske; Lebedyn:*** St. Nicholas Cathedral (19th century), St. Elijah the Prophet (18th century), Transfiguration (19th century); ***Lyubytove:*** Holy Trinity; ***Okhtyrka:*** Holy Trinity (18th century), Dormition Cathedral (17th century); ***Ozarychi:*** St. Nicholas; churches in ***Pidlypne*** and ***Popivka; Putyvl:*** Transfiguration Cathedral (17th century), Nativity of the Mother of God (18th century), St. John the Theologian, Ascension (18th century), Protection of the Blessed Virgin Mary (18th century); ***Romny:*** Holy Trinity Cathedral (17th century), Protection of the Blessed Virgin Mary (19th century), Nativity of the Mother of God (19th century); church in ***Vilkhove; Vilshana:*** Nativity of the Mother of God (19th century), St. Onufrius (19th century); ***Zholdaky:*** SS. Peter and Paul (1918), new church (1920).

Not a single church from the 11th-16th centuries remains in the oblast. 31 churches from the 17th-19th centuries remain in the oblast.

TERNOPIL OBLAST. Ternopil: Dormition; ***Pidhoryany:*** Monastery church.

Ten churches from the 12th-16th centuries and 36 from the 17th-19th centuries remain in the oblast.

VINNYTSYA OBLAST. Vinnytsya: Resurrection (19th century), Ascension, in Zamist; ***Bar:*** Cathedral of the Nunnery of the Nativity of the Mother of God (17th century), St. John the Theologian (18th century), Holy Trinity (19th century); ***Bershad:*** Cathedral of the Savior-Transfiguration Monastery (18th century), SS. Peter and Paul Refectory Church; ***Bratslav:*** Dormition Cathedral (17th century), Elevation of the Cross (18th century), St. Paraskeva (18th century); ***Busha:*** St. Michael the Archangel (17th century); ***Chetvertynivka:*** Holy Friday Paraskeva (17th century); ***Dzhulynka:*** Protection of the Blessed Virgin Mary (19th century); ***Haysyn:*** St. Nicholas Cathedral (19th century), Holy Trinity (18th century); ***Hnivan:*** SS. Peter and Paul (19th century); ***Holodky:*** St. Nicholas (18th century); ***Hryshkivtsi:*** Nativity of the Mother of God (19th century); ***Ivankivtsi:*** St. John the Theologian (19th century); ***Kalnyk:*** Nativity of the Mother of God (1698-1700); ***Khomutyntsi:*** St. John the Theologian (18th century); ***Krasne:*** Elevation of the Cross (18th century), Protection of the Blessed Virgin Mary (19th century); ***Krasnosilka:*** St. John the Theologian (19th century); ***Lityn:*** Transfiguration (19th century), Presentation of the Virgin Mary at the Temple (19th century), ***Luka:*** Nativity of the Mother of God; ***Lyadova:*** Cave Church of the Beheading of St. John the Baptist (12th century); ***Mankivtsi:*** Protection of the Blessed Virgin Mary (19th century); ***Mohyliv-Podilsky:*** Holy Spirit (18th century), Dormition, SS. Peter and Paul (18th century), Transfiguration (19th century); ***Myakokhid:*** St. Michael the Archangel (20th century); ***Nemyriv:*** Protection of the Blessed Virgin Mary (1657-1659), St. Nicholas (17th century), Ascension (18th century), St. Michael the Archangel (19th century); ***Olhopil:*** St. Philip the Apostle (18th century), Dormition; ***Pyrohiv:*** St. Nicholas (1843-1846); ***Radivka:*** St. Michael the Archangel (19th century); ***Rakhny-Polovy:*** Nativity of the Mother of God (19th century); ***Sharhorod:*** Church of the Ascension Monastery (18th century), Refectory Church of St. John the Baptist; ***Sutysky:*** St. John the Theologian (19th century); ***Tomashpil:*** Elevation of the Cross (19th century); ***Tulchyn:*** Cathedral of the Protection of the Blessed Virgin Mary (18th century), Nativity of the Mother of God (18th century); ***Tyvriv:*** Holy Trinity (18th century); ***Vasylivka:*** St. Onufrius (19th century); ***Veremiyivka:*** Holy Trinity (19th century); ***Voroshylivka:*** St. Michael the Archangel (18th century), Dormition (19th century); ***Yampil:*** Nativity of the Mother of God (19th century); ***Yaruha:*** Dormition (18th century).

One church from the 12th century and 23 from the 17th-19th centuries remain in the oblast.

VOLYNIA OBLAST. Churches destroyed or converted to other uses in the 1960s — ***Berestechko, Lypa, Mylushyn, Skobelka.***

Eight churches from the 10th-16th centuries and 81 from the 17th-20th centuries remain in the oblast.

VOROSHYLOVHRAD OBLAST. ***Brusivka:*** Protection of the Blessed Virgin Mary (19th century); ***Dadiyivka:*** Dormition Cathedral of the Svyatohirsky Monastery (17th century), SS. Peter and Paul (19th century); ***Lyman:*** Nativity of the Mother of God (19th century); churches in ***Stepanivka*** and ***Tsarivka; Osota:*** St. John the Baptist (18th century).

Only three churches from the 17th-19th centuries remain in the oblast; none remain as a museum or architectural monument.

ZAKARPATSKA OBLAST. Churches in villages of ***Danylivka, Oleksandrivka, Rososh, Ruske Pole*** and ***Sokornytsya.***

Seven churches from the 11th-16th centuries and 48 from the 17-19th centuries remain in the oblast.

ZAPORIZHZHYA OBLAST. ***Zaporizhzhya:*** Cathedral of the Protection of the Blessed Virgin Mary (18th century), Zaporizhzhya Cathedral, Ascension (18th century), St. Philip the Apostle (19th century); churches in ***Bilenke*** and ***Blahovishchenske; Petropavlivka:*** SS. Peter and Paul (18th century), Ascension (18th century), All Saints (19th century); ***Verbovske:*** Transfiguration (18th century), Theophany (18th century); ***Vesele:*** Protection of the Blessed Virgin Mary.

Only one church from the 19th century remains in the oblast as an architectural monument.

ZHYTOMYR OBLAST. ***Zhytomyr:*** Theophany (destroyed in 1975); ***Horodnytsya:*** St. George (1905); ***Meleni:*** St. Michael the Archangel (18th century); ***Serby:*** St. Michael the Archangel (18th century); ***Skuraty:*** Elevation of the Cross (19th century).

One church from the 12th-16th centuries and 8 from the 17th-19th centuries remain in the oblast.

DESTRUCTION OF UKRAINIAN ORTHODOX AND CATHOLIC CHURCHES ON UKRAINIAN TERRITORIES UNDER POLAND

After the end of World War I, a great part of the Ukrainian lands — Galicia, Volynia, Kholm, Pidlyashshya and the Lemko region — came under Polish rule.

In the Kholm and Pidlyashshya regions — the westernmost — there were 389 Ukrainian Orthodox churches in 1914. By September 1, 1939, the Polish government had burned or destroyed 189 churches, and forcibly transferred 149 churches to the Roman Catholic Church; thus, only 51 Ukrainian Orthodox churches remained in the regions.

After World War II, the Polish Communist government did not destroy Ukrainian Orthodox churches (with very few exceptions); Ukrainian Catholic churches, however, were frequent victims

On the Ukrainian territories now under Poland — Lemko and Peremyshl Regions — there were, in 1945, 514 Ukrainian Catholic churches, 311 of which were declared architectural monuments. Six churches were destroyed during the war. The Polish Communist government destroyed 158 churches during 1946-1956, 101 of which were architectural monuments. 57 churches were transferred, by the government, to the Roman Catholic Church 34 were converted into warehouses, 13 were maintained by the faithful, while the fate of 246 is not determined as yet. Of the 175 Ukrainian Catholic churches on other territories under Poland, especially in the Lemko Region, almost all were destroyed, transferred to the Roman Catholic Church or converted to other uses.

UKRAINIAN ORTHODOX CHURCHES DESTROYED BY THE POLISH AUTHORITIES IN 1938

(The year of construction in parentheses.)

Bartatychi (1886); Berezno (1914); Bila Pidlyaska (1929); Bisha (1930); Cherniyiv (1912); Chortovychi (1908); Depultychi (1908); Holube (1876); Hoya (1936); Holovno (1881); Horoshchytsi (1913); Husynne (1905) and (1909); Khmelok (1936); Kholm (1908); also Holy Spirit and former Military churches; Kmichyn (1892); Knyazhopil (1937); Kolekhovychi (1882); Kornytsya (1578); Klyatvy (1910); Kryliv (1911); Kulakovychi (1884); Kyyivets (1902) and (1936); Lahivtsi (1906); Lashchiv (1878); Laskiv (1980); Leshchany (1908); Lomazy (1889.); Lykoshyn (1908); Lypynky (1936); Lyuben (1938); Malkiv (1907); Mezhylystya (1907); Modryn (1596); Mohylnytsya (1912); Nabrozh (1907); Obsha (1937); Oshchiv (1909); Ostriv (1890); Perehorile (1907); Pidhirya (1596); Rozvadivka (1910); Silets (1877); Sharovolya (1902); Shebreshyn (1184); Tarnovatka (1930); Topilcha (1912); Turkovychi (1930) and (1903); Turobyn (1882); Uhnyn (1911); Ukhanye (1883); Vilkhovets (1912); Vytychno (1930); Yaniv Lyublynsky (1879); Yaroslavets (1596); Yuriv (1912); Zabirtsi (1914); Zahorovo (1909); Zakrovets (1906); Zamkh (1936) Zberezhe (1908); Zernyky (1893).

UKRAINIAN ORTHODOX CHURCHES FORCIBLY TAKEN OVER BY THE POLISH CATHOLICS

(The year of construction in parentheses.)

Berizka (1890); Bila Pidlyaska (1582); Bishcha (1911); Bukovychi (1806); Hansk (1882); Hdeshyn (1899); Honyatychi (1896); Horbiv (1904); Horodok (1914); Horyshiv Polsky (1907); Khlopkiv (1890); Khodyvantsi (1911); Kholm Cathedral (16th century); Koden (16th century); Kurmaniv (1907); Lysiv (1881); Maydan Knyazhy (1905); Monastyrok (1885); Mshana (1914); Neverkiv (1889); Ortel Knyazhy (1879); Pashenky (1894); Radche (1892); Radyn (1882); Sahryn (1878); Sedlyshche (1910); Shistka (1890); Tarnovatka (1890) and (1897); Tuchapy (1877); Voskrenychi Velyki (1902); Voyin (1893); Zamostya (1589).

A total of 66 churches were destroyed and 34 forcibly transferred to the Roman Catholic Church in 1938.

UKRAINIAN CATHOLIC CHURCHES DESTROYED BY THE POLISH COMMUNISTS 1946-1956

Listed below are 101* churches destroyed by the Polish Communists during 1946-1956. All these churches were historical architectural monuments. The year of construction is given in parentheses.

Bakhiv (1848); Balnytsya (1856); Besko (1892); Bircha (1829); Bukovets (1865); Bystre (1825); Chertyzhne (18th century); Deshna (1738); Dmytrovychi (1634); Dovzhytsya (1840); Dusivtsi (1641); Dvernyk (1765); Dzvonyach Dolishniy (1800); Fredropol (1866); Habkivtsi (1833); Horodok (1790); Hrab (1808); Hulske (1820); Izdebky (1660); Kalnytsya by Tisna (1842); Kaminka (1854); Karlykiv (1840); Kelchava (1837); Khrevt (1670); Kolonytsi (1832); Kopysko (1821); Korenytsya (1649); Kotan (early 19th century); Krayna (1882); Kryve (1842); Kryve by Tisna (1845); Kvashenytsya (1777); Lishna (1833); Lisko (16th century); Loboziv (1844); Lodynka Dolishnya (1824); Lopenka (1757); Luh (1864); Lupkiv (1820); Maniv (1841); Monastyr, County Lyubachiv (1723); Monastyr, County Yaroslav (1719); Moshanets (1834); Mshana (1865); Myakysh Novy (1869); Nebeshchany (1854); Novosilky Dydynski (1740); Orly (18th century); Ozhenna (1857); Polyany Surovychni (1728); Preluky (1831); Prusye (1793); Prybyshiv (1840); Pulavy (1831); Radava (1850); Rozstayne (17th century); Ruske (1848); Serednye Velyke (1810); Serednytsya (1765); Shcherbanivka (1857); Sinyavka (1877); Smerek (18th century); Stankova (1888); Strubovyska (1843); Stuposyany (1787); Stuzhnytsya (1826); Sukovate (1826); Tarnavka (1834); Telesnytsya Oshvarova (1826); Tisna (1825); Trostyanets (1822); Tsarynske (1778); Tvorylne (1876); Tykhanya (1790); Tysovets (1830); Uhertsi (1834); Ustiyanova Horishnya (1790); Veremen (1850); Volkovyya (1853); Volosate (1837); Volya Chervona (1753); Volya Sukova (1864); Volya Tseklynska (1768); Vyshovatka (18th century); Vyslochok (1818); Vyslok Horishniy (1834); Vysochany (1805); Yamna Horishnya (1843); Yankivtsi (1850); Yasel (1825); Yavirets (1846); Yavirnyk (1843); Zaluzh (1807); Zatvornytsya (1774); Zavadka, County Syanik (1856); Zavadka, County Ustryky (1838); Zaviy (1868); Zharnivka (1860); Zhernytsya Nyzhnya; Zhydivske (16th century); Zubenko (1789).

---

* Compiled from: Ryszard Brykowski, *W sprawie architektury cerkiewnej wojewodstwa rzeszowskiego* (*On the church architecture in the Rzeszow Region*). "Ochrana Zabytkow," Warszawa, 1957, No. 2 (37).

UKRAINIAN ORTHODOX AND CATHOLIC MONASTERIES

There were 117 Orthodox monasteries (66 monasteries and 51 nunneries with a population of 6,392 monks and 8,533 nuns on Ukrainian territories within the Russian Empire in the 1900s).

Nine Orthodox monasteries and five nunneries were in Poland in 1938. There remained one monastery and one nunnery in 1984.

There were 195 Ukrainian Catholic monasteries on Ukrainian territories under Poland in 1939 and eight in the Pryashiv Region in Czechoslovakia. By 1950, all Ukrainian Catholic monasteries were liquidated by the Communists — destroyed, converted to other uses (e.g., prisons, schools, warehouses, clubs) or transferred to the Russian Orthodox Church. By 1950, however, the number of Ukrainian Catholic monasteries in the Pryashiv Region had grown to 15.

By 1939 not a single monastery remained open in the Ukrainian S.S.R.; 40 monasteries were restored and reopened during the war.

According to statistics for 1986, out of 117 Ukrainian Orthodox monasteries and 195 Ukrainian Catholic monasteries that were located on Ukrainian territories under Soviet rule, only nine Orthodox monasteries were open (3 monasteries and 6 nunneries), 33 had been converted into museums or remained as historical architectural monuments, and 270 had been either destroyed or converted to other uses.

Listed below are Ukrainian Orthodox and Catholic monasteries that were destroyed by the Soviets, converted to other uses or into museums, or remain as historical architectural monuments, and 9 monasteries that remain open (it is possible, however, that some have been closed in the interim.)

Dates of founding or construction of the monasteries are shown as the first figure, and the number of Orthodox monks or nuns as of 1917 as the second figure in parentheses.

UKRAINIAN ORTHODOX MONASTERIES DESTROYED OR CONVERTED TO OTHER USES BY THE SOVIETS, 1920-1988

KIEV OBLAST. Kiev: Hospital Holy Trinity Monastery (12th century/507), Brotherhood Theophany Monastery (1615/78), Feofaniy Monastery (1786/103), St. Michael Golden-domed Monastery (1108/236), St. Nicholas Slupsky Monastery (1113/150), Mizhhirsky Transfiguration Monastery (1523/ unknown), Presentation of the Virgin Mary at the Temple convent (1898/99), Mother of God Monastery (1913/119); ***Bohuslav:*** St. Nicholas Monastery (1575/90); ***Lebedyn:*** St. Nicholas Convent (1779/312); ***Pereyaslav-Khmelnytsky:*** Ascension Monastery (19th century/33); ***Rzhyshiv:*** Transfiguration (1649/262).

OPEN MONASTERIES IN KIEV OBLAST. ***Kiev:*** Florivsky

Ascension Convent (1556/1001), Protection of the Blessed Virgin Mary (1889/694).

CHERKASY OBLAST. Chyhyryn: Holy Trinity Convent (1627/282), Mashnohorsky Ascension Monastery (17th century/53); ***Korsun-Shevchenkivsky:*** St. Onufriy Hulyanytsky Monastery (17th century/99); ***Medvedivka:*** St. Nicholas Monastery (1661/75); ***Melnykivka:*** Motronynsky Holy Trinity Monastery (13th century/92); ***Vynohrad:*** Dormition Monastery (18th century/35); ***Zhabotyn:*** St. Onufrious Monastery (1706/98).

OPEN MONASTERIES IN CHERKASY OBLAST. ***Chervonohirka:*** Protection of the Blessed Virgin Mary Convent (unknown/unknown).

CHERNIHIV OBLAST. Baturyn: St. Nicholas Monastery (15th century/13); ***Chernihiv:*** Kamensky Dormition Monastery (1681/95); ***Domnytsya:*** Nativity of the Mother of God Monastery (1696/38); ***Kozelets:*** St. George Monastery (1654/9), Nativity of the Mother of God Convent (1885/161); ***Maksaky:*** Holy Trinity Convent (1642/36); ***Mhlyn:*** Rozvytovsky Holy Trinity-Protection of the Blessed Virgin Mary Convent (1900/unknown); ***Mytkiv:*** Klymovsky Protection of the Blessed Virgin Mary Monastery (1847/10); ***Nizhyn:*** Annunciation Monastery (1716/11), Presentation of the Virgin Mary at the Temple Convent (18th century/196); ***Polissya:*** Malynoostrivsky Nativity of the Mother of God Convent (1768/16); ***Rykhly:*** St. Nicholas of the Desert Monastery (1666/90).

CRIMEA OBLAST. Burunduk: Toplova St. Paraskeva Monastery (1858/241); ***Kerch:*** Katerlez St. George Convent (1857/23); ***Sevastopol:*** Khersones St. Volodymyr Monastery (1850/158), ***Inkerman:*** St. Clement Pope Monastery (1852/177), ***Balaklava:*** St. George Monastery (1891/unknown); ***Sudak:*** Kyzeltash St. Stephen of Surozh Monastery (1851/36); ***Simferopol:*** SS. Cosmas and Damian Convent (1856/86).

DNIPROPETROVSK OBLAST. Dnipropetrovsk: Joy of the All Sorrowful Convent (1873/86), Tykhvynsky Convent (1886/169); ***Ivanivka:*** Znamensky Convent (1903/100), Three Holy Hierarchs Svitlivsky Convent (1897/97); ***Kokhanivka:*** Samarsky Holy Trinity Monastery (1885/85); ***Mariyivka:*** St. Joseph Convent (1873/287); ***Oleksandriya:*** Chechelevsky St. John the Baptist Convent (1870/86).

KHARKIV OBLAST. Kharkiv: Kuryazhsky Transfiguration Monastery (1663/29), Verkhnyekharkivsky St. Nicholas Monastery (1845/335), Ryasnensky St. Demetrius Monastery (1867/149); ***Bohodukhiv:*** Holy Trinity Convent (1889/308); ***Izyum:*** Svyatohirsky Dormition Monastery (13th century/398); ***Khoroshevsk:*** Ascension Convent (17th century/729); ***Kupyansk:*** Dormition-Seraphim Convent (1897/309); ***Zmiyiv:*** Vysochynovsky Kazansky Monastery (1886/99), Holy Savior (1889/64).

KHERSON OBLAST. Kherson: Annunciation Convent (1866/377); Beryslav: St. Gregory-Byzyukivsky Monastery (1783/76); ***Dniprovsk:*** Oleshkivsky Dormition Convent (1901/130).

KHMELNYTSKY OBLAST. Holovchyntsi: Transfiguration Convent (1540/82); ***Horodyshche:*** Nativity of the Mother of God Monastery (1538/225); ***Kamyanets-Podilsky:*** Holy Trinity Monastery (17th century/11); ***Korzhivtsi:*** Nativity of the Mother of God Monastery (1742/15).

ODESSA OBLAST. Balta: St. Theodosius Monastery (1908/83).

OPEN MONASTERIES IN ODESSA OBLAST. ***Odessa:*** Dormition Monastery (1824/31), St. Michael the Archangel Convent (1841/183).

POLTAVA OBLAST. Poltava: Elevation of the Cross Monastery (1650/58); ***Dykanka:*** Holy Trinity Velykobudyshchynsky Monastery (17th century/184); ***Ladyn:*** Protection of the Blessed Virgin Mary Convent (16th century/326); ***Mhar:*** Mhar Transfiguration Monastery (1624/59); ***Zolotonosha:*** St. John the Theologian Convent (17th century/228).

ROVNO OBLAST. Derman: Holy Trinity Monastery (15th century/18); ***Dubno:*** Elevation of the Cross Monastery (15th century/26), Dubno Convent (1909/60).

OPEN MONASTERIES IN THE ROVNO OBLAST. ***Korets:*** Holy Trinity Convent (17th century).

SUMY OBLAST. Hlukhiv: SS. Peter and Paul Monastery (17th century/53); ***Okhtyrka:*** Holy Trinity Monastery (1654/120), Kazansky Monastery (1904/25); ***Putyvl:*** Movchansky Monastery (17th century/unknown).

OPEN MONASTERIES IN THE TERNOPIL OBLAST. ***Pochayiv:*** Pochayiv Dormition Monastery (1240/196).

VINNYTSYA OBLAST. Bar: Protection of the Blessed Virgin Mary Convent (1881/110); ***Bershad:*** Transfiguration Monastery (1616/34); ***Brayiliv:*** Holy Trinity Convent (1635/113); ***Hraniv:*** Transfiguration Monastery (17th century/34); ***Nemyriv:*** St. Nicholas Convent (18th century/183).

VOLYNIA OBLAST. Novy Zahoriv: Nativity of the Mother of God Monastery (15th century/22); ***Kovel:*** Melets St. Nicholas Monastery (16th century/26); ***Volodymyr-Volynsky:*** Nativity Monastery (1755/36).

VOROSHYLOVHRAD OBLAST. Starobilsk: Sorrowful Virgin Convent (1862/357).

ZHYTOMYR OBLAST. Lyubar: St. George Convent (1666/133); ***Zhytomyr:*** Theophany Monastery (1898/17).

UKRAINIAN CATHOLIC MONASTERIES DESTROYED OR CONVERTED TO OTHER USES BY THE SOVIETS, 1939-1988

According to statistics for 1939, on Ukrainian territories under Poland there were 195 Ukrainian Catholic monasteries (including monastery buildings with only a few monks or nuns). After the occupation of these Western Ukrainian territories by the Soviet Army in 1939 and 1944, all Ukrainian Catholic monasteries were at first closed and in 1945-1950 all were either destroyed or converted to other uses. Only a few remain as historical monuments.

Below is a partial list compiled according to the administrative division of the present Ukrainian S.S.R. The year of founding of the monastery is shown in parentheses.

IVANO-FRANKIVSK OBLAST. Hoshiv: Transfiguration Monastery (1570); ***Pohonya:*** Dormition Monastery (1634).

LVIV OBLAST. Lviv: St. Onufriy Monastery (13th century), Immaculate Conception Convent, St. Macrina Convent, St. John the Studite Convent; ***Chervonohrad (formerly***

Krystynopil): St. George Monastery (1771-1776); ***Dobromyl:*** St. Onufrious Monastery (16th century); ***Drohobych:*** Holy Trinity Monastery (1774); ***Kryvchychi:*** St. John the Baptist Convent; ***Pidmykhaylivtsi:*** Holy Trinity Convent; ***Slovita:*** Elevation of the Cross Convent; ***Yaktoriv:*** Protection of the Blessed Virgin Mary Convent; ***Zboyiska:*** Our Lady of Perpetual Help Convent; ***Zolochiv:*** Ascension Monastery (1665).

TERNOPIL OBLAST. ***Ternopil:*** Dormition Monastery; ***Krasnopushcha:*** St. John the Baptist Monastery (1665); ***Mizhhirya:*** St. Basil Monastery (16th century); ***Ulashkivtsi:*** St. John Monastery (1738).

VOLYNIA OBLAST. ***Lutsk:*** St. Basil Monastery (17th century) was destroyed. Only monks' cells remain.

ZAKARPATSKA OBLAST. ***Boronyava:*** Annunciation Monastery (1716); ***Krasnobrid:*** Holy Spirit Monastery (15th century); ***Uzhhorod:*** St. Basil Monastery (17th century).

OPEN AS ORTHODOX MONASTERIES. ***Bukove:*** Elevation of the Cross Monastery (1742); ***Mukachiv:*** St. Nicholas Convent (1360).

Hierarchies of the Ukrainian Churches

Orthodox Metropolitans

METROPOLITANS OF KIEV

Mykhayil.. 988-922
Leontiy 992-1008
Ioann 1008-35
Theopemptos 1035-49
Ilarion (Hilarion) 1051-54
Yefrem I 1054
Heorhiy 1062-72
Ioann II 1077-88
Ioann III 1089-90
Yefrem II 1090-96
Mykolay 1097-1102
Nykyfor I 1104-21
Nykyta 1121-26
Mykhayil I 1130-45
Klym Smolyatych 1147-54
Konstantyn I 1155-58
Teodor 1161-62
Ioann IV 1164-66
Konstantyn II 1167-72
Mykhayil II 1171-82
Nykyfor II 1182-97
Matviy 1200-20
Kyrylo I 1223-33
Yosyf I 1237-40

METROPOLITANS OF KIEV AND ALL RUS'

Petro Akerovych 1241-42
Kyrylo II 1250-81
Maksym 1283-1305
Petro 1308-26
Teognost 1328-53
Teodoryt 1352-55
Aleksey 1354-1378
Cyprian 1375-1406
Fotiy 1407-14
Hryhoriy Tsamblak 1415-19
Fotiy 1420-31
Herasym 1432-35
Isidore (Izydor) 1436-39
Mysayil Drutsky 1475-80
Symon 1481-88
Iona Hlezna 1492-94
Makariy I 1495-97
Yosyf I Bolharynovych 1498-1501
Iona II 1503-07
Yosyf II Soltan 1507-21
Yosyf III 1522-34
Makariy II 1534-56
Sylvester Byelkevych 1556-67
Iona III Protasovych-Ostrovsky 1568-76
Illya Kucha 1576-79
Onysyfor Divochka 1579-89
Mykhaylo Rohoza 1589-96
Yov Boretsky 1620-31
Isaya Kopynsky 1631-33
Petro Mohyla 1632-47
Sylvester Kosiv 1647-57
Dionysiy Balaban 1657-63
Yosyf Nelyubovych-Tukalsky 1663-75
Antoniy Vynnytsky 1677-79
Hedeon Svyatopolk Chetvertynsky 1685-90
Varlaam Yasynsky 1690-1707
Yoakym Krokovsky 1707-18
Raphael Zaborovsky 1742-47
Tymofiy Shcherbatsky 1748-57
Arseniy Mohylyansky 1757-70
Havryyil Kremyanetsky 1770-83
Samuyil Myslavsky 1783-96
Yerofey Malytsky 1796-99

METROPOLITANS OF GALICIA

Nifont 1302-03, 1305
Petro, also Metropolitan of Kiev and All Rus' .. 1308-26
Havryil 1317-26, 1328
Teodor 1331-47
Roman, also the Lithuanian Metropolitan 1355-61
Antoniy 1371-91
Ioann 1393-97, 98

METROPOLITANS OF BUKOVYNA AND DALMATIA

Yevheniy Hakman 1873
Sylvester Andriyevych-Morar 1880-95
Volodymyr Repta 1902-25

METROPOLITANS OF KIEV AND ALL UKRAINE

Vasyl Lypkivsky 1921-27
Mykola Boretsky 1927-30

METROPOLITANS OF KHARKIV AND ALL UKRAINE

Ivan Pavlovsky 1930-36

METROPOLITANS OF THE UAOC IN THE DIASPORA

Polikarp Sikorsky 1945-58
Nikanor Abramovych 1953-69
Mstyslav Skrypnyk 1969-

METROPOLITANS OF THE UOC IN THE U.S.

Ioann Teodorovych 1950-71
Mstyslav Skrypnyk 1971-

METROPOLITANS OF THE UGOC IN CANADA

Hermanos 1919-24
Ilarion Ohiyenko 1951-72
Mykhayil Khoroshy 1972-75
Andriy Metyuk 1975-83
Vasyliy Fedak 1983-

METROPOLITAN OF THE CONCILIAR UAOC

Hryhoriy Ohiychuk 1971-1985

Catholic Metropolitans

METROPOLITANS OF KIEV AND ALL RUS'

Isidore (Izydor) 1439-42
Hryhoriy II 1458-72
Mykhaylo Rohoza 1596-99
Ipatiy Potiy 1600-13
Velyamyn Rutsky 1614-37
Raphael Korsak 1637-40
Antin Selyava 1641-55
Havryyil Kolenda 1665-74
Cyprian Zhokhovsky 1674-93
Lev Zalensky-Slyubych 1694-1708
Yuriy Vynnytsky 1708-13
Lev Kishka 1714-28
Atanasiy Sheptytsky 1729-46
Florian Hrebnytsky 1746-62
Pylyp Volodkovych 1762-78
Lev Sheptytsky 1778-79
Yason Smogozhevsky 1780-88
Teodosiy Rostotsky 1788-1805

UKRAINIAN METROPOLITANS OF GALICIA

Antin Anhelovych 1807-14
Mykhaylo Levytsky 1818-58
Hryhoriy Yakhymovych 1860-63
Spyrydon Lytvynovych 1863-69
Yosyf Sembratovych 1870-82
Sylvester Sembratovych 1885-98
Yuliyan Sas-Kuyilovsky 1899-1900
Andrey Sheptytsky 1900-1944

UKRAINIAN METROPOLITANS OF GALICIA AND ARCHBISHOPS-MAJOR

Yosyf Slipyj 1944-84
Myroslav Ivan Lubachivsky 1984-

METROPOLITANS OF THE UKRAINIAN CATHOLIC CHURCH IN THE U.S.

Konstantyn Bohachevsky 1958-61
Ambrose Senyshyn 1961-76
Yosyf Shmondyuk 1976-79
Myroslav Lubachivsky 1979-80
Stefan Sulyk 1981-

METROPOLITANS OF THE UKRAINIAN CATHOLIC CHURCH IN CANADA

Maksym Hermanyuk 1956-

UKRAINIAN CATHOLIC CARDINALS

Mykhaylo Levytsky .... nominated in 1856
Sylvester Sembratovych .... nominated in 1895
Yosyf Slipyj .... nominated in 1965
Myroslav Lubachivsky .... nominated in 1985

Orthodox Bishops

BILHOROD

Stefan 1072
Luke 1089
Mykyta 1115-21
Teodor (Fedir) .... ca. 1147
Epyfaniy Tykhorsky 1722-31

CHERNIHIV

Neofit 992
Neofit 1072
Ioann 1090-1112
Teoktyst 1112-20
Heraklid .... n.d.
Panteleymon 1140
Onufriy 1143-47
Teotekh 1147
Yevfymiy 1148
Antoniy 1158-68
Porfyriy 1187
Porfyriy 1230-38
Neofit 1238
Yevtymiy 1464
Nektariy 1499
Iona 1500
Isaya Kopynsky 1633-40
Zosym Prokopovych 1650-57
Lazar Baranovych 1657-93
Teodosiy Uhlytsky 1693-96
Ioan Maksymovych 1697-1712

HALYCH

Cosma . . . ca. 1165
Oleksiy . . . ante 1165
Teodor . . . 1330
Makariy . . . 1458

KAMYANETS-PODILSKY

Pankratiy . . . 1679
Hryhoriy . . . 1328
Kharyton . . . 1414

KHOLM

Hryhoriy Depolnytsky . . . 1446-67
Sylvester (Sava) . . . 1468-70
Herasym (Hrytsko Okyshkovych) Bozky . . . 1471-89
Symeon Buhak . . . 1492-94
Filaret (Ploshchansky) Oblaznytsky . . . 1507-33
Iona (Ivashko) Sosnovsky . . . 1504-07; 1533-54
Mykhaylo Sosnovsky, bishop elect . . . 1543
Vassiyan (Vasyl) Baka . . . 1546-52
Teodosiy Lazovsky . . . 1552-65
Zakharya (Zenko) Illyashevych . . . 1566-77
Teodor (Terentiy Onnys) Lazovsky, bishop-elect . . . 1566
Leontiy (Levko) Pelchytsky . . . 1577-85
Dionysiy (Dmytro) Zbiruysky . . . 1585-96
Payisiy Ipolytovych . . . 1621-33
Dionysiy Balaban . . . 1650-57

KIEV

Archbishops

Varlaam Vanatovych . . . 1722-30
Rafayil Zaborovsky . . . 1731-42

LUTSK

Teodosiy . . . 1328
Tryfon . . . 1331
Ioann . . . 1393
Teodor . . . 1397
Sava . . . 1401
Dionysiy . . . 1414
Martynyan . . . 1459
Nykyfor I . . . 1490
Iona . . . 1492-95
Kyrylo . . . 1495-1526
Pafnutiy . . . 1521-28
Makariy . . . 1528-34
Arseniy . . . 1540
Teodosiy . . . 1545-48
Tymotey . . . 1548
Nykyfor II . . . 1564
Marko Zharovnytsky . . . 1564-67
Kyrylo Terletsky . . . 1585-96
Isaakiy Boryskovych . . . 1620-33
Afanasiy (Oleksander) Puzyna . . . 1632-50
Yosyf Chaplych . . . 1650-54
Dionysiy Balaban . . . 1654-57
Hedeon (Svyatopolk) Chetvertynsky . . . 1663-85
Atanasiy Shumlyansky . . . 1685-94
Kyrylo Shumlansky . . . 1710-1712

LVIV

Makariy Tuchapsky . . . 1540-49
Arseniy (Mark) Balaban . . . 1549-68
Ivan (Lopatka) Ostalovsky . . . 1570-76
Hedeon Balaban . . . 1568-1607
Yeremiya (Yevstakhiy) Tysarovsky . . . 1606-41
Arseniy Zheliborsky . . . 1641-58
Atanasiy Zheliborsky . . . 1658-67
Yevstakhiy (Yeremiya) Svystelnytsky . . . 1667-76
Yosyf (Ivan) Shumlyansky . . . 1676-1700

MUKACHIV

Ivan . . . 1490
Vasyliy . . . 1551
Yevtymiy Amfiloniy . . . 1596-1606
Serhiy . . . 1601-16
Sofroniy Yuska . . . 1614-48
Yevtymiy . . . 1618
Sofroniy Rechko . . . 1620
Petroniy . . . 1623-27
Ivan Hryhorovych . . . 1627-33
Vasyl Tarasovych . . . 1633-46
Yoanykiy Zeykan . . . 1651-86
Yosyf Voloshynovsky . . . 1667-75
Metodiy Rakovetsky . . . 1687-88

PEREMYSHL

Antoniy Dobrynya Yadrenkovych . . . 1218-25
Ilarion . . . 1254
Avraam . . . 1271
Yeremiya . . . 1282
Serhiy . . . 1283-87
Memnon . . . 1288
Ilarion . . . 1292-1302
Heorhiy . . . 1315
Marko . . . 1330-41
Kyrylo Voloshyn . . . 1353
Ilarion . . . 1366-85
Vasyliy . . . 1385
Atanasiy . . . 1391-1407
Pavlo . . . 1415
Atanasiy Drohoyovsky . . . 1422
Iliya . . . 1422-42
Oleksander . . . 1442-67
Ioann Boretsky . . . 1442-76
Atañasiy (Oleksander) Biretsky . . . 1446-67
Ioann (Ivan) Biretsky . . . 1467-76
Yoannikiy . . . 1491-98
Antoniy Onykiy . . . 1498-1521
Yoakym . . . 1522-28
Lavrentiy (Arseniy) Terletsky . . . 1528-49
Antoniy (Yatsko) Radylovsky . . . 1549-81
Arseniy (Stefan) Brylynsky . . . 1581-91
Mykhaylo (Matey) Kopystynsky . . . 1591-1610
Ivan Khlopecky . . . 1610-11
Isaya Kopynsky . . . 1620-31
Ivan Popel . . . 1633-35
Sylvester (Semen) Hulevych-Voyutynsky . . . 1633-45
Antoniy Vynnytsky . . . 1677-79
Yuriy Hoshovsky . . . 1667-79
Innokentiy Vynnytsky . . . 1679-81

PEREYASLAV

Petro . . . 1072
Yefrem . . . 1090

Lazar ... 1105-18
Sylvester ... 1118-23
Ioann I ... 1123-25
Mark or Markel ... 1126-34
Yevfymiy ... 1141
Symeon ... 1239
Zakhariy Kornylovych ... 1701-16
Kyrylo Shumlansky ... 1716-26
Ioakym Strukov ... 1727-30
Varlaam Lenytsky ... 1730-31
Arseniy Berlo ... 1733-44
Nikodym Shryabnytsky ... 1745-51
Ivan Kozlovych ... 1753-57
Hevrasiy Lyntsevsky ... 1757-69
Yov Bazylevych ... 1770-76
Ilarion Kondratovsky ... 1776-85
Viktor Sadkovsky ... 1785-93
Dmytro Ustynovych ... 1793-95

SLOVYANO-KHERSON

Yevheniy Bulharyn ... 1775-79
Nykyfor Feotoky ... 1779-86
Amvroziy Serebrenikov ... 1786-93
Havryyil Banulesko-Bodoni ... 1793-99

VOLODYMYR-VOLYNSKY

Stefan ... 992
Amfilokhiy ... 1105-22
Teodor ... 1130-47
Atanasiy ... 1328
Yona ... 1389
Hohol ... 1405
Danylo ... 1446-49
Nykyfor II ... 1458
Porfyriy ... 1470
Teodosiy ... 1485
Damyan ... 1487
Vassiyan I ... 1487-94
Vassiyan II ... 1507-11
Pafnutiy ... 1513-21
Iona ... 1523-35
Hennadiy ... 1536-47
Yosyf ... 1565
Teodosiy Lazovsky ... 1565-79
Meletiy Khrebtovych-Bohurynsky ... 1580-93
Ipatiy Potiy ... 1593-96
Ezekiyil Kurtsevych ... 1620-25

VOLYNIA

Varlaam Shyshatsky ... 1799-1805

YURIYIV

Mykhayil ... 1072
Antoniy ... 1098
Maryn ... 1091
Danylo ... 1114-22
Damyan ... ca. 1147

ZAPORIZHZHYA HOST

Anatoliy Melas ... 1754-60

BUKOVYNA AND DALMATIA

Danylo Blakhovych ... 1789-1822
Yevhen Hakman ... 1835-73

UKRAINIAN AUTOCEPHALOUS ORTHODOX CHURCH
1921-1936

Archbishops

Anton Hrynevych ... 1923-30
Konstantyn Krotevych ... 1922-30
Konstantyn Malyushkevych ... 1922-34
Yuriy Mikhnovsky ... 1921-34
Stepan Orlyk ... 1921-28
Yosyp Oksiyuk ... 1922-33
Mykola Pyvovariv ... 1922-29
Volodymyr Samborsky ... 1923-32
Nestor Sharayivsky ... 1921-29
Feodosiy Serhiyiv ... 1924-30
Ioann Teodorovych ... 1021-24
Oleksander Yareshchenko ... 1921-26
Yuriy Zhevchenko ... 1922-29

Bishops

Konon Bey ... 1922-28
Volodymyr Brzhosnyovsky ... 1921-30
Pylyp Buchylo ... 1922-23
Oleksander Chervinsky ... 1925-34
Yakiv Chulayivsky ... 1928-31
Volodymyr Dakhivnyk-Dakhivsky ... 1922-30
Marko Hrushevsky ... 1922-26
Yukhym Kalishevsky ... 1922-30
Mykola Karabinevych ... 1922-30
Mykhaylo Malyarevsky ... 1921-36
Hryhoriy Mozolevsky ... 1924-26
Yuriy Prokopovych ... 1926
Petro Romodanov ... 1923-26
Mykola Shyryay ... 1922-30
Hryhoriy Storozhenko ... 1921-25
Petro Tarnavsky ... 1922-30s
Yuriy Teslenko ... 1925-30
Maksym Zadvirnyak ... 1923-30

UKRAINIAN ORTHODOX CHURCHES

ARCHBISHOPS AND BISHOPS

UKRAINIAN ORTHODOX AUTOCEPHALOUS CHURCH
1942

Archbishops and Bishops

Archbishop Polikarp Sikorsky
ADMINISTRATOR

Nikanor Abramovych
REPRESENTATIVE IN THE EASTERN LANDS OF UKRAINE

DNIPROPETROVSK AND SICHESLAV
Hennadiy Shyprykevych

LUTSK AND KOVEL
Archbishop Polikarp Sikorsky
Platon (Artymyuk) of Rovno
Vyacheslav Lisytsky of Dubno

MYKOLAYIV AND KHERSON
Mykhayil (Fedir) Khoroshy of Kirovohrad
Volodymyr (Vasyl) Malets of Cherkasy

POLISSYA
Archbishop Oleksander Inozemtsev

UMAN AND POLTAVA
Ihor Huba

Fotiy Tymoshchuk of Nizyn and Vinnytsya
Hryhoriy Ohiychuk of Zhytomyr
Sylvester Hayevsky of Lubny
Metropolitan Feofil Buldovky of Kharkiv
Mstyslav Skrypnyk of Pereyaslav

UKRAINIAN AUTOCEPHALOUS ORTHODOX CHURCH IN WESTERN EUROPE
1945-1949

Archbishops

Nikanor Abramovych of Chyhyryn
Mykhayil Khoroshy of Kirovohrad
Ihor Huba of Uman and Poltava
Hennadiy Shyprykevych of Dnipropetrovsk

Bishops

Volodymyr Malets of Cherkasy
Vyacheslav Lisytsky of Dubno
Sylvester Hayevsky of Lubny
Serhiy Okhotenko of Melitopol
Mstyslav Skrypnyk of Pereyaslav
Platon Artemyuk of Rovno
Hryhoriy Ohiychuk of Zhytomyr

UKRAINIAN AUTOCEPHALOUS ORTHODOX CHURCH IN THE DIASPORA
1949-1988

Archbishops

Sylvester Hayevsky of Australia and New Zealand .. 1949-75
Varlaam Soloviy of Australia and New Zealand 1957-66
Donat Burtan of Australia 1963-70
Orest Evanyuk of Western Europe 1970-80
Mykola Soloviy of South America 1952-53
Anatoliy Dublyansky of Western Europe 1982-
Volodymyr Didovych of London 1986-88

Bishops

Ivan Danylyuk of Australia and New Zealand 1952-54
Oleksiy Pylypenko of South America.............. 1952-69
Volodymyr Didovych of London 1984-86

UKRAINIAN ORTHODOX CHURCH IN THE UNITED STATES
1924-1988

Archbishops

Ioann Teodorovych of Philadelphia 1924-71
Mstyslav Skrypnyk of Philadelphia 1971-
Hennadiy Shyprykevych of Chicago............... 1950-61
Volodymyr Malets of Detroit 1950-66
Mstyslav Skrypnyk of New York 1950-70
Marko Hundyak of New York 1970-84
Iov Skakalsky of South America.................. 1970-74
Konstantyn Bagan of Chicago.................... 1979-

Bishops

Volodymyr Gay of South America 1947-77
Oleksander Novytsky of Chicago 1965-70
Konstantyn Bagan of Chicago.................... 1972-79
Antoniy Sharba of New York 1986-

UKRAINIAN GREEK ORTHODOX CHURCH IN CANADA
1924-1988

Archbishops

WINNIGEG

Ioann Teodorovych 1924-47
Mstyslav Skrypnyk 1947-49
Ilarion Ohiyenko 1949-51

EASTERN CANADA

Mykhayil Khoroshy 1952-77

CENTRAL CANADA

Borys Yakovkevych............................. 1962-83

WESTERN CANADA

Andriy Metyuk 1959-75

Bishops

EASTERN CANADA

Mykolay Debryn 1977-81

CENTRAL CANADA

Vasyliy Fedak............................... 1978-1983

WESTERN CANADA

Ivan Stinka 1984-

CONCILIAR UKRAINIAN AUTOCEPHALOUS ORTHODOX CHURCH

Archbishops

Hryhoriy Ohiychuk 1947-71
Hennadiy Shyprykevych 1961-72
Varlaam Dzyuba 1973-82
Oleksiy Pylypenko 1975-77

Bishops

ENGLAND

Ivan Hrytsenko 1969-85
Yosyf Burma 1981-

AUSTRALIA

Donat Burtan 1955-63

WINNIPEG

Mykola Urbanovych 1954-56

WESTERN EUROPE

Yevhen Bachynsky 1955-83

CHICAGO

Petro Kolesnyk 1975-

SAN FRANCISCO

Izyaslav Honchariv 1981-

UKRAINIAN ORTHODOX CHURCH IN THE U.S. AND CANADA

Yosyf Zhuk 1932-37
Bohdan Shpylka 1937-63
Metropolitan Andriy Kushchak 1967-86
Vsevolod Maydansky 1987-

UKRAINIAN AUTOCEPHALOUS ORTHODOX CHURCH IN EXILE

Archbishops

Palladiy Vydybida-Rudenko 1951-71
Ihor Huba 1954-67

Catholic Bishops in Ukrainian Lands

KHOLM

Dionysiy Zbiruysky 1596-1604
Arseniy Andriyevsky 1605-19
Atanasiy Pakosta 1619-25
Teodor Meleshko 1626
Metodiy Terletsky 1629-49
Andriy Furs 1649
Yakiv Susha 1652-86
Oleksander Lodzyata 1685-91
Ivan Malakhovsky 1691-92
Hedeon Oransky-Voyna 1693-1709
Yosyf Levytsky 1711-30
Pylyp Volodkovych 1730-58
Maksymilian Ryllo 1759-85
Teodosiy Rostotsky 1785-90
Porfyriy Vazhynsky 1790-1804
Ferdinand Tsyekhanovsky 1809-28
Felitsyan Shumborsky 1828-51
Ivan Terashkevych 1851-63
Ivan Kalinsky 1863-66
Yosyf Voytsitsky 1866-68
Mykhaylo Kuzemsky 1868-71
Markyl Popel 1871-75

LUTSK

Kyrylo Terletsky 1596-1607
Ostafiy Yelovych-Malynsky 1607-21
Yeremiya Pochapovsky 1621-36
Nykyfor Lasovsky 1637
Prokopiy Khmelyovsky 1660
Antoniy Terlecky 1662-66
Havryyil Kolenda 1666-74
Cyprian Zhokhovsky 1693
Lev Zalensky-Slyubych 1700
Dionysiy Zhabokrytsky 1702-15
Yosyf Vyhovsky 1716-30
Teodosiy Rudnytsky 1731-51
Sylvester Rudnytsky 1752-77
Cyprian Stetsky 1778-82
Mykhayil Stadnytsky 1783-87
Stefan Levynsky 1787-1809
Hryhoriy Kokhanovych 1807-13
Floryan Korsak 1810-11
Yakiv Martusevych 1817-26
Ivan Krasovsky 1826
Yosyf Botsyan 1914-24
Vasyl Velychkovsky 1963-72

LVIV

Makariy Tuchansky 1605-08
Velyamyn Rutsky 1608-13
Raphael Korsak 1626-32
Yosyf Shumlansky 1700-08
Varlaam Sheptytsky 1709-15
Atanasiy Sheptytsky 1715-46
Lev Sheptytsky 1749-79
Petro Byelansky 1780-98
Mykola Skorodynsky 1798-1805
Antin Anhelovych 1807-14
Hryhoriy Yakhymovych 1841-48
Ivan Bokhensky 1850-57
Spyrydon Lytvynovych 1857-59
Sylvester Sembratovych 1878-85
Andrey Sheptytsky 1900-44
Yosyf Botsyan 1924-26
Nykyta Budka 1928-49
Ivan Buchko 1929-40
Yosyf Slipyj 1939-44

MUKACHIV

Vasyl Tarasovych 1646-48
Parteniy Petrovych Rostoshynsky 1652-65
Yosyf Voloshynovych 1674
Theophanes Mavrocordato 1676-78

Porfyriy Kulchytsky 1683
Metodiy Rakovetsky 1687
Rafayil Habryelovych 1687-88
Joseph de Camelis 1689-1706
Yuriy Vynnytsky 1706
Ioann Hodermarsky (designate) 1707
Polikarp Fylypovych (designate) 1710
Yuriy Bizantsiy 1716-33
Symon Olshavsky 1734-37
Habriyel Blazhovsky 1737-42
Manuyil Olshavsky 1743-67
Ivan Bradach 1767-72
Andriy Bachynsky 1773-1809
Mykhaylo Bradach 1809-14
Oleksiy Povchiy 1815-31
Vasyl Popovych 1837-64
Stepan Pankovych 1867-74
Ivan Pasteliy 1875-91
Yuriy Firtsak 1891-1912
Antoniy Pap 1912-24
Oleksander Stoyka 1932-43
Dionysiy Nyaradi 1938-39
Mykola Dudash 1944
Teodor Romzha 1944-47

PEREMYSHL, SAMBIR AND SYANOK

Atanasiy Krupetsky 1610-52
Pavlo Ovluchynsky 1637-49
Prokopiy Khmilevsky 1652-64
Antoniy Terletsky 1664-69
Yakiv Susha 1667-69
Ivan Malakhovsky 1669-91
Yuriy (Havryyil) Vynnytsky 1700-13
Yeronim (Yuriy) Ustrytsky 1715-46
Onufriy (Yosyf) Shumlansky 1746-62
Maksymilian Ryllo 1785-93
Antin Anhelovych 1796-1807
Mykhaylo Levytsky 1813-16
Ivan Snihursky 1818-47
Hryhoriy Yakhymovych 1849-59
Toma Polyansky 1860-69
Yosyf Sembratovych 1869-72
Ivan Stupnytsky 1872-90
Yuliyan Sas-Kyuilovksy 1890-91

Yuliyan Pelesh 1891-96
Konstantyn Chekhovych 1896-1915
Yosafat Kotsylovsky 1916-47
Hryhoriy Lakota 1926-51

PRYASHIV

Hryhoriy Tarkovych 1818-41
Yosyf Hahanets 1843-75
Mykola Tovt 1876-82
Ivan Valiy 1882-1911
Stepan Novak 1913-20
Dionysiy Nyaradi 1922-27
Pavlo Goydych 1927-50
Vasyl Hopko 1947-50, 1968-69

STANYSLAVIV

Yuliyan Pelesh 1885-91
Yuliyan Sas-Kuyilovsky 1891-99
Andrey Sheptytsky 1899-1900
Hryhoriy Khomyshyn 1904-47
Ivan Lyatyshevsky 1929-57

VOLODYMYR-VOLYNSKY

Ipatiy Potiy 1596-1613
Yoakym (Atanasiy) Morokhovsky 1613-31
Yosyf Bakovetsky 1632-50
Ivan (Mykhaylo) Potiy 1655-66
Benedykt Hlynsky 1667-78
Lev Zalensky-Slyubych 1679-1708
Lev Kishka 1711-28
Kornel Lebetsky 1729-30
Teofil Godebsky 1730-56
Pylyp Volodkovych 1758-78
Antoniy Mlodovsky 1778
Symon Mlotsky 1778

VOLYNIA

Mykola Charnetsky 1931-59

CATACOMB UKRAINIAN CATHOLIC CHURCH

Oleksander Khira 1945-83
Vasyl Velychkovsky 1963-73

BISHOPS OF THE UKRAINIAN CATHOLIC CHURCH IN THE DIASPORA

ARGENTINA

Andriy Sapelak 1961-78

AUSTRALIA

Ivan Prashko 1958-

BRAZIL

Yosyf Martynets 1958-71
Yefrem Kryvy 1978-

CANADA

EDMONTON

Nil Savaryn 1948-86
Dmytro Greshchuk 1974-

NEW WESTMINSTER

Yeronim Khymiy 1974-

SASKATOON

Andriy Roboretsky 1951-82
Vasyl Filevych 1984-

TORONTO

Isydor Boretsky 1948-

WINNIPEG

Nykyta Budka 1912-28
Vasyl Ladyka 1929-56
Nil Savaryn 1943-48

Andriy Roboretsky 1948-51
Maksym Hermanyuk 1951-56
Myron Datsyuk 1982-

FRANCE

Volodymyr Malanchuk 1960-82
Mykhaylo Hrynchyshyn 1982-

GERMANY

Platon Kornylyak 1959-

GREAT BRITAIN

Avhustyn Hornyak 1961-87
Mykhaylo Hrynchyshyn 1987-

U.S.A.

CHICAGO

Yaroslav Gabro 1961-80
Innokentiy Lototsky 1981-

PARMA

Robert Moskal 1983-

PHILADELPHIA

Soter Ortynsky 1907-16
Konstantyn Bohachevsky 1924-58
Ambrose Senyshyn 1942-56
Yosyf Shmondyuk 1956-61
Ivan Stakh 1971-72
Vasyl Losten 1971-77
Robert Moskal 1981-83
Mykhyalo Kuchmyak 1988-

STAMFORD

Ambrose Senyshyn 1956-61
Yosyf Shmondyuk 1961-76
Vasyl Losten 1977-

YUGOSLAVIA

KRIZEVCI

Dionysiy Nyaradi 1914-24
Janko Shimrak 1942-46
Havryil Bukatko 1952-81
Ioakim Segedi 1963-84
Slavomir Miklovsh 1983-

Rulers of Ukraine

PRINCES AND GRAND PRINCES OF KIEVAN RUS'

Kyi .... ca. 560
Askold and Dyr .... ca. 860-82
Oleh 882-912
Ihor 912-45
Olha (Regent) 945-57
Svyatoslav Ihorevych 957-72
Yaropolk Svyatoslavych 972-78
Volodymyr Svyatoslavych 978-1015
Svyatopolk I Volodymyrovych the Damned 1015-19
Yaroslav I Volodymyrovych the Wise 1019-54
Izyaslav Yaroslavych 1054-68, 1069-73, 1976-77
Vseslav of Polotsk 1068-69
Svyatoslav Yaroslavych 1073-76
Vsevolod Yaroslavych 1077-93
Svyatopolk Izyaslavych 1093-1113
Volodymyr Vsevolodovych Monomakh 1113-25
Mstyslav I Volodymyrovych 1125-32
Yaropolk Volodymyrovych 1132-39
Vsevolod II Olhovych 1139-46
Ihor Olhovych 1146-47
Izyaslav II Mstyslavych 1147-54
Yuriy Volodymyrovych Dolgoruky 1154-57
Izyaslav Davydovych of Chernihiv 1157-58, 1161
Rostyslav Mstyslavych of Smolensk 1159-67
Mstyslav Izyaslavych of Volodymyr-Volynsky 1167-69
Hlib Yuriyevych 1169-71
Roman Rostyslavych of Smolensk 1171, 1175-76
Svyatoslav Vsevolodovych 1171-97
Ryuryk Rostyslavych 1197-1202, 1205-10
Roman Mstyslavych of Volodymyr-Volynsky 1202-05
Vsevolod Svyatoslavych of Chernihiv 1210-12
Mstyslav Romanovych (the Daring) of Smolensk ... 1212-23
Volodymyr Ryurykovych of Smolensk 1223-35, 1238-39
Yaroslav Vsevolodovych 1236-38
Mykhaylo Vsevolodovych of Chernihiv 1238-39
Rostyslav Mstyslavych of Smolensk 1239
Danylo Romanovych of Halych 1240
Mykhaylo Vsevolodovych 1241-46
Yaroslav of the Suzdal dynasty 1246

GRAND PRINCES AND KINGS
OF THE GALICIAN-VOLYNIAN PRINCIPALITY

Roman Mstyslavych 1198-1205
Volodymyr Ihorevych, Roman Ihorevych
Svyatoslav Ihorevych, Mstyslav Mstyslavych 1206-11
Volodyslav Kormylchych 1212-14
Mstyslav Udatny 1219-28
Danylo Romanovych, king 1228-33, 1237-64
Rostyslav Mykhaylovych 1233-37
Lev I Danylovych 1264-1301
Yuriy I Lvovych, king 1301-15
Andriy Yuriyevych, Lev II Yuriyevych 1315-23
Yuriy II Troydenovych 1323-40
Dmytro Detko 1340-49

HETMANS OF THE UKRAINIAN KOZAKS

Dmytro Vyshnevetsky .... ca. 1550-63
Bohdan Ruzhynsky 1575-76
Shakh 1576-77
Samiylo Zborovsky .... ca. 1581
Mykhaylo and Kyryk Ruzhynsky 1585
Voytykh Khanovytsky 1590
Khrystofer Kosynsky 1591-93
Hryhoriy Loboda 1593-96
Hnat Vasylevych 1596-97
Samiylo Kishka 1600-02
Havrylo Krutnevych, Ivan Koziy 1602-03
Hryhoriy Ivanovych 1606
Hryhoriy Tyshkevych 1610
Petro Sahaydachny 1613-22
Mykhaylo Doroshenko 1623-28
Hryhoriy Chorny 1628-29
Taras Fedorovych 1629-30
Ivan Sulyma 1633-35
Pavlo But 1637-38
Yakiv Ostryanyn 1638-41

HETMANS OF UKRAINE

Bohdan Khmelnytsky 1648-57
Ivan Vyhovsky 1657-59
Yuriy Khmelnytsky 1659-63
Pavlo Teterya 1663-65
Ivan Bryukhovetsky 1663-68
Petro Doroshenko 1666-76
Damyan Mnohohrishny 1668-72
Ivan Samoylovych 1672-87
Ivan Mazepa 1687-1709
Ivan Skoropadsky 1709-22
Pavlo Polubotok, Acting 1722-24
Pylyp Orlyk (in exile) 1710-42
Danylo Apostol 1727-34
Kyrylo Rozymovsky 1750-64

HEADS OF THE UKRAINIAN STATE

Mykhaylo Hrushevsky 1917-18
Pavlo Skoropadsky 1918
Symon Petlyura 1918-20

Bibliography

Aseev, Yu. S., editor. *Pamyatniki gradostroitelstva i arkhitektury Ukrainskoi SSR*. Vols. I-IV. Budivelnyk, Kiev, 1983-1986.

Barrett, David (ed.). *World Christian Encyclopaedia*. Oxford, 1982.

Blazejovskyj, Dmytro. *Byzantine Kyivan Rite Metropolitanates, Eparchies and Exarchates*. Nomenclature and Statistics. Ukrainian Catholic University, Rome, 1980.

Bociurkiw, Bohdan & Strong, John W. *Religion and Atheism in the USSR and Eastern Europe*. University of Toronto Press, Toronto-Buffalo, 1975.

Bociurkiw, Bohdan R. *Ukrainian Churches Under Soviet Rule: Two Case Studies*. Ukrainian Studies Fund, Harvard University, Cambridge, Massachusetts, 1984.

Boysak, B. *The Fate of the Holy Union in Carpatho-Ukraine*. Toronto-New York, 1963.

Braychevsky, Mykhaylo, *Bilya Dzherel Slovyanskoyi Derzhavnosti*. Naukova Dumka, Kiev, 1964.

———. *Kogda i kak voznik Kiev*. Naukova Dumka, Kiev, 1964.

———. *Pokhodzhennya Rusi*. Naukova Dumka, 1968.

Chadwick, Owen. *The Reformation*. 1982.

Chubaty, Mykola. *Istoriya Khrystyyanstva na Rusy-Ukrayini*. Vol. I-II. Ukrainian Catholic University, Rome-New York, 1965-1976.

Cross, Samuel H., & Sherbowitz-Wetzor, Olgerd P., translators and editors. *The Russian Primary Chronicle: Laurentian Text*. The Mediaeval Academy of America, Cambridge, Massachusetts, 1973.

Demkovych-Dobriansky, Mykhaylo. *Pototsky i Bobzhynsky, Tsisarski namisnyky Halychyny, 1903-1913*. Ukrainian Catholic University, Rome, 1987.

Denisov, L.I. *Pravoslavnyye Monastyri Rossiyskoi Imperii*. Moscow, 1908.

Domashovetz, Rev. G. *Narys Istoriyi Ukrayinskoyi Yevanhelsko-Baptystskoyi Tserkvy*. Irvington, New Jersey-Toronto, Ontario, 1967.

Dombrowsky, Alexander. *Narys istoriyi Ukrayinskoho Yevanhelsko-Reformavanoho Rukhu*. Ukrainian Evangelical Alliance of North America, New York-Toronto, 1979.

Doroshenko, Dmytro. *Narys Istorii Ukrainy*. Munich, 1966.

Fedoriw, George, Rev. *History of the Church in Ukraine*. Translated by Petro Krawchuk. Toronto, 1983.

Filaret (Gumilevsky). *Obzor russkoy dukhovnoy literatury*. (3rd. ed.) Books 1-2. I. L. Tuzov, S.-Peterburg, 1884.

Garaty, John A. & Gay, Peter (eds.). *The Columbia History of the World*. New York, 1972.

Golubinsky, E. *Istoriya Russkoy Tserkvi*. Vol. I (2nd ed.). Moscow, 1901-1904; Vol. II. Moscow, 1900-1911.

Hewryk, Titus D. *The Lost Architecture of Kiev*. The Ukrainian Museum, New York, 1982.

———. *Masterpieces in Wood: Houses of Worship in Ukraine*. The Ukrainian Museum, New York, 1987.

Heyer, F. *Die Orthodoxe Kirche in der Ukraine von 1917 bis 1945*. Verlagsgesellschaft Rudolf Muller, Koln-Braunsfeld, 1953.

Heymann, Frederick G. *Poland and Czechoslovakia*. Englewood Cliffs, N.J., 1966.

Himka, John-Paul. *The Greek Catholic Church and Ukrainian Society in Austrian Galicia*. Ukrainian Studies Fund, Harvard University, Cambridge, Massachusetts, 1986.

Hordynsky, Sviatoslav. *The Ukrainian Icon of the XIIth to XVIIIth Centuries*. Providence Association, Philadelphia, 1973.

Hrushevsky, Mykhaylo. *Istoriya Ukrayiny-Rusy*. Vol. I-X. Kiev-Lviv, 1898-1937.

———. *Z istoriyi relihiynoyi dumky na Ukrayini*. (2nd ed.) Ukrainian Evangelical Alliance of North America, Winnipeg-Munich-Detroit, 1962.

———. *A History of Ukraine*. O. J. Frederiksen (ed.). Archon Books, 1970.

Hussey, J. M., ed. *The Cambridge Medieval History*. Vol. IV, Pt. I. Cambridge, 1966.

Hvat, Ivan. *The Catacomb Ukrainian Catholic Church and Pope John Paul II*. Ukrainian Studies Fund, Harvard University, Cambridge, Massachusetts, 1984.

Ilarion, Metropolitan. *Pryyednannya Tserkvy Ukrayinskoyi do Moskovskoyi v 1686 rotsi*. (5th ed.) Mytropolitalny Sobor, Winnipeg, 1948.

———. *Ukrayinska Tserkva za Bohdana Khmelnytskoho, 1647-1657*. Ukrayinske Naukove Pravoslavne Bohoslovske Tovarystvo, Winnipeg, 1955.

Ilarion, Metropolitan. *Ukrayinska Tserkva za chas ruyiny (1657-1687).* Ukrayinske Naukove Bohoslovske Tovarystvo, Winnipeg, 1956.

Iwanusiw, Oleh. *Church in Ruins. The Demise of Ukrainian Churches in the Eparchy of Peremyshl.* St. Sophia Religious Association of Ukrainian Catholics in Canada, St. Catharines, 1987.

Kharlampovich, K.V. *Malorossiyskoye Vliyaniye na Velikorusskuyu Tserkovnuyu Zhyzn.* Kazan, 1914.

Khyzhnyak, Z. I. *Kyyevo-Mohylyanska Akademiya* (2nd ed.). Vyshcha Shkola, Kiev, 1981.

Korolevskij, C. *Metropolite Andre Szeptyckyj, 1865-1944.* Ukrayinske Bohoslovske Naukove Tovarystvo, Rome, 1964.

Kubijovyc, V. ed. *Ukraine: A Concise Encyclopedia.* Vol. I-II. University of Toronto Press, Toronto-New York, 1963-1971.

Kubinyi, Julius. *The History of Prjasiv Eparchy.* Opera Graeco-Catholicae Academiae Theologicae Vol. XXXII, Editiones Universitatis Catholicae Ucrainorum S. Clementis Papae, Romae, 1970.

Labunka, M. and Rudnytsky, L. (eds.). *The Ukrainian Catholic Church: 1945-1975.* St. Sophia Religious Association of Ukrainians, Philadelphia, 1976.

Letopis Nestora. So Vklyucheniyem Poucheniya Vladimira Monomakha. S.-Peterburg, 1903.

Likhachev, D.S., compiler. *Povest Vremennykh Let.* Parts I-II. Akademiya Nauk SSSR. Moskva-Leningrad, 1950.

Lohvyn, H. N. *Po Ukrayini: starodavni mystetski pamyatky.* Mystetstvo, Kyiv, 1968.

Lubachivsky, Myroslav Ivan, Cardinal. *Chy spravdi bulo khryshchennya Rosiyi 988 roku?* Rome-Munich, 1986.

Luzhnytsky, H. *Ukrayinska Tserkva mizh Skhodom i Zakhodom. Narys istoriyi Ukrayinskoyi Tserkvy.* Providence Association, Philadelphia, 1954.

Lypynsky, Vyacheslav. *Relihiya i Tserkva v Istoriyi Ukrayiny.* Bulava, New York, 1956.

Magosci, Paul R. *Ukraine: a Historical Atlas.* Toronto, 1985.

———. *Wooden Churches in the Carpathians.* W. Braumuller, Vienna, 1982.

Makary, Metropolitan of Moscow. *Istoriya Russkoi Tserkvi.* Vols. I-XI, S.-Peterburg, 1881-91.

Makhnovets, L. Ye., compiler (Biletsky, O.I., editor). *Ukrayinski pysmennyky.* Bio-bibliohrafichny slovnyk. Vol. I. Derzhavne vydavnytstvo khudozhnoyi literatury, Kiev, 1960.

Markus, Vasyl. *Religion and Nationalism in Soviet Ukraine after 1945.* Ukrainian Studies Fund, Harvard University, Cambridge, Massachusetts, 1985.

McEvedy, Colin. *The Penguin Atlas of Medieval History.* Harmondsworth, Middlesex, 1961.

———. *The Penguin Atlas of Modern History (to 1815).* n.l., 1972.

———. *The Penguin Atlas of Recent History.* Harmondsworth, Middlesex, 1982.

Monumenta Ucrainae Historica. Vols. I-X. Ukrainian Catholic University, Rome, 1964-1971.

Nazarko, Iryney I., Fr., OSBM. *Kyivski i Halytski Mytropolyty.* Biohrafichni narysy (1590-1960). Basilian Fathers, Toronto, 1962.

Orthodoxia 1986-1987. Ostkirchliches Institut. Regensburg, 1988.

Patrylo, Isydor I., OSBM. *Dzherela i bibliohrafiya istoriyi ukrayinskoyi tserkvy.* Series II Analecta OSBM Section I, Opera, vol. XXXIII. Basilian Fathers, Rome, 1975.

Pekar, A., OSBM. *Historic Background of the Eparchy of Pryashev.* Pittsburgh, 1968.

Pelesz, J. *Geschichte der Union der ruthenischen Kirche mit von den altesten Zeiten bis auf die Gegenwart.* Vols. I-II. Verlag der Mechitaristischen Buchdruckerei (W. Heinrich), Vienna, 1878-1880.

Polnoe Sobraniye Russkikh Letopisey. Vols. I-XII. Arkheograficheskaya Kommissiya, Vols. I-XII. 1841-1901.

Posnov, M. E. *Istoriya Khristianskoy Tserkvi (do razdeleniya Tserkvey — 1054 g.).* Zhyzn s Bogom, Brussels, 1964.

Potthast, August. *Bibliotheca Historica Medii Aevi: Wegweiser durch die Geschichtswerke des Europaischen Mittelalters bis 1500.* Berlin, 1896.

Powstenko, Olexa. *The Cathedral of St. Sophia in Kiev.* The Ukrainian Academy of Arts and Sciences in the U.S., New York, 1954.

Pravoslavnaya Bogoslovskaya Entsyklopediya. A. P. Lopukhin (ed.). Vols. I-XII. S.-Peterburg, 1900-1911.

Priselkov, M. D. *Ocherki po tserkovno-politicheskoy istoriyi Kievskoy Rusi X-XII vv.* S.-Peterburg, 1913.

Pritsak, Omeljan. *On the Writing of History in Kievan Rus'.* Ukrainian Studies Fund, Harvard University, Cambridge, Massachusetts, n.d.

———. *The Origin of Rus'.* Vol. I: *Old Scandinavian Sources other than the Sagas.* Harvard Ukrainian Research Institute, Cambridge, Massachusetts, 1981.

Romanyuk, Vasyl. *A Voice in the Wilderness.* Tr. and edited by Juriy Dobczansky. Wheaton, Illinois, 1980.

Senyk, S. *Women's Monasteries in Ukraine and Byelorussia to the Period of Suppressions.* Pontificum Institutum Studiorum Orientalium, Rome, 1983.

Shevelov, George Y. *Two Orthodox Ukrainian Churchmen of the Early Eighteenth Century: Teofan Prokopovych and Stefan Iavors'kyi.* Ukrainian Studies Fund, Harvard University, Cambridge, Massachusetts, 1985.

Sichnysky, Volodymyr. *Ukraine in Foreign Comments and Descriptions from the VIth to XXth Century.* Ukrainian Congress Committee of America, Inc., New York, 1953.

Sonevytsky, L. *Ukrayinsky Yepyskopat Peremyskoyi i Kholmskoyi Yeparkhiy v XV-XVI st.* Series II Analecta OSBM Sectio Opera Vol. VI, Rome, 1955.

Sorokowski, Andrew. *For My Name's Sake. Selections from the Writings of Iosyp Terelya.* Keston College, Keston, England, 1986.

Southern, R. W. *Western Society and the Church in the Middle Ages.* 1970.

Sysyn, Frank E. *The Ukrainian Orthodox Question in the USSR.* Ukrainian Studies Fund, Harvard University, Cambridge, Massachusetts, 1987.

Tapsell, R. F., compiler. *Monarchs, Rulers, Dynasties and Kingdoms of the World. Facts on File.* New York, 1983.

Tesla, Ivan & Tiutko, Evhen. (Wynar, Lubomyr, ed.) *Istorychny Atlas Ukrayiny.* Ukrainian Historical Association, Montreal-New York-Munich, 1980.

The Tragedy of the Greek Catholic Church in Czechoslovakia. Carpathian Alliance, New York, 1971.

Tolochko, Petro. *Kiev i Kievskaya Zemlya v Epokhu Feodalnoi Razdroblennosti XII-XIII Vekov.* Naukova Dumka, Kiev, 1980.

Truhart, Peter. *Regents of Nations.* Part II. Munich-New York-London-Paris, 1985.

Velyky, A. H., OSBM. *Z litopysu khrystyyanskoyi Ukrayiny.* Vols. I-VIII. Basilian Fathers, Rome, 1968-1976.

———. *Pecherskyi Pateryk abo pravedni staroyi Ukrayiny.* Basilian Fathers, Rome, 1973.

Vidler, Alec R. *The Church in an Age of Revolution.* 1971.

Vlasovsky, Ivan. *Narys istoriyi Ukrayinskoyi Pravoslavnoyi Tserkvy.* Vols. I-IV. Ukrainian Orthodox Church of U.S.A., New York-Bound Brook, 1956-1966.

Wace, Henry & Piercy, William C., eds. *A Dictionary of Christian Biography and Literature.* London, 1911.

Wolf, Josef, Maria, de. *Katholisch sein ist ein Verbrechen.* Aktionsgemeinschaft Kyrillos und Methodios e.V., Koln, n.d.

Yawdas, Mytrofan. *Ukrayinska Avtokefalna Pravoslavna Tserkva.* Munich-Ingolstadt, 1956.

Zinkewych, Osyp and Lonchyna, Taras R., Rev., editors. *Martyrolohiya Ukrayinskykh Tserkov.* Vol. II: *Ukrayinska Katolytska Tserkva.* Smoloskyp, Toronto-Baltimore, 1985.

Zinkewych, Osyp and Voronyn, Oleksander, editors. *Martyrolohiya Ukrayinskykh Tserkov.* Vol. I: *Ukrayinska Pravoslavna Tserkva.* Smoloskyp, Toronto-Baltimore, 1987.

Index

The index contains the names of only those hierarchs who are mentioned in the text. A complete list of Ukrainian metropolitans, bishops and rulers of Kievan Rus' and Hetmans is provided on pages 275-283.

Ignatius Antonius Hayek, Syrian Patriarch of Antioch, 252
Ignatius Petrus X Batanian, Armenian Patriarch, 252
Ihor (Huba), Ukrainian Orthodox Archbishop, 227, 229, 231
Ihor (Ingvar), Prince of Kiev (912-945), 14, 15, 19, 21, 27
Ihor Svyatoslavych, Prince of Novhorod-Siversky, 50, 225
Ihor Olhovych, Grand Prince of Kiev (1146-47), 51, 61
Ilarion, Bishop of Rostov (10th c.), 29, 35
Ilarion (Hilarion), Kievan Metropolitan (1051-54), 24, 28, 30, 33, 34
Ilarion, M., 125
Ilarion (Ohiyenko), Ukrainian Orthodox Metropolitan in Canada, 227, 232-234, 236
Illya, Bishop of Novgorod (1160s), 57
Illya (Kucha), Metropolitan of Kiev and Galicia (1576-79), 94, 96, 109
Ilmen, lake, 16
Immaculate Conception, proclamation of (1854), 180
Ingvar, see Ihor
"Initiative Group for the Defense of the Rights of Believers and the Church in Ukraine," 255
Inkerman, 17
In Memory and Praise of Volodymyr, Prince of Rus', 20, 27
Innocent III, Pope (1198-1216), 58, 66
Innocent IV, Pope (1243-54), 66, 76
Innocent XI, Pope (1676-89), 144
Innocent XII, Pope (1691-1700), 156
Inquisition, 88
Instructions to Children (1117), 50
International Eucharistic Congress (1881), 180
International Missionary Conference (1910), 180
International Sakharov Hearings in Rome (1977), 255
Ioakym Korsunyanyn, Bishop of Novgorod (992-1030), 35
Ioann, Bishop of Chernihiv (1080-1112), 60
Ioann, Bishop of Chernihiv (1335), 84
Ioann, Bishop of the Goths (4th c.), 17
Ioann, Bishop of Lutsk (1393), 70
Ioann I, Bishop of Pereyaslav (1123-25), 60
Ioann (Biretsky), Bishop of Peremyshl (1467-76), 110
Ioann (Maksymovych), Archbishop of Chernihiv, 156, 157
Ioann, Metropolitan of Kiev (1008-35), 30, 31, 34, 35
Ioann II, Metropolitan of Kiev (1077-88), 52, 59
Ioann III, Metropolitan of Kiev (1089-90), 52, 59
Ioann IV, Metropolitan of Kiev (1164-66), 57, 59
Ioann, Metropolitan of Galicia (1393, 1397-98), 70
Ioann (Teodorovych), Metropolitan of Ukrainian Orthodox Church in the U.S., 224, 232, 234, 236
Ioann (Sokolov), Russian Metropolitan of Kiev, 231, 244
Ioasaf (Lelyukhin), Russian Metropolitan of Kiev (1964-66), 234
Iona, Bishop of Chernihiv, 91
Iona, Bishop of Lutsk (1492-95), 91, 110
Iona, Bishop of Ryazan and Murom, 81
Iona, Bishop of Volynia, 79
Iona, Metropolitan of Moscow (1448-61), 83, 89
Iona (Hlezna), Metropolitan of Kiev (1492-94), 90, 109
Iona II, Metropolitan of Kiev (1503-07), 91, 109
Iona III (Protasovych-Ostrovsky), Metropolitan of Kiev (1568-76), 93, 94, 109
Iona, Patriarch of Moscow, 97
Ipolytovych, Paisiy, Orthodox Bishop of Kholm, 119, 124, 127
Ipatiy (Potiy), Bishop of Volodymyr-Volynsky (1593-96), 110
Irkutsk, 233
Iryna, Princess (11th c.), 34, 48
Isaakiy, Bishop of Chernihiv and Bryansk, 69, 80
Isaias, Patriarch of Constantinople (1323-32), 67, 77
Isakiy (Yatsko) Hdashytsky, Metropolitan's vicar in Lviv (1522-35), 109
Isidore, Metropolitan of Kiev (1436-42), Cardinal, 74, 81-83
Isidore I Kakkinos, Patriarch of Constantinople (1347-50), 67
Iskra, Ivan, 150
Islam, 13, 14, 74, 87, 88, 152, 206
Istanbul, see Constantinople
Istria, 23
Italy, Italians, 23, 50, 82, 87, 88, 151, 180
Ivan III, Grand Prince of Muscovy, 88, 90, 91
Ivan IV, Tsar of Muscovy, 162
Ivan V Romanov, Tsar of Muscovy, 153
Ivan the Terrible, Tsar of Muscovy, 87, 112
Ivan Kalita, Grand Prince of Muscovy, 67, 77
Ivan (Lavrynenko), Bishop of Orthodox Autonomous Church, 231
Ivan (Lopatka Ostalovsky), Bishop of Lviv, 94
Ivan Suchavsky, 77
Ivan Zatvornyk, 57
Ivano-Frankivsk, 254, 255
Ivanytsky, S., 196
Izborsk, 14
Izyaslav Davydovych of Chernihiv, Grand Prince of Kiev (1157-1158, 1161), 51, 61
Izyaslav II Mstyslavych, Grand Prince of Kiev (1147-54), 51, 55, 56, 60
Izyaslav Volodymyrovych, Prince, 32
Izyaslav Yaroslavych, Prince of Kiev (11th c.), 32, 50-52

Jacobus I, Patriarch of Constantinople (1679-83, 1685-86, 1687-88), 144, 146
Jadwiga, Queen of Poland, ruler of Galicia (1382-86), 66, 68, 73, 79
Jagiello, Grand Prince of Lithuania, ruler of Kievan Rus' (1377-1386), 73, 74, 75, 79
Jan Casimir, King of Poland, 132, 133
Jansenism, 152
Jehovah's Witnesses, 257
Jeremiah II, Patriarch of Constantinople, 94, 96-98
Jerome, St., 16
Jerusalem, 56-58, 60
Jerusalem Patriarchate, 17
Jesuits, 88, 94, 96, 106, 115, 117, 119, 130, 132, 151, 152, 167, 180, 181, 193, 195
Jews, 14, 24, 104, 205, 207, 242
Joachim, Patriarch of Antioch, 97
Joachimus, Metropolitan of Chalcedon, 216
Joasaph, Metropolitan of Corinthia, 132
John II Comnenus, Byzantine emperor (1118), 50
John VI Cantacuzene, Byzantine emperor (1347-54), 67
John VIII Palaeologus, Byzantine emperor (1425-48), 82
John X Camaterus, Patriarch of Constantinople (1198-1206), 66
John XII, Pope (955-64), 20
John XIII Glykys Patriarch of Constantinople (1315-19), 67, 77
John XV, Pope (985-996), 28, 29
John XVIII, Pope (1003-09), 30
John XXIII, Pope (1958-63), 206, 250, 251
John Chrysostom, St., 16, 17
John-Paul II, Pope (1978-), 207, 255, 256
Joseph II, Emperor of Austria, 152, 167-169, 182
Joseph II, Patriarch of Constantinople (1416-39), 81
Josephine Reforms, 167

GOSHEN COLLEGE - GOOD LIBRARY
3 9310 01018022 0